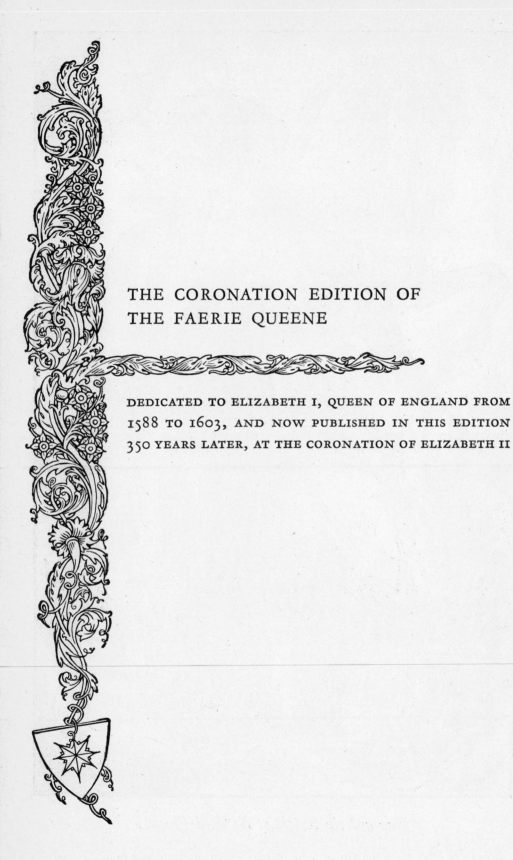

THE CORONATION EDITION OF
THE FAERIE QUEENE

DEDICATED TO ELIZABETH I, QUEEN OF ENGLAND FROM
1588 TO 1603, AND NOW PUBLISHED IN THIS EDITION
350 YEARS LATER, AT THE CORONATION OF ELIZABETH II

Una and the Knight of the Red Crosse

EDMUND SPENSER

The Faerie Queene

DISPOSED INTO TWELVE BOOKES
FASHIONING XII MORALL VERTUES

WITH AN INTRODUCTION BY JOHN HAYWARD
DECORATIONS DRAWN BY JOHN AUSTEN
AND ILLUSTRATIONS ENGRAVED IN WOOD
BY AGNES MILLER PARKER

THE HERITAGE PRESS, NEW YORK: IN THE YEAR
OF THE CORONATION OF QUEEN ELIZABETH II

THE ENTIRE TEXT COMPOSED AND PLATED BY CHARLES BATEY,
PRINTER TO THE UNIVERSITY, OXFORD

INTRODUCTION

IN recent years critics have frequently remarked that the present age is unfavourable to the writing of poetry. Whether this is equally true of the reading of poetry is another matter. But it can be said, I think, without fear of contradiction that the works of our older English poets are seldom read now outside the schools and universities and then only by those who are under some obligation to study what they wrote. In such circumstances an edition of this kind, of a poem which is now generally neglected, yet whose title to greatness has never seriously been questioned since it was first published three hundred and fifty years ago, may fairly be regarded as something more than a mere collector's piece. To reprint *The Faerie Queene* in this form and at this time is to do a service to English poetry; for it is unworthy of so great a poem that it should continue 'in print' only in the mean and unpleasing dress of the student's text-book or as part of its author's 'Collected Works'. Such an edition as this, to which the artist and designer have contributed in their kind no less than the scholar, and which aims at providing an exact and authoritative text in a fitting form, serves to perpetuate the poem in a manner not only appropriate to its importance but sympathetic and, it is to be hoped, alluring to an otherwise reluctant reader.

Edmund Spenser, whom Lamb first labelled 'the poets' poet' at the beginning of the last century, when the poets of the romantic revival in Europe found much of their inspiration in poems like *The Faerie Queene*, might be relabelled today and with scarcely less impropriety 'the scholars' poet'. It is deplorable and yet at the same time significant that when Spenser's grave in Westminster Abbey was disturbed in the summer of 1938 it was not for the purpose of recovering if possible the manuscript elegies which his fellow poets cast into his grave at his funeral, but with the futile and egregious hope of finding among those long-buried verses evidence that Bacon wrote Shakespeare. The pedant, hot for certainties, will lay hands on anything, unaware that in his eagerness to clear things up he may sometimes mar as much as he mends. I believe that part of the disinclination the average reader feels towards *The Faerie Queene* at the present time must be blamed on those commentators whose elaborate interpretations of its moral and political allegory, not to mention their learned glossaries, metrical appendixes, and other aids to study, have made the poem appear far more difficult and unapproachable than in fact it is. I do not wish to imply, however, that *The Faerie Queene* is easy to read or can be easily enjoyed without some practice and perseverance, or that it can be perfectly well understood without the help of some commentary; but I do contend that anyone who is prepared to take a little more trouble over it than he would over an equally long poem in comparatively modern English, like *Paradise Lost*, will be rewarded for his pains with an extraordinary sense of delight and wonder—a form of aesthetic pleasure that is rarely derived from any other poetry but Spenser's and of which he is the supreme begetter, and one, moreover, that has a peculiar value for our own spiritually and emotionally disorientated age.

It is probable that its composition provided Spenser himself with an escape from his own disillusion and discontent with the material world. There is, indeed, much in his life to suggest that he was frustrated in his worldly ambitions, by which, in common with Shakespeare and other poets of his time, he set greater store than by his literary attainments. The latter, it is true, were abundantly acknowledged by his contemporaries; he was immediately recognized as the first poet of his age, as much for his authorship of *The Shepheardes Calender* and other minor poems as of *The Faerie Queene*; he was pensioned by a grateful queen and at his death was buried at Chaucer's side in Westminster Abbey. In the former, however, he considered himself thwarted, much as Swift did a century and a half later.

Yet, by birth, though he claimed kinship with the renowned Spencers of Althorp, Spenser had no reason to expect worldly advancement. He was born in modest circumstances about the year 1552 in East Smithfield, close to the Tower of London. His education, first at the then newly founded school of the Merchant Taylors' Company, of which his father was a 'free journeyman', and later at Pembroke College, Cambridge, where he took his degree of M.A. in 1576, was partly subsidized by charitable grants. During his seven years' residence at the University, lack of money, which prevented him from cutting a figure in the world; indifferent health, which gave him leisure to read deeply in the classics as well as in modern French and Italian literature; and his association with the famous critic Gabriel Harvey, combined to direct his interests into literary channels. An unhappy love affair with an unidentified girl, whom he called Rosalind—a sorrow that was to keep him single until he was well over forty—deepened his love of poetry and prompted him to write on his own account. At that period and in such circumstances the most he could have expected of the future, without the help of a patron, was the decent obscurity of the life of an impecunious scholar or country parson.

Through Harvey's influence, however, Spenser was introduced to Queen Elizabeth's powerful favourite Robert Dudley, Earl of Leicester. This introduction was decisive as far as Spenser's future ambitions were concerned; for on Harvey's recommendation he was taken into Lord Leicester's household to serve, in the first place, as a secretary and courier. In such a position it would be natural for a young man to assume that sooner or later he would be advanced to a more important post. At the same time as his ambition was fired by the prospect of worldly preferment, he aspired, with his patron's encouragement and with the encouragement of his patron's friend Sir Philip Sidney, to write an epic that should outrival the celebrated *Orlando Furioso* and shed on English poetry a lustre even greater than that which Ariosto's poem had over Italian literature. Under such happy, hopeful auspices *The Faerie Queene* was begun at Leicester House in London. In due course Spenser was appointed to a position which, if it did not altogether come up to his expectations, must have seemed to him then to promise still further advancement. In the summer of 1580 he was sent to Ireland as secretary to Lord Grey

de Wilton, the Lord Deputy. With what high hopes he set out
we do not know; but he could not have foreseen, when he landed
in Dublin, that, with the exception of two short visits to England,
he was to be left to languish in Ireland until within a month of his
death nearly twenty years later.

Like Swift in not dissimilar circumstances, Spenser made the
best of a bad job. But he was unhappy and depressed; he disliked
Ireland and never felt any real sympathy for the 'savage nation' in
whose 'civilization' by fire and the sword he was to lend a sadly
insensitive hand; and he remained poor in spite of the purchase or
annexation of real estate. In the autumn of 1598, some four years
after his marriage to Elizabeth Boyle, Kilcolman Castle—part of
his 'share' of the Earl of Desmond's forfeited estates—was burnt
to the ground during Tyrone's rebellion and he was forced to flee
with his wife and four children, leaving behind him, according to
tradition, part of the manuscript of *The Faerie Queene*. He was
sent to London to report, but fell ill on arrival—from undernourish-
ment, according to some accounts, though more probably from
nervous exhaustion—and died in mean lodgings in Westminster
on 16 January 1599.

If Spenser's disappointment and brooding melancholy over the
way he was treated by his superiors had been combined, during
his exile, as Swift's was, with a burning indignation at the tyranny
and oppression of English rule in Ireland, it is possible that he
would have sought compensation, as Swift did, in writing satire
instead of a fairy tale. There is certainly no doubt that Spenser
could write satire when he wanted to; he satirized the Court, for
example, with considerable sting in his *Mother Hubbard's Tale*.
Since, however, he countenanced the conduct of his ruthless and
cruel master Grey in crushing the unfortunate Irish, there was no
occasion for him to answer savagery with satire. Instead, he was
to find consolation for the neglect and injustice of which he considered himself the victim, and solace for the life he was forced
to lead in an unsympathetic land, in the fabulous kingdom of his
'Faerie Queene'.

The remoteness of that fairyland from the real world still invites
the dreamer to forget the present and recall an idealized past. The
novel, it is true, and particularly the historical novel—two forms
of fiction unknown to Spenser's public—long ago displaced the
romantic epics that delighted European readers in the sixteenth
century; and with the tendency of the modern novel towards an
ever greater degree of realism the taste for pure fantasy, whether

in prose or verse, has correspondingly declined. Yet *The Faerie Queene*, notwithstanding the grave difficulties which the evolution of thought and sensibility and literary expression during the last three and a half centuries has created for its readers, still has the power to capture the imagination of those who, by what Coleridge described as 'a willing suspension of disbelief', are prepared to welcome its enchantment.

It would be foolish, none the less, to underestimate those difficulties.

If Spenser's masterpiece is now generally neglected by those who enjoy reading poetry it is because three obstacles, at once formidable and, to modern eyes, almost insuperable, stand in the way of its enjoyment. It is, in the first place, an immensely long work, originally planned to contain twelve 'Books'. *The Faerie Queene*, even in its unfinished state, is still one of the longest poems in modern European literature. The six complete Books and the superb fragment of a seventh, which were all that Spenser appears to have written before his death, account for some 35,000 lines of verse. One is forced to admit, moreover, that the 'Spenserian stanza'[1]—a crowning metrical achievement and purposely invented to give continuity to the poem—is incapable of sustaining the more pedestrian parts of the narrative. A generation that denies itself, in pursuit of communal amusements and activities, leisure for unhurried reading and time for contemplation, may not unreasonably quail before settling down to such a book. To make matters worse, *The Faerie Queene* is not a poem that can be read profitably or even conveniently by bits and pieces. It would not be difficult, indeed, for anyone who knows it well to pick out numerous passages of matchless beauty and ravishing charm; but these must be discovered in their context if their significance is to be properly understood and their poetic value correctly established.

The mere length of a poem, however, should not balk a determined reader. Vast as it is, *The Faerie Queene* might not seem so long, on first acquaintance, if it were not for the unfamiliar allegory with which Spenser points his moral and the archaic language with which he adorns his tale. These are the other two obstacles that confront the inexperienced reader and it must be confessed that they are extremely forbidding. Spenser's poetic diction was considered archaic even by his contemporaries. Ben Jonson, for example, failing to see that Spenser required a

---

[1] The Spenserian stanza consists of eight five-foot iambic lines followed by an iambic line of six feet rhyming a b a b b c b c c.

language remote from ordinary life in order to give an illusion of reality to the fairyland he had created, characteristically trounced it as no language at all. The fact remains, nevertheless, that much of Spenser's vocabulary in general and, in particular, the many new words or new forms he coined, not to mention his antique and capricious spelling, will baffle the unpractised eye and ear. Even so, it is surprising how, as one reads on, this feeling of bewilderment in the face of what seems at first almost a foreign tongue gradually diminishes and how, as one penetrates farther into Spenser's enchanted world, one almost insensibly picks up the meaning and cadence of his verses.

The last obstacle is the most redoubtable. To understand, let alone appreciate, the allegory of *The Faerie Queene* is too much to expect of anyone who has not made a particular study of the subject and who is not acquainted with the works of the allegorists, English, French, and Italian, from the Middle Ages onwards, whom Spenser took for his models. It is not particularly reassuring, for instance, to find that one of his most intelligent friends thought it 'tedious and confused'. Their trouble, like ours, was that the allegorical interpretation of life and conduct was already outmoded in Spenser's lifetime. Bunyan, it is true, was to revive the method, in a simpler form, in his *Pilgrim's Progress*, but its use in imaginative literature had begun to lose its attraction for writer and reader alike before the end of the sixteenth century. It is thus exceedingly difficult now—for most people perhaps impossible— to discover the meaning as well as the purport of the 'allegorical Devises' Spenser employed in his poem and with which, as he ingenuously observed, it is 'cloudily enwrapped'. They were sufficiently abstruse, in fact, to perplex Sir Walter Ralegh, who after reading the first three books was obliged to ask the poet to explain what he was trying to do. Spenser accepted the challenge and in a letter dated 23 January 1589 briefly indicated the aim and scope of *The Faerie Queene*.

'The generall end of all the booke,' he told Ralegh, 'is to fashion a gentleman or noble person in vertuous and gentle discipline.' This, at any rate, was its original intention; and the gentleman or noble person Spenser selected for his purpose was none other than the traditional English hero, King Arthur—or rather Prince Arthur, for, in order to dissociate the central figure of his romance from the familiar Arthur of legend and history, Spenser portrays him as he was or might have been before he became king. In him the reader is to recognize 'the image of a brave knight perfected in the twelve private morall vertues as Aristotle hath devised' and acquiring that perfection in twelve different adventures in each of which one particular moral Vertue was to triumph over its corresponding Vice. These twelve adventures were conceived as taking place during the twelve consecutive days during which Gloriana, the Fairy Queen, kept her Annual Feast, and a separate 'Book' was to be devoted to each; they were to conclude with the obvious climax to so exacting a trial—the marriage of Prince Arthur to the Queen of Fairyland. Unfortunately, as we have seen, Spenser succeeded in completing only six of these 'Books'—the poem, as it stands, recording the triumphs of only six of the twelve virtues: Holiness, Temperance, Chastity, Friendship, Justice, and Courtesy.

If, after the first three adventures (which were originally published separately in 1590), the reader begins to wonder, as Sir Walter Ralegh did, what they are all about and feels, as he did, the need for further elucidation of the general trend of the poem, it will be because Spenser's own analysis of it is far from satisfactory. Where, one may well ask, after reading them, does Prince Arthur come in; what has happened to the Fairy Queen and her festive Court; and who, moreover, are these Knights apparently engaged to do Prince Arthur's work for him? These questions arise for the simple reason that, in its unfinished form, *The Faerie Queene* is no more than an anticipation of the whole poem as Spenser originally planned it.

Unlike the historian, says Spenser, the poet 'thrusteth into the middest' of his tale. Granting himself this poetic licence, he began *The Faerie Queene,* not at the beginning one would expect, with an account of Gloriana's Annual Feast and of Prince Arthur sallying forth on his quest of the twelve virtues, but, without any preamble, without indeed any mention of Arthur or Gloriana, with one of the separate adventures in the course of which each particular virtue was to be acquired. After a time it will slowly dawn upon the reader that Arthur is not going to be personally responsible for acquiring any of them, but will merely appear at suitable moments to prompt and rally others to win them for him, until at last he becomes possessed of them all as it were by proxy. To this end Spenser created twelve Knights or delegates, each of whom was to represent a single virtue and to triumph over his enemies, sometimes with the Prince's moral support but more often without. For his vicarious share in their triumphs Arthur was ultimately to achieve in the twelfth and last 'Book' the highest virtue of all—'Magnificence' or, as we should say, magnanimity, which presupposes the possession of all the rest. Thus, in the six surviving books, the triumph of Holiness is achieved by the Red Cross Knight; of Temperance by Sir Guyon; of Chastity and Friendship by the lady Knight Britomartis (Sir Scudamour finding these two virtues too hard for a man to compass); of Justice by Sir Artegall; and of Courtesy, by which is now meant charity and humility, by Sir Calidore. Since there is apparently little to link together the extraordinary exploits of these champions beyond a common setting in Fairyland, the consequence of opening the poem with a detached episode, and continuing it with others in which completely different sets of characters appear, is extremely puzzling and prompts the ironical wish that Spenser had adapted to his fanciful end not only Aristotle's 'private morall vertues' but also Aristotle's view that a plot should have a beginning, a middle, and an end.

The elaborate ethical design of *The Faerie Queene* is further complicated by the introduction of an historical allegory. The scene is not only Fairyland but England as well, and not the legendary Britaine of Arthurian romance but the England of Queen Elizabeth and Leicester. Doubtless to Spenser's contemporaries it was amusing to be able to identify living persons in the characters of the poem; to recognize in Gloriana 'the most excellent and glorious person' of Elizabeth herself, in Sir Calidore an idealized portrait of Spenser's great and best-loved friend Sir Philip Sidney, in Sir Artegall Lord Grey de Wilton and in Prince Arthur, possibly, the Earl of Leicester. But to a modern reader it is a barren and tedious game which may safely be left for the pedants to play. As for the purely fictitious digressions from the main theme of each book, which are so numerous and often so involved that, in the third, fourth, and fifth books in particular, they coalesce into an almost inextricable tangle of wildly improbable stories, the modern reader to whom allegory, whether moral or historical, is distasteful will find in them, on the contrary, a recurrent source of entertainment and delight. No English poet and few foreign ones, besides Spenser's master Ariosto, have possessed so prodigiously fertile a gift of fantastic invention or a greater power of holding a reader spellbound. Indeed, under the hypnotic influence of the spell induced by Spenser's fabulous happenings and his perpetually changing and dissolving surrealist imagery; in the presence of his enchanted castles, magic wells, grotesque apparitions, fearful giants, bewitched trees, and horrible dragons; in a world where, as in a dream, there is no change of seasons and all sense of duration in time is lost, it is easy enough to forget his moral intention with its cumbrous allegorical cloak and to cease wondering if there is a plot or what, if anything, will happen in the end.

Very few people, I imagine, after waking from the long dream of *The Faerie Queene*, would dispute Saintsbury's contention 'that the accessories of Spenser's scheme have become of more importance in poetical appeal than those things which to him were perhaps the chief'. Yet it cannot be denied, I think, that interest and delight even in them flags from time to time. For there is no humour or irony, as there is in Ariosto, to relieve the high seriousness of Spenser's romantic epic; nor, for all his delicate and subtle observation of womanhood, is it possible to feel any real concern for his characters. Further, the smooth and languorous flow of the Spenserian stanza, running on from canto to canto, through Book after Book, though it moves forward with the dignity and inexorability of a great river tends, as one is carried along upon its placid surface, to become monotonous.

I have not attempted to conceal the difficulties which the inexperienced reader must face if he intends to read *The Faerie Queene* and is not merely content to leave his copy unopened on the shelf between Chaucer and Milton. It is better, I believe, that he should realize what they are and so perhaps be tempted to defy them, rather than that he should simply assume that *The Faerie Queene* is one of those great works, like *The Canterbury Tales* and *Paradise Lost*, which are known, by common consent, only by repute. I believe, moreover, even if Lord Macaulay was justified in generalizing from his own experience and maintaining that 'very few and very weary' are those who ever reach the end of the poem, that the 'very few' who do will not regret the labour or the time spent. For Spenser's fairyland is a sanctuary from the contentious world of the present, and the lulling harmony of his verse a sovereign remedy for the nervous strain of modern life.

JOHN HAYWARD

CONTENTS

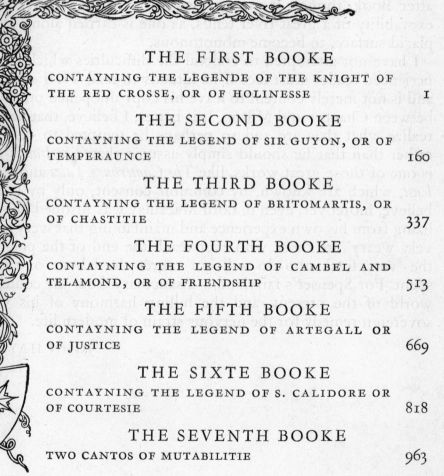

ILLUSTRATIONS

The sign † at I. iii. 32, I. viii. 44, and II. ii. 44
indicates that the 1596 edition has been followed
without emendation

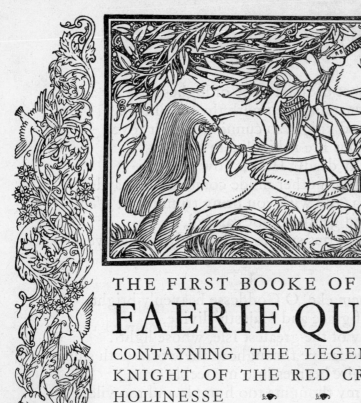

THE FIRST BOOKE OF THE
FAERIE QUEENE
CONTAYNING THE LEGENDE OF THE KNIGHT OF THE RED CROSSE, OR OF HOLINESSE

I

L O I the man, whose Muse whilome did maske,
As time her taught, in lowly Shepheards weeds;
Am now enforst a far unfitter taske,
For trumpets sterne to chaunge mine Oaten reeds,
And sing of Knights and Ladies gentle deeds;
Whose prayses having slept in silence long,
Me, all too meane, the sacred Muse areeds
To blazon broad emongst her learned throng:
Fierce warres and faithfull loves shall moralize my song.

2

Helpe then, O holy Virgin chiefe of nine,
Thy weaker Novice to performe thy will,
Lay forth out of thine everlasting scryne
The antique rolles, which there lye hidden still,
Of Faerie knights and fairest *Tanaquill*,
Whom that most noble Briton Prince so long
Sought through the world, and suffered so much ill,
That I must rue his undeserved wrong:
O helpe thou my weake wit, and sharpen my dull tong.

3

And thou most dreaded impe of highest *Jove*,
　Faire *Venus* sonne, that with thy cruell dart
At that good knight so cunningly didst rove,
　That glorious fire it kindled in his hart,
　Lay now thy deadly Heben bow apart,
And with thy mother milde come to mine ayde:
　Come both, and with you bring triumphant *Mart*,
　In loves and gentle jollities arrayd,
After his murdrous spoiles and bloudy rage allayd.

4

And with them eke, O Goddesse heavenly bright,
　Mirrour of grace and Majestie divine,
Great Lady of the greatest Isle, whose light
　Like *Phœbus* lampe throughout the world doth shine,
　Shed thy faire beames into my feeble eyne,
And raise my thoughts too humble and too vile,
　To thinke of that true glorious type of thine,
　The argument of mine afflicted stile:
The which to heare, vouchsafe, O dearest dred a-while.

CANTO I

The Patron of true Holinesse,
Foule Errour doth defeate:
Hypocrisie him to entrappe,
Doth to his home entreate.

I

A GENTLE Knight was pricking on the plaine,
　Y cladd in mightie armes and silver shielde,
Wherein old dints of deepe wounds did remaine,
　The cruell markes of many' a bloudy fielde;
　Yet armes till that time did he never wield:
His angry steede did chide his foming bitt,
　As much disdayning to the curbe to yield:
　Full jolly knight he seemd, and faire did sitt,
As one for knightly giusts and fierce encounters fitt.

2

But on his brest a bloudie Crosse he bore,
  The deare remembrance of his dying Lord,
  For whose sweete sake that glorious badge he wore,
  And dead as living ever him ador'd:
  Upon his shield the like was also scor'd,
  For soveraine hope, which in his helpe he had:
  Right faithfull true he was in deede and word,
  But of his cheere did seeme too solemne sad;
Yet nothing did he dread, but ever was ydrad.

3

Upon a great adventure he was bond,
  That greatest *Gloriana* to him gave,
  That greatest Glorious Queene of *Faerie* lond,
  To winne him worship, and her grace to have,
  Which of all earthly things he most did crave;
  And ever as he rode, his hart did earne
  To prove his puissance in battell brave
  Upon his foe, and his new force to learne;
Upon his foe, a Dragon horrible and stearne.

4

A lovely Ladie rode him faire beside,
  Upon a lowly Asse more white than snow,
  Yet she much whiter, but the same did hide
  Under a vele, that wimpled was full low,
  And over all a blacke stole she did throw,
  As one that inly mournd: so was she sad,
  And heavie sat upon her palfrey slow:
  Seemed in heart some hidden care she had,
And by her in a line a milke white lambe she lad.

5

So pure an innocent, as that same lambe,
  She was in life and every vertuous lore,
  And by descent from Royall lynage came
  Of ancient Kings and Queenes, that had of yore
  Their scepters stretcht from East to Westerne shore,
  And all the world in their subjection held;
  Till that infernall feend with foule uprore
  Forwasted all their land, and them expeld:
Whom to avenge, she had this Knight from far compeld.

6

Behind her farre away a Dwarfe did lag,
  That lasie seemd in being ever last,
  Or wearied with bearing of her bag
  Of needments at his backe. Thus as they past,
  The day with cloudes was suddeine overcast,
  And angry *Jove* an hideous storme of raine
  Did poure into his Lemans lap so fast,
  That every wight to shrowd it did constrain,
And this faire couple eke to shroud themselves were fain.

7

Enforst to seeke some covert nigh at hand,
  A shadie grove not far away they spide,
  That promist ayde the tempest to withstand:
  Whose loftie trees yclad with sommers pride,
  Did spred so broad, that heavens light did hide,
  Not perceable with power of any starre:
  And all within were pathes and alleies wide,
  With footing worne, and leading inward farre:
Faire harbour that them seemes; so in they entred arre.

8

And foorth they passe, with pleasure forward led,
  Joying to heare the birdes sweete harmony,
  Which therein shrouded from the tempest dred,
  Seemd in their song to scorne the cruell sky.
  Much can they prayse the trees so straight and hy,
  The sayling Pine, the Cedar proud and tall,
  The vine-prop Elme, the Poplar never dry,
  The builder Oake, sole king of forrests all,
The Aspine good for staves, the Cypresse funerall.

9

The Laurell, meed of mightie Conquerours
  And Poets sage, the Firre that weepeth still,
  The Willow worne of forlorne Paramours,
  The Eugh obedient to the benders will,
  The Birch for shaftes, the Sallow for the mill,
  The Mirrhe sweete bleeding in the bitter wound,
  The warlike Beech, the Ash for nothing ill,
  The fruitfull Olive, and the Platane round,
The carver Holme, the Maple seeldom inward sound.

10

Led with delight, they thus beguile the way,
  Untill the blustring storme is overblowne;
  When weening to returne, whence they did stray,
  They cannot finde that path, which first was showne,
  But wander too and fro in wayes unknowne,
  Furthest from end then, when they neerest weene,
  That makes them doubt, their wits be not their owne:
  So many pathes, so many turnings seene,
That which of them to take, in diverse doubt they been.

11

At last resolving forward still to fare,
  Till that some end they finde or in or out,
  That path they take, that beaten seemd most bare,
  And like to lead the labyrinth about;
  Which when by tract they hunted had throughout,
  At length it brought them to a hollow cave,
  Amid the thickest woods. The Champion stout
  Eftsoones dismounted from his courser brave,
And to the Dwarfe a while his needlesse spere he gave.

12

Be well aware, quoth then that Ladie milde,
  Least suddaine mischiefe ye too rash provoke:
  The danger hid, the place unknowne and wilde,
  Breedes dreadfull doubts: Oft fire is without smoke,
  And perill without show: therefore your stroke
  Sir knight with-hold, till further triall made.
  Ah Ladie (said he) shame were to revoke
  The forward footing for an hidden shade:
Vertue gives her selfe light, through darkenesse for to wade.

13

Yea but (quoth she) the perill of this place
  I better wot than you, though now too late
  To wish you backe returne with foule disgrace,
  Yet wisedome warnes, whilest foot is in the gate,
  To stay the steppe, ere forced to retrate.
  This is the wandring wood, this *Errours den*,
  A monster vile, whom God and man does hate:
  Therefore I read beware. Fly fly (quoth then
The fearefull Dwarfe:) this is no place for living men.

14

But full of fire and greedy hardiment,
  The youthfull knight could not for ought be staide,
  But forth unto the darksome hole he went,
  And looked in: his glistring armor made
  A litle glooming light, much like a shade,
  By which he saw the ugly monster plaine,
  Halfe like a serpent horribly displaide,
  But th'other halfe did womans shape retaine,
Most lothsom, filthie, foule, and full of vile disdaine.

15

And as she lay upon the durtie ground,
  Her huge long taile her den all overspred,
  Yet was in knots and many boughtes upwound,
  Pointed with mortall sting. Of her there bred
  A thousand yong ones, which she dayly fed,
  Sucking upon her poisonous dugs, eachone
  Of sundry shapes, yet all ill favored:
  Soone as that uncouth light upon them shone,
Into her mouth they crept, and suddain all were gone.

16

Their dam upstart, out of her den effraide,
  And rushed forth, hurling her hideous taile
  About her cursed head, whose folds displaid
  Were stretcht now forth at length without entraile.
  She lookt about, and seeing one in mayle
  Armed to point, sought backe to turne againe;
  For light she hated as the deadly bale,
  Ay wont in desert darknesse to remaine,
Where plaine none might her see, nor she see any plaine.

17

Which when the valiant Elfe perceiv'd, he lept
  As Lyon fierce upon the flying pray,
  And with his trenchand blade her boldly kept
  From turning backe, and forced her to stay:
  Therewith enrag'd she loudly gan to bray,
  And turning fierce, her speckled taile advaunst,
  Threatning her angry sting, him to dismay:
  Who nought aghast, his mightie hand enhaunst:
The stroke down from her head unto her shoulder glaunst.

18

Much daunted with that dint, her sence was dazd,
  Yet kindling rage, her selfe she gathered round,
  And all attonce her beastly body raizd
  With doubled forces high above the ground:
  Tho wrapping up her wrethed sterne arownd,
  Lept fierce upon his shield, and her huge traine
  All suddenly about his body wound,
  That hand or foot to stirre he strove in vaine:
God helpe the man so wrapt in *Errours* endlesse traine.

19

His Lady sad to see his sore constraint,
  Cride out, Now now Sir knight, shew what ye bee,
  Add faith unto your force, and be not faint:
  Strangle her, else she sure will strangle thee.
  That when he heard, in great perplexitie,
  His gall did grate for griefe and high disdaine,
  And knitting all his force got one hand free,
  Wherewith he grypt her gorge with so great paine,
That soone to loose her wicked bands did her constraine.

20

Therewith she spewd out of her filthy maw
  A floud of poyson horrible and blacke,
  Full of great lumpes of flesh and gobbets raw,
  Which stunck so vildly, that it forst him slacke
  His grasping hold, and from her turne him backe:
  Her vomit full of bookes and papers was,
  With loathly frogs and toades, which eyes did lacke,
  And creeping sought way in the weedy gras:
Her filthy parbreake all the place defiled has.

21

As when old father *Nilus* gins to swell
  With timely pride above the *Aegyptian* vale,
  His fattie waves do fertile slime outwell,
  And overflow each plaine and lowly dale:
  But when his later spring gins to avale,
  Huge heapes of mudd he leaves, wherein there breed
  Ten thousand kindes of creatures, partly male
  And partly female of his fruitfull seed;
Such ugly monstrous shapes elswhere may no man reed.

22

The same so sore annoyed has the knight,
    That welnigh choked with the deadly stinke,
    His forces faile, ne can no longer fight.
    Whose corage when the feend perceiv'd to shrinke,
    She poured forth out of her hellish sinke
    Her fruitfull cursed spawne of serpents small,
    Deformed monsters, fowle, and blacke as inke,
    Which swarming all about his legs did crall,
And him encombred sore, but could not hurt at all.

23

As gentle Shepheard in sweete even-tide,
    When ruddy *Phœbus* gins to welke in west,
    High on an hill, his flocke to vewen wide,
    Markes which do byte their hasty supper best;
    A cloud of combrous gnattes do him molest,
    All striving to infixe their feeble stings,
    That from their noyance he no where can rest,
    But with his clownish hands their tender wings
He brusheth oft, and oft doth mar their murmurings.

24

Thus ill bestedd, and fearefull more of shame,
    Than of the certaine perill he stood in,
    Halfe furious unto his foe he came,
    Resolv'd in minde all suddenly to win,
    Or soone to lose, before he once would lin;
    And strooke at her with more than manly force,
    That from her body full of filthie sin
    He raft her hatefull head without remorse;
A streame of cole black bloud forth gushed from her corse.

25

Her scattred brood, soone as their Parent deare
    They saw so rudely falling to the ground,
    Groning full deadly, all with troublous feare,
    Gathred themselves about her body round,
    Weening their wonted entrance to have found
    At her wide mouth: but being there withstood
    They flocked all about her bleeding wound,
    And sucked up their dying mothers blood,
Making her death their life, and eke her hurt their good.

26

That detestable sight him much amazde,
　To see th'unkindly Impes of heaven accurst,
　Devoure their dam; on whom while so he gazd,
　Having all satisfide their bloudy thurst,
　Their bellies swolne he saw with fulnesse burst,
　And bowels gushing forth: well worthy end
　Of such as drunke her life, the which them nurst;
　Now needeth him no lenger labour spend,
His foes have slaine themselves, with whom he should contend.

27

His Ladie seeing all, that chaunst, from farre
　Approcht in hast to greet his victorie,
　And said, Faire knight, borne under happy starre,
　Who see your vanquisht foes before you lye;
　Well worthy be you of that Armorie,
　Wherein ye have great glory wonne this day,
　And proov'd your strength on a strong enimie,
　Your first adventure: many such I pray,
And henceforth ever wish, that like succeed it may.

28

Then mounted he upon his Steede againe,
　And with the Lady backward sought to wend;
　That path he kept, which beaten was most plaine,
　Ne ever would to any by-way bend,
　But still did follow one unto the end,
　The which at last out of the wood them brought.
　So forward on his way (with God to frend)
　He passed forth, and new adventure sought;
Long way he travelled, before he heard of ought.

29

At length they chaunst to meet upon the way
　An aged Sire, in long blacke weedes yclad,
　His feete all bare, his beard all hoarie gray,
　And by his belt his booke he hanging had;
　Sober he seemde, and very sagely sad,
　And to the ground his eyes were lowly bent,
　Simple in shew, and voyde of malice bad,
　And all the way he prayed, as he went,
And often knockt his brest, as one that did repent.

30

He faire the knight saluted, louting low,
  Who faire him quited, as that courteous was:
  And after asked him, if he did know
  Of straunge adventures, which abroad did pas.
  Ah my deare Sonne (quoth he) how should, alas,
  Silly old man, that lives in hidden cell,
  Bidding his beades all day for his trespas,
  Tydings of warre and worldly trouble tell?
With holy father sits not with such things to mell.

31

But if of daunger which hereby doth dwell,
  And homebred evill ye desire to heare,
  Of a straunge man I can you tidings tell,
  That wasteth all this countrey farre and neare.
  Of such (said he) I chiefly do inquere,
  And shall you well reward to shew the place,
  In which that wicked wight his dayes doth weare:
  For to all knighthood it is foule disgrace,
That such a cursed creature lives so long a space.

32

Far hence (quoth he) in wastfull wildernesse
  His dwelling is, by which no living wight
  May ever passe, but thorough great distresse.
  Now (sayd the Lady) draweth toward night,
  And well I wote, that of your later fight
  Ye all forwearied be: for what so strong,
  But wanting rest will also want of might?
  The Sunne that measures heaven all day long,
At night doth baite his steedes the *Ocean* waves emong.

33

Then with the Sunne take Sir, your timely rest,
  And with new day new worke at once begin:
  Untroubled night they say gives counsell best.
  Right well Sir knight ye have advised bin,
  (Quoth then that aged man;) the way to win
  Is wisely to advise: now day is spent;
  Therefore with me ye may take up your In
  For this same night. The knight was well content:
So with that godly father to his home they went.

34

A little lowly Hermitage it was,
  Downe in a dale, hard by a forests side,
  Far from resort of people, that did pas
  In travell to and froe: a little wyde
  There was an holy Chappell edifyde,
  Wherein the Hermite dewly wont to say
  His holy things each morne and eventyde:
  Thereby a Christall streame did gently play,
Which from a sacred fountaine welled forth alway.

35

Arrived there, the little house they fill,
  Ne looke for entertainement, where none was:
  Rest is their feast, and all things at their will;
  The noblest mind the best contentment has.
  With faire discourse the evening so they pas:
  For that old man of pleasing wordes had store,
  And well could file his tongue as smooth as glas;
  He told of Saintes and Popes, and evermore
He strowd an *Ave-Mary* after and before.

36

The drouping Night thus creepeth on them fast,
  And the sad humour loading their eye liddes,
  As messenger of *Morpheus* on them cast
  Sweet slombring deaw, the which to sleepe them biddes.
  Unto their lodgings then his guestes he riddes:
  Where when all drownd in deadly sleepe he findes,
  He to his study goes, and there amiddes
  His Magick bookes and artes of sundry kindes,
He seekes out mighty charmes, to trouble sleepy mindes.

37

Then choosing out few wordes most horrible,
  (Let none them read) thereof did verses frame,
  With which and other spelles like terrible,
  He bad awake blacke *Plutoes* griesly Dame,
  And cursed heaven, and spake reprochfull shame
  Of highest God, the Lord of life and light;
  A bold bad man, that dar'd to call by name
  Great *Gorgon*, Prince of darknesse and dead night,
At which *Cocytus* quakes, and *Styx* is put to flight.

38

And forth he cald out of deepe darknesse dred
  Legions of Sprights, the which like little flyes
  Fluttring about his ever damned hed,
  A-waite whereto their service he applyes,
  To aide his friends, or fray his enimies:
  Of those he chose out two, the falsest twoo,
  And fittest for to forge true-seeming lyes;
  The one of them he gave a message too,
The other by him selfe staide other worke to doo.

39

He making speedy way through spersed ayre,
  And through the world of waters wide and deepe,
  To *Morpheus* house doth hastily repaire.
  Amid the bowels of the earth full steepe,
  And low, where dawning day doth never peepe,
  His dwelling is; there *Tethys* his wet bed
  Doth ever wash, and *Cynthia* still doth steepe
  In silver deaw his ever-drouping hed,
Whiles sad Night over him her mantle black doth spred.

40

Whose double gates he findeth locked fast,
  The one faire fram'd of burnisht Yvory,
  The other all with silver overcast;
  And wakefull dogges before them farre do lye,
  Watching to banish Care their enimy,
  Who oft is wont to trouble gentle Sleepe.
  By them the Sprite doth passe in quietly,
  And unto *Morpheus* comes, whom drowned deepe
In drowsie fit he findes: of nothing he takes keepe.

41

And more, to lulle him in his slumber soft,
  A trickling streame from high rocke tumbling downe
  And ever-drizling raine upon the loft,
  Mixt with a murmuring winde, much like the sowne
  Of swarming Bees, did cast him in a swowne:
  No other noyse, nor peoples troublous cryes,
  As still are wont t'annoy the walled towne,
  Might there be heard: but carelesse Quiet lyes,
Wrapt in eternall silence farre from enemyes.

42

The messenger approching to him spake,
    But his wast wordes returnd to him in vaine:
    So sound he slept, that nought mought him awake.
    Then rudely he him thrust, and pusht with paine,
    Whereat he gan to stretch: but he againe
    Shooke him so hard, that forced him to speake.
    As one then in a dreame, whose dryer braine
    Is tost with troubled sights and fancies weake,
He mumbled soft, but would not all his silence breake.

43

The Sprite then gan more boldly him to wake,
    And threatned unto him the dreaded name
    Of *Hecate*: whereat he gan to quake,
    And lifting up his lumpish head, with blame
    Halfe angry asked him, for what he came.
    Hither (quoth he) me *Archimago* sent,
    He that the stubborne Sprites can wisely tame,
    He bids thee to him send for his intent
A fit false dreame, that can delude the sleepers sent.

44

The God obayde, and calling forth straight way
    A diverse dreame out of his prison darke,
    Delivered it to him, and downe did lay
    His heavie head, devoide of carefull carke,
    Whose sences all were straight benumbd and starke.
    He backe returning by the Yvorie dore,
    Remounted up as light as chearefull Larke,
    And on his litle winges the dreame he bore
In hast unto his Lord, where he him left afore.

45

Who all this while with charmes and hidden artes,
    Had made a Lady of that other Spright,
    And fram'd of liquid ayre her tender partes
    So lively, and so like in all mens sight,
    That weaker sence it could have ravisht quight:
    The maker selfe for all his wondrous witt,
    Was nigh beguiled with so goodly sight:
    Her all in white he clad, and over it
Cast a blacke stole, most like to seeme for *Una* fit.

46

Now when that ydle dreame was to him brought,
    Unto that Elfin knight he bad him fly,
    Where he slept soundly void of evill thought,
    And with false shewes abuse his fantasy,
    In sort as he him schooled privily:
    And that new creature borne without her dew,
    Full of the makers guile, with usage sly
    He taught to imitate that Lady trew,
Whose semblance she did carrie under feigned hew.

47

Thus well instructed, to their worke they hast,
    And comming where the knight in slomber lay,
    The one upon his hardy head him plast,
    And made him dreame of loves and lustfull play,
    That nigh his manly hart did melt away,
    Bathed in wanton blis and wicked joy:
    Then seemed him his Lady by him lay,
    And to him playnd, how that false winged boy
Her chast hart had subdewd, to learne Dame pleasures toy.

48

And she her selfe of beautie soveraigne Queene,
    Faire *Venus* seemde unto his bed to bring
    Her, whom he waking evermore did weene
    To be the chastest flowre, that ay did spring
    On earthly braunch, the daughter of a king,
    Now a loose Leman to vile service bound:
    And eke the *Graces* seemed all to sing,
    Hymen ιὸ Hymen, dauncing all around,
Whilst freshest *Flora* her with Yvie girlond crownd.

49

In this great passion of unwonted lust,
    Or wonted feare of doing ought amis,
    He started up, as seeming to mistrust
    Some secret ill, or hidden foe of his:
    Lo there before his face his Lady is,
    Under blake stole hyding her bayted hooke,
    And as halfe blushing offred him to kis,
    With gentle blandishment and lovely looke,
Most like that virgin true, which for her knight him took.

50

All cleane dismayd to see so uncouth sight,
    And halfe enraged at her shamelesse guise,
    He thought have slaine her in his fierce despight:
    But hasty heat tempring with sufferance wise,
    He stayde his hand, and gan himselfe advise
    To prove his sense, and tempt her faigned truth.
    Wringing her hands in wemens pitteous wise,
    Tho can she weepe, to stirre up gentle ruth,
Both for her noble bloud, and for her tender youth.

51

And said, Ah Sir, my liege Lord and my love,
    Shall I accuse the hidden cruell fate,
    And mightie causes wrought in heaven above,
    Or the blind God, that doth me thus amate,
    For hoped love to winne me certaine hate?
    Yet thus perforce he bids me do, or die.
    Die is my dew: yet rew my wretched state
    You, whom my hard avenging destinie
Hath made judge of my life or death indifferently.

52

Your owne deare sake forst me at first to leave
    My Fathers kingdome, There she stopt with teares;
    Her swollen hart her speach seemd to bereave,
    And then againe begun, My weaker yeares
    Captiv'd to fortune and frayle worldly feares,
    Fly to your faith for succour and sure ayde:
    Let me not dye in languor and long teares.
    Why Dame (quoth he) what hath ye thus dismayd?
What frayes ye, that were wont to comfort me affrayd?

53

Love of your selfe, she said, and deare constraint
    Lets me not sleepe, but wast the wearie night
    In secret anguish and unpittied plaint,
    Whiles you in carelesse sleepe are drowned quight.
    Her doubtfull words made that redoubted knight
    Suspect her truth: yet since no' untruth he knew,
    Her fawning love with foule disdainefull spight
    He would not shend, but said, Deare dame I rew,
That for my sake unknowne such griefe unto you grew.

54

Assure your selfe, it fell not all to ground;
  For all so deare as life is to my hart,
  I deeme your love, and hold me to you bound;
  Ne let vaine feares procure your needlesse smart,
  Where cause is none, but to your rest depart.
  Not all content, yet seemd she to appease
  Her mournefull plaintes, beguiled of her art,
  And fed with words, that could not chuse but please,
So slyding softly forth, she turnd as to her ease.

55

Long after lay he musing at her mood,
  Much griev'd to thinke that gentle Dame so light,
  For whose defence he was to shed his blood.
  At last dull wearinesse of former fight
  Having yrockt a sleepe his irkesome spright,
  That troublous dreame gan freshly tosse his braine,
  With bowres, and beds, and Ladies deare delight:
  But when he saw his labour all was vaine,
With that misformed spright he backe returnd againe.

CANT. II

The guilefull great Enchaunter parts
The Redcrosse Knight from Truth:
Into whose stead faire falshood steps,
And workes him wofull ruth.

I

BY this the Northerne wagoner had set
  His sevenfold teme behind the stedfast starre,
  That was in Ocean waves yet never wet,
  But firme is fixt, and sendeth light from farre
  To all, that in the wide deepe wandring arre:
  And chearefull Chaunticlere with his note shrill
  Had warned once, that *Phœbus* fiery carre
  In hast was climbing up the Easterne hill,
Full envious that night so long his roome did fill.

2

When those accursed messengers of hell,
 That feigning dreame, and that faire-forged Spright
 Came to their wicked maister, and gan tell
 Their bootelesse paines, and ill succeeding night:
 Who all in rage to see his skilfull might
 Deluded so, gan threaten hellish paine
 And sad *Proserpines* wrath, them to affright.
 But when he saw his threatning was but vaine,
He cast about, and searcht his balefull bookes againe.

3

Eftsoones he tooke that miscreated faire,
 And that false other Spright, on whom he spred
 A seeming body of the subtile aire,
 Like a young Squire, in loves and lusty-hed
 His wanton dayes that ever loosely led,
 Without regard of armes and dreaded fight:
 Those two he tooke, and in a secret bed,
 Covered with darknesse and misdeeming night,
Them both together laid, to joy in vaine delight.

4

Forthwith he runnes with feigned faithfull hast
 Unto his guest, who after troublous sights
 And dreames, gan now to take more sound repast,
 Whom suddenly he wakes with fearefull frights,
 As one aghast with feends or damned sprights,
 And to him cals, Rise rise unhappy Swaine,
 That here wex old in sleepe, whiles wicked wights
 Have knit themselves in *Venus* shamefull chaine;
Come see, where your false Lady doth her honour staine.

5

All in amaze he suddenly up start
 With sword in hand, and with the old man went;
 Who soone him brought into a secret part,
 Where that false couple were full closely ment
 In wanton lust and lewd embracement:
 Which when he saw, he burnt with gealous fire,
 The eye of reason was with rage yblent,
 And would have slaine them in his furious ire,
But hardly was restreined of that aged sire.

6

Returning to his bed in torment great,
  And bitter anguish of his guiltie sight,
  He could not rest, but did his stout heart eat,
  And wast his inward gall with deepe despight,
  Yrksome of life, and too long lingring night.
  At last faire *Hesperus* in highest skie
  Had spent his lampe, and brought forth dawning light.
  Then up he rose, and clad him hastily;
The Dwarfe him brought his steed: so both away do fly.

7

Now when the rosy-fingred Morning faire,
  Weary of aged *Tithones* saffron bed,
  Had spred her purple robe through deawy aire,
  And the high hils *Titan* discovered,
  The royall virgin shooke off drowsy-hed,
  And rising forth out of her baser bowre,
  Lookt for her knight, who far away was fled,
  And for her Dwarfe, that wont to wait each houre;
Then gan she waile and weepe, to see that woefull stowre.

8

And after him she rode with so much speede
  As her slow beast could make; but all in vaine:
  For him so far had borne his light-foot steede,
  Pricked with wrath and fiery fierce disdaine,
  That him to follow was but fruitlesse paine;
  Yet she her weary limbes would never rest,
  But every hill and dale, each wood and plaine
  Did search, sore grieved in her gentle brest,
He so ungently left her, whom she loved best.

9

But subtill *Archimago*, when his guests
  He saw divided into double parts,
  And *Una* wandring in woods and forrests,
  Th'end of his drift, he praisd his divelish arts,
  That had such might over true meaning harts;
  Yet rests not so, but other meanes doth make,
  How he may worke unto her further smarts:
  For her he hated as the hissing snake,
And in her many troubles did most pleasure take.

Prince Arthur guided by the Dwarfe

10

He then devisde himselfe how to disguise;
  For by his mightie science he could take
  As many formes and shapes in seeming wise,
  As ever *Proteus* to himselfe could make:
  Sometime a fowle, sometime a fish in lake,
  Now like a foxe, now like a dragon fell,
  That of himselfe he oft for feare would quake,
  And oft would flie away. O who can tell
The hidden power of herbes, and might of Magicke spell?

11

But now seemde best, the person to put on
  Of that good knight, his late beguiled guest:
  In mighty armes he was yclad anon,
  And silver shield: upon his coward brest
  A bloudy crosse, and on his craven crest
  A bounch of haires discolourd diversly:
  Full jolly knight he seemde, and well addrest,
  And when he sate upon his courser free,
Saint George himself ye would have deemed him to be.

12

But he the knight, whose semblaunt he did beare,
  The true *Saint George* was wandred far away,
  Still flying from his thoughts and gealous feare;
  Will was his guide, and griefe led him astray.
  At last him chaunst to meete upon the way
  A faithlesse Sarazin all arm'd to point,
  In whose great shield was writ with letters gay
  Sans foy: full large of limbe and every joint
He was, and cared not for God or man a point.

13

He had a faire companion of his way,
  A goodly Lady clad in scarlot red,
  Purfled with gold and pearle of rich assay,
  And like a *Persian* mitre on her hed
  She wore, with crownes and owches garnished,
  The which her lavish lovers to her gave;
  Her wanton palfrey all was overspred
  With tinsell trappings, woven like a wave,
Whose bridle rung with golden bels and bosses brave.

14

With faire disport and courting dalliaunce
 She intertainde her lover all the way:
 But when she saw the knight his speare advaunce,
 She soone left off her mirth and wanton play,
 And bad her knight addresse him to the fray:
 His foe was nigh at hand. He prickt with pride
 And hope to winne his Ladies heart that day,
 Forth spurred fast: adowne his coursers side
The red bloud trickling staind the way, as he did ride.

15

The knight of the *Redcrosse* when him he spide,
 Spurring so hote with rage dispiteous,
 Gan fairely couch his speare, and towards ride:
 Soone meete they both, both fell and furious,
 That daunted with their forces hideous,
 Their steeds do stagger, and amazed stand,
 And eke themselves too rudely rigorous,
 Astonied with the stroke of their owne hand,
Do backe rebut, and each to other yeeldeth land.

16

As when two rams stird with ambitious pride,
 Fight for the rule of the rich fleeced flocke,
 Their horned fronts so fierce on either side
 Do meete, that with the terrour of the shocke
 Astonied both, stand sencelesse as a blocke,
 Forgetfull of the hanging victory:
 So stood these twaine, unmoved as a rocke,
 Both staring fierce, and holding idely
The broken reliques of their former cruelty.

17

The *Sarazin* sore daunted with the buffe
 Snatcheth his sword, and fiercely to him flies;
 Who well it wards, and quyteth cuff with cuff:
 Each others equall puissaunce envies,
 And through their iron sides with cruell spies
 Does seeke to perce: repining courage yields
 No foote to foe. The flashing fier flies
 As from a forge out of their burning shields,
And streames of purple bloud new dies the verdant fields.

18

Curse on that Crosse (quoth then the *Sarazin*)
  That keepes thy body from the bitter fit;
  Dead long ygoe I wote thou haddest bin,
  Had not that charme from thee forwarned it:
  But yet I warne thee now assured sitt,
  And hide thy head. Therewith upon his crest
  With rigour so outrageous he smitt,
  That a large share it hewd out of the rest,
And glauncing downe his shield, from blame him fairely blest.

19

Who thereat wondrous wroth, the sleeping spark
  Of native vertue gan eftsoones revive,
  And at his haughtie helmet making mark,
  So hugely stroke, that it the steele did rive,
  And cleft his head. He tumbling downe alive,
  With bloudy mouth his mother earth did kis,
  Greeting his grave: his grudging ghost did strive
  With the fraile flesh; at last it flitted is,
Whither the soules do fly of men, that live amis.

20

The Lady when she saw her champion fall,
  Like the old ruines of a broken towre,
  Staid not to waile his woefull funerall,
  But from him fled away with all her powre;
  Who after her as hastily gan scowre,
  Bidding the Dwarfe with him to bring away
  The *Sarazins* shield, signe of the conqueroure.
  Her soone he overtooke, and bad to stay,
For present cause was none of dread her to dismay.

21

She turning backe with ruefull countenaunce,
  Cride, Mercy mercy Sir vouchsafe to show
  On silly Dame, subject to hard mischaunce,
  And to your mighty will. Her humblesse low
  In so ritch weedes and seeming glorious show,
  Did much emmove his stout heroïcke heart,
  And said, Deare dame, your suddein overthrow
  Much rueth me; but now put feare apart,
And tell, both who ye be, and who that tooke your part.

22

Melting in teares, then gan she thus lament;
  The wretched woman, whom unhappy howre
  Hath now made thrall to your commandement,
  Before that angry heavens list to lowre,
  And fortune false betraide me to your powre
  Was, (O what now availeth that I was!)
  Borne the sole daughter of an Emperour,
  He that the wide West under his rule has,
And high hath set his throne, where *Tiberis* doth pas.

23

He in the first flowre of my freshest age,
  Betrothed me unto the onely haire
  Of a most mighty king, most rich and sage;
  Was never Prince so faithfull and so faire,
  Was never Prince so meeke and debonaire;
  But ere my hoped day of spousall shone,
  My dearest Lord fell from high honours staire,
  Into the hands of his accursed fone,
And cruelly was slaine, that shall I ever mone.

24

His blessed body spoild of lively breath,
  Was afterward, I know not how, convaid
  And fro me hid: of whose most innocent death
  When tidings came to me unhappy maid,
  O how great sorrow my sad soule assaid.
  Then forth I went his woefull corse to find,
  And many yeares throughout the world I straid,
  A virgin widow, whose deepe wounded mind
With love, long time did languish as the striken hind.

25

At last it chaunced this proud *Sarazin*
  To meete me wandring, who perforce me led
  With him away, but yet could never win
  The Fort, that Ladies hold in soveraigne dread.
  There lies he now with foule dishonour dead,
  Who whiles he liv'de, was called proud *Sans foy*,
  The eldest of three brethren, all three bred
  Of one bad sire, whose youngest is *Sans joy*,
And twixt them both was borne the bloudy bold *Sans loy*.

26

In this sad plight, friendlesse, unfortunate,
  Now miserable I *Fidessa* dwell,
  Craving of you in pitty of my state,
  To do none ill, if please ye not do well.
  He in great passion all this while did dwell,
  More busying his quicke eyes, her face to view,
  Than his dull eares, to heare what she did tell;
  And said, Faire Lady hart of flint would rew
The undeserved woes and sorrowes, which ye shew.

27

Henceforth in safe assuraunce may ye rest,
  Having both found a new friend you to aid,
  And lost an old foe, that did you molest:
  Better new friend than an old foe is said.
  With chaunge of cheare the seeming simple maid
  Let fall her eyen, as shamefast to the earth,
  And yeelding soft, in that she nought gain-said.
  So forth they rode, he feining seemely merth,
And she coy lookes: so dainty they say maketh derth.

28

Long time they thus together traveiled,
  Till weary of their way, they came at last,
  Where grew two goodly trees, that faire did spred
  Their armes abroad, with gray mosse overcast,
  And their greene leaves trembling with every blast,
  Made a calme shadow far in compasse round:
  The fearefull Shepheard often there aghast
  Under them never sat, ne wont there sound
His mery oaten pipe, but shund th'unlucky ground.

29

But this good knight soone as he them can spie,
  For the coole shade him thither hastly got:
  For golden *Phœbus* now ymounted hie,
  From fiery wheeles of his faire chariot
  Hurled his beame so scorching cruell hot,
  That living creature mote it not abide;
  And his new Lady it endured not.
  There they alight, in hope themselves to hide
From the fierce heat, and rest their weary limbs a tide.

30

Faire seemely pleasaunce each to other makes,
  With goodly purposes there as they sit:
  And in his falsed fancy he her takes
  To be the fairest wight, that lived yit;
  Which to expresse, he bends his gentle wit,
  And thinking of those braunches greene to frame
  A girlond for her dainty forehead fit,
  He pluckt a bough; out of whose rift there came
Small drops of gory bloud, that trickled downe the same.

31

Therewith a piteous yelling voyce was heard,
  Crying, O spare with guilty hands to teare
  My tender sides in this rough rynd embard,
  But fly, ah fly far hence away, for feare
  Least to you hap, that happened to me heare,
  And to this wretched Lady, my deare love,
  O too deare love, love bought with death too deare.
  Astond he stood, and up his haire did hove,
And with that suddein horror could no member move.

32

At last whenas the dreadfull passion
  Was overpast, and manhood well awake,
  Yet musing at the straunge occasion,
  And doubting much his sence, he thus bespake;
  What voyce of damned Ghost from *Limbo* lake,
  Or guilefull spright wandring in empty aire,
  Both which fraile men do oftentimes mistake,
  Sends to my doubtfull eares these speaches rare,
And ruefull plaints, me bidding guiltlesse bloud to spare?

33

Then groning deepe, Nor damned Ghost, (quoth he,)
  Nor guilefull sprite to thee these wordes doth speake,
  But once a man *Fradubio*, now a tree,
  Wretched man, wretched tree; whose nature weake,
  A cruell witch her cursed will to wreake,
  Hath thus transformd, and plast in open plaines,
  Where *Boreas* doth blow full bitter bleake,
  And scorching Sunne does dry my secret vaines:
For though a tree I seeme, yet cold and heat me paines.

34

Say on *Fradubio* then, or man, or tree,
  Quoth then the knight, by whose mischievous arts
  Art thou misshaped thus, as now I see?
  He oft finds med'cine, who his griefe imparts;
  But double griefs afflict concealing harts,
  As raging flames who striveth to suppresse.
  The author then (said he) of all my smarts,
  Is one *Duessa* a false sorceresse,
That many errant knights hath brought to wretchednesse.

35

In prime of youthly yeares, when corage hot
  The fire of love and joy of chevalree
  First kindled in my brest, it was my lot
  To love this gentle Lady, whom ye see,
  Now not a Lady, but a seeming tree;
  With whom as once I rode accompanyde,
  Me chaunced of a knight encountred bee,
  That had a like faire Lady by his syde,
Like a faire Lady, but did fowle *Duessa* hyde.

36

Whose forged beauty he did take in hand,
  All other Dames to have exceeded farre;
  I in defence of mine did likewise stand,
  Mine, that did then shine as the Morning starre:
  So both to battell fierce arraunged arre,
  In which his harder fortune was to fall
  Under my speare: such is the dye of warre;
  His Lady left as a prise martiall,
Did yield her comely person, to be at my call.

37

So doubly lov'd of Ladies unlike faire,
  Th'one seeming such, the other such indeede,
  One day in doubt I cast for to compare,
  Whether in beauties glorie did exceede;
  A Rosy girlond was the victors meede:
  Both seemde to win, and both seemde won to bee,
  So hard the discord was to be agreede.
  Frælissa was as faire, as faire mote bee,
And ever false *Duessa* seemde as faire as shee.

38

The wicked witch now seeing all this while
  The doubtfull ballaunce equally to sway,
  What not by right, she cast to win by guile,
  And by her hellish science raisd streight way
  A foggy mist, that overcast the day,
  And a dull blast, that breathing on her face,
  Dimmed her former beauties shining ray,
  And with foule ugly forme did her disgrace:
Then was she faire alone, when none was faire in place.

39

Then cride she out, Fye, fye, deformed wight,
  Whose borrowed beautie now appeareth plaine
  To have before bewitched all mens sight;
  O leave her soone, or let her soone be slaine.
  Her loathly visage viewing with disdaine,
  Eftsoones I thought her such, as she me told,
  And would have kild her; but with faigned paine,
  The false witch did my wrathfull hand withhold;
So left her, where she now is turned to treen mould.

40

Thens forth I tooke *Duessa* for my Dame,
  And in the witch unweeting joyd long time,
  Ne ever wist, but that she was the same,
  Till on a day (that day is every Prime,
  When Witches wont do penance for their crime)
  I chaunst to see her in her proper hew,
  Bathing her selfe in origane and thyme:
  A filthy foule old woman I did vew,
That ever to have toucht her, I did deadly rew.

41

Her neather partes misshapen, monstruous,
  Were hidd in water, that I could not see,
  But they did seeme more foule and hideous,
  Than womans shape man would beleeve to bee.
  Thens forth from her most beastly companie
  I gan refraine, in minde to slip away,
  Soone as appeard safe opportunitie:
  For danger great, if not assur'd decay
I saw before mine eyes, if I were knowne to stray.

42

The divelish hag by chaunges of my cheare
  Perceiv'd my thought, and drownd in sleepie night,
  With wicked herbes and ointments did besmeare
  My bodie all, through charmes and magicke might,
  That all my senses were bereaved quight:
  Then brought she me into this desert waste,
  And by my wretched lovers side me pight,
  Where now enclosd in wooden wals full faste,
Banisht from living wights, our wearie dayes we waste.

43

But how long time, said then the Elfin knight,
  Are you in this misformed house to dwell?
  We may not chaunge (quoth he) this evil plight
  Till we be bathed in a living well;
  That is the terme prescribed by the spell.
  O how, said he, mote I that well out find,
  That may restore you to your wonted well?
  Time and suffised fates to former kynd
Shall us restore, none else from hence may us unbynd.

44

The false *Duessa*, now *Fidessa* hight,
  Heard how in vaine *Fradubio* did lament,
  And knew well all was true. But the good knight
  Full of sad feare and ghastly dreriment,
  When all this speech the living tree had spent,
  The bleeding bough did thrust into the ground,
  That from the bloud he might be innocent,
  And with fresh clay did close the wooden wound:
Then turning to his Lady, dead with feare her found.

45

Her seeming dead he found with feigned feare,
  As all unweeting of that well she knew,
  And paynd himselfe with busie care to reare
  Her out of carelesse swowne. Her eylids blew
  And dimmed sight with pale and deadly hew
  At last she up gan lift: with trembling cheare
  Her up he tooke, too simple and too trew,
  And oft her kist. At length all passed feare,
He set her on her steede, and forward forth did beare.

CANT. III

Forsaken Truth long seekes her love,
And makes the Lyon mylde,
Marres blind Devotions mart, and fals
In hand of leachour vylde.

I

NOUGHT is there under heav'ns wide hollownesse,
  That moves more deare compassion of mind,
  Than beautie brought t'unworthy wretchednesse
  Through envies snares or fortunes freakes unkind:
  I, whether lately through her brightnesse blind,
  Or through alleageance and fast fealtie,
  Which I do owe unto all woman kind,
  Feele my heart perst with so great agonie,
When such I see, that all for pittie I could die.

2

And now it is empassioned so deepe,
  For fairest *Unaes* sake, of whom I sing,
  That my fraile eyes these lines with teares do steepe,
  To thinke how she through guilefull handeling,
  Though true as touch, though daughter of a king,
  Though faire as ever living wight was faire,
  Though nor in word nor deede ill meriting,
  Is from her knight divorced in despaire
And her due loves deriv'd to that vile witches share.

3

Yet she most faithfull Ladie all this while
  Forsaken, wofull, solitarie mayd
  Farre from all peoples prease, as in exile,
  In wildernesse and wastfull deserts strayd,
  To seeke her knight; who subtilly betrayd
  Through that late vision, which th'Enchaunter wrought,
  Had her abandond. She of nought affrayd,
  Through woods and wastnesse wide him daily sought;
Yet wished tydings none of him unto her brought.

4

One day nigh wearie of the yrksome way,
　From her unhastie beast she did alight,
　And on the grasse her daintie limbes did lay
　In secret shadow, farre from all mens sight:
　From her faire head her fillet she undight,
　And laid her stole aside. Her angels face
　As the great eye of heaven shyned bright,
　And made a sunshine in the shadie place;
Did never mortall eye behold such heavenly grace.

5

It fortuned out of the thickest wood
　A ramping Lyon rushed suddainly,
　Hunting full greedie after salvage blood;
　Soone as the royall virgin he did spy,
　With gaping mouth at her ran greedily,
　To have attonce devour'd her tender corse:
　But to the pray when as he drew more ny,
　His bloudie rage asswaged with remorse,
And with the sight amazd, forgat his furious forse.

6

In stead thereof he kist her wearie feet,
　And lickt her lilly hands with fawning tong,
　As he her wronged innocence did weet.
　O how can beautie maister the most strong,
　And simple truth subdue avenging wrong?
　Whose yeelded pride and proud submission,
　Still dreading death, when she had marked long,
　Her hart gan melt in great compassion,
And drizling teares did shed for pure affection.

7

The Lyon Lord of everie beast in field,
　Quoth she, his princely puissance doth abate,
　And mightie proud to humble weake does yield,
　Forgetfull of the hungry rage, which late
　Him prickt, in pittie of my sad estate:
　But he my Lyon, and my noble Lord,
　How does he find in cruell hart to hate
　Her that him lov'd, and ever most adord,
As the God of my life? why hath he me abhord?

8

Redounding teares did choke th'end of her plaint,
  Which softly ecchoed from the neighbour wood;
  And sad to see her sorrowfull constraint
  The kingly beast upon her gazing stood;
  With pittie calmd, downe fell his angry mood.
  At last in close hart shutting up her paine,
  Arose the virgin borne of heavenly brood,
  And to her snowy Palfrey got againe,
To seeke her strayed Champion, if she might attaine.

9

The Lyon would not leave her desolate,
  But with her went along, as a strong gard
  Of her chast person, and a faithfull mate
  Of her sad troubles and misfortunes hard:
  Still when she slept, he kept both watch and ward,
  And when she wakt, he waited diligent,
  With humble service to her will prepard:
  From her faire eyes he tooke commaundement,
And ever by her lookes conceived her intent.

10

Long she thus traveiled through deserts wyde,
  By which she thought her wandring knight shold pas,
  Yet never shew of living wight espyde;
  Till that at length she found the troden gras,
  In which the tract of peoples footing was,
  Under the steepe foot of a mountaine hore;
  The same she followes, till at last she has
  A damzell spyde slow footing her before,
That on her shoulders sad a pot of water bore.

11

To whom approching she to her gan call,
  To weet, if dwelling place were nigh at hand;
  But the rude wench her answer'd nought at all,
  She could not heare, nor speake, nor understand;
  Till seeing by her side the Lyon stand,
  With suddaine feare her pitcher downe she threw,
  And fled away: for never in that land
  Face of faire Ladie she before did vew,
And that dread Lyons looke her cast in deadly hew.

12

Full fast she fled, ne ever lookt behynd,
  As if her life upon the wager lay,
  And home she came, whereas her mother blynd
  Sate in eternall night: nought could she say,
  But suddaine catching hold, did her dismay
  With quaking hands, and other signes of feare:
  Who full of ghastly fright and cold affray,
  Gan shut the dore. By this arrived there
Dame *Una*, wearie Dame, and entrance did requere.

13

Which when none yeelded, her unruly Page
  With his rude clawes the wicket open rent,
  And let her in; where of his cruell rage
  Nigh dead with feare, and faint astonishment,
  She found them both in darkesome corner pent;
  Where that old woman day and night did pray
  Upon her beades devoutly penitent;
  Nine hundred *Pater nosters* every day,
And thrise nine hundred *Aves* she was wont to say.

14

And to augment her painefull pennance more,
  Thrise every weeke in ashes she did sit,
  And next her wrinkled skin rough sackcloth wore,
  And thrise three times did fast from any bit:
  But now for feare her beads she did forget.
  Whose needlesse dread for to remove away,
  Faire *Una* framed words and count'nance fit:
  Which hardly doen, at length she gan them pray,
That in their cotage small, that night she rest her may.

15

The day is spent, and commeth drowsie night,
  When every creature shrowded is in sleepe;
  Sad *Una* downe her laies in wearie plight,
  And at her feet the Lyon watch doth keepe:
  In stead of rest, she does lament, and weepe
  For the late losse of her deare loved knight,
  And sighes, and grones, and evermore does steepe
  Her tender brest in bitter teares all night,
All night she thinks too long, and often lookes for light.

16

Now when *Aldeboran* was mounted hie
    Above the shynie *Cassiopeias* chaire,
    And all in deadly sleepe did drowned lie,
    One knocked at the dore, and in would fare;
    He knocked fast, and often curst, and sware,
    That readie entrance was not at his call:
    For on his backe a heavy load he bare
    Of nightly stelths and pillage severall,
Which he had got abroad by purchase criminall.

17

He was to weete a stout and sturdie thiefe,
    Wont to robbe Churches of their ornaments,
    And poore mens boxes of their due reliefe,
    Which given was to them for good intents;
    The holy Saints of their rich vestiments
    He did disrobe, when all men carelesse slept,
    And spoild the Priests of their habiliments,
    Whiles none the holy things in safety kept;
Then he by cunning sleights in at the window crept.

18

And all that he by right or wrong could find,
    Unto this house he brought, and did bestow
    Upon the daughter of this woman blind,
    Abessa daughter of *Corceca* slow,
    With whom he whoredome usd, that few did know,
    And fed her fat with feast of offerings,
    And plentie, which in all the land did grow;
    Ne spared he to give her gold and rings:
And now he to her brought part of his stolen things.

19

Thus long the dore with rage and threats he bet,
    Yet of those fearefull women none durst rize,
    The Lyon frayed them, him in to let:
    He would no longer stay him to advize,
    But open breakes the dore in furious wize,
    And entring is; when that disdainfull beast
    Encountring fierce, him suddaine doth surprize,
    And seizing cruell clawes on trembling brest,
Under his Lordly foot him proudly hath supprest.

20

Him booteth not resist, nor succour call,
His bleeding hart is in the vengers hand,
Who streight him rent in thousand peeces small,
And quite dismembred hath: the thirstie land
Drunke up his life; his corse left on the strand.
His fearefull friends weare out the wofull night,
Ne dare to weepe, nor seeme to understand
The heavie hap, which on them is alight,
Affraid, least to themselves the like mishappen might.

21

Now when broad day the world discovered has,
Up *Una* rose, up rose the Lyon eke,
And on their former journey forward pas,
In wayes unknowne, her wandring knight to seeke,
With paines farre passing that long wandring *Greeke*,
That for his love refused deitie;
Such were the labours of this Lady meeke,
Still seeking him, that from her still did flie,
Then furthest from her hope, when most she weened nie.

22

Soone as she parted thence, the fearefull twaine,
That blind old woman and her daughter deare
Came forth, and finding *Kirkrapine* there slaine,
For anguish great they gan to rend their heare,
And beat their brests, and naked flesh to teare.
And when they both had wept and wayld their fill,
Then forth they ranne like two amazed deare,
Halfe mad through malice, and revenging will,
To follow her, that was the causer of their ill.

23

Whom overtaking, they gan loudly bray,
With hollow howling, and lamenting cry,
Shamefully at her rayling all the way,
And her accusing of dishonesty,
That was the flowre of faith and chastity;
And still amidst her rayling, she did pray,
That plagues, and mischiefs, and long misery
Might fall on her, and follow all the way,
And that in endlesse error she might ever stray.

24

But when she saw her prayers nought prevaile,
  She backe returned with some labour lost;
  And in the way as she did weepe and waile,
  A knight her met in mighty armes embost,
  Yet knight was not for all his bragging bost,
  But subtill *Archimag*, that *Una* sought
  By traynes into new troubles to have tost:
  Of that old woman tydings he besought,
If that of such a Ladie she could tellen ought.

25

Therewith she gan her passion to renew,
  And cry, and curse, and raile, and rend her heare,
  Saying, that harlot she too lately knew,
  That causd her shed so many a bitter teare,
  And so forth told the story of her feare:
  Much seemed he to mone her haplesse chaunce,
  And after for that Ladie did inquere;
  Which being taught, he forward gan advaunce
His fair enchaunted steed, and eke his charmed launce.

26

Ere long he came, where *Una* traveild slow,
  And that wilde Champion wayting her besyde:
  Whom seeing such, for dread he durst not show
  Himselfe too nigh at hand, but turned wyde
  Unto an hill; from whence when she him spyde,
  By his like seeming shield, her knight by name
  She weend it was, and towards him gan ryde:
  Approching nigh, she wist it was the same,
And with faire fearefull humblesse towards him shee came.

27

And weeping said, Ah my long lacked Lord,
  Where have ye bene thus long out of my sight?
  Much feared I to have bene quite abhord,
  Or ought have done, that ye displeasen might,
  That should as death unto my deare hart light:
  For since mine eye your joyous sight did mis,
  My chearefull day is turnd to chearelesse night,
  And eke my night of death the shadow is;
But welcome now my light, and shining lampe of blis.

28

He thereto meeting said, My dearest Dame,
  Farre be it from your thought, and fro my will,
  To thinke that knighthood I so much should shame,
  As you to leave, that have me loved still,
  And chose in Faery court of meere goodwill,
  Where noblest knights were to be found on earth:
  The earth shall sooner leave her kindly skill
  To bring forth fruit, and make eternall derth,
Than I leave you, my liefe, yborne of heavenly berth.

29

And sooth to say, why I left you so long,
  Was for to seeke adventure in strange place,
  Where *Archimago* said a felon strong
  To many knights did daily worke disgrace;
  But knight he now shall never more deface:
  Good cause of mine excuse; that mote ye please
  Well to accept, and evermore embrace
  My faithfull service, that by land and seas
Have vowd you to defend, now then your plaint appease.

30

His lovely words her seemd due recompence
  Of all her passed paines: one loving howre
  For many yeares of sorrow can dispence:
  A dram of sweet is worth a pound of sowre:
  She has forgot, how many a wofull stowre
  For him she late endur'd; she speakes no more
  Of past: true is, that true love hath no powre
  To looken backe; his eyes be fixt before.
Before her stands her knight, for whom she toyld so sore.

31

Much like, as when the beaten marinere,
  That long hath wandred in the *Ocean* wide,
  Oft soust in swelling *Tethys* saltish teare,
  And long time having tand his tawney hide
  With blustring breath of heaven, that none can bide,
  And scorching flames of fierce *Orions* hound,
  Soone as the port from farre he has espide,
  His chearefull whistle merrily doth sound,
And *Nereus* crownes with cups; his mates him pledg around.

32

Such joy made *Una*, when her knight she found;
　And eke th'enchaunter joyous seemd no lesse,
　Than the glad marchant, that does vew from ground
　His ship farre come from watrie wildernesse,
　He hurles out vowes, and *Neptune* oft doth blesse:
　So forth they past, and all the way they spent
　Discoursing of her dreadfull late distresse,
　In which he askt her, what the Lyon ment:
† Who told her all that fell in journey as she went.

33

They had not ridden farre, when they might see
　One pricking towards them with hastie heat,
　Full strongly armd, and on a courser free,
　That through his fiercenesse fomed all with sweat,
　And the sharpe yron did for anger eat,
　When his hot ryder spurd his chauffed side;
　His looke was sterne, and seemed still to threat
　Cruell revenge, which he in hart did hyde,
And on his shield *Sans loy* in bloudie lines was dyde.

34

When nigh he drew unto this gentle payre
　And saw the Red-crosse, which the knight did beare,
　He burnt in fire, and gan eftsoones prepare
　Himselfe to battell with his couched speare.
　Loth was that other, and did faint through feare,
　To taste th'untryed dint of deadly steele;
　But yet his Lady did so well him cheare,
　That hope of new good hap he gan to feele;
So bent his speare, and spurnd his horse with yron heele.

35

But that proud Paynim forward came so fierce,
　And full of wrath, that with his sharp-head speare
　Through vainely crossed shield he quite did pierce,
　And had his staggering steede not shrunke for feare,
　Through shield and bodie eke he should him beare:
　Yet so great was the puissance of his push,
　That from his saddle quite he did him beare:
　He tombling rudely downe to ground did rush,
And from his gored wound a well of bloud did gush.

36

Dismounting lightly from his loftie steed,
    He to him lept, in mind to reave his life,
    And proudly said, Lo there the worthie meed
    Of him, that slew *Sansfoy* with bloudie knife;
    Henceforth his ghost freed from repining strife,
    In peace may passen over *Lethe* lake,
    When mourning altars purgd with enemies life,
    The blacke infernall *Furies* doen aslake:
Life from *Sansfoy* thou tookst, *Sansloy* shall from thee take.

37

Therewith in haste his helmet gan unlace,
    Till *Una* cride, O hold that heavie hand,
    Deare Sir, what ever that thou be in place:
    Enough is, that thy foe doth vanquisht stand
    Now at thy mercy: Mercie not withstand:
    For he is one the truest knight alive,
    Though conquered now he lie on lowly land,
    And whilest him fortune favourd, faire did thrive
In bloudie field: therefore of life him not deprive.

38

Her piteous words might not abate his rage,
    But rudely rending up his helmet, would
    Have slaine him straight: but when he sees his age,
    And hoarie head of *Archimago* old,
    His hastie hand he doth amazed hold,
    And halfe ashamed, wondred at the sight:
    For the old man well knew he, though untold,
    In charmes and magicke to have wondrous might,
Ne ever wont in field, ne in round lists to fight.

39

And said, Why *Archimago*, lucklesse syre,
    What doe I see? what hard mishap is this,
    That hath thee hither brought to taste mine yre?
    Or thine the fault, or mine the error is,
    In stead of foe to wound my friend amis?
    He answered nought, but in a traunce still lay,
    And on those guilefull dazed eyes of his
    The cloud of death did sit. Which doen away,
He left him lying so, ne would no lenger stay.

40

But to the virgin comes, who all this while
  Amased stands, her selfe so mockt to see
  By him, who has the guerdon of his guile,
  For so misfeigning her true knight to bee:
  Yet is she now in more perplexitie,
  Left in the hand of that same Paynim bold,
  From whom her booteth not at all to flie;
  Who by her cleanly garment catching hold,
Her from her Palfrey pluckt, her visage to behold.

41

But her fierce servant full of kingly awe
  And high disdaine, whenas his soveraine Dame
  So rudely handled by her foe he sawe,
  With gaping jawes full greedy at him came,
  And ramping on his shield, did weene the same
  Have reft away with his sharpe rending clawes.
  But he was stout, and lust did now inflame
  His corage more, that from his griping pawes
He hath his shield redeem'd, and foorth his swerd he drawes.

42

O then too weake and feeble was the forse
  Of salvage beast, his puissance to withstand:
  For he was strong, and of so mightie corse,
  As ever wielded speare in warlike hand,
  And feates of armes did wisely understand.
  Eftsoones he perced through his chaufed chest
  With thrilling point of deadly yron brand,
  And launcht his Lordly hart: with death opprest
He roar'd aloud, whiles life forsooke his stubborne brest.

43

Who now is left to keepe the forlorne maid
  From raging spoile of lawlesse victors will?
  Her faithfull gard remov'd, her hope dismaid,
  Her selfe a yeelded pray to save or spill.
  He now Lord of the field, his pride to fill,
  With foule reproches, and disdainfull spight
  Her vildly entertaines, and will or nill,
  Beares her away upon his courser light:
Her prayers nought prevaile, his rage is more of might.

44

And all the way, with great lamenting paine,
  And piteous plaints she filleth his dull eares,
  That stony hart could riven have in twaine,
  And all the way she wets with flowing teares:
  But he enrag'd with rancor, nothing heares.
  Her servile beast yet would not leave her so,
  But followes her farre off, ne ought he feares,
  To be partaker of her wandring woe,
More mild in beastly kind, than that her beastly foe.

CANT. IIII

*To sinfull house of Pride, Duessa
guides the faithfull knight,
Where brothers death to wreak Sansjoy
doth chalenge him to fight.*

I

YOUNG knight, what ever that dost armes professe,
  And through long labours huntest after fame,
  Beware of fraud, beware of ficklenesse,
  In choice, and change of thy deare loved Dame,
  Least thou of her beleeve too lightly blame,
  And rash misweening doe thy hart remove:
  For unto knight there is no greater shame,
  Than lightnesse and inconstancie in love;
That doth this *Redcrosse* knights ensample plainly prove.

2

Who after that he had faire *Una* lorne,
  Through light misdeeming of her loialtie,
  And false *Duessa* in her sted had borne,
  Called *Fidess'*, and so supposd to bee;
  Long with her traveild, till at last they see
  A goodly building, bravely garnished,
  The house of mightie Prince it seemd to bee:
  And towards it a broad high way that led,
All bare through peoples feet, which thither traveiled.

3

Great troupes of people traveild thitherward
  Both day and night, of each degree and place,
  But few returned, having scaped hard,
  With balefull beggerie, or foule disgrace,
  Which ever after in most wretched case,
  Like loathsome lazars, by the hedges lay.
  Thither *Duessa* bad him bend his pace:
  For she is wearie of the toilesome way,
And also nigh consumed is the lingring day.

4

A stately Pallace built of squared bricke,
  Which cunningly was without morter laid,
  Whose wals were high, but nothing strong, nor thick,
  And golden foile all over them displaid,
  That purest skye with brightnesse they dismaid:
  High lifted up were many loftie towres,
  And goodly galleries farre over laid,
  Full of faire windowes, and delightfull bowres;
And on the top a Diall told the timely howres.

5

It was a goodly heape for to behould,
  And spake the praises of the workmans wit;
  But full great pittie, that so faire a mould
  Did on so weake foundation ever sit:
  For on a sandie hill, that still did flit,
  And fall away, it mounted was full hie,
  That every breath of heaven shaked it:
  And all the hinder parts, that few could spie,
Were ruinous and old, but painted cunningly.

6

Arrived there they passed in forth right;
  For still to all the gates stood open wide,
  Yet charge of them was to a Porter hight
  Cald *Malvenù*, who entrance none denide:
  Thence to the hall, which was on every side
  With rich array and costly arras dight:
  Infinite sorts of people did abide
  There waiting long, to win the wished sight
Of her, that was the Lady of that Pallace bright.

7

By them they passe, all gazing on them round,
  And to the Presence mount; whose glorious vew
  Their frayle amazed senses did confound:
  In living Princes court none ever knew
  Such endlesse richesse, and so sumptuous shew;
  Ne *Persia* selfe, the nourse of pompous pride
  Like ever saw. And there a noble crew
  Of Lordes and Ladies stood on every side,
Which with their presence faire, the place much beautifide.

8

High above all a cloth of State was spred,
  And a rich throne, as bright as sunny day,
  On which there sate most brave embellished
  With royall robes and gorgeous array,
  A mayden Queene, that shone as *Titans* ray,
  In glistring gold, and peerelesse pretious stone:
  Yet her bright blazing beautie did assay
  To dim the brightnesse of her glorious throne,
As envying her selfe, that too exceeding shone.

9

Exceeding shone, like *Phœbus* fairest childe,
  That did presume his fathers firie wayne,
  And flaming mouthes of steedes unwonted wilde
  Through highest heaven with weaker hand to rayne:
  Proud of such glory and advancement vaine,
  While flashing beames do daze his feeble eyen,
  He leaves the welkin way most beaten plaine,
  And rapt with whirling wheeles, inflames the skyen,
With fire not made to burne, but fairely for to shyne.

10

So proud she shyned in her Princely state,
  Looking to heaven; for earth she did disdayne,
  And sitting high; for lowly she did hate:
  Lo underneath her scornefull feete, was layne
  A dreadfull Dragon with an hideous trayne,
  And in her hand she held a mirrhour bright,
  Wherein her face she often vewed fayne,
  And in her selfe-lov'd semblance tooke delight;
For she was wondrous faire, as any living wight.

11

Of griesly *Pluto* she the daughter was,
  And sad *Proserpina* the Queene of hell;
  Yet did she thinke her pearelesse worth to pas
  That parentage, with pride so did she swell,
  And thundring *Jove*, that high in heaven doth dwell,
  And wield the world, she claymed for her syre,
  Or if that any else did *Jove* excell:
  For to the highest she did still aspyre,
Of if ought higher were than that, did it desyre.

12

And proud *Lucifera* men did her call,
  That made her selfe a Queene, and crownd to be,
  Yet rightfull kingdome she had none at all,
  Ne heritage of native soveraintie,
  But did usurpe with wrong and tyrannie
  Upon the scepter, which she now did hold:
  Ne ruld her Realmes with lawes, but pollicie,
  And strong advizement of six wisards old,
That with their counsels bad her kingdome did uphold.

13

Soone as the Elfin knight in presence came,
  And false *Duessa* seeming Lady faire,
  A gentle Husher, *Vanitie* by name
  Made rowme, and passage for them did prepaire:
  So goodly brought them to the lowest staire
  Of her high throne, where they on humble knee
  Making obeyssance, did the cause declare,
  Why they were come, her royall state to see,
To prove the wide report of her great Majestee.

14

With loftie eyes, halfe loth to looke so low,
  She thanked them in her disdainefull wise,
  Ne other grace vouchsafed them to show
  Of Princesse worthy, scarse them bad arise.
  Her Lordes and Ladies all this while devise
  Themselves to setten forth to straungers sight:
  Some frounce their curled haire in courtly guise,
  Some prancke their ruffes, and others trimly dight
Their gay attire: each others greater pride does spight.

15

Goodly they all that knight do entertaine,
  Right glad with him to have increast their crew:
But to *Duess'* each one himself did paine
All kindnesse and faire courtesie to shew;
For in that court whylome her well they knew:
Yet the stout Faerie mongst the middest crowd
Thought all their glorie vaine in knightly vew,
  And that great Princesse too exceeding prowd,
That to strange knight no better countenance allowd.

16

Suddein upriseth from her stately place
  The royall Dame, and for her coche doth call:
All hurtlen forth, and she with Princely pace,
As faire *Aurora* in her purple pall,
Out of the East the dawning day doth call:
So forth she comes: her brightnesse brode doth blaze;
The heapes of people thronging in the hall,
  Do ride each other, upon her to gaze:
Her glorious glitterand light doth all mens eyes amaze.

17

So forth she comes, and to her coche does clyme,
  Adorned all with gold, and girlonds gay,
That seemd as fresh as *Flora* in her prime,
And strove to match, in royall rich array,
Great *Junoes* golden chaire, the which they say
The Gods stand gazing on, when she does ride
To *Joves* high house through heavens bras-paved way
  Drawne of faire Pecocks, that excell in pride,
And full of *Argus* eyes their tailes dispredden wide.

18

But this was drawne of six unequall beasts,
  On which her six sage Counsellours did ryde,
Taught to obey their bestiall beheasts,
With like conditions to their kinds applyde:
Of which the first, that all the rest did guyde,
Was sluggish *Idlenesse* the nourse of sin;
Upon a slouthfull Asse he chose to ryde,
  Arayd in habit blacke, and amis thin,
Like to an holy Monck, the service to begin.

19

And in his hand his Portesse still he bare,
  That much was worne, but therein little red,
  For of devotion he had little care,
  Still drownd in sleepe, and most of his dayes ded;
  Scarse could he once uphold his heavie hed,
  To looken, whether it were night or day:
  May seeme the wayne was very evill led,
  When such an one had guiding of the way,
That knew not, whether right he went, or else astray.

20

From worldly cares himselfe he did esloyne,
  And greatly shunned manly exercise,
  From every worke he chalenged essoyne,
  For contemplation sake: yet otherwise,
  His life he led in lawlesse riotise;
  By which he grew to grievous malady;
  For in his lustlesse limbs through evill guise
  A shaking fever raignd continually:
Such one was *Idlenesse*, first of this company.

21

And by his side rode loathsome *Gluttony*,
  Deformed creature, on a filthie swyne,
  His belly was up-blowne with luxury,
  And eke with fatnesse swollen were his eyne,
  And like a Crane his necke was long and fyne,
  With which he swallowd up excessive feast,
  For want whereof poore people oft did pyne;
  And all the way, most like a brutish beast,
He spued up his gorge, that all did him deteast.

22

In greene vine leaves he was right fitly clad;
  For other clothes he could not weare for heat,
  And on his head an yvie girland had,
  From under which fast trickled downe the sweat:
  Still as he rode, he somewhat still did eat,
  And in his hand did beare a bouzing can,
  Of which he supt so oft, that on his seat
  His dronken corse he scarse upholden can,
In shape and life more like a monster, than a man.

23

Unfit he was for any worldly thing,
  And eke unhable once to stirre or go,
  Not meet to be of counsell to a king,
  Whose mind in meat and drinke was drowned so,
  That from his friend he seldome knew his fo:
  Full of diseases was his carcas blew,
  And a dry dropsie through his flesh did flow:
  Which by misdiet daily greater grew:
Such one was *Gluttony*, the second of that crew.

24

And next to him rode lustfull *Lechery*,
  Upon a bearded Goat, whose rugged haire,
  And whally eyes (the signe of gelosy,)
  Was like the person selfe, whom he did beare:
  Who rough, and blacke, and filthy did appeare,
  Unseemely man to please faire Ladies eye;
  Yet he of Ladies oft was loved deare,
  When fairer faces were bid standen by:
O who does know the bent of womens fantasy?

25

In a greene gowne he clothed was full faire,
  Which underneath did hide his filthinesse,
  And in his hand a burning hart he bare,
  Full of vaine follies, and new fanglenesse:
  For he was false, and fraught with ficklenesse,
  And learned had to love with secret lookes,
  And well could daunce, and sing with ruefulnesse,
  And fortunes tell, and read in loving bookes,
And thousand other wayes, to bait his fleshly hookes.

26

Inconstant man, that loved all he saw,
  And lusted after all, that he did love,
  Ne would his looser life be tide to law,
  But joyd weake wemens hearts to tempt and prove
  If from their loyall loves he might then move;
  Which lewdnesse fild him with reprochfull paine
  Of that fowle evill, which all men reprove,
  That rots the marrow, and consumes the braine:
Such one was *Lecherie*, the third of all this traine.

27

And greedy *Avarice* by him did ride,
　Upon a Camell loaden all with gold;
　Two iron coffers hong on either side,
　With precious mettall full, as they might hold,
　And in his lap an heape of coine he told;
　For of his wicked pelfe his God he made,
　And unto hell him selfe for money sold;
　Accursed usurie was all his trade,
And right and wrong ylike in equall ballaunce waide.

28

His life was nigh unto deaths doore yplast,
　And thred-bare cote, and cobled shoes he ware,
　Ne scarse good morsell all his life did tast,
　But both from backe and belly still did spare,
　To fill his bags, and richesse to compare;
　Yet chylde ne kinsman living had he none
　To leave them to; but thorough daily care
　To get, and nightly feare to lose his owne,
He led a wretched life unto him selfe unknowne.

29.

Most wretched wight, whom nothing might suffise,
　Whose greedy lust did lacke in greatest store,
　Whose need had end, but no end covetise,
　Whose wealth was want, whose plenty made him pore,
　Who had enough, yet wished ever more;
　A vile disease, and eke in foote and hand
　A grievous gout tormented him full sore,
　That well he could not touch, nor go, nor stand:
Such one was *Avarice*, the fourth of this faire band.

30

And next to him malicious *Envie* rode,
　Upon a ravenous wolfe, and still did chaw
　Betweene his cankred teeth a venemous tode,
　That all the poison ran about his chaw;
　But inwardly he chawed his owne maw
　At neighbours wealth, that made him ever sad;
　For death it was, when any good he saw,
　And wept, that cause of weeping none he had,
But when he heard of harme, he wexed wondrous glad.

31

All in a kirtle of discolourd say
　He clothed was, ypainted full of eyes;
And in his bosome secretly there lay
An hatefull Snake, the which his taile uptyes
In many folds, and mortall sting implyes.
Still as he rode, he gnasht his teeth, to see
Those heapes of gold with griple Covetyse,
And grudged at the great felicitie
Of proud *Lucifera*, and his owne companie.

32

He hated all good workes and vertuous deeds,
　And him no lesse, that any like did use,
And who with gracious bread the hungry feeds,
His almes for want of faith he doth accuse;
So every good to bad he doth abuse:
And eke the verse of famous Poets witt
He does backebite, and spightfull poison spues
From leprous mouth on all, that ever writt:
Such one vile *Envie* was, that fifte in row did sitt.

33

And him beside rides fierce revenging *Wrath*,
　Upon a Lion, loth for to be led;
And in his hand a burning brond he hath,
The which he brandisheth about his hed;
His eyes did hurle forth sparkles fiery red,
And stared sterne on all, that him beheld,
As ashes pale of hew and seeming ded;
And on his dagger still his hand he held,
Trembling through hasty rage, when choler in him sweld.

34

His ruffin raiment all was staind with blood,
　Which he had spilt, and all to rags yrent,
Through unadvized rashnesse woxen wood;
For of his hands he had no governement,
Ne car'd for bloud in his avengement:
But when the furious fit was overpast,
His cruell facts he often would repent;
Yet wilfull man he never would forecast,
How many mischieves should ensue his heedlesse hast.

35

Full many mischiefes follow cruell *Wrath*;
  Abhorred bloudshed, and tumultuous strife,
  Unmanly murder, and unthrifty scath,
  Bitter despight, with rancours rusty knife,
  And fretting griefe the enemy of life;
  All these, and many evils moe haunt ire,
  The swelling Splene, and Frenzy raging rife,
  The shaking Palsey, and Saint *Fraunces* fire:
Such one was *Wrath*, the last of this ungodly tire.

36

And after all, upon the wagon beame
  Rode *Sathan*, with a smarting whip in hand,
  With which he forward lasht the laesie teme,
  So oft as *Slowth* still in the mire did stand.
  Huge routs of people did about them band,
  Showting for joy, and still before their way
  A foggy mist had covered all the land;
  And underneath their feet, all scattered lay
Dead sculs and bones of men, whose life had gone astray.

37

So forth they marchen in this goodly sort,
  To take the solace of the open aire,
  And in fresh flowring fields themselves to sport;
  Emongst the rest rode that false Lady faire,
  The fowle *Duessa*, next unto the chaire
  Of proud *Lucifera*, as one of the traine:
  But that good knight would not so nigh repaire,
  Him selfe estraunging from their joyaunce vaine,
Whose fellowship seemd far unfit for warlike swaine.

38

So having solaced themselves a space
  With pleasaunce of the breathing fields yfed,
  They backe returned to the Princely Place;
  Whereas an errant knight in armes ycled,
  And heathnish shield, wherein with letters red
  Was writ *Sans joy*, they new arrived find:
  Enflam'd with fury and fiers hardy-hed,
  He seemd in hart to harbour thoughts unkind,
And nourish bloudy vengeaunce in his bitter mind.

39

Who when the shamed shield of slaine *Sans foy*
   He spide with that same Faery champions page,
   Bewraying him, that did of late destroy
   His eldest brother, burning all with rage
   He to him leapt, and that same envious gage
   Of victors glory from him snatcht away:
   But th'Elfin knight, which ought that warlike wage,
   Disdaind to loose the meed he wonne in fray,
And him rencountring fierce, reskewd the noble pray.

40

Therewith they gan to hurtlen greedily,
   Redoubted battaile ready to darrayne,
   And clash their shields, and shake their swords on hy,
   That with their sturre they troubled all the traine;
   Till that great Queene upon eternall paine
   Of high displeasure, that ensewen might,
   Commaunded them their fury to refraine,
   And if that either to that shield had right,
In equall lists they should the morrow next it fight.

41

Ah dearest Dame, (quoth then the Paynim bold,)
   Pardon the errour of enraged wight,
   Whom great griefe made forget the raines to hold
   Of reasons rule, to see this recreant knight,
   No knight, but treachour full of false despight
   And shamefull treason, who through guile hath slayn
   The prowest knight, that ever field did fight,
   Even stout *Sans foy* (O who can then refrayn?)
Whose shield he beares renverst, the more to heape disdayn.

42

And to augment the glorie of his guile,
   His dearest love the faire *Fidessa* loe
   Is there possessed of the traytour vile,
   Who reapes the harvest sowen by his foe,
   Sowen in bloudy field, and bought with woe:
   That brothers hand shall dearely well requight
   So be, O Queene, you equall favour showe.
   Him litle answerd th'angry Elfin knight;
He never meant with words, but swords to plead his right.

43

But threw his gauntlet as a sacred pledge,
　　His cause in combat the next day to try:
　　So been they parted both, with harts on edge,
　　To be aveng'd each on his enimy.
　　That night they pas in joy and jollity,
　　Feasting and courting both in bowre and hall;
　　For Steward was excessive *Gluttonie*,
　　That of his plenty poured forth to all;
Which doen, the Chamberlain *Slowth* did to rest them call.

44

Now whenas darkesome night had all displayd
　　Her coleblacke curtein over brightest skye,
　　The warlike youthes on dayntie couches layd,
　　Did chace away sweet sleepe from sluggish eye,
　　To muse on meanes of hoped victory.
　　But whenas *Morpheus* had with leaden mace
　　Arrested all that courtly company,
　　Up-rose *Duessa* from her resting place,
And to the Paynims lodging comes with silent pace.

45

Whom broad awake she finds, in troublous fit,
　　Forecasting, how his foe he might annoy,
　　And him amoves with speaches seeming fit:
　　Ah deare *Sans joy*, next dearest to *Sans foy*,
　　Cause of my new griefe, cause of my new joy,
　　Joyous, to see his ymage in mine eye,
　　And greev'd, to thinke how foe did him destroy,
　　That was the flowre of grace and chevalrye;
Lo his *Fidessa* to thy secret faith I flye.

46

With gentle wordes he can her fairely greet,
　　And bad say on the secret of her hart.
　　Then sighing soft, I learne that litle sweet
　　Oft tempred is (quoth she) with muchell smart:
　　For since my brest was launcht with lovely dart
　　Of deare *Sansfoy*, I never joyed howre,
　　But in eternall woes my weaker hart
　　Have wasted, loving him with all my powre,
And for his sake have felt full many an heavie stowre.

47

At last when perils all I weened past,
  And hop'd to reape the crop of all my care,
  Into new woes unweeting I was cast,
  By this false faytor, who unworthy ware
  His worthy shield, whom he with guilefull snare
  Entrapped slew, and brought to shamefull grave.
  Me silly maid away with him he bare,
  And ever since hath kept in darksome cave,
For that I would not yeeld, that to *Sans-foy* I gave.

48

But since faire Sunne hath sperst that lowring clowd,
  And to my loathed life now shewes some light,
  Under your beames I will me safely shrowd,
  From dreaded storme of his disdainfull spight:
  To you th'inheritance belongs by right
  Of brothers prayse, to you eke longs his love.
  Let not his love, let not his restlesse spright
  Be unreveng'd, that calles to you above
From wandring *Stygian* shores, where it doth endlesse move.

49

Thereto said he, Faire Dame be nought dismaid
  For sorrowes past; their griefe is with them gone:
  Ne yet of present perill be affraid;
  For needlesse feare did never vantage none,
  And helplesse hap it booteth not to mone.
  Dead is *Sans-foy*, his vitall paines are past,
  Though greeved ghost for vengeance deepe do grone:
  He lives, that shall him pay his dewties last,
And guiltie Elfin bloud shall sacrifice in hast.

50

O but I feare the fickle freakes (quoth shee)
  Of fortune false, and oddes of armes in field.
  Why dame (quoth he) what oddes can ever bee,
  Where both do fight alike, to win or yield?
  Yea but (quoth she) he beares a charmed shield,
  And eke enchaunted armes, that none can perce,
  Ne none can wound the man, that does them wield.
  Charmd or enchaunted (answerd he then ferce)
I no whit reck, ne you the like need to reherce.

51

But faire *Fidessa*, sithens fortunes guile,
 Or enimies powre hath now captived you,
 Returne from whence ye came, and rest a while
 Till morrow next, that I the Elfe subdew,
 And with *Sans-foyes* dead dowry you endew.
 Ay me, that is a double death (she said)
 With proud foes sight my sorrow to renew:
 Where ever yet I be, my secrete aid
Shall follow you. So passing forth she him obaid.

CANT. V

The faithfull knight in equall field
subdewes his faithlesse foe,
Whom false Duessa saves, and for
his cure to hell does goe.

1

THE noble hart, that harbours vertuous thought,
 And is with child of glorious great intent,
 Can never rest, until it forth have brought
 Th'eternall brood of glorie excellent:
 Such restlesse passion did all night torment
 The flaming corage of that Faery knight,
 Devizing, how that doughtie turnament
 With greatest honour he atchieven might;
Still did he wake, and still did watch for dawning light.

2

At last the golden Orientall gate
 Of greatest heaven gan to open faire,
 And *Phœbus* fresh, as bridegrome to his mate,
 Came dauncing forth, shaking his deawie haire:
 And hurld his glistring beames through gloomy aire.
 Which when the wakeful Elfe perceiv'd, streight way
 He started up, and did him selfe prepaire,
 In sun-bright armes, and battailous array:
For with that Pagan proud he combat will that day.

3

And forth he comes into the commune hall,
  Where earely waite him many a gazing eye,
  To weet what end to straunger knights may fall.
  There many Minstrales maken melody,
  To drive away the dull melancholy,
  And many Bardes, that to the trembling chord
  Can tune their timely voyces cunningly,
  And many Chroniclers, that can record
Old loves, and warres for Ladies doen by many a Lord.

4

Soone after comes the cruell Sarazin,
  In woven maile all armed warily,
  And sternly lookes at him, who not a pin
  Does care for looke of living creatures eye.
  They bring them wines of *Greece* and *Araby*,
  And daintie spices fetcht from furthest *Ynd*,
  To kindle heat of corage privily:
  And in the wine a solemne oth they bynd
T'observe the sacred lawes of armes, that are assynd.

5

At last forth comes that far renowmed Queene,
  With royall pomp and Princely majestie;
  She is ybrought unto a paled greene,
  And placed under stately canapee,
  The warlike feates of both those knights to see.
  On th'other side in all mens open vew
  Duessa placed is, and on a tree
  Sans-foy his shield is hangd with bloudy hew:
Both those the lawrell girlonds to the victor dew.

6

A shrilling trompet sownded from on hye,
  And unto battaill bad them selves addresse:
  Their shining shieldes about their wrestes they tye,
  And burning blades about their heads do blesse,
  The instruments of wrath and heavinesse:
  With greedy force each other doth assayle,
  And strike so fiercely, that they do impresse
  Deepe dinted furrowes in the battred mayle;
The yron walles to ward their blowes are weake and fraile.

7

The Sarazin was stout, and wondrous strong,
  And heaped blowes like yron hammers great:
  For after bloud and vengeance he did long.
  The knight was fiers, and full of youthly heat:
  And doubled strokes, like dreaded thunders threat:
  For all for prayse and honour he did fight.
  Both stricken strike, and beaten both do beat,
  That from their shields forth flyeth firie light,
And helmets hewen deepe, shew marks of eithers might.

8

So th'one for wrong, the other strives for right:
  As when a Gryfon seized of his pray,
  A Dragon fiers encountreth in his flight,
  Through widest ayre making his ydle way,
  That would his rightfull ravine rend away:
  With hideous horrour both together smight,
  And souce so sore, that they the heavens affray:
  The wise Southsayer seeing so sad sight,
Th'amazed vulgar tels of warres and mortall fight.

9

So th'one for wrong, the other strives for right,
  And each to deadly shame would drive his foe:
  The cruell steele so greedily doth bight
  In tender flesh, that streames of bloud down flow,
  With which the armes, that earst so bright did show,
  Into a pure vermillion now are dyde:
  Great ruth in all the gazers harts did grow,
  Seeing the gored woundes to gape so wyde,
That victory they dare not wish to either side.

10

At last the Paynim chaunst to cast his eye,
  His suddein eye, flaming with wrathfull fyre,
  Upon his brothers shield, which hong thereby:
  Therewith redoubled was his raging yre,
  And said, Ah wretched sonne of wofull syre,
  Doest thou sit wayling by black *Stygian* lake,
  Whilest here thy shield is hangd for victors hyre,
  And sluggish german doest thy forces slake,
To after-send his foe, that him may overtake?

11

Goe caytive Elfe, him quickly overtake,
    And soone redeeme from his long wandring woe;
    Goe guiltie ghost, to him my message make,
    That I his shield have quit from dying foe.
    Therewith upon his crest he stroke him so,
    That twise he reeled, readie twise to fall;
    End of the doubtfull battell deemed tho
    The lookers on, and lowd to him gan call
The false *Duessa*, Thine the shield, and I, and all.

12

Soone as the Faerie heard his Ladie speake,
    Out of his swowning dreame he gan awake,
    And quickning faith, that earst was woxen weake,
    The creeping deadly cold away did shake:
    Tho mov'd with wrath, and shame, and Ladies sake,
    Of all attonce he cast avengd to bee,
    And with so'exceeding furie at him strake,
    That forced him to stoupe upon his knee;
Had he not stouped so, he should have cloven bee.

13

And to him said, Goe now proud Miscreant,
    Thy selfe thy message doe to german deare,
    Alone he wandring thee too long doth want:
    Goe say, his foe thy shield with his doth beare.
    Therewith his heavie hand he high gan reare,
    Him to have slaine; when loe a darkesome clowd
    Upon him fell: he no where doth appeare,
    But vanisht is. The Elfe him cals alowd,
But answer none receives: the darknes him does shrowd.

14

In haste *Duessa* from her place arose,
    And to him running said, O prowest knight,
    That ever Ladie to her love did chose,
    Let now abate the terror of your might,
    And quench the flame of furious despight,
    And bloudie vengeance; lo th'infernall powres
    Covering your foe with cloud of deadly night,
    Have borne him hence to *Plutoes* balefull bowres.
The conquest yours, I yours, the shield, and glory yours.

15

Not all so satisfide, with greedie eye
  He sought all round about, his thirstie blade
  To bath in bloud of faithlesse enemy;
  Who all that while lay hid in secret shade:
  He standes amazed, how he thence should fade.
  At last the trumpets Triumph sound on hie,
  And running Heralds humble homage made,
  Greeting him goodly with new victorie,
And to him brought the shield, the cause of enmitie.

16

Wherewith he goeth to that soveraine Queene,
  And falling her before on lowly knee,
  To her makes present of his service seene:
  Which she accepts, with thankes, and goodly gree,
  Greatly advauncing his gay chevalree.
  So marcheth home, and by her takes the knight,
  Whom all the people follow with great glee,
  Shouting, and clapping all their hands on hight,
That all the aire it fils, and flyes to heaven bright.

17

Home is he brought, and laid in sumptuous bed:
  Where many skilfull leaches him abide,
  To salve his hurts, that yet still freshly bled.
  In wine and oyle they wash his woundes wide,
  And softly can embalme on every side.
  And all the while, most heavenly melody
  About the bed sweet musicke did divide,
  Him to beguile of griefe and agony:
And all the while *Duessa* wept full bitterly.

18

As when a wearie traveller that strayes
  By muddy shore of broad seven-mouthed *Nile*,
  Unweeting of the perillous wandring wayes,
  Doth meet a cruell craftie Crocodile,
  Which in false griefe hyding his harmefull guile,
  Doth weepe full sore, and sheddeth tender teares:
  The foolish man, that pitties all this while
  His mournefull plight, is swallowd up unwares,
Forgetfull of his owne, that mindes anothers cares.

19

So wept *Duessa* untill eventide,
  That shyning lampes in *Joves* high house were light:
  Then forth she rose, ne lenger would abide,
  But comes unto the place, where th'Hethen knight
  In slombring swownd nigh voyd of vitall spright,
  Lay cover'd with inchaunted cloud all day:
  Whom when she found, as she him left in plight,
  To wayle his woefull case she would not stay,
But to the easterne coast of heaven makes speedy way.

20

Where griesly *Night*, with visage deadly sad,
  That *Phœbus* chearefull face durst never vew,
  And in a foule blacke pitchie mantle clad,
  She findes forth comming from her darkesome mew,
  Where she all day did hide her hated hew.
  Before the dore her yron charet stood,
  Alreadie harnessed for journey new;
  And coleblacke steedes yborne of hellish brood,
That on their rustie bits did champ, as they were wood.

21

Who when she saw *Duessa* sunny bright,
  Adornd with gold and jewels shining cleare,
  She greatly grew amazed at the sight,
  And th'unacquainted light began to feare:
  For never did such brightnesse there appeare,
  And would have backe retyred to her cave,
  Untill the witches speech she gan to heare,
  Saying, Yet O thou dreaded Dame, I crave
Abide, till I have told the message, which I have.

22

She stayd, and foorth *Duessa* gan proceede,
  O thou most auncient Grandmother of all,
  More old than *Jove*, whom thou at first didst breede,
  Or that great house of Gods cælestiall,
  Which wast begot in *Dæmogorgons* hall,
  And sawst the secrets of the world unmade,
  Why suffredst thou thy Nephewes deare to fall
  With Elfin sword, most shamefully betrade?
Lo where the stout *Sansjoy* doth sleepe in deadly shade.

23

And him before, I saw with bitter eyes
  The bold *Sansfoy* shrinke underneath his speare;
  And now the pray of fowles in field he lyes,
  Nor wayld of friends, nor laid on groning beare,
  That whylome was to me too dearely deare.
  O what of Gods then boots it to be borne,
  If old *Aveugles* sonnes so evill heare?
  Or who shall not great *Nightes* children scorne,
When two of three her Nephews are so fowle forlorne.

24

Up then, up dreary Dame, of darknesse Queene,
  Go gather up the reliques of thy race,
  Or else goe them avenge, and let be seene,
  That dreaded *Night* in brightest day hath place,
  And can the children of faire light deface.
  Her feeling speeches some compassion moved
  In hart, and chaunge in that great mothers face:
  Yet pittie in her hart was never proved
Till then: for evermore she hated, never loved.

25

And said, Deare daughter rightly may I rew
  The fall of famous children borne of mee,
  And good successes, which their foes ensew:
  But who can turne the streame of destinee,
  Or breake the chayne of strong necessitee,
  Which fast is tyde to *Joves* eternall seat?
  The sonnes of Day he favoureth, I see,
  And by my ruines thinkes to make them great:
To make one great by others losse, is bad excheat.

26

Yet shall they not escape so freely all;
  For some shall pay the price of others guilt:
  And he the man that made *Sansfoy* to fall,
  Shall with his owne bloud price that he hath spilt.
  But what art thou, that telst of Nephews kilt?
  I that do seeme not I, *Duessa* am,
  (Quoth she) how ever now in garments gilt,
  And gorgeous gold arayd I to thee came;
Duessa I, the daughter of Deceipt and Shame.

27

Then bowing downe her aged backe, she kist
  The wicked witch, saying; In that faire face
  The false resemblance of Deceipt, I wist
  Did closely lurke; yet so true-seeming grace
  It carried, that I scarse in darkesome place
  Could it discerne, though I the mother bee
  Of falshood, and root of *Duessaes* race.
  O welcome child, whom I have longd to see,
And now have seene unwares. Lo now I go with thee.

28

Then to her yron wagon she betakes,
  And with her beares the fowle welfavourd witch:
  Through mirkesome aire her readie way she makes.
  Her twyfold Teme, of which two blacke as pitch,
  And two were browne, yet each to each unlich,
  Did softly swim away, ne ever stampe,
  Unlesse she chaunst their stubborne mouths to twitch;
  Then foming tarre, their bridles they would champe,
And trampling the fine element, would fiercely rampe.

29

So well they sped, that they be come at length
  Unto the place, whereas the Paynim lay,
  Devoid of outward sense, and native strength,
  Coverd with charmed cloud from vew of day,
  And sight of men, since his late luckelesse fray.
  His cruell wounds with cruddy bloud congealed,
  They binden up so wisely, as they may,
  And handle softly, till they can be healed:
So lay him in her charet, close in night concealed.

30

And all the while she stood upon the ground,
  The wakefull dogs did never cease to bay,
  As giving warning of th'unwonted sound,
  With which her yron wheeles did them affray,
  And her darke griesly looke them much dismay;
  The messenger of death, the ghastly Owle
  With drearie shriekes did also her bewray;
  And hungry Wolves continually did howle,
At her abhorred face, so filthy and so fowle.

31

Thence turning backe in silence soft they stole,
 And brought the heavie corse with easie pace
 To yawning gulfe of deepe *Avernus* hole.
 By that same hole an entrance darke and bace
 With smoake and sulphure hiding all the place,
 Descends to hell: there creature never past,
 That backe returned without heavenly grace;
 But dreadfull *Furies*, which their chaines have brast,
And damned sprights sent forth to make ill men aghast.

32

By that same way the direfull dames doe drive
 Their mournefull charet, fild with rusty blood,
 And downe to *Plutoes* house are come bilive:
 Which passing through, on every side them stood
 The trembling ghosts with sad amazed mood,
 Chattring their yron teeth, and staring wide
 With stonie eyes; and all the hellish brood
 Of feends infernall flockt on every side,
To gaze on earthly wight, that with the Night durst ride.

33

They pas the bitter waves of *Acheron*,
 Where many soules sit wailing woefully,
 And come to fiery flood of *Phlegeton*,
 Whereas the damned ghosts in torments fry,
 And with sharpe shrilling shriekes doe bootlesse cry,
 Cursing high *Jove*, the which them thither sent.
 The house of endlesse paine is built thereby,
 In which ten thousand sorts of punishment
The cursed creatures doe eternally torment.

34

Before the threshold dreadfull *Cerberus*
 His three deformed heads did lay along,
 Curled with thousand adders venemous,
 And lilled forth his bloudie flaming tong:
 At them he gan to reare his bristles strong,
 And felly gnarre, untill dayes enemy
 Did him appease; then downe his taile he hong
 And suffered them to passen quietly:
For she in hell and heaven had power equally.

35

There was *Ixion* turned on a wheele,
　For daring tempt the Queene of heaven to sin;
　And *Sisyphus* an huge round stone did reele
　Against an hill, ne might from labour lin;
　There thirstie *Tantalus* hong by the chin;
　And *Tityus* fed a vulture on his maw;
　Typhæus joynts were stretched on a gin,
　Theseus condemned to endlesse slouth by law,
And fifty sisters water in leake vessels draw.

36

They all beholding worldly wights in place,
　Leave off their worke, unmindfull of their smart,
　To gaze on them; who forth by them doe pace,
　Till they be come unto the furthest part:
　Where was a Cave ywrought by wondrous art,
　Deepe, darke, uneasie, dolefull, comfortlesse,
　In which sad *Æsculapius* farre a part
　Emprisond was in chaines remedilesse,
For that *Hippolytus* rent corse he did redresse.

37

Hippolytus a jolly huntsman was,
　That wont in charet chace the foming Bore;
　He all his Peeres in beautie did surpas,
　But Ladies love as losse of time forbore:
　His wanton stepdame loved him the more,
　But when she saw her offred sweets refused
　Her love she turnd to hate, and him before
　His father fierce of treason false accused,
And with her gealous termes his open eares abused.

38

Who all in rage his Sea-god syre besought,
　Some cursed vengeance on his sonne to cast:
　From surging gulf two monsters straight were brought,
　With dread whereof his chasing steedes aghast,
　Both charet swift and huntsman overcast.
　His goodly corps on ragged cliffs yrent,
　Was quite dismembred, and his members chast
　Scattered on every mountaine, as he went,
That of *Hippolytus* was left no moniment.

39

His cruell stepdame seeing what was donne,
   Her wicked dayes with wretched knife did end,
   In death avowing th'innocence of her sonne.
   Which hearing his rash Syre, began to rend
   His haire, and hastie tongue, that did offend:
   Tho gathering up the relicks of his smart
   By *Dianes* meanes, who was *Hippolyts* frend,
   Them brought to *Æsculape*, that by his art
Did heale them all againe, and joyned every part.

40

Such wondrous science in mans wit to raine
   When *Jove* avizd, that could the dead revive,
   And fates expired could renew againe,
   Of endlesse life he might him not deprive,
   But unto hell did thrust him downe alive,
   With flashing thunderbolt ywounded sore:
   Where long remaining, he did alwaies strive
   Himselfe with salves to health for to restore,
And slake the heavenly fire, that raged evermore.

41

There auncient Night arriving, did alight
   From her nigh wearie waine, and in her armes
   To *Æsculapius* brought the wounded knight:
   Whom having softly disarayd of armes,
   Tho gan to him discover all his harmes,
   Beseeching him with prayer, and with praise,
   If either salves, or oyles, or herbes, or charmes
   A fordonne wight from dore of death mote raise,
He would at her request prolong her nephews daies.

42

Ah Dame (quoth he) thou temptest me in vaine,
   To dare the thing, which daily yet I rew,
   And the old cause of my continued paine
   With like attempt to like end to renew.
   Is not enough, that thrust from heaven dew
   Here endlesse penance for one fault I pay,
   But that redoubled crime with vengence new
   Thou biddest me to eeke? Can Night defray
The wrath of thundring *Jove*, that rules both night and day?

43

Not so (quoth she) but sith that heavens king
  From hope of heaven hath thee excluded quight,
  Why fearest thou, that canst not hope for thing,
  And fearest not, that more thee hurten might,
  Now in the powre of everlasting Night?
  Goe to then, O thou farre renowmed sonne
  Of great *Apollo*, shew thy famous might
  In medicine, that else hath to thee wonne
Great paines, and greater praise, both never to be donne.

44

Her words prevaild: And then the learned leach
  His cunning hand gan to his wounds to lay,
  And all things else, the which his art did teach:
  Which having seene, from thence arose away
  The mother of dread darknesse, and let stay
  Aveugles sonne there in the leaches cure,
  And backe returning tooke her wonted way,
  To runne her timely race, whilst *Phœbus* pure
In westerne waves his wearie wagon did recure.

45

The false *Duessa* leaving noyous Night,
  Returned to stately pallace of dame Pride;
  Where when she came, she found the Faery knight
  Departed thence, albe his woundes wide
  Not throughly heald, unreadie were to ride.
  Good cause he had to hasten thence away;
  For on a day his wary Dwarfe had spide,
  Where in a dongeon deepe huge numbers lay
Of caytive wretched thrals, that wayled night and day.

46

A ruefull sight, as could be seene with eie;
  Of whom he learned had in secret wise
  The hidden cause of their captivitie,
  How mortgaging their lives to *Covetise*,
  Through wastfull Pride, and wanton Riotise,
  They were by law of that proud Tyrannesse
  Provokt with *Wrath*, and *Envies* false surmise,
  Condemned to that Dongeon mercilesse,
Where they should live in woe, and die in wretchednesse.

47

There was that great proud king of *Babylon,*
    That would compell all nations to adore,
    And him as onely God to call upon,
    Till through celestiall doome throwne out of dore,
    Into an Oxe he was transform'd of yore:
    There also was king *Cræsus,* that enhaunst
    His heart too high through his great riches store;
    And proud *Antiochus,* the which advaunst
His cursed hand gainst God, and on his altars daunst.

48

And them long time before, great *Nimrod* was,
    That first the world with sword and fire warrayd;
    And after him old *Ninus* farre did pas
    In princely pompe, of all the world obayd;
    There also was that mightie Monarch layd
    Low under all, yet above all in pride,
    That name of native syre did fowle upbrayd,
    And would as *Ammons* sonne be magnifide,
Till scornd of God and man a shamefull death he dide.

49

All these together in one heape were throwne,
    Like carkases of beasts in butchers stall.
    And in another corner wide were strowne
    The antique ruines of the *Romaines* fall:
    Great *Romulus* the Grandsyre of them all,
    Proud *Tarquin,* and too lordly *Lentulus,*
    Stout *Scipio,* and stubborne *Hanniball,*
    Ambitious *Sylla,* and sterne *Marius,*
High *Cæsar,* great *Pompey,* and fierce *Antonius.*

50

Amongst these mighty men were wemen mixt,
    Proud wemen, vaine, forgetfull of their yoke:
    The bold *Semiramis,* whose sides transfixt
    With sonnes owne blade, her fowle reproches spoke;
    Faire *Sthenobœa,* that her selfe did choke
    With wilfull cord, for wanting of her will;
    High minded *Cleopatra,* that with stroke
    Of Aspes sting her selfe did stoutly kill:
And thousands moe the like, that did that dongeon fill.

51

Besides the endlesse routs of wretched thralles,
　Which thither were assembled day by day,
　From all the world after their wofull falles,
　Through wicked pride, and wasted wealthes decay.
　But most of all, which in that Dongeon lay
　Fell from high Princes courts, or Ladies bowres,
　Where they in idle pompe, or wanton play,
　Consumed had their goods, and thriftlesse howres,
And lastly throwne themselves into these heavy stowres.

52

Whose case when as the carefull Dwarfe had tould,
　And made ensample of their mournefull sight
　Unto his maister, he no lenger would
　There dwell in perill of like painefull plight,
　But early rose, and ere that dawning light
　Discovered had the world to heaven wyde,
　He by a privie Posterne tooke his flight,
　That of no envious eyes he mote be spyde:
For doubtlesse death ensewd, if any him descryde.

53

Scarse could he footing find in that fowle way,
　For many corses, like a great Lay-stall
　Of murdred men which therein strowed lay,
　Without remorse, or decent funerall:
　Which all through that great Princesse pride did fall
　And came to shamefull end. And them beside
　Forth ryding underneath the castell wall,
　A donghill of dead carkases he spide,
The dreadfull spectacle of that sad house of *Pride*.

CANT. VI

From lawlesse lust by wondrous grace
fayre Una is releast:
Whom salvage nation does adore,
and learnes her wise beheast.

I

AS when a ship, that flyes faire under saile,
   An hidden rocke escaped hath unwares,
   That lay in waite her wrack for to bewaile,
   The Marriner yet halfe amazed stares
   At perill past, and yet in doubt ne dares
   To joy at his foole-happie oversight:
   So doubly is distrest twixt joy and cares
   The dreadlesse courage of this Elfin knight,
Having escapt so sad ensamples in his sight.

2

Yet sad he was that his too hastie speed
   The faire *Duess'* had forst him leave behind;
   And yet more sad, that *Una* his deare dreed
   Her truth had staind with treason so unkind;
   Yet crime in her could never creature find,
   But for his love, and for her owne selfe sake,
   She wandred had from one to other *Ynd*,
   Him for to seeke, ne ever would forsake,
Till her unwares the fierce *Sansloy* did overtake.

3

Who after *Archimagoes* fowle defeat,
   Led her away into a forrest wilde,
   And turning wrathfull fire to lustfull heat,
   With beastly sin thought her to have defilde,
   And made the vassall of his pleasures vilde.
   Yet first he cast by treatie, and by traynes,
   Her to perswade, that stubborne fort to yilde:
   For greater conquest of hard love he gaynes,
That workes it to his will, than he that it constraines.

4

With fawning wordes he courted her a while,
  And looking lovely, and oft sighing sore,
  Her constant hart did tempt with diverse guile:
  But wordes, and lookes, and sighes she did abhore,
  As rocke of Diamond stedfast evermore.
  Yet for to feed his fyrie lustfull eye,
  He snatcht the vele, that hong her face before;
  Then gan her beautie shine, as brightest skye,
And burnt his beastly hart t'efforce her chastitye.

5

So when he saw his flatt'ring arts to fayle,
  And subtile engines bet from batteree,
  With greedy force he gan the fort assayle,
  Whereof he weend possessed soone to bee,
  And win rich spoile of ransackt chastetee.
  Ah heavens, that do this hideous act behold,
  And heavenly virgin thus outraged see,
  How can ye vengeance just so long withhold,
And hurle not flashing flames upon that Paynim bold?

6

The pitteous maiden carefull comfortlesse,
  Does throw out thrilling shriekes, and shrieking cryes,
  The last vaine helpe of womens great distresse,
  And with loud plaints importuneth the skyes,
  That molten starres do drop like weeping eyes;
  And *Phœbus* flying so most shamefull sight,
  His blushing face in foggy cloud implyes,
  And hides for shame. What wit of mortall wight
Can now devise to quit a thrall from such a plight?

7

Eternall providence exceeding thought,
  Where none appeares can make her selfe a way:
  A wondrous way it for this Lady wrought,
  From Lyons clawes to pluck the griped pray.
  Her shrill outcryes and shriekes so loud did bray,
  That all the woodes and forestes did resownd;
  A troupe of *Faunes* and *Satyres* far away
  Within the wood were dauncing in a rownd,
Whiles old *Sylvanus* slept in shady arber sownd.

8

Who when they heard that pitteous strained voice,
    In hast forsooke their rurall meriment,
    And ran towards the far rebownded noyce,
    To weet, what wight so loudly did lament.
    Unto the place they come incontinent:
    Whom when the raging Sarazin espide,
    A rude, misshapen, monstrous rablement,
    Whose like he never saw, he durst not bide,
But got his ready steed, and fast away gan ride.

9

The wyld woodgods arrived in the place,
    There find the virgin dolefull desolate,
    With ruffled rayments, and faire blubbred face,
    As her outrageous foe had left her late,
    And trembling yet through feare of former hate;
    All stand amazed at so uncouth sight,
    And gin to pittie her unhappie state,
    All stand astonied at her beautie bright,
In their rude eyes unworthie of so wofull plight.

10

She more amaz'd, in double dread doth dwell;
    And every tender part for feare does shake:
    As when a greedie Wolfe through hunger fell
    A seely Lambe farre from the flocke does take,
    Of whom he meanes his bloudie feast to make,
    A Lyon spyes fast running towards him,
    The innocent pray in hast he does forsake,
    Which quit from death yet quakes in every lim
With chaunge of feare, to see the Lyon looke so grim.

11

Such fearefull fit assaid her trembling hart,
    Ne word to speake, ne joynt to move she had:
    The salvage nation feele her secret smart,
    And read her sorrow in her count'nance sad;
    Their frowning forheads with rough hornes yclad,
    And rusticke horror all a side doe lay,
    And gently grenning, shew a semblance glad
    To comfort her, and feare to put away,
Their backward bent knees teach her humbly to obay.

12

The doubtfull Damzell dare not yet commit
    Her single person to their barbarous truth,
    But still twixt feare and hope amazd does sit,
    Late learnd what harme to hastie trust ensu'th,
    They in compassion of her tender youth,
    And wonder of her beautie soveraine,
    Are wonne with pitty and unwonted ruth,
    And all prostrate upon the lowly plaine,
Do kisse her feete, and fawne on her with count'nance faine.

13

Their harts she ghesseth by their humble guise,
    And yieldes her to extremitie of time;
    So from the ground she fearelesse doth arise,
    And walketh forth without suspect of crime:
    They all as glad, as birdes of joyous Prime,
    Thence lead her forth, about her dauncing round,
    Shouting, and singing all a shepheards ryme,
    And with greene braunches strowing all the ground,
Do worship her, as Queene, with olive girlond cround.

14

And all the way their merry pipes they sound,
    That all the woods with doubled Eccho ring,
    And with their horned feet do weare the ground,
    Leaping like wanton kids in pleasant Spring.
    So towards old *Sylvanus* they her bring;
    Who with the noyse awaked, commeth out,
    To weet the cause, his weake steps governing,
    And aged limbs on Cypresse stadle stout,
And with an yvie twyne his wast is girt about.

15

Far off he wonders, what them makes so glad,
    Or *Bacchus* merry fruit they did invent,
    Or *Cybeles* franticke rites have made them mad;
    They drawing nigh, unto their God present
    That flowre of faith and beautie excellent.
    The God himselfe vewing that mirrhour rare,
    Stood long amazd, and burnt in his intent;
    His owne faire *Dryope* now he thinkes not faire,
And *Pholoe* fowle, when her to this he doth compaire.

16

The woodborne people fall before her flat,
 And worship her as Goddesse of the wood;
 And old *Sylvanus* selfe bethinkes not, what
 To thinke of wight so faire, but gazing stood,
 In doubt to deeme her borne of earthly brood;
 Sometimes Dame *Venus* selfe he seemes to see,
 But *Venus* never had so sober mood;
 Sometimes *Diana* he her takes to bee,
But misseth bow, and shaftes, and buskins to her knee.

17

By vew of her he ginneth to revive
 His ancient love, and dearest *Cyparisse*,
 And calles to mind his pourtraiture alive,
 How faire he was, and yet not faire to this,
 And how he slew with glauncing dart amisse
 A gentle Hynd, the which the lovely boy
 Did love as life, above all worldly blisse;
 For griefe whereof the lad n'ould after joy,
But pynd away in anguish and selfe-wild annoy.

18

The wooddy Nymphes, faire *Hamadryades*
 Her to behold do thither runne apace,
 And all the troupe of light-foot *Naiades*,
 Flocke all about to see her lovely face:
 But when they vewed have her heavenly grace,
 They envie her in their malitious mind,
 And fly away for feare of fowle disgrace:
 But all the *Satyres* scorne their woody kind,
And henceforth nothing faire, but her on earth they find.

19

Glad of such lucke, the luckelesse lucky maid,
 Did her content to please their feeble eyes,
 And long time with that salvage people staid,
 To gather breath in many miseries.
 During which time her gentle wit she plyes,
 To teach them truth, which worshipt her in vaine,
 And made her th'Image of Idolatryes;
 But when their bootlesse zeale she did restraine
From her own worship, they her Asse would worship fayn.

20

It fortuned a noble warlike knight
  By just occasion to that forrest came,
  To seeke his kindred, and the lignage right,
  From whence he tooke his well deserved name:
  He had in armes abroad wonne muchell fame,
  And fild far landes with glorie of his might,
  Plaine, faithfull, true, and enimy of shame,
  And ever lov'd to fight for Ladies right,
But in vaine glorious frayes he litle did delight.

21

A Satyres sonne yborne in forrest wyld,
  By straunge adventure as it did betyde,
  And there begotten of a Lady myld,
  Faire *Thyamis* the daughter of *Labryde*,
  That was in sacred bands of wedlocke tyde
  To *Therion*, a loose unruly swayne;
  Who had more joy to raunge the forrest wyde,
  And chase the salvage beast with busie payne,
Than serve his Ladies love, and wast in pleasures vayne.

22

The forlorne mayd did with loves longing burne,
  And could not lacke her lovers company,
  But to the wood she goes, to serve her turne,
  And seeke her spouse, that from her still does fly,
  And followes other game and venery:
  A Satyre chaunst her wandring for to find,
  And kindling coles of lust in brutish eye,
  The loyall links of wedlocke did unbind,
And made her person thrall unto his beastly kind.

23

So long in secret cabin there he held
  Her captive to his sensuall desire,
  Till that with timely fruit her belly sweld,
  And bore a boy unto that salvage sire:
  Then home he suffred her for to retire,
  For ransome leaving him the late borne childe;
  Whom till to ryper yeares he gan aspire,
  He noursled up in life and manners wilde,
Emongst wild beasts and woods, from lawes of men exilde.

24

For all he taught the tender ymp, was but
　　To banish cowardize and bastard feare;
　　His trembling hand he would him force to put
　　Upon the Lyon and the rugged Beare,
　　And from the she Beares teats her whelps to teare;
　　And eke wyld roring Buls he would him make
　　To tame, and ryde their backes not made to beare;
　　And the Robuckes in flight to overtake,
That every beast for feare of him did fly and quake.

25

Thereby so fearelesse, and so fell he grew,
　　That his owne sire and maister of his guise
　　Did often tremble at his horrid vew,
　　And oft for dread of hurt would him advise,
　　The angry beasts not rashly to despise,
　　Nor too much to provoke; for he would learne
　　The Lyon stoup to him in lowly wise,
　　(A lesson hard) and make the Libbard sterne
Leave roaring, when in rage he for revenge did earne.

26

And for to make his powre approved more,
　　Wyld beasts in yron yokes he would compell;
　　The spotted Panther, and the tusked Bore,
　　The Pardale swift, and the Tigre cruell;
　　The Antelope, and Wolfe both fierce and fell;
　　And them constraine in equall teme to draw.
　　Such joy he had, their stubborne harts to quell,
　　And sturdie courage tame with dreadfull aw,
That his beheast they feared, as a tyrans law.

27

His loving mother came upon a day
　　Unto the woods, to see her little sonne;
　　And chaunst unwares to meet him in the way,
　　After his sportes, and cruell pastime donne,
　　When after him a Lyonesse did runne,
　　That roaring all with rage, did lowd requere
　　Her children deare, whom he away had wonne:
　　The Lyon whelpes she saw how he did beare,
And lull in rugged armes, withouten childish feare.

28

The fearefull Dame all quaked at the sight,
　And turning backe, gan fast to fly away,
　Untill with love revokt from vaine affright,
　She hardly yet perswaded was to stay,
　And then to him these womanish words gan say;
　Ah *Satyrane*, my dearling, and my joy,
　For love of me leave off this dreadfull play;
　To dally thus with death, is no fit toy,
Go find some other play-fellowes, mine own sweet boy.

29

In these and like delights of bloudy game
　He trayned was, till ryper yeares he raught,
　And there abode, whilst any beast of name
　Walkt in that forest, whom he had not taught
　To feare his force: and then his courage haught
　Desird of forreine foemen to be knowne,
　And far abroad for straunge adventures sought:
　In which his might was never overthrowne,
But through all Faery lond his famous worth was blown.

30

Yet evermore it was his manner faire,
　After long labours and adventures spent,
　Unto those native woods for to repaire,
　To see his sire and ofspring auncient.
　And now he thither came for like intent;
　Where he unwares the fairest *Una* found,
　Straunge Lady, in so straunge habiliment,
　Teaching the Satyres, which her sat around,
Trew sacred lore, which from her sweet lips did redound.

31

He wondred at her wisedome heavenly rare,
　Whose like in womens wit he never knew;
　And when her curteous deeds he did compare,
　Gan her admire, and her sad sorrowes rew,
　Blaming of Fortune, which such troubles threw,
　And joyd to make proofe of her crueltie
　On gentle Dame, so hurtlesse, and so trew:
　Thenceforth he kept her goodly company,
And learnd her discipline of faith and veritie.

32

But she all vowd unto the *Redcrosse* knight,
His wandring perill closely did lament,
Ne in this new acquaintaunce could delight,
But her deare heart with anguish did torment,
And all her wit in secret counsels spent,
How to escape. At last in privie wise
To *Satyrane* she shewed her intent;
Who glad to gain such favour, gan devise,
How with that pensive Maid he best might thence arise.

33

So on a day when Satyres all were gone,
To do their service to *Sylvanus* old,
The gentle virgin left behind alone
He led away with courage stout and bold.
Too late it was, to Satyres to be told,
Or ever hope recover her againe:
In vaine he seekes that having cannot hold.
So fast he carried her with carefull paine,
That they the woods are past, and come now to the plaine.

34

The better part now of the lingring day,
They traveild had, when as they farre espide
A wearie wight forwandring by the way,
And towards him they gan in hast to ride,
To weet of newes, that did abroad betide,
Or tydings of her knight of the *Redcrosse*.
But he them spying, gan to turne aside,
For feare as seemd, or for some feigned losse;
More greedy they of newes, fast towards him do crosse.

35

A silly man, in simple weedes forworne,
And soild with dust of the long dried way;
His sandales were with toilesome travell torne,
And face all tand with scorching sunny ray,
As he had traveild many a sommers day,
Through boyling sands of *Arabie* and *Ynde*;
And in his hand a *Jacobs* staffe, to stay
His wearie limbes upon: and eke behind,
His scrip did hang, in which his needments he did bind.

36

The knight approching nigh, of him inquerd
  Tydings of warre, and of adventures new;
  But warres, nor new adventures none he herd.
  Then *Una* gan to aske, if ought he knew,
  Or heard abroad of that her champion trew,
  That in his armour bare a croslet red.
  Aye me, Deare dame (quoth he) well may I rew
  To tell the sad sight, which mine eies have red:
These eyes did see that knight both living and eke ded.

37

That cruell word her tender hart so thrild,
  That suddein cold did runne through every vaine,
  And stony horrour all her sences fild
  With dying fit, that downe she fell for paine.
  The knight her lightly reared up againe,
  And comforted with curteous kind reliefe:
  Then wonne from death, she bad him tellen plaine
  The further processe of her hidden griefe;
The lesser pangs can beare, who hath endur'd the chiefe.

38

Then gan the Pilgrim thus, I chaunst this day,
  This fatall day, that shall I ever rew,
  To see two knights in travell on my way
  (A sory sight) arraung'd in battell new,
  Both breathing vengeaunce, both of wrathfull hew:
  My fearefull flesh did tremble at their strife,
  To see their blades so greedily imbrew,
  That drunke with bloud, yet thristed after life:
What more? the *Redcrosse* knight was slaine with Paynim knife.

39

Ah dearest Lord (quoth she) how might that bee,
  And he the stoutest knight, that ever wonne?
  Ah dearest dame (quoth he) how might I see
  The thing, that might not be, and yet was donne?
  Where is (said *Satyrane*) that Paynims sonne,
  That him of life, and us of joy hath reft?
  Not far away (quoth he) he hence doth wonne
  Foreby a fountaine, where I late him left
Washing his bloudy wounds, that through the steele were cleft.

40

Therewith the knight thence marched forth in hast,
 Whiles *Una* with huge heavinesse opprest,
 Could not for sorrow follow him so fast;
 And soone he came, as he the place had ghest,
 Whereas that *Pagan* proud him selfe did rest,
 In secret shadow by a fountaine side:
 Even he it was, that earst would have supprest
 Fair *Una*: whom when *Satyrane* espide,
With fowle reprochfull words he boldly him defide.

41

And said, Arise thou cursed Miscreaunt,
 That hast with knightlesse guile and trecherous train
 Faire knighthood fowly shamed, and doest vaunt
 That good knight of the *Redcrosse* to have slain:
 Arise, and with like treason now maintain
 Thy guilty wrong, or else thee guilty yield.
 The Sarazin this hearing, rose amain,
 And catching up in hast his three square shield,
And shining helmet, soone him buckled to the field.

42

And drawing nigh him said, Ah misborne Elfe,
 In evill houre thy foes thee hither sent,
 Anothers wrongs to wreake upon thy selfe:
 Yet ill thou blamest me, for having blent
 My name with guile and traiterous intent;
 That *Redcrosse* knight, perdie, I never slew,
 But had he beene, where earst his armes were lent,
 Th'enchaunter vaine his errour should not rew:
But thou his errour shalt, I hope now proven trew.

43

Therewith they gan, both furious and fell,
 To thunder blowes, and fiersly to assaile
 Each other bent his enimy to quell,
 That with their force they perst both plate and maile,
 And made wide furrowes in their fleshes fraile,
 That it would pitty any living eie.
 Large floods of bloud adowne their sides did raile:
 But floods of bloud could not them satisfie:
Both hungred after death: both chose to win, or die.

44

So long they fight, and fell revenge pursue,
  That fainting each, themselves to breathen let,
  And oft refreshed, battell oft renue:
  As when two Bores with rancling malice met,
  Their gory sides fresh bleeding fiercely fret,
  Til breathlesse both them selves aside retire,
  Where foming wrath, their cruell tuskes they whet,
  And trample th'earth, the whiles they may respire;
Then backe to fight againe, new breathed and entire.

45

So fiersly, when these knights had breathed once,
  They gan to fight returne, increasing more
  Their puissant force, and cruell rage attonce,
  With heaped strokes more hugely, than before,
  That with their drerie wounds and bloudy gore
  They both deformed, scarsely could be known.
  By this sad *Una* fraught with anguish sore,
  Led with their noise, which through the aire was thrown,
Arriv'd, where they in erth their fruitles bloud had sown.

46

Whom all so soone as that proud Sarazin
  Espide, he gan revive the memory
  Of his lewd lusts, and late attempted sin,
  And left the doubtfull battell hastily,
  To catch her, newly offred to his eie:
  But *Satyrane* with strokes him turning, staid,
  And sternely bad him other businesse plie,
  Than hunt the steps of pure unspotted Maid:
Wherewith he all enrag'd, these bitter speaches said.

47

O foolish faeries sonne, what furie mad
  Hath thee incenst, to hast thy dolefull fate?
  Were it not better, I that Lady had,
  Than that thou hadst repented it too late?
  Most sencelesse man he, that himselfe doth hate,
  To love another. Lo then for thine ayd
  Here take thy lovers token on thy pate.
  So they to fight; the whiles the royall Mayd
Fled farre away, of that proud Paynim sore affrayd.

48

But that false *Pilgrim*, which that leasing told,
   Being in deed old *Archimage*, did stay
   In secret shadow, all this to behold,
   And much rejoyced in their bloudy fray:
   But when he saw the Damsell passe away
   He left his stond, and her pursewd apace,
   In hope to bring her to her last decay.
   But for to tell her lamentable cace,
And eke this battels end, will need another place.

CANT. VII

The Redcrosse knight is captive made
By Gyaunt proud opprest,
Prince Arthur meets with Una great-
ly with those newes distrest.

1

WHAT man so wise, what earthly wit so ware,
   As to descry the crafty cunning traine,
   By which deceipt doth maske in visour faire,
   And cast her colours dyed deepe in graine,
   To seeme like Truth, whose shape she well can faine,
   And fitting gestures to her purpose frame,
   The guiltlesse man with guile to entertaine?
   Great maistresse of her art was that false **Dame**,
The false *Duessa*, cloked with *Fidessaes* name.

2

Who when returning from the drery *Night*,
   She fownd not in that perilous house of *Pryde*,
   Where she had left, the noble *Redcrosse* knight,
   Her hoped pray, she would no lenger bide,
   But forth she went, to seeke him far and wide.
   Ere long she fownd, whereas he wearie sate,
   To rest him selfe, foreby a fountaine side,
   Disarmed all of yron-coted Plate,
And by his side his steed the grassy forage ate.

3

He feedes upon the cooling shade, and bayes
  His sweatie forehead in the breathing wind,
  Which through the trembling leaves full gently playes
  Wherein the cherefull birds of sundry kind
  Do chaunt sweet musick, to delight his mind:
  The Witch approching gan him fairely greet,
  And with reproch of carelesnesse unkind
  Upbrayd, for leaving her in place unmeet,
With fowle words tempring faire, soure gall with hony sweet.

4

Unkindnesse past, they gan of solace treat,
  And bathe in pleasaunce of the joyous shade,
  Which shielded them against the boyling heat,
  And with greene boughes decking a gloomy glade,
  About the fountaine like a girlond made;
  Whose bubbling wave did ever freshly well,
  Ne ever would through fervent sommer fade:
  The sacred Nymph, which therein wont to dwell,
Was out of *Dianes* favour, as it then befell.

5

The cause was this: one day when *Phœbe* fayre
  With all her band was following the chace,
  This Nymph, quite tyr'd with heat of scorching ayre
  Sat downe to rest in middest of the race:
  The goddesse wroth gan fowly her disgrace,
  And bad the waters, which from her did flow,
  Be such as she her selfe was then in place.
  Thenceforth her waters waxed dull and slow,
And all that drunke thereof, did faint and feeble grow.

6

Hereof this gentle knight unweeting was,
  And lying downe upon the sandie graile,
  Drunke of the streame, as cleare as cristall glas;
  Eftsoones his manly forces gan to faile,
  And mightie strong was turnd to feeble fraile.
  His chaunged powres at first them selves not felt,
  Till crudled cold his corage gan assaile,
  And chearefull bloud in faintnesse chill did melt,
Which like a fever fit through all his body swelt.

7

Yet goodly court he made still to his Dame,
　Pourd out in loosnesse on the grassy grownd,
　Both carelesse of his health, and of his fame:
　Till at the last he heard a dreadfull sownd,
　Which through the wood loud bellowing, did rebownd,
　That all the earth for terrour seemd to shake,
　And trees did tremble. Th'Elfe therewith astownd,
　Upstarted lightly from his looser make,
And his unready weapons gan in hand to take.

8

But ere he could his armour on him dight,
　Or get his shield, his monstrous enimy
　With sturdie steps came stalking in his sight,
　An hideous Geant horrible and hye,
　That with his talnesse seemd to threat the skye,
　The ground eke groned under him for dreed;
　His living like saw never living eye,
　Ne durst behold: his stature did exceed
The hight of three the tallest sonnes of mortall seed.

9

The greatest Earth his uncouth mother was,
　And blustring *Æolus* his boasted sire,
　Who with his breath, which through the world doth pas,
　Her hollow womb did secretly inspire,
　And fild her hidden caves with stormie yre,
　That she conceiv'd; and trebling the dew time,
　In which the wombes of women do expire,
　Brought forth this monstrous masse of earthly slime,
Puft up with emptie wind, and fild with sinfull crime.

10

So growen great through arrogant delight
　Of th'high descent, whereof he was yborne,
　And through presumption of his matchlesse might,
　All other powres and knighthood he did scorne.
　Such now he marcheth to this man forlorne,
　And left to losse: his stalking steps are stayde
　Upon a snaggy Oke, which he had torne
　Out of his mothers bowelles, and it made
His mortall mace, wherewith his foemen he dismayde.

11

That when the knight he spide, he gan advance
　With huge force and insupportable mayne,
　And towardes him with dreadfull fury praunce;
　Who haplesse, and eke hopelesse, all in vaine
　Did to him pace, sad battaile to darrayne,
　Disarmd, disgrast, and inwardly dismayde,
　And eke so faint in every joynt and vaine,
　Through that fraile fountaine, which him feeble made,
That scarsely could he weeld his bootlesse single blade.

12

The Geaunt strooke so maynly mercilesse,
　That could have overthrowne a stony towre,
　And were not heavenly grace, that him did blesse,
　He had beene pouldred all, as thin as flowre:
　But he was wary of that deadly stowre,
　And lightly lept from underneath the blow:
　Yet so exceeding was the villeins powre,
　That with the wind it did him overthrow,
And all his sences stound, that still he lay full low.

13

As when that divelish yron Engin wrought
　In deepest Hell, and framd by *Furies* skill,
　With windy Nitre and quick Sulphur fraught,
　And ramd with bullet round, ordaind to kill,
　Conceiveth fire, the heavens it doth fill
　With thundring noyse, and all the ayre doth choke,
　That none can breath, nor see, nor heare at will,
　Through smouldry cloud of duskish stincking smoke,
That th'onely breath him daunts, who hath escapt the stroke.

14

So daunted when the Geaunt saw the knight,
　His heavie hand he heaved up on hye,
　And him to dust thought to have battred quight,
　Untill *Duessa* loud to him gan crye;
　O great *Orgoglio*, greatest under skye,
　O hold thy mortall hand for Ladies sake,
　Hold for my sake, and do him not to dye,
　But vanquisht thine eternall bondslave make,
And me thy worthy meed unto thy Leman take.

15

He hearkned, and did stay from further harmes,
  To gayne so goodly guerdon, as she spake:
  So willingly she came into his armes,
  Who her as willingly to grace did take,
  And was possessed of his new found make.
  Then up he tooke the slombred sencelesse corse,
  And ere he could out of his swowne awake,
  Him to his castle brought with hastie forse,
And in a Dongeon deepe him threw without remorse.

16

From that day forth *Duessa* was his deare,
  And highly honourd in his haughtie eye,
  He gave her gold and purple pall to weare,
  And triple crowne set on her head full hye,
  And her endowd with royall majestye:
  Then for to make her dreaded more of men,
  And peoples harts with awfull terrour tye,
  A monstrous beast ybred in filthy fen
He chose, which he had kept long time in darksome den.

17

Such one it was, as that renowmed Snake
  Which great *Alcides* in *Stremona* slew,
  Long fostred in the filth of *Lerna* lake,
  Whose many heads out budding ever new,
  Did breed him endlesse labour to subdew:
  But this same Monster much more ugly was;
  For seven great heads out of his body grew,
  An yron brest, and backe of scaly bras,
And all embrewd in bloud, his eyes did shine as glas.

18

His tayle was stretched out in wondrous length,
  That to the house of heavenly gods it raught,
  And with extorted powre, and borrow'd strength,
  The ever-burning lamps from thence it brought,
  And prowdly threw to ground, as things of nought;
  And underneath his filthy feet did tread
  The sacred things, and holy heasts foretaught.
  Upon this dreadfull Beast with sevenfold head
He set the false *Duessa*, for more aw and dread.

19

The wofull Dwarfe, which saw his maisters fall,
  Whiles he had keeping of his grasing steed,
  And valiant knight become a caytive thrall,
  When all was past, tooke up his forlorne weed,
  His mightie armour, missing most at need;
  His silver shield, now idle maisterlesse;
  His poynant speare, that many made to bleed,
  The ruefull moniments of heavinesse,
And with them all departes, to tell his great distresse.

20

He had not travaild long, when on the way
  He wofull Ladie, wofull *Una* met,
  Fast flying from the Paynims greedy pray,
  Whilest *Satyrane* him from pursuit did let:
  Who when her eyes she on the Dwarfe had set,
  And saw the signes, that deadly tydings spake,
  She fell to ground for sorrowfull regret,
  And lively breath her sad brest did forsake,
Yet might her pitteous hart be seene to pant and quake.

21

The messenger of so unhappie newes
  Would faine have dyde: dead was his hart within,
  Yet outwardly some little comfort shewes:
  At last recovering hart, he does begin
  To rub her temples, and to chaufe her chin,
  And every tender part does tosse and turne:
  So hardly he the flitted life does win,
  Unto her native prison to retourne:
Then gins her grieved ghost thus to lament and mourne.

22

Ye dreary instruments of dolefull sight,
  That doe this deadly spectacle behold,
  Why do ye lenger feed on loathed light,
  Or liking find to gaze on earthly mould,
  Sith cruell fates the carefull threeds unfould,
  The which my life and love together tyde?
  Now let the stony dart of senselesse cold
  Perce to my hart, and pas through every side,
And let eternall night so sad sight fro me hide.

23

O lightsome day, the lampe of highest *Jove*,
  First made by him, mens wandring wayes to guyde,
  When darknesse he in deepest dongeon drove,
  Henceforth thy hated face for ever hyde,
  And shut up heavens windowes shyning wyde:
  For earthly sight can nought but sorrow breed,
  And late repentance, which shall long abyde.
  Mine eyes no more on vanitie shall feed,
But seeled up with death, shall have their deadly meed.

24

Then downe againe she fell unto the ground;
  But he her quickly reared up againe:
  Thrise did she sinke adowne in deadly swownd,
  And thrise he her reviv'd with busie paine:
  At last when life recover'd had the raine,
  And over-wrestled his strong enemie,
  With foltring tong, and trembling every vaine,
  Tell on (quoth she) the wofull Tragedie,
The which these reliques sad present unto mine eie.

25

Tempestuous fortune hath spent all her spight,
  And thrilling sorrow throwne his utmost dart;
  Thy sad tongue cannot tell more heavy plight,
  Than that I feele, and harbour in mine hart:
  Who hath endur'd the whole, can beare each part.
  If death it be, it is not the first wound,
  That launched hath my brest with bleeding smart.
  Begin, and end the bitter balefull stound;
If lesse, than that I feare, more favour I have found.

26

Then gan the Dwarfe the whole discourse declare,
  The subtill traines of *Archimago* old;
  The wanton loves of false *Fidessa* faire,
  Bought with the bloud of vanquisht Paynim bold:
  The wretched payre transform'd to treen mould;
  The house of Pride, and perils round about;
  The combat, which he with *Sansjoy* did hould;
  The lucklesse conflict with the Gyant stout,
Wherein captiv'd, of life or death he stood in doubt.

27

She heard with patience all unto the end,
  And strove to maister sorrowfull assay,
  Which greater grew, the more she did contend,
  And almost rent her tender hart in tway;
  And love fresh coles unto her fire did lay:
  For greater love, the greater is the losse.
  Was never Ladie loved dearer day,
  Than she did love the knight of the *Redcrosse*;
For whose deare sake so many troubles her did tosse.

28

At last when fervent sorrow slaked was,
  She up arose, resolving him to find
  Alive or dead: and forward forth doth pas,
  All as the Dwarfe the way to her assynd:
  And evermore in constant carefull mind
  She fed her wound with fresh renewed bale;
  Long tost with stormes, and bet with bitter wind,
  High over hils, and low adowne the dale,
She wandred many a wood, and measurd many a vale.

29

At last she chaunced by good hap to meet
  A goodly knight, faire marching by the way
  Together with his Squire, arrayed meet:
  His glitterand armour shined farre away,
  Like glauncing light of *Phœbus* brightest ray;
  From top to toe no place appeared bare,
  That deadly dint of steele endanger may:
  Athwart his brest a bauldrick brave he ware,
That shynd, like twinkling stars, with stons most pretious rare.

30

And in the midst thereof one pretious stone
  Of wondrous worth, and eke of wondrous mights,
  Shapt like a Ladies head, exceeding shone,
  Like *Hesperus* emongst the lesser lights,
  And strove for to amaze the weaker sights;
  Thereby his mortall blade full comely hong
  In yvory sheath, ycarv'd with curious slights;
  Whose hilts were burnisht gold, and handle strong
Of mother pearle, and buckled with a golden tong.

31

His haughtie helmet, horrid all with gold,
　Both glorious brightnesse, and great terrour bred;
　For all the crest a Dragon did enfold
　With greedie pawes, and over all did spred
　His golden wings: his dreadfull hideous hed
　Close couched on the bever, seem'd to throw
　From flaming mouth bright sparkles fierie red,
　That suddeine horror to faint harts did show;
And scaly tayle was stretcht adowne his backe full low.

32

Upon the top of all his loftie crest,
　A bunch of haires discolourd diversly,
　With sprincled pearle, and gold full richly drest,
　Did shake, and seem'd to daunce for jollity,
　Like to an Almond tree ymounted hye
　On top of greene *Selinis* all alone,
　With blossomes brave bedecked daintily;
　Whose tender locks do tremble every one
At every little breath, that under heaven is blowne.

33

His warlike shield all closely cover'd was,
　Ne might of mortall eye be ever seene;
　Not made of steele, nor of enduring bras,
　Such earthly mettals soone consumed bene:
　But all of Diamond perfect pure and cleene
　It framed was, one massie entire mould,
　Hewen out of Adamant rocke with engines keene,
　That point of speare it never percen could,
Ne dint of direfull sword divide the substance would.

34

The same to wight he never wont disclose,
　But when as monsters huge he would dismay,
　Or daunt unequall armies of his foes,
　Or when the flying heavens he would affray;
　For so exceeding shone his glistring ray,
　That *Phœbus* golden face it did attaint,
　As when a cloud his beames doth over-lay;
　And silver *Cynthia* wexed pale and faint,
As when her face is staynd with magicke arts constraint.

35

No magicke arts hereof had any might,
  Nor bloudie wordes of bold Enchaunters call,
  But all that was not such, as seemd in sight,
  Before that shield did fade, and suddeine fall:
  And when him list the raskall routes appall,
  Men into stones therewith he could transmew,
  And stones to dust, and dust to nought at all;
  And when him list the prouder lookes subdew,
He would them gazing blind, or turne to other hew.

36

Ne let it seeme, that credence this exceedes,
  For he that made the same, was knowne right well
  To have done much more admirable deedes.
  It *Merlin* was, which whylome did excell
  All living wightes in might of magicke spell:
  Both shield, and sword, and armour all he wrought
  For this young Prince, when first to armes he fell;
  But when he dyde, the Faerie Queene it brought
To Faerie lond, where yet it may be seene, if sought.

37

A gentle youth, his dearely loved Squire
  His speare of heben wood behind him bare,
  Whose harmefull head, thrice heated in the fire,
  Had riven many a brest with pikehead square;
  A goodly person, and could menage faire
  His stubborne steed with curbed canon bit,
  Who under him did trample as the aire,
  And chauft, that any on his backe should sit;
The yron rowels into frothy fome he bit.

38

When as this knight nigh to the Ladie drew,
  With lovely court he gan her entertaine;
  But when he heard her answeres loth, he knew
  Some secret sorrow did her heart distraine:
  Which to allay, and calme her storming paine,
  Faire feeling words he wisely gan display,
  And for her humour fitting purpose faine,
  To tempt the cause it selfe for to bewray;
Wherewith emmov'd, these bleeding words she gan to say.

39

What worlds delight, or joy of living speach
  Can heart, so plung'd in sea of sorrowes deepe,
  And heaped with so huge misfortunes, reach?
  The carefull cold beginneth for to creepe,
  And in my heart his yron arrow steepe,
  Soone as I thinke upon my bitter bale:
  Such helplesse harmes yts better hidden keepe,
  Than rip up griefe, where it may not availe,
My last left comfort is, my woes to weepe and waile.

40

Ah Ladie deare, quoth then the gentle knight,
  Well may I weene, your griefe is wondrous great;
  For wondrous great griefe groneth in my spright,
  Whiles thus I heare you of your sorrowes treat.
  But wofull Ladie let me you intrete,
  For to unfold the anguish of your hart:
  Mishaps are maistred by advice discrete,
  And counsell mittigates the greatest smart;
Found never helpe, who never would his hurts impart.

41

O but (quoth she) great griefe will not be tould,
  And can more easily be thought, than said.
  Right so; (quoth he) but he, that never would,
  Could never: will to might gives greatest aid.
  But griefe (quoth she) does greater grow displaid,
  If then it find not helpe, and breedes despaire.
  Despaire breedes not (quoth he) where faith is staid.
  No faith so fast (quoth she) but flesh does paire.
Flesh may empaire (quoth he) but reason can repaire.

42

His goodly reason, and well guided speach
  So deepe did settle in her gratious thought,
  That her perswaded to disclose the breach,
  Which love and fortune in her heart had wrought,
  And said; Faire Sir, I hope good hap hath brought
  You to inquire the secrets of my griefe,
  Or that your wisedome will direct my thought,
  Or that your prowesse can me yield reliefe:
Then heare the storie sad, which I shall tell you briefe.

43

The forlorne Maiden, whom your eyes have seene
  The laughing stocke of fortunes mockeries,
  Am th'only daughter of a King and Queene,
  Whose parents deare, whilest equall destinies
  Did runne about, and their felicities
  The favourable heavens did not envy,
  Did spread their rule through all the territories,
  Which *Phison* and *Euphrates* floweth by,
And *Gehons* golden waves doe wash continually.

44

Till that their cruell cursed enemy,
  An huge great Dragon horrible in sight,
  Bred in the loathly lakes of *Tartary*,
  With murdrous ravine, and devouring might
  Their kingdome spoild, and countrey wasted quight:
  Themselves, for feare into his jawes to fall,
  He forst to castle strong to take their flight,
  Where fast embard in mightie brasen wall,
He has them now foure yeres besiegd to make them thrall.

45

Full many knights adventurous and stout
  Have enterprizd that Monster to subdew;
  From every coast that heaven walks about,
  Have thither come the noble Martiall crew,
  That famous hard atchievements still pursew,
  Yet never any could that girlond win,
  But all still shronke, and still he greater grew:
  All they for want of faith, or guilt of sin,
The pitteous pray of his fierce crueltie have bin.

46

At last yledd with farre reported praise,
  Which flying fame throughout the world had spred,
  Of doughtie knights, whom Faery land did raise,
  That noble order hight of Maidenhed,
  Forthwith to court of *Gloriane* I sped,
  Of *Gloriane* great Queene of glory bright,
  Whose kingdomes seat *Cleopolis* is red,
  There to obtaine some such redoubted knight,
That Parents deare from tyrants powre deliver might.

47

It was my chance (my chance was faire and good)
  There for to find a fresh unproved knight,
  Whose manly hands imbrew'd in guiltie blood
  Had never bene, ne ever by his might
  Had throwne to ground the unregarded right:
  Yet of his prowesse proofe he since hath made
  (I witnesse am) in many a cruell fight;
  The groning ghosts of many one dismaide
Have felt the bitter dint of his avenging blade.

48

And ye the forlorne reliques of his powre,
  His byting sword, and his devouring speare,
  Which have endured many a dreadfull stowre,
  Can speake his prowesse, that did earst you beare,
  And well could rule: now he hath left you heare,
  To be the record of his ruefull losse,
  And of my dolefull disaventurous deare:
  O heavie record of the good *Redcrosse*,
Where have you left your Lord, that could so well you tosse?

49

Well hoped I, and faire beginnings had,
  That he my captive langour should redeeme,
  Till all unweeting, an Enchaunter bad
  His sence abusd, and made him to misdeeme
  My loyalty, not such as it did seeme;
  That rather death desire, than such despight.
  Be judge ye heavens, that all things right esteeme,
  How I him lov'd, and love with all my might,
So thought I eke of him, and thinke I thought aright.

50

Thenceforth me desolate he quite forsooke,
  To wander, where wilde fortune would me lead,
  And other bywaies he himselfe betooke,
  Where never foot of living wight did tread,
  That brought not backe the balefull body dead;
  In which him chaunced false *Duessa* meete,
  Mine onely foe, mine onely deadly dread,
  Who with her witchcraft and misseeming sweete,
Inveigled him to follow her desires unmeete.

51

At last by subtill sleights she him betraid
  Unto his foe, a Gyant huge and tall,
Who him disarmed, dissolute, dismaid,
Unwares surprised, and with mightie mall
The monster mercilesse him made to fall,
Whose fall did never foe before behold;
And now in darkesome dungeon, wretched thrall,
Remedilesse, for aie he doth him hold;
This is my cause of griefe, more great, than may be told.

52

Ere she had ended all, she gan to faint:
  But he her comforted and faire bespake,
Certes, Madame, ye have great cause of plaint,
That stoutest heart, I weene, could cause to quake.
But be of cheare, and comfort to you take:
For till I have acquit your captive knight,
Assure your selfe, I will you not forsake.
His chearefull words reviv'd her chearelesse spright,
So forth they went, the Dwarfe them guiding ever right.

CANT. VIII

Faire virgin to redeeme her deare
brings Arthur to the fight:
Who slayes the Gyant, wounds the beast,
and strips Duessa quight.

I

AY me, how many perils doe enfold
  The righteous man, to make him daily fall?
Were not, that heavenly grace doth him uphold,
And stedfast truth acquite him out of all.
Her love is firme, her care continuall,
So oft as he through his owne foolish pride,
Or weaknesse is to sinfull bands made thrall:
Else should this *Redcrosse* knight in bands have dyde,
For whose deliverance she this Prince doth thither guide.

2

They sadly traveild thus, untill they came
  Nigh to a castle builded strong and hie:
  Then cryde the Dwarfe, lo yonder is the same,
  In which my Lord my liege doth lucklesse lie,
  Thrall to that Gyants hatefull tyrannie:
  Therefore, deare Sir, your mightie powres assay.
  The noble knight alighted by and by
  From loftie steede, and bad the Ladie stay,
To see what end of fight should him befall that day.

3

So with the Squire, th'admirer of his might,
  He marched forth towards that castle wall;
  Whose gates he found fast shut, ne living wight
  To ward the same, nor answere commers call.
  Then tooke that Squire an horne of bugle small,
  Which hong adowne his side in twisted gold,
  And tassels gay. Wyde wonders over all
  Of that same hornes great vertues weren told,
Which had approved bene in uses manifold.

4

Was never wight, that heard that shrilling sound,
  But trembling feare did feele in every vaine;
  Three miles it might be easie heard around,
  And Ecchoes three answerd it selfe againe:
  No false enchauntment, nor deceiptfull traine
  Might once abide the terror of that blast,
  But presently was voide and wholly vaine:
  No gate so strong, no locke so firme and fast,
But with that percing noise flew open quite, or brast.

5

The same before the Geants gate he blew,
  That all the castle quaked from the ground,
  And every dore of freewill open flew.
  The Gyant selfe dismaied with that sownd,
  Where he with his *Duessa* dalliance fownd,
  In hast came rushing forth from inner bowre,
  With staring countenance sterne, as one astownd,
  And staggering steps, to weet, what suddein stowre
Had wrought that horror strange, and dar'd his dreaded powre.

6

And after him the proud *Duessa* came,
  High mounted on her manyheaded beast,
  And every head with fyrie tongue did flame,
  And every head was crowned on his creast,
  And bloudie mouthed with late cruell feast.
  That when the knight beheld, his mightie shild
  Upon his manly arme he soone addrest,
  And at him fiercely flew, with courage fild,
And eger greedinesse through every member thrild.

7

Therewith the Gyant buckled him to fight,
  Inflam'd with scornefull wrath and high disdaine,
  And lifting up his dreadfull club on hight,
  All arm'd with ragged snubbes and knottie graine,
  Him thought at first encounter to have slaine.
  But wise and warie was that noble Pere,
  And lightly leaping from so monstrous maine,
  Did faire avoide the violence him nere;
It booted nought, to thinke, such thunderbolts to beare.

8

Ne shame he thought to shunne so hideous might:
  The idle stroke, enforcing furious way,
  Missing the marke of his misaymed sight
  Did fall to ground, and with his heavie sway
  So deepely dinted in the driven clay,
  That three yardes deepe a furrow up did throw:
  The sad earth wounded with so sore assay,
  Did grone full grievous underneath the blow,
And trembling with strange feare, did like an earthquake show.

9

As when almightie *Jove* in wrathfull mood,
  To wreake the guilt of mortall sins is bent,
  Hurles forth his thundring dart with deadly food,
  Enrold in flames, and smouldring dreriment,
  Through riven cloudes and molten firmament;
  The fierce threeforked engin making way,
  Both loftie towres and highest trees hath rent,
  And all that might his angrie passage stay,
And shooting in the earth, casts up a mount of clay.

10

His boystrous club, so buried in the ground,
  He could not rearen up againe so light,
  But that the knight him at avantage found,
  And whiles he strove his combred clubbe to quight
  Out of the earth, with blade all burning bright
  He smote off his left arme, which like a blocke
  Did fall to ground, depriv'd of native might;
  Large streames of bloud out of the truncked stocke
Forth gushed, like fresh water streame from riven rocke.

11

Dismaied with so desperate deadly wound,
  And eke impatient of unwonted paine,
  He loudly brayd with beastly yelling sound,
  That all the fields rebellowed againe;
  As great a noyse, as when in Cymbrian plaine
  An heard of Bulles, whom kindly rage doth sting,
  Do for the milkie mothers want complaine,
  And fill the fields with troublous bellowing,
The neighbour woods around with hollow murmur ring.

12

That when his deare *Duessa* heard, and saw
  The evill stownd, that daungerd her estate,
  Unto his aide she hastily did draw
  Her dreadfull beast, who swolne with bloud of late
  Came ramping forth with proud presumpteous gate,
  And threatned all his heads like flaming brands.
  But him the Squire made quickly to retrate,
  Encountring fierce with single sword in hand,
And twixt him and his Lord did like a bulwarke stand.

13

The proud *Duessa* full of wrathfull spight,
  And fierce disdaine, to be affronted so,
  Enforst her purple beast with all her might
  That stop out of the way to overthroe,
  Scorning the let of so unequall foe:
  But nathemore would that courageous swayne
  To her yeeld passage, gainst his Lord to goe,
  But with outrageous strokes did him restraine,
And with his bodie bard the way atwixt them twaine.

14

Then tooke the angrie witch her golden cup,
  Which still she bore, replete with magicke artes;
  Death and despeyre did many thereof sup,
  And secret poyson through their inner parts,
  Th'eternall bale of heavie wounded harts;
  Which after charmes and some enchauntments said,
  She lightly sprinkled on his weaker parts;
  Therewith his sturdie courage soone was quayd,
And all his senses were with suddeine dread dismayd.

15

So downe he fell before the cruell beast,
  Who on his necke his bloudie clawes did seize,
  That life nigh crusht out of his panting brest:
  No powre he had to stirre, nor will to rize.
  That when the carefull knight gan well avise,
  He lightly left the foe, with whom he fought,
  And to the beast gan turne his enterprise;
  For wondrous anguish in his hart it wrought,
To see his loved Squire into such thraldome brought.

16

And high advauncing his bloud-thirstie blade,
  Stroke one of those deformed heads so sore,
  That of his puissance proud ensample made;
  His monstrous scalpe downe to his teeth it tore,
  And that misformed shape mis-shaped more:
  A sea of bloud gusht from the gaping wound,
  That her gay garments staynd with filthy gore,
  And overflowed all the field around;
That over shoes in bloud he waded on the ground.

17

Thereat he roared for exceeding paine,
  That to have heard, great horror would have bred,
  And scourging the'emptie ayre with his long traine,
  Through great impatience of his grieved hed
  His gorgeous ryder from her loftie sted
  Would have cast downe, and trod in durtie myre,
  Had not the Gyant soone her succoured;
  Who all enrag'd with smart and franticke yre,
Came hurtling in full fierce, and forst the knight retyre.

18

The force, which wont in two to be disperst,
  In one alone left hand he now unites,
  Which is through rage more strong than both were erst;
  With which his hideous club aloft he dites,
  And at his foe with furious rigour smites,
  That strongest Oake might seeme to overthrow:
  The stroke upon his shield so heavie lites,
  That to the ground it doubleth him full low:
What mortall wight could ever beare so monstrous blow?

19

And in his fall his shield, that covered was,
  Did loose his vele by chaunce, and open flew:
  The light whereof, that heavens light did pas,
  Such blazing brightnesse through the aier threw,
  That eye mote not the same endure to vew.
  Which when the Gyaunt spyde with staring eye,
  He downe let fall his arme, and soft withdrew
  His weapon huge, that heaved was on hye
For to have slaine the man, that on the ground did lye.

20

And eke the fruitfull-headed beast, amaz'd
  At flashing beames of that sunshiny shield,
  Became starke blind, and all his senses daz'd,
  That downe he tumbled on the durtie field,
  And seem'd himselfe as conquered to yield.
  Whom when his maistresse proud perceiv'd to fall,
  Whiles yet his feeble feet for faintnesse reeld,
  Unto the Gyant loudly she gan call,
O helpe *Orgoglio*, helpe, or else we perish all.

21

At her so pitteous cry was much amoov'd
  Her champion stout, and for to ayde his frend,
  Againe his wonted angry weapon proov'd:
  But all in vaine: for he has read his end
  In that bright shield, and all their forces spend
  Themselves in vaine: for since that glauncing sight,
  He hath no powre to hurt, nor to defend;
  As where th'Almighties lightning brond does light,
It dimmes the dazed eyen, and daunts the senses quight.

22

Whom when the Prince, to battell new addrest,
  And threatning high his dreadfull stroke did see,
  His sparkling blade about his head he blest,
  And smote off quite his right leg by the knee,
  That downe he tombled; as an aged tree,
  High growing on the top of rocky clift,
  Whose hartstrings with keene steele nigh hewen be,
  The mightie trunck halfe rent, with ragged rift
Doth roll adowne the rocks, and fall with fearefull drift.

23

Or as a Castle reared high and round,
  By subtile engins and malitious slight
  Is undermined from the lowest ground,
  And her foundation forst, and feebled quight,
  At last downe falles, and with her heaped hight
  Her hastie ruine does more heavie make,
  And yields it selfe unto the victours might;
  Such was this Gyaunts fall, that seemd to shake
The stedfast globe of earth, as it for feare did quake.

24

The knight then lightly leaping to the pray,
  With mortall steele him smot againe so sore,
  That headlesse his unweldy bodie lay,
  All wallowd in his owne fowle bloudy gore,
  Which flowed from his wounds in wondrous store.
  But soone as breath out of his breast did pas,
  That huge great body, which the Gyaunt bore,
  Was vanisht quite, and of that monstrous mas
Was nothing left, but like an emptie bladder was.

25

Whose grievous fall, when false *Duessa* spide,
  Her golden cup she cast unto the ground,
  And crowned mitre rudely threw aside;
  Such percing griefe her stubborne hart did wound,
  That she could not endure that dolefull stound,
  But leaving all behind her, fled away:
  The light-foot Squire her quickly turnd around,
  And by hard meanes enforcing her to stay,
So brought unto his Lord, as his deserved pray.

26

The royall Virgin, which beheld from farre,
  In pensive plight, and sad perplexitie,
  The whole atchievement of this doubtfull warre,
  Came running fast to greet his victorie,
  With sober gladnesse, and myld modestie,
  And with sweet joyous cheare him thus bespake;
  Faire braunch of noblesse, flowre of chevalrie,
  That with your worth the world amazed make,
How shall I quite the paines, ye suffer for my sake?

27

And you fresh bud of vertue springing fast,
  Whom these sad eyes saw nigh unto deaths dore,
  What hath poore Virgin for such perill past,
  Wherewith you to reward? Accept therefore
  My simple selfe, and service evermore;
  And he that high does sit, and all things see
  With equall eyes, their merites to restore,
  Behold what ye this day have done for mee,
And what I cannot quite, requite with usuree.

28

But sith the heavens, and your faire handeling
  Have made you maister of the field this day,
  Your fortune maister eke with governing,
  And well begun end all so well, I pray,
  Ne let that wicked woman scape away;
  For she it is, that did my Lord bethrall,
  My dearest Lord, and deepe in dongeon lay,
  Where he his better dayes hath wasted all.
O heare, how piteous he to you for ayd does call.

29

Forthwith he gave in charge unto his Squire,
  That scarlot whore to keepen carefully;
  Whiles he himselfe with greedie great desire
  Into the Castle entred forcibly,
  Where living creature none he did espye;
  Then gan he lowdly through the house to call:
  But no man car'd to answere to his crye.
  There raignd a solemne silence over all,
Nor voice was heard, nor wight was seene in bowre or hall.

30

At last with creeping crooked pace forth came
　An old old man, with beard as white as snow,
　That on a staffe his feeble steps did frame,
　And guide his wearie gate both too and fro:
　For his eye sight him failed long ygo,
　And on his arme a bounch of keyes he bore,
　The which unused rust did overgrow:
　Those were the keyes of every inner dore,
But he could not them use, but kept them still in store.

31

But very uncouth sight was to behold,
　How he did fashion his untoward pace,
　For as he forward moov'd his footing old,
　So backward still was turnd his wrincled face,
　Unlike to men, who ever as they trace,
　Both feet and face one way are wont to lead.
　This was the auncient keeper of that place,
　And foster father of the Gyant dead;
His name *Ignaro* did his nature right aread.

32

His reverend haires and holy gravitie
　The knight much honord, as beseemed well,
　And gently askt, where all the people bee,
　Which in that stately building wont to dwell.
　Who answerd him full soft, he could not tell.
　Againe he askt, where that same knight was layd,
　Whom great *Orgoglio* with his puissaunce fell
　Had made his caytive thrall; againe he sayde,
He could not tell: ne ever other answere made.

33

Then asked he, which way he in might pas:
　He could not tell, againe he answered.
　Thereat the curteous knight displeased was,
　And said, Old sire, it seemes thou hast not red
　How ill it sits with that same silver hed
　In vaine to mocke, or mockt in vaine to bee:
　But if thou be, as thou art pourtrahed
　With natures pen, in ages grave degree,
Aread in graver wise, what I demaund of thee.

34

His answere likewise was, he could not tell.
  Whose sencelesse speach, and doted ignorance
  When as the noble Prince had marked well,
  He ghest his nature by his countenance,
  And calmd his wrath with goodly temperance.
  Then to him stepping, from his arme did reach
  Those keyes, and made himselfe free enterance.
  Each dore he opened without any breach;
There was no barre to stop, nor foe him to empeach.

35

There all within full rich arayd he found,
  With royall arras and resplendent gold.
  And did with store of every thing abound,
  That greatest Princes presence might behold.
  But all the floore (too filthy to be told)
  With bloud of guiltlesse babes, and innocents trew,
  Which there were slaine, as sheepe out of the fold,
  Defiled was, that dreadfull was to vew,
And sacred ashes over it was strowed new.

36

And there beside of marble stone was built
  An Altare, carv'd with cunning imagery,
  On which true Christians bloud was often spilt,
  And holy Martyrs often doen to dye,
  With cruell malice and strong tyranny:
  Whose blessed sprites from underneath the stone
  To God for vengeance cryde continually,
  And with great griefe were often heard to grone,
That hardest heart would bleede, to heare their piteous mone.

37

Through every rowme he sought, and every bowr,
  But no where could he find that wofull thrall:
  At last he came unto an yron doore,
  That fast was lockt, but key found not at all
  Emongst that bounch, to open it withall;
  But in the same a little grate was pight,
  Through which he sent his voyce, and lowd did call
  With all his powre, to weet, if living wight
Were housed therewithin, whom he enlargen might.

38

Therewith an hollow, dreary, murmuring voyce
  These piteous plaints and dolours did resound;
  O who is that, which brings me happy choyce
  Of death, that here lye dying every stound,
  Yet live perforce in balefull darkenesse bound?
  For now three Moones have changed thrice their hew,
  And have beene thrice hid underneath the ground,
  Since I the heavens chearefull face did vew,
O welcome thou, that doest of death bring tydings trew.

39

Which when that Champion heard, with percing point
  Of pitty deare his hart was thrilled sore,
  And trembling horrour ran through every joynt,
  For ruth of gentle knight so fowle forlore:
  Which shaking off, he rent that yron dore,
  With furious force, and indignation fell;
  Where entred in, his foot could find no flore,
  But all a deepe descent, as darke as hell,
That breathed ever forth a filthie banefull smell.

40

But neither darkenesse fowle, nor filthy bands,
  Nor noyous smell his purpose could withhold,
  (Entire affection hateth nicer hands)
  But that with constant zeale, and courage bold,
  After long paines and labours manifold,
  He found the meanes that Prisoner up to reare;
  Whose feeble thighes, unhable to uphold
  His pined corse, him scarse to light could beare,
A ruefull spectacle of death and ghastly drere.

41

His sad dull eyes deepe sunck in hollow pits,
  Could not endure th'unwonted sunne to view;
  His bare thin cheekes for want of better bits,
  And empty sides deceived of their dew,
  Could make a stony hart his hap to rew;
  His rawbone armes, whose mighty brawned bowrs
  Were wont to rive steele plates, and helmets hew,
  Were cleane consum'd, and all his vitall powres
Decayd, and all his flesh shronk up like withered flowres.

42

Whom when his Lady saw, to him she ran
  With hasty joy: to see him made her glad,
  And sad to view his visage pale and wan,
  Who earst in flowres of freshest youth was clad.
  Tho when her well of teares she wasted had,
  She said, Ah dearest Lord, what evill starre
  On you hath fround, and pourd his influence bad,
  That of your selfe ye thus berobbed arre,
And this misseeming hew your manly looks doth marre?

43

But welcome now my Lord, in wele or woe,
  Whose presence I have lackt too long a day;
  And fie on Fortune mine avowed foe,
  Whose wrathfull wreakes them selves do now alay.
  And for these wrongs shall treble penaunce pay
  Of treble good: good growes of evils priefe.
  The chearelesse man, whom sorrow did dismay,
  Had no delight to treaten of his griefe;
His long endured famine needed more reliefe.

44

Faire Lady, then said that victorious knight,
  The things, that grievous were to do, or beare,
  Them to renew, I wote, breeds no delight;
  Best musicke breeds †delight in loathing eare:
  But th'onely good, that growes of passed feare,
  Is to be wise, and ware of like agein.
  This dayes ensample hath this lesson deare
  Deepe written in my heart with yron pen,
That blisse may not abide in state of mortall men.

45

Henceforth sir knight, take to you wonted strength,
  And maister these mishaps with patient might;
  Loe where your foe lyes stretcht in monstrous length,
  And loe that wicked woman in your sight,
  The roote of all your care, and wretched plight,
  Now in your powre, to let her live, or dye.
  To do her dye (quoth *Una*) were despight,
  And shame t'avenge so weake an enimy;
But spoile her of her scarlot robe, and let her fly.

46

So as she bad, that witch they disaraid,
  And robd of royall robes, and purple pall,
  And ornaments that richly were displaid;
  Ne spared they to strip her naked all.
  Then when they had despoild her tire and call,
  Such as she was, their eyes might her behold,
  That her misshaped parts did them appall,
  A loathly, wrinckled hag, ill favoured, old,
Whose secret filth good manners biddeth not be told.

47

Her craftie head was altogether bald,
  And as in hate of honorable eld,
  Was overgrowne with scurfe and filthy scald;
  Her teeth out of her rotten gummes were feld,
  And her sowre breath abhominably smeld;
  Her dried dugs, like bladders lacking wind,
  Hong downe, and filthy matter from them weld;
  Her wrizled skin as rough, as maple rind,
So scabby was, that would have loathd all womankind.

48

Her neather parts, the shame of all her kind,
  My chaster Muse for shame doth blush to write;
  But at her rompe she growing had behind
  A foxes taile, with dong all fowly dight;
  And eke her feete most monstrous were in sight;
  For one of them was like an Eagles claw,
  With griping talaunts armd to greedy fight,
  The other like a Beares uneven paw:
More ugly shape yet never living creature saw.

49

Which when the knights beheld, amazd they were,
  And wondred at so fowle deformed wight.
  Such then (said *Una*) as she seemeth here,
  Such is the face of falshood, such the sight
  Of fowle *Duessa*, when her borrowed light
  Is laid away, and counterfesaunce knowne.
  Thus when they had the witch disrobed quight,
  And all her filthy feature open showne,
They let her goe at will, and wander wayes unknowne.

50

She flying fast from heavens hated face,
    And from the world that her discovered wide,
    Fled to the wastfull wildernesse apace,
    From living eyes her open shame to hide,
    And lurkt in rocks and caves long unespide.
    But that faire crew of knights, and *Una* faire
    Did in that castle afterwards abide,
    To rest them selves, and weary powres repaire,
Where store they found of all, that dainty was and rare.

CANT. IX

His loves and lignage Arthur tells:
The knights knit friendly bands:
Sir Trevisan flies from Despayre,
Whom Redcrosse knight withstands.

1

O GOODLY golden chaine, wherewith yfere
    The vertues linked are in lovely wize:
    And noble minds of yore allyed were,
    In brave poursuit of chevalrous emprize,
    That none did others safety despize,
    Nor aid envy to him, in need that stands,
    But friendly each did others prayse devize
    How to advaunce with favourable hands,
As this good Prince redeemd the *Redcrosse* knight from bands.

2

Who when their powres, empaird through labour long,
    With dew repast they had recured well,
    And that weake captive wight now wexed strong,
    Them list no lenger there at leasure dwell,
    But forward fare, as their adventures fell,
    But ere they parted, *Una* faire besought
    That straunger knight his name and nation tell;
    Least so great good, as he for her had wrought,
Should die unknown, and buried be in thanklesse thought.

3

Faire virgin (said the Prince) ye me require
  A thing without the compas of my wit:
  For both the lignage and the certain Sire,
  From which I sprong, from me are hidden yit.
  For all so soone as life did me admit
  Into this world, and shewed heavens light,
  From mothers pap I taken was unfit:
  And streight delivered to a Faery knight,
To be upbrought in gentle thewes and martiall might.

4

Unto old *Timon* he me brought bylive,
  Old *Timon*, who in youthly yeares hath beene
  In warlike feates th'expertest man alive,
  And is the wisest now on earth I weene;
  His dwelling is low in a valley greene,
  Under the foot of *Rauran* mossy hore,
  From whence the river *Dee* as silver cleene
  His tombling billowes rolls with gentle rore:
There all my dayes he traind me up in vertuous lore.

5

Thither the great Magicien *Merlin* came,
  As was his use, ofttimes to visit me:
  For he had charge my discipline to frame,
  And Tutours nouriture to oversee.
  Him oft and oft I askt in privitie,
  Of what loines and what lignage I did spring:
  Whose aunswere bad me still assured bee,
  That I was sonne and heire unto a king,
As time in her just terme the truth to light should bring.

6

Well worthy impe, said then the Lady gent,
  And Pupill fit for such a Tutours hand.
  But what adventure, or what high intent
  Hath brought you hither into Faery land,
  Aread Prince *Arthur*, crowne of Martiall band?
  Full hard it is (quoth he) to read aright
  The course of heavenly cause, or understand
  The secret meaning of th'eternall might,
That rules mens wayes, and rules the thoughts of living wight.

7

For whither he through fatall deepe foresight
  Me hither sent, for cause to me unghest,
  Or that fresh bleeding wound, which day and night
  Whilome doth rancle in my riven brest,
  With forced fury following his behest,
  Me hither brought by wayes yet never found,
  You to have helpt I hold my selfe yet blest.
  Ah curteous knight (quoth she) what secret wound
Could ever find, to grieve the gentlest hart on ground?

8

Deare Dame (quoth he) you sleeping sparkes awake,
  Which troubled once, into huge flames will grow,
  Ne ever will their fervent fury slake,
  Till living moysture into smoke do flow,
  And wasted life do lye in ashes low.
  Yet sithens silence lesseneth not my fire,
  But told it flames, and hidden it does glow,
  I will revele, what ye so much desire:
Ah Love, lay downe thy bow, the whiles I may respire.

9

It was in freshest flowre of youthly yeares,
  When courage first does creepe in manly chest,
  Then first the coale of kindly heat appeares
  To kindle love in every living brest;
  But me had warnd old *Timons* wise behest,
  Those creeping flames by reason to subdew,
  Before their rage grew to so great unrest,
  As miserable lovers use to rew,
Which still wex old in woe, whiles woe still wexeth new.

10

That idle name of love, and lovers life,
  As losse of time, and vertues enimy
  I ever scornd, and joyd to stirre up strife,
  In middest of their mournfull Tragedy,
  Ay wont to laugh, when them I heard to cry,
  And blow the fire, which them to ashes brent:
  Their God himselfe, griev'd at my libertie,
  Shot many a dart at me with fiers intent,
But I them warded all with wary government.

11

But all in vaine: no fort can be so strong,
  Ne fleshly brest can armed be so sound,
  But will at last be wonne with battrie long,
  Or unawares at disavantage found;
  Nothing is sure, that growes on earthly ground:
  And who most trustes in arme of fleshly might,
  And boasts, in beauties chaine not to be bound,
  Doth soonest fall in disaventrous fight,
And yeeldes his caytive neck to victours most despight.

12

Ensample make of him your haplesse joy,
  And of my selfe now mated, as ye see;
  Whose prouder vaunt that proud avenging boy
  Did soone pluck downe, and curbd my libertie.
  For on a day prickt forth with jollitie
  Of looser life, and heat of hardiment,
  Raunging the forest wide on courser free,
  The fields, the floods, the heavens with one consent
Did seeme to laugh on me, and favour mine intent.

13

For-wearied with my sports, I did alight
  From loftie steed, and downe to sleepe me layd;
  The verdant gras my couch did goodly dight,
  And pillow was my helmet faire displayd:
  Whiles every sence the humour sweet embayd,
  And slombring soft my hart did steale away,
  Me seemed, by my side a royall Mayd
  Her daintie limbes full softly down did lay:
So faire a creature yet saw never sunny day.

14

Most goodly glee and lovely blandishment
  She to me made, and bad me love her deare,
  For dearely sure her love was to me bent,
  As when just time expired should appeare.
  But whether dreames delude, or true it were,
  Was never hart so ravisht with delight,
  Ne living man like words did ever heare,
  As she to me delivered all that night;
And at her parting said, She Queene of Faeries hight.

15

When I awoke, and found her place devoyd,
And nought but pressed gras, where she had lyen,
I sorrowed all so much, as earst I joyd,
And washed all her place with watry eyen.
From that day forth I lov'd that face divine;
From that day forth I cast in carefull mind,
To seeke her out with labour, and long tyne,
And never vow to rest, till her I find,
Nine monethes I seeke in vaine yet ni'll that vow unbind.

16

Thus as he spake, his visage wexed pale,
And chaunge of hew great passion did bewray;
Yet still he strove to cloke his inward bale,
And hide the smoke, that did his fire display,
Till gentle *Una* thus to him gan say;
O happy Queene of Faeries, that hast found
Mongst many, one that with his prowesse may
Defend thine honour, and thy foes confound:
True Loves are often sown, but seldom grow on ground.

17

Thine, O then, said the gentle *Redcrosse* knight,
Next to that Ladies love, shalbe the place,
O fairest virgin, full of heavenly light,
Whose wondrous faith, exceeding earthly race,
Was firmest fixt in mine extremest case.
And you, my Lord, the Patrone of my life,
Of that great Queene may well gaine worthy grace:
For onely worthy you through prowes priefe
Yf living man mote worthy be, to be her liefe.

18

So diversly discoursing of their loves,
The golden Sunne his glistring head gan shew,
And sad remembraunce now the Prince amoves,
With fresh desire his voyage to pursew:
Als *Una* earnd her traveill to renew.
Then those two knights, fast friendship for to bynd,
And love establish each to other trew,
Gave goodly gifts, the signes of gratefull mynd,
And eke as pledges firme. right hands together joynd.

19

Prince *Arthur* gave a boxe of Diamond sure,
　Embowd with gold and gorgeous ornament,
　Wherein were closd few drops of liquor pure,
　Of wondrous worth, and vertue excellent,
　That any wound could heale incontinent:
　Which to requite, the *Redcrosse* knight him gave
　A booke, wherein his Saveours testament
　Was writ with golden letters rich and brave;
A worke of wondrous grace, and able soules to save.

20

Thus beene they parted, *Arthur* on his way
　To seeke his love, and th'other for to fight
　With *Unaes* foe, that all her realme did pray.
　But she now weighing the decayed plight,
　And shrunken synewes of her chosen knight,
　Would not a while her forward course pursew,
　Ne bring him forth in face of dreadfull fight,
　Till he recovered had his former hew:
For him to be yet weake and wearie well she knew.

21

So as they traveild, lo they gan espy
　An armed knight towards them gallop fast,
　That seemed from some feared foe to fly,
　Or other griesly thing, that him agast.
　Still as he fled, his eye was backward cast,
　As if his feare still followed him behind;
　Als flew his steed, as he his bands had brast,
　And with his winged heeles did tread the wind,
As he had beene a fole of *Pegasus* his kind.

22

Nigh as he drew, they might perceive his head
　To be unarmd, and curld uncombed heares
　Upstaring stiffe, dismayd with uncouth dread;
　Nor drop of bloud in all his face appeares
　Nor life in limbe: and to increase his feares,
　In fowle reproch of knighthoods faire degree,
　About his neck an hempen rope he weares,
　That with his glistring armes does ill agree;
But he of rope or armes has now no memoree.

23

The *Redcrosse* knight toward him crossed fast,
　To weet, what mister wight was so dismayd:
　There him he finds all sencelesse and aghast,
　That of him selfe he seemd to be afrayd;
　Whom hardly he from flying forward stayd,
　Till he these wordes to him deliver might;
　Sir knight, aread who hath ye thus arayd,
　And eke from whom make ye this hasty flight:
For never knight I saw in such misseeming plight.

24

He answerd nought at all, but adding new
　Feare to his first amazment, staring wide
　With stony eyes, and hartlesse hollow hew,
　Astonisht stood, as one that had aspide
　Infernall furies, with their chaines untide.
　Him yet againe, and yet againe bespake
　The gentle knight; who nought to him replide,
　But trembling every joynt did inly quake,
And foltring tongue at last these words seemd forth to shake.

25

For Gods deare love, Sir knight, do me not stay;
　For loe he comes, he comes fast after mee.
　Eft looking backe would faine have runne away;
　But he him forst to stay, and tellen free
　The secret cause of his perplexitie:
　Yet nathemore by his bold hartie speach,
　Could his bloud-frosen hart emboldned bee,
　But through his boldnesse rather feare did reach,
Yet forst, at last he made through silence suddein breach.

26

And am I now in safetie sure (quoth he)
　From him, that would have forced me to dye?
　And is the point of death now turned fro mee,
　That I may tell this haplesse history?
　Feare nought: (quoth he) no daunger now is nye.
　Then shall I you recount a ruefull cace,
　(Said he) the which with this unlucky eye
　I late beheld, and had not greater grace
Me reft from it, had bene partaker of the place.

27

I lately chaunst (Would I had never chaunst)
 With a faire knight to keepen companee,
 Sir *Terwin* hight, that well himselfe advaunst
 In all affaires, and was both bold and free,
 But not so happie as mote happie bee:
 He lov'd, as was his lot, a Ladie gent,
 That him againe lov'd in the least degree:
 For she was proud, and of too high intent,
And joyd to see her lover languish and lament.

28

From whom returning sad and comfortlesse,
 As on the way together we did fare,
 We met that villen (God from him me blesse)
 That cursed wight, from whom I scapt whyleare,
 A man of hell, that cals himselfe *Despaire*:
 Who first us greets, and after faire areedes
 Of tydings strange, and of adventures rare:
 So creeping close, as Snake in hidden weedes,
Inquireth of our states, and of our knightly deedes.

29

Which when he knew, and felt our feeble harts
 Embost with bale, and bitter byting griefe,
 Which love had launched with his deadly darts,
 With wounding words and termes of foule repriefe
 He pluckt from us all hope of due reliefe,
 That earst us held in love of lingring life;
 Then hopelesse hartlesse, gan the cunning thiefe
 Perswade us die, to stint all further strife:
To me he lent this rope, to him a rustie knife.

30

With which sad instrument of hastie death,
 That wofull lover, loathing lenger light,
 A wide way made to let forth living breath.
 But I more fearefull, or more luckie wight,
 Dismayd with that deformed dismall sight,
 Fled fast away, halfe dead with dying feare:
 Ne yet assur'd of life by you, Sir knight,
 Whose like infirmitie like chaunce may beare:
But God you never let his charmed speeches heare.

31

How may a man (said he) with idle speach
  Be wonne, to spoyle the Castle of his health?
  I wote (quoth he) whom triall late did teach,
  That like would not for all this worldes wealth:
  His subtill tongue, like dropping honny, mealt'th
  Into the hart, and searcheth every vaine,
  That ere one be aware, by secret stealth
  His powre is reft, and weaknesse doth remaine.
O never Sir desire to try his guilefull traine.

32

Certes (said he) hence shall I never rest,
  Till I that treachours art have heard and tride;
  And you Sir knight, whose name mote I request,
  Of grace do me unto his cabin guide.
  I that hight *Trevisan* (quoth he) will ride
  Against my liking backe, to doe you grace:
  But nor for gold nor glee will I abide
  By you, when ye arrive in that same place;
For lever had I die, than see his deadly face.

33

Ere long they come, where that same wicked wight
  His dwelling has, low in an hollow cave,
  Farre underneath a craggie clift ypight,
  Darke, dolefull, drearie, like a greedie grave,
  That still for carrion carcases doth crave:
  On top whereof aye dwelt the ghastly Owle,
  Shrieking his balefull note, which ever drave
  Farre from that haunt all other chearefull fowle;
And all about it wandring ghostes did waile and howle.

34

And all about old stockes and stubs of trees,
  Whereon nor fruit, nor leafe was ever seene,
  Did hang upon the ragged rocky knees;
  On which had many wretches hanged beene,
  Whose carcases were scattered on the greene,
  And throwne about the cliffs. Arrived there,
  That bare-head knight for dread and dolefull teene,
  Would faine have fled, ne durst approchen neare,
But th'other forst him stay, and comforted in feare.

35

That darkesome cave they enter, where they find
  That cursed man, low sitting on the ground,
  Musing full sadly in his sullein mind;
  His griesie lockes, long growen, and unbound,
  Disordred hong about his shoulders round,
  And hid his face; through which his hollow eyne
  Lookt deadly dull, and stared as astound;
  His raw-bone cheekes through penurie and pine,
Were shronke into his jawes, as he did never dine.

36

His garment nought but many ragged clouts,
  With thornes together pind and patched was,
  The which his naked sides he wrapt abouts;
  And him beside there lay upon the gras
  A drearie corse, whose life away did pas,
  All wallowd in his owne yet luke-warme blood,
  That from his wound yet welled fresh alas;
  In which a rustie knife fast fixed stood,
And made an open passage for the gushing flood.

37

Which piteous spectacle, approving trew
  The wofull tale that *Trevisan* had told,
  When as the gentle *Redcrosse* knight did vew,
  With firie zeale he burnt in courage bold,
  Him to avenge, before his bloud were cold,
  And to the villein said, Thou damned wight,
  The author of this fact, we here behold,
  What justice can but judge against thee right,
With thine owne bloud to price his bloud, here shed in sight?

38

What franticke fit (quoth he) hath thus distraught
  Thee, foolish man, so rash a doome to give?
  What justice ever other judgement taught,
  But he should die, who merites not to live?
  None else to death this man despayring drive,
  But his owne guiltie mind deserving death.
  Is then unjust to each his due to give?
  Or let him die, that loatheth living breath?
Or let him die at ease, that liveth here uneath?

39

Who travels by the wearie wandring way,
    To come unto his wished home in haste,
    And meetes a flood, that doth his passage stay,
    Is not great grace to helpe him over past,
    Or free his feet, that in the myre sticke fast?
    Most envious man, that grieves at neighbours good,
    And fond, that joyest in the woe thou hast,
    Why wilt not let him passe, that long hath stood
Upon the banke, yet wilt thy selfe not passe the flood?

40

He there does now enjoy eternall rest
    And happie ease, which thou doest want and crave,
    And further from it daily wanderest:
    What if some litle paine the passage have,
    That makes fraile flesh to feare the bitter wave?
    Is not short paine well borne, that brings long ease,
    And layes the soule to sleepe in quiet grave?
    Sleepe after toyle, port after stormie seas,
Ease after warre, death after life does greatly please.

41

The knight much wondred at his suddeine wit,
    And said, The terme of life is limited,
    Ne may a man prolong, nor shorten it;
    The souldier may not move from watchfull sted,
    Nor leave his stand, untill his Captaine bed.
    Who life did limit by almightie doome,
    (Quoth he) knowes best the termes established;
    And he, that points the Centonell his roome,
Doth license him depart at sound of morning droome.

42

Is not his deed, what ever thing is donne,
    In heaven and earth? did not he all create
    To die againe? all ends that was begonne.
    Their times in his eternall booke of fate
    Are written sure, and have their certaine date.
    Who then can strive with strong necessitie,
    That holds the world in his still chaunging state,
    Or shunne the death ordaynd by destinie?
When houre of death is come, let none aske whence, nor why.

43

The lenger life, I wote the greater sin,
　The greater sin, the greater punishment:
　All those great battels, which thou boasts to win,
　Through strife, and bloud-shed, and avengement,
　Now praysd, hereafter deare thou shalt repent:
　For life must life, and bloud must bloud repay.
　Is not enough thy evill life forespent?
　For he, that once hath missed the right way,
The further he doth goe, the further he doth stray.

44

Then do no further goe, no further stray,
　But here lie downe, and to thy rest betake,
　Th'ill to prevent, that life ensewen may.
　For what hath life, that may it loved make,
　And gives not rather cause it to forsake?
　Feare, sicknesse, age, losse, labour, sorrow, strife,
　Paine, hunger, cold, that makes the hart to quake;
　And ever fickle fortune rageth rife,
All which, and thousands mo do make a loathsome life.

45

Thou wretched man, of death hast greatest need,
　If in true ballance thou wilt weigh thy state:
　For never knight, that dared warlike deede,
　More lucklesse disaventures did amate:
　Witnesse the dongeon deepe, wherein of late
　Thy life shut up, for death so oft did call;
　And though good lucke prolonged hath thy date,
　Yet death then, would the like mishaps forestall,
Into the which hereafter thou maiest happen fall.

46

Why then doest thou, O man of sin, desire
　To draw thy dayes forth to their last degree?
　Is not the measure of thy sinfull hire
　High heaped up with huge iniquitie,
　Against the day of wrath, to burden thee?
　Is not enough, that to this Ladie milde
　Thou falsed hast thy faith with perjurie,
　And sold thy selfe to serve *Duessa* vilde,
With whom in all abuse thou hast thy selfe defilde?

47

Is not he just, that all this doth behold
    From highest heaven, and beares an equall eye?
    Shall he thy sins up in his knowledge fold,
    And guiltie be of thine impietie?
    Is not his law, Let every sinner die:
    Die shall all flesh? what then must needs be donne,
    Is it not better to doe willinglie,
    Than linger, till the glasse be all out ronne?
Death is the end of woes: die soone, O faeries sonne.

48

The knight was much enmoved with his speach,
    That as a swords point through his hart did perse,
    And in his conscience made a secret breach,
    Well knowing true all, that he did reherse
    And to his fresh remembrance did reverse
    The ugly vew of his deformed crimes,
    That all his manly powres it did disperse,
    As he were charmed with inchaunted rimes,
That oftentimes he quakt, and fainted oftentimes.

49

In which amazement, when the Miscreant
    Perceived him to waver weake and fraile,
    Whiles trembling horror did his conscience dant,
    And hellish anguish did his soule assaile,
    To drive him to despaire, and quite to quaile,
    He shew'd him painted in a table plaine,
    The damned ghosts, that doe in torments waile,
    And thousand feends that doe them endlesse paine
With fire and brimstone, which for ever shall remaine.

50

The sight whereof so throughly him dismaid,
    That nought but death before his eyes he saw,
    And ever burning wrath before him laid,
    By righteous sentence of th'Almighties law:
    Then gan the villein him to overcraw,
    And brought unto him swords, ropes, poison, fire,
    And all that might him to perdition draw;
    And bad him choose, what death he would desire:
For death was due to him, that had provokt Gods ire.

51

But when as none of them he saw him take,
  He to him raught a dagger sharpe and keene,
  And gave it him in hand: his hand did quake,
  And tremble like a leafe of Aspin greene,
  And troubled bloud through his pale face was seene
  To come, and goe with tydings from the hart,
  As it a running messenger had beene.
  At last resolv'd to worke his finall smart,
He lifted up his hand, that backe againe did start.

52

Which when as *Una* saw, through every vaine
  The crudled cold ran to her well of life,
  As in a swowne: but soone reliv'd againe,
  Out of his hand she snatcht the cursed knife,
  And threw it to the ground, enraged rife,
  And to him said, Fie, fie, faint harted knight,
  What meanest thou by this reprochfull strife?
  Is this the battell, which thou vauntst to fight
With that fire-mouthed Dragon, horrible and bright?

53

Come, come away, fraile, feeble, fleshly wight,
  Ne let vaine words bewitch thy manly hart,
  Ne divelish thoughts dismay thy constant spright.
  In heavenly mercies hast thou not a part?
  Why shouldst thou then despeire, that chosen art?
  Where justice growes, there grows eke greater grace,
  The which doth quench the brond of hellish smart,
  And that accurst hand-writing doth deface.
Arise, Sir knight arise, and leave this cursed place.

54

So up he rose, and thence amounted streight.
  Which when the carle beheld, and saw his guest
  Would safe depart, for all his subtill sleight,
  He chose an halter from among the rest,
  And with it hung himselfe, unbid unblest.
  But death he could not worke himselfe thereby;
  For thousand times he so himselfe had drest,
  Yet nathelesse it could not doe him die,
Till he should die his last, that is eternally.

CANT. X

*Her faithfull knight faire Una brings
to house of Holinesse,
Where he is taught repentance, and
the way to heavenly blesse.*

I

WHAT man is he, that boasts of fleshly might,
    And vaine assurance of mortality,
    Which all so soone, as it doth come to fight,
    Against spirituall foes, yeelds by and by,
    Or from the field most cowardly doth fly?
    Ne let the man ascribe it to his skill,
    That thorough grace hath gained victory.
    If any strength we have, it is to ill,
But all the good is Gods, both power and eke will.

2

By that, which lately hapned, *Una* saw,
    That this her knight was feeble, and too faint;
    And all his sinews woxen weake and raw,
    Through long enprisonment, and hard constraint,
    Which he endured in his late restraint,
    That yet he was unfit for bloudie fight:
    Therefore to cherish him with diets daint,
    She cast to bring him, where he chearen might,
Till he recovered had his late decayed plight.

3

There was an auntient house not farre away,
    Renowmd throughout the world for sacred lore,
    And pure unspotted life: so well they say
    It governd was, and guided evermore,
    Through wisedome of a matrone grave and hore;
    Whose onely joy was to relieve the needes
    Of wretched soules, and helpe the helpelesse pore:
    All night she spent in bidding of her bedes,
And all the day in doing good and godly deedes.

4

Dame *Cælia* men did her call, as thought
  From heaven to come, or thither to arise,
  The mother of three daughters, well upbrought
  In goodly thewes, and godly exercise:
  The eldest two most sober, chast, and wise,
  Fidelia and *Speranza* virgins were,
  Though spousd, yet wanting wedlocks solemnize;
  But faire *Charissa* to a lovely fere
Was lincked, and by him had many pledges dere.

5

Arrived there, the dore they find fast lockt;
  For it was warely watched night and day,
  For feare of many foes: but when they knockt,
  The Porter opened unto them streight way:
  He was an aged syre, all hory gray,
  With lookes full lowly cast, and gate full slow,
  Wont on a staffe his feeble steps to stay,
  Hight *Humiltá*. They passe in stouping low;
For streight and narrow was the way, which he did show.

6

Each goodly thing is hardest to begin,
  But entred in a spacious court they see,
  Both plaine, and pleasant to be walked in,
  Where them does meete a francklin faire and free,
  And entertaines with comely courteous glee,
  His name was *Zele*, that him right well became,
  For in his speeches and behaviour hee
  Did labour lively to expresse the same,
And gladly did them guide, till to the Hall they came.

7

There fairely them receives a gentle Squire,
  Of milde demeanure, and rare courtesie,
  Right cleanly clad in comely sad attire;
  In word and deede that shew'd great modestie,
  And knew his good to all of each degree,
  Hight *Reverence*. He them with speeches meet
  Does faire entreat; no courting nicetie,
  But simple true, and eke unfained sweet,
As might become a Squire so great persons to greet.

8

And afterwards them to his Dame he leades,
  That aged Dame, the Ladie of the place:
  Who all this while was busie at her beades:
  Which doen, she up arose with seemely grace,
  And toward them full matronely did pace.
  Where when that fairest *Una* she beheld,
  Whom well she knew to spring from heavenly race,
  Her hart with ioy unwonted inly sweld,
As feeling wondrous comfort in her weaker eld.

9

And her embracing said, O happie earth,
  Whereon thy innocent feet doe ever tread,
  Most vertuous virgin borne of heavenly berth,
  That to redeeme thy woefull parents head,
  From tyrans rage, and ever-dying dread,
  Hast wandred through the world now long a day;
  Yet ceasest not thy wearie soles to lead,
  What grace hath thee now hither brought this way?
Or doen thy feeble feet unweeting hither stray?

10

Strange thing it is an errant knight to see
  Here in this place, or any other wight,
  That hither turnes his steps. So few there bee,
  That chose the narrow path, or seeke the right:
  All keepe the broad high way, and take delight
  With many rather for to go astray,
  And be partakers of their evill plight,
  Than with a few to walke the rightest way;
O foolish men, why haste ye to your owne decay?

11

Thy selfe to see, and tyred limbs to rest,
  O matrone sage (quoth she) I hither came,
  And this good knight his way with me addrest,
  Led with thy prayses and broad-blazed fame,
  That up to heaven is blowne. The auncient Dame
  Him goodly greeted in her modest guise,
  And entertaynd them both, as best became,
  With all the court'sies, that she could devise,
Ne wanted ought, to shew her bounteous or wise.

12

Thus as they gan of sundry things devise,
  Loe two most goodly virgins came in place,
  Ylinked arme in arme in lovely wise,
  With countenance demure, and modest grace,
  They numbred even steps and equall pace:
  Of which the eldest, that *Fidelia* hight,
  Like sunny beames threw from her Christall face,
  That could have dazd the rash beholders sight,
And round about her head did shine like heavens light.

13

She was araied all in lilly white,
  And in her right hand bore a cup of gold,
  With wine and water fild up to the hight,
  In which a Serpent did himselfe enfold,
  That horrour made to all, that did behold;
  But she no whit did chaunge her constant mood:
  And in her other hand she fast did hold
  A booke, that was both signd and seald with blood,
Wherein darke things were writ, hard to be understood.

14

Her younger sister, that *Speranza* hight,
  Was clad in blew, that her beseemed well;
  Not all so chearefull seemed she of sight,
  As was her sister; whether dread did dwell,
  Or anguish in her hart, is hard to tell:
  Upon her arme a silver anchor lay,
  Whereon she leaned ever, as befell:
  And ever up to heaven, as she did pray,
Her stedfast eyes were bent, ne swarved other way.

15

They seeing *Una*, towards her gan wend,
  Who them encounters with like courtesie;
  Many kind speeches they betwene them spend,
  And greatly joy each other well to see:
  Then to the knight with shamefast modestie
  They turne themselves, at *Unaes* meeke request,
  And him salute with well beseeming glee;
  Who faire them quites, as him beseemed best,
And goodly gan discourse of many a noble gest.

16

Then *Una* thus; But she your sister deare;
  The deare *Charissa* where is she become?
  Or wants she health, or busie is elsewhere?
  Ah no, said they, but forth she may not come:
  For she of late is lightned of her wombe,
  And hath encreast the world with one sonne more,
  That her to see should be but troublesome.
  Indeede (quoth she) that should her trouble sore,
But thankt be God, and her encrease so evermore.

17

Then said the aged *Cælia*, Deare dame,
  And you good Sir, I wote that of your toyle,
  And labours long, through which ye hither came,
  Ye both forwearied be: therefore a whyle
  I read you rest, and to your bowres recoyle.
  Then called she a Groome, that forth him led
  Into a goodly lodge, and gan despoile
  Of puissant armes, and laid in easie bed;
His name was meeke *Obedience* rightfully ared.

18

Now when their wearie limbes with kindly rest,
  And bodies were refresht with due repast,
  Faire *Una* gan *Fidelia* faire request,
  To have her knight into her schoolehouse plaste,
  That of her heavenly learning he might taste,
  And heare the wisedome of her words divine.
  She graunted, and that knight so much agraste,
  That she him taught celestiall discipline,
And opened his dull eyes, that light mote in them shine.

19

And that her sacred Booke, with bloud ywrit,
  That none could read, except she did them teach,
  She unto him disclosed every whit,
  And heavenly documents thereout did preach,
  That weaker wit of man could never reach,
  Of God, of grace, of justice, of free will,
  That wonder was to heare her goodly speach:
  For she was able, with her words to kill,
And raise againe to life the hart, that she did thrill.

20

And when she list poure out her larger spright,
  She would commaund the hastie Sunne to stay,
  Or backward turne his course from heavens hight;
  Sometimes great hostes of men she could dismay,
  Dry-shod to passe, she parts the flouds in tway;
  And eke huge mountaines from their native seat
  She would commaund, themselves to beare away,
  And throw in raging sea with roaring threat.
Almightie God her gave such powre, and puissance great.

21

The faithfull knight now grew in litle space,
  By hearing her, and by her sisters lore,
  To such perfection of all heavenly grace,
  That wretched world he gan for to abhore,
  And mortall life gan loath, as thing forlore,
  Greev'd with remembrance of his wicked wayes,
  And prickt with anguish of his sinnes so sore,
  That he desirde to end his wretched dayes:
So much the dart of sinfull guilt the soule dismayes.

22

But wise *Speranza* gave him comfort sweet,
  And taught him how to take assured hold
  Upon her silver anchor, as was meet;
  Else had his sinnes so great, and manifold
  Made him forget all that *Fidelia* told.
  In this distressed doubtfull agonie,
  When him his dearest *Una* did behold,
  Disdeining life, desiring leave to die,
She found her selfe assayld with great perplexitie.

23

And came to *Cælia* to declare her smart,
  Who well acquainted with that commune plight,
  Which sinfull horror workes in wounded hart,
  Her wisely comforted all that she might,
  With goodly counsell and advisement right;
  And streightway sent with carefull diligence.
  To fetch a Leach, the which had great insight
  In that disease of grieved conscience,
And well could cure the same; His name was *Patience*.

24

Who comming to that soule-diseased knight,
　　Could hardly him intreat, to tell his griefe:
　　Which knowne, and all that noyd his heavie spright
　　Well searcht, eftsoones he gan apply reliefe
　　Of salves and med'cines, which had passing priefe,
　　And thereto added words of wondrous might:
　　By which to ease he him recured briefe,
　　And much asswag'd the passion of his plight,
That he his paine endur'd, as seeming now more light.

25

But yet the cause and root of all his ill,
　　Inward corruption, and infected sin,
　　Not purg'd nor heald, behind remained still,
　　And festring sore did rankle yet within,
　　Close creeping twixt the marrow and the skin.
　　Which to extirpe, he laid him privily
　　Downe in a darkesome lowly place farre in,
　　Whereas he meant his corrosives to apply,
And with streight diet tame his stubborne malady.

26

In ashes and sackcloth he did array
　　His daintie corse, proud humors to abate,
　　And dieted with fasting every day,
　　The swelling of his wounds to mitigate,
　　And made him pray both earely and eke late:
　　And ever as superfluous flesh did rot
　　Amendment readie still at hand did wayt,
　　To pluck it out with pincers firie whot,
That soone in him was left no one corrupted jot.

27

And bitter *Penance* with an yron whip,
　　Was wont him once to disple every day:
　　And sharpe *Remorse* his hart did pricke and nip,
　　That drops of bloud thence like a well did play;
　　And sad *Repentance* used to embay
　　His bodie in salt water smarting sore,
　　The filthy blots of sinne to wash away.
　　So in short space they did to health restore
The man that would not live, but earst lay at deathes dore.

28

In which his torment often was so great,
  That like a Lyon he would cry and rore,
  And rend his flesh, and his owne synewes eat.
  His owne deare *Una* hearing evermore
  His ruefull shriekes and gronings, often tore
  Her guiltlesse garments, and her golden heare,
  For pitty of his paine and anguish sore;
  Yet all with patience wisely she did beare;
For well she wist, his crime could else be never cleare.

29

Whom thus recover'd by wise Patience,
  And trew *Repentance* they to *Una* brought:
  Who joyous of his cured conscience,
  Him dearely kist, and fairely eke besought
  Himselfe to chearish, and consuming thought
  To put away out of his carefull brest.
  By this *Charissa*, late in child-bed brought,
  Was woxen strong, and left her fruitfull nest;
To her faire *Una* brought this unacquainted guest.

30

She was a woman in her freshest age,
  Of wondrous beauty, and of bountie rare,
  With goodly grace and comely personage,
  That was on earth not easie to compare;
  Full of great love, but *Cupids* wanton snare
  As hell she hated, chast in worke and will;
  Her necke and breasts were ever open bare,
  That ay thereof her babes might sucke their fill;
The rest was all in yellow robes arayed still.

31

A multitude of babes about her hong,
  Playing their sports, that joyd her to behold,
  Whom still she fed, whiles they were weake and young,
  But thrust them forth still, as they wexed old:
  And on her head she wore a tyre of gold,
  Adornd with gemmes and owches wondrous faire,
  Whose passing price uneath was to be told;
  And by her side there sate a gentle paire
Of turtle doves, she sitting in an yvorie chaire.

32

The knight and *Una* entring, faire her greet,
   And bid her joy of that her happie brood;
   Who them requites with court'sies seeming meet,
   And entertaines with friendly chearefull mood.
   Then *Una* her besought, to be so good,
   As in her vertuous rules to schoole her knight,
   Now after all his torment well withstood,
   In that sad house of *Penaunce*, where his spright
Had past the paines of hell, and long enduring night.

33

She was right joyous of her just request,
   And taking by the hand that Faeries sonne,
   Gan him instruct in every good behest,
   Of love, and righteousnesse, and well to donne,
   And wrath, and hatred warely to shonne,
   That drew on men Gods hatred, and his wrath,
   And many soules in dolours had fordonne:
   In which when him she well instructed hath,
From thence to heaven she teacheth him the ready path.

34

Wherein his weaker wandring steps to guide,
   An auncient matrone she to her does call,
   Whose sober lookes her wisedome well describe:
   Her name was *Mercie*, well knowne over all,
   To be both gratious, and eke liberall:
   To whom the carefull charge of him she gave,
   To lead aright, that he should never fall
   In all his wayes through this wide worldes wave,
That Mercy in the end his righteous soule might save.

35

The godly Matrone by the hand him beares
   Forth from her presence, by a narrow way,
   Scattred with bushy thornes, and ragged breares,
   Which still before him she remov'd away,
   That nothing might his ready passage stay:
   And ever when his feet encombred were,
   Or gan to shrinke, or from the right to stray,
   She held him fast, and firmely did upbeare,
As carefull Nourse her child from falling oft does reare.

36

Eftsoones unto an holy Hospitall,
  That was fore by the way, she did him bring,
  In which seven Bead-men that had vowed all
  Their life to service of high heavens king
  Did spend their dayes in doing godly thing:
  Their gates to all were open evermore,
  That by the wearie way were traveiling,
  And one sate wayting ever them before,
To call in commers-by, that needy were and pore.

37

The first of them that eldest was, and best,
  Of all the house had charge and governement,
  As Guardian and Steward of the rest:
  His office was to give entertainement
  And lodging, unto all that came, and went:
  Not unto such, as could him feast againe,
  And double quite, for that he on them spent,
  But such, as want of harbour did constraine:
Those for Gods sake his dewty was to entertaine.

38

The second was as Almner of the place,
  His office was, the hungry for to feed,
  And thristy give to drinke, a worke of grace:
  He feard not once him selfe to be in need,
  Ne car'd to hoord for those, whom he did breede:
  The grace of God he layd up still in store,
  Which as a stocke he left unto his seede;
  He had enough, what need him care for more?
And had he lesse, yet some he would give to the pore.

39

The third had of their wardrobe custodie,
  In which were not rich tyres, nor garments gay,
  The plumes of pride, and wings of vanitie,
  But clothes meet to keepe keene could away,
  And naked nature seemely to aray;
  With which bare wretched wights he dayly clad,
  The images of God in earthly clay;
  And if that no spare cloths to give he had,
His owne coate he would cut, and it distribute glad.

40

The fourth appointed by his office was,
  Poore prisoners to relieve with gratious ayd,
  And captives to redeeme with price of bras,
  From Turkes and Sarazins, which them had stayd;
  And though they faultie were, yet well he wayd,
  That God to us forgiveth every howre
  Much more than that, why they in bands were layd,
  And he that harrowd hell with heavie stowre,
The faultie soules from thence brought to his heavenly bowre.

41

The fift had charge sicke persons to attend,
  And comfort those, in point of death which lay;
  For them most needeth comfort in the end,
  When sin, and hell, and death do most dismay
  The feeble soule departing hence away.
  All is but lost, that living we bestow,
  If not well ended at our dying day.
  O man have mind of that last bitter throw;
For as the tree does fall, so lyes it ever low.

42

The sixt had charge of them now being dead,
  In seemely sort their corses to engrave,
  And deck with dainty flowres their bridall bed,
  That to their heavenly spouse both sweet and brave
  They might appeare, when he their soules shall save.
  The wondrous workemanship of Gods owne mould,
  Whose face he made, all beasts to feare, and gave
  All in his hand, even dead we honour should.
Ah dearest God me graunt, I dead be not defould.

43

The seventh now after death and buriall done,
  Had charge the tender Orphans of the dead
  And widowes ayd, least they should be undone:
  In face of judgement he their right would plead,
  Ne ought the powre of mighty men did dread
  In their defence, nor would for gold or fee
  Be wonne their rightfull causes downe to tread:
  And when they stood in most necessitee,
He did supply their want, and gave them ever free.

44

There when the Elfin knight arrived was,
  The first and chiefest of the seven, whose care
  Was guests to welcome, towardes him did pas:
  Where seeing *Mercie*, that his steps up bare,
  And always led, to her with reverence rare
  He humbly louted in meeke lowlinesse,
  And seemely welcome for her did prepare:
  For of their order she was Patronesse,
Albe *Charissa* were their chiefest founderesse.

45

There she awhile him stayes, him selfe to rest,
  That to the rest more able he might bee:
  During which time, in every good behest
  And godly worke of Almes and charitee
  She him instructed with great industree;
  Shortly therein so perfect he became,
  That from the first unto the last degree,
  His mortall life he learned had to frame
In holy righteousnesse, without rebuke or blame.

46

Thence forward by that painfull way they pas,
  Forth to an hill, that was both steepe and hy;
  On top whereof a sacred chappell was,
  And eke a litle Hermitage thereby,
  Wherein an aged holy man did lye,
  That day and night said his devotion,
  Ne other worldly busines did apply;
  His name was heavenly *Contemplation*;
Of God and goodnesse was his meditation.

47

Great grace that old man to him given had;
  For God he often saw from heavens hight,
  All were his earthly eyen both blunt and bad,
  And through great age had lost their kindly sight,
  Yet wondrous quick and persant was his spright,
  As Eagles eye, that can behold the Sunne:
  That hill they scale with all their powre and might,
  That his frayle thighes nigh wearie and fordonne
Gan faile, but by her helpe the top at last he wonne.

48

There they do finde that godly aged Sire,
 With snowy lockes adowne his shoulders shed,
 As hoarie frost with spangles doth attire
 The mossy braunches of an Oke halfe ded.
 Each bone might through his body well be red,
 And every sinew seene through his long fast:
 For nought he car'd his carcas long unfed;
 His mind was full of spirituall repast,
And pyn'd his flesh, to keepe his body low and chast.

49

Who when these two approching he aspide,
 At their first presence grew agrieved sore,
 That forst him lay his heavenly thoughts aside;
 And had he not that Dame respected more,
 Whom highly he did reverence and adore,
 He would not once have moved for the knight.
 They him saluted standing far afore;
 Who well them greeting, humbly did requight,
And asked, to what end they clomb that tedious height.

50

What end (quoth she) should cause us take such paine,
 But that same end, which every living wight
 Should make his marke, high heaven to attaine?
 Is not from hence the way, that leadeth right
 To that most glorious house, that glistreth bright
 With burning starres, and everliving fire,
 Whereof the keyes are to thy hand behight
 By wise *Fidelia*? she doth thee require,
To shew it to this knight, according his desire.

51

Thrise happy man, said then the father grave,
 Whose staggering steps thy steady hand doth lead,
 And shewes the way, his sinfull soule to save.
 Who better can the way to heaven aread,
 Than thou thy selfe, that was both borne and bred
 In heavenly throne, where thousand Angels shine?
 Thou doest the prayers of the righteous sead
 Present before the majestie divine,
And his avenging wrath to clemencie incline.

52

Yet since thou bidst, thy pleasure shalbe donne.
  Then come thou man of earth, and see the way,
  That never yet was seene of Faeries sonne,
  That never leads the traveiler astray,
  But after labours long, and sad delay,
  Brings them to joyous rest and endlesse blis.
  But first thou must a season fast and pray,
  Till from her bands the spright assoiled is,
And have her strength recur'd from fraile infirmitis.

53

That done, he leads him to the highest Mount;
  Such one, as that same mighty man of God,
  That bloud-red billowes like a walled front
  On either side disparted with his rod,
  Till that his army dry-foot through them yod,
  Dwelt fortie dayes upon; where writ in stone
  With bloudy letters by the hand of God,
  The bitter doome of death and balefull mone
He did receive, whiles flashing fire about him shone.

54

Or like that sacred hill, whose head full hie,
  Adornd with fruitfull Olives all arownd,
  Is, as it were for endlesse memory
  Of that deare Lord, who oft thereon was fownd,
  For ever with a flowring girlond crownd:
  Or like that pleasaunt Mount, that is for ay
  Through famous Poets verse each where renownd,
  On which the thrise three learned Ladies play
Their heavenly notes, and make full many a lovely lay.

55

From thence, far off he unto him did shew
  A litle path, that was both steepe and long,
  Which to a goodly Citie led his vew;
  Whose wals and towres were builded high and strong
  Of perle and precious stone, that earthly tong
  Cannot describe, nor wit of man can tell;
  Too high a ditty for my simple song;
  The Citie of the great king hight it well,
Wherein eternall peace and happinesse doth dwell.

56

As he thereon stood gazing, he might see
  The blessed Angels to and fro descend
  From highest heaven, in gladsome companee,
  And with great joy into that Citie wend,
  As commonly as friend does with his frend.
  Whereat he wondred much, and gan enquere,
  What stately building durst so high extend
  Her loftie towres unto the starry sphere,
And what unknowen nation there empeopled were.

57

Faire knight (quoth he) *Hierusalem* that is,
  The new *Hierusalem*, that God has built
  For those to dwell in, that are chosen his,
  His chosen people purg'd from sinfull guilt,
  With pretious bloud, which cruelly was spilt
  On cursed tree, of that unspotted lam,
  That for the sinnes of all the world was kilt:
  Now are they Saints all in that Citie sam,
More deare unto their God, than younglings to their dam.

58

Till now, said then the knight, I weened well,
  That great *Cleopolis*, where I have beene,
  In which that fairest *Faerie Queene* doth dwell,
  The fairest Citie was, that might be seene;
  And that bright towre all built of christall cleene,
  Panthea, seemd the brightest thing, that was:
  But now by proofe all otherwise I weene;
  For this great Citie that does far surpas,
And this bright Angels towre quite dims that towre of glas.

59

Most trew, then said the holy aged man;
  Yet is *Cleopolis* for earthly frame,
  The fairest peece, that eye beholden can:
  And well beseemes all knights of noble name,
  That covet in th'immortall booke of fame
  To be eternized, that same to haunt,
  And doen their service to that soveraigne Dame,
  That glorie does to them for guerdon graunt:
For she is heavenly borne, and heaven may justly vaunt.

60

And thou faire ymp, sprong out from English race,
  How ever now accompted Elfins sonne,
  Well worthy doest thy service for her grace,
  To aide a virgin desolate foredonne.
  But when thou famous victorie hast wonne,
  And high emongst all knights hast hong thy shield,
  Thenceforth the suit of earthly conquest shonne,
  And wash thy hands from guilt of bloudy field:
For bloud can nought but sin, and wars but sorrowes yield.

61

Then seeke this path, that I to thee presage,
  Which after all to heaven shall thee send;
  Then peaceably thy painefull pilgrimage
  To yonder same *Hierusalem* do bend,
  Where is for thee ordaind a blessed end:
  For thou emongst those Saints, whom thou doest see,
  Shalt be a Saint, and thine owne nations frend
  And Patrone: thou Saint *George* shalt called bee,
Saint *George* of mery England, the signe of victoree.

62

Unworthy wretch (quoth he) of so great grace,
  How dare I thinke such glory to attaine?
  These that have it attaind, were in like cace
  (Quoth he) as wretched, and liv'd in like paine.
  But deeds of armes must I at last be faine,
  And Ladies love to leave so dearely bought?
  What need of armes, where peace doth ay remaine,
  (Said he) and battailes none are to be fought?
As for loose loves are vaine, and vanish into nought.

63

O let me not (quoth he) then turne againe
  Backe to the world, whose joyes so fruitlesse are;
  But let me here for aye in peace remaine,
  Or streight way on that last long voyage fare,
  That nothing may my present hope empare.
  That may not be (said he) ne maist thou yit
  Forgo that royall maides bequeathed care,
  Who did her cause into thy hand commit,
Till from her cursed foe thou have her freely quit.

64

Then shall I soone, (quoth he) so God me grace,
  Abet that virgins cause disconsolate,
  And shortly backe returne unto this place,
  To walke this way in Pilgrims poore estate.
  But now aread, old father, why of late
  Didst thou behight me borne of English blood,
  Whom all a Faeries sonne doen nominate?
  That word shall I (said he) avouchen good,
Sith to thee is unknowne the cradle of thy brood.

65

For well I wote, thou springst from ancient race
  Of *Saxon* kings, that have with mightie hand
  And many bloudie battailes fought in place
  High reard their royall throne in *Britane* land,
  And vanquisht them, unable to withstand:
  From thence a Faerie thee unweeting reft,
  There as thou slepst in tender swadling band,
  And her base Elfin brood there for thee left.
Such men do Chaungelings call, so chaungd by Faeries theft.

66

Thence she thee brought into this Faerie lond,
  And in an heaped furrow did thee hyde,
  Where thee a Ploughman all unweeting fond,
  As he his toylesome teme that way did guyde,
  And brought thee up in ploughmans state to byde,
  Whereof *Georgos* he thee gave to name;
  Till prickt with courage, and thy forces pryde,
  To Faery court thou cam'st to seeke for fame,
And prove thy puissaunt armes, as seemes thee best became.

67

O holy Sire (quoth he) how shall I quight
  The many favours I with thee have found,
  That hast my name and nation red aright,
  And taught the way that does to heaven bound?
  This said, adowne he looked to the ground,
  To have returnd, but dazed were his eyne,
  Through passing brightnesse, which did quite confound
  His feeble sence, and too exceeding shyne.
So darke are earthly things compard to things divine.

68

At last whenas himselfe he gan to find,
　To *Una* back he cast him to retire;
　Who him awaited still with pensive mind.
　Great thankes and goodly meed to that good syre,
　He thence departing gave for his paines hyre.
　So came to *Una*, who him joyd to see,
　And after litle rest, gan him desire,
　Of her adventure mindfull for to bee.
So leave they take of *Cælia*, and her daughters three.

CANT. XI

*The knight with that old Dragon fights
two dayes incessantly:
The third him overthrowes, and gayns
most glorious victory.*

I

HIGH time now gan it wex for *Una* faire,
　To thinke of those her captive Parents deare,
　And their forwasted kingdome to repaire:
　Whereto whenas they now approched neare,
　With hartie words her knight she gan to cheare,
　And in her modest manner thus bespake;
　Deare knight, as deare, as ever knight was deare,
　That all these sorrowes suffer for my sake,
High heaven behold the tedious toyle, ye for me take.

2

Now are we come unto my native soyle,
　And to the place, where all our perils dwell;
　Here haunts that feend, and does his dayly spoyle,
　Therefore henceforth be at your keeping well,
　And ever ready for your foeman fell.
　The sparke of noble courage now awake,
　And strive your excellent selfe to excell;
　That shall ye evermore renowmed make,
Above all knights on earth, that batteill undertake.

3

And pointing forth, lo yonder is (said she)
 The brasen towre in which my parents deare
 For dread of that huge feend emprisond be,
 Whom I from far see on the walles appeare,
 Whose sight my feeble soule doth greatly cheare:
 And on the top of all I do espye
 The watchman wayting tydings glad to heare,
 That O my parents might I happily
Unto you bring, to ease you of your misery.

4

With that they heard a roaring hideous sound,
 That all the ayre with terrour filled wide,
 And seemd uneath to shake the stedfast ground.
 Eftsoones that dreadfull Dragon they espide,
 Where stretcht he lay upon the sunny side
 Of a great hill, himselfe like a great hill.
 But all so soone, as he from far descride
 Those glistring armes, that heaven with light did fill,
He rousd himselfe full blith, and hastned them untill.

5

Then bad the knight his Lady yede aloofe,
 And to an hill her selfe with draw aside,
 From whence she might behold that battailles proof
 And eke be safe from daunger far descryde:
 She him obayd, and turnd a little wyde.
 Now O thou sacred Muse, most learned Dame,
 Faire ympe of *Phœbus*, and his aged bride,
 The Nourse of time, and everlasting fame,
That warlike hands ennoblest with immortall name;

6

O gently come into my feeble brest,
 Come gently, but not with that mighty rage,
 Wherewith the martiall troupes thou doest infest,
 And harts of great Heroes doest enrage,
 That nought their kindled courage may aswage,
 Soone as thy dreadfull trompe begins to sownd;
 The God of warre with his fiers equipage
 Thou doest awake, sleepe never he so sownd,
And scared nations doest with horrour sterne astownd.

7

Faire Goddesse lay that furious fit aside,
  Till I of warres and bloudy *Mars* do sing,
  And Briton fields with Sarazin bloud bedyde,
  Twixt that great faery Queene and Paynim king,
  That with their horrour heaven and earth did ring,
  A worke of labour long, and endlesse prayse:
  But now a while let downe that haughtie string,
  And to my tunes thy second tenor rayse,
That I this man of God his godly armes may blaze.

8

By this the dreadfull Beast drew nigh to hand,
  Halfe flying, and halfe footing in his hast,
  That with his largenesse measured much land,
  And made wide shadow under his huge wast;
  As mountaine doth the valley overcast.
  Approching nigh, he reared high afore
  His body monstrous, horrible, and vast,
  Which to increase his wondrous greatnesse more,
Was swolne with wrath, and poyson, and with bloudy gore.

9

And over, all with brasen scales was armd,
  Like plated coate of steele, so couched neare,
  That nought mote perce, ne might his corse be harmd
  With dint of sword, nor push of pointed speare;
  Which as an Eagle, seeing pray appeare,
  His aery plumes doth rouze, full rudely dight,
  So shaked he, that horrour was to heare,
  For as the clashing of an Armour bright,
Such noyse his rouzed scales did send unto the knight.

10

His flaggy wings when forth he did display,
  Were like two sayles, in which the hollow wynd
  Is gathered full, and worketh speedy way:
  And eke the pennes, that did his pineons bynd,
  Were like mayne-yards, with flying canvas lynd,
  With which whenas him list the ayre to beat,
  And there by force unwonted passage find,
  The cloudes before him fled for terrour great,
And all the heavens stood still amazed with his threat.

11

His huge long tayle wound up in hundred foldes,
  Does overspred his long bras-scaly backe,
  Whose wreathed boughts when ever he unfoldes,
  And thicke entangled knots adown does slacke,
  Bespotted as with shields of red and blacke,
  It sweepeth all the land behind him farre,
  And of three furlongs does but litle lacke;
  And at the point two stings in-fixed arre,
Both deadly sharpe, that sharpest steele exceeden farre.*

12

But stings and sharpest steele did far exceed
  The sharpnesse of his cruell rending clawes;
  Dead was it sure, as sure as death in deed,
  Whatever thing does touch his ravenous pawes,
  Or what within his reach he ever drawes.
  But his most hideous head my toung to tell
  Does tremble: for his deepe devouring jawes
  Wide gaped, like the griesly mouth of hell,
Through which into his darke abisse all ravin fell.

13

And that more wondrous was, in either jaw
  Three ranckes of yron teeth enraunged were,
  In which yet trickling bloud and gobbets raw
  Of late devoured bodies did appeare,
  That sight thereof bred cold congealed feare:
  Which to increase, and all atonce to kill,
  A cloud of smoothering smoke and sulphur seare
  Out of his stinking gorge forth steemed still,
That all the ayre about with smoke and stench did fill.

14

His blazing eyes, like two bright shining shields,
  Did burne with wrath, and sparkled living fyre;
  As two broad Beacons, set in open fields,
  Send forth their flames farre off to every shyre,
  And warning give, that enemies conspyre,
  With fire and sword the region to invade;
  So flam'd his eyne with rage and rancorous yre:
  But farre within, as in a hollow glade,
Those glaring lampes were set, that made a dreadfull shade.

15

So dreadfully he towards him did pas,
Forelifting up aloft his speckled brest,
And often bounding on the brused gras,
As for great joyance of his newcome guest.
Eftsoones he gan advance his haughtie crest,
As chauffed Bore his bristles doth upreare,
And shoke his scales to battell readie drest;
That made the *Redcrosse* knight nigh quake for feare,
As bidding bold defiance to his foeman neare.

16

The knight gan fairely couch his steadie speare,
And fiercely ran at him with rigorous might:
The pointed steele arriving rudely theare,
His harder hide would neither perce, nor bight,
But glauncing by forth passed forward right;
Yet sore amoved with so puissant push,
The wrathfull beast about him turned light,
And him so rudely passing by, did brush
With his long tayle, that horse and man to ground did rush.

17

Both horse and man up lightly rose againe,
And fresh encounter towards him addrest:
But th'idle stroke yet backe recoyld in vaine,
And found no place his deadly point to rest.
Exceeding rage enflam'd the furious beast,
To be avenged of so great despight;
For never felt his imperceable brest
So wondrous force, from hand of living wight;
Yet had he prov'd the powre of many a puissant knight.

18

Then with his waving wings displayed wyde,
Himselfe up high he lifted from the ground,
And with strong flight did forcibly divide
The yielding aire, which nigh too feeble found
Her flitting partes, and element unsound,
To beare so great a weight: he cutting way
With his broad sayles, about him soared round:
At last low stouping with unweldie sway,
Snatcht up both horse and man, to beare them quite away.

19

Long he them bore above the subject plaine,
  So farre as Ewghen bow a shaft may send,
Till struggling strong did him at last constraine,
To let them downe before his flightes end:
As hagard hauke presuming to contend
With hardie fowle, above his hable might,
His wearie pounces all in vaine doth spend,
To trusse the pray too heavie for his flight;
Which comming downe to ground, does free it selfe by fight.

20

He so disseized of his gryping grosse,
  The knight his thrillant speare againe assayd
In his bras-plated body to embosse,
And three mens strength unto the stroke he layd;
Wherewith the stiffe beame quaked, as affrayd,
And glauncing from his scaly necke, did glyde
Close under his left wing, then broad displayd.
The percing steele there wrought a wound full wyde,
That with the uncouth smart the Monster lowdly cryde.

21

He cryde, as raging seas are wont to rore,
  When wintry storme his wrathfull wreck does threat,
The rolling billowes beat the ragged shore,
As they the earth would shoulder from her seat,
And greedie gulfe does gape, as he would eat
His neighbour element in his revenge:
Then gin the blustring brethren boldly threat,
To move the world from off his stedfast henge,
And boystrous battell make, each other to avenge.

22

The steely head stucke fast still in his flesh,
  Till with his cruell clawes he snatcht the wood,
And quite a sunder broke. Forth flowed fresh
A gushing river of blacke goarie blood,
That drowned all the land, whereon he stood;
The streame thereof would drive a water-mill.
Trebly augmented was his furious mood
With bitter sense of his deepe rooted ill,
That flames of fire he threw forth from his large nosethrill.

23

His hideous tayle then hurled he about,
  And therewith all enwrapt the nimble thyes
  Of his froth-fomy steed, whose courage stout
  Striving to loose the knot, that fast him tyes,
  Himselfe in streighter bandes too rash implyes,
  That to the ground he is perforce constraynd
  To throw his rider: who can quickly ryse
  From off the earth, with durty bloud distaynd,
For that reprochfull fall right fowly he disdaynd.

24

And fiercely tooke his trenchand blade in hand,
  With which he stroke so furious and so fell,
  That nothing seemd the puissance could withstand:
  Upon his crest the hardned yron fell,
  But his more hardned crest was armd so well,
  That deeper dint therein it would not make;
  Yet so extremely did the buffe him quell,
  That from thenceforth he shund the like to take,
But when he saw them come, he did them still forsake.

25

The knight was wrath to see his stroke beguyld,
  And smote againe with more outrageous might;
  But backe againe the sparckling steele recoyld,
  And left not any marke, where it did light;
  As if in Adamant rocke it had bene pight.
  The beast impatient of his smarting wound,
  And of so fierce and forcible despight,
  Thought with his wings to stye above the ground;
But his late wounded wing unserviceable found.

26

Then full of griefe and anguish vehement,
  He lowdly brayd, that like was never heard,
  And from his wide devouring oven sent
  A flake of fire, that flashing in his beard,
  Him all amazd, and almost made affeard:
  The scorching flame sore swinged all his face,
  And through his armour all his bodie seard,
  That he could not endure so cruell cace,
But thought his armes to leave, and helmet to unlace.

27

Not that great Champion of the antique world,
  Whom famous Poetes verse so much doth vaunt,
  And hath for twelve huge labours high extold,
  So many furies and sharpe fits did haunt,
  When him the poysoned garment did enchaunt
  With *Centaures* bloud, and bloudie verses charm'd,
  As did this knight twelve thousand dolours daunt,
  Whom fyrie steele now burnt, that earst him arm'd,
That erst him goodly arm'd, now most of all him harm'd.

28

Faint, wearie, sore, emboyled, grieved, brent
  With heat, toyle, wounds, armes, smart, and inward fire
  That never man such mischiefes did torment;
  Death better were, death did he oft desire,
  But death will never come, when needes require.
  Whom so dismayd when that his foe beheld,
  He cast to suffer him no more respire,
  But gan his sturdie sterne about to weld,
And him so strongly stroke, that to the ground him feld.

29

It fortuned (as faire it then befell)
  Behind his backe unweeting, where he stood,
  Of auncient time there was a springing well,
  From which fast trickled forth a silver flood,
  Full of great vertues, and for med'cine good.
  Whylome, before that cursed Dragon got
  That happie land, and all with innocent blood
  Defyld those sacred waves, it rightly hot
The well of life, ne yet his vertues had forgot.

30

For unto life the dead it could restore,
  And guilt of sinfull crimes cleane wash away,
  Those that with sicknesse were infected sore,
  It could recure, and aged long decay
  Renew, as one were borne that very day.
  Both *Silo* this, and *Jordan* did excell,
  And th'English *Bath*, and eke the german *Spau*,
  Ne can *Cephise*, nor *Hebrus* match this well:
Into the same the knight backe overthrowen, fell.

31

Now gan the golden *Phœbus* for to steepe
　His fierie face in billowes of the west,
　And his faint steedes watred in Ocean deepe,
　Whiles from their journall labours they did rest,
　When that infernall Monster, having kest
　His wearie foe into that living well,
　Can high advance his broad discoloured brest,
　Above his wonted pitch, with countenance fell,
And clapt his yron wings, as victor he did dwell.

32

Which when his pensive Ladie saw from farre,
　Great woe and sorrow did her soule assay,
　As weening that the sad end of the warre,
　And gan to highest God entirely pray,
　That feared chance from her to turne away;
　With folded hands and knees full lowly bent
　All night she watcht, ne once adowne would lay
　Her daintie limbs in her sad dreriment,
But praying still did wake, and waking did lament.

33

The morrow next gan early to appeare,
　That *Titan* rose to runne his daily race;
　But early ere the morrow next gan reare
　Out of the sea faire *Titans* deawy face,
　Up rose the gentle virgin from her place,
　And looked all about, if she might spy
　Her loved knight to move his manly pace:
　For she had great doubt of his safety,
Since late she saw him fall before his enemy.

34

At last she saw, where he upstarted brave
　Out of the well, wherein he drenched lay;
　As Eagle fresh out of the Ocean wave,
　Where he hath left his plumes all hoary gray,
　And deckt himselfe with feathers youthly gay,
　Like Eyas hauke up mounts unto the skies,
　His newly budded pineons to assay,
　And marveiles at himselfe, still as he flies:
So new this new-borne knight to battell new did rise.

35

Whom when the damned feend so fresh did spy,
　No wonder if he wondred at the sight,
　And doubted, whether his late enemy
　It were, or other new supplied knight.
　He, now to prove his late renewed might,
　High brandishing his bright deaw-burning blade,
　Upon his crested scalpe so sore did smite,
　That to the scull a yawning wound it made:
The deadly dint his dulled senses all dismaid.

36

I wote not, whether the revenging steele
　Were hardned with that holy water dew,
　Wherein he fell, or sharper edge did feele,
　Or his baptized hands now greater grew;
　Or other secret vertue did ensew;
　Else never could the force of fleshly arme,
　Ne molten mettall in his bloud embrew:
　For till that stownd could never wight him harme,
By subtilty, nor slight, nor might, nor mighty charme.

37

The cruell wound enraged him so sore,
　That loud he yelled for exceeding paine;
　As hundred ramping Lyons seem'd to rore,
　Whom ravenous hunger did thereto constraine:
　Then gan he tosse aloft his stretched traine,
　And therewith scourge the buxome aire so sore,
　That to his force to yeelden it was faine;
　Ne ought his sturdie strokes might stand afore,
That high trees overthrew, and rocks in peeces tore.

38

The same advauncing high above his head,
　With sharpe intended sting so rude him smot,
　That to the earth him drove, as stricken dead,
　Ne living wight would have him life behot:
　The mortall sting his angry needle shot
　Quite through his shield, and in his shoulder seasd,
　Where fast it stucke, ne would there out be got:
　The greife thereof him wondrous sore diseasd,
Ne might his ranckling paine with patience be appeasd.

39

But yet more mindfull of his honour deare,
  Than of the grievous smart, which him did wring,
  From loathed soile he can him lightly reare,
  And strove to loose the farre infixed sting:
  Which when in vaine he tryde with struggeling,
  Inflam'd with wrath, his raging blade he heft,
  And strooke so strongly, that the knotty string
  Of his huge taile he quite a sunder cleft,
Five joynts thereof he hewd, and but the stump him left.

40

Hart cannot thinke, what outrage, and what cryes,
  With foule enfouldred smoake and flashing fire,
  The hell-bred beast threw forth unto the skyes,
  That all was covered with darknesse dire:
  Then fraught with rancour, and engorged ire,
  He cast at once him to avenge for all,
  And gathering up himselfe out of the mire,
  With his uneven wings did fiercely fall
Upon his sunne-bright shield, and gript it fast withall.

41

Much was the man encombred with his hold,
  In feare to lose his weapon in his paw,
  Ne wist yet, how his talants to unfold;
  Nor harder was from *Cerberus* greedie jaw
  To plucke a bone, than from his cruell claw
  To reave by strength the griped gage away:
  Thrise he assayd it from his foot to draw,
  And thrise in vaine to draw it did assay,
It booted nought to thinke, to robbe him of his pray.

42

Tho when he saw no power might prevaile,
  His trustie sword he cald to his last aid,
  Wherewith he fiercely did his foe assaile,
  And double blowes about him stoutly laid,
  That glauncing fire out of the yron plaid;
  As sparckles from the Andvile use to fly,
  When heavie hammers on the wedge are swaid;
  Therewith at last he forst him to unty
One of his grasping feete, him to defend thereby.

43

The other foot, fast fixed on his shield,
  Whenas no strength, nor stroks mote him constraine
  To loose, ne yet the warlike pledge to yield,
  He smot thereat with all his might and maine,
  That nought so wondrous puissance might sustaine;
  Upon the joynt the lucky steele did light,
  And made such way, that hewd it quite in twaine;
  The paw yet missed not his minisht might,
But hong still on the shield, as it at first was pight.

44

For griefe thereof, and divelish despight,
  From his infernall fournace forth he threw
  Huge flames, that dimmed all the heavens light,
  Enrold in duskish smoke and brimstone blew;
  As burning *Aetna* from his boyling stew
  Doth belch out flames, and rockes in peeces broke,
  And ragged ribs of mountaines molten new,
  Enwrapt in coleblacke clouds and filthy smoke,
That all the land with stench, and heaven with horror choke.

45

The heate whereof, and harmefull pestilence
  So sore him noyd, that forst him to retire
  A little backward for his best defence,
  To save his bodie from the scorching fire,
  Which he from hellish entrailes did expire.
  It chaunst (eternall God that chaunce did guide)
  As he recoyled backward, in the mire
  His nigh forwearied feeble feet did slide,
And downe he fell, with dread of shame sore terrifide.

46

There grew a goodly tree him faire beside,
  Loaden with fruit and apples rosie red,
  As they in pure vermilion had beene dide,
  Whereof great vertues over all were red:
  For happie life to all, which thereon fed,
  And life eke everlasting did befall:
  Great God it planted in that blessed sted
  With his almightie hand, and did it call
The tree of life, the crime of our first fathers fall.

Redcrosse Knight and Dragon

47

In all the world like was not to be found,
  Save in that soile, where all good things did grow,
  And freely sprong out of the fruitfull ground,
  As incorrupted Nature did them sow,
  Till that dread Dragon all did overthrow.
  Another like faire tree eke grew thereby,
  Whereof who so did eat, eftsoones did know
  Both good and ill: O mornefull memory:
That tree through one mans fault hath doen us all to dy.

48

From that first tree forth flowd, as from a well,
  A trickling streame of Balme, most soveraine
  And daintie deare, which on the ground still fell,
  And overflowed all the fertill plaine,
  As it had deawed bene with timely raine:
  Life and long health that gratious ointment gave,
  And deadly woundes could heale, and reare againe
  The senselesse corse appointed for the grave.
Into that same he fell: which did from death him save.

49

For nigh thereto the ever damned beast
  Durst not approch, for he was deadly made,
  And all that life preserved, did detest:
  Yet he it oft adventur'd to invade.
  By this the drouping day-light gan to fade,
  And yeeld his roome to sad succeeding night,
  Who with her sable mantle gan to shade
  The face of earth, and wayes of living wight,
And high her burning torch set up in heaven bright.

50

When gentle *Una* saw the second fall
  Of her deare knight, who wearie of long fight,
  And faint through losse of bloud, mov'd not at all,
  But lay as in a dreame of deepe delight,
  Besmeard with pretious Balme, whose vertuous might
  Did heale his wounds, and scorching heat alay,
  Againe she stricken was with sore affright,
  And for his safetie gan devoutly pray;
And watch the noyous night, and wait for joyous day.

51

The joyous day gan early to appeare,
  And faire *Aurora* from the deawy bed
  Of aged *Tithone* gan her selfe to reare,
  With rosie cheekes, for shame as blushing red;
  Her golden lockes for haste were loosely shed
  About her eares, when *Una* her did marke
  Clymbe to her charet, all with flowers spred,
  From heaven high to chase the chearelesse darke;
With merry note her loud salutes the mounting larke.

52

Then freshly up arose the doughtie knight,
  All healed of his hurts and woundes wide,
  And did himselfe to battell readie dight;
  Whose early foe awaiting him beside
  To have devourd, so soone as day he spyde,
  When now he saw himselfe so freshly reare,
  As if late fight had nought him damnifyde,
  He woxe dismayd, and gan his fate to feare;
Nathlesse with wonted rage he him advaunced neare.

53

And in his first encounter, gaping wide,
  He thought attonce him to have swallowd quight,
  And rusht upon him with outragious pride;
  Who him r'encountring fierce, as hauke in flight,
  Perforce rebutted backe. The weapon bright
  Taking advantage of his open jaw,
  Ran through his mouth with so importune might,
  That deepe emperst his darksome hollow maw,
And back retyrd, his life bloud forth with all did draw.

54

So downe he fell, and forth his life did breath,
  That vanisht into smoke and cloudes swift;
  So downe he fell, that th'earth him underneath
  Did grone, as feeble so great load to lift;
  So downe he fell, as an huge rockie clift,
  Whose false foundation waves have washt away,
  With dreadfull poyse is from the mayneland rift,
  And rolling downe, great *Neptune* doth dismay;
So downe he fell, and like an heaped mountaine lay.

55

The knight himselfe even trembled at his fall,
　So huge and horrible a masse it seem'd;
　And his deare Ladie, that beheld it all,
　Durst not approch for dread, which she misdeem'd,
　But yet at last, when as the direfull feend
　She saw not stirre, off-shaking vaine affright,
　She nigher drew, and saw that joyous end:
　Then God she praysd, and thankt her faithfull knight,
That had atchiev'd so great a conquest by his might.

CANT. XII

Faire Una to the Redcrosse knight
betrouthed is with joy:
Though false Duessa it to barre
her false sleights doe imploy.

I

BEHOLD I see the haven nigh at hand,
　To which I meane my wearie course to bend;
　Vere the maine shete, and beare up with the land,
　The which afore is fairely to be kend,
　And seemeth safe from stormes, that may offend;
　There this faire virgin wearie of her way
　Must landed be, now at her journeyes end:
　There eke my feeble barke a while may stay,
Till merry wind and weather call her thence away.

2

Scarsely had *Phœbus* in the glooming East
　Yet harnessed his firie-footed teeme,
　Ne reard above the earth his flaming creast,
　When the last deadly smoke aloft did steeme,
　That signe of last outbreathed life did seeme
　Unto the watchman on the castle wall;
　Who thereby dead that balefull Beast did deeme,
　And to his Lord and Ladie lowd gan call,
To tell, how he had seene the Dragons fatall fall.

3

Uprose with hastie joy, and feeble speed
  That aged Sire, the Lord of all that land,
  And looked forth, to weet, if true indeede
  Those tydings were, as he did understand,
  Which whenas true by tryall he out fond,
  He bad to open wyde his brazen gate,
  Which long time had bene shut, and out of hond
  Proclaymed joy and peace through all his state;
For dead now was their foe, which them forrayed late.

4

Then gan triumphant Trompets sound on hie,
  That sent to heaven the ecchoed report
  Of their new joy, and happie victorie
  Gainst him, that had them long opprest with tort,
  And fast imprisoned in sieged fort.
  Then all the people, as in solemne feast,
  To him assembled with one full consort,
  Rejoycing at the fall of that great beast,
From whose eternall bondage now they were releast.

5

Forth came that auncient Lord and aged Queene,
  Arayd in antique robes downe to the ground,
  And sad habiliments right well beseene;
  A noble crew about them waited round
  Of sage and sober Peres, all gravely gownd;
  Whom farre before did march a goodly band
  Of tall young men, all hable armes to sownd,
  But now they laurell braunches bore in hand;
Glad signe of victorie and peace in all their land.

6

Unto that doughtie Conquerour they came,
  And him before themselves prostrating low,
  Their Lord and Patrone loud did him proclame,
  And at his feet their laurell boughes did throw.
  Soone after them all dauncing on a row
  The comely virgins came, with girlands dight,
  As fresh as flowres in medow greene do grow,
  When morning deaw upon their leaves doth light:
And in their hands sweet Timbrels all upheld on hight.

7

And them before, the fry of children young
  Their wanton sports and childish mirth did play,
  And to the Maydens sounding tymbrels sung
  In well attuned notes, a joyous lay,
  And made delightfull musicke all the way,
  Untill they came, where that faire virgin stood;
  As faire *Diana* in fresh sommers day
  Beholds her Nymphes, enraung'd in shadie wood,
Some wrestle, some do run, some bathe in christall flood.

8

So she beheld those maydens meriment
  With chearefull vew; who when to her they came,
  Themselves to ground with gratious humblesse bent,
  And her ador'd by honorable name,
  Lifting to heaven her everlasting fame:
  Then on her head they set a girland greene,
  And crowned her twixt earnest and twixt game;
  Who in her selfe-resemblance well beseene,
Did seeme such, as she was, a goodly maiden Queene.

9

And after, all the raskall many ran,
  Heaped together in rude rablement,
  To see the face of that victorious man:
  Whom all admired, as from heaven sent,
  And gazd upon with gaping wonderment.
  But when they came, where that dead Dragon lay,
  Stretcht on the ground in monstrous large extent,
  The sight with idle feare did them dismay,
Ne durst approch him nigh, to touch, or once assay.

10

Some feard, and fled; some feard and well it faynd;
  One that would wiser seeme, than all the rest,
  Warnd him not touch, for yet perhaps remaynd
  Some lingring life within his hollow brest,
  Or in his wombe might lurke some hidden nest
  Of many Dragonets, his fruitfull seed;
  Another said, that in his eyes did rest
  Yet sparckling fire, and bad thereof take heed;
Another said, he saw him move his eyes indeed.

11

One mother, when as her foolehardie chyld
  Did come too neare, and with his talants play,
  Halfe dead through feare, her litle babe revyld,
  And to her gossips gan in counsell say;
  How can I tell, but that his talants may
  Yet scratch my sonne, or rend his tender hand?
  So diversly themselves in vaine they fray;
  Whiles some more bold, to measure him nigh stand,
To prove how many acres he did spread of land.

12

Thus flocked all the folke him round about,
  The whiles that hoarie king, with all his traine,
  Being arrived, where that champion stout
  After his foes defeasance did remaine,
  Him goodly greetes, and faire does entertaine,
  With princely gifts of yvorie and gold,
  And thousand thankes him yeelds for all his paine.
  Then when his daughter deare he does behold,
Her dearely doth imbrace, and kisseth manifold.

13

And after to his Pallace he them brings,
  With shaumes, and trompets, and with Clarions sweet;
  And all the way the joyous people sings,
  And with their garments strowes the paved street:
  Whence mounting up, they find purveyance meet
  Of all, that royall Princes court became,
  And all the floore was underneath their feet
  Bespred with costly scarlot of great name,
On which they lowly sit, and fitting purpose frame.

14

What needs me tell their feast and goodly guize,
  In which was nothing riotous nor vaine?
  What needs of daintie dishes to devize,
  Of comely services, or courtly trayne?
  My narrow leaves cannot in them containe
  The large discourse of royall Princes state.
  Yet was their manner then but bare and plaine:
  For th'antique world excesse and pride did hate;
Such proud luxurious pompe is swollen up but late.

15

Then when with meates and drinkes of every kinde
  Their fervent appetites they quenched had,
  That auncient Lord gan fit occasion finde,
  Of straunge adventures, and of perils sad,
  Which in his travell him befallen had,
  For to demaund of his renowmed guest:
  Who then with utt'rance grave, and count'nance sad,
  From point to point, as is before exprest,
Discourst his voyage long, according his request.

16

Great pleasure mixt with pittifull regard,
  That godly King and Queene did passionate,
  Whiles they his pittifull adventures heard,
  That oft they did lament his lucklesse state,
  And often blame the too importune fate,
  That heapd on him so many wrathfull wreakes:
  For never gentle knight, as he of late,
  So tossed was in fortunes cruell freakes;
And all the while salt teares bedeawd the hearers cheaks.

17

Then said that royall Pere in sober wise;
  Deare Sonne, great beene the evils, which ye bore
  From first to last in your late enterprise,
  That I note, whether prayse, or pitty more:
  For never living man, I weene, so sore
  In sea of deadly daungers was distrest;
  But since now safe ye seised have the shore,
  And well arrived are, (high God be blest)
Let us devize of ease and everlasting rest.

18

Ah dearest Lord, said then that doughty knight,
  Of ease or rest I may not yet devize;
  For by the faith, which I to armes have plight,
  I bounden am streight after this emprize,
  As that your daughter can ye well advize,
  Backe to returne to that great Faerie Queene,
  And her to serve six yeares in warlike wize,
  Gainst that proud Paynim king, that workes her teene:
Therefore I ought crave pardon, till I there have beene.

19

Unhappie falles that hard necessitie,
  (Quoth he) the troubler of my happie peace,
  And vowed foe of my felicitie;
  Ne I against the same can justly preace:
  But since that band ye cannot now release,
  Nor doen undo; (for vowes may not be vaine)
  Soone as the terme of those six yeares shall cease,
  Ye then shall hither backe returne againe,
The marriage to accomplish vowd betwixt you twain.

20

Which for my part I covet to performe,
  In sort as through the world I did proclame,
  That who so kild that monster most deforme,
  And him in hardy battaile overcame,
  Should have mine onely daughter to his Dame,
  And of my kingdome heire apparaunt bee:
  Therefore since now to thee perteines the same,
  By dew desert of noble chevalree,
Both daughter and eke kingdome, lo I yield to thee.

21

Then forth he called that his daughter faire,
  The fairest *Un'* his onely daughter deare,
  His onely daughter, and his onely heyre;
  Who forth proceeding with sad sober cheare,
  As bright as doth the morning starre appeare
  Out of the East, with flaming lockes bedight,
  To tell that dawning day is drawing neare,
  And to the world does bring long wished light;
So faire and fresh that Lady shewd her selfe in sight.

22

So faire and fresh, as freshest flowre in May;
  For she had layd her mournefull stole aside,
  And widow-like sad wimple throwne away,
  Wherewith her heavenly beautie she did hide,
  Whiles on her wearie journey she did ride;
  And on her now a garment she did weare,
  All lilly white, withoutten spot, or pride,
  That seemd like silke and silver woven neare,
But neither silke nor silver therein did appeare.

23

The blazing brightnesse of her beauties beame,
  And glorious light of her sunshyny face
To tell, were as to strive against the streame.
My ragged rimes are all too rude and bace,
Her heavenly lineaments for to enchace.
Ne wonder; for her owne deare loved knight,
All were she dayly with himselfe in place,
Did wonder much at her celestiall sight:
Oft had he seene her faire, but never so faire dight.

24

So fairely dight, when she in presence came,
  She to her Sire made humble reverence,
And bowed low, that her right well became,
And added grace unto her excellence:
Who with great wisedome, and grave eloquence
Thus gan to say. But eare he thus had said,
With flying speede, and seeming great pretence,
Came running in, much like a man dismaid,
A Messenger with letters, which his message said.

25

All in the open hall amazed stood,
  At suddeinnesse of that unwarie sight,
And wondred at his breathlesse hastie mood.
But he for nought would stay his passage right
Till fast before the king he did alight;
Where falling flat, great humblesse he did make,
And kist the ground, whereon his foot was pight;
Then to his hands that writ he did betake,
Which he disclosing, red thus, as the paper spake.

26

To thee, most mighty king of *Eden* faire,
  Her greeting sends in these sad lines addrest,
The wofull daughter, and forsaken heire
Of that great Emperour of all the West;
And bids thee be advized for the best,
Ere thou thy daughter linck in holy band
Of wedlocke to that new unknowen guest:
For he already plighted his right hand
Unto another love, and to another land.

27

To me sad mayd, or rather widow sad,
  He was affiaunced long time before,
  And sacred pledges he both gave, and had,
  False erraunt knight, infamous, and forswore:
  Witnesse the burning Altars, which he swore,
  And guiltie heavens of his bold perjury,
  Which though he hath polluted oft of yore,
  Yet I to them for judgement just do fly,
And them conjure t'avenge this shamefull injury.

28

Therefore since mine he is, or free or bond,
  Or false or trew, or living or else dead,
  Withhold, O soveraine Prince, your hasty hond
  From knitting league with him, I you aread;
  Ne weene my right with strength adowne to tread,
  Through weakenesse of my widowhed, or woe:
  For truth is strong, her rightfull cause to plead,
  And shall find friends, if need requireth soe,
So bids thee well to fare, Thy neither friend, nor foe, *Fidessa*.

29

When he these bitter byting words had red,
  The tydings straunge did him abashed make,
  That still he sate long time astonished
  As in great muse, ne word to creature spake.
  At last his solemne silence thus he brake,
  With doubtfull eyes fast fixed on his guest;
  Redoubted knight, that for mine onely sake
  Thy life and honour late adventurest,
Let nought be hid from me, that ought to be exprest.

30

What meane these bloudy vowes, and idle threats,
  Throwne out from womanish impatient mind?
  What heavens? what altars? what enraged heates
  Here heaped up with termes of love unkind,
  My conscience cleare with guilty bands would bind?
  High God be witnesse, that I guiltlesse ame.
  But if your selfe, Sir knight, ye faultie find,
  Or wrapped be in loves of former Dame,
With crime do not it cover, but disclose the same.

31

To whom the *Redcrosse* knight this answere sent,
  My Lord, my King, be nought hereat dismayd,
  Till well ye wote by grave intendiment,
  What woman, and wherefore doth me upbrayd
  With breach of love, and loyalty betrayd.
  It was in my mishaps, as hitherward
  I lately traveild, that unwares I strayd
  Out of my way, through perils straunge and hard;
That day should faile me, ere I had them all declard.

32

There did I find, or rather I was found
  Of this false woman, that *Fidessa* hight,
  Fidessa hight the falsest Dame on ground,
  Most false *Duessa*, royall richly dight,
  That easie was t'invegle weaker sight:
  Who by her wicked arts, and wylie skill,
  Too false and strong for earthly skill or might,
  Unwares me wrought unto her wicked will,
And to my foe betrayd, when least I feared ill.

33

Then stepped forth the goodly royall Mayd,
  And on the ground her selfe prostrating low,
  With sober countenaunce thus to him sayd;
  O pardon me, my soveraigne Lord, to show
  The secret treasons, which of late I know
  To have bene wroght by that false sorceresse.
  She onely she it is, that earst did throw
  This gentle knight into so great distresse,
That death him did awaite in dayly wretchednesse.

34

And now it seemes, that she suborned hath
  This craftie messenger with letters vaine,
  To worke new woe and improvided scath,
  By breaking of the band betwixt us twaine;
  Wherein she used hath the practicke paine
  Of this false footman, clokt with simplenesse,
  Whom if ye please for to discover plaine,
  Ye shall him *Archimago* find, I ghesse,
The falsest man alive; who tries shall find no lesse.

35

The king was greatly moved at her speach,
  And all with suddein indignation fraight,
  Bad on that Messenger rude hands to reach.
  Eftsoones the Gard, which on his state did wait,
  Attacht that faitor false, and bound him strait:
  Who seeming sorely chauffed at his band,
  As chained Beare, whom cruell dogs do bait,
  With idle force did faine them to withstand,
And often semblaunce made to scape out of their hand.

36

But they him layd full low in dungeon deepe,
  And bound him hand and foote with yron chaines.
  And with continuall watch did warely keepe;
  Who then would thinke, that by his subtile trains
  He could escape fowle death or deadly paines?
  Thus when that Princes wrath was pacifide,
  He gan renew the late forbidden banes,
  And to the knight his daughter deare he tyde,
With sacred rites and vowes for ever to abyde.

37

His owne two hands the holy knots did knit,
  That none but death for ever can devide;
  His owne two hands, for such a turne most fit,
  The housling fire did kindle and provide,
  And holy water thereon sprinckled wide;
  At which the bushy Teade a groome did light,
  And sacred lampe in secret chamber hide,
  Where it should not be quenched day nor night,
For feare of evill fates, but burnen ever bright.

38

Then gan they sprinckle all the posts with wine,
  And made great feast to solemnize that day;
  They all perfumde with frankencense divine,
  And precious odours fetcht from far away,
  That all the house did sweat with great aray:
  And all the while sweete Musicke did apply
  Her curious skill, the warbling notes to play,
  To drive away the dull Melancholy;
The whiles one sung a song of love and jollity.

39

During the which there was an heavenly noise
  Heard sound through all the Pallace pleasantly,
  Like as it had bene many an Angels voice,
  Singing before th'eternall majesty,
  In their trinall triplicities on hye;
  Yet wist no creature, whence that heavenly sweet
  Proceeded, yet each one felt secretly
  Himselfe thereby reft of his sences meet,
And ravished with rare impression in his sprite.

40

Great joy was made that day of young and old,
  And solemne feast proclaimd throughout the land,
  That their exceeding merth may not be told:
  Suffice it heare by signes to understand
  The usuall joyes at knitting of loves band.
  Thrise happy man the knight himselfe did hold,
  Possessed of his Ladies hart and hand,
  And ever, when his eye did her behold,
His heart did seeme to melt in pleasures manifold.

41

Her joyous presence and sweet company
  In full content he there did long enjoy,
  Ne wicked envie, ne vile gealosy
  His deare delights were able to annoy:
  Yet swimming in that sea of blisfull joy,
  He nought forgot, how he whilome had sworne,
  In case he could that monstrous beast destroy,
  Unto his Farie Queene backe to returne:
The which he shortly did, and *Una* left to mourne.

42

Now strike your sailes ye jolly Mariners,
  For we be come unto a quiet rode,
  Where we must land some of our passengers,
  And light this wearie vessell of her lode.
  Here she a while may make her safe abode,
  Till she repaired have her tackles spent,
  And wants supplide. And then againe abroad
  On the long voyage whereto she is bent:
Well may she speede and fairely finish her intent.

FINIS LIB. I

THE SECOND BOOKE OF THE

FAERIE QUEENE

CONTAYNING THE LEGEND OF SIR GUYON, OR OF TEMPERAUNCE

1

RIGHT well I wote most mighty Soveraine,
    That all this famous antique history,
    Of some th'aboundance of an idle braine
    Will judged be, and painted forgery,
    Rather than matter of just memory,
    Sith none, that breatheth living aire, does know,
    Where is that happy land of Faery,
    Which I so much do vaunt, yet no where show,
But vouch antiquities, which no body can know.

2

But let that man with better sence advize,
    That of the world least part to us is red:
    And dayly how through hardy enterprize,
    Many great Regions are discovered,
    Which to late age were never mentioned.
    Who ever heard of th'Indian *Peru* ?
    Or who in venturous vessell measured
    The *Amazons* huge river now found trew?
Or fruitfullest *Virginia* who did ever vew?

3

Yet all these were, when no man did them know;
  Yet have from wisest ages hidden beene:
  And later times things more unknowne shall show.
  Why then should witlesse man so much misweene
  That nothing is, but that which he hath seene?
  What if within the Moones faire shining spheare?
  What if in every other starre unseene
  Of other worldes he happily should heare?
He wonder would much more: yet such to some appeare.

4

Of Faerie lond yet if he more inquire,
  By certaine signes here set in sundry place
  He may it find; ne let him then admire,
  But yield his sence to be too blunt and bace,
  That no'te without an hound fine footing trace.
  And thou, O fairest Princesse under sky,
  In this faire mirrhour maist behold thy face,
  And thine owne realmes in lond of Faery,
And in this antique Image thy great auncestry.

5

The which O pardon me thus to enfold
  In covert vele, and wrap in shadowes light,
  That feeble eyes your glory may behold,
  Which else could not endure those beames bright,
  But would be dazled with exceeding light.
  O pardon, and vouchsafe with patient eare
  The brave adventures of this Faery knight
  The good Sir *Guyon* gratiously to heare,
In whom great rule of Temp'raunce goodly doth appeare.

CANT. I

Guyon by Archimage abusd,
The Redcrosse knight awaytes,
Findes Mordant and Amavia slaine
With pleasures poisoned baytes.

I

THAT cunning Architect of cancred guile,
  Whom Princes late displeasure left in bands,
  For falsed letters and suborned wile,
  Soone as the *Redcrosse* knight he understands
  To beene departed out of *Eden* lands,
  To serve againe his soveraine Elfin Queene,
  His artes he moves, and out of caytives hands
  Himselfe he frees by secret meanes unseene;
His shackles emptie left, him selfe escaped cleene.

2

And forth he fares full of malicious mind,
  To worken mischiefe and avenging woe,
  Where ever he that godly knight may find,
  His onely hart sore, and his onely foe,
  Sith *Una* now he algates must forgoe,
  Whom his victorious hands did earst restore
  To native crowne and kingdome late ygoe:
  Where she enjoyes sure peace for evermore,
As weather-beaten ship arriv'd on happie shore.

3

Him therefore now the object of his spight
  And deadly food he makes: him to offend
  By forged treason, or by open fight
  He seekes, of all his drift the aymed end:
  Thereto his subtile engins he does bend,
  His practick wit, and his faire filed tong,
  With thousand other sleights: for well he kend,
  His credit now in doubtfull ballaunce hong;
For hardly could be hurt, who was already stong.

4

Still as he went, he craftie stales did lay,
　With cunning traines him to entrap unwares,
　And privie spials plast in all his way,
　To weete what course he takes, and how he fares;
　To ketch him at a vantage in his snares.
　But now so wise and warie was the knight
　By triall of his former harmes and cares,
　That he descride, and shonned still his slight:
The fish that once was caught, new bait will hardly bite.

5

Nath'lesse th'Enchaunter would not spare his paine,
　In hope to win occasion to his will;
　Which when he long awaited had in vaine,
　He chaungd his minde from one to other ill:
　For to all good he enimy was still.
　Upon the way him fortuned to meet,
　Faire marching underneath a shady hill,
　A goodly knight, all armd in harnesse meete,
That from his head no place appeared to his feete.

6

His carriage was full comely and upright,
　His countenaunce demure and temperate,
　But yet so sterne and terrible in sight,
　That cheard his friends, and did his foes amate:
　He was an Elfin borne of noble state,
　And mickle worship in his native land;
　Well could he tourney and in lists debate,
　And knighthood tooke of good Sir *Huons* hand,
When with king *Oberon* he came to Faerie land.

7

Him als accompanyd upon the way
　A comely Palmer, clad in blacke attire,
　Of ripest yeares, and haires all hoarie gray,
　That with a staffe his feeble steps did stire,
　Least his long way his aged limbes should tire:
　And if by lookes one may the mind aread,
　He seemd to be a sage and sober sire,
　And ever with slow pace the knight did lead,
Who taught his trampling steed with equall steps to tread.

8

Such whenas *Archimago* them did view,
  He weened well to worke some uncouth wile,
  Eftsoones untwisting his deceiptfull clew,
  He gan to weave a web of wicked guile,
  And with faire countenance and flattring stile,
  To them approching, thus the knight bespake:
  Faire sonne of *Mars*, that seeke with warlike spoile,
  And great atchiev'ments great your selfe to make,
Vouchsafe to stay your steed for humble misers sake.

9

He stayd his steed for humble misers sake,
  And bad tell on the tenor of his plaint;
  Who feigning then in every limbe to quake,
  Through inward feare, and seeming pale and faint
  With piteous mone his percing speach gan paint;
  Deare Lady how shall I declare thy cace,
  Whom late I left in langourous constraint?
  Would God thy selfe now present were in place,
To tell this ruefull tale; thy sight could win thee grace.

10

Or rather would, O would it so had chaunst,
  That you, most noble Sir, had present beene,
  When that lewd ribauld with vile lust advaunst
  Layd first his filthy hands on virgin cleene,
  To spoile her daintie corse so faire and sheene,
  As on the earth, great mother of us all,
  With living eye more faire was never seene,
  Of chastitie and honour virginall:
Witnesse ye heavens, whom she in vaine to helpe did call.

11

How may it be, (said then the knight halfe wroth,)
  That knight should knighthood ever so have shent?
  None but that saw (quoth he) would weene for troth,
  How shamefully that Maid he did torment.
  Her looser golden lockes he rudely rent,
  And drew her on the ground, and his sharpe sword
  Against her snowy brest he fiercely bent,
  And threatned death with many a bloudie word;
Toung hates to tell the rest, that eye to see abhord.

12

Therewith amoved from his sober mood,
  And lives he yet (said he) that wrought this act,
  And doen the heavens afford him vitall food?
  He lives, (quoth he) and boasteth of the fact,
  Ne yet hath any knight his courage crackt.
  Where may that treachour then (said he) be found,
  Or by what meanes may I his footing tract?
  That shall I shew (said he) as sure, as hound
The stricken Deare doth chalenge by the bleeding wound.

13

He staid not lenger talke, but with fierce ire
  And zealous hast away is quickly gone
  To seeke that knight, where him that craftie Squire
  Supposd to be. They do arrive anone,
  Where sate a gentle Lady all alone,
  With garments rent, and haire discheveled,
  Wringing her hands, and making piteous mone;
  Her swollen eyes were much disfigured,
And her faire face with teares was fowly blubbered.

14

The knight approching nigh, thus to her said,
  Faire Ladie, through foule sorrow ill bedight,
  Great pittie is to see you thus dismaid,
  And marre the blossome of your beautie bright:
  Forthy appease your griefe and heavie plight,
  And tell the cause of your conceived paine.
  For if he live, that hath you doen despight,
  He shall you doe due recompence againe,
Or else his wrong with greater puissance maintaine.

15

Which when she heard, as in despightfull wise,
  She wilfully her sorrow did augment,
  And offred hope of comfort did despise:
  Her golden lockes most cruelly she rent,
  And scratcht her face with ghastly dreriment,
  Ne would she speake, ne see, ne yet be seene,
  But hid her visage, and her head downe bent,
  Either for grievous shame, or for great teene,
As if her hart with sorrow had transfixed beene.

16

Till her that Squire bespake, Madame my liefe,
  For Gods deare love be not so wilfull bent,
  But doe vouchsafe now to receive reliefe,
  The which good fortune doth to you present.
  For what bootes it to weepe and to wayment,
  When ill is chaunst, but doth the ill increase,
  And the weake mind with double woe torment?
  When she her Squire heard speake, she gan appease
Her voluntarie paine, and feele some secret ease.

17

Eftsoone she said, Ah gentle trustie Squire,
  What comfort can I wofull wretch conceave,
  Or why should ever I henceforth desire
  To see faire heavens face, and life not leave,
  Sith that false Traytour did my honour reave?
  False traytour certes (said the Faerie knight)
  I read the man, that ever would deceave
  A gentle Ladie, or her wrong through might:
Death were too little paine for such a foule despight.

18

But now, faire Ladie, comfort to you make,
  And read, who hath ye wrought this shamefull plight;
  That short revenge the man may overtake,
  Where so he be, and soone upon him light.
  Certes (saide she) I wote not how he hight,
  But under him a gray steede did he wield,
  Whose sides with dapled circles weren dight;
  Upright he rode, and in his silver shield
He bore a bloudie Crosse, that quartred all the field.

19

Now by my head (said *Guyon*) much I muse,
  How that same knight should do so foule amis,
  Or ever gentle Damzell so abuse:
  For may I boldly say, he surely is
  A right good knight, and true of word ywis:
  I present was, and can it witnesse well,
  When armes he swore, and streight did enterpris
  Th'adventure of the *Errant damozell*,
In which he hath great glorie wonne, as I heare tell.

20

Nathlesse he shortly shall againe be tryde,
And fairely quite him of th'imputed blame,
Else be ye sure he dearely shall abyde,
Or make you good amendment for the same:
All wrongs have mends, but no amends of shame.
Now therefore Ladie, rise out of your paine,
And see the salving of your blotted name.
Full loth she seemd thereto, but yet did faine;
For she was inly glad her purpose so to gaine.

21

Her purpose was not such, as she did faine,
Ne yet her person such, as it was seene,
But under simple shew and semblant plaine
Lurckt false *Duessa* secretly unseene,
As a chast Virgin, that had wronged beene:
So had false *Archimago* her disguisd,
To cloke her guile with sorrow and sad teene;
And eke himselfe had craftily devisd
To be her Squire, and do her service well aguisd.

22

Her late forlorne and naked he had found,
Where she did wander in waste wildernesse,
Lurking in rockes and caves farre under ground,
And with greene mosse cov'ring her nakednesse,
To hide her shame and loathly filthinesse;
Sith her Prince *Arthur* of proud ornaments
And borrow'd beautie spoyld. Her nathelesse
Th'enchaunter finding fit for his intents,
Did thus revest, and deckt with due habiliments.

23

For all he did, was to deceive good knights,
And draw them from pursuit of praise and fame,
To slug in slouth and sensuall delights,
And end their daies with irrenowmed shame.
And now exceeding griefe him overcame,
To see the *Redcrosse* thus advaunced hye;
Therefore this craftie engine he did frame,
Against his praise to stirre up enmitye
Of such, as vertues like mote unto him allye.

24

So now he *Guyon* guides an uncouth way
    Through woods and mountaines, till they came at last
    Into a pleasant dale, that lowly lay
    Betwixt two hils, whose high heads overplast,
    The valley did with coole shade overcast,
    Through midst thereof a little river rold,
    By which there sate a knight with helme unlast,
    Himselfe refreshing with the liquid cold,
After his travell long, and labours manifold.

25

Loe yonder he, cryde *Archimage* alowd,
    That wrought the shamefull fact, which I did shew;
    And now he doth himselfe in secret shrowd,
    To flie the vengeance for his outrage dew;
    But vaine: for ye shall dearely do him rew,
    So God ye speed, and send you good successe;
    Which we farre off will here abide to vew.
    So they him left, inflam'd with wrathfulnesse,
That streight against that knight his speare he did addresse.

26

Who seeing him from farre so fierce to pricke,
    His warlike armes about him gan embrace,
    And in the rest his readie speare did sticke;
    Tho when as still he saw him towards pace,
    He gan rencounter him in equall race.
    They bene ymet, both readie to affrap,
    When suddenly that warriour gan abace
    His threatned speare, as if some new mishap
Had him betidde, or hidden daunger did entrap.

27

And cryde, Mercie Sir knight, and mercie Lord,
    For mine offence and heedlesse hardiment,
    That had almost committed crime abhord,
    And with reprochfull shame mine honour shent,
    Whiles cursed steele against that badge I bent,
    The sacred badge of my Redeemers death,
    Which on your shield is set for ornament:
    But his fierce foe his steede could stay uneath,
Who prickt with courage kene, did cruell battell breath.

28

But when he heard him speake, streight way he knew
  His error, and himselfe inclyning sayd;
  Ah deare Sir *Guyon*, well becommeth you,
  But me behoveth rather to upbrayd,
  Whose hastie hand so farre from reason strayd,
  That almost it did haynous violence
  On that faire image of that heavenly Mayd,
  That decks and armes your shield with faire defence:
Your court'sie takes on you anothers due offence.

29

So bene they both attone, and doen upreare
  Their bevers bright, each other for to greete;
  Goodly comportance each to other beare,
  And entertaine themselves with court'sies meet.
  Then said the *Redcrosse* knight, Now mote I weet,
  Sir *Guyon*, why with so fierce saliaunce,
  And fell intent ye did at earst me meet;
  For sith I know your goodly governaunce,
Great cause, I weene, you guided, or some uncouth chaunce.

30

Certes (said he) well mote I shame to tell
  The fond encheason, that me hither led.
  A false infamous faitour late befell
  Me for to meet, that seemed ill bested,
  And playnd of grievous outrage, which he red
  A knight had wrought against a Ladie gent;
  Which to avenge, he to this place me led,
  Where you he made the marke of his intent,
And now is fled; foule shame him follow, where he went.

31

So can he turne his earnest unto game,
  Through goodly handling and wise temperance.
  By this his aged guide in presence came;
  Who soone as on that knight his eye did glance,
  Eft soones of him had perfect cognizance,
  Sith him in Faerie court he late avizd;
  And said, Faire sonne, God give you happie chance,
  And that deare Crosse upon your shield devizd,
Wherewith above all knights ye goodly seeme aguizd.

32

Joy may you have, and everlasting fame,
  Of late most hard atchiev'ment by you donne,
For which enrolled is your glorious name
  In heavenly Registers above the Sunne,
Where you a Saint with Saints your seat have wonne:
  But wretched we, where ye have left your marke,
  Must now anew begin, like race to runne;
God guide thee, *Guyon*, well to end thy warke,
And to the wished haven bring thy weary barke.

33

Palmer, (him answered the *Redcrosse* knight)
  His be the praise, that this atchiev'ment wrought,
Who made my hand the organ of his might;
  More than goodwill to me attribute nought:
For all I did, I did but as I ought.
  But you, faire Sir, whose pageant next ensewes,
  Well mote yee thee, as well can wish your thought,
That home ye may report thrise happie newes;
For well ye worthie bene for worth and gentle thewes.

34

So courteous congé both did give and take,
  With right hands plighted, pledges of good will.
Then *Guyon* forward gan his voyage make,
  With his blacke Palmer, that him guided still.
Still he him guided over dale and hill,
  And with his steedie staffe did point his way:
  His race with reason, and with words his will,
From foule intemperance he oft did stay,
And suffred not in wrath his hastie steps to stray.

35

In this faire wize they traveild long yfere,
  Through many hard assayes, which did betide;
Of which he honour still away did beare,
  And spred his glorie through all countries wide.
At last as chaunst them by a forest side
  To passe, for succour from the scorching ray,
  They heard a ruefull voice, that dearnly cride
With percing shriekes, and many a dolefull lay;
Which to attend, a while their forward steps they stay.

36

But if that carelesse heavens (quoth she) despise
  The doome of just revenge, and take delight
  To see sad pageants of mens miseries,
  As bound by them to live in lives despight,
  Yet can they not warne death from wretched wight.
  Come then, come soone, come sweetest death to mee,
  And take away this long lent loathed light:
  Sharpe be thy wounds, but sweet the medicines bee,
That long captived soules from wearie thraldome free.

37

But thou, sweet Babe, whom frowning froward fate
  Hath made sad witnesse of thy fathers fall,
  Sith heaven thee deignes to hold in living state,
  Long maist thou live, and better thrive withall,
  Than to thy lucklesse parents did befall:
  Live thou, and to thy mother dead attest,
  That cleare she dide from blemish criminall;
  Thy litle hands embrewd in bleeding brest
Loe I for pledges leave. So give me leave to rest.

38

With that a deadly shrieke she forth did throw,
  That through the wood reecchoed againe,
  And after gave a grone so deepe and low,
  That seemd her tender heart was rent in twaine,
  Or thrild with point of thorough piercing paine;
  As gentle Hynd, whose sides with cruell steele
  Through launched, forth her bleeding life does raine,
  Whiles the sad pang approching she does feele,
Brayes out her latest breath, and up her eyes doth seele.

39

Which when that warriour heard, dismounting straict
  From his tall steed, he rusht into the thicke,
  And soone arrived, where that sad pourtraict
  Of death and dolour lay, halfe dead, halfe quicke,
  In whose white alabaster brest did sticke
  A cruell knife, that made a griesly wound,
  From which forth gusht a streme of gorebloud thick,
  That all her goodly garments staind around,
And into a deepe sanguine dide the grassie ground.

40

Pittifull spectacle of deadly smart,
  Beside a bubbling fountaine low she lay,
  Which she increased with her bleeding hart,
  And the cleane waves with purple gore did ray;
  Als in her lap a lovely babe did play
  His cruell sport, in stead of sorrow dew;
  For in her streaming blood he did embay
  His litle hands, and tender joynts embrew;
Pitifull spectacle, as ever eye did view.

41

Besides them both, upon the soiled gras
  The dead corse of an armed knight was spred,
  Whose armour all with bloud besprinckled was;
  His ruddie lips did smile, and rosy red
  Did paint his chearefull cheekes, yet being ded:
  Seemd to have beene a goodly personage,
  Now in his freshest flowre of lustie hed,
  Fit to inflame faire Lady with loves rage,
But that fiers fate did crop the blossome of his age.

42

Whom when the good Sir *Guyon* did behold,
  His hart gan wexe as starke, as marble stone,
  And his fresh bloud did frieze with fearefull cold,
  That all his senses seemd bereft attone:
  At last his mightie ghost gan deepe to grone,
  As Lyon grudging in his great disdaine,
  Mournes inwardly, and makes to himselfe mone,
  Till ruth and fraile affection did constraine
His stout courage to stoupe, and shew his inward paine.

43

Out of her gored wound the cruell steele
  He lightly snatcht, and did the floudgate stop
  With his faire garment: then gan softly feele
  Her feeble pulse, to prove if any drop
  Of living bloud yet in her veynes did hop;
  Which when he felt to move, he hoped faire
  To call backe life to her forsaken shop;
  So well he did her deadly wounds repaire,
That at the last she gan to breath out living aire.

44

Which he perceiving greatly gan rejoice,
  And goodly counsell, that for wounded hart
  Is meetest med'cine, tempred with sweet voice;
  Ay me, deare Lady, which the image art
  Of ruefull pitie, and impatient smart,
  What direfull chance, armd with revenging fate,
  Or cursed hand hath plaid this cruell part,
  Thus fowle to hasten your untimely date;
Speake, O deare Lady. speake: help never comes too late.

45

Therewith her dim eie-lids she up gan reare,
  On which the drery death did sit, as sad
  As lump of lead, and made darke clouds appeare;
  But when as him all in bright armour clad
  Before her standing she espied had,
  As one out of a deadly dreame affright,
  She weakely started, yet she nothing drad:
  Streight downe againe her selfe in great despight
She groveling threw to ground, as hating life and light.

46

The gentle knight her soone with carefull paine
  Uplifted light, and softly did uphold:
  Thrise he her reard, and thrise she sunke againe,
  Till he his armes about her sides gan fold,
  And to her said; Yet if the stony cold
  Have not all seized on your frozen hart,
  Let one word fall that may your griefe unfold,
  And tell the secret of your mortall smart;
He oft finds present helpe, who does his griefe impart.

47

Then casting up a deadly looke, full low
  Shee sight from bottome of her wounded brest,
  And after, many bitter throbs did throw
  With lips full pale and foltring tongue opprest,
  These words she breathed forth from riven chest;
  Leave, ah leave off, what ever wight thou bee,
  To let a wearie wretch from her dew rest,
  And trouble dying soules tranquilitee.
Take not away now got, which none would give to me.

48

Ah farre be it (said he) Deare dame fro mee,
  To hinder soule from her desired rest,
  Or hold sad life in long captivitee:
  For all I seeke, is but to have redrest
  The bitter pangs, that doth your heart infest.
  Tell then, O Lady tell, what fatall priefe
  Hath with so huge misfortune you opprest?
  That I may cast to compasse your reliefe,
Or die with you in sorrow, and partake your griefe.

49

With feeble hands then stretched forth on hye,
  As heaven accusing guiltie of her death,
  And with dry drops congealed in her eye,
  In these sad words she spent her utmost breath:
  Heare then, O man, the sorrowes that uneath
  My tongue can tell, so farre all sense they pas:
  Loe this dead corpse, that lies here underneath,
  The gentlest knight, that ever on greene gras
Gay steed with spurs did pricke, the good Sir *Mordant* was.

50

Was, (ay the while, that he is not so now)
  My Lord my love; my deare Lord, my deare love,
  So long as heavens just with equall brow
  Vouchsafed to behold us from above,
  One day when him high courage did emmove,
  As wont ye knights to seeke adventures wilde,
  He pricked forth, his puissant force to prove,
  Me then he left enwombed of this child,
This lucklesse child, whom thus ye see with bloud defild.

51

Him fortuned (hard fortune ye may ghesse)
  To come, where vile *Acrasia* does wonne,
  Acrasia a false enchaunteresse,
  That many errant knights hath foule fordonne:
  Within a wandring Island, that doth ronne
  And stray in perilous gulfe, her dwelling is;
  Faire Sir, if ever there ye travell, shonne
  The cursed land where many wend amis,
And know it by the name; it hight the *Bowre of blis*.

52

Her blisse is all in pleasure and delight,
  Wherewith she makes her lovers drunken mad,
  And then with words and weedes of wondrous might,
  On them she workes her will to uses bad:
  My lifest Lord she thus beguiled had;
  For he was flesh: (all flesh doth frailtie breed.)
  Whom when I heard to beene so ill bestad,
  Weake wretch I wrapt my selfe in Palmers weed,
And cast to seeke him forth through daunger and great dreed.

53

Now had faire *Cynthia* by even tournes
  Full measured three quarters of her yeare,
  And thrise three times had fild her crooked hornes,
  Whenas my wombe her burdein would forbeare,
  And bad me call *Lucina* to me neare.
  Lucina came: a manchild forth I brought:
  The woods, the Nymphes, my bowres, my midwives weare,
  Hard helpe at need. So deare thee babe I bought,
Yet nought too deare I deemd, while so my dear I sought.

54

Him so I sought, and so at last I found,
  Where him that witch had thralled to her will,
  In chaines of lust and lewd desires ybound,
  And so transformed from his former skill,
  That me he knew not, neither his owne ill;
  Till through wise handling and faire governance,
  I him recured to a better will,
  Purged from drugs of foule intemperance:
Then meanes I gan devise for his deliverance.

55

Which when the vile Enchaunteresse perceiv'd,
  How that my Lord from her I would reprive,
  With cup thus charmd, him parting she deceiv'd;
  Sad verse, give death to him that death does give,
  And losse of love, to her that loves to live,
  So soone as Bacchus with the Nymphe does lincke:
  So parted we and on our journey drive,
  Till comming to this well, he stoupt to drincke:
The charme fulfild, dead suddenly he downe did sincke.

56

Which when I wretch, Not one word more she sayd
   But breaking off the end for want of breath,
   And slyding soft, as downe to sleepe her layd,
   And ended all her woe in quiet death.
   That seeing good Sir *Guyon*, could uneath
   From teares abstaine, for griefe his hart did grate,
   And from so heavie sight his head did wreath,
   Accusing fortune, and too cruell fate,
Which plunged had faire Ladie in so wretched state.

57

Then turning to his Palmer said, Old syre
   Behold the image of mortalitie,
   And feeble nature cloth'd with fleshly tyre,
   When raging passion with fierce tyrannie
   Robs reason of her due regalitie,
   And makes it servant to her basest part:
   The strong it weakens with infirmitie,
   And with bold furie armes the weakest hart;
The strong through pleasure soonest falles, the weake through smart.

58

But temperance (said he) with golden squire
   Betwixt them both can measure out a meane,
   Neither to melt in pleasures whot desire,
   Nor fry in hartlesse griefe and dolefull teene.
   Thrise happie man, who fares them both atweene:
   But sith this wretched woman overcome
   Of anguish, rather than of crime hath beene,
   Reserve her cause to her eternall doome,
And in the meane vouchsafe her honorable toombe.

59

Palmer (quoth he) death is an equall doome
   To good and bad, the common Inne of rest;
   But after death the tryall is to come,
   When best shall be to them, that lived best:
   But both alike, when death hath both supprest,
   Religious reverence doth buriall teene,
   Which who so wants, wants so much of his rest:
   For all so great shame after death I weene,
As selfe to dyen bad, unburied bad to beene.

60

So both agree their bodies to engrave;
  The great earthes wombe they open to the sky,
  And with sad Cypresse seemely it embrave,
  Then covering with a clod their closed eye,
  They lay therein those corses tenderly,
  And bid them sleepe in everlasting peace.
  But ere they did their utmost obsequy,
  Sir *Guyon* more affection to increace,
Bynempt a sacred vow, which none should aye releace.

61

The dead knights sword out of his sheath he drew,
  With which he cut a locke of all their heare,
  Which medling with their bloud and earth, he threw
  Into the grave, and gan devoutly sweare;
  Such and such evill God on *Guyon* reare,
  And worse and worse young Orphane be thy paine,
  If I or thou dew vengeance doe forbeare,
  Till guiltie bloud her guerdon doe obtaine:
So shedding many teares, they closd the earth againe.

CANT. II

Babes bloudie hands may not be clensd:
the face of golden Meane.
Her sisters two Extremities
strive her to banish cleane.

I

THUS when Sir *Guyon* with his faithfull guide
  Had with due rites and dolorous lament
  The end of their sad Tragedie uptyde,
  The litle babe up in his armes he hent;
  Who with sweet pleasance and bold blandishment
  Gan smyle on them, that rather ought to weepe,
  As carelesse of his woe, or innocent
  Of that was doen, that ruth emperced deepe
In that knights heart, and wordes with bitter teares did steepe.

2

Ah lucklesse babe, borne under cruell starre,
  And in dead parents balefull ashes bred,
  Full litle weenest thou, what sorrowes are
  Left thee for portion of thy livelihed,
  Poore Orphane in the wide world scattered,
  As budding braunch rent from the native tree,
  And throwen forth, till it be withered:
  Such is the state of men: thus enter wee
Into this life with woe, and end with miseree.

3

Then soft himselfe inclyning on his knee
  Downe to that well, did in the water weene
  (So love does loath disdainfull nicitee)
  His guiltie hands from bloudie gore to cleene.
  He washt them oft and oft, yet nought they beene
  For all his washing cleaner. Still he strove,
  Yet still the litle hands were bloudie seene;
  The which him into great amaz'ment drove,
And into diverse doubt his wavering wonder clove.

4

He wist not whether blot of foule offence
  Might not be purgd with water nor with bath;
  Or that high God, in lieu of innocence,
  Imprinted had that token of his wrath,
  To shew how sore bloudguiltinesse he hat'th;
  Or that the charme and venim, which they druncke,
  Their bloud with secret filth infected hath,
  Being diffused through the senselesse truncke,
That through the great contagion direfull deadly stunck,

5

Whom thus at gaze, the Palmer gan to bord
  With goodly reason, and thus faire bespake;
  Ye bene right hard amated, gratious Lord,
  And of your ignorance great marvell make,
  Whiles cause not well conceived ye mistake.
  But know, that secret vertues are infusd
  In every fountaine, and in every lake,
  Which who hath skill them rightly to have chusd,
To proofe of passing wonders hath full often usd.

Sir Guyon and Palmer

6

Of those some were so from their sourse indewd
  By great Dame Nature, from whose fruitfull pap
  Their welheads spring, and are with moisture deawd;
  Which feedes each living plant with liquid sap,
  And filles with flowres faire *Floraes* painted lap:
  But other some by gift of later grace,
  Or by good prayers, or by other hap,
  Had vertue pourd into their waters bace,
And thenceforth were renowmd, and sought from place to place.

7

Such is this well, wrought by occasion straunge,
  Which to her Nymph befell. Upon a day,
  As she the woods with bow and shafts did raunge,
  The hartlesse Hind and Robucke to dismay,
  Dan Faunus chaunst to meet her by the way,
  And kindling fire at her faire burning eye,
  Inflamed was to follow beauties chace,
  And chaced her, that fast from him did fly;
As Hind from her, so she fled from her enimy.

8

At last when fayling breath began to faint,
  And saw no meanes to scape, of shame affrayd,
  She set her downe to weepe for sore constraint,
  And to *Diana* calling lowd for ayde,
  Her deare besought, to let her dye a mayd.
  The goddesse heard, and suddeine where she sate,
  Welling out streames of teares, and quite dismayd
  With stony feare of that rude rustick mate,
Transformd her to a stone from stedfast virgins state.

9

Lo now she is that stone, from whose two heads,
  As from two weeping eyes, fresh streames do flow,
  Yet cold through feare, and old conceived dreads;
  And yet the stone her semblance seemes to show,
  Shapt like a maid, that such ye may her know;
  And yet her vertues in her water byde:
  For it is chast and pure, as purest snow,
  Ne lets her waves with any filth be dyde,
But ever like her selfe unstained hath beene tryde.

10

From thence it comes, that this babes bloudy hand
　　May not be clensd with water of this well:
　　Ne certes Sir strive you it to withstand,
　　But let them still be bloudy, as befell,
　　That they his mothers innocence may tell,
　　As she bequeathd in her last testament;
　　That as a sacred Symbole it may dwell
　　In her sonnes flesh, to minde revengement,
And be for all chast Dames an endlesse moniment.

11

He hearkned to his reason, and the childe
　　Uptaking, to the Palmer gave to beare;
　　But his sad fathers armes with bloud defilde,
　　An heavie load himselfe did lightly reare,
　　And turning to that place, in which whyleare
　　He left his loftie steed with golden sell,
　　And goodly gorgeous barbes, him found not theare.
　　By other accident that earst befell,
He is convaide, but how or where, here fits not tell.

12

Which when Sir *Guyon* saw, all were he wroth,
　　Yet algates mote he soft himselfe appease,
　　And fairely fare on foot, how ever loth;
　　His double burden did him sore disease.
　　So long they traveiled with litle ease,
　　Till that at last they to a Castle came,
　　Built on a rocke adjoyning to the seas;
　　It was an auncient worke of antique fame,
And wondrous strong by nature, and by skilfull frame.

13

Therein three sisters dwelt of sundry sort,
　　The children of one sire by mothers three;
　　Who dying whylome did divide this fort
　　To them by equall shares in equall fee:
　　But strifull minde, and diverse qualitee
　　Drew them in parts, and each made others foe:
　　Still did they strive, and dayly disagree;
　　The eldest did against the youngest goe,
And both against the middest meant to worken woe.

14

Where when the knight arriv'd, he was right well
  Receiv'd, as knight of so much worth became,
  Of second sister, who did far excell
  The other two; *Medina* was her name,
  A sober sad, and comely curteous Dame;
  Who rich arayd, and yet in modest guize,
  In goodly garments, that her well became,
  Faire marching forth in honorable wize,
Him at the threshold met, and well did enterprize.

15

She led him up into a goodly bowre,
  And comely courted with meet modestie,
  Ne in her speach, ne in her haviour,
  Was lightnesse seene, or looser vanitie,
  But gratious womanhood, and gravitie,
  Above the reason of her youthly yeares:
  Her golden lockes she roundly did uptye
  In breaded tramels, that no looser heares
Did out of order stray about her daintie eares.

16

Whilest she her selfe thus busily did frame,
  Seemely to entertaine her new-come guest,
  Newes hereof to her other sisters came,
  Who all this while were at their wanton rest,
  Accourting each her friend with lavish fest:
  They were two knights of perelesse puissance,
  And famous far abroad for warlike gest,
  Which to these Ladies love did countenaunce,
And to his mistresse each himselfe strove to advaunce.

17

He that made love unto the eldest Dame,
  Was hight Sir *Huddibras*, an hardy man;
  Yet not so good of deedes, as great of name,
  Which he by many rash adventures wan,
  Since errant armes to sew he first began;
  More huge in strength, than wise in workes he was,
  And reason with foole-hardize over ran;
  Sterne melancholy did his courage pas,
And was for terrour more, all armd in shyning bras.

18

But he that lov'd the youngest, was *Sans-loy*,
    He that faire *Una* late fowle outraged,
    The most unruly, and the boldest boy,
    That ever warlike weapons menaged,
    And to all lawlesse lust encouraged,
    Through strong opinion of his matchlesse might:
    Ne ought he car'd, whom he endamaged
    By tortious wrong, or whom bereav'd of right.
He now this Ladies champion chose for love to fight.

19

These two gay knights, vowd to so diverse loves,
    Each other does envie with deadly hate,
    And dayly warre against his foeman moves,
    In hope to win more favour with his mate,
    And th'others pleasing service to abate,
    To magnifie his owne. But when they heard,
    How in that place straunge knight arrived late,
    Both knights and Ladies forth right angry far'd,
And fiercely unto battell sterne themselves prepar'd.

20

But ere they could proceede unto the place,
    Where he abode, themselves at discord fell,
    And cruell combat joynd in middle space:
    With horrible assault, and furie fell,
    They heapt huge strokes, the scorned life to quell,
    That all on uprore from her settled seat
    The house was raysd, and all that in did dwell;
    Seemd that lowde thunder with amazement great
Did rend the ratling skyes with flames of fouldring heat.

21

The noyse thereof cald forth that straunger knight,
    To weet, what dreadfull thing was there in hand;
    Where when as two brave knights in bloudy fight
    With deadly rancour he enraunged fond,
    His sunbroad shield about his wrest he bond,
    And shyning blade unsheathd, with which he ran
    Unto that stead, their strife to understond;
    And at his first arrivall, them began
With goodly meanes to pacifie, well as he can.

22

But they him spying, both with greedy forse
  Attonce upon him ran, and him beset
  With strokes of mortall steele without remorse,
  And on his shield like yron sledges bet:
  As when a Beare and Tygre being met
  In cruell fight on lybicke Ocean wide,
  Espye a traveiler with feet surbet,
  Whom they in equall pray hope to devide,
They stint their strife, and him assaile on every side.

23

But he, not like a wearie traveilere,
  Their sharpe assault right boldly did rebut,
  And suffred not their blowes to byte him nere,
  But with redoubled buffes them backe did put:
  Whose grieved mindes, which choler did englut,
  Against themselves turning their wrathfull spight,
  Gan with new rage their shields to hew and cut;
  But still when *Guyon* came to part their fight,
With heavie load on him they freshly gan to smight.

24

As a tall ship tossed in troublous seas,
  Whom raging windes threatning to make the pray
  Of the rough rockes, do diversly disease,
  Meetes two contrary billowes by the way,
  That her on either side do sore assay,
  And boast to swallow her in greedy grave;
  She scorning both their spights, does make wide way,
  And with her brest breaking the fomy wave,
Does ride on both their backs, and faire her selfe doth save.

25

So boldly he him beares, and rusheth forth
  Betweene them both, by conduct of his blade.
  Wondrous great prowesse and heroick worth
  He shewd that day, and rare ensample made,
  When two so mighty warriours he dismade:
  Attonce he wards and strikes, he takes and payes,
  Now forst to yield, now forcing to invade,
  Before, behind, and round about him layes:
So double was his paines, so double be his prayse.

26

Straunge sort of fight, three valiaunt knights to see
  Three combats joyne in one, and to darraine
  A triple warre with triple enmitee,
  All for their Ladies froward love to gaine,
  Which gotten was but hate. So love does raine
  In stoutest minds, and maketh monstrous warre;
  He maketh warre, he maketh peace againe,
  And yet his peace is but continuall jarre:
O miserable men, that to him subject arre.

27

Whilst thus they mingled were in furious armes,
  The faire *Medina* with her tresses torne,
  And naked brest, in pitty of their harmes,
  Emongst them ran, and falling them beforne,
  Besought them by the womb, which them had borne,
  And by the loves, which were to them most deare,
  And by the knighthood, which they sure had sworne,
  Their deadly cruell discord to forbeare,
And to her just conditions of faire peace to heare.

28

But her two other sisters standing by,
  Her lowd gainsaid, and both their champions bad
  Pursew the end of their strong enmity,
  As ever of their loves they would be glad.
  Yet she with pitthy words and counsell sad,
  Still strove their stubborne rages to revoke,
  That at the last suppressing fury mad,
  They gan abstaine from dint of direfull stroke,
And hearken to the sober speaches, which she spoke.

29

Ah puissaunt Lords, what cursed evill Spright,
  Or fell *Erinnys*, in your noble harts
  Her hellish brond hath kindled with despight,
  And stird you up to worke your wilfull smarts?
  Is this the joy of armes? be these the parts
  Of glorious knighthood, after bloud to thrust,
  And not regard dew right and just desarts?
  Vaine is the vaunt, and victory unjust,
That more to mighty hands, than rightfull cause doth trust.

30

And were there rightfull cause of difference,
  Yet were not better, faire it to accord,
  Than with bloud guiltinesse to heape offence,
  And mortall vengeaunce joyne to crime abhord?
  O fly from wrath, fly, O my liefest Lord:
  Sad be the sights, and bitter fruits of warre,
  And thousand furies wait on wrathfull sword;
  Ne ought the prayse of prowesse more doth marre,
Than fowle revenging rage, and base contentious jarre.

31

But lovely concord, and most sacred peace
  Doth nourish vertue, and fast friendship breeds;
  Weake she makes strong, and strong thing does increace,
  Till it the pitch of highest prayse exceeds:
  Brave be her warres, and honorable deeds,
  By which she triumphes over ire and pride,
  And winnes an Olive girlond for her meeds:
  Be therefore, O my deare Lords, pacifide,
And this misseeming discord meekely lay aside.

32

Her gracious wordes their rancour did appall,
  And suncke so deepe into their boyling brests,
  That downe they let their cruell weapons fall,
  And lowly did abase their loftie crests
  To her faire presence, and discrete behests.
  Then she began a treatie to procure,
  And stablish termes betwixt both their requests,
  That as a law for ever should endure;
Which to observe in word of knights they did assure.

33

Which to confirme, and fast to bind their league,
  After their wearie sweat and bloudy toile,
  She them besought, during their quiet treague,
  Into her lodging to repaire a while,
  To rest themselves, and grace to reconcile.
  They soone consent: so forth with her they fare,
  Where they are well receiv'd, and made to spoile
  Themselves of soiled armes, and to prepare
Their minds to pleasure, and their mouthes to dainty fare.

34

And those two froward sisters, their faire loves
  Came with them eke, all were they wondrous loth,
  And fained cheare, as for the time behoves,
  But could not colour yet so well the troth,
  But that their natures bad appeard in both:
  For both did at their second sister grutch,
  And inly grieve, as doth an hidden moth
  The inner garment fret, not th'utter touch;
One thought their cheare too litle, th'other thought too mutch.

35

Elissa (so the eldest hight) did deeme
  Such entertainment base, ne ought would eat,
  Ne ought would speake, but evermore did seeme
  As discontent for want of merth or meat;
  No solace could her Paramour intreat
  Her once to show, ne court, nor dalliance,
  But with bent lowring browes, as she would threat,
  She scould, and frownd with froward countenaunce,
Unworthy of faire Ladies comely governaunce.

36

But young *Perissa* was of other mind,
  Full of disport, still laughing, loosely light,
  And quite contrary to her sisters kind;
  No measure in her mood, no rule of right,
  But poured out in pleasure and delight;
  In wine and meats she flowd above the bancke,
  And in excesse exceeded her owne might;
  In sumptuous tire she joyd her selfe to prancke,
But of her love too lavish (litle have she thancke.)

37

Fast by her side did sit the bold *Sans-loy*,
  Fit mate for such a mincing mineon,
  Who in her loosenesse tooke exceeding joy;
  Might not be found a franker franion,
  Of her lewd parts to make companion;
  But *Huddibras*, more like a Malecontent,
  Did see and grieve at his bold fashion;
  Hardly could he endure his hardiment,
Yet still he sat, and inly did him selfe torment.

38

Betwixt them both the faire *Medina* sate
  With sober grace, and goodly carriage:
  With equall measure she did moderate
  The strong extremities of their outrage;
  That forward paire she ever would asswage,
  When they would strive dew reason to exceed;
  But that same froward twaine would accourage,
  And of her plenty adde unto their need:
So kept she them in order, and her selfe in heed.

39

Thus fairely she attempered her feast,
  And pleasd them all with meete satietie,
  At last when lust of meat and drinke was ceast,
  She *Guyon* deare besought of curtesie,
  To tell from whence he came through jeopardie,
  And whither now on new adventure bound.
  Who with bold grace, and comely gravitie,
  Drawing to him the eyes of all around,
From lofty siege began these words aloud to sound.

40

This thy demaund, O Lady, doth revive
  Fresh memory in me of that great Queene,
  Great and most glorious virgin Queene alive,
  That with her soveraigne powre, and scepter shene
  All Faery lond does peaceably sustene.
  In widest Ocean she her throne does reare,
  That over all the earth it may be seene;
  As morning Sunne her beames dispredden cleare,
And in her face faire peace, and mercy doth appeare.

41

In her the richesse of all heavenly grace
  In chiefe degree are heaped up on hye:
  And all that else this worlds enclosure bace
  Hath great or glorious in mortall eye,
  Adornes the person of her Majestie;
  That men beholding so great excellence,
  And rare perfection in mortalitie,
  Do her adore with sacred reverence,
As th'Idole of her makers great magnificence.

42

To her I homage and my service owe,
  In number of the noblest knights on ground,
  Mongst whom on me she deigned to bestowe
  Order of *Maydenhead*, the most renownd,
  That may this day in all the world be found:
  An yearely solemne feast she wontes to make
  The day that first doth lead the yeare around;
  To which all knights of worth and courage bold
Resort, to heare of straunge adventures to be told.

43

There this old Palmer shewed himselfe that day,
  And to that mighty Princesse did complaine
  Of grievous mischiefes, which a wicked Fay
  Had wrought, and many whelmd in deadly paine,
  Whereof he crav'd redresse. My Soveraine,
  Whose glory is in gracious deeds, and joyes
  Throughout the world her mercy to maintaine,
  Eftsoones devisd redresse for such annoyes;
Me all unfit for so great purpose she employes.

44

Now hath faire *Phœbe* with her silver face
  Thrise seene the shadowes of the neather world,
  Sith last I left that honorable place,
  In which her royall presence is †introld;
  Ne ever shall I rest in house nor hold,
  Till I that false *Acrasia* have wonne;
  Of whose fowle deedes, too hideous to be told,
  I witnesse am, and this their wretched sonne,
Whose wofull parents she hath wickedly fordonne.

45

Tell on, faire Sir, said she, that dolefull tale,
  From which sad ruth does seeme you to restraine,
  That we may pitty such unhappy bale,
  And learne from pleasures poyson to abstaine:
  Ill by ensample good doth often gayne.
  Then forward he his purpose gan pursew,
  And told the storie of the mortall payne,
  Which *Mordant* and *Amavia* did rew;
As with lamenting eyes him selfe did lately vew.

46

Night was far spent, and now in *Ocean* deepe
    Orion, flying fast from hissing snake,
    His flaming head did hasten for to steepe,
    When of his pitteous tale he end did make;
    Whilest with delight of that he wisely spake,
    Those guestes beguiled, did beguile their eyes
    Of kindly sleepe, that did them overtake.
    At last when they had markt the chaunged skyes,
They wist their houre was spent; then each to rest him hyes.

CANT. III

*Vaine Braggadocchio getting Guyons
horse is made the scorne
Of knighthood trew, and is of fayre
Belphœbe fowle forlorne.*

I

Soone as the morrow faire with purple beames
    Disperst the shadowes of the mistie night,
    And *Titan* playing on the eastern streames,
    Gan cleare the deawy ayre with springing light,
    Sir *Guyon* mindfull of his vow yplight,
    Uprose from drowsie couch, and him addrest
    Unto the journey which he had behight:
    His puissaunt armes about his noble brest,
And many-folded shield he bound about his wrest.

2

Then taking *Congé* of that virgin pure,
    The bloudy-handed babe unto her truth
    Did earnestly commit, and her conjure,
    In vertuous lore to traine his tender youth,
    And all that gentle noriture ensu'th:
    And that so soone as ryper yeares he raught,
    He might for memorie of that dayes ruth,
    Be called *Ruddymane*, and thereby taught,
T'avenge his Parents death on them, that had it wrought.

3

So forth he far'd, as now befell, on foot,
  Sith his good steed is lately from him gone;
  Patience perforce; helpelesse what may it boot
  To fret for anger, or for griefe to mone?
  His Palmer now shall foot no more alone:
  So fortune wrought, as under greene woods syde
  He lately heard that dying Lady grone,
  He left his steed without, and speare besyde,
And rushed in on foot to ayd her, ere she dyde.

4

The whiles a losell wandring by the way,
  One that to bountie never cast his mind,
  Ne thought of honour ever did assay
  His baser brest, but in his kestrell kind
  A pleasing vaine of glory vaine did find,
  To which his flowing toung, and troublous spright
  Gave him great ayd, and made him more inclind:
  He that brave steed there finding ready dight,
Purloynd both steed and speare, and ran away full light.

5

Now gan his hart all swell in jollitie,
  And of him selfe great hope and helpe conceiv'd,
  That puffed up with smoke of vanitie,
  And with selfe-loved personage deceiv'd,
  He gan to hope, of men to be receiv'd
  For such, as he him thought, or faine would bee:
  But for in court gay portaunce he perceiv'd
  And gallant shew to be in greatest gree,
Eftsoones to court he cast t'avaunce his first degree.

6

And by the way he chaunced to espy
  One sitting idle on a sunny bancke,
  To whom avaunting in great bravery,
  As Peacocke, that his painted plumes doth prancke,
  He smote his courser in the trembling flancke,
  And to him threatned his hart-thrilling speare:
  The seely man seeing him ryde so rancke,
  And ayme at him, fell flat to ground for feare,
And crying Mercy lowd, his pitious hands gan reare.

7

Thereat the Scarcrow wexed wondrous prowd,
　Through fortune of his first adventure faire,
　And with big thundring voyce revyld him lowd;
　Vile Caytive, vassall of dread and despaire,
　Unworthie of the commune breathed aire,
　Why livest thou, dead dog, a lenger day,
　And doest not unto death thy selfe prepaire.
　Dye, or thy selfe my captive yield for ay;
Great favour I thee graunt, for aunswere thus to stay.

8

Hold, O deare Lord, hold your dead-doing hand,
　Then loud he cryde, I am your humble thrall.
　Ah wretch (quoth he) thy destinies withstand
　My wrathfull will, and do for mercy call.
　I give thee life: therefore prostrated fall,
　And kisse my stirrup; that thy homage bee.
　The Miser threw him selfe, as an Offall,
　Streight at his foot in base humilitee,
And cleeped him his liege, to hold of him in fee.

9

So happy peace they made and faire accord:
　Eftsoones this liege-man gan to wexe more bold,
　And when he felt the folly of his Lord,
　In his owne kind he gan him selfe unfold:
　For he was wylie witted, and growne old
　In cunning sleights and practick knavery.
　From that day forth he cast for to uphold
　His idle humour with fine flattery,
And blow the bellowes to his swelling vanity.

10

Trompart fit man for *Braggadocchio*,
　To serve at court in view of vaunting eye;
　Vaine-glorious man, when fluttring wind does blow
　In his light wings, is lifted up to skye:
　The scorne of knighthood and trew chevalrye,
　To thinke without desert of gentle deed,
　And noble worth to be advaunced hye:
　Such prayse is shame; but honour vertues meed
Doth beare the fairest flowre in honorable seed.

11

So forth they pas, a well consorted paire,
  Till that at length with *Archimage* they meet:
  Who seeing one that shone in armour faire,
  On goodly courser thundring with his feet,
  Eftsoones supposed him a person meet,
  Of his revenge to make the instrument:
  For since the *Redcrosse* knight he earst did weet,
  To beene with *Guyon* knit in one consent,
The ill, which earst to him, he now to *Guyon* ment.

12

And comming close to *Trompart* gan inquere
  Of him, what mighty warriour that mote bee,
  That rode in golden sell with single spere,
  But wanted sword to wreake his enmitee.
  He is a great adventurer, (said he)
  That hath his sword through hard assay forgone,
  And now hath vowd, till he avenged bee,
  Of that despight, never to wearen none;
That speare is him enough to doen a thousand grone.

13

Th'enchaunter greatly joyed in the vaunt,
  And weened well ere long his will to win,
  And both his foen with equall foyle to daunt.
  Tho to him louting lowly, did begin
  To plaine of wrongs, which had committed bin
  By *Guyon*, and by that false *Redcrosse* knight,
  Which two through treason and deceiptfull gin,
  Had slaine Sir *Mordant*, and his Lady bright:
That mote him honour win, to wreake so foule despight.

14

Therewith all suddeinly he seemd enraged,
  And threatned death with dreadfull countenaunce,
  As if their lives had in his hand beene gaged;
  And with stiffe force shaking his mortall launce,
  To let him weet his doughtie valiaunce,
  Thus said; Old man, great sure shalbe thy meed,
  If where those knights for feare of dew vengeaunce
  Do lurke, thou certainly to me areed,
That I may wreake on them their hainous hatefull deed.

15

Certes, my Lord, (said he) that shall I soone,
  And give you eke good helpe to their decay,
  But mote I wisely you advise to doon;
  Give no ods to your foes, but do purvay
  Your selfe of sword before that bloudy day:
  For they be two the prowest knights on ground,
  And oft approv'd in many hard assay,
  And eke of surest steele, that may be found,
Do arme your selfe against that day, them to confound.

16

Dotard (said he) let be thy deepe advise;
  Seemes that through many yeares thy wits thee faile,
  And that weake eld hath left thee nothing wise,
  Else never should thy judgement be so fraile,
  To measure manhood by the sword or maile.
  Is not enough foure quarters of a man,
  Withouten sword or shield, an host to quaile?
  Thou little wotest, what this right hand can:
Speake they, which have beheld the battailes, which it wan.

17

The man was much abashed at his boast;
  Yet well he wist, that who so would contend
  With either of those knights on even coast,
  Should need of all his armes, him to defend;
  Yet feared least his boldnesse should offend,
  When *Braggadocchio* said, Once I did sweare,
  When with one sword seven knights I brought to end,
  Thence forth in battell never sword to beare,
But it were that, which noblest knight on earth doth weare.

18

Perdie Sir knight, said then th'enchaunter blive,
  That shall I shortly purchase to your hond:
  For now the best and noblest knight alive
  Prince *Arthur* is, that wonnes in Faerie lond;
  He hath a sword, that flames like burning brond,
  The same by my device I undertake
  Shall by to morrow by thy side be fond.
  At which bold word that boaster gan to quake,
And wondred in his mind, what mote that monster make.

19

He stayd not for more bidding, but away
  Was suddein vanished out of his sight:
  The Northerne wind his wings did broad display
  At his commaund, and reared him up light
  From off the earth to take his aerie flight.
  They lookt about, but no where could espie
  Tract of his foot: then dead through great affright
  They both nigh were, and each bad other flie:
Both fled attonce, ne ever backe returned eie.

20

Till that they come unto a forrest greene,
  In which they shrowd themselves from causelesse feare;
  Yet feare them followes still, where so they beene,
  Each trembling leafe, and whistling wind they heare,
  As ghastly bug their haire on end does reare:
  Yet both doe strive their fearfulnesse to faine.
  At last they heard a horne, that shrilled cleare
  Throughout the wood, that ecchoed againe,
And made the forrest ring, as it would rive in twaine.

21

Eft through the thicke they heard one rudely rush;
  With noyse whereof he from his loftie steed
  Downe fell to ground, and crept into a bush,
  To hide his coward head from dying dreed.
  But *Trompart* stoutly stayd to taken heed
  Of what might hap. Eftsoone there stepped forth
  A goodly Ladie clad in hunters weed,
  That seemd to be a woman of great worth,
And by her stately portance, borne of heavenly birth.

22

Her face so faire as flesh it seemed not,
  But heavenly pourtraict of bright Angels hew,
  Cleare as the skie, withouten blame or blot,
  Through goodly mixture of complexions dew;
  And in her cheekes the vermeill red did shew
  Like roses in a bed of lillies shed,
  The which ambrosiall odours from them threw,
  And gazers sense with double pleasure fed,
Hable to heale the sicke, and to revive the ded.

23

In her faire eyes two living lamps did flame,
  Kindled above at th'heavenly makers light,
  And darted fyrie beames out of the same,
  So passing persant, and so wondrous bright,
  That quite bereav'd the rash beholders sight:
  In them the blinded god his lustfull fire
  To kindle oft assayd, but had no might;
  For with dredd Majestie, and awfull ire,
She broke his wanton darts, and quenched base desire.

24

Her ivorie forhead, full of bountie brave,
  Like a broad table did it selfe dispred,
  For Love his loftie triumphes to engrave,
  And write the battels of his great godhed:
  All good and honour might therein be red:
  For there their dwelling was. And when she spake,
  Sweet words, like dropping honny she did shed,
  And twixt the perles and rubins softly brake
A silver sound, that heavenly musicke seemd to make.

25

Upon her eyelids many Graces sate,
  Under the shadow of her even browes,
  Working belgards, and amorous retrate,
  And every one her with a grace endowes:
  And every one with meekenesse to her bowes.
  So glorious mirrhour of celestiall grace,
  And soveraine moniment of mortall vowes,
  How shall fraile pen descrive her heavenly face,
For feare through want of skill her beautie to disgrace?

26

So faire, and thousand thousand times more faire
  She seemd, when she presented was to sight,
  And was yclad, for heat of scorching aire,
  All in a silken Camus lylly whight,
  Purfled upon with many a folded plight,
  Which all above besprinckled was throughout
  With golden aygulets, that glistred bright,
  Like twinckling starres, and all the skirt about
Was hemd with golden fringe.

27

Below her ham her weed did somewhat traine,
　And her streight legs most bravely were embayld
In gilden buskins of costly Cordwaine,
　All bard with golden bendes, which were entayld
With curious antickes, and full faire aumayld:
　Before they fastned were under her knee
In a rich Jewell, and therein entrayld
　The ends of all their knots, that none might see,
How they within their fouldings close enwrapped bee.

28

Like two faire marble pillours they were seene,
　Which doe the temple of the Gods support,
Whom all the people decke with girlands greene,
　And honour in their festivall resort;
Those same with stately grace, and princely port
　She taught to tread, when she her selfe would grace,
But with the wooddie Nymphes when she did play,
　Or when the flying Libbard she did chace,
She could them nimbly move, and after fly apace.

29

And in her hand a sharpe bore-speare she held,
　And at her backe a bow and quiver gay,
Stuft with steele-headed darts, wherewith she queld
　The salvage beastes in her victorious play,
Knit with a golden bauldricke, which forelay
　Athwart her snowy brest, and did divide
Her daintie paps; which like young fruit in May
　Now little gan to swell, and being tide,
Through her thin weed their places only signifide.

30

Her yellow lockes crisped, like golden wyre,
　About her shoulders weren loosely shed,
And when the winde emongst them did inspyre,
　They waved like a penon wide dispred,
And low behinde her backe were scattered:
　And whether art it were, or heedlesse hap,
As through the flouring forrest rash she fled,
　In her rude haires sweet flowres themselves did lap,
And flourishing fresh leaves and blossomes did enwrap.

31

Such as *Diana* by the sandie shore
　Of swift *Eurotas*, or on *Cynthus* greene,
　Where all the Nymphes have her unwares forlore,
　Wandreth alone with bow and arrowes keene,
　To seeke her game: Or as that famous Queene
　Of *Amazons*, whom *Pyrrhus* did destroy,
　The day that first of *Priame* she was seene,
　Did shew her selfe in great triumphant joy,
To succour the weake state of sad afflicted *Troy*.

32

Such when as hartlesse *Trompart* did her vew,
　He was dismayed in his coward mind,
　And doubted, whether he himselfe should shew,
　Or fly away, or bide alone behind:
　Both feare and hope he in her face did find,
　When she at last him spying thus bespake;
　Hayle Groome; didst not thou see a bleeding Hind,
　Whose right haunch earst my stedfast arrow strake?
If thou didst, tell me, that I may her overtake.

33

Wherewith reviv'd, this answere forth he threw;
　O Goddesse, (for such I thee take to bee)
　For neither doth thy face terrestriall shew,
　Nor voyce sound mortall; I avow to thee,
　Such wounded beast, as that, I did not see,
　Sith earst into this forrest wild I came.
　But mote thy goodlyhed forgive it mee,
　To weet, which of the Gods I shall thee name,
That unto thee due worship I may rightly frame.

34

To whom she thus; but ere her words ensewed,
　Unto the bush her eye did suddein glaunce,
　In which vaine *Braggadocchio* was mewed,
　And saw it stirre: she left her percing launce,
　And towards gan a deadly shaft advaunce,
　In mind to marke the beast. At which sad stowre,
　Trompart forth stept, to stay the mortall chaunce,
　Out crying, O what ever heavenly powre,
Or earthly wight thou be, withhold this deadly howre.

35

O stay thy hand, for yonder is no game
  For thy fierce arrowes, them to exercize,
  But loe my Lord, my liege, whose warlike name
  Is farre renowmd through many bold emprize;
  And now in shade he shrowded yonder lies.
  She staid: with that he crauld out of his nest,
  Forth creeping on his caitive hands and thies,
  And standing stoutly up, his loftie crest
Did fiercely shake, and rowze, as comming late from rest.

36

As fearefull fowle, that long in secret cave
  For dread of soaring hauke her selfe hath hid,
  Not caring how, her silly life to save,
  She her gay painted plumes disorderid,
  Seeing at last her selfe from daunger rid,
  Peepes foorth, and soone renewes her native pride;
  She gins her feathers foule disfigured
  Proudly to prune, and set on every side,
So shakes off shame, ne thinks how erst she did her hide.

37

So when her goodly visage he beheld,
  He gan himselfe to vaunt: but when he vewed
  Those deadly tooles, which in her hand she held,
  Soone into other fits he was transmewed,
  Till she to him her gratious speach renewed;
  All haile, Sir knight, and well may thee befall,
  As all the like, which honour have pursewed
  Through deedes of armes and prowesse martiall;
All vertue merits praise, but such the most of all.

38

To whom he thus; O fairest under skie,
  True be thy words, and worthy of thy praise,
  That warlike feats doest highest glorifie.
  Therein have I spent all my youthly daies,
  And many battailes fought, and many fraies
  Throughout the world, wher so they might be found,
  Endevouring my dreadded name to raise
  Above the Moone, that fame may it resound
In her eternall trompe, with laurell girland cround.

39

But what art thou, O Ladie, which doest raunge
  In this wilde forrest, where no pleasure is,
  And doest not it for joyous court exchaunge,
  Emongst thine equall peres, where happie blis
  And all delight does raigne, much more than this?
  There thou maist love, and dearely loved bee,
  And swim in pleasure, which thou here doest mis;
  There maist thou best be seene, and best maist see:
The wood is fit for beasts, the court is fit for thee.

40

Who so in pompe of proud estate (quoth she)
  Does swim, and bathes himselfe in courtly blis,
  Does waste his dayes in darke obscuritee,
  And in oblivion ever buried is:
  Where ease abounds, yt's eath to doe amis;
  But who his limbs with labours, and his mind
  Behaves with cares, cannot so easie mis.
  Abroad in armes, at home in studious kind
Who seekes with painfull toile, shall honor soonest find.

41

In woods, in waves, in warres she wonts to dwell,
  And will be found with perill and with paine;
  Ne can the man, that moulds in idle cell,
  Unto her happie mansion attaine:
  Before her gate high God did Sweat ordaine,
  And wakefull watches ever to abide:
  But easie is the way, and passage plaine
  To pleasures pallace; it may soone be spide,
And day and night her dores to all stand open wide.

42

In Princes court, The rest she would have said,
  But that the foolish man, fild with delight
  Of her sweet words, that all his sence dismaid,
  And with her wondrous beautie ravisht quight,
  Gan burne in filthy lust, and leaping light,
  Thought in his bastard armes her to embrace.
  With that she swarving backe, her Javelin bright
  Against him bent, and fiercely did menace
So turned her about, and fled away apace.

43

Which when the Peasant saw, amazd he stood,
 And grieved at her flight; yet durst he not
Pursew her steps, through wild unknowen wood;
Besides he feard her wrath, and threatned shot
Whiles in the bush he lay, not yet forgot:
Ne car'd he greatly for her presence vaine,
But turning said to *Trompart*, What foule blot
Is this to knight, that Ladie should againe
Depart to woods untoucht, and leave so proud disdaine?

44

Perdie (said *Trompart*) let her passe at will,
 Least by her presence daunger mote befall.
For who can tell (and sure I feare it ill)
But that she is some powre celestiall?
For whiles she spake, her great words did apall
My feeble courage, and my hart oppresse,
That yet I quake and tremble over all.
And I (said *Braggadocchio*) thought no lesse,
When first I heard her horne sound with such ghastlinesse.

45

For from my mothers wombe this grace I have
 Me given by eternall destinie,
That earthly thing may not my courage brave
Dismay with feare, or cause one foot to flie:
But either hellish feends, or powres on hie:
Which was the cause, when earst that horne I heard,
Weening it had beene thunder in the skie,
I hid my selfe from it, as one affeard;
But when I other knew, my selfe I boldly reard.

46

But now for feare of worse, that may betide,
 Let us soone hence depart. They soone agree;
So to his steed he got, and gan to ride,
As one unfit therefore, that all might see
He had not trayned bene in chevalree.
Which well that valiant courser did discerne;
For he despysd to tread in dew degree,
But chaufd and fom'd, with courage fierce and sterne,
And to be easd of that base burden still did erne.

CANT. IIII

Guyon does Furor bind in chaines,
and stops Occasion:
Delivers Phedon, and therefore
by Strife is rayld upon.

1

IN brave pursuit of honorable deed,
 There is I know not what great difference
 Betweene the vulgar and the noble seed,
 Which unto things of valorous pretence
 Seemes to be borne by native influence;
 As feates of armes, and love to entertaine,
 But chiefly skill to ride, seemes a science
 Proper to gentle bloud: some others faine
To menage steeds, as did this vaunter; but in vaine.

2

But he the rightfull owner of that steed,
 Who well could menage and subdew his pride,
 The whiles on foot was forced for to yeed,
 With that blacke Palmer, his most trusty guide;
 Who suffred not his wandring feet to slide.
 But when strong passion, or weake fleshlinesse
 Would from the right way seeke to draw him wide,
 He would through temperance and stedfastnesse,
Teach him the weake to strengthen, and the strong suppresse.

3

It fortuned forth faring on his way,
 He saw from farre, or seemed for to see
 Some troublous uprore or contentious fray,
 Whereto he drew in haste it to agree.
 A mad man, or that feigned mad to bee,
 Drew by the haire along upon the ground,
 A handsome stripling with great crueltee,
 Whom sore he bett, and gor'd with many a wound,
That cheekes with teares, and sides with bloud did all abound.

4

And him behind, a wicked Hag did stalke,
　　In ragged robes, and filthy disaray,
　　Her other leg was lame, that she no'te walke,
　　But on a staffe her feeble steps did stay;
　　Her lockes, that loathly were and hoarie gray,
　　Grew all afore, and loosely hong unrold,
　　But all behind was bald, and worne away,
　　That none thereof could ever taken hold,
And eke her face ill favour, full of wrinckles old.

5

And ever as she went, her tongue did walke
　　In foule reproch, and termes of vile despight,
　　Provoking him by her outrageous talke,
　　To heape more vengeance on that wretched wight;
　　Sometimes she raught him stones, wherwith to smite,
　　Sometimes her staffe, though it her one leg were,
　　Withouten which she could not go upright;
　　Ne any evill meanes she did forbeare,
That might him move to wrath, and indignation reare.

6

The noble *Guyon* mov'd with great remorse,
　　Approching, first the Hag did thrust away,
　　And after adding more impetuous forse,
　　His mightie hands did on the madman lay,
　　And pluckt him backe; who all on fire streight way,
　　Against him turning all his fell intent,
　　With beastly brutish rage gan him assay,
　　And smot, and bit, and kickt, and scratcht, and rent,
And did he wist not what in his avengement.

7

And sure he was a man of mickle might,
　　Had he had governance, it well to guide:
　　But when the franticke fit inflamd his spright,
　　His force was vaine, and strooke more often wide,
　　Than at the aymed marke, which he had eide:
　　And oft himselfe he chaunst to hurt unwares,
　　Whilst reason blent through passion, nought descride,
　　But as a blindfold Bull at randon fares,
And where he hits, nought knowes, and whom he hurts, nought cares.

8

His rude assault and rugged handeling
    Straunge seemed to the knight, that aye with foe
    In faire defence and goodly menaging
    Of armes was wont to fight, yet nathemoe
    Was he abashed now not fighting so,
    But more enfierced through his currish play,
    Him sternely grypt, and haling to and fro,
    To overthrow him strongly did assay,
But overthrew himselfe unwares, and lower lay.

9

And being downe the villein sore did beat,
    And bruze with clownish fistes his manly face:
    And eke the Hag with many a bitter threat,
    Still cald upon to kill him in the place.
    With whose reproch and odious menace
    The knight emboyling in his haughtie hart,
    Knit all his forces, and gan soone unbrace
    His grasping hold: so lightly did upstart,
And drew his deadly weapon, to maintaine his part.

10

Which when the Palmer saw, he loudly cryde,
    Not so, O *Guyon*, never thinke that so
    That Monster can be maistred or destroyd:
    He is not, ah, he is not such a foe,
    As steele can wound, or strength can overthroe.
    That same is *Furor*, cursed cruell wight,
    That unto knighthood workes much shame and woe;
    And that same Hag, his aged mother, hight
Occasion, the root of all wrath and despight.

11

With her, who so will raging *Furor* tame,
    Must first begin, and well her amenage:
    First her restraine from her reprochfull blame,
    And evill meanes, with which she doth enrage
    Her franticke sonne, and kindles his courage,
    Then when she is withdrawen, or strong withstood,
    It's eath his idle furie to asswage,
    And calme the tempest of his passion wood;
The bankes are overflowen, when stopped is the flood.

12

Therewith Sir *Guyon* left his first emprise,
  And turning to that woman, fast her hent
  By the hoare lockes, that hong before her eyes,
  And to the ground her threw: yet n'ould she stent
  Her bitter rayling and foule revilement,
  But still provokt her sonne to wreake her wrong;
  But nathelesse he did her still torment,
  And catching hold of her ungratious tong,
Thereon an yron lock did fasten firme and strong.

13

Then when as use of speach was from her reft,
  With her two crooked handes she signes did make,
  And beckned him, the last helpe she had left:
  But he that last left helpe away did take,
  And both her hands fast bound unto a stake,
  That she note stirre. Then gan her sonne to flie
  Full fast away, and did her quite forsake;
  But *Guyon* after him in haste did hie,
And soone him overtooke in sad perplexitie.

14

In his strong armes he stiffely him embraste,
  Who him gainstriving, nought at all prevaild:
  For all his power was utterly defaste,
  And furious fits at earst quite weren quaild:
  Oft he re'nforst, and oft his forces fayld,
  Yet yield he would not, nor his rancour slacke.
  Then him to ground he cast, and rudely hayld,
  And both his hands fast bound behind his backe,
And both his feet in fetters to an yron racke.

15

With hundred yron chaines he did him bind,
  And hundred knots that did him sore constraine:
  Yet his great yron teeth he still did grind,
  And grimly gnash, threatning revenge in vaine;
  His burning eyen, whom bloudie strakes did staine,
  Stared full wide, and threw forth sparkes of fire,
  And more for ranck despight, than for great paine,
  Shakt his long lockes, colourd like copper-wire,
And bit his tawny beard to shew his raging ire.

16

Thus when as *Guyon Furor* had captiv'd,
 Turning about he saw that wretched Squire,
 Whom that mad man of life nigh late depriv'd,
 Lying on ground, all soild with bloud and mire:
 Whom when as he perceived to respire,
 He gan to comfort, and his wounds to dresse.
 Being at last recured, he gan inquire,
 What hard mishap him brought to such distresse,
And made that caitives thral, the thral of wretchednesse.

17

With hart then throbbing, and with watry eyes,
 Faire Sir (quoth he) what man can shun the hap,
 That hidden lyes unwares him to surpryse?
 Misfortune waites advantage to entrap
 The man most warie in her whelming lap.
 So me weake wretch, of many weakest one,
 Unweeting, and unware of such mishap,
 She brought to mischiefe through occasion,
Where this same wicked villein did me light upon.

18

It was a faithlesse Squire, that was the sourse
 Of all my sorrow, and of these sad teares,
 With whom from tender dug of commune nourse,
 Attonce I was upbrought, and eft when yeares
 More rype us reason lent to chose our Peares,
 Our selves in league of vowed love we knit:
 In which we long time without gealous feares,
 Or faultie thoughts continewd, as was fit;
And for my part I vow, dissembled not a whit.

19

It was my fortune commune to that age,
 To love a Ladie faire of great degree,
 The which was borne of noble parentage,
 And set in highest seat of dignitee,
 Yet seemd no lesse to love, than loved to bee:
 Long I her serv'd, and found her faithfull still,
 Ne ever thing could cause us disagree:
 Love that two harts makes one, makes eke one will:
Each strove to please, and others pleasure to fulfill.

20

My friend, hight *Philemon*, I did partake
  Of all my love and all my privitie;
  Who greatly joyous seemed for my sake,
  And gratious to that Ladie, as to mee,
  Ne ever wight, that mote so welcome bee,
  As he to her, withouten blot or blame,
  Ne ever thing, that she could thinke or see,
  But unto him she would impart the same:
O wretched man, that would abuse so gentle Dame.

21

At last such grace I found, and meanes I wrought,
  That I that Ladie to my spouse had wonne;
  Accord of friends, consent of parents sought,
  Affiance made, my happinesse begonne,
  There wanted nought but few rites to be donne,
  Which mariage make; that day too farre did seeme:
  Most joyous man, on whom the shining Sunne
  Did shew his face, my selfe I did esteeme,
And that my falser friend did no lesse joyous deeme.

22

But ere that wished day his beame disclosd,
  He either envying my toward good,
  Or of himselfe to treason ill disposd,
  One day unto me came in friendly mood,
  And told for secret how he understood
  That Ladie whom I had to me assynd,
  Had both distaind her honorable blood,
  And eke the faith, which she to me did bynd;
And therfore wisht me stay, till I more truth should fynd.

23

The gnawing anguish and sharpe gelosy,
  Which his sad speech infixed in my brest,
  Ranckled so sore, and festred inwardly,
  That my engreeved mind could find no rest,
  Till that the truth thereof I did outwrest,
  And him besought by that same sacred band
  Betwixt us both, to counsell me the best.
  He then with solemne oath and plighted hand
Assur'd, ere long the truth to let me understand.

24

Ere long with like againe he boorded mee,
  Saying, he now had boulted all the floure,
  And that it was a groome of base degree,
  Which of my love was partner Paramoure:
  Who used in a darkesome inner bowre
  Her oft to meet: which better to approve,
  He promised to bring me at that howre,
  When I should see, that would me nearer move,
And drive me to withdraw my blind abused love.

25

This gracelesse man for furtherance of his guile,
  Did court the handmayd of my Lady deare,
  Who glad t'embosome his affection vile,
  Did all she might, more pleasing to appeare.
  One day to worke her to his will more neare,
  He woo'd her thus: *Pryene* (so she hight)
  What great despight doth fortune to thee beare,
  Thus lowly to abase thy beautie bright,
That it should not deface all others lesser light?

26

But if she had her least helpe to thee lent,
  T'adorne thy forme according thy desart,
  Their blazing pride thou wouldest soone have blent,
  And staynd their prayses with thy least good part;
  Ne should faire *Claribell* with all her art,
  Though she thy Lady be, approch thee neare:
  For proofe thereof, this evening, as thou art,
  Aray thy selfe in her most gorgeous geare,
That I may more delight in thy embracement deare.

27

The Maiden proud through prayse, and mad through love
  Him hearkned to, and soone her selfe arayd,
  The whiles to me the treachour did remove
  His craftie engin, and as he had sayd,
  Me leading, in a secret corner layd,
  The sad spectatour of my Tragedie;
  Where left, he went, and his owne false part playd,
  Disguised like that groome of base degree,
Whom he had feignd th'abuser of my love to bee.

28

Eftsoones he came unto th'appointed place,
 And with him brought *Pryene*, rich arayd,
 In *Claribellaes* clothes. Her proper face
 I not descerned in that darkesome shade,
 But weend it was my love, with whom he playd.
 Ah God, what horrour and tormenting griefe
 My hart, my hands, mine eyes, and all assayd?
 Me liefer were ten thousand deathes priefe,
Than wound of gealous worme, and shame of such repriefe.

29

I home returning, fraught with fowle despight,
 And chawing vengeance all the way I went,
 Soone as my loathed love appeard in sight,
 With wrathfull hand I slew her innocent;
 That after soone I dearely did lament:
 For when the cause of that outrageous deede
 Demaunded, I made plaine and evident,
 Her faultie Handmayd, which that bale did breede,
Confest, how *Philemon* her wrought to chaunge her weede.

30

Which when I heard, with horrible affright
 And hellish fury all enragd, I sought
 Upon my selfe that vengeable despight
 To punish: yet it better first I thought,
 To wreake my wrath on him, that first it wrought.
 To *Philemon*, false faytour *Philemon*
 I cast to pay, that I so dearely bought;
 Of deadly drugs I gave him drinke anon,
And washt away his guilt with guiltie potion.

31

Thus heaping crime on crime, and griefe on griefe,
 To losse of love adjoyning losse of frend,
 I meant to purge both with a third mischiefe,
 And in my woes beginner it to end:
 That was *Pryene*; she did first offend,
 She last should smart: with which cruell intent,
 When I at her my murdrous blade did bend,
 She fled away with ghastly dreriment,
And I pursewing my fell purpose, after went.

32

Feare gave her wings, and rage enforst my flight;
  Through woods and plaines so long I did her chace,
  Till this mad man, whom your victorious might
  Hath now fast bound, me met in middle space,
  As I her, so he me pursewd apace,
  And shortly overtooke: I, breathing yre,
  Sore chauffed at my stay in such a cace,
  And with my heat kindled his cruell fyre;
Which kindled once, his mother did more rage inspyre.

33

Betwixt them both, they have me doen to dye,
  Through wounds, and strokes, and stubborne handeling,
  That death were better, than such agony,
  As griefe and furie unto me did bring;
  Of which in me yet stickes the mortall sting,
  That during life will never be appeasd.
  When he thus ended had his sorrowing,
  Said *Guyon*, Squire, sore have ye beene diseasd;
But all your hurts may soone through temperance be easd.

34

Then gan the Palmer thus, Most wretched man,
  That to affections does the bridle lend;
  In their beginning they are weake and wan,
  But soone through suff'rance grow to fearefull end;
  Whiles they are weake betimes with them contend:
  For when they once to perfect strength do grow,
  Strong warres they make, and cruell battry bend
  Gainst fort of Reason, it to overthrow:
Wrath, gelosie, griefe, love this Squire have layd thus low.

35

Wrath, gealosie, griefe, love do thus expell:
  Wrath is a fire, and gealosie a weede,
  Griefe is a flood, and love a monster fell;
  The fire of sparkes, the weede of little seede,
  The flood of drops, the Monster filth did breede:
  But sparks, seed, drops, and filth do thus delay;
  The sparks soone quench, the springing seed outweed,
  The drops dry up, and filth wipe cleane away:
So shall wrath, gealosie, griefe, love dye and decay.

36

Unlucky Squire (said *Guyon*) sith thou hast
Falne into mischiefe through intemperaunce,
Henceforth take heede of that thou now hast past,
And guide thy wayes with warie governaunce,
Least worse betide thee by some later chaunce.
But read how art thou nam'd, and of what kin.
Phedon I hight (quoth he) and do advaunce
Mine auncestry from famous *Coradin*,
Who first to rayse our house to honour did begin.

37

Thus as he spake, lo far away they spyde
A varlet running towards hastily,
Whose flying feet so fast their way applyde,
That round about a cloud of dust did fly,
Which mingled all with sweate, did dim his eye.
He soone approched, panting, breathlesse, whot,
And all so soyld, that none could him descry;
His countenaunce was bold, and bashed not
For *Guyons* lookes, but scornefull eyglaunce at him shot.

38

Behind his backe he bore a brasen shield,
On which was drawen faire, in colours fit,
A flaming fire in midst of bloudy field,
And round about the wreath this word was writ,
Burnt I do burne. Right well beseemed it,
To be the shield of some redoubted knight;
And in his hand two darts exceeding flit,
And deadly sharpe he held, whose heads were dight
In poyson and in bloud, of malice and despight.

39

When he in presence came, to *Guyon* first
He boldly spake, Sir knight, if knight thou bee,
Abandon this forestalled place at erst,
For feare of further harme, I counsell thee,
Or bide the chaunce at thine owne jeoperdie.
The knight at his great boldnesse wondered,
And though he scornd his idle vanitie,
Yet mildly him to purpose answered;
For not to grow of nought he it conjectured.

40

Varlet, this place most dew to me I deeme,
  Yielded by him, that held it forcibly.
  But whence should come that harme, which thou doest seeme
  To threat to him, that minds his chaunce t'abye?
  Perdy (said he) here comes, and is hard by
  A knight of wondrous powre, and great assay,
  That never yet encountred enemy,
  But did him deadly daunt, or fowle dismay;
Ne thou for better hope, if thou his presence stay.

41

How hight he then (said *Guyon*) and from whence?
  Pyrochles is his name, renowmed farre
  For his bold feats and hardy confidence,
  Full oft approv'd in many a cruell warre,
  The brother of *Cymochles*, both which arre
  The sonnes of old *Acrates* and *Despight*,
  Acrates sonne of *Phlegeton* and *Jarre*;
  But *Phlegeton* is sonne of *Herebus* and *Night*;
But *Herebus* sonne of *Aeternitie* is hight.

42

So from immortall race he does proceede,
  That mortall hands may not withstand his might,
  Drad for his derring do, and bloudy deed;
  For all in bloud and spoile is his delight.
  His am I *Atin*, his in wrong and right,
  That matter make for him to worke upon
  And stirre him up to strife and cruell fight.
  Fly therefore, fly this fearefull stead anon,
Least thy foolhardize worke thy sad confusion.

43

His be that care, whom most it doth concerne,
  (Said he) but whither with such hasty flight
  Art thou now bound? for well mote I discerne
  Great cause, that carries thee so swift and light.
  My Lord (quoth he) me sent, and streight behight
  To seeke *Occasion*, where so she bee:
  For he is all disposd to bloudy fight,
  And breathes out wrath and hainous crueltie;
Hard is his hap, that first fals in his jeopardie.

44

Madman (said then the Palmer) that does seeke
  Occasion to wrath, and cause of strife;
  She comes unsought, and shonned followes eke.
  Happy, who can abstaine, when Rancour rife
  Kindles Revenge, and threats his rusty knife;
  Woe never wants, where every cause is caught,
  And rash *Occasion* makes unquiet life.
  Then loe, where bound she sits, whom thou hast sought,
(Said *Guyon*,) let that message to thy Lord be brought.

45

That when the varlet heard and saw, streight way
  He wexed wondrous wroth, and said, Vile knight,
  That knights and knighthood doest with shame upbray,
  And shewst th'ensample of thy childish might,
  With silly weake old woman thus to fight.
  Great glory and gay spoile sure hast thou got,
  And stoutly prov'd thy puissaunce here in sight;
  That shall *Pyrochles* well requite, I wot,
And with thy bloud abolish so reprochfull blot.

46

With that one of his thrillant darts he threw,
  Headed with ire and vengeable despight;
  The quivering steele his aymed end well knew,
  And to his brest it selfe intended right:
  But he was warie, and ere it empight
  In the meant marke, advaunst his shield atweene,
  On which it seizing, no way enter might,
  But backe rebounding, left the forckhead keene;
Eftsoones he fled away, and might no where be seene.

CANT. V

Pyrochles does with Guyon fight,
And Furors chayne unbinds:
Of whom sore hurt, for his revenge
Atin Cymochles finds.

1

WHO ever doth to temperaunce apply
  His stedfast life, and all his actions frame,
  Trust me, shall find no greater enimy,
  Than stubborne perturbation, to the same;
  To which right well the wise do give that name,
  For it the goodly peace of stayed mindes
  Does overthrow, and troublous warre proclame:
  His owne woes authour, who so bound it findes,
As did *Pyrochles*, and it wilfully unbindes.

2

After that varlets flight, it was not long,
  Ere on the plaine fast pricking *Guyon* spide
  One in bright armes embatteiled full strong,
  That as the Sunny beames do glaunce and glide
  Upon the trembling wave, so shined bright,
  And round about him threw forth sparkling fire,
  That seemd him to enflame on every side:
  His steed was bloudy red, and fomed ire,
When with the maistring spur he did him roughly stire.

3

Approching nigh, he never stayd to greete,
  Ne chaffar words, prowd courage to provoke,
  But prickt so fiers, that underneath his feete
  The smouldring dust did round about him smoke,
  Both horse and man nigh able for to choke;
  And fairly couching his steele-headed speare,
  Him first saluted with a sturdy stroke;
  It booted nought Sir *Guyon* comming neare
To thinke, such hideous puissaunce on foot to beare.

4

But lightly shunned it, and passing by,
　With his bright blade did smite at him so fell,
　That the sharpe steele arriving forcibly
　On his broad shield, bit not, but glauncing fell
　On his horse necke before the quilted sell,
　And from the head the body sundred quight.
　So him dismounted low, he did compell
　On foot with him to matchen equall fight;
The truncked beast fast bleeding, did him fowly dight.

5

Sore bruzed with the fall, he slow uprose,
　And all enraged, thus him loudly shent;
　Disleall knight, whose coward courage chose
　To wreake it selfe on beast all innocent,
　And shund the marke, at which it should be ment,
　Thereby thine armes seeme strong, but manhood fraile;
　So hast thou oft with guile thine honour blent;
　But litle may such guile thee now availe,
If wonted force and fortune do not much me faile.

6

With that he drew his flaming sword, and strooke
　At him so fiercely, that the upper marge
　Of his sevenfolded shield away it tooke,
　And glauncing on his helmet, made a large
　And open gash therein: were not his targe,
　That broke the violence of his intent,
　The weary soule from thence it would discharge;
　Nathelesse so sore a buff to him it lent,
That made him reele, and to his brest his bever bent.

7

Exceeding wroth was *Guyon* at that blow,
　And much ashamd, that stroke of living arme
　Should him dismay, and make him stoup so low,
　Though otherwise it did him litle harme:
　Tho hurling high his yron braced arme,
　He smote so manly on his shoulder plate,
　That all his left side it did quite disarme;
　Yet there the steele stayd not, but inly bate
Deepe in his flesh, and opened wide a red floodgate.

8

Deadly dismayd, with horrour of that dint
  Pyrochles was, and grieved eke entyre;
  Yet nathemore did it his fury stint,
  But added flame unto his former fire,
  That welnigh molt his hart in raging yre,
  Ne thenceforth his approved skill, to ward,
  Or strike, or hurtle round in warlike gyre,
  Remembred he, ne car'd for his saufgard,
But rudely rag'd, and like a cruell Tygre far'd.

9

He hewd, and lasht, and foynd, and thundred blowes,
  And every way did seeke into his life,
  Ne plate, ne male could ward so mighty throwes,
  But yielded passage to his cruell knife.
  But *Guyon*, in the heat of all his strife,
  Was warie wise, and closely did awayt
  Avauntage, whilest his foe did rage most rife;
  Sometimes a thwart, sometimes he strooke him strayt,
And falsed oft his blowes, t'illude him with such bayt.

10

Like as a Lyon, whose imperiall powre
  A prowd rebellious Unicorne defies,
  T'avoide the rash assault and wrathfull stowre
  Of his fiers foe, him to a tree applies,
  And when him running in full course he spies,
  He slips aside; the whiles that furious beast
  His precious horne, sought of his enimies,
  Strikes in the stocke, ne thence can be releast,
But to the mighty victour yields a bounteous feast.

11

With such faire slight him *Guyon* often faild,
  Till at the last all breathlesse, wearie, faint
  Him spying, with fresh onset he assaild,
  And kindling new his courage seeming queint,
  Strooke him so hugely, that through great constraint
  He made him stoup perforce unto his knee,
  And do unwilling worship to the Saint,
  That on his shield depainted he did see;
Such homage till that instant never learned hee.

12

Whom *Guyon* seeing stoup, pursewed fast
  The present offer of faire victory,
  And soone his dreadfull blade about he cast,
  Wherewith he smote his haughty crest so hye,
  That streight on ground made him full low to lye;
  Then on his brest his victour foote he thrust,
  With that he cryde, Mercy, do me not dye,
  Ne deeme thy force by fortunes doome unjust,
That hath (maugre her spight) thus low me laid in dust.

13

Eftsoones his cruell hand Sir *Guyon* stayd,
  Tempring the passion with advizement slow,
  And maistring might on enimy dismayd:
  For th'equall dye of warre he well did know;
  Then to him said, Live and allegaunce owe,
  To him that gives thee life and libertie,
  And henceforth by this dayes ensample trow,
  That hasty wroth, and heedlesse hazardrie
Do breede repentaunce late, and lasting infamie.

14

So up he let him rise, who with grim looke
  And count'naunce sterne upstanding, gan to grind
  His grated teeth for great disdeigne, and shooke
  His sandy lockes, long hanging downe behind,
  Knotted in bloud and dust, for griefe of mind,
  That he in ods of armes was conquered;
  Yet in himselfe some comfort he did find,
  That him so noble knight had maistered,
Whose bounty more than might, yet both he wondered.

15

Which *Guyon* marking said, Be nought agriev'd,
  Sir knight, that thus ye now subdewed arre:
  Was never man, who most conquestes atchiev'd,
  But sometimes had the worse, and lost by warre,
  Yet shortly gaynd, that losse exceeded farre:
  Losse is no shame, nor to be lesse than foe,
  But to be lesser, than himselfe, doth marre
  Both loosers lot, and victours prayse alsoe.
Vaine others overthrowes, who selfe doth overthrowe.

16

Fly, O *Pyrochles*, fly the dreadfull warre,
  That in thy selfe thy lesser parts do move,
  Outrageous anger, and woe-working jarre,
  Direfull impatience, and hart murdring love;
  Those, those thy foes, those warriours far remove,
  Which thee to endlesse bale captived lead.
  But sith in might thou didst my mercy prove,
  Of curtesie to me the cause aread,
That thee against me drew with so impetuous dread.

17

Dreadlesse (said he) that shall I soone declare:
  It was complaind, that thou hadst done great tort
  Unto an aged woman, poore and bare,
  And thralled her in chaines with strong effort,
  Voide of all succour and needfull comfort:
  That ill beseemes thee, such as I thee see,
  To worke such shame. Therefore I thee exhort,
  To chaunge thy will, and set *Occasion* free,
And to her captive sonne yield his first libertee.

18

Thereat Sir *Guyon* smilde, And is that all
  (Said he) that thee so sore displeased hath?
  Great mercy sure, for to enlarge a thrall,
  Whose freedome shall thee turne to greatest scath.
  Nath'lesse now quench thy whot emboyling wrath:
  Loe there they be; to thee I yield them free.
  Thereat he wondrous glad, out of the path
  Did lightly leape, where he them bound did see,
And gan to breake the bands of their captivitee.

19

Soone as *Occasion* felt her selfe untyde,
  Before her sonne could well assoyled bee,
  She to her use returnd, and streight defyde
  Both *Guyon* and *Pyrochles*: th'one (said shee)
  Bycause he wonne; the other because hee
  Was wonne: So matter did she make of nought,
  To stirre up strife, and do them disagree:
  But soone as *Furor* was enlargd, she sought
To kindle his quencht fire, and thousand causes wrought.

20

It was not long, ere she inflam'd him so,
　That he would algates with *Pyrochles* fight,
　And his redeemer chalengd for his foe,
　Because he had not well mainteind his right,
　But yielded had to that same straunger knight:
　Now gan *Pyrochles* wex as wood, as hee,
　And him affronted with impatient might:
　So both together fiers engrasped bee,
Whiles *Guyon* standing by, their uncouth strife does see.

21

Him all that while *Occasion* did provoke
　Against *Pyrochles*, and new matter framed
　Upon the old, him stirring to be wroke
　Of his late wrongs, in which she oft him blamed
　For suffering such abuse, as knighthood shamed,
　And him dishabled quite. But he was wise
　Ne would with vaine occasions be inflamed;
　Yet others she more urgent did devise:
Yet nothing could him to impatience entise.

22

Their fell contention still increased more,
　And more thereby increased *Furors* might,
　That he his foe has hurt, and wounded sore,
　And him in bloud and durt deformed quight.
　His mother eke, more to augment his spight,
　Now brought to him a flaming fire brond,
　Which she in *Stygian* lake, ay burning bright,
　Had kindled: that she gave into his hond,
That armd with fire, more hardly he mote him withstond.

23

Tho gan that villein wex so fiers and strong,
　That nothing might sustaine his furious forse;
　He cast him downe to ground, and all along
　Drew him through durt and myre without remorse,
　And fowly battered his comely corse,
　That *Guyon* much disdeignd so loathly sight.
　At last he was compeld to cry perforse,
　Helpe, O Sir *Guyon*, helpe most noble knight,
To rid a wretched man from hands of hellish wight.

24

The knight was greatly moved at his plaint,
  And gan him dight to succour his distresse,
  Till that the Palmer, by his grave restraint,
  Him stayd from yielding pitifull redresse;
  And said, Deare sonne, thy causelesse ruth represse,
  Ne let thy stout hart melt in pitty vayne:
  He that his sorrow sought through wilfulnesse,
  And his foe fettred would release agayne,
Deserves to tast his follies fruit, repented payne.

25

Guyon obayd; So him away he drew
  From needlesse trouble of renewing fight
  Already fought, his voyage to pursew.
  But rash *Pyrochles* varlet, *Atin* hight,
  When late he saw his Lord in heavy plight,
  Under Sir *Guyons* puissaunt stroke to fall,
  Him deeming dead, as then he seemd in sight,
  Fled fast away, to tell his funerall
Unto his brother, whom *Cymochles* men did call.

26

He was a man of rare redoubted might,
  Famous throughout the world for warlike prayse,
  And glorious spoiles, purchast in perilous fight:
  Full many doughtie knights he in his dayes
  Had doen to death, subdewde in equall frayes,
  Whose carkases, for terrour of his name,
  Of fowles and beastes he made the piteous prayes,
  And hong their conquered armes for more defame
On gallow trees, in honour of his dearest Dame.

27

His dearest Dame is that Enchaunteresse,
  The vile *Acrasia*, that with vaine delightes,
  And idle pleasures in her *Bowre* of *Blisse*,
  Does charme her lovers, and the feeble sprightes
  Can call out of the bodies of fraile wightes:
  Whom then she does transforme to monstrous hewes,
  And horribly misshapes with ugly sightes,
  Captiv'd eternally in yron mewes,
And darksom dens, where *Titan* his face never shewes.

28

There *Atin* found *Cymochles* sojourning,
　To serve his Lemans love: for he, by kind,
　Was given all to lust and loose living,
　When ever his fiers hands he free mote find:
　And now he has pourd out his idle mind
　In daintie delices, and lavish joyes,
　Having his warlike weapons cast behind,
　And flowes in pleasures, and vaine pleasing toyes,
Mingled emongst loose Ladies and lascivious boyes.

29

And over him, art striving to compaire
　With nature, did an Arber greene dispred,
　Framed of wanton Yvie, flouring faire,
　Through which the fragrant Eglantine did spred
　His pricking armes, entrayld with roses red,
　Which daintie odours round about them threw,
　And all within with flowres was garnished,
　That when myld *Zephyrus* emongst them blew,
Did breath out bounteous smels, and painted colors shew.

30

And fast beside, there trickled softly downe
　A gentle streame, whose murmuring wave did play
　Emongst the pumy stones, and made a sowne,
　To lull him soft a sleepe, that by it lay;
　The wearie Traveiler, wandring that way,
　Therein did often quench his thristy heat,
　And then by it his wearie limbes display,
　Whiles creeping slomber made him to forget
His former paine, and wypt away his toylsom sweat.

31

And on the other side a pleasaunt grove
　Was shot up high, full of the stately tree,
　That dedicated is t'*Olympicke Jove*,
　And to his sonne *Alcides*, whenas hee
　Gaynd in *Nemea* goodly victoree;
　Therein the mery birds of every sort
　Chaunted alowd their chearefull harmonie:
　And made emongst themselves a sweet consort,
That quickned the dull spright with musicall comfort.

32

There he him found all carelesly displayd,
  In secret shadow from the sunny ray,
  On a sweet bed of lillies softly layd,
  Amidst a flocke of Damzels fresh and gay,
  That round about him dissolute did play
  Their wanton follies, and light meriment;
  Every of which did loosely disaray
  Her upper parts of meet habiliments,
And shewd them naked, deckt with many ornaments.

33

And every of them strove, with most delights,
  Him to aggrate, and greatest pleasures shew;
  Some framd faire lookes, glancing like evening lights,
  Others sweet words, dropping like honny dew;
  Some bathed kisses, and did soft embrew
  The sugred licour through his melting lips:
  One boastes her beautie, and does yeeld to vew
  Her daintie limbes above her tender hips;
Another her out boastes, and all for tryall strips.

34

He, like an Adder, lurking in the weeds,
  His wandring thought in deepe desire does steepe,
  And his fraile eye with spoyle of beautie feedes;
  Sometimes he falsely faines himselfe to sleepe,
  Whiles through their lids his wanton eies do peepe,
  To steale a snatch of amorous conceipt,
  Whereby close fire into his heart does creepe:
  So, them deceives, deceiv'd in his deceipt,
Made drunke with drugs of deare voluptuous receipt.

35

Atin arriving there, when him he spide,
  Thus in still waves of deepe delight to wade,
  Fiercely approching, to him lowdly cride,
  Cymochles; oh no, but *Cymochles* shade,
  In which that manly person late did fade,
  What is become of great *Acrates* sonne?
  Or where hath he hong up his mortall blade,
  That hath so many haughtie conquests wonne?
Is all his force forlorne, and all his glory donne?

36

Then pricking him with his sharpe-pointed dart,
  He said; Up, up, thou womanish weake knight,
  That here in Ladies lap entombed art,
  Unmindfull of thy praise and prowest might,
  And weetlesse eke of lately wrought despight,
  Whiles sad *Pyrochles* lies on senselesse ground,
  And groneth out his utmost grudging spright,
  Through many a stroke, and many a streaming wound,
Calling thy helpe in vaine, that here in joyes art dround.

37

Suddeinly out of his delightfull dreame
  The man awoke, and would have questiond more;
  But he would not endure that wofull theame
  For to dilate at large, but urged sore
  With percing words, and pittifull implore,
  Him hastie to arise. As one affright
  With hellish feends, or *Furies* mad uprore,
  He then uprose, inflam'd with fell despight,
And called for his armes; for he would algates fight.

38

They bene ybrought; he quickly does him dight,
  And lightly mounted, passeth on his way,
  Ne Ladies loves, ne sweete entreaties might
  Appease his heat, or hastie passage stay;
  For he has vowd, to beene aveng'd that day,
  (That day it selfe him seemed all too long:)
  On him, that did *Pyrochles* deare dismay:
  So proudly pricketh on his courser strong,
And *Atin* aie him pricks with spurs of shame and wrong.

CANT. VI

*Guyon is of immodest Merth
led into loose desire,
Fights with Cymochles, whiles his brother burnes in furious fire.*

I

A HARDER lesson, to learne Continence
  In joyous pleasure, than in grievous paine:
  For sweetnesse doth allure the weaker sence
  So strongly, that uneathes it can refraine
  From that, which feeble nature covets faine;
  But griefe and wrath, that be her enemies,
  And foes of life, she better can restraine;
  Yet vertue vaunts in both their victories,
And *Guyon* in them all shewes goodly maisteries.

2

Whom bold *Cymochles* travelling to find,
  With cruell purpose bent to wreake on him
  The wrath, which *Atin* kindled in his mind,
  Came to a river, by whose utmost brim
  Wayting to passe, he saw whereas did swim
  A long the shore, as swift as glaunce of eye,
  A litle Gondelay, bedecked trim
  With boughes and arbours woven cunningly,
That like a litle forrest seemed outwardly.

3

And therein sate a Ladie fresh and faire,
  Making sweet solace to her selfe alone;
  Sometimes she sung, as loud as larke in aire,
  Sometimes she laught, that nigh her breth was gone,
  Yet was there not with her else any one,
  That might to her move cause of meriment:
  Matter of merth enough, though there were none,
  She could devise, and thousand waies invent,
To feede her foolish humour, and vaine jolliment.

4

Which when farre off *Cymochles* heard, and saw,
 He loudly cald to such, as were a bord,
 The little barke unto the shore to draw,
 And him to ferrie over that deepe ford:
 The merry marriner unto his word
 Soone hearkned, and her painted bote streightway
 Turnd to the shore, where that same warlike Lord
 She in receiv'd; but *Atin* by no way
She would admit, albe the knight her much did pray.

5

Eftsoones her shallow ship away did slide,
 More swift, than swallow sheres the liquid skie,
 Withouten oare or Pilot it to guide,
 Or winged canvas with the wind to flie,
 Only she turn'd a pin, and by and by
 It cut away upon the yielding wave,
 Ne cared she her course for to apply:
 For it was taught the way, which she would have,
And both from rocks and flats it selfe could wisely save.

6

And all the way, the wanton Damzell found
 New merth, her passenger to entertaine:
 For she in pleasant purpose did abound,
 And greatly joyed merry tales to faine,
 Of which a store-house did with her remaine,
 Yet seemed, nothing well they her became;
 For all her words she drownd with laughter vaine,
 And wanted grace in utt'ring of the same,
That turned all her pleasance to a scoffing game.

7

And other whiles vaine toyes she would devize
 As her fantasticke wit did most delight,
 Sometimes her head she fondly would aguize
 With gaudie girlonds, or fresh flowrets dight
 About her necke, or rings of rushes plight;
 Sometimes to doe him laugh, she would assay
 To laugh at shaking of the leaves light,
 Or to behold the water worke, and play
About her litle frigot, therein making way.

8

Her light behaviour, and loose dalliaunce
Gave wondrous great contentment to the knight,
That of his way he had no sovenaunce,
Nor care of vow'd revenge, and cruell fight,
But to weake wench did yeeld his martiall might.
So easie was to quench his flamed mind
With one sweet drop of sensuall delight,
So easie is, t'appease the stormie wind
Of malice in the calme of pleasant womankind.

9

Diverse discourses in their way they spent,
Mongst which *Cymochles* of her questioned,
Both what she was, and what that usage ment,
Which in her cot she daily practised.
Vaine man (said she) that wouldest be reckoned
A straunger in thy home, and ignoraunt
Of *Phædria* (for so my name is red)
Of *Phædria*, thine owne fellow servaunt;
For thou to serve *Acrasia* thy selfe doest vaunt.

10

In this wide Inland sea, that hight by name
The *Idle lake*, my wandring ship I row,
That knowes her port, and thither sailes by ayme,
Ne care, ne feare I, how the wind do blow,
Or whether swift I wend, or whether slow:
Both slow and swift a like do serve my tourne,
Ne swelling *Neptune*, ne loud thundring *Jove*
Can chaunge my cheare, or make me ever mourne;
My litle boat can safely passe this perilous bourne.

11

Whiles thus she talked, and whiles thus she toyd,
They were farre past the passage, which he spake,
And come unto an Island, waste and voyd,
That floted in the midst of that great lake,
There her small Gondelay her port did make,
And that gay paire issuing on the shore
Disburdned her. Their way they forward take
Into the land, that lay them faire before,
Whose pleasaunce she him shew'd, and plentifull great store.

12

It was a chosen plot of fertile land,
　　Emongst wide waves set, like a litle nest,
　　As if it had by Natures cunning hand
　　Bene choisely picked out from all the rest,
　　And laid forth for ensample of the best:
　　No daintie flowre or herbe, that growes on ground,
　　No arboret with painted blossomes drest,
　　And smelling sweet, but there it might be found
To bud out faire, and her sweet smels throw all around.

13

No tree, whose braunches did not bravely spring;
　　No braunch, whereon a fine bird did not sit:
　　No bird, but did her shrill notes sweetly sing;
　　No song but did containe a lovely dit:
　　Trees, braunches, birds, and songs were framed fit,
　　For to allure fraile mind to carelesse ease.
　　Carelesse the man soone woxe, and his weake wit
　　Was overcome of thing, that did him please;
So pleased, did his wrathfull purpose faire appease.

14

Thus when she had his eyes and senses fed
　　With false delights, and fild with pleasures vaine,
　　Into a shadie dale she soft him led,
　　And laid him downe upon a grassie plaine;
　　And her sweet selfe without dread, or disdaine,
　　She set beside, laying his head disarm'd
　　In her loose lap, it softly to sustaine,
　　Where soone he slumbred, fearing not be harm'd,
The whiles with a loud lay she thus him sweetly charm'd.

15

Behold, O man, that toilesome paines doest take,
　　The flowres, the fields, and all that pleasant growes,
　　How they themselves doe thine ensample make,
　　Whiles nothing envious nature them forth throwes
　　Out of her fruitfull lap; how, no man knowes,
　　They spring, they bud, they blossome fresh and faire,
　　And deck the world with their rich pompous showes;
　　Yet no man for them taketh paines or care,
Yet no man to them can his carefull paines compare.

16

The lilly, Ladie of the flowring field,
  The Flowre-deluce, her lovely Paramoure,
  Bid thee to them thy fruitlesse labours yield,
  And soone leave off this toylesome wearie stoure;
  Loe loe how brave she decks her bounteous boure,
  With silken curtens and gold coverlets,
  Therein to shrowd her sumptuous Belamoure,
  Yet neither spinnes nor cardes, ne cares nor frets,
But to her mother Nature all her care she lets.

17

Why then dost thou, O man, that of them all
  Art Lord, and eke of nature Soveraine,
  Wilfully make thy selfe a wretched thrall,
  And wast thy joyous houres in needlesse paine,
  Seeking for daunger and adventures vaine?
  What bootes it all to have, and nothing use?
  Who shall him rew, that swimming in the maine,
  Will die for thirst, and water doth refuse?
Refuse such fruitlesse toile, and present pleasures chuse.

18

By this she had him lulled fast a sleepe,
  That of no worldly thing he care did take;
  Then she with liquors strong his eyes did steepe,
  That nothing should him hastily awake:
  So she him left, and did her selfe betake
  Unto her boat againe, with which she cleft
  The slouthfull wave of that great griesly lake;
  Soone she that Island farre behind her left,
And now is come to that same place, where first she weft.

19

By this time was the worthy *Guyon* brought
  Unto the other side of that wide strond,
  Where she was rowing, and for passage sought:
  Him needed not long call, she soone to hond
  Her ferry brought, where him she byding fond,
  With his sad guide; himselfe she tooke a boord,
  But the *Blacke Palmer* suffred still to stond,
  Ne would for price, or prayers once affoord,
To ferry that old man over the perlous foord.

20

Guyon was loath to leave his guide behind,
  Yet being entred, might not backe retyre;
  For the flit barke, obaying to her mind,
  Forth launched quickly, as she did desire,
  Ne gave him leave to bid that aged sire
  Adieu, but nimbly ran her wonted course
  Through the dull billowes thicke as troubled mire,
  Whom neither wind out of their seat could forse,
Nor timely tides did drive out of their sluggish sourse.

21

And by the way, as was her wonted guize,
  Her merry fit she freshly gan to reare,
  And did of joy and jollitie devize,
  Her selfe to cherish, and her guest to cheare:
  The knight was courteous, and did not forbeare
  Her honest merth and pleasaunce to partake;
  But when he saw her toy, and gibe, and geare,
  And passe the bonds of modest merimake,
Her dalliance he despisd, and follies did forsake.

22

Yet she still followed her former stile,
  And said, and did all that mote him delight,
  Till they arrived in that pleasant Ile,
  Where sleeping late she left her other knight.
  But when as Guyon of that land had sight,
  He wist himselfe amisse, and angry said;
  Ah Dame, perdie ye have not doen me right,
  Thus to mislead me, whiles I you obaid:
Me litle needed from my right way to have straid.

23

Faire Sir (quoth she) be not displeasd at all;
  Who fares on sea, may not commaund his way,
  Ne wind and weather at his pleasure call:
  The sea is wide, and easie for to stray;
  The wind unstable, and doth never stay.
  But here a while ye may in safety rest,
  Till season serve new passage to assay;
  Better safe port, than be in seas distrest.
Therewith she laught, and did her earnest end in jest.

24

But he halfe discontent, mote nathelesse
  Himselfe appease, and issewd forth on shore:
  The joyes whereof, and happie fruitfulnesse,
  Such as he saw, she gan him lay before,
  And all though pleasant, yet she made much more:
  The fields did laugh, the flowres did freshly spring,
  The trees did bud, and earely blossomes bore,
  And all the quire of birds did sweetly sing,
And told that gardins pleasures in their caroling.

25

And she more sweet, than any bird on bough,
  Would oftentimes emongst them beare a part,
  And strive to passe (as she could well enough)
  Their native musicke by her skilfull art:
  So did she all, that might his constant hart
  Withdraw from thought of warlike enterprize,
  And drowne in dissolute delights apart,
  Where noyse of armes, or vew of martiall guize
Might not revive desire of knightly exercize.

26

But he was wise, and warie of her will,
  And ever held his hand upon his hart:
  Yet would not seeme so rude, and thewed ill,
  As to despise so courteous seeming part,
  That gentle Ladie did to him impart,
  But fairely tempring fond desire subdewd,
  And ever her desired to depart.
  She list not heare, but her disports poursewd,
And ever bad him stay, till time the tide renewd.

27

And now by this, *Cymochles* howre was spent,
  That he awoke out of his idle dreme,
  And shaking off his drowzie dreriment,
  Gan him avize, how ill did him beseeme,
  In slouthfull sleepe his molten hart to steme,
  And quench the brond of his conceived ire.
  Tho up he started, stird with shame extreme,
  Ne staied for his Damzell to inquire,
But marched to the strond, there passage to require.

28

And in the way he with Sir *Guyon* met,
　Accompanyde with *Phædria* the faire,
　Eftsoones he gan to rage, and inly fret,
　Crying, Let be that Ladie debonaire,
　Thou recreant knight, and soone thy selfe prepaire
　To battell, if thou meane her love to gaine:
　Loe, loe alreadie, how the fowles in aire
　Doe flocke, awaiting shortly to obtaine
Thy carcasse for their pray, the guerdon of thy paine.

29

And therewithall he fiercely at him flew,
　And with importune outrage him assayld;
　Who soone prepard to field, his sword forth drew,
　And him with equall value countervayld:
　Their mightie strokes their haberjeons dismayld,
　And naked made each others manly spalles;
　The mortall steele despiteously entayld
　Deepe in their flesh, quite through the yron walles,
That a large purple streme adown their giambeux falles.

30

Cymochles, that had never met before
　So puissant foe, with envious despight
　His proud presumed force increased more,
　Disdeigning to be held so long in fight;
　Sir *Guyon* grudging not so much his might,
　As those unknightly raylings, which he spoke,
　With wrathfull fire his courage kindled bright,
　Thereof devising shortly to be wroke,
And doubling all his powres, redoubled every stroke.

31

Both of them high attonce their hands enhaunst,
　And both attonce their huge blowes downe did sway;
　Cymochles sword on *Guyons* shield yglaunst,
　And thereof nigh one quarter sheard away;
　But *Guyons* angry blade so fierce did play
　On th'others helmet, which as *Titan* shone,
　That quite it clove his plumed crest in tway,
　And bared all his head unto the bone;
Wherewith astonisht, still he stood, as senselesse stone.

32

Still as he stood, faire *Phædria*, that beheld
  That deadly daunger, soone atweene them ran;
  And at their feet her selfe most humbly feld,
  Crying with pitteous voice, and count'nance wan;
  Ah well away, most noble Lords, how can
  Your cruell eyes endure so pitteous sight,
  To shed your lives on ground? wo worth the man,
  That first did teach the cursed steele to bight
In his owne flesh, and make way to the living spright.

33

If ever love of Ladie did empierce
  Your yron brestes, or pittie could find place,
  Withhold your bloudie hands from battell fierce,
  And sith for me ye fight, to me this grace
  Both yeeld, to stay your deadly strife a space.
  They stayd a while: and forth she gan proceed:
  Most wretched woman, and of wicked race,
  That am the author of this hainous deed,
And cause of death betweene two doughtie knights doe breed.

34

But if for me ye fight, or me will serve,
  Not this rude kind of battell, nor these armes
  Are meet, the which doe men in bale to sterve,
  And dolefull sorrow heape with deadly harmes:
  Such cruell game my scarmoges disarmes:
  Another warre, and other weapons I
  Doe love, where love does give his sweet alarmes,
  Without bloudshed, and where the enemy
Does yeeld unto his foe a pleasant victory.

35

Debatefull strife, and cruell enmitie
  The famous name of knighthood fowly shend;
  But lovely peace, and gentle amitie,
  And in Amours the passing houres to spend,
  The mightie martiall hands doe most commend:
  Of love they ever greater glory bore,
  Than of their armes: *Mars* is *Cupidoes* frend,
  And is for *Venus* loves renowmed more,
Than all his wars and spoiles, the which he did of yore.

36

Therewith she sweetly smyld. They though full bent
  To prove extremities of bloudie fight,
  Yet at her speach their rages gan relent,
  And calme the sea of their tempestuous spight,
  Such powre have pleasing words: such is the might
  Of courteous clemencie in gentle hart.
  Now after all was ceast, the Faery knight
  Besought that Damzell suffer him depart,
And yield him readie passage to that other part.

37

She no lesse glad, than he desirous was
  Of his departure thence; for of her joy
  And vaine delight she saw he light did pas,
  A foe of folly and immodest toy,
  Still solemne sad, or still disdainfull coy,
  Delighting all in armes and cruell warre,
  That her sweet peace and pleasures did annoy,
  Troubled with terrour and unquiet jarre,
That she well pleased was thence to amove him farre.

38

Tho him she brought abord, and her swift bote
  Forthwith directed to that further strand;
  The which on the dull waves did lightly flote
  And soone arrived on the shallow sand,
  Where gladsome *Guyon* salied forth to land,
  And to that Damzell thankes gave for reward.
  Upon that shore he spied *Atin* stand,
  There by his maister left, when late he far'd
In *Phædrias* flit barke over that perlous shard.

39

Well could he him remember, sith of late
  He with *Pyrochles* sharp debatement made;
  Streight gan he him revile, and bitter rate,
  As shepheards curre, that in darke evenings shade
  Hath tracted forth some salvage beastes trade;
  Vile Miscreant (said he) whither doest thou flie
  The shame and death, which will thee soone invade?
  What coward hand shall doe thee next to die,
That art thus foully fled from famous enemie?

40

With that he stiffely shooke his steelehead dart:
  But sober *Guyon*, hearing him so raile,
  Though somewhat moved in his mightie hart,
  Yet with strong reason maistred passion fraile,
  And passed fairely forth. He turning taile,
  Backe to the strond retyrd, and there still stayd,
  Awaiting passage, which him late did faile;
  The whiles *Cymochles* with that wanton mayd
The hastie heat of his avowd revenge delayd.

41

Whylest there the varlet stood, he saw from farre
  An armed knight, that towards him fast ran,
  He ran on foot, as if in lucklesse warre
  His forlorne steed from him the victour wan;
  He seemed breathlesse, hartlesse, faint, and wan,
  And all his armour sprinckled was with bloud,
  And soyld with durtie gore, that no man can
  Discerne the hew thereof. He never stood,
But bent his hastie course towards the idle flood.

42

The varlet saw, when to the flood he came,
  How without stop or stay he fiercely lept,
  And deepe him selfe beducked in the same,
  That in the lake his loftie crest was steept,
  Ne of his safetie seemed care he kept,
  But with his raging armes he rudely flasht
  The waves about, and all his armour swept,
  That all the bloud and filth away was washt,
Yet still he bet the water, and the billowes dasht.

43

Atin drew nigh, to weet what it mote bee;
  For much he wondred at that uncouth sight;
  Whom should he, but his owne deare Lord, there see,
  His owne deare Lord *Pyrochles*, in sad plight,
  Readie to drowne himselfe for fell despight.
  Harrow now out, and well away, he cryde,
  What dismall day hath lent this cursed light,
  To see my Lord so deadly damnifyde?
Pyrochles, O *Pyrochles*, what is thee betyde?

44

I burne, I burne, I burne, then loud he cryde,
 O how I burne with implacable fire,
 Yet nought can quench mine inly flaming syde,
 Nor sea of licour cold, nor lake of mire,
 Nothing but death can doe me to respire.
 Ah be it (said he) from *Pyrochles* farre
 After pursewing death once to require,
 Or think, that ought those puissant hands may marre:
Death is for wretches borne under unhappie starre.

45

Perdie, then is it fit for me (said he)
 That am, I weene, most wretched man alive,
 Burning in flames, yet no flames can I see,
 And dying daily, daily yet revive:
 O *Atin*, helpe to me last death to give.
 The varlet at his plaint was grieved so sore,
 That his deepe wounded hart in two did rive,
 And his owne health remembring now no more,
Did follow that ensample, which he blam'd afore.

46

Into the lake he lept, his Lord to ayd,
 (So Love the dread of daunger doth despise)
 And of him catching hold him strongly stayd
 From drowning. But more happie he, than wise
 Of that seas nature did him not avise.
 The waves thereof so slow and sluggish were,
 Engrost with mud, which did them foule agrise,
 That every weightie thing they did upbeare,
Ne ought mote ever sinke downe to the bottome there.

47

Whiles thus they strugled in that idle wave,
 And strove in vaine, the one himselfe to drowne,
 The other both from drowning for to save,
 Lo, to that shore one in an auncient gowne,
 Whose hoarie locks great gravitie did crowne,
 Holding in hand a goodly arming sword,
 By fortune came, led with the troublous sowne:
 Where drenched deepe he found in that dull ford
The carefull servant, striving with his raging Lord.

48

Him *Atin* spying, knew right well of yore,
  And loudly cald, Helpe helpe, O *Archimage*;
  To save my Lord, in wretched plight forlore;
  Helpe with thy hand, or with thy counsell sage:
  Weake hands, but counsell is most strong in age.
  Him when the old man saw, he wondred sore,
  To see *Pyrochles* there so rudely rage:
  Yet sithens helpe, he saw, he needed more
Than pittie, he in hast approched to the shore.

49

And cald, *Pyrochles*, what is this, I see?
  What hellish furie hath at earst thee hent?
  Furious ever I thee knew to bee,
  Yet never in this straunge astonishment.
  These flames, these flames (he cryde) do me torment.
  What flames (quoth he) when I thee present see,
  In daunger rather to be drent, than brent?
  Harrow, the flames, which me consume (said hee)
Ne can be quencht, within my secret bowels bee.

50

That cursed man, that cruell feend of hell,
  Furor, oh *Furor* hath me thus bedight:
  His deadly wounds within my livers swell,
  And his whot fire burnes in mine entrails bright,
  Kindled through his infernall brond of spight,
  Sith late with him I batteil vaine would boste;
  That now I weene *Joves* dreaded thunder light
  Does scorch not halfe so sore, nor damned ghoste
In flaming *Phlegeton* does not so felly roste.

51

Which when as *Archimago* heard, his griefe
  He knew right well, and him attonce disarmd:
  Then searcht his secret wounds, and made a priefe
  Of every place, that was with brusing harmd,
  Or with the hidden fire too inly warmd.
  Which done, he balmes and herbes thereto applyde,
  And evermore with mighty spels them charmd,
  That in short space he has them qualifyde,
And him restor'd to health, that would have algates dyde.

CANT. VII

Guyon findes Mammon in a delve,
Sunning his threasure hore:
Is by him tempted, and led downe,
To see his secret store.

1

AS Pilot well expert in perilous wave,
  That to a stedfast starre his course hath bent,
  When foggy mistes, or cloudy tempests have
  The faithfull light of that faire lampe yblent,
  And cover'd heaven with hideous dreriment,
  Upon his card and compas firmes his eye,
  The maisters of his long experiment,
  And to them does the steddy helme apply,
Bidding his winged vessell fairely forward fly:

2

So *Guyon* having lost his trusty guide,
  Late left beyond that *Ydle lake*, proceedes
  Yet on his way, of none accompanide;
  And evermore himselfe with comfort feedes,
  Of his owne vertues, and prayse-worthy deedes.
  So long he yode, yet no adventure found,
  Which fame of her shrill trompet worthy reedes:
  For still he traveild through wide wastfull ground,
That nought but desert wildernesse shew'd all around.

3

At last he came unto a gloomy glade,
  Cover'd with boughes and shrubs from heavens light,
  Whereas he sitting found in secret shade
  An uncouth, salvage, and uncivile wight,
  Of griesly hew, and fowle ill favour'd sight;
  His face with smoke was tand, and eyes were bleard,
  His head and beard with sout were ill bedight,
  His cole-blacke hands did seeme to have beene seard
In smithes fire-spitting forge, and nayles like clawes appeard.

4

His yron coate all overgrowne with rust,
　Was underneath enveloped with gold,
　Whose glistring glosse darkned with filthy dust,
　Well yet appeared, to have beene of old
　A worke of rich entayle, and curious mould,
　Woven with antickes and wild Imagery:
　And in his lap a masse of coyne he told,
　And turned upsidowne, to feede his eye
And covetous desire with his huge threasury.

5

And round about him lay on every side
　Great heapes of gold, that never could be spent:
　Of which some were rude owre, not purifide
　Of *Mulcibers* devouring element;
　Some others were new driven, and distent
　Into great Ingoes, and to wedges square;
　Some in round plates withouten moniment;
　But most were stampt, and in their metall bare
The antique shapes of kings and kesars straunge and rare.

6

Soone as he *Guyon* saw, in great affright
　And hast he rose, for to remove aside
　Those pretious hils from straungers envious sight,
　And downe them poured through an hole full wide,
　Into the hollow earth, them there to hide.
　But *Guyon* lightly to him leaping, stayd
　His hand, that trembled, as one terrifyde;
　And though him selfe were at the sight dismayd,
Yet him perforce restraynd, and to him doubtfull sayd.

7

What art thou man, (if man at all thou art)
　That here in desert hast thine habitaunce,
　And these rich heapes of wealth doest hide apart
　From the worldes eye, and from her right usaunce?
　Thereat with staring eyes fixed askaunce,
　In great disdaine, he answerd; Hardy Elfe,
　That darest vew my direfull countenaunce,
　I read thee rash, and heedlesse of thy selfe,
To trouble my still seate, and heapes of pretious pelfe.

8

God of the world and worldlings I me call,
  Great *Mammon*, greatest god below the skye,
  That of my plenty poure out unto all,
  And unto none my graces do envye:
  Riches, renowme, and principality,
  Honour, estate, and all this worldes good,
  For which men swinck and sweat incessantly,
  Fro me do flow into an ample flood,
And in the hollow earth have their eternall brood.

9

Wherefore if me thou deigne to serve and sew,
  At thy commaund lo all these mountaines bee;
  Of if to thy great mind, or greedy vew
  All these may not suffise, there shall to thee
  Ten times so much be numbred francke and free.
  Mammon (said he) thy godheades vaunt is vaine,
  And idle offers of thy golden fee;
  To them, that covet such eye-glutting gaine,
Proffer thy giftes, and fitter servaunts entertaine.

10

Me ill besits, that in der-doing armes,
  And honours suit my vowed dayes do spend,
  Unto thy bounteous baytes, and pleasing charmes,
  With which weake men thou witchest, to attend:
  Regard of worldly mucke doth fowly blend,
  And low abase the high heroicke spright,
  That joyes for crownes and kingdomes to contend;
  Faire shields, gay steedes, bright armes be my delight:
Those be the riches fit for an advent'rous knight.

11

Vaine glorious Elfe (said he) doest not thou weet,
  That money can thy wantes at will supply?
  Sheilds, steeds, and armes, and all things for thee meet
  It can purvay in twinckling of an eye;
  And crownes and kingdomes to thee multiply.
  Do not I kings create, and throw the crowne
  Sometimes to him, that low in dust doth ly?
  And him that raignd, into his rowme thrust downe,
And whom I lust, do heape with glory and renowne?

12

All otherwise (said he) I riches read,
 And deeme them roote of all disquietnesse;
First got with guile, and then preserv'd with dread,
And after spent with pride and lavishnesse,
Leaving behind them griefe and heavinesse.
Infinite mischiefes of them do arize,
Strife, and debate, bloudshed, and bitternesse,
Outrageous wrong, and hellish covetize,
That noble heart as great dishonour doth despize.

13

Ne thine be kingdomes, ne the scepters thine;
 But realmes and rulers thou doest both confound,
And loyall truth to treason doest incline;
Witnesse the guiltlesse bloud pourd oft on ground,
The crowned often slaine, the slayer cround,
The sacred Diademe in peeces rent,
And purple robe gored with many a wound;
Castles surprizd, great cities sackt and brent:
So mak'st thou kings, and gaynest wrongfull governement.

14

Long were to tell the troublous stormes, that tosse
 The private state, and make the life unsweet:
Who swelling sayles in Caspian sea doth crosse,
And in frayle wood on *Adrian* gulfe doth fleet,
Doth not, I weene, so many evils meet.
Then *Mammon* wexing wroth, And why then, said,
Are mortall men so fond and undiscreet,
So evill thing to seeke unto their ayd,
And having not complaine, and having it upbraid?

15

Indeede (quoth he) through fowle intemperaunce,
 Frayle men are oft captiv'd to covetise:
But would they thinke, with how small allowaunce
Untroubled Nature doth her selfe suffise,
Such superfluities they would despise,
Which with sad cares empeach our native joyes:
At the well head the purest streames arise:
But mucky filth his braunching armes annoyes,
And with uncomely weedes the gentle wave accloyes.

16

The antique world, in his first flowring youth,
　　Found no defect in his Creatours grace,
　　But with glad thankes, and unreproved truth,
　　The gifts of soveraigne bountie did embrace:
　　Like Angels life was then mens happy cace;
　　But later ages pride, like corn-fed steed,
　　Abusd her plenty, and fat swolne encreace
　　To all licentious lust, and gan exceed
The measure of her meane, and naturall first need.

17

Then gan a cursed hand the quiet wombe
　　Of his great Grandmother with steele to wound,
　　And the hid treasures in her sacred tombe,
　　With Sacriledge to dig.　Therein he found
　　Fountaines of gold and silver to abound,
　　Of which the matter of his huge desire
　　And pompous pride eftsoones he did compound;
　　Then avarice gan through his veines inspire
His greedy flames, and kindled life-devouring fire.

18

Sonne (said he then) let be thy bitter scorne,
　　And leave the rudenesse of that antique age
　　To them, that liv'd therein in state forlorne;
　　Thou that doest live in later times, must wage
　　Thy workes for wealth, and life for gold engage.
　　If then thee list my offred grace to use,
　　Take what thou please of all this surplusage;
　　If thee list not, leave have thou to refuse:
But thing refused, do not afterward accuse.

19

Me list not (said the Elfin knight) receave
　　Thing offred, till I know it well be got,
　　Ne wote I, but thou didst these goods bereave
　　From rightfull owner by unrighteous lot,
　　Or that bloud guiltinesse or guile them blot.
　　Perdy (quoth he) yet never eye did vew,
　　Ne toung did tell, ne hand these handled not,
　　But safe I have them kept in secret mew,
From heavens sight, and powre of all which them pursew.

20

What secret place (quoth he) can safely hold
  So huge a masse, and hide from heavens eye?
  Or where hast thou thy wonne, that so much gold
  Thou canst preserve from wrong and robbery?
  Come thou (quoth he) and see. So by and by
  Through that thicke covert he him led, and found
  A darkesome way, which no man could descry,
  That deepe descended through the hollow ground,
And was with dread and horrour compassed around.

21

At length they came into a larger space,
  That stretcht it selfe into an ample plaine,
  Through which a beaten broad high way did trace,
  That streight did lead to *Plutoes* griesly raine:
  By that wayes side, there sate infernall Payne,
  And fast beside him sat tumultuous Strife:
  The one in hand an yron whip did straine,
  The other brandished a bloudy knife,
And both did gnash their teeth, and both did threaten life.

22

On thother side in one consort there sate,
  Cruell Revenge, and rancorous Despight,
  Disloyall Treason, and hart-burning Hate,
  But gnawing Gealosie out of their sight
  Sitting alone, his bitter lips did bight,
  And trembling Feare still to and fro did fly,
  And found no place, where safe he shroud him might,
  Lamenting Sorrow did in darknesse lye,
And Shame his ugly face did hide from living eye.

23

And over them sad Horrour with grim hew,
  Did alwayes sore, beating his yron wings;
  And after him Owles and Night-ravens flew,
  The hatefull messengers of heavy things,
  Of death and dolour telling sad tidings;
  Whiles sad *Celeno*, sitting on a clift,
  A song of bale and bitter sorrow sings,
  That hart of flint a sunder could have rift:
Which having ended, after him she flyeth swift.

24

All these before the gates of *Pluto* lay,
　By whom they passing, spake unto them nought.
　But th'Elfin knight with wonder all the way
　Did feed his eyes, and fild his inner thought.
　At last him to a litle dore he brought,
　That to the gate of Hell, which gaped wide,
　Was next adjoyning, ne them parted ought:
　Betwixt them both was but a litle stride,
That did the house of Richesse from hell-mouth divide.

25

Before the dore sat selfe-consuming Care,
　Day and night keeping wary watch and ward,
　For feare least Force or Fraud should unaware
　Breake in, and spoile the treasure there in gard:
　Ne would he suffer Sleepe once thither-ward
　Approch, albe his drowsie den were next;
　For next to death is Sleepe to be compard:
　Therefore his house is unto his annext;
Here Sleep, there Richesse, and Hel-gate them both betwext.

26

So soone as *Mammon* there arriv'd, the dore
　To him did open, and affoorded way;
　Him followed eke Sir *Guyon* evermore,
　Ne darkenesse him, ne daunger might dismay.
　Soone as he entred was, the dore streight way
　Did shut, and from behind it forth there lept
　An ugly feend, more fowle than dismall day,
　The which with monstrous stalke behind him stept,
And ever as he went, dew watch upon him kept.

27

Well hoped he, ere long that hardy guest,
　If ever covetous hand, or lustfull eye,
　Or lips he layd on thing, that likt him best,
　Or ever sleepe his eye-strings did untye,
　Should be his pray. And therefore still on hye
　He over him did hold his cruell clawes,
　Threatning with greedy gripe to do him dye
　And rend in peeces with his ravenous pawes,
If ever he transgrest the fatall *Stygian* lawes.

28

That houses forme within was rude and strong,
  Like an huge cave, hewne out of rocky clift,
  From whose rough vaut the ragged breaches hong,
  Embost with massy gold of glorious gift,
  And with rich metall loaded every rift,
  That heavy ruine they did seeme to threat;
  And over them *Arachne* high did lift
  Her cunning web, and spred her subtile net,
Enwrapped in fowle smoke and clouds more blacke than Jet.

29

Both roofe, and floore, and wals were all of gold,
  But overgrowne with dust and old decay,
  And hid in darkenesse, that none could behold
  The hew thereof: for vew of chearefull day
  Did never in that house it selfe display,
  But a faint shadow of uncertain light;
  Such as a lamp, whose life does fade away:
  Or as the Moone cloathed with clowdy night,
Does shew to him, that walkes in feare and sad affright.

30

In all that rowme was nothing to be seene,
  But huge great yron chests and coffers strong,
  All bard with double bends, that none could weene
  Them to efforce by violence or wrong;
  On every side they placed were along.
  But all the ground with sculs was scattered,
  And dead mens bones, which round about were flong,
  Whose lives, it seemed, whilome there were shed,
And their vile carcases now left unburied.

31

They forward passe, ne *Guyon* yet spoke word,
  Till that they came unto an yron dore,
  Which to them opened of his owne accord,
  And shewd of richesse such exceeding store,
  As eye of man did never see before;
  Ne ever could within one place be found,
  Though all the wealth, which is, or was of yore,
  Could gathered be through all the world around,
And that above were added to that under ground.

32

The charge thereof unto a covetous Spright
  Commaunded was, who thereby did attend,
  And warily awaited day and night,
  From other covetous feends it to defend,
  Who it to rob and ransacke did intend.
  Then *Mammon* turning to that warriour, said;
  Loe here the worldes blis, loe here the end,
  To which all men do ayme, rich to be made:
Such grace now to be happy, is before thee laid.

33

Certes (said he) I n'ill thine offred grace,
  Ne to be made so happy do intend:
  Another blis before mine eyes I place,
  Another happinesse, another end.
  To them, that list, these base regardes I lend:
  But I in armes, and in atchievements brave,
  Do rather choose my flitting houres to spend,
  And to be Lord of those, that riches have,
Than them to have my selfe, and be their servile sclave.

34

Thereat the feend his gnashing teeth did grate,
  And griev'd, so long to lacke his greedy pray;
  For well he weened, that so glorious bayte
  Would tempt his guest, to take thereof assay:
  Had he so doen, he had him snatcht away,
  More light than Culver in the Faulcons fist.
  Eternall God thee save from such decay.
  But whenas *Mammon* saw his purpose mist,
Him to entrap unwares another way he wist.

35

Thence forward he him led, and shortly brought
  Unto another rowme, whose dore forthright,
  To him did open, as it had beene taught:
  Therein an hundred raunges weren pight,
  And hundred fornaces all burning bright;
  By every fornace many feends did bide,
  Deformed creatures, horrible in sight,
  And every feend his busie paines applide,
To melt the golden metall, ready to be tride.

36

One with great bellowes gathered filling aire,
  And with forst wind the fewell did inflame;
  Another did the dying bronds repaire
  With yron toungs, and sprinckled oft the same
  With liquid waves, fiers *Vulcans* rage to tame,
  Who maistring them, renewd his former heat;
  Some scumd the drosse, that from the metall came;
  Some stird the molten owre with ladles great;
And every one did swincke, and every one did sweat.

37

But when as earthly wight they present saw,
  Glistring in armes and battailous aray,
  From their whot worke they did themselves withdraw
  To wonder at the sight: for till that day,
  They never creature saw, that came that way.
  Their staring eyes sparckling with fervent fire,
  And ugly shapes did nigh the man dismay,
  That were it not for shame, he would retire,
Till that him thus bespake their soveraigne Lord and sire.

38

Behold, thou Faeries sonne, with mortall eye,
  That living eye before did never see:
  The thing, that thou didst crave so earnestly,
  To weet, whence all the wealth late shewd by mee,
  Proceeded, lo now is reveald to thee.
  Here is the fountaine of the worldes good:
  Now therefore, if thou wilt enriched bee,
  Avise thee well, and chaunge thy wilfull mood,
Least thou perhaps hereafter wish, and be withstood.

39

Suffise it then, thou Money God (quoth hee)
  That all thine idle offers I refuse.
  All that I need I have; what needeth mee
  To covet more, than I have cause to use?
  With such vaine shewes thy worldlings vile abuse:
  But give me leave to follow mine emprise.
  Mammon was much displeasd, yet no'te he chuse,
  But beare the rigour of his bold mesprise,
And thence him forward led, him further to entise.

40

He brought him through a darksome narrow strait,
  To a broad gate, all built of beaten gold:
  The gate was open, but therein did wait
  A sturdy villein, striding stiffe and bold,
  As if that highest God defie he would;
  In his right hand an yron club he held,
  But he himselfe was all of golden mould,
  Yet had both life and sence, and well could weld
That cursed weapon, when his cruell foes he queld.

41

Disdayne he called was, and did disdaine
  To be so cald, and who so did him call:
  Sterne was his looke, and full of stomacke vaine,
  His portaunce terrible, and stature tall,
  Far passing th'hight of men terrestriall;
  Like an huge Gyant of the *Titans* race,
  That made him scorne all creatures great and small,
  And with his pride all others powre deface:
More fit amongst blacke fiendes, than men to have his place.

42

Soone as those glitterand armes he did espye,
  That with their brightnesse made that darknesse light,
  His harmefull club he gan to hurtle hye,
  And threaten batteill to the Faery knight;
  Who likewise gan himselfe to batteill dight,
  Till *Mammon* did his hasty hand withhold,
  And counseld him abstaine from perilous fight:
  For nothing might abash the villein bold,
Ne mortall steele emperce his miscreated mould.

43

So having him with reason pacifide,
  And the fiers Carle commaunding to forbeare,
  He brought him in. The rowme was large and wide,
  As it some Gyeld or solemne Temple weare:
  Many great golden pillours did upbeare
  The massy roofe, and riches huge sustayne,
  And every pillour decked was full deare
  With crownes and Diademes, and titles vaine,
Which mortall Princes wore, whiles they on earth did rayne.

44

A route of people there assembled were,
  Of every sort and nation under skye,
  Which with great uprore preaced to draw nere
  To th'upper part, where was advaunced hye
  A stately siege of soveraigne majestye;
  And thereon sat a woman gorgeous gay,
  And richly clad in robes of royaltye,
  That never earthly Prince in such aray
His glory did enhaunce, and pompous pride display.

45

Her face right wondrous faire did seeme to bee,
  That her broad beauties beam great brightnes threw
  Through the dim shade, that all men might it see:
  Yet was not that same her owne native hew,
  But wrought by art and counterfetted shew,
  Thereby more lovers unto her to call;
  Nath'lesse most heavenly faire in deed and vew
  She by creation was, till she did fall;
Thenceforth she sought for helps, to cloke her crime withall.

46

There, as in glistring glory she did sit,
  She held a great gold chaine ylincked well,
  Whose upper end to highest heaven was knit,
  And lower part did reach to lowest Hell;
  And all that preace did round about her swell,
  To catchen hold of that long chaine, thereby
  To clime aloft, and others to excell:
  That was *Ambition*, rash desire to sty,
And every lincke thereof a step of dignity.

47

Some thought to raise themselves to high degree,
  By riches and unrighteous reward,
  Some by close shouldring, some by flatteree;
  Others through friends, others for base regard;
  And all by wrong wayes for themselves prepard.
  Those that were up themselves, kept others low,
  Those that were low themselves, held others hard,
  Ne suffred them to rise or greater grow,
But every one did strive his fellow downe to throw.

48

Which whenas *Guyon* saw, he gan inquire,
  What meant that preace about that Ladies throne,
  And what she was that did so high aspire.
  Him *Mammon* answered; That goodly one,
  Whom all that folke with such contention,
  Do flocke about, my deare, my daughter is;
  Honour and dignitie from her alone
  Derived are, and all this worldes blis
For which ye men do strive: few get, but many mis.

49

And faire *Philotime* she rightly hight,
  The fairest wight that wonneth under skye,
  But that this darksome neather world her light
  Doth dim with horrour and deformitie,
  Worthy of heaven and hye felicitie,
  From whence the gods have her for envy thrust:
  But sith thou hast found favour in mine eye,
  Thy spouse I will her make, if that thou lust,
That she may thee advance for workes and merites just.

50

Gramercy *Mammon* (said the gentle knight)
  For so great grace and offred high estate;
  But I, that am fraile flesh and earthly wight,
  Unworthy match for such immortall mate
  My selfe well wote, and mine unequall fate;
  And were I not, yet is my trouth yplight,
  And love avowd to other Lady late,
  That to remove the same I have no might:
To chaunge love causelesse is reproch to warlike knight.

51

Mammon emmoved was with inward wrath;
  Yet forcing it to faine, him forth thence led
  Through griesly shadowes by a beaten path,
  Into a gardin goodly garnished
  With hearbs and fruits, whose kinds mote not be red:
  Not such, as earth out of her fruitfull woomb
  Throwes forth to men, sweet and well savoured,
  But direfull deadly blacke both leafe and bloom,
Fit to adorne the dead, and decke the drery toombe.

52

There mournfull *Cypresse* grew in greatest store,
   And trees of bitter *Gall*, and *Heben* sad,
   Dead sleeping *Poppy*, and blacke *Hellebore*,
   Cold *Coloquintida*, and *Tetra* mad,
   Mortall *Samnitis*, and *Cicuta* bad,
   With which th'unjust *Atheniens* made to dy
   Wise *Socrates*, who thereof quaffing glad
   Pourd out his life, and last Philosophy
To the faire *Critias* his dearest Belamy.

53

The *Gardin* of *Proserpina* this hight;
   And in the midst thereof a silver seat,
   With a thicke Arber goodly over dight,
   In which she often usd from open heat
   Her selfe to shroud, and pleasures to entreat.
   Next thereunto did grow a goodly tree,
   With braunches broad dispred and body great,
   Clothed with leaves, that none the wood mote see
And loaden all with fruit as thicke as it might bee.

54

Their fruit were golden apples glistring bright,
   That goodly was their glory to behold,
   On earth like never grew, ne living wight
   Like ever saw, but they from hence were sold;
   For those, which *Hercules* with conquest bold
   Got from great *Atlas* daughters, hence began,
   And planted there, did bring forth fruit of gold:
   And those with which th'*Eubæan* young man wan
Swift *Atalanta*, when through craft he her out ran.

55

Here also sprong that goodly golden fruit,
   With which *Acontius* got his lover trew,
   Whom he had long time sought with fruitlesse suit:
   Here eke that famous golden Apple grew,
   The which emongst the gods false *Ate* threw;
   For which th'*Idæan* Ladies disagreed,
   Till partiall *Paris* dempt it *Venus* dew,
   And had of her, faire *Helen* for his meed,
That many noble *Greekes* and *Trojans* made to bleed.

56

The warlike Elfe much wondred at this tree,
  So faire and great, that shadowed all the ground,
  And his broad braunches, laden with rich fee,
  Did stretch themselves without the utmost bound
  Of this great gardin, compast with a mound,
  Which over-hanging, they themselves did steepe,
  In a blacke flood which flow'd about it round;
  That is the river of *Cocytus* deepe,
In which full many soules do endlesse waile and weepe.

57

Which to behold, he clomb up to the banke,
  And looking downe, saw many damned wights,
  In those sad waves, which direfull deadly stanke,
  Plonged continually of cruell Sprights,
  That with their pitteous cryes, and yelling shrights,
  They made the further shore resounden wide:
  Emongst the rest of those same ruefull sights,
  One cursed creature he by chaunce espide,
That drenched lay full deepe, under the Garden side.

58

Deepe was he drenched to the upmost chin,
  Yet gaped still, as coveting to drinke
  Of the cold liquor, which he waded in,
  And stretching forth his hand, did often thinke
  To reach the fruit, which grew upon the brincke:
  But both the fruit from hand, and floud from mouth
  Did flie abacke, and made him vainely swinke:
  The whiles he sterv'd with hunger and with drouth
He daily dyde, yet never throughly dyen couth.

59

The knight him seeing labour so in vaine,
  Askt who he was, and what he ment thereby:
  Who groning deepe, thus answerd him againe;
  Most cursed of all creatures under skye,
  Lo *Tantalus*, I here tormented lye:
  Of whom high *Jove* wont whylome feasted bee,
  Lo here I now for want of food doe dye:
  But if that thou be such, as I thee see,
Of grace I pray thee, give to eat and drinke to mee.

60

Nay, nay, thou greedie *Tantalus* (quoth he)
  Abide the fortune of thy present fate,
  And unto all that live in high degree,
  Ensample be of mind intemperate,
  To teach them how to use their present state.
  Then gan the cursed wretch aloud to cry,
  Accusing highest *Jove* and gods ingrate,
  And eke blaspheming heaven bitterly,
As authour of unjustice, there to let him dye.

61

He lookt a little further, and espyde
  Another wretch, whose carkasse deepe was drent
  Within the river, which the same did hyde:
  But both his hands most filthy feculent,
  Above the water were on high extent,
  And faynd to wash themselves incessantly;
  Yet nothing cleaner were for such intent,
  But rather fowler seemed to the eye;
So lost his labour vaine and idle industry.

62

The knight him calling, asked who he was,
  Who lifting up his head, him answerd thus:
  I *Pilate* am the falsest Judge, alas,
  And most unjust, that by unrighteous
  And wicked doome, to Jewes despiteous
  Delivered up the Lord of life to die,
  And did acquite a murdrer felonous:
  The whiles my hands I washt in puritie,
The whiles my soule was soyld with foule iniquitie.

63

Infinite moe, tormented in like paine
  He there beheld, too long here to be told:
  Ne *Mammon* would there let him long remaine,
  For terrour of the tortures manifold,
  In which the damned soules he did behold,
  But roughly him bespake. Thou fearefull foole,
  Why takest not of that same fruit of gold,
  Ne sittest downe on that same silver stoole,
To rest thy wearie person, in the shadow coole.

64

All which he did, to doe him deadly fall
  In frayle intemperance through sinfull bayt;
  To which if he inclined had at all,
  That dreadfull feend, which did behind him wayt,
  Would him have rent in thousand peeces strayt:
  But he was warie wise in all his way,
  And well perceived his deceiptfull sleight,
  Ne suffred lust his safetie to betray;
So goodly did beguile the Guyler of the pray.

65

And now he has so long remained there,
  That vitall powres gan wexe both weake and wan,
  For want of food, and sleepe, which two upbeare,
  Like mightie pillours, this fraile life of man,
  That none without the same enduren can.
  For now three dayes of men were full outwrought,
  Since he this hardie enterprize began:
  For thy great *Mammon* fairely he besought,
Into the world to guide him backe, as he him brought.

66

The God, though loth, yet was constraind t'obay,
  For lenger time, than that, no living wight
  Below the earth, might suffred be to stay:
  So backe againe, him brought to living light.
  But all so soone as his enfeebled spright
  Gan sucke this vitall aire into his brest,
  As overcome with too exceeding might,
  The life did flit away out of her nest,
And all his senses were with deadly fit opprest.

CANT. VIII

Sir Guyon laid in swowne is by
Acrates sonnes despoyld,
Whom Arthur soone hath reskewed
And Paynim brethren foyld.

I

And is there care in heaven? and is there love
  In heavenly spirits to these creatures bace,
  That may compassion of their evils move?
  There is: else much more wretched were the cace
  Of men, than beasts. But O th'exceeding grace
  Of highest God, that loves his creatures so,
  And all his workes with mercy doth embrace,
  That blessed Angels, he sends to and fro,
To serve to wicked man, to serve his wicked foe.

2

How oft do they, their silver bowers leave,
  To come to succour us, that succour want?
  How oft do they with golden pineons, cleave
  The flitting skyes, like flying Pursuivant,
  Against foule feends to aide us millitant?
  They for us fight, they watch and dewly ward,
  And their bright Squadrons round about us plant,
  And all for love, and nothing for reward:
Ó why should heavenly God to men have such regard?

3

During the while, that *Guyon* did abide
  In *Mammons* house, the Palmer, whom whyleare
  That wanton Mayd of passage had denide,
  By further search had passage found elsewhere,
  And being on his way, approched neare,
  Where *Guyon* lay in traunce, when suddenly
  He heard a voice, that called loud and cleare,
  Come hither, come hither, O come hastily;
That all the fields resounded with the ruefull cry.

4

The Palmer lent his eare unto the noyce,
　To weet, who called so importunely:
Againe he heard a more efforced voyce,
That bad him come in haste. He by and by
His feeble feet directed to the cry;
Which to that shadie delve him brought at last,
Where *Mammon* earst did sunne his threasury:
There the good *Guyon* he found slumbring fast
In senselesse dreame; which sight at first him sore aghast.

5

Beside his head there sate a faire young man,
　Of wondrous beautie, and of freshest yeares,
Whose tender bud to blossome new began,
And flourish faire above his equall peares;
His snowy front curled with golden heares,
Like *Phœbus* face adornd with sunny rayes,
Divinely shone, and two sharpe winged sheares,
Decked with diverse plumes, like painted Jayes,
Were fixed at his backe, to cut his ayerie wayes.

6

Like as *Cupido* on *Idæan* hill,
　When having laid his cruell bow away,
And mortall arrowes, wherewith he doth fill
The world with murdrous spoiles and bloudie pray,
With his faire mother he him dights to play,
And with his goodly sisters, *Graces* three;
The Goddesse pleased with his wanton play,
Suffers her selfe through sleepe beguild to bee,
The whiles the other Ladies mind their merry glee.

7

Whom when the Palmer saw, abasht he was
　Through fear and wonder, that he nought could say,
Till him the child bespoke, Long lackt, alas,
Hath bene thy faithfull aide in hard assay,
Whiles deadly fit thy pupill doth dismay;
Behold this heavie sight, thou reverend Sire,
But dread of death and dolour doe away;
For life ere long shall to her home retire,
And he that breathlesse seemes, shal corage bold respire.

8

The charge, which God doth unto me arret,
  Of his deare safetie, I to thee commend;
  Yet will I not forgoe, ne yet forget
  The care thereof my selfe unto the end,
  But evermore him succour, and defend
  Against his foe and mine: watch thou I pray;
  For evill is at hand him to offend.
  So having said, eftsoones he gan display
His painted nimble wings, and vanisht quite away.

9

The Palmer seeing his left empty place,
  And his slow eyes beguiled of their sight,
  Woxe sore affraid, and standing still a space,
  Gaz'd after him, as fowle escapt by flight;
  At last him turning to his charge behight,
  With trembling hand his troubled pulse gan try;
  Where finding life not yet dislodged quight,
  He much rejoyst, and courd it tenderly,
As chicken newly hatcht, from dreaded destiny.

10

At last he spide, where towards him did pace
  Two Paynim knights, all armd as bright as skie,
  And them beside an aged Sire did trace,
  And farre before a light-foot Page did flie,
  That breathed strife and troublous enmitie;
  Those were the two sonnes of *Acrates* old,
  Who meeting earst with *Archimago* slie,
  Foreby that idle strond, of him were told,
That he, which earst them combatted, was *Guyon* bold.

11

Which to avenge on him they dearely vowd,
  Where ever that on ground they mote him fynd;
  False *Archimage* provokt their courage prowd,
  And stryfull *Atin* in their stubborne mynd
  Coles of contention and whot vengeance tynd.
  Now bene they come, whereas the Palmer sate,
  Keeping that slombred corse to him assynd;
  Well knew they both his person, sith of late
With him in bloudie armes they rashly did debate.

12

Whom when *Pyrochles* saw, inflam'd with rage,
  That sire he foule bespake, Thou dotard vile,
  That with thy brutenesse shendst thy comely age,
  Abandone soone, I read, the caitive spoile
  Of that same outcast carkasse, that erewhile
  Made it selfe famous through false trechery,
  And crownd his coward crest with knightly stile;
  Loe where he now inglorious doth lye,
To prove he lived ill, that did thus foully dye.

13

To whom the Palmer fearelesse answered;
  Certes, Sir knight, ye bene too much to blame,
  Thus for to blot the honour of the dead,
  And with foule cowardize his carkasse shame,
  Whose living hands immortalizd his name.
  Vile is the vengeance on the ashes cold,
  And envie base, to barke at sleeping fame:
  Was never wight, that treason of him told;
Your selfe his prowesse prov'd and found him fiers and bold.

14

Then said *Cymochles*; Palmer, thou doest dote,
  Ne canst of prowesse, ne of knighthood deeme,
  Save as thou seest or hearst. But well I wote,
  That of his puissance tryall made extreeme;
  Yet gold all is not, that doth golden seeme,
  Ne all good knights, that shake well speare and shield:
  The worth of all men by their end esteeme,
  And then due praise, or due reproch them yield;
Bad therefore I him deeme, that thus lies dead on field.

15

Good or bad (gan his brother fierce reply)
  What doe I recke, sith that he dyde entire?
  Or what doth his bad death now satisfy
  The greedy hunger of revenging ire,
  Sith wrathfull hand wrought not her owne desire?
  Yet since no way is left to wreake my spight,
  I will him reave of armes, the victors hire,
  And of that shield, more worthy of good knight;
For why should a dead dog be deckt in armour bright?

16

Faire Sir, said then the Palmer suppliaunt,
  For knighthoods love, do not so foule a deed,
  Ne blame your honour with so shamefull vaunt
  Of vile revenge. To spoile the dead of weed
  Is sacrilege, and doth all sinnes exceed;
  But leave these relicks of his living might,
  To decke his herce, and trap his tomb-blacke steed.
  What herce or steed (said he) should he have dight,
But be entombed in the raven or the kight?

17

With that, rude hand upon his shield he laid,
  And th'other brother gan his helme unlace,
  Both fiercely bent to have him disaraid;
  Till that they spide, where towards them did pace
  An armed knight, of bold and bounteous grace,
  Whose squire bore after him an heben launce,
  And coverd shield. Well kend him so farre space
  Th'enchaunter by his armes and amenaunce,
When under him he saw his Lybian steed to praunce.

18

And to those brethren said, Rise rise by live,
  And unto battell doe your selves addresse;
  For yonder comes the prowest knight alive,
  Prince *Arthur*, flowre of grace and nobilesse,
  That hath to Paynim knights wrought great distresse,
  And thousand Sar'zins foully donne to dye.
  That word so deepe did in their harts impresse,
  That both eftsoones upstarted furiously,
And gan themselves prepare to battell greedily.

19

But fierce *Pyrochles*, lacking his owne sword,
  The want thereof now greatly gan to plaine,
  And *Archimage* besought, him that afford,
  Which he had brought for *Braggadocchio* vaine.
  So would I (said th'enchaunter) glad and faine
  Beteeme to you this sword, you to defend,
  Or ought that else your honour might maintaine,
  But that this weapons powre I well have kend,
To be contrarie to the worke, which ye intend.

20

For that same knights owne sword this is of yore,
  Which *Merlin* made by his almightie art
  For that his noursling, when he knighthood swore,
  Therewith to doen his foes eternall smart.
  The metall first he mixt with *Medæwart*,
  That no enchauntment from his dint might save;
  Then it in flames of *Aetna* wrought apart,
  And seven times dipped in the bitter wave
Of hellish *Styx*, which hidden vertue to it gave.

21

The vertue is, that neither steele, nor stone
  The stroke thereof from entrance may defend;
  Ne ever may be used by his fone,
  Ne forst his rightfull owner to offend,
  Ne ever will it breake, ne ever bend.
  Wherefore *Morddure* it rightfully is hight.
  In vaine therefore, *Pyrochles*, should I lend
  The same to thee, against his lord to fight,
For sure it would deceive thy labour, and thy might.

22

Foolish old man, said then the Pagan wroth,
  That weenest words or charmes may force withstond:
  Soone shalt thou see, and then beleeve for troth,
  That I can carve with this inchaunted brond
  His Lords owne flesh. Therewith out of his hond
  That vertuous steele he rudely snatcht away,
  And *Guyons* shield about his wrest he bond;
  So readie dight, fierce battaile to assay,
And match his brother proud in battailous array.

23

By this that straunger knight in presence came,
  And goodly salued them; who nought againe
  Him answered, as courtesie became,
  But with sterne lookes, and stomachous disdaine,
  Gave signes of grudge and discontentment vaine:
  Then turning to the Palmer, he gan spy
  Where at his feete, with sorrowfull demaine
  And deadly hew, an armed corse did lye,
In whose dead face he red great magnanimity.

Arthur fights Pyrochles and Cymochles

24

Said he then to the Palmer, Reverend syre,
  What great misfortune hath betidd this knight?
  Or did his life her fatall date expyre,
  Or did he fall by treason, or by fight?
  How ever, sure I rew his pitteous plight.
  Not one, nor other, (said the Palmer grave)
  Hath him befalne, but cloudes of deadly night
  A while his heavie eylids cover'd have,
And all his senses drowned in deepe senselesse wave.

25

Which, those his cruell foes, that stand hereby,
  Making advantage, to revenge their spight,
  Would him disarme, and treaten shamefully,
  Unworthy usage of redoubted knight.
  But you, faire Sir, whose honorable sight
  Doth promise hope of helpe, and timely grace,
  Mote I beseech to succour his sad plight,
  And by your powre protect his feeble cace.
First praise of knighthood is, foule outrage to deface.

26

Palmer, (said he) no knight so rude, I weene,
  As to doen outrage to a sleeping ghost:
  Ne was there ever noble courage seene,
  That in advauntage would his puissance bost:
  Honour is least, where oddes appeareth most.
  May be, that better reason will asswage
  The rash revengers heat. Words well dispost
  Have secret powre, t'appease inflamed rage:
If not, leave unto me thy knights last patronage.

27

Tho turning to those brethren, thus bespoke,
  Ye warlike payre, whose valorous great might
  It seemes, just wrongs to vengeance doe provoke,
  To wreake your wrath on this dead seeming knight,
  Mote ought allay the storme of your despight,
  And settle patience in so furious heat?
  Not to debate the chalenge of your right,
  But for this carkasse pardon I entreat,
Whom fortune hath alreadie laid in lowest seat.

28

To whom *Cymochles* said; For what art thou,
  That mak'st thy selfe his dayes-man, to prolong
  The vengeance prest? Or who shall let me now,
  On this vile bodie from to wreake my wrong,
  And make his carkasse as the outcast dong?
  Why should not that dead carrion satisfie
  The guilt, which if he lived had thus long,
  His life for due revenge should deare abie?
The trespasse still doth live, albe the person die.

29

Indeed (then said the Prince) the evill donne
  Dyes not, when breath the bodie first doth leave,
  But from the grandsyre to the Nephewes sonne,
  And all his seed the curse doth often cleave,
  Till vengeance utterly the guilt bereave:
  So streightly God doth judge. But gentle knight,
  That doth against the dead his hand upreare,
  His honour staines with rancour and despight,
And great disparagment makes to his former might.

30

Pyrochles gan reply the second time,
  And to him said, Now felon sure I read,
  How that thou art partaker of his crime:
  Therefore by *Termagaunt* thou shalt be dead.
  With that his hand, more sad than lomp of lead,
  Uplifting high, he weened with *Morddure*,
  His owne good sword *Morddure*, to cleave his head.
  The faithfull steele such treason no'uld endure,
But swarving from the marke, his Lords life did assure.

31

Yet was the force so furious and so fell,
  That horse and man it made to reele aside;
  Nath'lesse the Prince would not forsake his sell:
  For well of yore he learned had to ride,
  But full of anger fiercely to him cride;
  False traitour miscreant, thou broken hast
  The law of armes, to strike foe undefide.
  But thou thy treasons fruit, I hope, shalt taste
Right sowre, and feele the law, the which thou hast defast.

32

With that his balefull speare he fiercely bent
  Against the Pagans brest, and therewith thought
  His cursed life out of her lodge have rent:
  But ere the point arrived, where it ought,
  That seven-fold shield, which he from *Guyon* brought
  He cast betwene to ward the bitter stound:
  Through all those foldes the steelehead passage wrought
  And through his shoulder pierst; wherwith to ground
He groveling fell, all gored in his gushing wound.

33

Which when his brother saw, fraught with great griefe
  And wrath, he to him leaped furiously,
  And fowly said, By *Mahoune*, cursed thiefe,
  That direfull stroke thou dearely shalt aby.
  Then hurling up his harmefull blade on hye,
  Smote him so hugely on his haughtie crest,
  That from his saddle forced him to fly:
  Else mote it needes downe to his manly brest
Have cleft his head in twaine, and life thence dispossest.

34

Now was the Prince in daungerous distresse,
  Wanting his sword, when he on foot should fight:
  His single speare could doe him small redresse,
  Against two foes of so exceeding might,
  The least of which was match for any knight.
  And now the other, whom he earst did daunt,
  Had reard himselfe againe to cruell fight,
  Three times more furious, and more puissaunt,
Unmindfull of his wound, of his fate ignoraunt.

35

So both attonce him charge on either side,
  With hideous strokes, and importable powre,
  That forced him his ground to traverse wide,
  And wisely watch to ward that deadly stowre:
  For in his shield, as thicke as stormie showre,
  Their strokes did raine, yet did he never quaile,
  Ne backward shrinke, but as a stedfast towre,
  Whom foe with double battry doth assaile,
Them on her bulwarke beares, and bids them nought availe.

36

So stoutly he withstood their strong assay,
  Till that at last, when he advantage spyde,
His poinant speare he thrust with puissant sway
At proud *Cymochles*, whiles his shield was wyde,
That through his thigh the mortall steele did gryde:
He swarving with the force, within his flesh
Did breake the launce, and let the head abyde:
Out of the wound the red bloud flowed fresh,
That underneath his feet soone made a purple plesh.

37

Horribly then he gan to rage, and rayle,
  Cursing his Gods, and himselfe damning deepe:
Als when his brother saw the red bloud rayle
Adowne so fast, and all his armour steepe,
For very felnesse lowd he gan to weepe,
And said, Caytive, cursse on thy cruell hond,
That twise hath sped; yet shall it not thee keepe
From the third brunt of this my fatall brond:
Loe where the dreadfull Death behind thy backe doth stond.

38

With that he strooke, and th'other strooke withall,
  That nothing seem'd mote beare so monstrous might:
The one upon his covered shield did fall,
And glauncing downe would not his owner byte:
But th'other did upon his troncheon smyte,
Which hewing quite a sunder, further way
It made, and on his hacqueton did lyte,
The which dividing with importune sway,
It seizd in his right side, and there the dint did stay.

39

Wyde was the wound, and a large lukewarme flood,
  Red as the Rose, thence gushed grievously;
That when the Paynim spyde the streaming blood,
Gave him great hart, and hope of victory.
On th'other side, in huge perplexity,
The Prince now stood, having his weapon broke;
Nought could he hurt, but still at ward did ly:
Yet with his troncheon he so rudely stroke
Cymochles twise, that twise him forst his foot revoke.

40

Whom when the Palmer saw in such distresse,
  Sir *Guyons* sword he lightly to him raught,
  And said; Faire Son, great God thy right hand blesse,
  To use that sword so wisely as it ought.
  Glad was the knight, and with fresh courage fraught,
  When as againe he armed felt his hond;
  Then like a Lion, which hath long time saught
  His robbed whelpes, and at the last them fond
Emongst the shepheard swaynes, then wexeth wood and yond.

41

So fierce he laid about him, and dealt blowes
  On either side, that neither mayle could hold,
  Ne shield defend the thunder of his throwes:
  Now to *Pyrochles* many strokes he told;
  Eft to *Cymochles* twise so many fold:
  Then backe againe turning his busie hond,
  Them both attonce compeld with courage bold,
  To yield wide way to his hart-thrilling brond;
And though they both stood stiffe, yet could not both withstond.

42

As salvage Bull, whom two fierce mastives bayt,
  When rancour doth with rage him once engore,
  Forgets with warie ward them to awayt,
  But with his dreadfull hornes them drives afore,
  Or flings aloft, or treads downe in the flore,
  Breathing out wrath, and bellowing disdaine,
  That all the forrest quakes to heare him rore:
  So rag'd Prince *Arthur* twixt his foemen twaine,
That neither could his mightie puissance sustaine.

43

But ever at *Pyrochles* when he smit,
  Who *Guyons* shield cast ever him before,
  Whereon the Faery Queenes pourtract was writ,
  His hand relented, and the stroke forbore,
  And his deare hart the picture gan adore,
  Which oft the Paynim sav'd from deadly stowre.
  But him henceforth the same can save no more;
  For now arrived is his fatall howre,
That no'te avoyded be by earthly skill or powre.

44

For when *Cymochles* saw the fowle reproch,
  Which them appeached, prickt with guilty shame,
  And inward griefe, he fiercely gan approch,
  Resolv'd to put away that loathly blame,
  Or dye with honour and desert of fame;
  And on the hauberk stroke the Prince so sore,
  That quite disparted all the linked frame,
  And pierced to the skin, but bit no more,
Yet made him twise to reele, that never moov'd afore.

45

Whereat renfierst with wrath and sharpe regret,
  He stroke so hugely with his borrowd blade,
  That it empierst the Pagans burganet,
  And cleaving the hard steele, did deepe invade
  Into his head, and cruell passage made
  Quite through his braine. He tombling downe on ground,
  Breathd out his ghost, which to th'infernall shade
  Fast flying, there eternall torment found,
For all the sinnes, wherewith his lewd life did abound.

46

Which when his german saw, the stony feare
  Ran to his hart, and all his sence dismayd,
  Ne thenceforth life ne courage did appeare,
  But as a man, whom hellish feends have frayd,
  Long trembling still he stood: at last thus sayd;
  Traytour what hast thou doen? how ever may
  Thy cursed hand so cruelly have swayd
  Against that knight: Harrow and well away,
After so wicked deed why liv'st thou lenger day?

47

With that all desperate as loathing light,
  And with revenge desiring soone to dye,
  Assembling all his force and utmost might,
  With his owne sword he fierce at him did flye,
  And strooke, and foynd, and lasht outrageously,
  Withouten reason or regard. Well knew
  The Prince, with patience and sufferaunce sly
  So hasty heat soone cooled to subdew:
Tho when this breathlesse woxe, that batteil gan renew.

48

As when a windy tempest bloweth hye,
  That nothing may withstand his stormy stowre,
  The cloudes, as things affrayd, before him flye;
  But all so soone as his outrageous powre
  Is layd, they fiercely then begin to shoure,
  And as in scorne of his spent stormy spight,
  Now all attonce their malice forth do poure;
  So did Prince *Arthur* beare himselfe in fight,
And suffred rash *Pyrochles* wast his idle might.

49

At last when as the Sarazin perceiv'd,
  How that straunge sword refusd, to serve his need,
  But when he stroke most strong, the dint deceiv'd,
  He flong it from him, and devoyd of dreed,
  Upon him lightly leaping without heed,
  Twixt his two mighty armes engrasped fast,
  Thinking to overthrow and downe him tred:
  But him in strength and skill the Prince surpast,
And through his nimble sleight did under him down cast.

50

Nought booted it the Paynim then to strive;
  For as a Bittur in the Eagles claw,
  That may not hope by flight to scape alive,
  Still waites for death with dread and trembling aw;
  So he now subject to the victours law,
  Did not once move, nor upward cast his eye,
  For vile disdaine and rancour, which did gnaw
  His hart in twaine with sad melancholy,
As one that loathed life, and yet despisd to dye.

51

But full of Princely bounty and great mind,
  The Conquerour nought cared him to slay,
  But casting wrongs and all revenge behind,
  More glory thought to give life, than decay,
  And said, Paynim, this is thy dismall day;
  Yet if thou wilt renounce thy miscreaunce,
  And my trew liegeman yield thy selfe for ay,
  Life will I graunt thee for thy valiaunce,
And all thy wrongs will wipe out of my sovenaunce.

52

Foole (said the Pagan) I thy gift defye,
  But use thy fortune, as it doth befall,
  And say, that I not overcome do dye,
  But in despight of life, for death do call.
  Wroth was the Prince, and sory yet withall,
  That he so wilfully refused grace;
  Yet sith his fate so cruelly did fall,
  His shining Helmet he gan soone unlace,
And left his headlesse body bleeding all the place.

53

By this Sir *Guyon* from his traunce awakt,
  Life having maistered her sencelesse foe;
  And looking up, when as his shield he lakt,
  And sword saw not, he wexed wondrous woe:
  But when the Palmer, whom he long ygoe
  Had lost, he by him spide, right glad he grew,
  And said, Deare sir, whom wandring to and fro
  I long have lackt, I joy thy face to vew;
Firme is thy faith, whom daunger never fro me drew.

54

But read what wicked hand hath robbed mee
  Of my good sword and shield? The Palmer glad,
  With so fresh hew uprising him to see,
  Him answered; Faire sonne, be no whit sad
  For want of weapons, they shall soone be had.
  So gan he to discourse the whole debate,
  Which that straunge knight for him sustained had,
  And those two Sarazins confounded late,
Whose carcases on ground were horribly prostrate.

55

Which when he heard, and saw the tokens trew,
  His hart with great affection was embayd,
  And to the Prince bowing with reverence dew,
  As to the Patrone of his life, thus sayd;
  My Lord, my liege, by whose most gratious ayd
  I live this day, and see my foes subdewd,
  What may suffise, to be for meede repayd
  Of so great graces, as ye have me shewd,
But to be ever bound

56

To whom the Infant thus, Faire Sir, what need
  Good turnes be counted, as a servile bond,
  To bind their doers, to receive their meede?
  Are not all knights by oath bound, to withstond
  Oppressours powre by armes and puissant hond?
  Suffise, that I have done my dew in place.
  So goodly purpose they together fond,
  Of kindnesse and of curteous aggrace;
The whiles false *Archimage* and *Atin* fled apace.

CANT. IX

*The house of Temperance, in which
doth sober Alma dwell,
Besiegd of many foes, whom straunger
knightes to flight compell.*

I

Of all Gods workes, which do this world adorne,
  There is no one more faire and excellent,
  Than is mans body both for powre and forme,
  Whiles it is kept in sober government;
  But none than it, more fowle and indecent,
  Distempred through misrule and passions bace:
  It growes a Monster, and incontinent
  Doth loose his dignitie and native grace.
Behold, who list, both one and other in this place.

2

After the Paynim brethren conquer'd were,
  The *Briton* Prince recov'ring his stolne sword,
  And *Guyon* his lost shield, they both yfere
  Forth passed on their way in faire accord,
  Till him the Prince with gentle court did bord;
  Sir knight, mote I of you this curt'sie read,
  To weet why on your shield so goodly scord
  Beare ye the picture of that Ladies head?
Full lively is the semblaunt, though the substance dead.

3

Faire Sir (said he) if in that picture dead
  Such life ye read, and vertue in vaine shew,
  What mote ye weene, if the trew lively-head
  Of that most glorious visage ye did vew?
  But if the beautie of her mind ye knew,
  That is her bountie, and imperiall powre,
  Thousand times fairer than her mortall hew,
  O how great wonder would your thoughts devoure,
And infinite desire into your spirite poure!

4

She is the mighty Queene of *Faerie*,
  Whose faire retrait I in my shield do beare;
  She is the flowre of grace and chastitie,
  Throughout the world renowmed far and neare,
  My liefe, my liege, my Soveraigne, my deare,
  Whose glory shineth as the morning starre,
  And with her light the earth enlumines cleare;
  Far reach her mercies, and her prayses farre,
As well in state of peace, as puissaunce in warre.

5

Thrise happy man, (said then the *Briton* knight)
  Whom gracious lot, and thy great valiaunce
  Have made thee souldier of that Princesse bright,
  Which with her bounty and glad countenance
  Doth blesse her servaunts, and them high advaunce.
  How may straunge knight hope ever to aspire,
  By faithfull service, and meet amenance,
  Unto such blisse? sufficient were that hire
For losse of thousand lives, to dye at her desire.

6

Said *Guyon*, Noble Lord, what meed so great,
  Or grace of earthly Prince so soveraine,
  But by your wondrous worth and warlike feat
  Ye well may hope, and easely attaine?
  But were your will, her sold to entertaine,
  And numbred be mongst knights of *Maydenhed*,
  Great guerdon, well I wote, should you remaine,
  And in her favour high be reckoned,
As *Arthegall*, and *Sophy* now beene honored.

7

Certes (then said the Prince) I God avow,
  That sith I armes and knighthood first did plight,
  My whole desire hath beene, and yet is now,
  To serve that Queene with all my powre and might.
  Now hath the Sunne with his lamp-burning light,
  Walkt round about the world, and I no lesse,
  Sith of that Goddesse I have sought the sight,
  Yet no where can her find: such happinesse
Heaven doth to me envy, and fortune favourlesse.

8

Fortune, the foe of famous chevisaunce
  Seldome (said *Guyon*) yields to vertue aide,
  But in her way throwes mischiefe and mischaunce,
  Whereby her course is stopt, and passage staid.
  But you, faire Sir, be not herewith dismaid,
  But constant keepe the way, in which ye stand;
  Which were it not, that I am else delaid
  With hard adventure, which I have in hand,
I labour would to guide you through all Faery land.

9

Gramercy Sir (said he) but mote I weete,
  What straunge adventure do ye now pursew?
  Perhaps my succour, or advizement meete
  Mote stead you much your purpose to subdew.
  Then gan Sir *Guyon* all the story shew
  Of false *Acrasia*, and her wicked wiles,
  Which to avenge, the Palmer him forth drew
  From Faery court. So talked they, the whiles
They wasted had much way, and measurd many miles.

10

And now faire *Phœbus* gan decline in hast
  His weary wagon to the Westerne vale,
  Whenas they spide a goodly castle, plast
  Foreby a river in a pleasaunt dale,
  Which choosing for that evenings hospitale,
  They thither marcht: but when they came in sight,
  And from their sweaty Coursers did avale,
  They found the gates fast barred long ere night,
And every loup fast lockt, as fearing foes despight.

11

Which when they saw, they weened fowle reproch
  Was to them doen, their entrance to forstall,
  Till that the Squire gan nigher to approch;
  And wind his horne under the castle wall,
  That with the noise it shooke, as it would fall:
  Eftsoones forth looked from the highest spire
  The watch, and lowd unto the knights did call,
  To weete, what they so rudely did require.
Who gently answered, They entrance did desire.

12

Fly fly, good knights, (said he) fly fast away
  If that your lives ye love, as meete ye should;
  Fly fast, and save your selves from neare decay,
  Here may ye not have entraunce, though we would:
  We would and would againe, if that we could;
  But thousand enemies about us rave,
  And with long siege us in this castle hould:
  Seven yeares this wize they us besieged have,
And many good knights slaine, that have us sought to save.

13

Thus as he spoke, loe with outragious cry
  A thousand villeins round about them swarmd
  Out of the rockes and caves adjoyning nye,
  Vile caytive wretches, ragged, rude, deformd,
  All threatning death, all in straunge manner armd,
  Some with unweldy clubs, some with long speares,
  Some rusty knives, some staves in fire warmd.
  Sterne was their looke, like wild amazed steares,
Staring with hollow eyes, and stiffe upstanding heares.

14

Fiersly at first those knights they did assaile,
  And drove them to recoile: but when againe
  They gave fresh charge, their forces gan to faile,
  Unhable their encounter to sustaine;
  For with such puissaunce and impetuous maine
  Those Champions broke on them, that forst them fly,
  Like scattered Sheepe, whenas the Shepheards swaine
  A Lyon and a Tigre doth espye,
With greedy pace forth rushing from the forest nye.

15

A while they fled, but soone returnd againe
  With greater fury, than before was found;
  And evermore their cruell Capitaine
  Sought with his raskall routs t'enclose them round,
  And overrun to tread them to the ground.
  But soone the knights with their bright-burning blades
  Broke their rude troupes, and orders did confound,
  Hewing and slashing at their idle shades;
For though they bodies seeme, yet substance from them fades.

16

As when a swarme of Gnats at eventide
  Out of the fennes of Allan do arise,
  Their murmuring small trompets sounden wide,
  Whiles in the aire their clustring army flies,
  That as a cloud doth seeme to dim the skies;
  Ne man nor beast may rest, or take repast,
  For their sharpe wounds, and noyous injuries,
  Till the fierce Northerne wind with blustring blast
Doth blow them quite away, and in the *Ocean* cast.

17

Thus when they had that troublous rout disperst,
  Unto the castle gate they come againe,
  And entraunce crav'd, which was denied erst.
  Now when report of that their perilous paine,
  And combrous conflict, which they did sustaine,
  Came to the Ladies eare, which there did dwell,
  She forth issewed with a goodly traine
  Of Squires and Ladies equipaged well,
And entertained them right fairely, as befell.

18

Alma she called was, a virgin bright;
  That had not yet felt *Cupides* wanton rage,
  Yet was she woo'd of many a gentle knight,
  And many a Lord of noble parentage,
  That sought with her to lincke in marriage:
  For she was faire, as faire mote ever bee,
  And in the flowre now of her freshest age;
  Yet full of grace and goodly modestee,
That even heaven rejoyced her sweete face to see.

19

In robe of lilly white she was arayd,
  That from her shoulder to her heele downe raught,
  The traine whereof loose far behind her strayd,
  Braunched with gold and pearle, most richly wrought,
  And borne of two faire Damsels, which were taught
  That service well. Her yellow golden heare
  Was trimly woven, and in tresses wrought,
  Ne other tyre she on her head did weare,
But crowned with a garland of sweete Rosiere.

20

Goodly she entertaind those noble knights,
  And brought them up into her castle hall;
  Where gentle court and gracious delight
  She to them made, with mildnesse virginall,
  Shewing her selfe both wise and liberall:
  There when they rested had a season dew,
  They her besought of favour speciall,
  Of that faire Castle to affoord them vew;
She graunted, and them leading forth, the same did shew.

21

First she them led up to the Castle wall,
  That was so high, as foe might not it clime,
  And all so faire, and fensible withall,
  Not built of bricke, ne yet of stone and lime,
  But of thing like to that *Ægyptian* slime,
  Whereof king *Nine* whilome built *Babell* towre;
  But O great pitty, that no lenger time
  So goodly workemanship should not endure:
Soone it must turne to earth; no earthly thing is sure.

22

The frame thereof seemd partly circulare,
  And part triangulare, O worke divine;
  Those two the first and last proportions are,
  The one imperfect, mortall, fœminine;
  Th'other immortall, perfect, masculine,
  And twixt them both a quadrate was the base
  Proportioned equally by seven and nine;
  Nine was the circle set in heavens place,
All which compacted made a goodly diapase.

23

Therein two gates were placed seemly well:
  The one before, by which all in did pas,
  Did th'other far in workmanship excell;
  For not of wood, nor of enduring bras,
  But of more worthy substance fram'd it was;
  Doubly disparted, it did locke and close,
  That when it locked, none might thorough pas,
  And when it opened, no man might it close,
Still open to their friends, and closed to their foes.

24

Of hewen stone the porch was fairely wrought,
  Stone more of valew, and more smooth and fine,
  Than Jet or Marble far from Ireland brought;
  Over the which was cast a wandring vine,
  Enchaced with a wanton yvie twine.
  And over it a faire Portcullis hong,
  Which to the gate directly did incline,
  With comely compasse, and compacture strong,
Neither unseemely short, nor yet exceeding long.

25

Within the Barbican a Porter sate,
  Day and night duely keeping watch and ward,
  Nor wight, nor word mote passe out of the gate,
  But in good order, and with dew regard;
  Utterers of secrets he from thence debard,
  Bablers of folly, and blazers of crime.
  His larumbell might lowd and wide be hard,
  When cause requird, but never out of time;
Early and late it rong, at evening and at prime.

26

And round about the porch on every side
  Twise sixteen warders sat, all armed bright
  In glistring steele, and strongly fortifide:
  Tall yeomen seemed they, and of great might,
  And were enraunged ready, still for fight.
  By them as *Alma* passed with her guestes,
  They did obeysaunce, as beseemed right,
  And then againe returned to their restes:
The Porter eke to her did lout with humble gestes.

27

Thence she them brought into a stately Hall,
  Wherein were many tables faire dispred,
  And ready dight with drapets festivall,
  Against the viaundes should be ministred,
  At th'upper end there sate, yclad in red
  Downe to the ground, a comely personage,
  That in his hand a white rod menaged,
  He Steward was hight *Diet*; rype of age,
And in demeanure sober, and in counsell sage.

28

And through the Hall there walked to and fro
  A jolly yeoman, Marshall of the same,
  Whose name was *Appetite*; he did bestow
  Both guestes and meate, when ever in they came,
  And knew them how to order without blame,
  As him the Steward bad. They both attone
  Did dewty to their Lady, as became;
  Who passing by, forth led her guestes anone
Into the kitchin rowme, ne spard for nicenesse none.

29

It was a vaut ybuilt for great dispence,
  With many raunges reard along the wall;
  And one great chimney, whose long tonnell thence
  The smoke forth threw. And in the midst of all
  There placed was a caudron wide and tall,
  Upon a mighty furnace, burning whot,
  More whot, than *Aetn'*, or flaming *Mongiball*:
  For day and night it brent, ne ceased not,
So long as any thing it in the caudron got.

30

But to delay the heat, least by mischaunce
  It might breake out, and set the whole on fire,
  There added was by goodly ordinaunce,
  An huge great paire of bellowes, which did styre
  Continually, and cooling breath inspyre.
  About the Caudron many Cookes accoyld,
  With hookes and ladles, as need did require;
  The whiles the viandes in the vessell boyld
They did about their businesse sweat, and sorely toyld.

31

The maister Cooke was cald *Concoction*,
  A carefull man, and full of comely guise:
  The kitchin Clerke, that hight *Digestion*,
  Did order all th'Achates in seemely wise,
  And set them forth, as well he could devise.
  The rest had severall offices assind,
  Some to remove the scum, as it did rise;
  Others to beare the same away did mind;
And others it to use according to his kind.

32

But all the liquour, which was fowle and wast,
  Not good nor serviceable else for ought,
  They in another great round vessell plast,
  Till by a conduit pipe it thence were brought:
  And all the rest, that noyous was, and nought,
  By secret wayes, that none might it espy,
  Was close convaid, and to the back-gate brought,
  That cleped was *Port Esquiline*, whereby
It was avoided quite, and throwne out privily.

33

Which goodly order, and great workmans skill
  Whenas those knights beheld, with rare delight,
  And gazing wonder they their minds did fill;
  For never had they seene so straunge a sight.
  Thence backe againe faire *Alma* led them right,
  And soone into a goodly Parlour brought,
  That was with royall arras richly dight,
  In which was nothing pourtrahed, nor wrought,
Not wrought, nor pourtrahed, but easie to be thought.

34

And in the midst thereof upon the floure,
  A lovely bevy of faire Ladies sate,
  Courted of many a jolly Paramoure,
  The which them did in modest wise amate,
  And eachone sought his Lady to aggrate:
  And eke emongst them litle *Cupid* playd
  His wanton sports, being returned late
  From his fierce warres, and having from him layd
His cruell bow, wherewith he thousands hath dismayd.

35

Diverse delights they found them selves to please;
  Some song in sweet consort, some laught for joy,
  Some plaid with strawes, some idly sat at ease;
  But other some could not abide to toy,
  All pleasaunce was to them griefe and annoy:
  This fround, that faund, the third for shame did blush,
  Another seemed envious, or coy,
  Another in her teeth did gnaw a rush:
But at these straungers presence every one did hush.

36

Soone as the gracious *Alma* came in place
  They all attonce out of their seates arose,
  And to her homage made, with humble grace:
  Whom when the knights beheld, they gan dispose
  Themselves to court, and each a Damsell chose:
  The Prince by chaunce did on a Lady light,
  That was right faire and fresh as morning rose,
  But somwhat sad, and solemne eke in sight,
As if some pensive thought constraind her gentle spright.

37

In a long purple pall, whose skirt with gold
  Was fretted all about, she was arayd;
  And in her hand a Poplar braunch did hold:
  To whom the Prince in curteous manner said;
  Gentle Madame, why beene ye thus dismaid,
  And your faire beautie do with sadnesse spill?
  Lives any, that you hath thus ill apaid?
  Or doen you love, or doen you lacke your will?
What ever be the cause, it sure beseemes you ill.

38

Faire Sir, (said she halfe in disdainefull wise,)
  How is it, that this mood in me ye blame,
  And in your selfe do not the same advise?
  Him ill beseemes, anothers fault to name,
  That may unwares be blotted with the same:
  Pensive I yeeld I am, and sad in mind,
  Through great desire of glory and of fame;
  Ne ought I weene are ye therein behind,
That have twelve moneths sought one, yet no where can her find.

39

The Prince was inly moved at her speach,
  Well weeting trew, what she had rashly told;
  Yet with faire semblaunt sought to hide the breach,
  Which chaunge of colour did perforce unfold,
  Now seeming flaming whot, now stony cold.
  Tho turning soft aside, he did inquire,
  What wight she was, that Poplar braunch did hold:
  It answered was, her name was *Prays-desire*,
That by well doing sought to honour to aspire.

40

The whiles, the *Faerie* knight did entertaine
  Another Damsell of that gentle crew,
  That was right faire, and modest of demaine,
  But that too oft she chaung'd her native hew:
  Straunge was her tyre, and all her garment blew,
  Close round about her tuckt with many a plight:
  Upon her fist the bird, which shonneth vew,
  And keepes in coverts close from living wight,
Did sit, as yet ashamd, how rude *Pan* did her dight.

41

So long as *Guyon* with her commoned,
  Unto the ground she cast her modest eye,
  And ever and anone with rosie red
  The bashfull bloud her snowy cheekes did dye,
  That her became, as polisht yvory,
  Which cunning Craftesmans hand hath overlayd
  With faire vermilion or pure Castory.
  Great wonder had the knight, to see the mayd
So straungely passioned, and to her gently sayd,

42

Faire Damzell, seemeth, by your troubled cheare,
  That either me too bold ye weene, this wise
  You to molest, or other ill to feare
  That in the secret of your hart close lyes,
  From whence it doth, as cloud from sea arise.
  If it be I, of pardon I you pray;
  But if ought else that I mote not devise,
  I will, if please you it discure, assay,
To ease you of that ill, so wisely as I may.

43

She answerd nought, but more abasht for shame,
  Held downe her head, the whiles her lovely face
  The flashing bloud with blushing did inflame,
  And the strong passion mard her modest grace,
  That *Guyon* mervayld at her uncouth cace:
  Till *Alma* him bespake, Why wonder yee
  Faire Sir at that, which ye so much embrace?
  She is the fountaine of your modestee;
You shamefast are, but *Shamefastnesse* it selfe is shee.

44

Thereat the Elfe did blush in privitee,
  And turnd his face away; but she the same
  Dissembled faire, and faynd to oversee.
  Thus they awhile with court and goodly game,
  Themselves did solace each one with his Dame,
  Till that great Ladie thence away them sought,
  To vew her castles other wondrous frame.
  Up to a stately Turret she them brought,
Ascending by ten steps of Alablaster wrought.

45

That Turrets frame most admirable was,
  Like highest heaven compassed around,
  And lifted high above this earthly masse,
  Which it survew'd, as hils doen lower ground;
  But not on ground mote like to this be found,
  Not that, which antique *Cadmus* whylome built
  In *Thebes*, which *Alexander* did confound;
  Nor that proud towre of *Troy*, though richly guilt,
From which young *Hectors* bloud by cruell *Greekes* was spilt.

46

The roofe hereof was arched over head,
  And deckt with flowers and herbars daintily;
  Two goodly Beacons, set in watches stead,
  Therein gave light, and flam'd continually:
  For they of living fire most subtilly
  Were made, and set in silver sockets bright,
  Cover'd with lids deviz'd of substance sly,
  That readily they shut and open might.
O who can tell the prayses of that makers might!

47

Ne can I tell, ne can I stay to tell
  This parts great workmanship, and wondrous powre,
  That all this other worlds worke doth excell,
  And likest is unto that heavenly towre,
  That God hath built for his owne blessed bowre.
  Therein were diverse roomes, and diverse stages,
  But three the chiefest, and of greatest powre,
  In which there dwelt three honorable sages,
The wisest men, I weene, that lived in their ages.

48

Not he, whom *Greece*, the Nourse of all good arts,
  By *Phœbus* doome, the wisest thought alive,
  Might be compar'd to these by many parts:
  Nor that sage *Pylian* syre, which did survive
  Three ages, such as mortall men contrive,
  By whose advise old *Priams* cittie fell,
  With these in praise of pollicies mote strive.
  These three in these three roomes did sundry dwell,
And counselled faire *Alma*, how to governe well.

49

The first of them could things to come foresee:
  The next could of things present best advize;
  The third things past could keepe in memoree,
  So that no time, nor reason could arize,
  But that the same could one of these comprize.
  For thy the first did in the forepart sit,
  That nought mote hinder his quicke prejudize:
  He had a sharpe foresight, and working wit,
That never idle was, ne once could rest a whit.

50

His chamber was dispainted all within,
  With sundry colours, in the which were writ
  Infinite shapes of things dispersed thin;
  Some such as in the world were never yit,
  Ne can devized be of mortall wit;
  Some daily seene, and knowen by their names,
  Such as in idle fantasies doe flit:
  Infernall Hags, *Centaurs*, feendes, *Hippodames*,
Apes, Lions, Ægles, Owles, fooles, lovers, children, Dames.

51

And all the chamber filled was with flyes,
   Which buzzed all about, and made such sound,
   That they encombred all mens eares and eyes,
   Like many swarmes of Bees assembled round,
   After their hives with honny do abound:
   All those were idle thoughts and fantasies,
   Devices, dreames, opinions unsound,
   Shewes, visions, sooth-sayes, and prophesies;
And all that fained is, as leasings, tales, and lies.

52

Emongst them all sate he, which wonned there,
   That hight *Phantastes* by his nature trew;
   A man of yeares yet fresh, as mote appere,
   Of swarth complexion, and of crabbed hew,
   That him full of melancholy did shew;
   Bent hollow beetle browes, sharpe staring eyes,
   That mad or foolish seemd: one by his vew
   Mote deeme him borne with ill disposed skyes,
When oblique *Saturne* sate in the house of agonyes.

53

Whom *Alma* having shewed to her guestes,
   Thence brought them to the second roome, whose wals
   Were painted faire with memorable gestes,
   Of famous Wisards, and with picturals
   Of Magistrates, of courts, of tribunals,
   Of commen wealthes, of states, of pollicy,
   Of lawes, of judgements, and of decretals;
   All artes, all science, all Philosophy,
And all that in the world was aye thought wittily.

54

Of those that roome was full, and them among
   There sate a man of ripe and perfect age,
   Who did them meditate all his life long,
   That through continuall practise and usage,
   He now was growne right wise, and wondrous sage.
   Great pleasure had those stranger knights, to see
   His goodly reason, and grave personage,
   That his disciples both desir'd to bee;
But *Alma* thence them led to th'hindmost roome of three.

55

That chamber seemed ruinous and old,
   And therefore was removed farre behind,
   Yet were the wals, that did the same uphold,
   Right firme and strong, though somewhat they declind;
   And therein sate an old oldman, halfe blind,
   And all decrepit in his feeble corse,
   Yet lively vigour rested in his mind,
   And recompenst him with a better scorse:
Weake body well is chang'd for minds redoubled forse.

56

This man of infinite remembrance was,
   And things foregone through many ages held,
   Which he recorded still, as they did pas,
   Ne suffred them to perish through long eld,
   As all things else, the which this world doth weld,
   But laid them up in his immortall scrine,
   Where they for ever incorrupted dweld:
   The warres he well remembred of king *Nine*,
Of old *Assaracus*, and *Inachus* divine.

57

The yeares of *Nestor* nothing were to his,
   Ne yet *Mathusalem*, though longest liv'd;
   For he remembred both their infancies:
   Ne wonder then, if that he were depriv'd
   Of native strength now, that he them surviv'd.
   His chamber all was hangd about with rolles,
   And old records from auncient times deriv'd,
   Some made in books, some in long parchment scrolles,
That were all worme-eaten, and full of canker holes.

58

Amidst them all he in a chaire was set,
   Tossing and turning them withouten end;
   But for he was unhable them to fet,
   A litle boy did on him still attend,
   To reach, when ever he for ought did send;
   And oft when things were lost, or laid amis,
   That boy them sought, and unto him did lend.
   Therefore he *Anamnestes* cleped is,
And that old man *Eumnestes*, by their propertis.

59

The knights there entring, did him reverence dew
    And wondred at his endlesse exercise,
    Then as they gan his Librarie to vew,
    And antique Registers for to avise,
    There chaunced to the Princes hand to rize,
    An auncient booke, hight *Briton moniments*,
    That of this lands first conquest did devize,
    And old division into Regiments,
Till it reduced was to one mans governments.

60

Sir *Guyon* chaunst eke on another booke,
    That hight *Antiquitie* of *Faerie* lond,
    In which when as he greedily did looke,
    Th'off-spring of Elves and Faries there he fond,
    As it delivered was from hond to hond:
    Whereat they burning both with fervent fire,
    Their countries auncestry to understond,
    Crav'd leave of *Alma*, and that aged sire,
To read those bookes; who gladly graunted their desire.

CANT. X.

A chronicle of Briton kings,
*   from Brute to Uthers rayne.*
And rolles of Elfin Emperours,
*   till time of Gloriane.*

I

WHO now shall give unto me words and sound,
    Equall unto this haughtie enterprise?
    Or who shall lend me wings, with which from ground
    My lowly verse may loftily arise,
    And lift it selfe unto the highest skies?
    More ample spirit, than hitherto was wount,
    Here needes me, whiles the famous auncestries
    Of my most dreaded Soveraigne I recount,
By which all earthly Princes she doth farre surmount.

2

Ne under Sunne, that shines so wide and faire,
  Whence all that lives, does borrow life and light,
  Lives ought, that to her linage may compaire,
  Which though from earth it be derived right,
  Yet doth it selfe stretch forth to heavens hight,
  And all the world with wonder overspred;
  A labour huge, exceeding farre my might:
  How shall fraile pen, with feare disparaged,
Conceive such soveraine glory, and great bountihed?

3

Argument worthy of *Mæonian* quill,
  Or rather worthy of great *Phœbus* rote,
  Whereon the ruines of great *Ossa* hill,
  And triumphes of *Phlegræan Jove* he wrote,
  That all the Gods admird his loftie note.
  But if some relish of that heavenly lay
  His learned daughters would to me report,
  To decke my song withall, I would assay,
Thy name, O soveraine Queene, to blazon farre away.

4

Thy name O soveraine Queene, thy realme and race,
  From this renowmed Prince derived arre,
  Who mightily upheld that royall mace,
  Which now thou bear'st, to thee descended farre
  From mightie kings and conquerours in warre,
  Thy fathers and great Grandfathers of old,
  Whose noble deedes above the Northerne starre
  Immortall fame for ever hath enrold;
As in that old mans booke they were in order told.

5

The land, which warlike Britons now possesse,
  And therein have their mightie empire raysd,
  In antique times was salvage wildernesse,
  Unpeopled, unmanurd, unprov'd, unpraysd,
  Ne was it Island then, ne was it paysd
  Amid the *Ocean* waves, ne was it sought
  Of marchants farre, for profits therein praysd,
  But was all desolate, and of some thought
By sea to have bene from the *Celticke* maynland brought.

6

Ne did it then deserve a name to have,
  Till that the venturous Mariner that way
  Learning his ship from those white rocks to save,
  Which all along the Southerne sea-coast lay,
  Threatning unheedie wrecke and rash decay,
  For safeties sake that same his sea-marke made,
  And namd it *Albion*. But later day
  Finding in it fit ports for fishers trade,
Gan more the same frequent, and further to invade.

7

But farre in land a salvage nation dwelt,
  Of hideous Giants, and halfe beastly men,
  That never tasted grace, nor goodnesse felt,
  But like wild beasts lurking in loathsome den,
  And flying fast as Roebucke through the fen,
  All naked without shame, or care of cold,
  By hunting and by spoiling lived then;
  Of stature huge, and eke of courage bold,
That sonnes of men amazd their sternnesse to behold.

8

But whence they sprong, or how they were begot,
  Uneath is to assure; uneath to wene
  That monstrous error, which doth some assot,
  That *Dioclesians* fiftie daughters shene
  Into this land by chaunce have driven bene,
  Where companing with feends and filthy Sprights,
  Through vaine illusion of their lust unclene,
  They brought forth Giants and such dreadfull wights,
As farre exceeded men in their immeasurd mights.

9

They held this land, and with their filthinesse
  Polluted this same gentle soyle long time:
  That their owne mother loathd their beastlinesse,
  And gan abhorre her broods unkindly crime,
  All were they borne of her owne native slime,
  Untill that *Brutus* anciently deriv'd
  From royall stocke of old *Assaracs* line,
  Driven by fatall error, here arriv'd,
And them of their unjust possession depriv'd.

10

But ere he had established his throne,
  And spred his empire to the utmost shore,
  He fought great battels with his salvage fone;
  In which he them defeated evermore,
  And many Giants left on groning flore;
  That well can witnesse yet unto this day
  The westerne Hogh, besprincled with the gore
  Of mightie *Goëmot*, whom in stout fray
Corineus conquered, and cruelly did slay.

11

And eke that ample Pit, yet farre renownd,
  For the large leape, which *Debon* did compell
  Coulin to make, being eight lugs of grownd;
  Into the which returning backe, he fell,
  But those three monstrous stones doe most excell
  Which that huge sonne of hideous *Albion*,
  Whose father *Hercules* in Fraunce did quell,
  Great *Godmer* threw, in fierce contention,
At bold *Canutus*; but of him was slaine anon.

12

In meed of these great conquests by them got,
  Corineus had that Province utmost west,
  To him assigned for his worthy lot,
  Which of his name and memorable gest
  He called *Cornewaile*, yet so called best:
  And *Debons* shayre was, that is *Devonshyre*:
  But *Canute* had his portion from the rest,
  The which he cald *Canutium*, for his hyre;
Now *Cantium*, which Kent we commenly inquire.

13

Thus *Brute* this Realme unto his rule subdewd,
  And raigned long in great felicitie,
  Lov'd of his friends, and of his foes eschewd,
  He left three sonnes, his famous progeny,
  Borne of faire *Inogene* of *Italy*;
  Mongst whom he parted his imperiall state,
  And *Locrine* left chiefe Lord of *Britany*.
  At last ripe age bad him surrender late
His life, and long good fortune unto finall fate.

14

Locrine was left the soveraine Lord of all;
　But *Albanact* had all the Northrene part,
　Which of himselfe *Albania* he did call;
　And *Camber* did possesse the Westerne quart,
　Which *Severne* now from *Logris* doth depart:
　And each his portion peaceably enjoyd,
　Ne was there outward breach, nor grudge in hart,
　That once their quiet government annoyd,
But each his paines to others profit still employd.

15

Untill a nation straung, with visage swart,
　And courage fierce, that all men did affray,
　Which through the world then swarmd in every part,
　And overflow'd all countries farre away,
　Like *Noyes* great flood, with their importune sway,
　This land invaded with like violence,
　And did themselves through all the North display:
　Untill that *Locrine* for his Realmes defence,
Did head against them make, and strong munifience.

16

He them encountred, a confused rout,
　Foreby the River, that whylome was hight
　The auncient *Abus*, where with courage stout
　He them defeated in victorious fight,
　And chaste so fiercely after fearfull flight,
　That forst their Chieftaine, for his safeties sake,
　(Their Chieftaine *Humber* named was aright)
　Unto the mightie streame him to betake,
Where he an end of battell, and of life did make.

17

The king returned proud of victorie,
　And insolent wox through unwonted ease,
　That shortly he forgot the jeopardie,
　Which in his land he lately did appease,
　And fell to vaine voluptuous disease:
　He lov'd faire Ladie *Estrild*, lewdly lov'd,
　Whose wanton pleasures him too much did please,
　That quite his hart from *Guendolene* remov'd,
From *Guendolene* his wife, though alwaies faithfull prov'd.

18

The noble daughter of *Corineus*
　Would not endure to be so vile disdaind,
　But gathering force, and courage valorous,
　Encountred him in battell well ordaind,
　In which him vanquisht she to fly constraind:
　But she so fast pursewd, that him she tooke,
　And threw in bands, where he till death remaind;
　Als his faire Leman, flying through a brooke,
She overhent, nought moved with her piteous looke.

19

But both her selfe, and eke her daughter deare,
　Begotten by her kingly Paramoure,
　The faire *Sabrina* almost dead with feare,
　She there attached, farre from all succoure;
　The one she slew in that impatient stoure,
　But the sad virgin innocent of all,
　Adowne the rolling river she did poure,
　Which of her name now *Severne* men do call:
Such was the end, that to disloyall love did fall.

20

Then for her sonne, which she to *Locrin* bore,
　Madan was young, unmeet the rule to sway,
　In her owne hand the crowne she kept in store,
　Till ryper yeares he raught, and stronger stay:
　During which time her powre she did display
　Through all this realme, the glorie of her sex,
　And first taught men a woman to obay:
　But when her sonne to mans estate did wex,
She it surrendred, ne her selfe would lenger vex.

21

Tho *Madan* raignd, unworthie of his race
　For with all shame that sacred throne he fild:
　Next *Memprise*, as unworthy of that place,
　In which being consorted with *Manild*,
　For thirst of single kingdome him he kild.
　But *Ebranck* salved both their infamies
　With noble deedes, and warreyd on *Brunchild*
　In *Henault*, where yet of his victories
Brave moniments remaine, which yet that land envies.

22

An happie man in his first dayes he was,
  And happie father of faire progeny:
  For all so many weekes as the yeare has,
  So many children he did multiply;
  Of which were twentie sonnes, which did apply
  Their minds to praise, and chevalrous desire:
  Those germans did subdew all Germany,
  Of whom it hight; but in the end their Sire
With foule repulse from Fraunce was forced to retire.

23

Which blot his sonne succeeding in his seat,
  The second *Brute*, the second both in name,
  And eke in semblance of his puissance great,
  Right well recur'd, and did away that blame
  With recompence of everlasting fame.
  He with his victour sword first opened
  The bowels of wide Fraunce, a forlorne Dame,
  And taught her first how to be conquered;
Since which, with sundrie spoiles she hath beene ransacked.

24

Let *Scaldis* tell, and let tell *Hania*,
  And let the marsh of *Estham bruges* tell,
  What colour were their waters that same day,
  And all the moore twixt *Elversham* and *Dell*,
  With bloud of *Henalois*, which therein fell.
  How oft that day did sad *Brunchildis* see
  The greene shield dyde in dolorous vermell?
  That not *Scuith guiridh* it mote seeme to bee,
But rather *y Scuith gogh*, signe of sad crueltee.

25

His sonne king *Leill* by fathers labour long,
  Enjoyd an heritage of lasting peace,
  And built *Cairleill*, and built *Cairleon* strong.
  Next *Huddibras* his realme did not encrease,
  But taught the land from wearie warres to cease.
  Whose footsteps *Bladud* following, in arts
  Exceld at *Athens* all the learned preace,
  From whence he brought them to these salvage parts,
And with sweet science mollifide their stubborne harts.

26

Ensample of his wondrous faculty,
  Behold the boyling Bathes at *Cairbadon*,
  Which seeth with secret fire eternally,
  And in their entrails, full of quicke Brimston,
  Nourish the flames, which they are warm'd upon,
  That to their people wealth they forth do well,
  And health to every forreine nation:
  Yet he at last contending to excell
The reach of men, through flight into fond mischief fell.

27

Next him king *Leyr* in happie peace long raind,
  But had no issue male him to succeed,
  But three faire daughters, which were well uptraind,
  In all that seemed fit for kingly seed:
  Mongst whom his realme he equally decreed
  To have divided. Tho when feeble age
  Nigh to his utmost date he saw proceed,
  He cald his daughters; and with speeches sage
Inquyrd, which of them most did love her parentage.

28

The eldest *Gonorill* gan to protest,
  That she much more than her owne life him lov'd:
  And *Regan* greater love to him profest,
  Than all the world, when ever it were proov'd;
  But *Cordeill* said she lov'd him, as behoov'd:
  Whose simple answere, wanting colours faire
  To paint it forth, him to displeasance moov'd,
  That in his crowne he counted her no haire,
But twixt the other twaine his kingdome whole did shaire.

29

So wedded th'one to *Maglan* king of Scots,
  And th'other to the king of *Cambria*,
  And twixt them shayrd his realme by equall lots:
  But without dowre the wise *Cordelia*
  Was sent to *Aganip* of *Celtica*.
  Their aged Syre, thus eased of his crowne,
  A private life led in *Albania*,
  With *Gonorill*, long had in great renowne,
That nought him griev'd to bene from rule deposed downe.

30

But true it is, that when the oyle is spent,
  The light goes out, and weeke is throwne away;
  So when he had resigned his regiment,
  His daughter gan despise his drouping day,
  And wearie waxe of his continuall stay.
  Tho to his daughter *Regan* he repayrd,
  Who him at first well used every way;
  But when of his departue she despayrd,
Her bountie she abated, and his cheare empayrd.

31

The wretched man gan then avise too late,
  That love is not, where most it is profest,
  Too truely tryde in his extreamest state;
  At last resolv'd likewise to prove the rest,
  He to *Cordelia* him selfe addrest,
  Who with entire affection him receav'd,
  As for her Syre and king her seemed best;
  And after all an army strong she leav'd,
To war on those, which him had of his realme bereav'd.

32

So to his crowne she him restor'd againe,
  In which he dyde, made ripe for death by eld,
  And after wild, it should to her remaine:
  Who peaceably the same long time did weld:
  And all mens harts in dew obedience held:
  Till that her sisters children, woxen strong
  Through proud ambition, against her rebeld,
  And overcommen kept in prison long,
Till wearie of that wretched life, her selfe she hong.

33

Then gan the bloudie brethren both to raine:
  But fierce *Cundah* gan shortly to envie
  His brother *Morgan*, prickt with proud disdaine,
  To have a pere in part of soveraintie,
  And kindling coles of cruell enmitie,
  Raisd warre, and him in battell overthrew:
  Whence as he to those woodie hils did flie,
  Which hight of him *Glamorgan*, there him slew:
Then did he raigne alone, when he none equall knew.

34

His sonne *Rivallo* his dead roome did supply,
  In whose sad time bloud did from heaven raine:
  Next great *Gurgustus*, then faire *Cæcily*
  In constant peace their kingdomes did containe,
  After whom *Lago*, and *Kinmarke* did raine,
  And *Gorbogud*, till farre in yeares he grew:
  Then his ambitious sonnes unto them twaine
  Arraught the rule, and from their father drew,
Stout *Ferrex* and sterne *Porrex* him in prison threw.

35

But O, the greedy thirst of royall crowne,
  That knowes no kinred, nor regardes no right,
  Stird *Porrex* up to put his brother downe;
  Who unto him assembling forreine might,
  Made warre on him, and fell him selfe in fight:
  Whose death t'avenge, his mother mercilesse,
  Most mercilesse of women, *Wyden* hight,
  Her other sonne fast sleeping did oppresse,
And with most cruell hand him murdred pittilesse.

36

Here ended *Brutus* sacred progenie,
  Which had seven hundred yeares this scepter borne,
  With high renowme, and great felicitie;
  The noble braunch from th'antique stocke was torne
  Through discord, and the royall throne forlorne:
  Thenceforth this Realme was into factions rent,
  Whilest each of *Brutus* boasted to be borne,
  That in the end was left no moniment
Of *Brutus*, nor of Britons glory auncient.

37

Then up arose a man of matchlesse might,
  And wondrous wit to menage high affaires,
  Who stird with pitty of the stressed plight
  Of this sad Realme, cut into sundry shaires
  By such, as claymd themselves *Brutes* rightfull haires.
  Gathered the Princes of the people loose,
  To taken counsell of their common cares;
  Who with his wisdom won, him streight did choose
Their king, and swore him fealty to win or loose.

38

Then made he head against his enimies,
  And *Ymner* slew, of *Logris* miscreate;
  Then *Ruddoc* and proud *Stater*, both allyes,
  This of *Albanie* newly nominate,
  And that of *Cambry* king confirmed late,
  He overthrew through his owne valiaunce;
  Whose countreis he redus'd to quiet state,
  And shortly brought to civill governaunce,
Now one, which earst were many, made through variaunce.

39

Then made he sacred lawes, which some men say
  Were unto him reveald in vision,
  By which he freed the Traveilers high way,
  The Churches part, and Ploughmans portion,
  Restraining stealth, and strong extortion;
  The gracious *Numa* of great *Britanie*:
  For till his dayes, the chiefe dominion
  By strength was wielded without pollicie;
Therefore he first wore crowne of gold for dignitie.

40

Donwallo dyde (for what may live for ay?)
  And left two sonnes, of pearelesse prowesse both;
  That sacked *Rome* too dearely did assay,
  The recompence of their perjured oth,
  And ransackt *Greece* well tryde, when they were wroth;
  Besides subjected *Fraunce*, and *Germany*,
  Which yet their prayses speake, all be they loth,
  And inly tremble at the memory
Of *Brennus* and *Bellinus*, kings of Britany.

41

Next them did *Gurgunt*, great *Bellinus* sonne
  In rule succeede, and eke in fathers prayse;
  He Easterland subdewd, and Danmarke wonne,
  And of them both did foy and tribute raise,
  The which was dew in his dead fathers dayes:
  He also gave to fugitives of *Spayne*,
  Whom he at sea found wandring from their wayes,
  A seate in *Ireland* safely to remayne,
Which they should hold of him, as subject to *Britayne*.

42

After him raigned *Guitheline* his hayre,
  The justest man and trewest in his dayes,
Who had to wife Dame *Mertia* the fayre,
A woman worthy of immortall prayse,
Which for this Realme found many goodly layes,
And wholesome Statutes to her husband brought;
Her many deemd to have beene of the *Fayes*,
As was *Aegerie*, that *Numa* tought;
Those yet of her be *Mertian* lawes both nam'd and thought.

43

Her sonne *Sisillus* after her did rayne,
  And then *Kimarus*, and then *Danius*;
Next whom *Morindus* did the crowne sustaine,
Who, had he not with wrath outrageous,
And cruell rancour dim'd his valorous
And mightie deeds, should matched have the best:
As well in that same field victorious
Against the forreine *Morands* he exprest;
Yet lives his memorie, though carcas sleepe in rest.

44

Five sonnes he left begotten of one wife,
  All which successively by turnes did raine;
First *Gorboman* a man of vertuous life;
Next *Archigald*, who for his proud disdaine,
Deposed was from Princedome soveraine,
And pitteous *Elidure* put in his sted;
Who shortly it to him restord againe,
Till by his death he it recovered;
But *Peridure* and *Vigent* him disthronized.

45

In wretched prison long he did remaine,
  Till they outraigned had their utmost date,
And then therein reseized was againe,
And ruled long with honorable state,
Till he surrendred Realme and life to fate.
Then all the sonnes of these five brethren raynd
By dew successe, and all their Nephewes late,
Even thrise eleven descents the crowne retaynd,
Till aged *Hely* by dew heritage it gaynd.

46

He had two sonnes, whose eldest called *Lud*
  Left of his life most famous memory,
  And endlesse moniments of his great good:
  The ruin'd wals he did reædifye
  Of *Troynovant*, gainst force of enimy,
  And built that gate, which of his name is hight,
  By which he lyes entombed solemnly.
  He left two sonnes, too young to rule aright,
Androgeus and *Tenantius*, pictures of his might.

47

Whilst they were young, *Cassibalane* their Eme
  Was by the people chosen in their sted,
  Who on him tooke the royall Diademe,
  And goodly well long time it governed,
  Till the prowd *Romanes* him disquieted,
  And warlike *Cæsar*, tempted with the name
  Of this sweet Island, never conquered,
  And envying the Britons blazed fame,
(O hideous hunger of dominion) hither came.

48

Yet twise they were repulsed backe againe,
  And twise renforst, backe to their ships to fly,
  The whiles with bloud they all the shore did staine,
  And the gray *Ocean* into purple dy:
  Ne had they footing found at last perdie,
  Had not *Androgeus*, false to native soyle,
  And envious of Uncles soveraintie,
  Betrayd his contrey unto forreine spoyle:
Nought else, but treason, from the first this land did foyle.

49

So by him *Cæsar* got the victory,
  Through great bloudshed, and many a sad assay,
  In which him selfe was charged heavily
  Of hardy *Nennius*, whom he yet did slay,
  But lost his sword, yet to be seene this day.
  Thenceforth this land was tributarie made
  T'ambitious *Rome*, and did their rule obay,
  Till *Arthur* all that reckoning defrayd;
Yet oft the Briton kings against them strongly swayd.

50

Next him *Tenantius* raigned, then *Kimbeline*,
  What time th'eternall Lord in fleshly slime
  Enwombed was, from wretched *Adams* line
  To purge away the guilt of sinfull crime:
  O joyous memorie of happy time,
  That heavenly grace so plenteously displayd;
  (O too high ditty for my simple rime.)
  Soone after this the *Romanes* him warrayd;
For that their tribute he refusd to let be payd.

51

Good *Claudius*, that next was Emperour,
  An army brought, and with him battell fought,
  In which the king was by a Treachetour
  Disguised slaine, ere any thereof thought:
  Yet ceased not the bloudy fight for ought;
  For *Arvirage* his brothers place supplide,
  Both in his armes, and crowne, and by that draught
  Did drive the *Romanes* to the weaker side,
That they to peace agreed. So all was pacifide.

52

Was never king more highly magnifide,
  Nor dred of *Romanes*, than was *Arvirage*,
  For which the Emperour to him allide
  His daughter *Genuiss'* in marriage:
  Yet shortly he renounst the vassalage
  Of *Rome* againe, who hither hastly sent
  Vespasian, that with great spoile and rage
  Forwasted all, till *Genuissa* gent
Perswaded him to ceasse, and her Lord to relent.

53

He dyde; and him succeeded *Marius*,
  Who joyd his dayes in great tranquillity,
  Then *Coyll*, and after him good *Lucius*,
  That first received Christianitie,
  The sacred pledge of Christes Evangely;
  Yet true it is, that long before that day
  Hither came *Joseph* of *Arimathy*,
  Who brought with him the holy grayle, (they say)
And preacht the truth, but since it greatly did decay.

54

This good king shortly without issew dide,
  Whereof great trouble in the kingdome grew,
  That did her selfe in sundry parts divide,
  And with her powre her owne selfe overthrew,
  Whilest *Romanes* dayly did the weake subdew:
  Which seeing stout *Bunduca*, up arose,
  And taking armes, the *Britons* to her drew;
  With whom she marched streight against her foes,
And them unwares besides the *Severne* did enclose.

55

There she with them a cruell battell tride,
  Not with so good successe, as she deserv'd;
  By reason that the Captaines on her side,
  Corrupted by *Paulinus*, from her swerv'd:
  Yet such, as were through former flight preserv'd,
  Gathering againe, her Host she did renew,
  And with fresh courage on the victour serv'd:
  But being all defeated, save a few,
Rather than fly, or be captiv'd her selfe she slew.

56

O famous moniment of womens prayse,
  Matchable either to *Semiramis*,
  Whom antique history so high doth raise,
  Or to *Hypsiphil'* or to *Thomiris*:
  Her Host two hundred thousand numbred is;
  Who whiles good fortune favoured her might,
  Triumphed oft against her enimis;
  And yet though overcome in haplesse fight,
She triumphed on death, in enemies despight.

57

Her reliques *Fulgent* having gathered,
  Fought with *Severus*, and him overthrew;
  Yet in the chace was slaine of them, that fled:
  So made them victours, whom he did subdew.
  Then gan *Carausius* tirannize anew,
  And gainst the *Romanes* bent their proper powre,
  But him *Allectus* treacherously slew,
  And took on him the robe of Emperoure:
Nath'lesse the same enjoyed but short happy howre:

58

For *Asclepiodate* him overcame,
    And left inglorious on the vanquisht playne,
    Without or robe, or rag, to hide his shame.
    Then afterwards he in his stead did rayne;
    But shortly was by *Coyll* in battell slaine:
    Who after long debate, since *Lucies* time,
    Was of the *Britons* first crownd Soveraine:
    Then gan this Realme renewe her passed prime:
He of his name *Coylchester* built of stone and lime.

59

Which when the *Romanes* heard, they hither sent
    Constantius, a man of mickle might,
    With whom king *Coyll* made an agreement,
    And to him gave for wife his daughter bright,
    Faire *Helena*, the fairest living wight;
    Who in all godly thewes, and goodly prayse
    Did far excell, but was most famous hight
    For skill in Musicke of all in her dayes,
Aswell in curious instruments, as cunning layes.

60

Of whom he did great *Constantine* beget,
    Who afterward was Emperour of *Rome*;
    To which whiles absent he his mind did set,
    Octavius here lept into his roome,
    And it usurped by unrighteous doome:
    But he his title justifide by might,
    Slaying *Traherne*, and having overcome
    The *Romane* legion in dreadfull fight:
So settled he his kingdome, and confirmd his right.

61

But wanting issew male, his daughter deare
    He gave in wedlocke to *Maximian*,
    And him with her made of his kingdome heyre,
    Who soone by meanes thereof the Empire wan,
    Till murdred by the friends of *Gratian*;
    Then gan the Hunnes and Picts invade this land,
    During the raigne of *Maximinian*;
    Who dying left none heire them to withstand,
But that they overran all parts with easie hand.

62

The weary *Britons*, whose war-hable youth
  Was by *Maximian* lately led away,
  With wretched miseries, and woefull ruth,
  Were to those Pagans made an open pray,
  And dayly spectacle of sad decay:
  Whom *Romane* warres, which now foure hundred yeares,
  And more had wasted, could no whit dismay;
  Till by consent of Commons and of Peares,
They crownd the second *Constantine* with joyous teares,

63

Who having oft in battell vanquished
  Those spoilefull Picts, and swarming Easterlings,
  Long time in peace his Realme established,
  Yet oft annoyd with sundry bordragings
  Of neighbour Scots, and forrein Scatterlings,
  With which the world did in those dayes abound:
  Which to outbarre, with painefull pyonings
  From sea to sea he heapt a mightie mound,
Which from *Alcluid* to *Panwelt* did that border bound.

64

Three sonnes he dying left, all under age;
  By meanes whereof, their uncle *Vortigere*
  Usurpt the crowne, during their pupillage;
  Which th'Infants tutors gathering to feare,
  Them closely into *Armorick* did beare:
  For dread of whom, and for those Picts annoyes,
  He sent to *Germanie*, straunge aid to reare,
  From whence eftsoones arrived here three hoyes
Of *Saxons*, whom he for his safetie imployes.

65

Two brethren were their Capitains, which hight
  Hengist and *Horsus*, well approv'd in warre,
  And both of them men of renowmed might;
  Who making vantage of their civill jarre,
  And of those forreiners, which came from farre,
  Grew great, and got large portions of land,
  That in the Realme ere long they stronger arre,
  Than they which sought at first their helping hand,
And *Vortiger* enforst the kingdome to aband.

66

But by the helpe of *Vortimere* his sonne,
  He is againe unto his rule restord,
  And *Hengist* seeming sad, for that was donne,
  Received is to grace and new accord,
  Through his faire daughters face, and flattring word;
  Soone after which, three hundred Lordes he slew
  Of British bloud, all sitting at his bord;
  Whose dolefull moniments who list to rew,
Th'eternall markes of treason may at *Stonheng* vew.

67

By this the sonnes of *Constantine*, which fled,
  Ambrose and *Uther* did ripe yeares attaine,
  And here arriving, strongly challenged
  The crowne, which *Vortiger* did long detaine:
  Who flying from his guilt, by them was slaine,
  And *Hengist* eke soone brought to shamefull death.
  Thenceforth *Aurelius* peaceably did rayne,
  Till that through poyson stopped was his breath;
So now entombed lyes at Stoneheng by the heath.

68

After him *Uther*, which *Pendragon* hight,
  Succeding There abruptly it did end,
  Without full point, or other Cesure right,
  As if the rest some wicked hand did rend,
  Or th'Authour selfe could not at least attend
  To finish it: that so untimely breach
  The Prince him selfe halfe seemeth to offend,
  Yet secret pleasure did offence empeach,
And wonder of antiquitie long stopt his speach.

69

At last quite ravisht with delight, to heare
  The royall Ofspring of his native land,
  Cryde out, Deare countrey, O how dearely deare
  Ought thy remembraunce, and perpetuall band
  Be to thy foster Childe, that from thy hand
  Did commun breath and nouriture receave?
  How brutish is it not to understand,
  How much to her we owe, that all us gave,
That gave unto us all, what ever good we have.

70

But *Guyon* all this while his booke did read,
  Ne yet has ended: for it was a great
  And ample volume, that doth far excead
  My leasure, so long leaves here to repeat:
  It told, how first *Prometheus* did create
  A man, of many partes from beasts derived,
  And then stole fire from heaven, to animate
  His worke, for which he was by *Jove* deprived
Of life him selfe, and hart-strings of an Ægle rived.

71

That man so made, he called *Elfe*, to weet
  Quick, the first authour of all Elfin kind:
  Who wandring through the world with wearie feet,
  Did in the gardins of *Adonis* find
  A goodly creature, whom he deemd in mind
  To be no earthly wight, but either Spright,
  Or Angell, th'authour of all woman kind;
  Therefore a *Fay* he her according hight,
Of whom all *Faeryes* spring, and fetch their lignage right.

72

Of these a mightie people shortly grew,
  And puissaunt kings, which all the world warrayd,
  And to them selves all Nations did subdew:
  The first and eldest, which that scepter swayd,
  Was *Elfin*; him all *India* obayd,
  And all that now *America* men call:
  Next him was noble *Elfinan*, who layd
  Cleopolis foundation first of all:
But *Elfiline* enclosd it with a golden wall.

73

His sonne was *Elfinell*, who overcame
  The wicked *Gobbelines* in bloudy field:
  But *Elfant* was of most renowmed fame,
  Who all of Christall did *Panthea* build:
  Then *Elfar*, who two brethren gyants kild,
  The one of which had two heads, th'other three:
  Then *Elfinor*, who was in Magick skild;
  He built by art upon the glassy See
A bridge of bras, whose sound heavens thunder seem'd to bee.

74

He left three sonnes, the which in order raynd,
  And all their Ofspring, in their dew descents,
  Even seven hundred Princes, which maintaynd
  With mightie deedes their sundry governments;
  That were too long their infinite contents
  Here to record, ne much materiall:
  Yet should they be most famous moniments,
  And brave ensample, both of martiall,
And civill rule to kings and states imperiall.

75

After all these *Elficleos* did rayne,
  The wise *Elficleos* in great Majestie,
  Who mightily that scepter did sustayne,
  And with rich spoiles and famous victorie,
  Did high advaunce the crowne of *Faery*:
  He left two sonnes, of which faire *Elferon*
  The eldest brother did untimely dy;
  Whose emptie place the mightie *Oberon*
Doubly supplide, in spousall, and dominion.

76

Great was his power and glorie over all,
  Which him before, that sacred seate did fill,
  That yet remaines his wide memoriall:
  He dying left the fairest *Tanaquill*,
  Him to succeede therein, by his last will:
  Fairer and nobler liveth none this howre,
  Ne like in grace, ne like in learned skill;
  Therefore they *Glorian* call that glorious flowre,
Long mayst thou *Glorian* live, in glory and great powre.

77

Beguild thus with delight of novelties,
  And naturall desire of countreys state,
  So long they red in those antiquities,
  That how the time was fled, they quite forgate,
  Till gentle *Alma* seeing it so late,
  Perforce their studies broke, and them besought
  To thinke, how supper did them long awaite.
  So halfe unwilling from their bookes them brought,
And fairely feasted, as so noble knights she ought.

CANT. XI

*The enimies of Temperaunce
besiege her dwelling place:
Prince Arthur them repelles, and fowle
Maleger doth deface.*

1

WHAT warre so cruell, or what siege so sore,
  As that, which strong affections do apply
  Against the fort of reason evermore
  To bring the soule into captivitie:
  Their force is fiercer through infirmitie
  Of the fraile flesh, relenting to their rage,
  And exercise most bitter tyranny
  Upon the parts, brought into their bondage:
No wretchednesse is like to sinfull vellenage.

2

But in a body, which doth freely yeeld
  His partes to reasons rule obedient,
  And letteth her that ought the scepter weeld,
  All happy peace and goodly government
  Is setled there in sure establishment;
  There *Alma* like a virgin Queene most bright,
  Doth florish in all beautie excellent:
  And to her guestes doth bounteous banket dight,
Attempred goodly well for health and for delight.

3

Early before the Morne with cremosin ray,
  The windowes of bright heaven opened had,
  Through which into the world the dawning day
  Might looke, that maketh every creature glad,
  Uprose Sir *Guyon*, in bright armour clad,
  And to his purposd journey him prepar'd:
  With him the Palmer eke in habit sad,
  Him selfe addrest to that adventure hard:
So to the rivers side they both together far'd.

4

Where them awaited ready at the ford
  The *Ferriman*, as *Alma* had behight,
  With his well rigged boate: They go abord,
  And he eftsoones gan launch his barke forthright.
  Ere long they rowed were quite out of sight,
  And fast the land behind them fled away.
  But let them pas, whiles wind and weather right
  Do serve their turnes: here I a while must stay,
To see a cruell fight doen by the Prince this day.

5

For all so soone, as *Guyon* thence was gon
  Upon his voyage with his trustie guide,
  That wicked band of villeins fresh begon
  That castle to assaile on every side,
  And lay strong siege about it far and wide.
  So huge and infinite their numbers were,
  That all the land they under them did hide;
  So fowle and ugly, that exceeding feare
Their visages imprest, when they approched neare.

6

Them in twelve troupes their Captain did dispart
  And round about in fittest steades did place,
  Where each might best offend his proper part,
  And his contrary object most deface,
  As every one seem'd meetest in that cace.
  Seven of the same against the Castle gate,
  In strong entrenchments he did closely place,
  Which with incessaunt force and endlesse hate,
They battred day and night, and entraunce did awate.

7

The other five, five sundry wayes he set,
  Against the five great Bulwarkes of that pile,
  And unto each a Bulwarke did arret,
  T'assayle with open force or hidden guile,
  In hope thereof to win victorious spoile.
  They all that charge did fervently apply,
  With greedie malice and importune toyle,
  And planted there their huge artillery,
With which they dayly made most dreadfull battery.

8

The first troupe was a monstrous rablement
　　Of fowle misshapen wights, of which some were
　　Headed like Owles, with beckes uncomely bent,
　　Others like Dogs, others like Gryphons dreare,
　　And some had wings, and some had clawes to teare,
　　And every one of them had Lynces eyes,
　　And every one did bow and arrowes beare:
　　All those were lawlesse lustes, corrupt envies,
And covetous aspectes, all cruell enimies.

9

Those same against the bulwarke of the *Sight*
　　Did lay strong siege, and battailous assault,
　　Ne once did yield it respit day nor night,
　　But soone as *Titan* gan his head exault,
　　And soone againe as he his light with hault,
　　Their wicked engins they against it bent:
　　That is each thing, by which the eyes may fault,
　　But two than all more huge and violent,
Beautie, and money, they that Bulwarke sorely rent.

10

The second Bulwarke was the *Hearing* sence,
　　Gainst which the second troupe dessignment makes;
　　Deformed creatures, in straunge difference,
　　Some having heads like Harts, some like to Snakes,
　　Some like wild Bores late rouzd out of the brakes;
　　Slaunderous reproches, and fowle infamies,
　　Leasings, backbytings, and vaine-glorious crakes,
　　Bad counsels, prayses, and false flatteries.
All those against that fort did bend their batteries.

11

Likewise that same third Fort, that is the *Smell*
　　Of that third troupe was cruelly assayd:
　　Whose hideous shapes were like to feends of hell,
　　Some like to hounds, some like to Apes, dismayd,
　　Some like to Puttockes, all in plumes arayd:
　　All shap't according their conditions,
　　For by those ugly formes weren pourtrayd,
　　Foolish delights and fond abusions,
Which do that sence besiege with light illusions.

12

And that fourth band, which cruell battry bent,
  Against the fourth Bulwarke, that is the *Tast*,
  Was as the rest, a grysie rablement,
  Some mouth'd like greedy Oystriges, some fast
  Like loathly Toades, some fashioned in the wast
  Like swine; for so deformd is luxury,
  Surfeat, misdiet, and unthriftie wast,
  Vaine feasts, and idle superfluity:
All those this sences Fort assayle incessantly.

13

But the fift troupe most horrible of hew,
  And fierce of force, was dreadfull to report:
  For some like Snailes, some did like spyders shew,
  And some like ugly Urchins thicke and short:
  Cruelly they assayled that fift Fort,
  Armed with darts of sensuall delight,
  With stings of carnall lust, and strong effort
  Of feeling pleasures, with which day and night
Against that same fift bulwarke they continued fight.

14

Thus these twelve troupes with dreadfull puissance
  Against that Castle restlesse siege did lay,
  And evermore their hideous Ordinance
  Upon the Bulwarkes cruelly did play,
  That now it gan to threaten neare decay:
  And evermore their wicked Capitaine
  Provoked them the breaches to assay,
  Somtimes with threats, somtimes with hope of gaine,
Which by the ransack of that peece they should attaine.

15

On th'other side, th'assieged Castles ward
  Their stedfast stonds did mightily maintaine,
  And many bold repulse, and many hard
  Atchievement wrought with perill and with paine,
  That goodly frame from ruine to sustaine:
  And those two brethren Giants did defend
  The walles so stoutly with their sturdie maine,
  That never entrance any durst pretend,
But they to direfull death their groning ghosts did send.

16

The noble virgin, Ladie of the place,
　Was much dismayed with that dreadfull sight:
　For never was she in so evill cace,
　Till that the Prince seeing her wofull plight,
　Gan her recomfort from so sad affright,
　Offring his service, and his dearest life
　For her defence, against that Carle to fight,
　Which was their chiefe and th'author of that strife:
She him remercied as the Patrone of her life.

17

Eftsoones himselfe in glitterand armes he dight,
　And his well proved weapons to him hent;
　So taking courteous conge he behight,
　Those gates to be unbar'd, and forth he went.
　Faire mote he thee, the prowest and most gent,
　That ever brandished bright steele on hye:
　Whom soone as that unruly rablement,
　With his gay Squire issuing did espy,
They reard a most outrageous dreadfull yelling cry.

18

And therewith all attonce at him let fly
　Their fluttring arrowes, thicke as flakes of snow,
　And round about him flocke impetuously,
　Like a great water flood, that tombling low
　From the high mountaines, threats to overflow
　With suddein fury all the fertile plaine,
　And the sad husbandmans long hope doth throw
　A downe the streame, and all his vowes make vaine,
Nor bounds nor banks his headlong ruine may sustaine.

19

Upon his shield their heaped hayle he bore,
　And with his sword disperst the raskall flockes,
　Which fled a sunder, and him fell before,
　As withered leaves drop from their dried stockes,
　When the wroth Western wind does reave their locks;
　And under neath him his courageous steed,
　The fierce *Spumador* trode them downe like docks,
　The fierce *Spumador* borne of heavenly seed:
Such as *Laomedon* of *Phœbus* race did breed.

Guyon overthrows the Bowre of Blisse

20

Which suddeine horrour and confused cry,
  When as their Captaine heard, in haste he yode,
  The cause to weet, and fault to remedy;
  Upon a Tygre swift and fierce he rode,
  That as the winde ran underneath his lode,
  Whiles his long legs nigh raught unto the ground;
  Full large he was of limbe, and shoulders brode,
  But of such subtile substance and unsound,
That like a ghost he seem'd, whose grave-clothes were unbound.

21

And in his hand a bended bow was seene,
  And many arrowes under his right side,
  All deadly daungerous, all cruell keene,
  Headed with flint, and feathers bloudie dide,
  Such as the *Indians* in their quivers hide;
  Those could he well direct and streight as line,
  And bid them strike the marke, which he had eyde,
  Ne was there salve, ne was there medicine,
That mote recure their wounds: so inly they did tine.

22

As pale and wan as ashes was his looke,
  His bodie leane and meagre as a rake,
  And skin all withered like a dryed rooke,
  Thereto as cold and drery as a Snake,
  That seem'd to tremble evermore, and quake:
  All in a canvas thin he was bedight,
  And girded with a belt of twisted brake,
  Upon his head he wore an Helmet light,
Made of a dead mans skull, that seem'd a ghastly sight.

23

Maleger was his name, and after him,
  There follow'd fast at hand two wicked Hags,
  With hoarie lockes all loose, and visage grim;
  Their feet unshod, their bodies wrapt in rags,
  And both as swift on foot, as chased Stags;
  And yet the one her other legge had lame,
  Which with a staffe, all full of litle snags
  She did support, and *Impotence* her name:
But th'other was *Impatience*, arm'd with raging flame.

24

Soone as the Carle from farre the Prince espyde,
 Glistring in armes and warlike ornament,
 His Beast he felly prickt on either syde,
 And his mischievous bow full readie bent,
 With which at him a cruell shaft he sent:
 But he was warie, and it warded well
 Upon his shield, that it no further went,
 But to the ground the idle quarrell fell:
Then he another and another did expell.

25

Which to prevent, the Prince his mortall speare
 Soone to him raught, and fierce at him did ride,
 To be avenged of that shot whyleare:
 But he was not so hardie to abide
 That bitter stownd, but turning quicke aside
 His light-foot beast, fled fast away for feare:
 Whom to pursue, the Infant after hide,
 So fast as his good Courser could him beare,
But labour lost it was, to weene approch him neare.

26

For as the winged wind his Tigre fled,
 That vew of eye could scarse him overtake,
 Ne scarse his feet on ground were seene to tred;
 Through hils and dales he speedie way did make,
 Ne hedge ne ditch his readie passage brake,
 And in his flight the villein turn'd his face,
 (As wonts the *Tartar* by the *Caspian* lake,
 When as the *Russian* him in fight does chace)
Unto his Tygres taile, and shot at him apace.

27

Apace he shot, and yet he fled apace,
 Still as the greedy knight nigh to him drew,
 And oftentimes he would relent his pace,
 That him his foe more fiercely should pursew:
 Who when his uncouth manner he did vew,
 He gan avize to follow him no more,
 But keepe his standing, and his shaftes eschew,
 Untill he quite had spent his perlous store,
And then assayle him fresh, ere he could shift for more.

28

But that lame Hag, still as abroad he strew
  His wicked arrowes, gathered them againe,
  And to him brought, fresh battell to renew:
  Which he espying, cast her to restraine
  From yielding succour to that cursed Swaine,
  And her attaching, thought her hands to tye;
  But soone as him dismounted on the plaine,
  That other Hag did farre away espy
Binding her sister, she to him ran hastily.

29

And catching hold of him, as downe he lent,
  Him backward overthrew, and downe him stayd
  With their rude hands and griesly graplement,
  Till that the villein comming to their ayd,
  Upon him fell, and lode upon him layd;
  Full litle wanted, but he had him slaine,
  And of the battell balefull end had made,
  Had not his gentle Squire beheld his paine,
And commen to his reskew, ere his bitter bane.

30

So greatest and most glorious thing on ground
  May often need the helpe of weaker hand;
  So feeble is mans state, and life unsound,
  That in assurance it may never stand,
  Till it dissolved be from earthly band.
  Proofe be thou Prince, the prowest man alive,
  And noblest borne of all in *Britayne* land;
  Yet thee fierce Fortune did so nearely drive,
That had not grace thee blest, thou shouldest not survive.

31

The Squire arriving, fiercely in his armes
  Snatcht first the one, and then the other Jade,
  His chiefest lets and authors of his harmes,
  And them perforce withheld with threatned blade,
  Least that his Lord they should behind invade;
  The whiles the Prince prickt with reprochfull shame,
  As one awakt out of long slombring shade,
  Reviving thought of glorie and of fame,
United all his powres to purge himselfe from blame.

32

Like as a fire, the which in hollow cave
  Hath long bene underkept, and downe supprest,
  With murmurous disdaine doth inly rave,
  And grudge, in so streight prison to be prest,
  At last breakes forth with furious unrest,
  And strives to mount unto his native seat;
  All that did earst it hinder and molest,
  It now devoures with flames and scorching heat,
And carries into smoake with rage and horror great.

33

So mightily the *Briton* Prince him rouzd
  Out of his hold, and broke his caitive bands,
  And as a Beare whom angry curres have touzd,
  Having off-shakt them, and escapt their hands,
  Becomes more fell, and all that him withstands
  Treads downe and overthrowes. Now had the Carle
  Alighted from his Tigre, and his hands
  Discharged of his bow and deadly quar'le,
To seize upon his foe flat lying on the marle.

34

Which now him turnd to disavantage deare;
  For neither can he fly, nor other harme,
  But trust unto his strength and manhood meare,
  Sith now he is farre from his monstrous swarme,
  And of his weapons did himselfe disarme.
  The knight yet wrothfull for his late disgrace,
  Fiercely advaunst his valorous right arme,
  And him so sore smote with his yron mace,
That groveling to the ground he fell, and fild his place.

35

Well weened he, that field was then his owne,
  And all his labour brought to happie end,
  When suddein up the villein overthrowne,
  Out of his swowne arose, fresh to contend,
  And gan himselfe to second battell bend,
  As hurt he had not bene. Thereby there lay
  An huge great stone, which stood upon one end,
  And had not bene removed many a day;
Some land-marke seem'd to be, or signe of sundry way.

36

The same he snatcht, and with exceeding sway
 Threw at his foe, who was right well aware
 To shunne the engin of his meant decay;
 It booted not to thinke that throw to beare,
 But ground he gave, and lightly leapt areare:
 Eft fierce returning, as a Faulcon faire
 That once hath failed of her souse full neare,
 Remounts againe into the open aire,
And unto better fortune doth her selfe prepaire.

37

So brave returning, with his brandisht blade,
 He to the Carle himselfe againe addrest,
 And strooke at him so sternely, that he made
 An open passage through his riven brest,
 That halfe the steele behind his back did rest;
 Which drawing backe, he looked evermore
 When the hart bloud should gush out of his chest,
 Or his dead corse should fall upon the flore;
But his dead corse upon the flore fell nathemore.

38

Ne drop of bloud appeared shed to bee,
 All were the wounde so wide and wonderous,
 That through his carkasse one might plainely see:
 Halfe in a maze with horror hideous,
 And halfe in rage, to be deluded thus,
 Againe through both the sides he strooke him quight,
 That made his spright to grone full piteous:
 Yet nathemore forth fled his groning spright,
But freshly as at first, prepard himselfe to fight.

39

Thereat he smitten was with great affright,
 And trembling terror did his hart apall,
 Ne wist he, what to thinke of that same sight,
 Ne what to say, ne what to doe at all;
 He doubted, least it were some magicall
 Illusion, that did beguile his sense,
 Or wandring ghost, that wanted funerall,
 Or aerie spirit under false pretence,
Or hellish feend raysd up through divelish science.

40

His wonder farre exceeded reasons reach,
That he began to doubt his dazeled sight,
And oft of error did himselfe appeach:
Flesh without bloud, a person without spright,
Wounds without hurt, a bodie without might,
That could doe harme, yet could not harmed bee,
That could not die, yet seem'd a mortall wight,
That was most strong in most infirmitee;
Like did he never heare, like did he never see.

41

A while he stood in this astonishment,
Yet would he not for all his great dismay
Give over to effect his first intent,
And th'utmost meanes of victorie assay,
Or th'utmost issew of his owne decay.
His owne good sword *Morddure*, that never fayld
At need, till now, he lightly threw away,
And his bright shield, that nought him now avayld,
And with his naked hands him forcibly assayld.

42

Twixt his two mightie armes him up he snatcht,
And crusht his carkasse so against his brest,
That the disdainfull soule he thence dispatcht,
And th'idle breath all utterly exprest:
Tho when he felt him dead, a downe he kest
The lumpish corse unto the senselesse grownd;
Adowne he kest it with so puissant wrest,
That backe againe it did aloft rebownd,
And gave against his mother earth a gronefull sownd.

43

As when *Joves* harnesse-bearing Bird from hie
Stoupes at a flying heron with proud disdaine,
The stone-dead quarrey fals so forciblie,
That it rebounds against the lowly plaine,
A second fall redoubling backe againe.
Then thought the Prince all perill sure was past,
And that he victor onely did remaine;
No sooner thought, than that the Carle as fast
Gan heap huge strokes on him as ere he downe was cast.

44

Nigh his wits end then woxe th'amazed knight,
  And thought his labour lost and travell vaine,
  Against this lifelesse shadow so to fight:
  Yet life he saw, and felt his mightie maine,
  That whiles he marveild still, did still him paine:
  For thy he gan some other wayes advize,
  How to take life from that dead-living swaine,
  Whom still he marked freshly to arize
From th'earth, and from her wombe new spirits to reprize.

45

He then remembred well, that had bene sayd,
  How th'Earth his mother was, and first him bore;
  She eke so often, as his life decayd,
  Did life with usury to him restore,
  And raysd him up much stronger than before,
  So soone as he unto her wombe did fall;
  Therefore to ground he would him cast no more,
  Ne him commit to grave terrestriall,
But beare him farre from hope of succour usuall.

46

Tho up he caught him twixt his puissant hands,
  And having scruzd out of his carrion corse
  The lothfull life, now loosd from sinfull bands,
  Upon his shoulders carried him perforse
  Above three furlongs, taking his full course,
  Untill he came unto a standing lake;
  Him thereinto he threw without remorse,
  Ne stird, till hope of life did him forsake;
So end of that Carles dayes, and his owne paines did make.

47

Which when those wicked Hags from farre did spy,
  Like two mad dogs they ran about the lands,
  And th'one of them with dreadfull yelling cry,
  Throwing away her broken chaines and bands,
  And having quencht her burning fier brands,
  Hedlong her selfe did cast into that lake;
  But *Impotence* with her owne wilfull hands,
  One of *Malegers* cursed darts did take,
So riv'd her trembling hart, and wicked end did make.

48

Thus now alone he conquerour remaines;
　Tho comming to his Squire, that kept his steed,
　Thought to have mounted, but his feeble vaines
　Him faild thereto, and served not his need,
　Through losse of bloud, which from his wounds did bleed,
　That he began to faint, and life decay:
　But his good Squire him helping up with speed,
　With stedfast hand upon his horse did stay,
And led him to the Castle by the beaten way.

49

Where many Groomes and Squiers readie were,
　To take him from his steed full tenderly,
　And eke the fairest *Alma* met him there
　With balme and wine and costly spicery,
　To comfort him in his infirmity;
　Eftsoones she causd him up to be convayd,
　And of his armes despoyled easily,
　In sumptuous bed she made him to be layd,
And all the while his wounds were dressing, by him stayd.

CANT. XII

Guyon, by Palmers governance,
　passing through perils great,
Doth overthrow the Bowre of blisse,
　and Acrasie defeat.

I

NOW gins this goodly frame of Temperance
　Fairely to rise, and her adorned hed
　To pricke of highest praise forth to advance,
　Formerly grounded, and fast setteled
　On firme foundation of true bountihed;
　And this brave knight, that for that vertue fights,
　Now comes to point of that same perilous sted,
　Where Pleasure dwelles in sensuall delights,
Mongst thousand dangers, and ten thousand magick mights.

2

Two dayes now in that sea he sayled has,
  Ne ever land beheld, ne living wight,
  Ne ought save perill, still as he did pas:
  Tho when appeared the third *Morrow* bright,
  Upon the waves to spred her trembling light,
  An hideous roaring farre away they heard,
  That all their senses filled with affright,
  And streight they saw the raging surges reard
Up to the skyes, that them of drowning made affeard.

3

Said then the Boteman, Palmer stere aright,
  And keepe an even course; for yonder way
  We needes must passe (God do us well acquight,)
  That is the *Gulfe of Greedinesse*, they say,
  That deepe engorgeth all this worldes pray:
  Which having swallowd up excessively,
  He soone in vomit up againe doth lay,
  And belcheth forth his superfluity,
That all the seas for feare do seeme away to fly.

4

On th'other side an hideous Rocke is pight,
  Of mightie *Magnes* stone, whose craggie clift
  Depending from on high, dreadfull to sight,
  Over the waves his rugged armes doth lift,
  And threatneth downe to throw his ragged rift
  On who so commeth nigh; yet nigh it drawes
  All passengers, that none from it can shift:
  For whiles they fly that Gulfes devouring jawes,
They on this rock are rent, and sunck in helplesse wawes.

5

Forward they passe, and strongly he them rowes,
  Untill they nigh unto that Gulfe arrive,
  Where streame more violent and greedy growes:
  Then he with all his puissance doth strive
  To strike his oares, and mightily doth drive
  The hollow vessell through the threatfull wave,
  Which gaping wide, to swallow them alive,
  In th'huge abysse of his engulfing grave,
Doth rore at them in vaine, and with great terror rave.

6

They passing by, that griesly mouth did see,
    Sucking the seas into his entralles deepe,
    That seem'd more horrible than hell to bee,
    Or that darke dreadfull hole of *Tartare* steepe,
    Through which the damned ghosts doen often creepe
    Backe to the world, bad livers to torment:
    But nought that falles into this direfull deepe,
    Ne that approcheth nigh the wide descent,
May backe returne, but is condemned to be drent.

7

On th'other side, they saw that perilous Rocke,
    Threatning it selfe on them to ruinate,
    On whose sharpe clifts the ribs of vessels broke,
    And shivered ships, which had bene wrecked late,
    Yet stuck, with carkasses exanimate
    Of such, as having all their substance spent
    In wanton joyes, and lustes intemperate,
    Did afterwards make shipwracke violent,
Both of their life, and fame for ever fowly blent.

8

For thy, this hight *The Rocke* of vile *Reproch,*
    A daungerous and detestable place,
    To which nor fish nor fowle did once approch,
    But yelling Meawes, with Seagulles hoarse and bace,
    And Cormoyrants, with birds of ravenous race,
    Which still sate waiting on that wastfull clift,
    For spoyle of wretches, whose unhappie cace,
    After lost credite and consumed thrift,
At last them driven hath to this despairefull drift.

9

The Palmer seeing them in safetie past,
    Thus said; Behold th'ensamples in our sights,
    Of lustfull luxurie and thriftlesse wast:
    What now is left of miserable wights,
    Which spent their looser daies in lewd delights,
    But shame and sad reproch, here to be red,
    By these rent reliques, speaking their ill plights?
    Let all that live, hereby be counselled,
To shunne *Rocke of Reproch,* and it as death to dred.

10

So forth they rowed, and that *Ferryman*
　　With his stiffe oares did brush the sea so strong,
　　That the hoare waters from his frigot ran,
　　And the light bubbles daunced all along,
　　Whiles the salt brine out of the billowes sprong.
　　At last farre off they many Islands spy,
　　On every side floting the floods emong:
　　Then said the knight, Loe I the land descry,
Therefore old Syre thy course do thereunto apply.

11

That may not be, said then the *Ferryman*
　　Least we unweeting hap to be fordonne:
　　For those same Islands, seeming now and than,
　　Are not firme lande, nor any certein wonne,
　　But straggling plots, which to and fro do ronne
　　In the wide waters: therefore are they hight
　　The *wandring Islands*. Therefore doe them shonne;
　　For they have oft drawne many a wandring wight
Into most deadly daunger and distressed plight.

12

Yet well they seeme to him, that farre doth vew,
　　Both faire and fruitfull, and the ground dispred
　　With grassie greene of delectable hew,
　　And the tall trees with leaves apparelled,
　　Are deckt with blossomes dyde in white and red,
　　That mote the passengers thereto allure;
　　But whosoever once hath fastened
　　His foot thereon, may never it recure,
But wandreth ever more uncertein and unsure.

13

As th'Isle of *Delos* whylome men report
　　Amid th'*Aegaean* sea long time did stray,
　　Ne made for shipping any certaine port,
　　Till that *Latona* traveiling that way,
　　Flying from *Junoes* wrath and hard assay,
　　Of her faire twins was there delivered,
　　Which afterwards did rule the night and day;
　　Thenceforth it firmely was established,
And for *Apolloes* honor highly herried.

14

They to him hearken, as beseemeth meete,
  And passe on forward: so their way does ly,
  That one of those same Islands, which doe fleet
  In the wide sea, they needes must passen by,
  Which seemd so sweet and pleasant to the eye,
  That it would tempt a man to touchen there:
  Upon the banck they sitting did espy
  A daintie damzell, dressing of her heare,
By whom a litle skippet floting did appeare.

15

She them espying, loud to them can call,
  Bidding them nigher draw unto the shore;
  For she had cause to busie them withall;
  And therewith loudly laught: But nathemore
  Would they once turne, but kept on as afore:
  Which when she saw, she left her lockes undight,
  And running to her boat withouten ore
  From the departing land it launched light,
And after them did drive with all her power and might.

16

Whom overtaking, she in merry sort
  Them gan to bord, and purpose diversly,
  Now faining dalliance and wanton sport,
  Now throwing forth lewd words immodestly;
  Till that the Palmer gan full bitterly
  Her to rebuke, for being loose and light:
  Which not abiding, but more scornefully
  Scoffing at him, that did her justly wite,
She turnd her bote about, and from them rowed quite.

17

That was the wanton *Phædria*, which late
  Did ferry him over the *Idle lake*:
  Whom nought regarding, they kept on their gate,
  And all her vaine allurements did forsake,
  When them the wary Boateman thus bespake;
  Here now behoveth us well to avyse,
  And of our safetie good heede to take;
  For here before a perlous passage lyes,
Where many Mermayds haunt, making false melodies.

18

But by the way, there is a great Quicksand,
  And a whirlepoole of hidden jeopardy,
  Therefore, Sir Palmer, keepe an even hand;
  For twixt them both the narrow way doth ly.
  Scarse had he said, when hard at hand they spy
  That quicksand nigh with water covered;
  But by the checked wave they did descry
  It plaine, and by the sea discoloured:
It called was the quicksand of *Unthriftyhed*.

19

They passing by, a goodly Ship did see,
  Laden from far with precious merchandize,
  And bravely furnished, as ship might bee,
  Which through great disaventure, or mesprize,
  Her selfe had runne into that hazardize;
  Whose mariners and merchants with much toyle,
  Labour'd in vaine, to have recur'd their prize,
  And the rich wares to save from pitteous spoyle,
But neither toyle nor travell might her backe recoyle.

20

On th'other side they see that perilous Poole,
  That called was the *Whirlepoole of decay*,
  In which full many had with haplesse doole
  Beene suncke, of whom no memorie did stay:
  Whose circled waters rapt with whirling sway,
  Like to a restlesse wheele, still running round,
  Did covet, as they passed by that way,
  To draw their boate within the utmost bound
Of his wide *Labyrinth*, and then to have them dround.

21

But th'heedfull Boateman strongly forth did stretch
  His brawnie armes, and all his body straine,
  That th'utmost sandy breach they shortly fetch,
  Whiles the dred daunger does behind remaine.
  Suddeine they see from midst of all the Maine,
  The surging waters like a mountaine rise,
  And the great sea puft up with proud disdaine,
  To swell above the measure of his guise,
As threatning to devoure all, that his powre despise.

22

The waves come rolling, and the billowes rore
   Outragiously, as they enraged were,
   Or wrathfull *Neptune* did them drive before
   His whirling charet, for exceeding feare:
   For not one puffe of wind there did appeare,
   That all the three thereat woxe much afrayd,
   Unweeting, what such horrour straunge did reare.
   Eftsoones they saw an hideous hoast arrayd,
Of huge Sea monsters, such as living sence dismayd.

23

Most ugly shapes, and horrible aspects,
   Such as Dame Nature selfe mote feare to see,
   Or shame, that ever should so fowle defects
   From her most cunning hand escaped bee;
   All dreadfull pourtraicts of deformitee:
   Spring-headed *Hydraes*, and sea-shouldring Whales,
   Great whirlpooles, which all fishes make to flee,
   Bright Scolopendraes, arm'd with silver scales,
Mighty *Monoceros*, with immeasured tayles.

24

The dreadfull Fish, that hath deserv'd the name
   Of Death, and like him lookes in dreadfull hew,
   The griesly Wasserman, that makes his game
   The flying ships with swiftnesse to pursew,
   The horrible Sea-satyre, that doth shew
   His fearefull face in time of greatest storme,
   Huge *Ziffius*, whom Mariners eschew
   No lesse, than rockes, (as travellers informe,)
And greedy *Rosmarines* with visages deforme.

25

All these, and thousand thousands many more,
   And more deformed Monsters thousand fold,
   With dreadfull noise, and hollow rombling rore,
   Came rushing in the fomy waves enrold,
   Which seem'd to fly for feare, them to behold:
   Ne wonder, if these did the knight appall;
   For all that here on earth we dreadfull hold,
   Be but as bugs to fearen babes withall,
Compared to the creatures in the seas entrall.

26

Feare nought, (then said the Palmer well aviz'd;)
   For these same Monsters are not these in deed,
   But are into these fearefull shapes disguiz'd
   By that same wicked witch, to worke us dreed,
   And draw from on this journey to proceede.
   Tho lifting up his vertuous staffe on hye,
   He smote the sea, which calmed was with speed,
   And all that dreadfull Armie fast gan flye
Into great *Tethys* bosome, where they hidden lye.

27

Quit from that daunger, forth their course they kept,
   And as they went, they heard a ruefull cry
   Of one, that wayld and pittifully wept,
   That through the sea the resounding plaints did fly:
   At last they in an Island did espy
   A seemely Maiden, sitting by the shore,
   That with great sorrow and sad agony,
   Seemed some great misfortune to deplore,
And lowd to them for succour called evermore.

28

Which *Guyon* hearing, streight his Palmer bad,
   To stere the boate towards that dolefull Mayd,
   That he might know, and ease her sorrow sad:
   Who him avizing better, to him sayd;
   Faire Sir, be not displeasd, if disobayd:
   For ill it were to hearken to her cry;
   For she is inly nothing ill apayd,
   But onely womanish fine forgery,
Your stubborne hart t'affect with fraile infirmity.

29

To which when she your courage hath inclind
   Through foolish pitty, then her guilefull bayt
   She will embosome deeper in your mind,
   And for your ruine at the last awayt.
   The knight was ruled, and the Boateman strayt
   Held on his course with stayed stedfastnesse,
   Ne ever shruncke, ne ever sought to bayt
   His tyred armes for toylesome wearinesse,
But with his oares did sweepe the watry wildernesse.

30

And now they nigh approched to the sted,
　　Where as those Mermayds dwelt: it was a still
　　And calmy bay, on th'one side sheltered
　　With the brode shadow of an hoarie hill,
　　On th'other side an high rocke toured still,
　　That twixt them both a pleasaunt port they made,
　　And did like an halfe Theatre fulfill:
　　There those five sisters had continuall trade,
And usd to bath themselves in that deceiptfull shade.

31

They were faire Ladies, till they fondly striv'd
　　With th'*Heliconian* maides for maistery;
　　Of whom they over-comen, were depriv'd
　　Of their proud beautie, and th'one moyity
　　Transform'd to fish, for their bold surquedry,
　　But th'upper halfe their hew retained still,
　　And their sweet skill in wonted melody;
　　Which ever after they abusd to ill,
T'allure weake travellers, whom gotten they did kill.

32

So now to *Guyon*, as he passed by,
　　Their pleasaunt tunes they sweetly thus applide;
　　O thou faire sonne of gentle Faery,
　　That art in mighty armes most magnifide
　　Above all knights, that ever battell tride,
　　O turne thy rudder hither-ward a while:
　　Here may thy storme-bet vessell safely ride;
　　This is the Port of rest from troublous toyle,
The worlds sweet In, from paine and wearisome turmoyle.

33

With that the rolling sea resounding soft,
　　In his big base them fitly answered,
　　And on the rocke the waves breaking aloft,
　　A solemne Meane unto them measured,
　　The whiles sweet *Zephirus* lowd whisteled
　　His treble, a straunge kinde of harmony;
　　Which *Guyons* senses softly tickeled,
　　That he the boateman bad row easily,
And let him beare some part of their rare melody.

34

But him the Palmer from that vanity,
With temperate advice discounselled,
That they it past, and shortly gan descry
The land, to which their course they leveled;
When suddeinly a grosse fog over spred
With his dull vapour all that desert has,
And heavens chearefull face enveloped,
That all things one, and one as nothing was,
And this great Universe seemd one confused mas.

35

Thereat they greatly were dismayd, ne wist
How to direct their way in darkenesse wide,
But feard to wander in that wastfull mist,
For tombling into mischiefe unespide.
Worse is the daunger hidden, than descride.
Suddeinly an innumerable flight
Of harmefull fowles about them fluttering, cride,
And with their wicked wings them oft did smight,
And sore annoyed, groping in that griesly night.

36

Even all the nation of unfortunate
And fatall birds about them flocked were,
Such as by nature men abhorre and hate,
The ill-faste Owle, deaths dreadfull messengere,
The hoars Night-raven, trump of dolefull drere,
The lether-winged Bat, dayes enimy,
The ruefull Strich, still waiting on the bere,
The Whistler shrill, that who so heares, doth dy,
The hellish Harpies, prophets of sad destiny.

37

All those, and all that else does horrour breed,
About them flew, and fild their sayles with feare:
Yet stayd they not, but forward did proceed,
Whiles th'one did row, and th'other stifly steare;
Till that at last the weather gan to cleare,
And the faire land it selfe did plainly show.
Said then the Palmer, Lo where does appeare
The sacred soile, where all our perils grow;
Therefore, Sir knight, your ready armes about you throw.

38

He hearkned, and his armes about him tooke,
　The whiles the nimble boate so well her sped,
　That with her crooked keele the land she strooke,
　Then forth the noble *Guyon* sallied,
　And his sage Palmer, that him governed;
　But th'other by his boate behind did stay.
　They marched fairly forth, of nought ydred,
　Both firmely armd for every hard assay,
With constancy and care, gainst daunger and dismay.

39

Ere long they heard an hideous bellowing
　Of many beasts, that roard outrageously,
　As if that hungers point, or *Venus* sting
　Had them enraged with fell surquedry;
　Yet nought they feard, but past on hardily,
　Untill they came in vew of those wild beasts:
　Who all attonce, gaping full greedily,
　And rearing fiercely their upstarting crests,
Ran towards, to devoure those unexpected guests.

40

But soone as they approcht with deadly threat,
　The Palmer over them his staffe upheld,
　His mighty staffe, that could all charmes defeat:
　Eftsoones their stubborne courages were queld,
　And high advaunced crests downe meekely feld,
　In stead of fraying, they them selves did feare,
　And trembled, as them passing they beheld:
　Such wondrous powre did in that staffe appeare,
All monsters to subdew to him, that did it beare.

41

Of that same wood it fram'd was cunningly,
　Of which *Caduceus* whilome was made,
　Caduceus the rod of *Mercury*,
　With which he wonts the *Stygian* realmes invade,
　Through ghastly horrour, and eternall shade;
　Th'infernall feends with it he can asswage,
　And *Orcus* tame, whom nothing can perswade,
　And rule the *Furyes*, when they most do rage:
Such vertue in his staffe had eke this Palmer sage.

42

Thence passing forth, they shortly do arrive,
  Whereas the Bowre of *Blisse* was situate;
  A place pickt out by choice of best alive,
  That natures worke by art can imitate:
  In which what ever in this worldly state
  Is sweet, and pleasing unto living sense,
  Or that may dayntiest fantasie aggrate,
  Was poured forth with plentifull dispence,
And made there to abound with lavish affluence.

43

Goodly it was enclosed round about,
  Aswell their entred guestes to keepe within,
  As those unruly beasts to hold without;
  Yet was the fence thereof but weake and thin;
  Nought feard their force, that fortilage to win,
  But wisedomes powre, and temperaunces might,
  By which the mightiest things efforced bin:
  And eke the gate was wrought of substaunce light,
Rather for pleasure, than for battery or fight.

44

Yt framed was of precious yvory,
  That seemd a worke of admirable wit;
  And therein all the famous history
  Of *Jason* and *Medæa* was ywrit;
  Her mighty charmes, her furious loving fit,
  His goodly conquest of the golden fleece,
  His falsed faith, and love too lightly flit,
  The wondred *Argo*, which in venturous peece
First through the *Euxine* seas bore all the flowr of *Greece*.

45

Ye might have seene the frothy billowes fry
  Under the ship, as thorough them she went,
  That seemd the waves were into yvory,
  Or yvory into the waves were sent;
  And other where the snowy substaunce sprent
  With vermell, like the boyes bloud therein shed,
  A piteous spectacle did represent,
  And otherwhiles with gold besprinkeled;
Yt seemd th'enchaunted flame, which did *Creüsa* wed.

46

All this, and more might in that goodly gate
　　Be red; that ever open stood to all,
　　Which thither came: but in the Porch there sate
　　A comely personage of stature tall,
　　And semblaunce pleasing, more than naturall,
　　That travellers to him seemd to entize;
　　His looser garment to the ground did fall,
　　And flew about his heeles in wanton wize,
Not fit for speedy pace, or manly exercize.

47

They in that place him *Genius* did call:
　　Not that celestiall powre, to whom the care
　　Of life, and generation of all
　　That lives, pertaines in charge particulare,
　　Who wondrous things concerning our welfare,
　　And straunge phantomes doth let us oft forsee,
　　And oft of secret ill bids us beware:
　　That is our Selfe, whom though we do not see,
Yet each doth in him selfe it well perceive to bee.

48

Therefore a God him sage Antiquity
　　Did wisely make, and good *Agdistes* call:
　　But this same was to that quite contrary,
　　The foe of life, that good envyes to all,
　　That secretly doth us procure to fall,
　　Through guilefull semblaunts, which he makes us see.
　　He of this Gardin had the governall,
　　And Pleasures porter was devizd to bee,
Holding a staffe in hand for more formalitee.

49

With diverse flowres he daintily was deckt,
　　And strowed round about, and by his side
　　A mighty Mazer bowle of wine was set,
　　As if it had to him bene sacrifide;
　　Wherewith all new-come guests he gratifide:
　　So did he eke Sir *Guyon* passing by:
　　But he his idle curtesie defide,
　　And overthrew his bowle disdainfully;
And broke his staffe, with which he charmed semblants sly.

50

Thus being entred, they behold around
　A large and spacious plaine, on every side
　Strowed with pleasauns, whose faire grassy ground
　Mantled with greene, and goodly beautifide
　With all the ornaments of *Floraes* pride,
　Wherewith her mother Art, as halfe in scorne
　Of niggard Nature, like a pompous bride
　Did decke her, and too lavishly adorne,
When forth from virgin bowre she comes in th'early morne.

51

Thereto the Heavens alwayes Joviall,
　Lookt on them lovely, still in stedfast state,
　Ne suffred storme nor frost on them to fall,
　Their tender buds or leaves to violate,
　Nor scorching heat, nor cold intemperate
　T'afflict the creatures, which therein did dwell,
　But the milde aire with season moderate
　Gently attempred, and disposd so well,
That still it breathed forth sweet spirit and holesome smell.

52

More sweet and holesome, than the pleasaunt hill
　Of *Rhodope*, on which the Nimphe, that bore
　A gyaunt babe, her selfe for griefe did kill;
　Or the Thessalian *Tempe*, where of yore
　Faire *Daphne Phœbus* hart with love did gore;
　Or *Ida*, where the Gods lov'd to repaire,
　When ever they their heavenly bowres forlore;
　Or sweet *Parnasse*, the haunt of Muses faire;
Or *Eden* selfe, if ought with *Eden* mote compaire.

53

Much wondred *Guyon* at the faire aspect
　Of that sweet place, yet suffred no delight
　To sincke into his sence, nor mind affect,
　But passed forth, and lookt still forward right,
　Bridling his will, and maistering his might:
　Till that he came unto another gate;
　No gate, but like one, being goodly dight
　With boughes and braunches, which did broad dilate
Their clasping armes, in wanton wreathings intricate.

54

So fashioned a Porch with rare device,
  Archt over head with an embracing vine,
  Whose bounches hanging downe, seemed to entice
  All passers by, to tast their lushious wine,
  And did themselves into their hands incline,
  As freely offering to be gathered:
  Some deepe empurpled as the *Hyacint*,
  Some as the Rubine, laughing sweetly red,
Some like faire Emeraudes, not yet well ripened.

55

And them amongst, some were of burnisht gold,
  So made by art, to beautifie the rest,
  Which did themselves emongst the leaves enfold,
  As lurking from the vew of covetous guest,
  That the weake bowes, with so rich load opprest,
  Did bow adowne, as over-burdened.
  Under that Porch a comely dame did rest,
  Clad in faire weedes, but fowle disordered,
And garments loose, that seemd unmeet for womanhed.

56

In her left hand a Cup of gold she held,
  And with her right the riper fruit did reach,
  Whose sappy liquor, that with fulnesse sweld,
  Into her cup she scruzd, with daintie breach
  Of her fine fingers, without fowle empeach,
  That so faire wine-presse made the wine more sweet:
  Thereof she usd to give to drinke to each,
  Whom passing by she happened to meet:
It was her guise, all Straungers goodly so to greet.

57

So she to *Guyon* offred it to tast;
  Who taking it out of her tender hond,
  The cup to ground did violently cast,
  That all in peeces it was broken fond,
  And with the liquor stained all the lond:
  Whereat *Excesse* exceedingly was wroth,
  Yet no'te the same amend, ne yet withstond,
  But suffered him to passe, all were she loth;
Who nought regarding her displeasure forward goth.

58

There the most daintie Paradise on ground,
  It selfe doth offer to his sober eye,
  In which all pleasures plenteously abound,
  And none does others happinesse envye:
  The painted flowres, the trees upshooting hye,
  The dales for shade, the hilles for breathing space,
  The trembling groves, the Christall running by;
  And that, which all faire workes doth most aggrace,
The art, which all that wrought, appeared in no place.

59

One would have thought, (so cunningly, the rude,
  And scorned parts were mingled with the fine,)
  That nature had for wantonesse ensude
  Art, and that Art at nature did repine;
  So striving each th'other to undermine,
  Each did the others worke more beautifie;
  So diff'ring both in willes, agreed in fine:
  So all agreed through sweete diversitie,
This Gardin to adorne with all varietie.

60

And in the midst of all, a fountaine stood,
  Of richest substaunce, that on earth might bee,
  So pure and shiny, that the silver flood
  Through every channell running one might see;
  Most goodly it with curious imageree
  Was over-wrought, and shapes of naked boyes,
  Of which some seemd with lively jollitee,
  To fly about, playing their wanton toyes,
Whilest others did them selves embay in liquid joyes.

61

And over all, of purest gold was spred,
  A trayle of yvie in his native hew:
  For the rich mettall was so coloured,
  That wight, who did not well avis'd it vew,
  Would surely deeme it to be yvie trew:
  Low his lascivious armes adown did creepe,
  That themselves dipping in the silver dew,
  Their fleecy flowres they tenderly did steepe,
Which drops of Christall seemd for wantones to weepe.

62

Infinit streames continually did well
  Out of this fountaine, sweet and faire to see,
  The which into an ample laver fell,
  And shortly grew to so great quantitie,
  That like a little lake it seemd to bee;
  Whose depth exceeded not three cubits hight,
  That through the waves one might the bottom see,
  All pav'd beneath with Jaspar shining bright,
That seemd the fountaine in that sea did sayle upright.

63

And all the margent round about was set,
  With shady Laurell trees, thence to defend
  The sunny beames, which on the billowes bet,
  And those which therein bathed, mote offend.
  As *Guyon* hapned by the same to wend,
  Two naked Damzelles he therein espyde,
  Which therein bathing, seemed to contend,
  And wrestle wantonly, ne car'd to hyde,
Their dainty parts from vew of any, which them eyde.

64

Sometimes the one would lift the other quight
  Above the waters, and then downe againe
  Her plong, as over maistered by might,
  Where both awhile would covered remaine,
  And each the other from to rise restraine;
  The whiles their snowy limbes, as through a vele,
  So through the Christall waves appeared plaine:
  Then suddeinly both would themselves unhele,
And th'amarous sweet spoiles to greedy eyes revele.

65

As that faire Starre, the messenger of morne,
  His deawy face out of the sea doth reare:
  Or as the *Cyprian* goddesse, newly borne
  Of th'Oceans fruitfull froth, did first appeare:
  Such seemed they, and so their yellow heare
  Christalline humour dropped downe apace.
  Whom such when *Guyon* saw, he drew him neare,
  And somewhat gan relent his earnest pace,
His stubborne brest gan secret pleasaunce to embrace.

66

The wanton Maidens him espying, stood
　Gazing a while at his unwonted guise;
　Then th'one her selfe low ducked in the flood,
　Abasht, that her a straunger did a vise:
　But th'other rather higher did arise,
　And her two lilly paps aloft displayd,
　And all, that might his melting hart entise
　To her delights, she unto him bewrayd:
The rest hid underneath, him more desirous made.

67

With that, the other likewise up arose,
　And her faire lockes, which formerly were bownd
　Up in one knot, she low adowne did lose:
　Which flowing long and thick, her cloth'd arownd,
　And th'yvorie in golden mantle gownd:
　So that faire spectacle from him was reft,
　Yet that, which reft it, no lesse faire was fownd:
　So hid in lockes and waves from lookers theft,
Nought but her lovely face she for his looking left.

68

Withall she laughed, and she blusht withall,
　That blushing to her laughter gave more grace,
　And laughter to her blushing, as did fall:
　Now when they spide the knight to slacke his pace,
　Them to behold, and in his sparkling face
　The secret signes of kindled lust appeare,
　Their wanton meriments they did encreace,
　And to him beckned, to approch more neare,
And shewd him many sights, that courage cold could reare.

69

On which when gazing him the Palmer saw,
　He much rebukt those wandring eyes of his,
　And counseld well, him forward thence did draw.
　Now are they come nigh to the *Bowre of blis*
　Of her fond favorites so nam'd amis:
　When thus the Palmer; Now Sir, well avise;
　For here the end of all our travell is:
　Here wonnes *Acrasia*, whom we must surprise,
Else she will slip away, and all our drift despise.

70

Eftsoones they heard a most melodious sound,
　Of all that mote delight a daintie eare,
　Such as attonce might not on living ground,
　Save in this Paradise, be heard elswhere:
　Right hard it was, for wight, which did it heare,
　To read, what manner musicke that mote bee:
　For all that pleasing is to living eare,
　Was there consorted in one harmonee,
Birdes, voyces, instruments, windes, waters, all agree.

71

The joyous birdes shrouded in chearefull shade,
　Their notes unto the voyce attempred sweet;
　Th'Angelicall soft trembling voyces made
　To th'instruments divine respondence meet:
　The silver sounding instruments did meet
　With the base murmure of the waters fall:
　The waters fall with difference discreet,
　Now soft, now loud, unto the wind did call:
The gentle warbling wind low answered to all.

72

There, whence that Musick seemed heard to bee,
　Was the faire Witch her selfe now solacing,
　With a new Lover, whom through sorceree
　And witchcraft, she from farre did thither bring:
　There she had him now layd a slombering,
　In secret shade, after long wanton joyes:
　Whilst round about them pleasauntly did sing
　Many faire Ladies, and lascivious boyes,
That ever mixt their song with light licentious toyes.

73

And all that while, right over him she hong,
　With her false eyes fast fixed in his sight,
　As seeking medicine, whence she was stong,
　Or greedily depasturing delight:
　And oft inclining downe with kisses light,
　For feare of waking him, his lips bedewd,
　And through his humid eyes did sucke his spright,
　Quite molten into lust and pleasure lewd;
Wherewith she sighed soft, as if his case she rewd.

74

The whiles some one did chaunt this lovely lay;
 Ah see, who so faire thing doest faine to see,
 In springing flowre the image of thy day;
 Ah see the Virgin Rose, how sweetly shee
 Doth first peepe forth with bashfull modestee,
 That fairer seemes, the lesse ye see her may;
 Lo see soone after, how more bold and free
 Her bared bosome she doth broad display;
Loe see soone after, how she fades, and falles away.

75

So passeth, in the passing of a day,
 Of mortall life the leafe, the bud, the flowre,
 Ne more doth flourish after first decay,
 That earst was sought to decke both bed and bowre,
 Of many a Ladie, and many a Paramowre:
 Gather therefore the Rose, whilest yet is prime,
 For soone comes age, that will her pride deflowre:
 Gather the Rose of love, whilest yet is time,
Whilest loving thou mayst loved be with equall crime.

76

He ceast, and then gan all the quire of birdes
 Their diverse notes t'attune unto his lay,
 As in approvance of his pleasing words.
 The constant paire heard all, that he did say,
 Yet swarved not, but kept their forward way,
 Through many covert groves, and thickets close,
 In which they creeping did at last display
 That wanton Ladie, with her lover lose,
Whose sleepie head she in her lap did soft dispose.

77

Upon a bed of Roses she was layd,
 As faint through heat, or dight to pleasant sin,
 And was arayd, or rather disarayd,
 All in a vele of silke and silver thin,
 That hid no whit her alablaster skin,
 But rather shewd more white, if more might bee:
 More subtile web *Arachne* cannot spin,
 Nor the fine nets, which oft we woven see
Of scorched deaw, do not in th'aire more lightly flee.

78

Her snowy brest was bare to readie spoyle
  Of hungry eies, which n'ote therewith be fild,
  And yet through languour of her late sweet toyle,
  Few drops, more cleare than Nectar, forth distild,
  That like pure Orient perles adowne it trild,
  And her faire eyes sweet smyling in delight,
  Moystened their fierie beames, with which she thrild
  Fraile harts, yet quenched not; like starry light
Which sparckling on the silent waves, does seeme more bright.

79

The young man sleeping by her, seemd to bee
  Some goodly swayne of honorable place,
  That certes it great pittie was to see
  Him his nobilitie so foule deface;
  A sweet regard, and amiable grace,
  Mixed with manly sternnesse did appeare
  Yet sleeping, in his well proportiond face,
  And on his tender lips the downy heare
Did now but freshly spring, and silken blossomes beare.

80

His warlike armes, the idle instruments
  Of sleeping praise, were hong upon a tree,
  And his brave shield, full of old moniments,
  Was fowly ra'st, that none the signes might see;
  Ne for them, ne for honour cared hee,
  Ne ought, that did to his advauncement tend,
  But in lewd loves, and wastfull luxuree,
  His dayes, his goods, his bodie he did spend:
O horrible enchantment, that him so did blend.

81

The noble Elfe, and carefull Palmer drew
  So nigh them, minding nought, but lustfull game,
  That suddein forth they on them rusht, and threw
  A subtile net, which onely for the same
  The skilfull Palmer formally did frame.
  So held them under fast, the whiles the rest
  Fled all away for feare of fowler shame.
  The faire Enchauntresse, so unwares opprest,
Tryde all her arts, and all her sleights, thence out to wrest.

82

And eke her lover strove: but all in vaine;
For that same net so cunningly was wound,
That neither guile, nor force might it distraine.
They tooke them both, and both them strongly bound
In captive bandes, which there they readie found:
But her in chaines of adamant he tyde;
For nothing else might keepe her safe and sound;
But *Verdant* (so he hight) he soone untyde,
And counsell sage in steed thereof to him applyde.

83

But all those pleasant bowres and Pallace brave,
Guyon broke downe, with rigour pittilesse;
Ne ought their goodly workmanship might save
Them from the tempest of his wrathfulnesse,
But that their blisse he turn'd to balefulnesse:
Their groves he feld, their gardins did deface,
Their arbers spoyle, their Cabinets supresse,
Their banket houses burne, their buildings race,
And of the fairest late, now made the fowlest place.

84

Then led they her away, and eke that knight
They with them led, both sorrowfull and sad:
The way they came, the same retourn'd they right,
Till they arrived, where they lately had
Charm'd those wild-beasts, that rag'd with furie mad.
Which now awaking, fierce at them gan fly,
As in their mistresse reskew, whom they lad;
But them the Palmer soone did pacify.
Then *Guyon* askt, what meant those beastes, which there did ly.

85

Said he, These seeming beasts are men indeed,
Whom this Enchauntresse hath transformed thus,
Whylome her lovers, which her lusts did feed,
Now turned into figures hideous,
According to their mindes like monstruous.
Sad end (quoth he) of life intemperate,
And mournefull meed of joyes delicious:
But Palmer, if it mote thee so aggrate,
Let them returned be unto their former state.

86

Streight way he with his vertuous staffe them strooke,
And streight of beasts they comely men became;
Yet being men they did unmanly looke,
And stared ghastly, some for inward shame,
And some for wrath, to see their captive Dame:
But one above the rest in speciall,
That had an hog beene late, hight *Grille* by name,
Repined greatly, and did him miscall,
That had from hoggish forme him brought to naturall.

87

Said *Guyon*, See the mind of beastly man,
That hath so soone forgot the excellence
Of his creation, when he life began,
That now he chooseth, with vile difference,
To be a beast, and lacke intelligence.
To whom the Palmer thus, The donghill kind
Delights in filth and foule incontinence:
Let *Grill* be *Grill*, and have his hoggish mind,
But let us hence depart, whilest wether serves and wind.

THE THIRD BOOKE OF THE
FAERIE QUEENE
CONTAYNING THE LEGEND
OF BRITOMARTIS, OR OF CHASTITIE

I

IT falls me here to write of Chastity,
 That fairest vertue, farre above the rest;
 For which what needs me fetch from *Faery*
 Forreine ensamples, it to have exprest?
 Sith it is shrined in my Soveraines brest,
 And form'd so lively in each perfect part,
 That to all Ladies, which have it profest,
 Need but behold the pourtraict of her hart,
If pourtrayd it might be by any living art.

2

But living art may not least part expresse,
 Nor life-resembling pencill it can paint,
 All were it *Zeuxis* or *Praxiteles:*
 His dædale hand would faile, and greatly faint,
 And her perfections with his error taint:
 Ne Poets wit, that passeth Painter farre
 In picturing the parts of beautie daint,
 So hard a workmanship adventure darre,
For fear through want of words her excellence to marre.

3

How then shall I, Apprentice of the skill,
That whylome in divinest wits did raine,
Presume so high to stretch mine humble quill?
Yet now my lucklesse lot doth me constraine
Hereto perforce. But O dred Soveraine
Thus farre forth pardon, sith that choicest wit
Cannot your glorious pourtraict figure plaine
That I in colourd showes may shadow it,
And antique praises unto present persons fit.

4

But if in living colours, and right hew,
Your selfe you covet to see pictured,
Who can it doe more lively, or more trew,
Than that sweet verse, with *Nectar* sprinckeled,
In which a gracious servant pictured
His *Cynthia*, his heavens fairest light?
That with his melting sweetnesse ravished,
And with the wonder of her beames bright,
My senses lulled are in slomber of delight.

5

But let that same delitious Poet lend
A little leave unto a rusticke Muse
To sing his mistresse prayse, and let him mend,
If ought amis her liking may abuse:
Ne let his fairest *Cynthia* refuse,
In mirrours more than one her selfe to see,
But either *Gloriana* let her chuse,
Or in *Belphœbe* fashioned to bee:
In th'one her rule, in th'other her rare chastitee.

Britomart

CANT. I

Guyon encountreth Britomart,
faire Florimell is chaced:
Duessaes traines and Malecastaes
champions are defaced.

I

THE famous Briton Prince and Faerie knight,
　After long wayes and perilous paines endured,
　Having their wearie limbes to perfect plight
　Restord, and sory wounds right well recured,
　Of the faire *Alma* greatly were procured,
　To make there lenger sojourne and abode;
　But when thereto they might not be allured,
　From seeking praise, and deeds of armes abrode,
They courteous conge tooke, and forth together yode.

2

But the captiv'd *Acrasia* he sent,
　Because of travell long, a nigher way,
　With a strong gard, all reskew to prevent,
　And her to Faerie court safe to convay,
　That her for witnesse of his hard assay,
　Unto his *Faerie* Queene he might present:
　But he him selfe betooke another way,
　To make more triall of his hardiment,
And seeke adventures, as he with Prince *Arthur* went.

3

Long so they travelled through wastefull wayes,
　Where daungers dwelt, and perils most did wonne,
　To hunt for glorie and renowmed praise;
　Full many Countries they did overronne,
　From the uprising to the setting Sunne,
　And many hard adventures did atchieve;
　Of all the which they honour ever wonne,
　Seeking the weake oppressed to relieve,
And to recover right for such, as wrong did grieve.

4

At last as through an open plaine they yode,
  They spide a knight, that towards pricked faire,
  And him beside an aged Squire there rode,
  That seem'd to couch under his shield three-square,
  As if that age bad him that burden spare,
  And yield it those, that stouter could it wield:
  He them espying, gan himselfe prepare,
  And on his arme addresse his goodly shield
That bore a Lion passant in a golden field.

5

Which seeing good Sir *Guyon*, deare besought
  The Prince of grace, to let him runne that turne.
  He graunted: then the Faery quickly raught
  His poinant speare, and sharpely gan to spurne
  His fomy steed, whose fierie feete did burne
  The verdant grasse, as he thereon did tread;
  Ne did the other backe his foot returne,
  But fiercely forward came withouten dread,
And bent his dreadfull speare against the others head.

6

They bene ymet, and both their points arrived,
  But *Guyon* drove so furious and fell,
  That seem'd both shield and plate it would have rived;
  Nathelesse it bore his foe not from his sell,
  But made him stagger, as he were not well:
  But *Guyon* selfe, ere well he was aware,
  Nigh a speares length behind his crouper fell,
  Yet in his fall so well him selfe he bare,
That mischievous mischance his life and limbes did spare.

7

Great shame and sorrow of that fall he tooke;
  For never yet, sith warlike armes he bore,
  And shivering speare in bloudie field first shooke,
  He found himselfe dishonored so sore.
  Ah gentlest knight, that ever armour bore,
  Let not thee grieve dismounted to have beene,
  And brought to ground, that never wast before;
  For not thy fault, but secret powre unseene,
That speare enchaunted was, which layd thee on the greene.

8

But weenedst thou what wight thee overthrew,
  Much greater griefe and shamefuller regret
  For thy hard fortune then thou wouldst renew,
  That of a single damzell thou wert met
  On equall plaine, and there so hard beset;
  Even the famous *Britomart* it was,
  Whom straunge adventure did from *Britaine* fet,
  To seeke her lover (love farre sought alas,)
Whose image she had seene in *Venus* looking glas.

9

Full of disdainefull wrath, he fierce uprose,
  For to revenge that foule reprochfull shame,
  And snatching his bright sword began to close
  With her on foot, and stoutly forward came;
  Die rather would he, than endure that same.
  Which when his Palmer saw, he gan to feare
  His toward perill and untoward blame,
  Which by that new rencounter he should reare:
For death sate on the point of that enchaunted speare.

10

And hasting towards him gan faire perswade,
  Not to provoke misfortune, nor to weene
  His speares default to mend with cruell blade;
  For by his mightie Science he had seene
  The secret vertue of that weapon keene,
  That mortall puissance mote not withstond:
  Nothing on earth mote alwaies happie beene.
  Great hazard were it, and adventure fond,
To loose long gotten honour with one evill hond.

11

By such good meanes he him discounselled,
  From prosecuting his revenging rage;
  And eke the Prince like treaty handeled,
  His wrathfull will with reason to asswage,
  And laid the blame, not to his carriage,
  But to his starting steed, that swarv'd asyde,
  And to the ill purveyance of his page,
  That had his furnitures not firmely tyde:
So is his angry courage fairely pacifyde.

12

Thus reconcilement was betweene them knit,
Through goodly temperance, and affection chaste,
And either vowd with all their power and wit,
To let not others honour be defaste,
Of friend or foe, who ever it embaste,
Ne armes to beare against the others syde:
In which accord the Prince was also plaste,
And with that golden chaine of concord tyde.
So goodly all agreed, they forth yfere did ryde.

13

O goodly usage of those antique times,
In which the sword was servant unto right;
When not for malice and contentious crimes,
But all for praise, and proofe of manly might,
The martiall brood accustomed to fight:
Then honour was the meed of victorie,
And yet the vanquished had no despight:
Let later age that noble use envie,
Vile rancour to avoid, and cruell surquedrie.

14

Long they thus travelled in friendly wise,
Through countries waste, and eke well edifyde,
Seeking adventures hard, to exercise
Their puissance, whylome full dernely tryde:
At length they came into a forrest wyde,
Whose hideous horror and sad trembling sound
Full griesly seem'd: Therein they long did ryde,
Yet tract of living creatures none they found,
Save Beares, Lions, and Buls, which romed them around.

15

All suddenly out of the thickest brush,
Upon a milk-white Palfrey all alone,
A goodly Ladie did foreby them rush,
Whose face did seeme as cleare as Christall stone,
And eke through feare as white as whales bone:
Her garments all were wrought of beaten gold,
And all her steed with tinsell trappings shone,
Which fled so fast, that nothing mote him hold,
And scarse them leasure gave, her passing to behold.

16

Still as she fled, her eye she backward threw,
As fearing evill, that pursewd her fast;
And her faire yellow locks behind her flew,
Loosely disperst with puffe of every blast:
All as a blazing starre doth farre outcast
His hearie beames, and flaming lockes dispred,
At sight whereof the people stand aghast:
But the sage wisard telles, as he has red,
That it importunes death and dolefull drerihed.

17

So as they gazed after her a while,
Lo where a griesly Foster forth did rush,
Breathing out beastly lust her to defile:
His tyreling jade he fiercely forth did push,
Through thicke and thin, both over banke and bush
In hope her to attaine by hooke or crooke,
That from his gorie sides the bloud did gush:
Large were his limbes, and terrible his looke,
And in his clownish hand a sharp bore speare he shooke.

18

Which outrage when those gentle knights did see,
Full of great envie and fell gealosy,
They stayd not to avise, who first should bee,
But all spurd after fast, as they mote fly,
To reskew her from shamefull villany.
The Prince and *Guyon* equally bylive
Her selfe pursewd, in hope to win thereby
Most goodly meede, the fairest Dame alive:
But after the foule foster *Timias* did strive.

19

The whiles faire *Britomart*, whose constant mind,
Would not so lightly follow beauties chace,
Ne reckt of Ladies Love, did stay behind,
And them awayted there a certaine space,
To weet if they would turne backe to that place:
But when she saw them gone, she forward went,
As lay her journey, through that perlous Pace,
With stedfast courage and stout hardiment;
Ne evill thing she fear'd, ne evill thing she ment.

20

At last as nigh out of the wood she came,
  A stately Castle farre away she spyde,
  To which her steps directly she did frame.
  That Castle was most goodly edifyde,
  And plaste for pleasure nigh that forrest syde:
  But faire before the gate a spatious plaine,
  Mantled with greene, it selfe did spredden wyde,
  On which she saw sixe knights, that did darraine
Fierce battell against one, with cruell might and maine.

21

Mainly they all attonce upon him laid,
  And sore beset on every side around,
  That nigh he breathlesse grew, yet nought dismaid,
  Ne ever to them yielded foot of ground
  All had he lost much bloud through many a wound,
  But stoutly dealt his blowes, and every way
  To which he turned in his wrathfull stound,
  Made them recoile, and fly from dred decay,
That none of all the sixe before, him durst assay.

22

Like dastard Curres, that having at a bay
  The salvage beast embost in wearie chace,
  Dare not adventure on the stubborne pray,
  Ne byte before, but rome from place to place,
  To get a snatch, when turned is his face.
  In such distresse and doubtfull jeopardy,
  When *Britomart* him saw, she ran a pace
  Unto his reskew, and with earnest cry,
Bad those same sixe forbeare that single enimy.

23

But to her cry they list not lenden eare,
  Ne ought the more their mightie strokes surceasse,
  But gathering him round about more neare,
  Their direfull rancour rather did encreasse;
  Till that she rushing through the thickest preasse,
  Perforce disparted their compacted gyre,
  And soone compeld to hearken unto peace:
  Tho gan she myldly of them to inquyre
The cause of their dissention and outrageous yre.

24

Whereto that single knight did answere frame;
　These sixe would me enforce by oddes of might,
　To chaunge my liefe, and love another Dame,
　That death me liefer were, than such despight,
　So unto wrong to yield my wrested right:
　For I love one, the truest one on ground,
　Ne list me chaunge; she th'*Errant Damzell* hight,
　For whose deare sake full many a bitter stownd,
I have endur'd, and tasted many a bloudy wound.

25

Certes (said she) then bene ye sixe to blame,
　To weene your wrong by force to justifie:
　For knight to leave his Ladie were great shame,
　That faithfull is, and better were to die.
　All losse is lesse, and lesse the infamie,
　Than losse of love to him, that loves but one;
　Ne may love be compeld by maisterie;
　For soone as maisterie comes, sweet love anone
Taketh his nimble wings, and soone away is gone.

26

Then spake one of those sixe, There dwelleth here
　Within this castle wall a Ladie faire,
　Whose soveraine beautie hath no living pere,
　Thereto so bounteous and so debonaire,
　That never any mote with her compaire.
　She hath ordaind this law, which we approve,
　That every knight, which doth this way repaire,
　In case he have no Ladie, nor no love,
Shall doe unto her service never to remove.

27

But if he have a Ladie or a Love,
　Then must he her forgoe with foule defame,
　Or else with us by dint of sword approve,
　That she is fairer, than our fairest Dame,
　As did this knight, before ye hither came.
　Perdie (said *Britomart*) the choise is hard:
　But what reward had he, that overcame?
　He should advaunced be to high regard,
(Said they) and have our Ladies love for his reward.

28

Therefore aread Sir, if thou have a love.
  Love have I sure, (quoth she) but Lady none;
  Yet will I not fro mine owne love remove,
  Ne to your Lady will I service done,
  But wreake your wrongs wrought to this knight alone,
  And prove his cause. With that her mortall speare
  She mightily aventred towards one,
  And downe him smot, ere well aware he weare,
Then to the next she rode, and downe the next did beare.

29

Ne did she stay, till three on ground she layd
  That none of them himselfe could reare againe,
  The fourth was by that other knight dismayd,
  All were he wearie of his former paine,
  That now there do but two of six remaine;
  Which two did yield, before she did them smight.
  Ah (said she then) now may ye all see plaine,
  That truth is strong, and trew love most of might,
That for his trusty servaunts doth so strongly fight.

30

Too well we see, (said they) and prove too well
  Our faulty weaknesse, and your matchlesse might:
  For thy, faire Sir, yours be the Damozell,
  Which by her owne law to your lot doth light,
  And we your liege men faith unto you plight.
  So underneath her feet their swords they mard,
  And after her besought, well as they might,
  To enter in, and reape the dew reward:
She graunted, and then in they all together far'd.

31

Long were it to describe the goodly frame,
  And stately port of *Castle Joyeous*,
  (For so that Castle hight by commune name)
  Where they were entertaind with curteous
  And comely glee of many gracious
  Faire Ladies, and of many a gentle knight,
  Who through a Chamber long and spacious,
  Eftsoones them brought unto their Ladies sight,
That of them cleeped was the *Lady of delight*.

32

But for to tell the sumptuous aray
  Of that great chamber, should be labour lost:
  For living wit, I weene, cannot display
  The royall riches and exceeding cost,
  Of every pillour and of every post;
  Which all of purest bullion framed were,
  And with great pearles and pretious stones embost,
  That the bright glister of their beames cleare
Did sparckle forth great light, and glorious did appeare.

33

These straunger knights through passing, forth were led
  Into an inner rowme, whose royaltee
  And rich purveyance might uneath be red;
  Mote Princes place beseeme so deckt to bee.
  Which stately manner when as they did see,
  The image of superfluous riotize,
  Exceeding much the state of meane degree,
  They greatly wondred, whence so sumptuous guize
Might be maintaynd, and each gan diversely devize.

34

The wals were round about apparelled
  With costly clothes of *Arras* and of *Toure*,
  In which with cunning hand was pourtrahed
  The love of *Venus* and her Paramoure
  The faire *Adonis*, turned to a flowre,
  A worke of rare device, and wondrous wit.
  First did it shew the bitter balefull stowre,
  Which her assayd with many a fervent fit,
When first her tender hart was with his beautie smit.

35

Then with what sleights and sweet allurements she
  Entyst the Boy, as well that art she knew,
  And wooed him her Paramoure to be;
  Now making girlonds of each flowre that grew,
  To crowne his golden lockes with honour dew;
  Now leading him into a secret shade
  From his Beauperes, and from bright heavens vew,
  Where him to sleepe she gently would perswade,
Or bathe him in a fountaine by some covert glade.

36

And whilst he slept, she over him would spred
　Her mantle, colour'd like the starry skyes,
　And her soft arme lay underneath his hed,
　And with ambrosiall kisses bathe his eyes;
　And whilest he bath'd, with her two crafty spyes,
　She secretly would search each daintie lim,
　And throw into the well sweet Rosemaryes,
　And fragrant violets, and Pances trim,
And ever with sweet Nectar she did sprinkle him.

37

So did she steale his heedelesse hart away,
　And joyd his love in secret unespyde.
　But for she saw him bent to cruell play,
　To hunt the salvage beast in forrest wyde,
　Dreadfull of daunger, that mote him betyde,
　She oft and oft adviz'd him to refraine
　From chase of greater beasts, whose brutish pryde
　Mote breede him scath unwares: but all in vaine;
For who can shun the chaunce, that dest'ny doth ordaine?

38

Lo, where beyond he lyeth languishing,
　Deadly engored of a great wild Bore,
　And by his side the Goddesse groveling
　Makes for him endlesse mone, and evermore
　With her soft garment wipes away the gore,
　Which staines his snowy skin with hatefull hew:
　But when she saw no helpe might him restore,
　Him to a dainty flowre she did transmew,
Which in that cloth was wrought, as if it lively grew.

39

So was that chamber clad in goodly wize,
　And round about it many beds were dight,
　As whilome was the antique worldes guize,
　Some for untimely ease, some for delight,
　As pleased them to use, that use it might:
　And all was full of Damzels, and of Squires,
　Dauncing and reveling both day and night,
　And swimming deepe in sensuall desires,
And *Cupid* still emongst them kindled lustfull fires.

40

And all the while sweet Musicke did divide
  Her looser notes with *Lydian* harmony;
  And all the while sweet birdes thereto applide
  Their daintie layes and dulcet melody,
  Ay caroling of love and jollity,
  That wonder was to heare their trim consort.
  Which when those knights beheld, with scornefull eye,
  They sdeigned such lascivious disport,
And loath'd the loose demeanure of that wanton sort.

41

Thence they were brought to that great Ladies vew,
  Whom they found sitting on a sumptuous bed,
  That glistred all with gold and glorious shew,
  As the proud *Persian* Queenes accustomed:
  She seemd a woman of great bountihed,
  And of rare beautie, saving that askaunce
  Her wanton eyes, ill signes of womanhed,
  Did roll too lightly, and too often glaunce,
Without regard of grace, or comely amenaunce.

42

Long worke it were, and needlesse to devize
  Their goodly entertainement and great glee:
  She caused them be led in curteous wize
  Into a bowre, disarmed for to bee,
  And cheared well with wine and spiceree:
  The *Redcrosse* Knight was soone disarmed there,
  But the brave Mayd would not disarmed bee,
  But onely vented up her umbriere,
And so did let her goodly visage to appere.

43

As when faire *Cynthia*, in darkesome night,
  Is in a noyous cloud enveloped,
  Where she may find the substaunce thin and light,
  Breakes forth her silver beames, and her bright hed
  Discovers to the world discomfited;
  Of the poore traveller, that went astray,
  With thousand blessings she is heried;
  Such was the beautie and the shining ray,
With which faire *Britomart* gave light unto the day.

44

And eke those six, which lately with her fought,
  Now were disarmd, and did them selves present
  Unto her vew, and company unsoght;
  For they all seemed curteous and gent,
  And all sixe brethren, borne of one parent,
  Which had them traynd in all civilitee,
  And goodly taught to tilt and turnament;
  Now were they liegemen to this Lady free,
And her knights service ought, to hold of her in fee.

45

The first of them by name *Gardante* hight,
  A jolly person, and of comely vew;
  The second was *Parlante*, a bold knight,
  And next to him *Jocante* did ensew;
  Basciante did him selfe most curteous shew;
  But fierce *Bacchante* seemd too fell and keene;
  And yet in armes *Noctante* greater grew:
  All were faire knights, and goodly well beseene,
But to faire *Britomart* they all but shadowes beene.

46

For she was full of amiable grace,
  And manly terrour mixed therewithall,
  That as the one stird up affections bace,
  So th'other did mens rash desires apall,
  And hold them backe, that would in errour fall;
  As he, that hath espide a vermeill Rose,
  To which sharpe thornes and breres the way forstall,
  Dare not for dread his hardy hand expose,
But wishing it far off, his idle wish doth lose.

47

Whom when the Lady saw so faire a wight,
  All ignoraunt of her contrary sex,
  (For she her weend a fresh and lusty knight)
  She greatly gan enamoured to wex,
  And with vaine thoughts her falsed fancy vex:
  Her fickle hart conceived hasty fire,
  Like sparkes of fire, which fall in sclender flex,
  That shortly brent into extreme desire,
And ransackt all her veines with passion entire.

48

Eftsoones she grew to great impatience
  And into termes of open outrage brust,
  That plaine discovered her incontinence,
  Ne reckt she, who her meaning did mistrust;
  For she was given all to fleshly lust,
  And poured forth in sensuall delight,
  That all regard of shame she had discust,
  And meet respect of honour put to flight:
So shamelesse beauty soone becomes a loathly sight.

49

Faire Ladies, that to love captived arre,
  And chaste desires do nourish in your mind,
  Let not her fault your sweet affections marre,
  Ne blot the bounty of all womankind;
  'Mongst thousands good one wanton Dame to find:
  Emongst the Roses grow some wicked weeds;
  For this was not to love, but lust inclind;
  For love does alwayes bring forth bounteous deeds,
And in each gentle hart desire of honour breeds.

50

Nought so of love this looser Dame did skill,
  But as a coale to kindle fleshly flame,
  Giving the bridle to her wanton will,
  And treading under foote her honest name:
  Such love is hate, and such desire is shame.
  Still did she rove at her with crafty glaunce
  Of her false eyes, that at her hart did ayme,
  And told her meaning in her countenaunce;
But *Britomart* dissembled it with ignoraunce.

51

Supper was shortly dight and downe they sat,
  Where they were served with all sumptuous fare,
  Whiles fruitfull *Ceres*, and *Lyæus* fat
  Pourd out their plenty, without spight or spare:
  Nought wanted there, that dainty was and rare;
  And aye the cups their bancks did overflow,
  And aye betweene the cups, she did prepare
  Way to her love, and secret darts did throw;
But *Britomart* would not such guilfull message know.

52

So when they slaked had the fervent heat
  Of appetite with meates of every sort,
  The Lady did faire *Britomart* entreat,
  Her to disarme, and with delightfull sport
  To loose her warlike limbs and strong effort,
  But when she mote not thereunto be wonne,
  (For she her sexe under that straunge purport
  Did use to hide, and plaine apparaunce shonne:)
In plainer wise to tell her grievaunce she begonne.

53

And all attonce discovered her desire
  With sighes, and sobs, and plaints, and piteous griefe,
  The outward sparkes of her in burning fire;
  Which spent in vaine, at last she told her briefe,
  That but if she did lend her short reliefe,
  And do her comfort, she mote algates dye.
  But the chaste damzell, that had never priefe
  Of such malengine and fine forgerie,
Did easily beleeve her strong extremitie.

54

Full easie was for her to have beliefe,
  Who by self-feeling of her feeble sexe,
  And by long triall of the inward griefe,
  Wherewith imperious love her hart did vexe,
  Could judge what paines do loving harts perplexe.
  Who meanes no guile, be guiled soonest shall,
  And to faire semblaunce doth light faith annexe;
  The bird, that knowes not the false fowlers call,
Into his hidden net full easily doth fall.

55

For thy she would not in discourteise wise,
  Scorne the faire offer of good will profest;
  For great rebuke it is, love to despise,
  Or rudely sdeigne a gentle harts request;
  But with faire countenaunce, as beseemed best,
  Her entertaynd; nath'lesse she inly deemd
  Her love too light, to wooe a wandring guest:
  Which she misconstruing, thereby esteemd
That from like inward fire that outward smoke had steemd.

56

Therewith a while she her flit fancy fed,
  Till she mote winne fit time for her desire,
  But yet her wound still inward freshly bled,
  And through her bones the false instilled fire
  Did spred it selfe, and venime close inspire.
  Tho were the tables taken all away,
  And every knight, and every gentle Squire
  Gan choose his dame with *Basciomani* gay,
With whom he meant to make his sport and courtly play.

57

Some fell to daunce, some fell to hazardry,
  Some to make love, some to make meriment,
  As diverse wits to divers things apply;
  And all the while faire *Malecasta* bent
  Her crafty engins to her close intent.
  By this th'eternall lampes, wherewith high *Jove*
  Doth light the lower world, were halfe yspent,
  And the moist daughters of huge *Atlas* strove
Into the *Ocean* deepe to drive their weary drove.

58

High time it seemed then for every wight
  Them to betake unto their kindly rest;
  Eftsoones long waxen torches weren light,
  Unto their bowres to guiden every guest:
  Tho when the Britonesse saw all the rest
  Avoided quite, she gan her selfe despoile,
  And safe commit to her soft fethered nest,
  Where through long watch, and late dayes weary toile,
She soundly slept, and carefull thoughts did quite assoile.

59

Now whenas all the world in silence deepe
  Yshrowded was, and every mortall wight
  Was drowned in the depth of deadly sleepe,
  Faire *Malecasta*, whose engrieved spright
  Could find no rest in such perplexed plight,
  Lightly arose out of her wearie bed,
  And under the blacke vele of guilty Night,
  Her with a scarlot mantle covered,
That was with gold and Ermines faire enveloped.

60

Then panting soft, and trembling everie joynt,
   Her fearfull feete towards the bowre she moved;
   Where she for secret purpose did appoynt
   To lodge the warlike mayd unwisely loved,
   And to her bed approching, first she prooved,
   Whether she slept or wakt, with her soft hand
   She softly felt, if any member mooved,
   And lent her wary eare to understand,
If any puffe of breath, or signe of sence she fond.

61

Which whenas none she fond, with easie shift,
   For feare least her unwares she should abrayd,
   Th'embroderd quilt she lightly up did lift,
   And by her side her selfe she softly layd,
   Of every finest fingers touch affrayd;
   Ne any noise she made, ne word she spake,
   But inly sigh'd. At last the royall Mayd
   Out of her quiet slomber did awake,
And chaungd her weary side, the better ease to take.

62

Where feeling one close couched by her side,
   She lightly lept out of her filed bed,
   And to her weapon ran, in minde to gride
   The loathed leachour. But the Dame halfe ded
   Through suddein feare and ghastly drerihed,
   Did shrieke alowd, that through the house it rong,
   And the whole family therewith adred,
   Rashly out of their rouzed couches sprong,
And to the troubled chamber all in armes did throng.

63

And those six Knights that Ladies Champions,
   And eke the *Redcrosse* knight ran to the stownd,
   Halfe armd and halfe unarmd, with them attons:
   Where when confusedly they came, they fownd
   Their Lady lying on the sencelesse grownd;
   On th'other side, they saw the warlike Mayd
   All in her snow-white smocke, with locks unbownd,
   Threatning the point of her avenging blade,
That with so troublous terrour they were all dismayde.

64

About their Lady first they flockt arownd,
  Whom having laid in comfortable couch,
  Shortly they reard out of her frosen swownd;
  And afterwards they gan with fowle reproch
  To stirre up strife, and troublous contecke broch:
  But by ensample of the last dayes losse,
  None of them rashly durst to her approch,
  Ne in so glorious spoile themselves embosse;
Her succourd eke the Champion of the bloudy Crosse.

65

But one of those sixe knights, *Gardante* hight,
  Drew out a deadly bow and arrow keene,
  Which forth he sent with felonous despight,
  And fell intent against the virgin sheene:
  The mortall steele stayd not, till it was seene
  To gore her side, yet was the wound not deepe,
  But lightly rased her soft silken skin,
  That drops of purple bloud thereout did weepe,
Which did her lilly smock with staines of vermeil steepe.

66

Wherewith enrag'd she fiercely at them flew,
  And with her flaming sword about her layd,
  That none of them foule mischiefe could eschew,
  But with her dreadfull strokes were all dismayd:
  Here, there, and every where about her swayd
  Her wrathfull steele, that none mote it abide;
  And eke the *Redcrosse* knight gave her good aid,
  Ay joyning foot to foot, and side to side,
That in short space their foes they have quite terrifide.

67

Tho whenas all were put to shamefull flight,
  The noble *Britomartis* her arayd,
  And her bright armes about her body dight:
  For nothing would she lenger there be stayd,
  Where so loose life, and so ungentle trade
  Was usd of Knights and Ladies seeming gent:
  So earely ere the grosse Earthes gryesy shade
  Was all disperst out of the firmament,
They tooke their steeds, and forth upon their journey went.

CANT. II

The Redcrosse knight to Britomart
describeth Artegall:
The wondrous myrrhour, by which she
in love with him did fall.

1

HERE have I cause, in men just blame to find,
That in their proper prayse too partiall bee,
And not indifferent to woman kind,
To whom no share in armes and chevalrie
They do impart, ne maken memorie
Of their brave gestes and prowesse martiall;
Scarse do they spare to one or two or three,
Rowme in their writs; yet the same writing small
Does all their deeds deface, and dims their glories all.

2

But by record of antique times I find,
That women wont in warres to beare most sway,
And to all great exploits them selves inclind:
Of which they still the girlond bore away,
Till envious Men fearing their rules decay,
Gan coyne streight lawes to curb their liberty;
Yet sith they warlike armes have layd away,
They have exceld in artes and pollicy,
That now we foolish men that prayse gin eke t'envy.

3

Of warlike puissaunce in ages spent,
Be thou faire *Britomart*, whose prayse I write,
But of all wisedome be thou precedent,
O soveraigne Queene, whose prayse I would endite,
Endite I would as dewtie doth excite;
But ah my rimes too rude and rugged arre,
When in so high an object they do lite,
And striving, fit to make, I feare do marre:
Thy selfe thy prayses tell, and make them knowen farre.

4

She travelling with *Guyon* by the way,
  Of sundry things faire purpose gan to find,
  T'abridg their journey long, and lingring day;
  Mongst which it fell into that Faeries mind,
  To aske this Briton Mayd, what uncouth wind,
  Brought her into those parts, and what inquest
  Made her dissemble her disguised kind:
  Faire Lady she him seemd, like Lady drest,
But fairest knight alive, when armed was her brest.

5

Thereat she sighing softly, had no powre
  To speake a while, ne ready answere make,
  But with hart-thrilling throbs and bitter stowre,
  As if she had a fever fit, did quake,
  And every daintie limbe with horrour shake;
  And ever and anone the rosy red,
  Flasht through her face, as it had been a flake
  Of lightning, through bright heaven fulmined;
At last the passion past she thus him answered.

6

Faire Sir, I let you weete, that from the howre
  I taken was from nourses tender pap,
  I have beene trained up in warlike stowre,
  To tossen speare and shield, and to affrap
  The warlike ryder to his most mishap;
  Sithence I loathed have my life to lead,
  As Ladies wont, in pleasures wanton lap,
  To finger the fine needle and nyce thread;
Me lever were with point of foemans speare be dead.

7

All my delight on deedes of armes is set,
  To hunt out perils and adventures hard,
  By sea, by land, where so they may be met,
  Onely for honour and for high regard,
  Without respect of richesse or reward.
  For such intent into these parts I came,
  Withouten compasse, or withouten card,
  Far fro my native soyle, that is by name
The greater *Britaine*, here to seeke for prayse and fame.

8

Fame blazed hath, that here in Faery lond
  Do many famous Knightes and Ladies wonne,
  And many straunge adventures to be fond,
  Of which great worth and worship may be wonne;
  Which I to prove, this voyage have begonne.
  But mote I weet of you, right curteous knight,
  Tydings of one, that hath unto me donne
  Late foule dishonour and reprochfull spight,
The which I seeke to wreake, and *Arthegall* he hight.

9

The word gone out, she backe againe would call,
  As her repenting so to have missayd,
  But that he it up-taking ere the fall,
  Her shortly answered; Faire martiall Mayd
  Certes ye misavised beene, t'upbrayd
  A gentle knight with so unknightly blame:
  For weet ye well of all, that ever playd
  At tilt or tourney, or like warlike game,
The noble *Arthegall* hath ever borne the name.

10

For thy great wonder were it, if such shame
  Should ever enter in his bounteous thought,
  Or ever do, that mote deserven blame:
  The noble courage never weeneth ought,
  That may unworthy of it selfe be thought.
  Therefore, faire Damzell, be ye well aware,
  Least that too farre ye have your sorrow sought:
  You and your countrey both I wish welfare,
And honour both; for each of other worthy are.

11

The royall Mayd woxe inly wondrous glad,
  To heare her Love so highly magnifide,
  And joyd that ever she affixed had,
  Her hart on knight so goodly glorifide,
  How ever finely she it faind to hide:
  The loving mother, that nine monethes did beare,
  In the deare closet of her painefull side,
  Her tender babe, it seeing safe appeare,
Doth not so much rejoyce, as she rejoyced theare.

12

But to occasion him to further talke,
  To feed her humour with his pleasing stile,
  Her list in strifull termes with him to balke,
  And thus replide, How ever, Sir, ye file
  Your curteous tongue, his prayses to compile,
  It ill beseemes a knight of gentle sort,
  Such as ye have him boasted, to beguile
  A simple mayd, and worke so haynous tort,
In shame of knighthood, as I largely can report.

13

Let be therefore my vengeaunce to disswade,
  And read, where I that faytour false may find.
  Ah, but if reason faire might you perswade,
  To slake your wrath, and mollifie your mind,
  (Said he) perhaps ye should it better find:
  For hardy thing it is, to weene by might,
  That man to hard conditions to bind,
  Or ever hope to match in equall fight,
Whose prowesse paragon saw never living wight.

14

Ne soothlich is it easie for to read,
  Where now on earth, or how he may be found;
  For he ne wonneth in one certaine stead,
  But restlesse walketh all the world around,
  Ay doing things, that to his fame redound,
  Defending Ladies cause, and Orphans right,
  Where so he heares, that any doth confound
  Them comfortlesse, through tyranny or might;
So is his soveraine honour raisde to heavens hight.

15

His feeling words her feeble sence much pleased,
  And softly sunck into her molten hart;
  Hart that is inly hurt, is greatly eased
  With hope of thing, that may allegge his smart;
  For pleasing words are like to Magick art,
  That doth the charmed Snake in slomber lay:
  Such secret ease felt gentle *Britomart*,
  Yet list the same efforce with faind gainesay;
So dischord oft in Musick makes the sweeter lay.

16

And said, Sir knight, these idle termes forbeare,
  And sith it is uneath to find his haunt,
  Tell me some markes, by which he may appeare,
  If chaunce I him encounter paravaunt;
  For perdie one shall other slay, or daunt:
  What shape, what shield, what armes, what steed, what sted,
  And what so else his person most may vaunt?
  All which the *Redcrosse* knight to point ared,
And him in every part before her fashioned.

17

Yet him in every part before she knew,
  How ever list her now her knowledge faine,
  Sith him whilome in *Britaine* she did vew,
  To her revealed in a mirrhour plaine,
  Whereof did grow her first engraffed paine;
  Whose root and stalke so bitter yet did tast,
  That but the fruit more sweetnesse did containe,
  Her wretched dayes in dolour she mote wast,
And yield the pray of love to lothsome death at last.

18

By strange occasion she did him behold,
  And much more strangely gan to love his sight,
  As it in bookes hath written bene of old.
  In *Deheubarth* that now South-wales is hight,
  What time king *Ryence* raign'd, and dealed right,
  The great Magitian *Merlin* had deviz'd,
  By his deepe science, and hell-dreaded might,
  A looking glasse, right wondrously aguiz'd,
Whose vertues through the wyde world soone were solemniz'd.

19

It vertue had, to shew in perfect sight,
  What ever thing was in the world contaynd,
  Betwixt the lowest earth and heavens hight,
  So that it to the looker appertaynd;
  What ever foe had wrought, or frend had faynd,
  Therein discovered was, ne ought mote pas,
  Ne ought in secret from the same remaynd;
  For thy it round and hollow shaped was,
Like to the world it selfe, and seem'd a world of glas.

20

Who wonders not, that reades so wonderous worke?
  But who does wonder, that has red the Towre,
  Wherein th'Ægyptian *Phao* long did lurke
  From all mens vew, that none might her discoure,
  Yet she might all men vew out of her bowre?
  Great *Ptolomæe* it for his lemans sake
  Ybuilded all of glasse, by Magicke powre,
  And also it impregnable did make;
Yet when his love was false, he with a peaze it brake.

21

Such was the glassie globe that *Merlin* made,
  And gave unto king *Ryence* for his gard,
  That never foes his kingdome might invade,
  But he it knew at home before he hard
  Tydings thereof, and so them still debar'd.
  It was a famous Present for a Prince,
  And worthy worke of infinite reward,
  That treasons could bewray, and foes convince;
Happie this Realme, had it remained ever since.

22

One day it fortuned, faire *Britomart*
  Into her fathers closet to repayre;
  For nothing he from her reserv'd apart,
  Being his onely daughter and his hayre:
  Where when she had espyde that mirrhour fayre,
  Her selfe a while therein she vewd in vaine;
  Tho her avizing of the vertues rare,
  Which thereof spoken were, she gan againe
Her to bethinke of, that mote to her selfe pertaine.

23

But as it falleth, in the gentlest harts
  Imperious Love hath highest set his throne,
  And tyrannizeth in the bitter smarts
  Of them, that to him buxome are and prone:
  So thought this Mayd (as maydens use to done)
  Whom fortune for her husband would allot,
  Not that she lusted after any one;
  For she was pure from blame of sinfull blot,
Yet wist her life at last must lincke in that same knot.

24

Eftsoones there was presented to her eye
  A comely knight, all arm'd in complete wize,
  Through whose bright ventayle lifted up on hye
  His manly face, that did his foes agrize,
  And friends to termes of gentle truce entize,
  Lookt foorth, as *Phœbus* face out of the east,
  Betwixt two shadie mountaines doth arize;
  Portly his person was, and much increast
Through his Heroicke grace, and honorable gest.

25

His crest was covered with a couchant Hound,
  And all his armour seem'd of antique mould,
  But wondrous massie and assured sound,
  And round about yfretted all with gold,
  In which there written was with cyphers old,
  Achilles armes, which Arthegall did win.
  And on his shield enveloped sevenfold
  He bore a crowned litle Ermilin,
That deckt the azure field with her faire pouldred skin.

26

The Damzell well did vew his personage,
  And liked well, ne further fastned not,
  But went her way; ne her unguilty age
  Did weene, unwares, that her unlucky lot
  Lay hidden in the bottome of the pot;
  Of hurt unwist most daunger doth redound:
  But the false Archer, which that arrow shot
  So slyly, that she did not feele the wound,
Did smyle full smoothly at her weetlesse wofull stound.

27

Thenceforth the feather in her loftie crest,
  Ruffed of love, gan lowly to availe,
  And her proud portance, and her princely gest,
  With which she earst tryumphed, now did quaile:
  Sad, solemne, sowre, and full of fancies fraile
  She woxe; yet wist she neither how, nor why,
  She wist not, silly Mayd, what she did aile,
  Yet wist, she was not well at ease perdy,
Yet thought it was not love, but some melancholy.

28

So soone as Night had with her pallid hew
  Defast the beautie of the shining sky,
  And reft from men the worlds desired vew,
  She with her Nourse adowne to sleepe did lye;
  But sleepe full farre away from her did fly:
  In stead thereof sad sighes, and sorrowes deepe
  Kept watch and ward about her warily,
  That nought she did but wayle, and often steepe
Her daintie couch with teares, which closely she did weepe.

29

And if that any drop of slombring rest
  Did chaunce to still into her wearie spright,
  When feeble nature felt her selfe opprest,
  Streight way with dreames, and with fantasticke sight
  Of dreadfull things the same was put to flight,
  That oft out of her bed she did astart,
  As one with vew of ghastly feends affright:
  Tho gan she to renew her former smart,
And thinke of that faire visage, written in her hart.

30

One night, when she was tost with such unrest,
  Her aged Nurse, whose name was *Glauce* hight,
  Feeling her leape out of her loathed nest,
  Betwixt her feeble armes her quickly keight,
  And downe againe in her warme bed her dight;
  Ah my deare daughter, ah my dearest dread,
  What uncouth fit (said she) what evill plight
  Hath thee opprest, and with sad drearyhead
Chaunged thy lively cheare, and living made thee dead?

31

For not of nought these suddeine ghastly feares
  All night afflict thy naturall repose,
  And all the day, when as thine equall peares
  Their fit disports with faire delight doe chose,
  Thou in dull corners doest thy selfe inclose,
  Ne tastest Princes pleasures, ne doest spred
  Abroad thy fresh youthes fairest flowre, but lose
  Both leafe and fruit, both too untimely shed,
As one in wilfull bale for ever buried.

32

The time, that mortall men their weary cares
  Do lay away, and all wilde beastes do rest,
And every river eke his course forbeares,
  Then doth this wicked evill thee infest,
  And rive with thousand throbs thy thrilled brest;
Like an huge *Aetn'* of deepe engulfed griefe,
  Sorrow is heaped in thy hollow chest,
Whence forth it breakes in sighes and anguish rife,
As smoke and sulphure mingled with confused strife.

33

Aye me, how much I feare, least love it bee;
  But if that love it be, as sure I read
By knowen signes and passions, which I see,
  Be it worthy of thy race and royall sead,
  Then I avow by this most sacred head
Of my deare foster child, to ease thy griefe,
  And win thy will: Therefore away doe dread;
For death nor daunger from thy dew reliefe
Shall me debarre, tell me therefore my liefest liefe.

34

So having said, her twixt her armes twaine
  She straightly straynd, and colled tenderly,
And every trembling joynt, and every vaine
  She softly felt, and rubbed busily,
  To doe the frosen cold away to fly;
And her faire deawy eies with kisses deare
  She oft did bath, and oft againe did dry;
And ever her importund, not to feare
To let the secret of her hart to her appeare.

35

The Damzell pauzd, and then thus fearefully;
  Ah Nurse, what needeth thee to eke my paine?
Is not enough, that I alone doe dye,
  But it must doubled be with death of twaine?
  For nought for me but death there doth remaine.
O daughter deare (said she) despaire no whit;
  For never sore, but might a salve obtaine:
That blinded God, which hath ye blindly smit,
Another arrow hath your lovers hart to hit.

36

But mine is not (quoth she) like others wound;
  For which no reason can find remedy.
  Was never such, but mote the like be found,
  (Said she) and though no reason may apply
  Salve to your sore, yet love can higher stye,
  Than reasons reach, and oft hath wonders donne.
  But neither God of love, nor God of sky
  Can doe (said she) that, which cannot be donne.
Things oft impossible (quoth she) seeme, ere begonne.

37

These idle words (said she) doe nought asswage
  My stubborne smart, but more annoyance breed,
  For no no usuall fire, no usuall rage
  It is, O Nurse, which on my life doth feed,
  And suckes the bloud, which from my hart doth bleed.
  But since thy faithfull zeale lets me not hyde
  My crime, (if crime it be) I will it reed.
  Nor Prince, nor pere it is, whose love hath gryde
My feeble brest of late, and launched this wound wyde.

38

Nor man it is, nor other living wight;
  For then some hope I might unto me draw,
  But th'only shade and semblant of a knight,
  Whose shape or person yet I never saw,
  Hath me subjected to loves cruell law:
  The same one day, as me misfortune led,
  I in my fathers wondrous mirrhour saw,
  And pleased with that seeming goodly-hed,
Unwares the hidden hooke with baite I swallowed.

39

Sithens it hath infixed faster hold
  Within my bleeding bowels, and so sore
  Now ranckleth in this same fraile fleshly mould,
  That all mine entrailes flow with poysnous gore,
  And th'ulcer groweth daily more and more;
  Ne can my running sore find remedie,
  Other than my hard fortune to deplore,
  And languish as the leafe falne from the tree,
Till death make one end of my dayes and miserie.

40

Daughter (said she) what need ye be dismayd,
　Or why make ye such Monster of your mind?
　Of much more uncouth thing I was affrayd;
　Of filthy lust, contrarie unto kind:
　But this affection nothing straunge I find;
　For who with reason can you aye reprove,
　To love the semblant pleasing most your mind,
　And yield your heart, whence ye cannot remove?
No guilt in you, but in the tyranny of love.

41

Not so th'*Arabian Myrrhe* did set her mind;
　Nor so did *Biblis* spend her pining hart,
　But lov'd their native flesh against all kind,
　And to their purpose used wicked art:
　Yet playd *Pasiphaë* a more monstrous part,
　That lov'd a Bull, and learnd a beast to bee;
　Such shamefull lusts who loaths not, which depart
　From course of nature and of modestie?
Sweet love such lewdnes bands from his faire companie.

42

But thine my Deare (welfare thy heart my deare)
　Though strange beginning had, yet fixed is
　On one, that worthy may perhaps appeare;
　And certes seemes bestowed not amis:
　Joy thereof have thou and eternall blis.
　With that upleaning on her elbow weake,
　Her alablaster brest she soft did kis,
　Which all that while she felt to pant and quake,
As it an Earth-quake were; at last she thus bespake.

43

Beldame, your words doe worke me litle ease;
　For though my love be not so lewdly bent,
　As those ye blame, yet may it nought appease
　My raging smart, ne ought my flame relent,
　But rather doth my helpelesse griefe augment.
　For they, how ever shamefull and unkind,
　Yet did possesse their horrible intent:
　Short end of sorrowes they thereby did find;
So was their fortune good, though wicked were their mind.

44

But wicked fortune mine, though mind be good,
  Can have no end, nor hope of my desire,
  But feed on shadowes, whiles I die for food,
  And like a shadow wexe, whiles with entire
  Affection, I doe languish and expire.
  I fonder, than *Cephisus* foolish child,
  Who having vewed in a fountaine shere
  His face, was with the love thereof beguild;
I fonder love a shade, the bodie farre exild.

45

Nought like (quoth she) for that same wretched boy
  Was of himselfe the idle Paramoure;
  Both love and lover, without hope of joy,
  For which he faded to a watry flowre.
  But better fortune thine, and better howre,
  Which lov'st the shadow of a warlike knight;
  No shadow, but a bodie hath in powre:
  That bodie, wheresoever that it light,
May learned be by cyphers, or by Magicke might.

46

But if thou may with reason yet represse
  The growing evill, ere it strength have got,
  And thee abandond wholly doe possesse,
  Against it strongly strive, and yield thee not,
  Till thou in open field adowne be smot.
  But if the passion mayster thy fraile might,
  So that needs love or death must be thy lot,
  Then I avow to thee, by wrong or right
To compasse thy desire, and find that loved knight.

47

Her chearefull words much cheard the feeble spright
  Of the sicke virgin, that her downe she layd
  In her warme bed to sleepe, if that she might;
  And the old-woman carefully displayd
  The clothes about her round with busie ayd;
  So that at last a little creeping sleepe
  Surprisd her sense: She therewith well apayd,
  The drunken lampe downe in the oyle did steepe,
And set her by to watch, and set her by to weepe.

48

Earely the morrow next, before that day
 His joyous face did to the world reveale,
 They both uprose and tooke their readie way
 Unto the Church, their prayers to appeale,
 With great devotion, and with litle zeale:
 For the faire Damzell from the holy herse
 Her love-sicke hart to other thoughts did steale;
 And that old Dame said many an idle verse,
Out of her daughters hart fond fancies to reverse.

49

Returned home, the royall Infant fell
 Into her former fit; for why, no powre
 Nor guidance of her selfe in her did dwell.
 But th'aged Nurse her calling to her bowre,
 Had gathered Rew, and Savine, and the flowre
 Of *Camphora*, and Calamint, and Dill,
 All which she in a earthen Pot did poure,
 And to the brim with Colt wood did it fill,
And many drops of milke and bloud through it did spill.

50

Then taking thrise three haires from off her head,
 Them trebly breaded in a threefold lace,
 And round about the pots mouth, bound the thread,
 And after having whispered a space
 Certaine sad words, with hollow voice and bace,
 She to the virgin said, thrise said she it;
 Come daughter come, come; spit upon my face,
 Spit thrise upon me, thrise upon me spit;
Th'uneven number for this businesse is most fit.

51

That sayd, her round about she from her turnd,
 She turned her contrarie to the Sunne,
 Thrise she her turnd contrary, and returnd,
 All contrary, for she the right did shunne,
 And ever what she did, was streight undonne.
 So thought she to undoe her daughters love:
 But love, that is in gentle brest begonne,
 No idle charmes so lightly may remove,
That well can witnesse, who by triall it does prove.

52

Ne ought it mote the noble Mayd avayle,
Ne slake the furie of her cruell flame,
But that she still did waste, and still did wayle,
That through long languour, and hart-burning brame
She shortly like a pyned ghost became,
Which long hath waited by the Stygian strond.
That when old *Glauce* saw, for feare least blame
Of her miscarriage should in her be fond,
She wist not how t'amend, nor how it to withstond.

CANT. III

Merlin bewrayes to Britomart,
the state of Artegall.
And shewes the famous Progeny
which from them springen shall.

I

Most sacred fire, that burnest mightily
In living brests, ykindled first above,
Emongst th'eternall spheres and lamping sky,
And thence pourd into men, which men call Love;
Not that same, which doth base affections move
In brutish minds, and filthy lust inflame,
But that sweet fit, that doth true beautie love,
And choseth vertue for his dearest Dame,
Whence spring all noble deeds and never dying fame:

2

Well did Antiquitie a God thee deeme,
That over mortall minds hast so great might,
To order them, as best to thee doth seeme,
And all their actions to direct aright;
The fatall purpose of divine foresight,
Thou doest effect in destined descents,
Through deepe impression of thy secret might,
And stirredst up th'Heroes high intents,
Which the late world admyres for wondrous moniments.

3

But thy dread darts in none doe triumph more,
    Ne braver proofe in any, of thy powre
    Shew'dst thou, than in this royall Maid of yore,
    Making her seeke an unknowne Paramoure,
    From the worlds end, through many a bitter stowre:
    From whose two loynes thou afterwards did rayse
    Most famous fruits of matrimoniall bowre,
    Which through the earth have spred their living prayse,
That fame in trompe of gold eternally displayes.

4

Begin then, O my dearest sacred Dame,
    Daughter of *Phœbus* and of *Memorie*,
    That doest ennoble with immortall name
    The warlike Worthies, from antiquitie,
    In thy great volume of Eternitie:
    Begin, O *Clio*, and recount from hence
    My glorious Soveraines goodly auncestrie,
    Till that by dew degrees and long protense,
Thou have it lastly brought unto her Excellence.

5

Full many wayes within her troubled mind,
    Old *Glauce* cast, to cure this Ladies griefe:
    Full many waies she sought, but none could find,
    Nor herbes, nor charmes, nor counsell, that is chiefe
    And choisest med'cine for sicke harts reliefe:
    For thy great care she tooke, and greater feare,
    Least that it should her turne to foule repriefe,
    And sore reproch, when so her father deare
Should of his dearest daughters hard misfortune heare.

6

At last she her avisd, that he, which made
    That mirrhour, wherein the sicke Damosell
    So straungely vewed her straunge lovers shade,
    To weet, the learned *Merlin*, well could tell,
    Under what coast of heaven the man did dwell,
    And by what meanes his love might best be wrought:
    For though beyond the *Africk Ismaell*,
    Or th'Indian *Peru* he were, she thought
Him forth through infinite endevour to have sought.

7

Forthwith themselves disguising both in straunge
  And base attyre, that none might them bewray,
  To *Maridunum*, that is now by chaunge
  Of name *Cayr-Merdin* cald, they tooke their way:
  There the wise *Merlin* whylome wont (they say)
  To make his wonne, low underneath the ground,
  In a deepe delve, farre from the vew of day,
  That of no living wight he mote be found,
When so he counseld with his sprights encompast round.

8

And if thou ever happen that same way
  To travell, goe to see that dreadfull place:
  It is an hideous hollow cave (they say)
  Under a rocke that lyes a little space
  From the swift *Barry*, tombling downe apace,
  Emongst the woodie hilles of *Dynevowre*:
  But dare thou not, I charge, in any cace,
  To enter into that same balefull Bowre,
For fear the cruell Feends should thee unwares devowre.

9

But standing high aloft, low lay thine eare,
  And there such ghastly noise of yron chaines,
  And brasen Caudrons thou shalt rombling heare,
  Which thousand sprights with long enduring paines
  Doe tosse, that it will stonne thy feeble braines,
  And oftentimes great grones, and grievous stounds,
  When too huge toile and labour them constraines:
  And oftentimes loud strokes, and ringing sounds
From under that deepe Rocke most horribly rebounds.

10

The cause some say is this: A litle while
  Before that *Merlin* dyde, he did intend,
  A brasen wall in compas to compile
  About *Cairmardin*, and did it commend
  Unto these Sprights, to bring to perfect end.
  During which worke the Ladie of the Lake,
  Whom long he lov'd, for him in hast did send,
  Who thereby forst his workemen to forsake,
Them bound till his returne, their labour not to slake.

11

In the meane time through that false Ladies traine,
  He was surprisd, and buried under beare,
  Ne ever to his worke returnd againe:
  Nath'lesse those feends may not their worke forbeare,
  So greatly his commaundement they feare,
  But there doe toyle and travell day and night,
  Untill that brasen wall they up doe reare:
  For *Merlin* had in Magicke more insight,
Than ever him before or after living wight.

12

For he by words could call out of the sky
  Both Sunne and Moone, and make them him obay:
  The land to sea, and sea to maineland dry,
  And darkesome night he eke could turne to day:
  Huge hostes of men he could alone dismay,
  And hostes of men of meanest things could frame,
  When so him list his enimies to fray:
  That to this day for terror of his fame,
The feends do quake, when any him to them does name.

13

And sooth, men say that he was not the sonne
  Of mortall Syre, or other living wight,
  But wondrously begotten, and begonne
  By false illusion of a guilefull Spright,
  On a faire Ladie Nonne, that whilome hight
  Matilda, daughter to *Pubidius*,
  Who was the Lord of *Mathravall* by right,
  And coosen unto king *Ambrosius*:
Whence he indued was with skill so marvellous.

14

They here ariving, staid a while without,
  Ne durst adventure rashly in to wend,
  But of their first intent gan make new dout
  For dread of daunger, which it might portend:
  Untill the hardie Mayd (with love to frend)
  First entering, the dreadfull Mage there found
  Deepe busied bout worke of wondrous end,
  And writing strange characters in the ground,
With which the stubborn feends he to his service bound.

15

He nought was moved at their entrance bold:
  For of their comming well he wist afore,
  Yet list them bid their businesse to unfold,
  As if ought in this world in secret store
  Were from him hidden, or unknowne of yore.
  Then *Glauce* thus, Let not it thee offend,
  That we thus rashly through thy darkesome dore,
  Unwares have prest: for either fatall end,
Or other mightie cause us two did hither send.

16

He bad tell on; And then she thus began.
  Now have three Moones with borrow'd brothers light,
  Thrice shined faire, and thrice seem'd dim and wan,
  Sith a sore evill, which this virgin bright
  Tormenteth, and doth plonge in dolefull plight,
  First rooting tooke; but what thing it mote bee,
  Or whence it sprong, I cannot read aright:
  But this I read, that but if remedee
Thou her afford, full shortly I her dead shall see.

17

Therewith th'Enchaunter softly gan to smyle
  At her smooth speeches, weeting inly well,
  That she to him dissembled womanish guyle,
  And to her said, Beldame, by that ye tell,
  More need of leach-craft hath your Damozell,
  Than of my skill: who helpe may have elsewhere,
  In vaine seekes wonders out of Magicke spell.
  Th'old woman wox half blanck, those words to heare;
And yet was loth to let her purpose plaine appeare.

18

And to him said, If any leaches skill,
  Or other learned meanes could have redrest
  This my deare daughters deepe engraffed ill,
  Certes I should be loth thee to molest:
  But this sad evill, which doth her infest,
  Doth course of naturall cause farre exceed,
  And housed is within her hollow brest,
  That either seemes some cursed witches deed,
Or evill spright, that in her doth such torment breed.

19

The wisard could no lenger beare her bord,
  But brusting forth in laughter, to her sayd;
  Glauce, what needs this colourable word,
  To cloke the cause, that hath it selfe bewrayd?
  Ne ye faire *Britomartis*, thus arayd,
  More hidden are, than Sunne in cloudy vele;
  Whom thy good fortune, having fate obayd,
  Hath hither brought, for succour to appele:
The which the powres to thee are pleased to revele.

20

The doubtfull Mayd, seeing her selfe descryde,
  Was all abasht, and her pure yvory
  Into a cleare Carnation suddeine dyde;
  As faire *Aurora* rising hastily,
  Doth by her blushing tell, that she did lye
  All night in old *Tithonus* frosen bed,
  Whereof she seemes ashamed inwardly.
  But her old Nourse was nought dishartened,
But vauntage made of that, which *Merlin* had ared.

21

And sayd, Sith then thou knowest all our griefe,
  (For what doest not thou know?) of grace I pray,
  Pitty our plaint, and yield us meet reliefe.
  With that the Prophet still awhile did stay,
  And then his spirite thus gan forth display;
  Most noble Virgin, that by fatall lore
  Hast learn'd to love, let no whit thee dismay
  The hard begin, that meets thee in the dore,
And with sharpe fits thy tender hart oppresseth sore.

22

For so must all things excellent begin,
  And eke enrooted deepe must be that Tree,
  Whose big embodied braunches shall not lin,
  Till they to heavens hight forth stretched bee.
  For from thy wombe a famous Progenie
  Shall spring, out of the auncient *Trojan* blood,
  Which shall revive the sleeping memorie
  Of those same antique Peres the heavens brood,
Which *Greeke* and *Asian* rivers stained with their blood.

23

Renowmed kings, and sacred Emperours,
  Thy fruitfull Ofspring, shall from thee descend;
  Brave Captaines, and most mighty warriours,
  That shall their conquests through all lands extend,
  And their decayed kingdomes shall amend:
  The feeble Britons, broken with long warre,
  They shall upreare, and mightily defend
  Against their forrein foe, that comes from farre,
Till universall peace compound all civill jarre.

24

It was not, *Britomart*, thy wandring eye,
  Glauncing unwares in charmed looking glas,
  But the streight course of heavenly destiny,
  Led with eternall providence, that has
  Guided thy glaunce, to bring his will to pas:
  Ne is thy fate, ne is thy fortune ill,
  To love the prowest knight, that ever was.
  Therefore submit thy wayes unto his will,
And do by all dew meanes thy destiny fulfill.

25

But read (said *Glauce*) thou Magitian
  What meanes shall she out seeke, or what wayes take?
  How shall she know, how shall she find the man?
  Or what needs her to toyle, sith fates can make
  Way for themselves, their purpose to partake?
  Then *Merlin* thus; Indeed the fates are firme,
  And may not shrinck, though all the world do shake:
  Yet ought mens good endevours them confirme,
And guide the heavenly causes to their constant terme.

26

The man whom heavens have ordaynd to bee
  The spouse of *Britomart*, is *Arthegall*:
  He wonneth in the land of *Fayeree*,
  Yet is no *Fary* borne, ne sib at all
  To Elfes, but sprong of seed terrestriall,
  And whilome by false *Faries* stolne away,
  Whiles yet in infant cradle he did crall;
  Ne other to himselfe is knowne this day,
But that he by an Elfe was gotten of a *Fay*.

27

But sooth he is the sonne of *Gorlois*,
  And brother unto *Cador* Cornish king,
  And for his warlike feates renowmed is,
  From where the day out of the sea doth spring,
  Untill the closure of the Evening.
  From thence, him firmely bound with faithfull band,
  To this his native soyle thou backe shalt bring,
  Strongly to aide his countrey, to withstand
The powre of forrein Paynims, which invade thy land.

28

Great aid thereto his mighty puissaunce,
  And dreaded name shall give in that sad day:
  Where also proofe of thy prow valiaunce
  Thou then shalt make, t'increase thy lovers pray.
  Long time ye both in armes shall beare great sway,
  Till thy wombes burden thee from them do call,
  And his last fate him from thee take away,
  Too rathe cut off by practise criminall
Of secret foes, that him shall make in mischiefe fall.

29

With thee yet shall he leave for memory
  Of his late puissaunce, his Image dead,
  That living him in all activity
  To thee shall represent. He from the head
  Of his coosin *Constantius* without dread
  Shall take the crowne, that was his fathers right,
  And therewith crowne himselfe in th'others stead:
  Then shall he issew forth with dreadfull might,
Against his Saxon foes in bloudy field to fight.

30

Like as a Lyon, that in drowsie cave
  Hath long time slept, himselfe so shall he shake,
  And comming forth, shall spred his banner brave
  Over the troubled South, that it shall make
  The warlike *Mertians* for feare to quake:
  Thrise shall he fight with them, and twise shall win,
  But the third time shall faire accordaunce make:
  And if he then with victorie can lin,
He shall his dayes with peace bring to his earthly In.

31

His sonne, hight *Vortipore*, shall him succeede
  In kingdome, but not in felicity;
  Yet shall he long time warre with happy speed,
  And with great honour many battels try:
  But at the last to th'importunity
  Of froward fortune shall be forst to yield.
  But his sonne *Malgo* shall full mightily
  Avenge his fathers losse, with speare and shield,
And his proud foes discomfit in victorious field.

32

Behold the man, and tell me *Britomart*,
  If ay more goodly creature thou didst see;
  How like a Gyaunt in each manly part
  Beares he himselfe with portly majestee,
  That one of th'old *Heroes* seemes to bee:
  He the six Islands, comprovinciall
  In auncient times unto great Britainee,
  Shall to the same reduce, and to him call
Their sundry kings to do their homage severall.

33

All which his sonne *Careticus* awhile
  Shall well defend, and *Saxons* powre suppresse,
  Untill a straunger king from unknowne soyle
  Arriving, him with multitude oppresse;
  Great *Gormond*, having with huge mightinesse
  Ireland subdewd, and therein fixt his throne,
  Like a swift Otter, fell through emptinesse,
  Shall overswim the sea with many one
Of his Norveyses, to assist the Britons fone.

34

He in his furie all shall overrunne,
  And holy Church with faithlesse hands deface,
  That thy sad people utterly fordonne,
  Shall to the utmost mountaines fly apace:
  Was never so great wast in any place,
  Nor so fowle outrage doen by living men:
  For all thy Cities they shall sacke and race,
  And the greene grasse, that groweth, they shall bren,
That even the wild beast shall dy in starved den.

35

Whiles thus thy Britons do in languour pine,
  Proud *Etheldred* shall from the North arise,
  Serving th'ambitious will of *Augustine*,
  And passing *Dee* with hardy enterprise,
  Shall backe repulse the valiaunt *Brockwell* twise,
  And *Bangor* with massacred Martyrs fill;
  But the third time shall rew his foolhardise:
  For *Cadwan* pittying his peoples ill,
Shall stoutly him defeat, and thousand *Saxons* kill.

36

But after him, *Cadwallin* mightily
  On his sonne *Edwin* all those wrongs shall wreake;
  Ne shall availe the wicked sorcery
  Of false *Pellite*, his purposes to breake,
  But him shall slay, and on a gallowes bleake
  Shall give th'enchaunter his unhappy hire;
  Then shall the Britons, late dismayd and weake,
  From their long vassalage gin to respire,
And on their Paynim foes avenge their ranckled ire.

37

Ne shall he yet his wrath so mitigate,
  Till both the sonnes of *Edwin* he have slaine,
  Offricke and *Osricke*, twinnes unfortunate,
  Both slaine in battell upon Layburne plaine,
  Together with the king of *Louthiane*,
  Hight *Adin*, and the king of *Orkeny*,
  Both joynt partakers of their fatall paine:
  But *Penda*, fearefull of like desteny,
Shall yield him selfe his liegeman, and sweare fealty.

38

Him shall he make his fatall Instrument,
  T'afflict the other *Saxons* unsubdewd;
  He marching forth with fury insolent
  Against the good king *Oswald*, who indewd
  With heavenly powre, and by Angels reskewd,
  All holding crosses in their hands on hye,
  Shall him defeate withouten bloud imbrewd:
  Of which, that field for endlesse memory,
Shall *Hevenfield* be cald to all posterity.

39

Where at *Cadwallin* wroth, shall forth issew,
  And an huge hoste into Northumber lead,
  With which he godly *Oswald* shall subdew,
  And crowne with martyrdome his sacred head.
  Whose brother *Oswin*, daunted with like dread,
  With price of silver shall his kingdome buy,
  And *Penda*, seeking him adowne to tread,
  Shall tread adowne, and do him fowly dye,
But shall with gifts his Lord *Cadwallin* pacify.

40

Then shall *Cadwallin* dye, and then the raine
  Of *Britons* eke with him attonce shall dye;
  Ne shall the good *Cadwallader* with paine,
  Or powre, be hable it to remedy,
  When the full time prefixt by destiny,
  Shalbe expird of *Britons* regiment.
  For heaven it selfe shall their successe envy,
  And them with plagues and murrins pestilent
Consume, till all their warlike puissaunce be spent.

41

Yet after all these sorrowes, and huge hills
  Of dying people, during eight yeares space,
  Cadwallader not yielding to his ills,
  From *Armoricke*, where long in wretched cace
  He liv'd, returning to his native place,
  Shalbe by vision staid from his intent:
  For th'heavens have decreed, to displace
  The *Britons*, for their sinnes dew punishment,
And to the *Saxons* over-give their government.

42

Then woe, and woe, and everlasting woe,
  Be to the Briton babe, that shalbe borne,
  To live in thraldome of his fathers foe;
  Late King, now captive, late Lord, now forlorne,
  The worlds reproch, the cruell victors scorne,
  Banisht from Princely howre to wastfull wood:
  O who shall helpe me to lament, and mourne
  The royall seed, the antique *Trojan* blood,
Whose Empire lenger here, than ever any stood.

43

The Damzell was full deepe empassioned,
  Both for his griefe, and for her peoples sake,
  Whose future woes so plaine he fashioned,
  And sighing sore, at length him thus bespake;
  Ah but will heavens fury never slake,
  Nor vengeaunce huge relent it selfe at last?
  Will not long misery late mercy make,
  But shall their name for ever be defast,
And quite from of the earth their memory be rast?

44

Nay but the terme (said he) is limited,
  That in this thraldome *Britons* shall abide,
  And the just revolution measured,
  That they as Straungers shalbe notifide.
  For twise foure hundreth yeares shalbe supplide,
  Ere they to former rule restor'd shalbee,
  And their importune fates all satisfide:
  Yet during this their most obscuritee,
Their beames shall oft breake forth, that men them faire may see.

45

For *Rhodoricke*, whose surname shalbe Great,
  Shall of him selfe a brave ensample shew,
  That Saxon kings his friendship shall intreat;
  And *Howell Dha* shall goodly well indew
  The salvage minds with skill of just and trew;
  Then *Griffyth Conan* also shall up reare
  His dreaded head, and the old sparkes renew
  Of native courage, that his foes shall feare,
Least backe againe the kingdome he from them should beare.

46

Ne shall the Saxons selves all peaceably
  Enjoy the crowne, which they from Britons wonne
  First ill, and after ruled wickedly:
  For ere two hundred yeares be full outronne,
  There shall a Raven far from rising Sunne,
  With his wide wings upon them fiercely fly,
  And bid his faithlesse chickens overronne
  The fruitfull plaines, and with fell cruelty,
In their avenge, tread downe the victours surquedry.

47

Yet shall a third both these, and thine subdew;
  There shall a Lyon from the sea-bord wood
  Of *Neustria* come roring, with a crew
  Of hungry whelpes, his battailous bold brood,
  Whose clawes were newly dipt in cruddy blood,
  That from the Daniske Tyrants head shall rend
  Th'usurped crowne, as if that he were wood,
  And the spoile of the countrey conquered
Emongst his young ones shall divide with bountyhed.

48

Tho when the terme is full accomplishid,
  There shall a sparke of fire, which hath longwhile
  Bene in his ashes raked up, and hid,
  Be freshly kindled in the fruitfull Ile
  Of *Mona*, where it lurked in exile;
  Which shall breake forth into bright burning flame,
  And reach into the house, that beares the stile
  Of royall majesty and soveraigne name;
So shall the Briton bloud their crowne againe reclame.

49

Thenceforth eternall union shall be made
  Betweene the nations different afore,
  And sacred Peace shall lovingly perswade
  The warlike minds, to learne her goodly lore,
  And civile armes to exercise no more:
  Then shall a royall virgin raine, which shall
  Stretch her white rod over the *Belgicke* shore,
  And the great Castle smite so sore with all,
That it shall make him shake, and shortly learne to fall.

50

But yet the end is not. There *Merlin* stayd,
  As overcomen of the spirites powre,
  Or other ghastly spectacle dismayd,
  That secretly he saw, yet note discoure:
  Which suddein fit, and halfe extatick stoure
  When the two fearefull women saw, they grew
  Greatly confused in behavioure;
  At last the fury past, to former hew
Hee turnd againe, and chearefull looks ⟨as earst⟩ did shew.

51

Then, when them selves they well instructed had
  Of all, that needed them to be inquird,
  They both conceiving hope of comfort glad,
  With lighter hearts unto their home retird;
  Where they in secret counsell close conspird,
  How to effect so hard an enterprize,
  And to possesse the purpose they desird:
  Now this, now that twixt them they did devise,
And diverse plots did frame, to maske in strange disguise.

52

At last the Nourse in her foolhardy wit
  Conceiv'd a bold devise, and thus bespake;
  Daughter, I deeme that counsell aye most fit,
  That of the time doth dew advauntage take;
  Ye see that good king *Uther* now doth make
  Strong warre upon the Paynim brethren, hight
  Octa and *Oza*, whom he lately brake
  Beside *Cayr Verolame*, in victorious fight,
That now all *Britanie* doth burne in armes bright.

53

That therefore nought our passage may empeach,
  Let us in feigned armes our selves disguize,
  And our weake hands (whom need new strength shall teach)
  The dreadfull speare and shield to exercize:
  Ne certes daughter that same warlike wize
  I weene, would you misseeme; for ye bene tall,
  And large of limbe, t'atchieve an hard emprize,
  Ne ought ye want, but skill, which practize small
Will bring, and shortly make you a mayd Martiall.

54

And sooth, it ought your courage much inflame,
  To heare so often, in that royall hous,
  From whence to none inferiour ye came,
  Bards tell of many women valorous
  Which have full many feats adventurous
  Performd, in paragone of proudest men:
  The bold *Bunduca*, whose victorious
  Exploits made *Rome* to quake, stout *Guendolen*,
Renowmed *Martia*, and redoubted *Emmilen*.

55

And that, which more than all the rest may sway,
  Late dayes ensample, which these eyes beheld,
  In the last field before *Menevia*
  Which *Uther* with those forrein Pagans held,
  I saw a *Saxon* Virgin, the which feld
  Great *Ulfin* thrise upon the bloudy plaine,
  And had not *Carados* her hand withheld
  From rash revenge, she had him surely slaine,
Yet *Carados* himselfe from her escapt with paine.

56

Ah read, (quoth *Britomart*) how is she hight?
  Faire *Angela* (quoth she) men do her call,
  No whit lesse faire, than terrible in fight:
  She hath the leading of a Martiall
  And mighty people, dreaded more than all
  The other *Saxons*, which do for her sake
  And love, themselves of her name *Angles* call.
  Therefore faire Infant her ensample make
Unto thy selfe, and equall courage to thee take.

57

Her harty words so deepe into the mynd
  Of the young Damzell sunke, that great desire
  Of warlike armes in her forthwith they tynd,
  And generous stout courage did inspire,
  That she resolv'd, unweeting to her Sire,
  Advent'rous knighthood on her selfe to don,
  And counseld with her Nourse, her Maides attire
  To turne into a massy habergeon,
And bad her all things put in readinesse anon.

58

Th'old woman nought, that needed, did omit;
  But all things did conveniently purvay:
  It fortuned (so time their turne did fit)
  A band of Britons ryding on forray
  Few dayes before, had gotten a great pray
  Of Saxon goods, emongst the which was seene
  A goodly Armour, and full rich aray,
  Which long'd to *Angela*, the Saxon Queene,
All fretted round with gold, and goodly well beseene.

59

The same, with all the other ornaments,
  King *Ryence* caused to be hanged hy
  In his chiefe Church, for endlesse moniments
  Of his successe and gladfull victory:
  Of which her selfe avising readily,
  In th'evening late old *Glauce* thither led
  Faire *Britomart*, and that same Armory
  Downe taking, her therein appareled,
Well as she might, and with brave bauldrick garnished.

60

Beside those armes there stood a mighty speare,
  Which *Bladud* made by Magick art of yore,
  And usd the same in battell aye to beare;
  Sith which it had bin here preserv'd in store,
  For his great vertues proved long afore:
  For never wight so fast in sell could sit,
  But him perforce unto the ground it bore:
  Both speare she tooke, and shield, which hong by it:
Both speare and shield of great powre, for her purpose fit.

61

Thus when she had the virgin all arayd,
  Another harnesse, which did hang thereby,
  About her selfe she dight, that the young Mayd
  She might in equall armes accompany,
  And as her Squire attend her carefully:
  Tho to their ready Steeds they clombe full light,
  And through back wayes, that none might them espy,
  Covered with secret cloud of silent night,
Themselves they forth convayd, and passed forward right.

62

Ne rested they, till that to Faery lond
  They came, as *Merlin* them directed late:
  Where meeting with this *Redcrosse* knight, she fond
  Of diverse things discourses to dilate,
  But most of *Arthegall*, and his estate.
  At last their wayes so fell, that they mote part:
  Then each to other well affectionate,
  Friendship professed with unfained hart,
The *Redcrosse* knight diverst, but forth rode *Britomart*.

CANT. IIII

Bold Marinell of Britomart,
Is throwne on the Rich strond:
Faire Florimell of Arthur is
Long followed, but not fond.

1

WHERE is the Antique glory now become,
  That whilome wont in women to appeare?
  Where be the brave atchievements doen by some?
  Where be the battels, where the shield and speare,
  And all the conquests, which them high did reare,
  That matter made for famous Poets verse,
  And boastfull men so oft abasht to heare?
  Bene they all dead, and laid in dolefull herse?
Or doen they onely sleepe, and shall againe reverse?

2

If they be dead, then woe is me therefore:
  But if they sleepe, O let them soone awake:
  For all too long I burne with envy sore,
  To heare the warlike feates, which *Homere* spake
  Of bold *Penthesilee*, which made a lake
  Of *Greekish* bloud so oft in *Trojan* plaine;
  But when I read, how stout *Debora* strake
  Proud *Sisera*, and how *Camill'* hath slaine
The huge *Orsilochus*, I swell with great disdaine.

3

Yet these, and all that else had puissaunce,
  Cannot with noble *Britomart* compare,
  Aswell for glory of great valiaunce,
  As for pure chastitie and vertue rare,
  That all her goodly deeds do well declare.
  Well worthy stock, from which the branches sprong,
  That in late yeares so faire a blossome bare,
  As thee, O Queene, the matter of my song,
Whose lignage from this Lady I derive along.

4

Who when through speaches with the *Redcrosse* knight,
  She learned had th'estate of *Arthegall*,
  And in each point her selfe informd aright,
  A friendly league of love perpetuall
  She with him bound, and *Congé* tooke withall.
  Then he forth on his journey did proceede,
  To seeke adventures, which mote him befall,
  And win him worship through his warlike deed,
Which alwayes of his paines he made the chiefest meed.

5

But *Britomart* kept on her former course,
  Ne ever dofte her armes, but all the way
  Grew pensive through that amorous discourse,
  By which the *Redcrosse* knight did earst display
  Her lovers shape, and chevalrous aray;
  A thousand thoughts she fashioned in her mind,
  And in her feigning fancie did pourtray
  Him such, as fittest she for love could find,
Wise, warlike, personable, curteous, and kind.

6

With such selfe-pleasing thoughts her wound she fed,
  And thought so to beguile her grievous smart;
  But so her smart was much more grievous bred,
  And the deepe wound more deepe engord her hart,
  That nought but death her dolour mote depart.
  So forth she rode without repose or rest,
  Searching all lands and each remotest part,
  Following the guidance of her blinded guest,
Till that to the sea-coast at length she her addrest.

7

There she alighted from her light-foot beast,
  And sitting downe upon the rocky shore,
  Bad her old Squire unlace her lofty creast;
  Tho having vewd a while the surges hore,
  That gainst the craggy clifts did loudly rore,
  And in their raging surquedry disdaynd,
  That the fast earth affronted them so sore,
  And their devouring covetize restraynd,
Thereat she sighed deepe, and after thus complaynd.

8

Huge sea of sorrow, and tempestuous griefe,
  Wherein my feeble barke is tossed long,
  Far from the hoped haven of reliefe,
  Why do thy cruell billowes beat so strong,
  And thy moyst mountaines each on others throng,
  Threatning to swallow up my fearefull life?
  O do thy cruell wrath and spightfull wrong
  At length allay, and stint thy stormy strife,
Which in these troubled bowels raignes, and rageth rife.

9

For else my feeble vessell crazd, and crackt
  Through thy strong buffets and outrageous blowes,
  Cannot endure, but needs it must be wrackt
  On the rough rocks, or on the sandy shallowes,
  The whiles that love it steres, and fortune rowes;
  Love my lewd Pilot hath a restlesse mind
  And fortune Boteswaine no assuraunce knowes,
  But saile withouten starres gainst tide and wind:
How can they other do, sith both are bold and blind?

10

Thou God of winds, that raignest in the seas,
  That raignest also in the Continent,
  At last blow up some gentle gale of ease,
  The which may bring my ship, ere it be rent,
  Unto the gladsome port of her intent:
  Then when I shall my selfe in safety see,
  A table for eternall moniment
  Of thy great grace, and my great jeopardee,
Great *Neptune*, I avow to hallow unto thee.

11

Then sighing softly sore, and inly deepe,
  She shut up all her plaint in privy griefe;
  For her great courage would not let her weepe,
  Till that old *Glauce* gan with sharpe repriefe,
  Her to restraine, and give her good reliefe,
  Through hope of those, which *Merlin* had her told
  Should of her name and nation be chiefe,
  And fetch their being from the sacred mould
Of her immortall wombe, to be in heaven enrold.

12

Thus as she her recomforted, she spyde,
  Where farre away one all in armour bright,
  With hastie gallop towards her did ryde;
  Her dolour soone she ceast, and on her dight
  Her Helmet, to her Courser mounting light:
  Her former sorrow into suddein wrath,
  Both coosen passions of distroubled spright,
  Converting, forth she beates the dustie path;
Love and despight attonce her courage kindled hath.

13

As when a foggy mist hath overcast
  The face of heaven, and the cleare aire engrost,
  The world in darkenesse dwels, till that at last
  The watry Southwinde from the seabord cost
  Upblowing, doth disperse the vapour lo'st,
  And poures it selfe forth in a stormy showre;
  So the faire *Britomart* having disclo'st
  Her clowdy care into a wrathfull stowre,
The mist of griefe dissolv'd, did into vengeance powre.

14

Eftsoones her goodly shield addressing faire,
  That mortall speare she in her hand did take,
  And unto battell did her selfe prepaire.
  The knight approching, sternely her bespake;
  Sir knight, that doest thy voyage rashly make
  By this forbidden way in my despight,
  Ne doest by others death ensample take,
  I read thee soone retyre, whiles thou hast might,
Least afterwards it be too late to take thy flight.

15

Ythrild with deepe disdaine of his proud threat,
  She shortly thus; Fly they, that need to fly;
  Words fearen babes. I meane not thee entreat
  To passe; but maugre thee will passe or dy.
  Ne lenger stayd for th'other to reply,
  But with sharpe speare the rest made dearly knowne.
  Strongly the straunge knight ran, and sturdily
  Strooke her full on the brest, that made her downe
Decline her head, and touch her crouper with her crowne.

16

But she againe him in the shield did smite
  With so fierce furie and great puissaunce,
  That through his threesquare scuchin percing quite,
  And through his mayled hauberque, by mischaunce
  The wicked steele through his left side did glaunce;
  Him so transfixed she before her bore
  Beyond his croupe, the length of all her launce,
  Till sadly soucing on the sandie shore,
He tombled on an heape, and wallowd in his gore.

17

Like as the sacred Oxe, that carelesse stands,
  With gilden hornes, and flowry girlonds crownd,
  Proud of his dying honor and deare bands,
  Whiles th'altars fume with frankincense arownd,
  All suddenly with mortall stroke astownd,
  Doth groveling fall, and with his streaming gore
  Distaines the pillours, and the holy grownd,
  And the faire flowres, that decked him afore;
So fell proud *Marinell* upon the pretious shore.

18

The martiall Mayd stayd not him to lament,
  But forward rode, and kept her readie way
  Along the strond, which as she over-went,
  She saw bestrowed all with rich aray
  Of pearles and pretious stones of great assay,
  And all the gravell mixt with golden owre;
  Whereat she wondred much, but would not stay
  For gold, or perles, or pretious stones an howre,
But them despised all; for all was in her powre.

19

Whiles thus he lay in deadly stonishment,
  Tydings hereof came to his mothers eare;
  His mother was the blacke-browd *Cymoent*,
  The daughter of great *Nereus*, which did beare
  This warlike sonne unto an earthly peare,
  The famous *Dumarin*; who on a day
  Finding the Nymph a sleepe in secret wheare,
  As he by chaunce did wander that same way,
Was taken with her love, and by her closely lay.

20

There he this knight of her begot, whom borne
   She of his father *Marinell* did name,
   And in a rocky cave as wight forlorne,
   Long time she fostred up, till he became
   A mightie man at armes, and mickle fame
   Did get through great adventures by him donne:
   For never man he suffred by that same
   Rich strond to travell, whereas he did wonne,
But that he must do battell with the Sea-nymphes sonne.

21

An hundred knights of honorable name
   He had subdew'd, and them his vassals madé,
   That through all Farie lond his noble fame
   Now blazed was, and feare did all invade,
   That none durst passen through that perilous glade.
   And to advance his name and glorie more,
   Her Sea-god syre she dearely did perswade,
   T'endow her sonne with threasure and rich store,
Bove all the sonnes, that were of earthly wombes ybore.

22

The God did graunt his daughters deare demaund,
   To doen his Nephew in all riches flow;
   Eftsoones his heaped waves he did commaund,
   Out of their hollow bosome forth to throw
   All the huge threasure, which the sea below
   Had in his greedie gulfe devoured deepe,
   And him enriched through the overthrow
   And wreckes of many wretches, which did weepe,
And often waile their wealth, which he from them did keepe.

23

Shortly upon that shore there heaped was,
   Exceeding riches and all pretious things,
   The spoyle of all the world, that it did pas
   The wealth of th'East, and pompe of *Persian* kings;
   Gold, amber, yvorie, perles, owches, rings,
   And all that else was pretious and deare,
   The sea unto him voluntary brings,
   That shortly he a great Lord did appeare,
As was in all the lond of Faery, or elsewheare.

24

Thereto he was a doughtie dreaded knight,
    Tryde often to the scath of many deare,
    That none in equall armes him matchen might,
    The which his mother seeing, gan to feare
    Least his too haughtie hardines might reare
    Some hard mishap, in hazard of his life:
    For thy she oft him counseld to forbeare
    The bloudie battell, and to stirre up strife,
But after all his warre, to rest his wearie knife.

25

And for his more assurance, she inquir'd
    One day of *Proteus* by his mightie spell,
    (For *Proteus* was with prophecie inspir'd)
    Her deare sonnes destinie to her to tell,
    And the sad end of her sweet *Marinell*.
    Who through foresight of his eternall skill,
    Bad her from womankind to keepe him well:
    For of a woman he should have much ill,
A virgin strange and stout him should dismay, or kill.

26

For thy she gave him warning every day,
    The love of women not to entertaine;
    A lesson too too hard for living clay,
    From love in course of nature to refraine:
    Yet he his mothers lore did well retaine,
    And ever from faire Ladies love did fly;
    Yet many Ladies faire did oft complaine,
    That they for love of him would algates dy:
Dy, who so list for him, he was loves enimy.

27

But ah, who can deceive his destiny,
    Or weene by warning to avoyd his fate?
    That when he sleepes in most security,
    And safest seemes, him soonest doth amate,
    And findeth dew effect or soone or late.
    So feeble is the powre of fleshly arme.
    His mother bad him womens love to hate,
    For she of womans force did feare no harme;
So weening to have arm'd him, she did quite disarme.

28

This was that woman, this that deadly wound,
  That *Proteus* prophecide should him dismay,
  The which his mother vainely did expound,
  To be hart-wounding love, which should assay
  To bring her sonne unto his last decay.
  So tickle be the termes of mortall state,
  And full of subtile sophismes, which do play
  With double senses, and with false debate,
T'approve the unknowen purpose of eternall fate.

29

Too true the famous *Marinell* it fownd,
  Who through late triall, on that wealthy Strond
  Inglorious now lies in senselesse swownd,
  Through heavy stroke of *Britomartis* hond.
  Which when his mother deare did understond,
  And heavy tydings heard, whereas she playd
  Amongst her watry sisters by a pond,
  Gathering sweet daffadillyes, to have made
Gay girlonds, from the Sun their forheads faire to shade;

30

Eftsoones both flowres and girlonds farre away
  She flong, and her faire deawy lockes yrent,
  To sorrow huge she turnd her former play,
  And gamesom merth to grievous dreriment:
  She threw her selfe downe on the Continent,
  Ne word did speake, but lay as in a swowne,
  Whiles all her sisters did for her lament,
  With yelling outcries, and with shrieking sowne;
And every one did teare her girlond from her crowne.

31

Soone as she up out of her deadly fit
  Arose, she bad her charet to be brought,
  And all her sisters, that with her did sit,
  Bad eke attonce their charets to be sought;
  Tho full of bitter griefe and pensive thought,
  She to her wagon clombe; clombe all the rest,
  And forth together went, with sorrow fraught.
  The waves obedient to their beheast,
Them yielded readie passage, and their rage surceast.

32

Great *Neptune* stood amazed at their sight,
  Whiles on his broad round backe they softly slid
  And eke himselfe mournd at their mournfull plight,
  Yet wist not what their wailing ment, yet did
  For great compassion of their sorrow, bid
  His mightie waters to them buxome bee:
  Eftsoones the roaring billowes still abid,
  And all the griesly Monsters of the See
Stood gaping at their gate, and wondred them to see.

33

A teme of Dolphins raunged in aray,
  Drew the smooth charet of sad *Cymoent*;
  They were all taught by *Triton*, to obay
  To the long raynes, at her commaundement:
  As swift as swallowes, on the waves they went,
  That their broad flaggie finnes no fome did reare,
  Ne bubbling roundell they behind them sent;
  The rest of other fishes drawen weare,
Which with their finny oars the swelling sea did sheare.

34

Soone as they bene arriv'd upon the brim
  Of the *Rich strond*, their charets they forlore,
  And let their temed fishes softly swim
  Along the margent of the fomy shore,
  Least they their finnes should bruze, and surbate sore
  Their tender feet upon the stony ground:
  And comming to the place, where all in gore
  And cruddy bloud enwallowed they found
The lucklesse *Marinell*, lying in deadly swound;

35

His mother swowned thrise, and the third time
  Could scarce recovered be out of her paine;
  Had she not bene devoyd of mortall slime,
  She should not then have bene reliv'd againe,
  But soone as life recovered had the raine,
  She made so piteous mone and deare wayment,
  That the hard rocks could scarse from teares refraine,
  And all her sister Nymphes with one consent
Supplide her sobbing breaches with sad complement.

36

Deare image of my selfe (she said) that is,
   The wretched sonne of wretched mother borne,
   Is this thine high advauncement, O is this
   Th'immortall name, with which thee yet unborne
   Thy Gransire *Nereus* promist to adorne?
   Now lyest thou of life and honor reft;
   Now lyest thou a lumpe of earth forlorne,
   Ne of thy late life memory is left,
Ne can thy irrevocable destiny be weft?

37

Fond *Proteus*, father of false prophecis,
   And they more fond, that credit to thee give,
   Not this the worke of womans hand ywis,
   That so deepe wound through these deare members drive.
   I feared love: but they that love do live,
   But they that die, doe neither love nor hate.
   Nath'lesse to thee thy folly I forgive,
   And to my selfe, and to accursed fate
The guilt I doe ascribe: deare wisedome bought too late.

38

O what availes it of immortall seed
   To beene ybred and never borne to die?
   Farre better I it deeme to die with speed,
   Than waste in woe and wailefull miserie.
   Who dyes the utmost dolour doth abye,
   But who that lives, is left to waile his losse:
   So life is losse, and death felicitie.
   Sad life worse than glad death: and greater crosse
To see friends grave, than dead the grave selfe to engrosse.

39

But if the heavens did his dayes envie,
   And my short blisse maligne, yet mote they well
   Thus much afford me, ere that he did die
   That the dim eyes of my deare *Marinell*
   I mote have closed, and him bed farewell,
   Sith other offices for mother meet
   They would not graunt.
   Yet maulgre them farewell, my sweetest sweet;
Farewell my sweetest sonne, sith we no more shall meet.

40

Thus when they all had sorrowed their fill,
  They softly gan to search his griesly wound:
  And that they might him handle more at will,
  They him disarm'd, and spredding on the ground
  Their watchet mantles frindgd with silver round,
  They softly wipt away the gelly blood
  From th'orifice; which having well upbound,
  They pourd in soveraine balme, and Nectar good,
Good both for earthly med'cine, and for heavenly food.

41

Tho when the lilly handed *Liagore*,
  (This *Liagore* whylome had learned skill
  In leaches craft, by great *Appolloes* lore,
  Sith her whylome upon high *Pindus* hill,
  He loved, and at last her wombe did fill
  With heavenly seed, whereof wise *Pæon* sprong)
  Did feele his pulse, she knew their staied still
  Some litle life his feeble sprites emong;
Which to his mother told, despeire she from her flong.

42

Tho up him taking in their tender hands,
  They easily unto her charet beare:
  Her teme at her commaundement quiet stands,
  Whiles they the corse into her wagon reare,
  And strow with flowres the lamentable beare:
  Then all the rest into their coches clim,
  And through the brackish waves their passage sheare;
  Upon great *Neptunes* necke they softly swim,
And to her watry chamber swiftly carry him.

43

Deepe in the bottome of the sea, her bowre
  Is built of hollow billowes heaped hye,
  Like to thicke cloudes, that threat a stormy showre,
  And vauted all within, like to the sky,
  In which the Gods do dwell eternally:
  There they him laid in easie couch well dight;
  And sent in haste for *Tryphon*, to apply
  Salves to his wounds, and medicines of might:
For *Tryphon* of sea gods the soveraine leach is hight.

44

The whiles the *Nymphes* sit all about him round,
　Lamenting his mishap and heavy plight;
And oft his mother vewing his wide wound,
　Cursed the hand, that did so deadly smight
　Her dearest sonne, her dearest harts delight.
But none of all those curses overtooke
　The warlike Maid, th'ensample of that might,
　But fairely well she thriv'd, and well did brooke
Her noble deeds, ne her right course for ought forsooke.

45

Yet did false *Archimage* her still pursew,
　To bring to passe his mischievous intent,
Now that he had her singled from the crew
　Of courteous knights, the Prince, and Faery gent,
　Whom late in chace of beautie excellent
She left, pursewing that same foster strong;
　Of whose foule outrage they impatient,
　And full of fiery zeale, him followed long,
To reskew her from shame, and to revenge her wrong.

46

Through thick and thin, through mountaines and through plains,
　Those two great champions did attonce pursew
The fearefull damzell, with incessant paines:
　Who from them fled, as light-foot hare from vew
　Of hunter swift, and sent of houndes trew.
At last they came unto a double way,
　Where, doubtfull which to take, her to reskew,
　Themselves they did dispart, each to assay,
Whether more happie were, to win so goodly pray.

47

But *Timias*, the Princes gentle Squire,
　That Ladies love unto his Lord forlent,
And with proud envy, and indignant ire,
　After that wicked foster fiercely went.
　So beene they three three sundry wayes ybent.
But fairest fortune to the Prince befell,
　Whose chaunce it was, that soone he did repent,
　To take that way, in which that Damozell
Was fled afore, affraid of him, as feend of hell.

48

At last of her farre off he gained vew:
  Then gan he freshly pricke his fomy steed,
  And ever as he nigher to her drew,
  So evermore he did increase his speed,
  And of each turning still kept warie heed:
  Aloud to her he oftentimes did call,
  To doe away vaine doubt, and needlesse dreed:
  Full myld to her he spake, and oft let fall
Many meeke wordes, to stay and comfort her withall.

49

But nothing might relent her hastie flight;
  So deepe the deadly feare of that foule swaine
  Was earst impressed in her gentle spright:
  Like as a fearefull Dove, which through the raine,
  Of the wide aire her way does cut amaine,
  Having farre off espyde a Tassell gent,
  Which after her his nimble wings doth straine,
  Doubleth her haste for feare to be for-hent,
And with her pineons cleaves the liquid firmament.

50

With no lesse haste, and eke with no lesse dreed,
  That fearefull Ladie fled from him, that ment
  To her no evill thought, nor evill deed;
  Yet former feare of being fowly shent,
  Carried her forward with her first intent:
  And though oft looking backward, well she vewd,
  Her selfe freed from that foster insolent,
  And that it was a knight, which now her sewd,
Yet she no lesse the knight feard, than that villein rude.

51

His uncouth shield and straunge armes her dismayd,
  Whose like in Faery lond were seldome seene,
  That fast she from him fled, no lesse affrayd,
  Than of wilde beastes if she had chased beene:
  Yet he her followd still with courage keene,
  So long that now the golden *Hesperus*
  Was mounted high in top of heaven sheene,
  And warnd his other brethren joyeous,
To light their blessed lamps in *Joves* eternall hous.

52

All suddenly dim woxe the dampish ayre,
  And griesly shadowes covered heaven bright,
  That now with thousand starres was decked fayre;
  Which when the Prince beheld, a lothfull sight,
  And that perforce, for want of lenger light,
  He mote surcease his suit, and lose the hope
  Of his long labour, he gan fowly wyte
  His wicked fortune, that had turnd aslope,
And cursed night, that reft from him so goodly scope.

53

Tho when her wayes he could no more descry,
  But to and fro at disaventure strayd;
  Like as a ship, whose Lodestarre suddenly
  Covered with cloudes, her Pilot hath dismayd;
  His wearisome pursuit perforce he stayd,
  And from his loftie steed dismounting low,
  Did let him forage. Downe himselfe he layd
  Upon the grassie ground, to sleepe a throw;
The cold earth was his couch, the hard steele his pillow.

54

But gentle Sleepe envyde him any rest;
  In stead thereof sad sorrow, and disdaine
  Of his hard hap did vexe his noble brest,
  And thousand fancies bet his idle braine
  With their light wings, the sights of semblants vaine:
  Oft did he wish, that Lady faire mote bee
  His Faery Queene, for whom he did complaine:
  Or that his Faery Queene were such, as shee:
And ever hastie Night he blamed bitterlie.

55

Night thou foule Mother of annoyance sad,
  Sister of heavie death, and nourse of woe,
  Which wast begot in heaven, but for thy bad
  And brutish shape thrust downe to hell below,
  Where by the grim floud of *Cocytus* slow
  Thy dwelling is, in *Herebus* blacke hous,
  (Blacke *Herebus* thy husband is the foe
  Of all the Gods) where thou ungratious,
Halfe of thy dayes doest lead in horrour hideous.

56

What had th'eternall Maker need of thee,
  The world in his continuall course to keepe,
  That doest all things deface, ne lettest see
  The beautie of his worke? Indeed in sleepe
  The slouthfull bodie, that doth love to steepe
  His lustlesse limbes, and drowne his baser mind,
  Doth praise thee oft, and oft from *Stygian* deepe
  Calles thee, his goddesse in his error blind,
And great Dame Natures handmaide, chearing every kind.

57

But well I wote, that to an heavy hart
  Thou art the root and nurse of bitter cares,
  Breeder of new, renewer of old smarts:
  In stead of rest thou lendest rayling teares,
  In stead of sleepe thou sendest troublous feares,
  And dreadfull visions, in the which alive
  The drearie image of sad death appeares:
  So from the wearie spirit thou doest drive
Desired rest, and men of happinesse deprive.

58

Under thy mantle blacke there hidden lye,
  Light-shonning theft, and traiterous intent,
  Abhorred bloudshed, and vile felony,
  Shamefull deceipt, and daunger imminent;
  Foule horror, and eke hellish dreriment:
  All these I wote in thy protection bee,
  And light doe shonne, for feare of being shent:
  For light ylike is loth'd of them and thee,
And all that lewdnesse love, doe hate the light to see.

59

For day discovers all dishonest wayes,
  And sheweth each thing, as it is indeed:
  The prayses of high God he faire displayes,
  And his large bountie rightly doth areed.
  Dayes dearest children be the blessed seed,
  Which darknesse shall subdew, and heaven win:
  Truth is his daughter; he her first did breed,
  Most sacred virgin, without spot of sin.
Our life is day, but death with darknesse doth begin.

60

O when will day then turne to me againe,
  And bring with him his long expected light?
  O *Titan*, haste to reare thy joyous waine:
  Speed thee to spred abroad thy beames bright,
  And chase away this too long lingring night,
  Chase her away, from whence she came, to hell.
  She, she it is, that hath me done despight:
  There let her with the damned spirits dwell,
And yeeld her roome to day, that can it governe well.

61

Thus did the Prince that wearie night outweare,
  In restlesse anguish and unquiet paine:
  And earely, ere the morrow did upreare
  His deawy head out of the *Ocean* maine,
  He up arose, as halfe in great disdaine,
  And clombe unto his steed. So forth he went,
  With heavie looke and lumpish pace, that plaine
  In him bewraid great grudge and maltalent:
His steed eke seem'd t'apply his steps to his intent.

CANT. V

Prince Arthur heares of Florimell:
  three fosters Timias wound,
Belphebe finds him almost dead,
  and reareth out of sownd.

1

WONDER it is to see, in diverse minds,
  How diversly love doth his pageants play,
  And shewes his powre in variable kinds:
  The baser wit, whose idle thoughts alway
  Are wont to cleave unto the lowly clay,
  It stirreth up to sensuall desire,
  And in lewd slouth to wast his carelesse day:
  But in brave sprite it kindles goodly fire,
That to all high desert and honour doth aspire.

2

Ne suffereth it uncomely idlenesse,
  In his free thought to build her sluggish nest:
  Ne suffereth it thought of ungentlenesse,
  Ever to creepe into his noble brest,
  But to the highest and the worthiest
  Lifteth it up, that else would lowly fall:
  It lets not fall, it lets it not to rest:
  It lets not scarse this Prince to breath at all,
But to his first poursuit him forward still doth call.

3

Who long time wandred through the forrest wyde,
  To finde some issue thence, till that at last
  He met a Dwarfe, that seemed terrifyde
  With some late perill, which he hardly past,
  Or other accident, which him aghast;
  Of whom he asked, whence he lately came,
  And whither now he travelled so fast:
  For sore he swat, and running through that same
Thicke forest, was bescratcht, and both his feet nigh lame.

4

Panting for breath, and almost out of hart,
  The Dwarfe him answerd, Sir, ill mote I stay
  To tell the same. I lately did depart
  From Faery court, where I have many a day
  Served a gentle Lady of great sway,
  And high accompt through out all Elfin land,
  Who lately left the same, and tooke this way:
  Her now I seeke, and if ye understand
Which way she fared hath, good Sir tell out of hand.

5

What mister wight (said he) and how arayd?
  Royally clad (quoth he) in cloth of gold,
  As meetest may beseeme a noble mayd;
  Her faire lockes in rich circlet be enrold,
  A fairer wight did never Sunne behold,
  And on a Palfrey rides more white than snow,
  Yet she her selfe is whiter manifold:
  The surest signe, whereby ye may her know,
Is, that she is the fairest wight alive, I trow.

6

Now certes swaine (said he) such one I weene,
  Fast flying through this forest from her fo,
  A foule ill favoured foster, I have seene;
  Her selfe, well as I might, I reskewd tho,
  But could not stay; so fast she did foregoe,
  Carried away with wings of speedy feare.
  Ah dearest God (quoth he) that is great woe,
  And wondrous ruth to all, that shall it heare.
But can ye read Sir, how I may her find, or where?

7

Perdy me lever were to weeten that,
  (Said he) than ransome of the richest knight,
  Or all the good that ever yet I gat:
  But froward fortune, and too forward Night
  Such happinesse did, maulgre, to me spight,
  And fro me reft both life and light attone.
  But Dwarfe aread, what is that Lady bright,
  That through this forest wandreth thus alone;
For of her errour straunge I have great ruth and mone.

8

That Lady is (quoth he) where so she bee,
  The bountiest virgin, and most debonaire,
  That ever living eye I weene did see;
  Lives none this day, that may with her compare
  In stedfast chastitie and vertue rare,
  The goodly ornaments of beautie bright;
  And is ycleped *Florimell* the faire,
  Faire *Florimell* belov'd of many a knight,
Yet she loves none but one, that *Marinell* is hight.

9

A Sea-nymphes sonne, that *Marinell* is hight,
  Of my deare Dame is loved dearely well;
  In other none, but him, she sets delight,
  All her delight is set on *Marinell*;
  But he sets nought at all by *Florimell*:
  For Ladies love his mother long ygoe
  Did him, they say, forwarne through sacred spell.
  But fame now flies, that of a forreine foe
He is yslaine, which is the ground of all our woe.

10

Five dayes there be, since he (they say) was slaine,
  And foure, since *Florimell* the Court for-went,
  And vowed never to returne againe,
  Till him alive or dead she did invent.
  Therefore, faire Sir, for love of knighthood gent,
  And honour of trew Ladies, if ye may
  By your good counsell, or bold hardiment,
  Or succour her, or me direct the way;
Do one, or other good, I you most humbly pray.

11

So may ye gaine to you full great renowme,
  Of all good Ladies through the world so wide,
  And haply in her hart find highest rowme,
  Of whom ye seeke to be most magnifide:
  At least eternall meede shall you abide.
  To whom the Prince; Dwarfe, comfort to thee take,
  For till thou tidings learne, what her betide,
  I here avow thee never to forsake.
Ill weares he armes, that nill them use for Ladies sake.

12

So with the Dwarfe he backe return'd againe,
  To seeke his Lady, where he mote her find;
  But by the way he greatly gan complaine
  The want of his good Squire late left behind,
  For whom he wondrous pensive grew in mind,
  For doubt of daunger, which mote him betide;
  For him he loved above all mankind,
  Having him trew and faithfull ever tride,
And bold, as ever Squire that waited by knights side.

13

Who all this while full hardly was assayd
  Of deadly daunger, which to him betid;
  For whiles his Lord pursewd that noble Mayd,
  After that foster fowle he fiercely rid,
  To bene avenged of the shame, he did
  To that faire Damzell: Him he chaced long
  Through the thicke woods, wherein he would have hid
  His shamefull head from his avengement strong,
And oft him threatned death for his outrageous wrong.

14

Nathlesse the villen sped him selfe so well,
  Whether through swiftnesse of his speedy beast,
  Or knowledge of those woods, where he did dwell,
  That shortly he from daunger was releast,
  And out of sight escaped at the least;
  Yet not escaped from the dew reward
  Of his bad deeds, which dayly he increast,
  Ne ceased not, till him oppressed hard
The heavy plague, that for such leachours is prepard.

15

For soone as he was vanisht out of sight,
  His coward courage gan emboldned bee,
  And cast t'avenge him of that fowle despight,
  Which he had borne of his bold enimee.
  Tho to his brethren came: for they were three
  Ungratious children of one gracelesse sire,
  And unto them complained, how that he
  Had used bene of that foolehardy Squire;
So them with bitter words he stird to bloudy ire.

16

Forthwith themselves with their sad instruments
  Of spoyle and murder they gan arme bylive,
  And with him forth into the forest went,
  To wreake the wrath, which he did earst revive
  In their sterne brests, on him which late did drive
  Their brother to reproch and shamefull flight:
  For they had vow'd, that never he alive
  Out of that forest should escape their might;
Vile rancour their rude harts had fild with such despight.

17

Within that wood there was a covert glade,
  Foreby a narrow foord, to them well knowne,
  Through which it was uneath for wight to wade;
  And now by fortune it was overflowne:
  By that same way they knew that Squire unknowne
  Mote algates passe; for thy themselves they set
  There in await, with thicke woods over growne,
  And all the while their malice they did whet
With cruell threats, his passage through the ford to let.

18

It fortuned, as they devized had,
  The gentle Squire came ryding that same way,
  Unweeting of their wile and treason bad,
  And through the ford to passen did assay;
  But that fierce foster, which late fled away,
  Stoutly forth stepping on the further shore,
  Him boldly bad his passage there to stay,
  Till he had made amends, and full restore
For all the damage, which he had him doen afore.

19

With that at him a quiv'ring dart he threw,
  With so fell force and villeinous despighte,
  That through his haberjeon the forkehead flew,
  And through the linked mayles empierced quite,
  But had no powre in his soft flesh to bite:
  That stroke the hardy Squire did sore displease,
  But more that him he could not come to smite;
  For by no meanes the high banke he could sease,
But labour'd long in that deepe ford with vaine disease.

20

And still the foster with his long bore-speare
  Him kept from landing at his wished will;
  Anone one sent out of the thicket neare
  A cruell shaft, headed with deadly ill,
  And fethered with an unlucky quill;
  The wicked steele stayd not, till it did light
  In his left thigh, and deepely did it thrill:
  Exceeding griefe that wound in him empight,
But more that with his foes he could not come to fight.

21

At last through wrath and vengeaunce making way,
  He on the bancke arriv'd with mickle paine,
  Where the third brother him did sore assay,
  And drove at him with all his might and maine
  A forrest bill, which both his hands did straine;
  But warily he did avoide the blow,
  And with his speare requited him againe,
  That both his sides were thrilled with the throw,
And a large streame of bloud out of the wound did flow.

22

He tombling downe, with gnashing teeth did bite
  The bitter earth, and bad to let him in
  Into the balefull house of endlesse night,
  Where wicked ghosts do waile their former sin.
  Tho gan the battell freshly to begin;
  For nathemore for that spectacle bad,
  Did th'other two their cruell vengeaunce blin,
  But both attonce on both sides him bestad,
And load upon him layd, his life for to have had.

23

Tho when that villain he aviz'd, which late
  Affrighted had the fairest *Florimell*,
  Full of fiers fury, and indignant hate,
  To him he turned, and with rigour fell
  Smote him so rudely on the Pannikell,
  That to the chin he cleft his head in twaine:
  Downe on the ground his carkas groveling fell;
  His sinfull soule with desperate disdaine,
Out of her fleshly ferme fled to the place of paine.

24

That seeing now the onely last of three,
  Who with that wicked shaft him wounded had,
  Trembling with horrour, as that did foresee
  The fearefull end of his avengement sad,
  Through which he follow should his brethren bad,
  His bootelesse bow in feeble hand upcaught,
  And therewith shot an arrow at the lad;
  Which faintly fluttring, scarce his helmet raught,
And glauncing fell to ground, but him annoyed naught.

25

With that he would have fled into the wood;
  But *Timias* him lightly overhent,
  Right as he entring was into the flood,
  And strooke at him with force so violent,
  That headlesse him into the foord he sent:
  The carkas with the streame was carried downe,
  But th'head fell backeward on the Continent.
  So mischief fel upon the meaners crowne;
They three be dead with shame, the Squire lives with renowne.

26

He lives, but takes small joy of his renowne;
  For of that cruell wound he bled so sore,
  That from his steed he fell in deadly swowne;
  Yet still the bloud forth gusht in so great store,
  That he lay wallowd all in his owne gore.
  Now God thee keepe, thou gentlest Squire alive,
  Else shall thy loving Lord thee see no more,
  But both of comfort him thou shalt deprive,
And eke thy selfe of honour, which thou didst atchive.

27

Providence heavenly passeth living thought,
  And doth for wretched mens reliefe make way;
  For loe great grace or fortune thither brought
  Comfort to him, that comfortlesse now lay.
  In those same woods, ye well remember may,
  How that a noble hunteresse did wonne,
  She, that base *Braggadochio* did affray,
  And made him fast out of the forrest runne;
Belphœbe was her name, as faire as *Phœbus* sunne.

28

She on a day, as she pursewd the chace
  Of some wild beast, which with her arrowes keene
  She wounded had, the same along did trace
  By tract of bloud, which she had freshly seene,
  To have besprinckled all the grassy greene;
  By the great persue, which she there perceav'd,
  Well hoped she the beast engor'd had beene,
  And made more hast, the life to have bereav'd:
But ah, her expectation greatly was deceav'd.

29

Shortly she came, whereas that woefull Squire
  With bloud deformed, lay in deadly swowitd:
  In whose faire eyes, like lamps of quenched fire,
  The Christall humour stood congealed rownd;
  His locks, like faded leaves fallen to grownd,
  Knotted with bloud, in bounches rudely ran,
  And his sweete lips, on which before that stownd
  The bud of youth to blossome faire began,
Spoild of their rosie red, were woxen pale and wan.

30

Saw never living eye more heavy sight,
　　That could have made a rocke of stone to rew,
　　Or rive in twaine: which when that Lady bright
　　Besides all hope with melting eyes did vew,
　　All suddeinly abasht she chaunged hew,
　　And with sterne horrour backward gan to start:
　　But when she better him beheld, she grew
　　Full of soft passion and unwonted smart:
The point of pitty perced through her tender hart.

31

Meekely she bowed downe, to weete if life
　　Yet in his frosen members did remaine,
　　And feeling by his pulses beating rife,
　　That the weake soule her seat did yet retaine,
　　She cast to comfort him with busie paine:
　　His double folded necke she reard upright,
　　And rubd his temples, and each trembling vaine;
　　His mayled haberjeon she did undight,
And from his head his heavy burganet did light.

32

Into the woods thenceforth in hast she went,
　　To seeke for hearbes, that mote him remedy;
　　For she of hearbes had great intendiment,
　　Taught of the Nymphe, which from her infancy
　　Her nourced had in trew Nobility:
　　There, whether it divine *Tobacco* were,
　　Or *Panachæa*, or *Polygony*,
　　She found, and brought it to her patient deare
Who al this while lay bleeding out his hart-bloud neare.

33

The soveraigne weede betwixt two marbles plaine
　　She pownded small, and did in peeces bruze,
　　And then atweene her lilly handes twaine,
　　Into his wound the juyce thereof did scruze,
　　And round about, as she could well it uze,
　　The flesh therewith she suppled and did steepe,
　　T'abate all spasme, and soke the swelling bruze,
　　And after having searcht the intuse deepe,
She with her scarfe did bind the wound from cold to keepe.

34

By this he had sweete life recur'd againe,
   And groning inly deepe, at last his eyes,
   His watry eyes, drizling like deawy raine,
   He up gan lift toward the azure skies,
   From whence descend all hopelesse remedies:
   Therewith he sigh'd, and turning him aside,
   The goodly Mayd full of divinities,
   And gifts of heavenly grace he by him spide,
Her bow and gilden quiver lying him beside.

35

Mercy deare Lord (said he) what grace is this,
   That thou hast shewed to me sinfull wight,
   To send thine Angell from her bowre of blis,
   To comfort me in my distressed plight?
   Angell, or Goddesse do I call thee right?
   What service may I do unto thee meete,
   That hast from darkenesse me returnd to light,
   And with thy heavenly salves and med'cines sweete,
Hast drest my sinfull wounds? I kisse thy blessed feete.

36

Thereat she blushing said, Ah gentle Squire,
   Nor Goddesse I, nor Angell, but the Mayd,
   And daughter of a woody Nymphe, desire
   No service, but thy safety and ayd;
   Which if thou gaine, I shalbe well apayd.
   We mortall wights whose lives and fortunes bee
   To commun accidents still open layd,
   Are bound with commun bond of frailtee,
To succour wretched wights, whom we captived see.

37

By this her Damzels, which the former chace
   Had undertaken after her, arriv'd,
   As did *Belphœbe*, in the bloudy place,
   And thereby deemd the beast had bene depriv'd
   Of life, whom late their Ladies arrow ryv'd:
   For thy the bloudy tract they follow fast,
   And every one to runne the swiftest stryv'd;
   But two of them the rest far overpast,
And where their Lady was, arrived at the last.

38

Where when they saw that goodly boy, with blood
  Defowled, and their Lady dresse his wownd,
  They wondred much, and shortly understood,
  How him in deadly case their Lady fownd,
  And reskewed out of the heavy stownd.
  Eftsoones his warlike courser, which was strayd
  Farre in the woods, whiles that he lay in swownd,
  She made those Damzels search, which being stayd,
They did him set thereon, and forth with them convayd.

39

Into that forest farre they thence him led,
  Where was their dwelling, in a pleasant glade,
  With mountaines round about environed,
  And mighty woods, which did the valley shade,
  And like a stately Theatre it made,
  Spreading it selfe into a spatious plaine.
  And in the midst a little river plaide
  Emongst the pumy stones, which seemd to plaine
With gentle murmure, that his course they did restraine.

40

Beside the same a dainty place there lay,
  Planted with mirtle trees and laurels greene,
  In which the birds song many a lovely lay
  Of gods high prayse, and of their loves sweet teene,
  As it an earthly Paradize had beene:
  In whose enclosed shadow there was pight
  A faire Pavilion, scarcely to be seene,
  The which was all within most richly dight,
That greatest Princes living it mote well delight.

41

Thither they brought that wounded Squire, and layd
  In easie couch his feeble limbes to rest,
  He rested him a while, and then the Mayd
  His ready wound with better salves new drest;
  Dayly she dressed him, and did the best
  His grievous hurt to garish, that she might,
  That shortly she his dolour hath redrest,
  And his foule sore reduced to faire plight:
It she reduced, but himselfe destroyed quight.

42

O foolish Physick, and unfruitfull paine,
  That heales up one and makes another wound:
  She his hurt thigh to him recur'd againe,
  But hurt his hart, the which before was sound,
  Through an unwary dart, which did rebound
  From her faire eyes and gracious countenaunce.
  What bootes it him from death to be unbound,
  To be captived in endlesse duraunce
Of sorrow and despaire without aleggeaunce?

43

Still as his wound did gather, and grow hole,
  So still his hart woxe sore, and health decayd:
  Madnesse to save a part, and lose the whole.
  Still whenas he beheld the heavenly Mayd,
  Whiles dayly plaisters to his wound she layd,
  So still his Malady the more increast,
  The whiles her matchlesse beautie him dismayd.
  Ah God, what other could he do at least,
But love so faire a Lady, that his life releast?

44

Long while he strove in his courageous brest,
  With reason dew the passion to subdew,
  And love for to dislodge out of his nest:
  Still when her excellencies he did vew,
  Her soveraigne bounty, and celestiall hew,
  The same to love he strongly was constraind:
  But when his meane estate he did revew,
  He from such hardy boldnesse was restraind,
And of his lucklesse lot and cruell love thus plaind.

45

Unthankfull wretch (said he) is this the meed,
  With which her soveraigne mercy thou doest quight?
  Thy life she saved by her gracious deed,
  But thou doest weene with villeinous despight,
  To blot her honour, and her heavenly light.
  Dye rather, dye, than so disloyally
  Deeme of her high desert, or seeme so light:
  Faire death it is to shonne more shame, to dy:
Dye rather, dy, than ever love disloyally.

46

But if to love disloyalty it bee,
  Shall I then hate her, that from deathes dore
  Me brought? ah farre be such reproch fro mee.
  What can I lesse do, than her love therefore,
  Sith I her dew reward cannot restore?
  Dye rather, dye, and dying do her serve,
  Dying her serve, and living her adore;
  Thy life she gave, thy life she doth deserve:
Dye rather, dye, than ever from her service swerve.

47

But foolish boy, what bootes thy service bace
  To her, to whom the heavens do serve and sew?
  Thou a meane Squire, of meeke and lowly place,
  She heavenly borne, and of celestiall hew.
  How then? of all love taketh equall vew:
  And doth not highest God vouchsafe to take
  The love and service of the basest crew?
  If she will not, dye meekly for her sake;
Dye rather, dye, than ever so faire love forsake.

48

Thus warreid he long time against his will,
  Till that through weaknesse he was forst at last,
  To yield himselfe unto the mighty ill:
  Which as a victour proud, gan ransack fast
  His inward parts, and all his entrayles wast,
  That neither bloud in face, nor life in hart
  It left, but both did quite drye up, and blast;
  As percing levin, which the inner part
Of every thing consumes, and calcineth by art.

49

Which seeing faire *Belphœbe* gan to feare,
  Least that his wound were inly well not healed,
  Or that the wicked steele empoysned were:
  Litle she weend, that love he close concealed;
  Yet still he wasted, as the snow congealed,
  When the bright sunne his beams thereon doth beat;
  Yet never he his hart to her revealed,
  But rather chose to dye for sorrow great,
Than with dishonorable termes her to entreat.

50

She gracious Lady, yet no paines did spare,
  To do him ease, or do him remedy:
  Many Restoratives of vertues rare,
  And costly Cordialles she did apply,
  To mitigate his stubborne mallady:
  But that sweet Cordiall, which can restore
  A love-sick hart, she did to him envy;
  To him, and to all th'unworthy world forlore
She did envy that soveraigne salve, in secret store.

51

That dainty Rose, the daughter of her Morne,
  More deare than life she tendered, whose flowre
  The girlond of her honour did adorne:
  Ne suffred she the Middayes scorching powre,
  Ne the sharp Northerne wind thereon to showre,
  But lapped up her silken leaves most chaire,
  When so the froward skye began to lowre:
  But soone as calmed was the Christall aire,
She did it faire dispred, and let to florish faire.

52

Eternall God in his almighty powre,
  To make ensample of his heavenly grace,
  In Paradize whilome did plant this flowre,
  Whence he it fetcht out of her native place,
  And did in stocke of earthly flesh enrace,
  That mortall men her glory should admire:
  In gentle Ladies brest, and bounteous race
  Of woman kind it fairest flowre doth spire,
And beareth fruit of honour and all chast desire.

53

Faire ympes of beautie, whose bright shining beames
  Adorne the world with like to heavenly light,
  And to your willes both royalties and Realmes
  Subdew, through conquest of your wondrous might,
  With this faire flowre your goodly girlonds dight,
  Of chastity and vertue virginall,
  That shall embellish more your beautie bright,
  And crowne your heades with heavenly coronall,
Such as the Angels weare before Gods tribunall.

54

To youre faire selves a faire ensample frame,
  Of this faire virgin, this *Belphœbe* faire,
  To whom in perfect love, and spotlesse fame
  Of chastitie, none living may compaire:
  Ne poysnous Envy justly can empaire
  The prayse of her fresh flowring Maidenhead;
  For thy she standeth on the highest staire
  Of th'honorable stage of womanhead,
That Ladies all may follow her ensample dead.

55

In so great prayse of stedfast chastity,
  Nathlesse she was so curteous and kind,
  Tempred with grace, and goodly modesty,
  That seemed those two vertues strove to find
  The higher place in her Heroick mind:
  So striving each did other more augment,
  And both encreast the prayse of woman kind,
  And both encreast her beautie excellent;
So all did make in her a perfect complement.

CANT. VI

The birth of faire Belphœbe and
Of Amoret is told.
The Gardins of Adonis fraught
With pleasures manifold.

1

Well may I weene, faire Ladies, all this while
  Ye wonder, how this noble Damozell
  So great perfections did in her compile,
  Sith that in salvage forests she did dwell,
  So farre from court and royall Citadell,
  The great schoolmistresse of all curtesy:
  Seemeth that such wild woods should far expell
  All civill usage and gentility,
And gentle sprite deforme with rude rusticity.

2

But to this faire *Belphœbe* in her berth
  The heavens so favourable were and free,
  Looking with myld aspect upon the earth,
  In th'*Horoscope* of her nativitee,
  That all the gifts of grace and chastitee
  On her they poured forth of plenteous horne;
  Jove laught on *Venus* from his soveraigne see,
  And *Phœbus* with faire beames did her adorne,
And all the *Graces* rockt her cradle being borne.

3

Her berth was of the wombe of Morning dew,
  And her conception of the joyous Prime,
  And all her whole creation did her shew
  Pure and unspotted from all loathly crime,
  That is ingenerate in fleshly slime.
  So was this virgin borne, so was she bred,
  So was she trayned up from time to time,
  In all chast vertue, and true bounti-hed
Till to her dew perfection she was ripened.

4

Her mother was the faire *Chrysogonee*,
  The daughter of *Amphisa*, who by race
  A Faerie was, yborne of high degree,
  She bore *Belphœbe*, she bore in like cace
  Faire *Amoretta* in the second place:
  These two were twinnes, and twixt them two did share
  The heritage of all celestiall grace.
  That all the rest it seem'd they robbed bare
Of bountie, and of beautie, and all vertues rare.

5

It were a goodly storie, to declare,
  By what straunge accident faire *Chrysogone*
  Conceiv'd these infants, and how them she bare,
  In this wild forrest wandring all alone,
  After she had nine moneths fulfild and gone:
  For not as other wemens commune brood,
  They were enwombed in the sacred throne
  Of her chaste bodie, nor with commune food,
As other wemens babes, they sucked vitall blood.

6

But wondrously they were begot, and bred
  Through influence of th'heavens fruitfull ray,
  As it in antique bookes is mentioned.
  It was upon a Sommers shynie day,
  When *Titan* faire his beames did display,
  In a fresh fountaine, farre from all mens vew,
  She bath'd her brest, the boyling heat t'allay;
  She bath'd with roses red, and violets blew,
And all the sweetest flowres, that in the forrest grew.

7

Till faint through irkesome wearinesse, adowne
  Upon the grassie ground her selfe she layd
  To sleepe, the whiles a gentle slombring swowne
  Upon her fell all naked bare displayd;
  The sunne-beames bright upon her body playd,
  Being through former bathing mollifide,
  And pierst into her wombe, where they embayd
  With so sweet sence and secret power unspide,
That in her pregnant flesh they shortly fructifide.

8

Miraculous may seeme to him, that reades
  So straunge ensample of conception;
  But reason teacheth that the fruitfull seades
  Of all things living, through impression
  Of the sunbeames in moyst complexion,
  Doe life conceive and quickned are by kynd:
  So after *Nilus* inundation,
  Infinite shapes of creatures men do fynd,
Informed in the mud, on which the Sunne hath shynd.

9

Great father he of generation
  Is rightly cald, th'author of life and light;
  And his faire sister for creation
  Ministreth matter fit, which tempred right
  With heate and humour, breedes the living wight.
  So sprong these twinnes in wombe of *Chrysogone*,
  Yet wist she nought thereof, but sore affright,
  Wondred to see her belly so upblone,
Which still increast, till she her terme had full outgone.

10

Whereof conceiving shame and foule disgrace,
  Albe her guiltlesse conscience her cleard,
  She fled into the wildernesse a space,
  Till that unweeldy burden she had reard,
  And shund dishonor, which as death she feard:
  Where wearie of long travell, downe to rest
  Her selfe she set, and comfortably cheard;
  There a sad cloud of sleepe her overkest,
And seized every sense with sorrow sore opprest.

11

It fortuned, faire *Venus* having lost
  Her little sonne, the winged god of love,
  Who for some light displeasure, which him crost,
  Was from her fled, as flit as ayerie Dove,
  And left her blisfull bowre of joy above,
  (So from her often he had fled away,
  When she for ought him sharpely did reprove,
  And wandred in the world in strange aray,
Disguiz'd in thousand shapes, that none might him bewray.)

12

Him for to seeke, she left her heavenly hous,
  The house of goodly formes and faire aspects,
  Whence all the world derives the glorious
  Features of beautie, and all shapes select,
  With which high God his workmanship hath deckt;
  And searched every way, through which his wings
  Had borne him, or his tract she mote detect:
  She promist kisses sweet, and sweeter things
Unto the man, that of him tydings to her brings.

13

First she him sought in Court, where most he used
  Whylome to haunt, but there she found him not;
  But many there she found, which sore accused
  His falsehood, and with foule infamous blot
  His cruell deedes and wicked wyles did spot:
  Ladies and Lords she every where mote heare
  Complayning, how with his empoysned shot
  Their wofull harts he wounded had whyleare,
And so had left them languishing twixt hope and feare.

14

She then the Citties sought from gate to gate,
  And every one did aske, did he him see;
  And every one her answerd, that too late
  He had him seene, and felt the crueltie
  Of his sharpe darts and whot artillerie;
  And every one threw forth reproches rife
  Of his mischievous deedes, and said, That hee
  Was the disturber of all civill life,
The enimy of peace, and author of all strife.

15

Then in the countrey she abroad him sought,
  And in the rurall cottages inquired,
  Where also many plaints to her were brought,
  How he their heedlesse harts with love had fyred,
  And his false venim through their veines inspyred;
  And eke the gentle shepheard swaynes, which sat
  Keeping their fleecie flockes, as they were hyred,
  She sweetly heard complaine, both how and what
Her sonne had to them doen; yet she did smile thereat.

16

But when in none of all these she him got,
  She gan avize, where else he mote him hyde:
  At last she her bethought, that she had not
  Yet sought the salvage woods and forrests wyde,
  In which full many lovely Nymphes abyde,
  Mongst whom might be, that he did closely lye,
  Or that the love of some of them him tyde:
  For thy she thither cast her course t'apply,
To search the secret haunts of *Dianes* company.

17

Shortly unto the wastefull woods she came,
  Whereas she found the Goddesse with her crew,
  After late chace of their embrewed game,
  Sitting beside a fountaine in a rew,
  Some of them washing with the liquid dew
  From off their dainty limbes the dustie sweat,
  And soyle which did deforme their lively hew;
  Others lay shaded from the scorching heat;
The rest upon her person gave attendance great.

18

She having hong upon a bough on high
  Her bow and painted quiver, had unlaste
  Her silver buskins from her nimble thigh,
  And her lancke loynes ungirt, and brests unbraste,
  After her heat the breathing cold to taste;
  Her golden lockes, that late in tresses bright
  Embreaded were for hindring of her haste,
  Now loose about her shoulders hong undight,
And were with sweet *Ambrosia* all besprinckled light.

19

Soone as she *Venus* saw behind her backe,
  She was asham'd to be so loose surprized,
  And woxe halfe wroth against her damzels slacke,
  That had not her thereof before avized,
  But suffred her so carelesly disguized
  Be overtaken. Soone her garments loose
  Upgath'ring, in her bosome she comprized,
  Well as she might, and to the Goddesse rose,
Whiles all her Nymphes did like a girlond her enclose.

20

Goodly she gan faire *Cytherea* greet,
  And shortly asked her, what cause her brought
  Into that wildernesse for her unmeet,
  From her sweete bowres, and beds with pleasures fraught:
  That suddein change she strange adventure thought.
  To whom halfe weeping, she thus answered,
  That she her dearest sonne *Cupido* sought,
  Who in his frowardnesse from her was fled;
That she repented sore, to have him angered.

21

Thereat *Diana* gan to smile, in scorne
  Of her vaine plaint, and to her scoffing sayd;
  Great pittie sure, that ye be so forlorne
  Of your gay sonne, that gives ye so good ayd
  To your disports: ill mote ye bene apayd.
  But she was more engrieved, and replide;
  Faire sister, ill beseemes it to upbrayd
  A dolefull heart with so disdainfull pride;
The like that mine, may be your paine another tide.

22

As you in woods and wanton wildernesse
   Your glory set, to chace the salvage beasts,
   So my delight is all in joyfulnesse,
   In beds, in bowres, in banckets, and in feasts:
   And ill becomes you with your loftie creasts,
   To scorne the joy, that *Jove* is glad to seeke;
   We both are bound to follow heavens beheasts,
   And tend our charges with obeisance meeke:
Spare, gentle sister, with reproch my paine to eeke.

23

And tell me, if that ye my sonne have heard,
   To lurke emongst your Nymphes in secret wize;
   Or keepe their cabins: much I am affeard,
   Least he like one of them him selfe disguize,
   And turne his arrowes to their exercize:
   So may he long himselfe full easie hide:
   For he is faire and fresh in face and guize,
   As any Nymph (let not it be envyde.)
So saying every Nymph full narrowly she eyde.

24

But *Phœbe* therewith sore was angered,
   And sharply said; Goe Dame, goe seeke your boy,
   Where you him lately left, in *Mars* his bed;
   He comes not here, we scorne his foolish joy,
   Ne lend we leisure to his idle toy:
   But if I catch him in this company,
   By *Stygian* lake I vow, whose sad annoy
   The Gods doe dread, he dearely shall abye:
Ile clip his wanton wings, that he no more shall fly.

25

Whom when as *Venus* saw so sore displeased,
   She inly sory was, and gan relent,
   What she had said: so her she soone appeased,
   With sugred words and gentle blandishment,
   Which as a fountaine from her sweet lips went,
   And welled goodly forth, that in short space
   She was well pleasd, and forth her damzels sent,
   Through all the woods, to search from place to place,
If any tract of him or tydings they mote trace.

26

To search the God of love, her Nymphes she sent
  Throughout the wandring forrest every where:
  And after them her selfe eke with her went
  To seeke the fugitive, both farre and nere,
  So long they sought, till they arrived were
  In that same shadie covert, whereas lay
  Faire *Crysogone* in slombry traunce whilere:
  Who in her sleepe (a wondrous thing to say)
Unwares had borne two babes, as faire as springing day.

27

Unwares she them conceiv'd, unwares she bore:
  She bore withouten paine, that she conceived
  Withouten pleasure: ne her need implore
  Lucinaes aide: which when they both perceived,
  They were through wonder nigh of sense bereaved,
  And gazing each on other, nought bespake:
  At last they both agreed, her seeming grieved
  Out of her heavy swowne not to awake,
But from her loving side the tender babes to take.

28

Up they them tooke, each one a babe uptooke,
  And with them carried, to be fostered;
  Dame *Phœbe* to a Nymph her babe betooke,
  To be upbrought in perfect Maydenhed,
  And of her selfe her name *Belphœbe* red:
  But *Venus* hers thence farre away convayd,
  To be upbrought in goodly womanhed,
  And in her litle loves stead, which was strayd,
Her *Amoretta* cald, to comfort her dismayd.

29

She brought her to her joyous Paradize,
  Where most she wonnes, when she on earth does dwel.
  So faire a place, as Nature can devize:
  Whether in *Paphos*, or *Cytheron* hill,
  Or it in *Gnidus* be, I wote not well;
  But well I wote by tryall, that this same
  All other pleasant places doth excell,
  And called is by her lost lovers name,
The *Gardin* of *Adonis*, farre renowmd by fame.

30

In that same Gardin all the goodly flowres,
  Wherewith dame Nature doth her beautifie,
  And decks the girlonds of her paramoures,
  Are fetcht: there is the first seminarie
  Of all things, that are borne to live and die,
  According to their kindes. Long worke it were,
  Here to account the endlesse progenie
  Of all the weedes, that bud and blossome there;
But so much as doth need, must needs be counted here.

31

It sited was in fruitfull soyle of old,
  And girt in with two walles on either side;
  The one of yron, the other of bright gold,
  That none might thorough breake, nor overstride:
  And double gates it had, which opened wide,
  By which both in and out men moten pas;
  Th'one faire and fresh, the other old and dride:
  Old *Genius* the porter of them was,
Old *Genius*, the which a double nature has.

32

He letteth in, he letteth out to wend,
  All that to come into the world desire;
  A thousand thousand naked babes attend
  About him day and night, which doe require,
  That he with fleshly weedes would them attire:
  Such as him list, such as eternall fate
  Ordained hath, he clothes with sinfull mire,
  And sendeth forth to live in mortall state,
Till they againe returne backe by the hinder gate.

33

After that they againe returned beene,
  They in that Gardin planted be againe;
  And grow afresh, as they had never seene
  Fleshly corruption, nor mortall paine.
  Some thousand yeares so doen they there remaine;
  And then of him are clad with other hew,
  Or sent into the chaungefull world againe,
  Till thither they returne, where first they grew:
So like a wheele around they runne from old to new.

34

Ne needs there Gardiner to set, or sow,
  To plant or prune: for of their owne accord
  All things, as they created were, doe grow,
  And yet remember well the mightie word,
  Which first was spoken by th'Almightie lord,
  That bad them to increase and multiply:
  Ne doe they need with water of the ford,
  Or of the clouds to moysten their roots dry;
For in themselves eternall moisture they imply.

35

Infinite shapes of creatures there are bred,
  And uncouth formes, which none yet ever knew,
  And every sort is in a sundry bed
  Set by it selfe, and ranckt in comely rew:
  Some fit for reasonable soules t'indew,
  Some made for beasts, some made for birds to weare,
  And all the fruitfull spawne of fishes hew
  In endlesse rancks along enraunged were,
That seem'd the *Ocean* could not containe them there.

36

Daily they grow, and daily forth are sent
  Into the world, it to replenish more;
  Yet is the stocke not lessened, nor spent,
  But still remaines in everlasting store,
  As it at first created was of yore.
  For in the wide wombe of the world there lyes,
  In hatefull darkenesse and in deepe horrore,
  An huge eternall *Chaos*, which supplyes
The substances of natures fruitfull progenyes.

37

All things from thence doe their first being fetch,
  And borrow matter, whereof they are made,
  Which when as forme and feature it does ketch,
  Becomes a bodie, and doth then invade
  The state of life, out of the griesly shade.
  That substance is eterne, and bideth so,
  Ne when the life decayes, and forme does fade,
  Doth it consume, and into nothing go,
But chaunged is, and often altred to and fro.

38

The substance is not chaunged, nor altered,
  But th'only forme and outward fashion;
  For every substance is conditioned
  To change her hew, and sundry formes to don,
  Meet for her temper and complexion:
  For formes are variable and decay,
  By course of kind, and by occasion;
  And that faire flowre of beautie fades away,
As doth the lilly fresh before the sunny ray.

39

Great enimy to it, and to all the rest,
  That in the *Gardin* of *Adonis* springs,
  Is wicked *Time*, who with his scyth addrest,
  Does mow the flowring herbes and goodly things,
  And all their glory to the ground downe flings,
  Where they doe wither, and are fowly mard:
  He flyes about, and with his flaggy wings
  Beates downe both leaves and buds without regard,
Ne ever pittie may relent his malice hard.

40

Yet pittie often did the gods relent,
  To see so faire things mard, and spoyled quight:
  And their great mother *Venus* did lament
  The losse of her deare brood, her deare delight:
  Her hart was pierst with pittie at the sight,
  When walking through the Gardin, them she spyde,
  Yet no'te she find redresse for such despight.
  For all that lives, is subject to that law:
All things decay in time, and to their end do draw.

41

But were it not, that *Time* their troubler is,
  All that in this delightfull Gardin growes,
  Should happie be, and have immortall blis,
  For here all plentie, and all pleasure flowes,
  And sweet love gentle fits emongst them throwes,
  Without fell rancor, or fond gealosie;
  Franckly each paramour his leman knowes,
  Each bird his mate, ne any does envie
Their goodly meriment, and gay felicitie.

42

There is continuall spring, and harvest there
    Continuall, both meeting at one time:
    For both the boughes doe laughing blossomes beare,
    And with fresh colours decke the wanton Prime,
    And eke attonce the heavy trees they clime,
    Which seeme to labour under their fruits lode:
    The whiles the joyous birdes make their pastime
    Emongst the shadie leaves, their sweet abode,
And their true loves without suspition tell abrode.

43

Right in the middest of that Paradise,
    There stood a stately Mount, on whose round top
    A gloomy grove of mirtle trees did rise,
    Whose shadie boughes sharpe steele did never lop,
    Nor wicked beasts their tender buds did crop,
    But like a girlond compassed the hight,
    And from their fruitfull sides sweet gum did drop,
    That all the ground with precious deaw bedight,
Threw forth most dainty odours, and most sweet delight.

44

And in the thickest covert of that shade,
    There was a pleasant arbour, not by art,
    But of the trees owne inclination made,
    Which knitting their rancke braunches part to part,
    With wanton yvie twyne entrayld athwart,
    And Eglantine, and Caprifole emong,
    Fashiond above within their inmost part,
    That nether *Phœbus* beams could through them throng,
Nor *Aeolus* sharp blast could worke them any wrong.

45

And all about grew every sort of flowre,
    To which sad lovers were transformd of yore;
    Fresh *Hyacinthus*, *Phœbus* paramoure,
    And dearest love,
    Foolish *Narcisse*, that likes the watry shore,
    Sad *Amaranthus*, made a flowre but late,
    Sad *Amaranthus*, in whose purple gore
    Me seemes I see *Amintas* wretched fate,
To whom sweet Poets verse hath given endlesse date.

46

There wont faire *Venus* often to enjoy
  Her deare *Adonis* joyous company,
  And reape sweet pleasure of the wanton boy;
  There yet, some say, in secret he does ly,
  Lapped in flowres and pretious spycery,
  By her hid from the world, and from the skill
  Of *Stygian* Gods, which doe her love envy;
  But she her selfe, when ever that she will,
Possesseth him, and of his sweetnesse takes her fil.

47

And sooth it seemes they say: for he may not
  For ever die, and ever buried bee
  In balefull night, where all things are forgot;
  All be he subject to mortalitie,
  Yet is eterne in mutabilitie,
  And by succession made perpetuall,
  Transformed oft, and chaunged diverslie:
  For him the Father of all formes they call;
Therefore needs mote he live, that living gives to all.

48

There now he liveth in eternall blis,
  Joying his goddesse, and of her enjoyd:
  Ne feareth he henceforth that foe of his,
  Which with his cruell tuske him deadly cloyd:
  For that wilde Bore, the which him once annoyd,
  She firmely hath emprisoned for ay,
  That her sweet love his malice mote avoyd,
  In a strong rocky Cave, which is they say,
Hewen underneath that Mount, that none him losen may.

49

There now he lives in everlasting joy,
  With many of the Gods in company,
  Which thither haunt, and with the winged boy
  Sporting himselfe in safe felicity:
  Who when he hath with spoiles and cruelty
  Ransackt the world, and in the wofull harts
  Of many wretches set his triumphes hye,
  Thither resorts, and laying his sad darts
Aside, with faire *Adonis* playes his wanton parts.

50

And his true love faire *Psyche* with him playes,
  Faire *Psyche* to him lately reconcyld,
  After long troubles and unmeet upbrayes,
  With which his mother *Venus* her revyld,
  And eke himselfe her cruelly exyld:
  But now in stedfast love and happy state
  She with him lives, and hath him borne a chyld,
  Pleasure, that doth both gods and men aggrate,
Pleasure, the daughter of *Cupid* and *Psyche* late.

51

Hither great *Venus* brought this infant faire,
  The younger daughter of *Chrysogonee*,
  And under *Psyche* with great trust and care
  Committed her, yfostered to bee,
  And trained up in true feminitee:
  Who no lesse carefully her tendered,
  Than her owne daughter *Pleasure*, to whom shee
  Made her companion, and her lessoned
In all the lore of love, and goodly womanhead.

52

In which when she to perfect ripenesse grew,
  Of grace and beautie noble Paragone,
  She brought her forth into the worldes vew,
  To be th'ensample of true love alone,
  And Lodestarre of all chaste affectione,
  To all faire Ladies, that doe live on ground.
  To Faery court she came, where many one
  Admyrd her goodly haveour, and found
His feeble hart wide launched with loves cruell wound.

53

But she to none of them her love did cast,
  Save to the noble knight Sir *Scudamore*,
  To whom her loving hart she linked fast
  In faithfull love, t'abide for evermore,
  And for his dearest sake endured sore,
  Sore trouble of an hainous enimy;
  Who her would forced have to have forlore
  Her former love, and stedfast loialty,
As ye may elsewhere read that ruefull history.

54

But well I weene, ye first desire to learne,
What end unto that fearefull Damozell,
Which fled so fast from that same foster stearne,
Whom with his brethren *Timias* slew, befell:
That was to weet, the goodly *Florimell*;
Who wandring for to seeke her lover deare,
Her lover deare, her dearest *Marinell*,
Into misfortune fell, as ye did heare,
And from Prince *Arthur* fled with wings of idle feare.

CANT. VII

The witches sonne loves Florimell:
she flyes, he faines to die.
Satyrane saves the Squire of Dames
from Gyants tyrannie.

1

LIKE as an Hynd forth singled from the heard,
That hath escaped from a ravenous beast,
Yet flyes away of her owne feet affeard,
And every leafe, that shaketh with the least
Murmure of winde, her terror hath encreast;
So fled faire *Florimell* from her vaine feare,
Long after she from perill was releast:
Each shade she saw, and each noyse she did heare,
Did seeme to be the same, which she escapt whyleare.

2

All that same evening she in flying spent,
And all that night her course continewed:
Ne did she let dull sleepe once to relent,
Nor wearinesse to slacke her hast, but fled
Ever alike, as if her former dred
Were hard behind, her readie to arrest:
And her white Palfrey having conquered
The maistring raines out of her weary wrest,
Perforce her carried, where ever he thought best.

3

So long as breath, and hable puissance
　Did native courage unto him supply,
　His pace he freshly forward did advaunce,
　And carried her beyond all jeopardy,
　But nought that wanteth rest, can long aby.
　He having through incessant travell spent
　His force, at last perforce a downe did ly,
　Ne foot could further move: The Lady gent
Thereat was suddein strooke with great astonishment.

4

And forst t'alight, on foot mote algates fare,
　A traveller unwonted to such way:
　Need teacheth her this lesson hard and rare,
　That fortune all in equall launce doth sway,
　And mortall miseries doth make her play.
　So long she travelled, till at length she came
　To an hilles side, which did to her bewray
　A little valley, subject to the same,
All coverd with thick woods, that quite it overcame.

5

Through the tops of the high trees she did descry
　A litle smoke, whose vapour thin and light,
　Reeking aloft, uprolled to the sky:
　Which, chearefull signe did send unto her sight,
　That in the same did wonne some living wight.
　Eftsoones her steps she thereunto applyde,
　And came at last in weary wretched plight
　Unto the place, to which her hope did guyde,
To find some refuge there, and rest her weary syde.

6

There in a gloomy hollow glen she found
　A little cottage, built of stickes and reedes
　In homely wize, and wald with sods around,
　In which a witch did dwell, in loathly weedes,
　And wilfull want, all carelesse of her needes;
　So choosing solitarie to abide,
　Far from all neighbours, that her devilish deedes
　And hellish arts from people she might hide,
And hurt far off unknowne, whom ever she envide.

7

The Damzell there arriving entred in;
  Where sitting on the flore the Hag she found,
  Busie (as seem'd) about some wicked gin:
  Who soone as she beheld that suddein stound,
  Lightly upstarted from the dustie ground,
  And with fell looke and hollow deadly gaze
  Stared on her awhile, as one astound,
  Ne had one word to speake, for great amaze,
But shewd by outward signes, that dread her sence did daze.

8

At last turning her feare to foolish wrath,
  She askt, what devill had her thither brought,
  And who she was, and what unwonted path
  Had guided her, unwelcomed, unsought?
  To which the Damzell full of doubtfull thought,
  Her mildly answer'd; Beldame be not wroth
  With silly Virgin by adventure brought
  Unto your dwelling, ignorant and loth,
That crave but rowme to rest, while tempest overblo'th.

9

With that adowne out of her Christall eyne
  Few trickling teares she softly forth let fall,
  That like two Orient pearles, did purely shyne
  Upon her snowy cheeke; and therewithall
  She sighed soft, that none so bestiall,
  Nor salvage hart, but ruth of her sad plight
  Would make to melt, or pitteously appall;
  And that vile Hag, all were her whole delight
In mischiefe, was much moved at so pitteous sight.

10

And gan recomfort her in her rude wyse,
  With womanish compassion of her plaint,
  Wiping the teares from her suffused eyes,
  And bidding her sit downe, to rest her faint
  And wearie limbs a while. She nothing quaint
  Nor s'deignfull of so homely fashion,
  Sith brought she was now to so hard constraint,
  Sate downe upon the dusty ground anon,
As glad of that small rest, as Bird of tempest gon.

11

Tho gan she gather up her garments rent,
  And her loose lockes to dight in order dew,
  With golden wreath and gorgeous ornament;
  Whom such whenas the wicked Hag did vew,
  She was astonisht at her heavenly hew,
  And doubted her to deeme an earthly wight,
  But or some Goddesse, or of *Dianes* crew,
  And thought her to adore with humble spright;
T'adore thing so divine as beauty, were but right.

12

This wicked woman had a wicked sonne,
  The comfort of her age and weary dayes,
  A laesie loord, for nothing good to donne,
  But stretched forth in idlenesse alwayes,
  Ne ever cast his mind to covet prayse,
  Or ply him selfe to any honest trade,
  But all the day before the sunny rayes
  He us'd to slug, or sleepe in slothfull shade:
Such laesinesse both lewd and poore attonce him made.

13

He comming home at undertime, there found
  The fairest creature, that he ever saw,
  Sitting beside his mother on the ground;
  The sight whereof did greatly him adaw,
  And his base thought with terrour and with aw
  So inly smot, that as one, which had gazed
  On the bright Sunne unwares, doth soone withdraw
  His feeble eyne, with too much brightnesse dazed,
So stared he on her, and stood long while amazed.

14

Softly at last he gan his mother aske,
  What mister wight that was, and whence derived,
  That in so straunge disguizement there did maske,
  And by what accident she there arrived:
  But she, as one nigh of her wits deprived,
  With nought but ghastly lookes him answered,
  Like to a ghost, that lately is revived
  From *Stygian* shores, where late it wandered;
So both at her, and each at other wondered.

15

But the faire Virgin was so meeke and mild,
　That she to them vouchsafed to embace
　Her goodly port, and to their senses vild,
　Her gentle speach applide, that in short space
　She grew familiare in that desert place.
　During which time, the Chorle through her so kind
　And curteise use conceiv'd affection bace,
　And cast to love her in his brutish mind;
No love, but brutish lust, that was so beastly tind.

16

Closely the wicked flame his bowels brent,
　And shortly grew into outrageous fire;
　Yet had he not the hart, nor hardiment,
　As unto her to utter his desire;
　His caytive thought durst not so high aspire,
　But with soft sighes, and lovely semblaunces,
　He ween'd that his affection entire
　She should aread; many resemblaunces
To her he made, and many kind remembraunces.

17

Oft from the forrest wildings he did bring,
　Whose sides empurpled were with smiling red,
　And oft young birds, which he had taught to sing
　His mistresse prayses, sweetly caroled,
　Girlonds of flowres sometimes for her faire hed
　He fine would dight; sometimes the squirell wild
　He brought to her in bands, as conquered
　To be her thrall, his fellow servant vild;
All which, she of him tooke with countenance meeke and mild.

18

But past awhile, when she fit season saw
　To leave that desert mansion, she cast
　In secret wize her selfe thence to withdraw,
　For feare of mischiefe, which she did forecast
　Might be by the witch or that her sonne compast:
　Her wearie Palfrey closely, as she might,
　Now well recovered after long repast,
　In his proud furnitures she freshly dight,
His late miswandred wayes now to remeasure right.

19

And earely ere the dawning day appeard,
    She forth issewed, and on her journey went;
    She went in perill, of each noyse affeard,
    And of each shade, that did it selfe present;
    For still she feared to be overhent,
    Of that vile hag, or her uncivile sonne:
    Who when too late awaking, well they kent,
    That their faire guest was gone, they both begonne
To make exceeding mone, as they had bene undonne.

20

But that lewd lover did the most lament
    For her depart, that ever man did heare;
    He knockt his brest with desperate intent,
    And scratcht his face, and with his teeth did teare
    His rugged flesh, and rent his ragged heare:
    That his sad mother seeing his sore plight,
    Was greatly woe begon, and gan to feare,
    Least his fraile senses were emperisht quight,
And love to frenzy turnd, sith love is franticke hight.

21

All wayes she sought, him to restore to plight,
    With herbs, with charms, with counsell, and with teares,
    But tears, nor charms, nor herbs, nor counsell might
    Asswage the fury, which his entrails teares:
    So strong is passion, that no reason heares.
    Tho when all other helpes she saw to faile,
    She turnd her selfe backe to her wicked leares
    And by her devilish arts thought to prevaile,
To bring her backe againe, or worke her finall bale.

22

Eftsoones out of her hidden cave she cald
    An hideous beast, of horrible aspect,
    That could the stoutest courage have appald;
    Monstrous mishapt, and all his backe was spect
    With thousand spots of colours queint elect,
    Thereto so swift, that it all beasts did pas:
    Like never yet did living eye detect;
    But likest it to an *Hyena* was,
That feeds on womens flesh, as others feede on gras.

23

It forth she cald, and gave it streight in charge,
  Through thicke and thin her to pursew apace,
  Ne once to stay to rest, or breath at large,
  Till her he had attaind, and brought in place,
  Or quite devourd her beauties scornefull grace.
  The Monster swift as word, that from her went,
  Went forth in hast, and did her footing trace
  So sure and swiftly, through his perfect sent,
And passing speede, that shortly he her overhent.

24

Whom when the fearefull Damzell nigh espide,
  No need to bid her fast away to flie;
  That ugly shape so sore her terrifide,
  That it she shund no lesse, than dread to die,
  And her flit Palfrey did so well apply
  His nimble feet to her conceived feare,
  That whilest his breath did strength to him supply,
  From perill free he her away did beare:
But when his force gan faile, his pace gan wex areare.

25

Which whenas she perceiv'd, she was dismayd
  At that same last extremitie full sore,
  And of her safetie greatly grew afrayd;
  And now she gan approch to the sea shore,
  As it befell, that she could flie no more,
  But yield her selfe to spoile of greedinesse.
  Lightly she leaped, as a wight forlore,
  From her dull horse, in desperate distresse,
And to her feet betooke her doubtfull sickernesse.

26

Not halfe so fast the wicked *Myrrha* fled
  From dread of her revenging fathers hond:
  Nor halfe so fast to save her maidenhed,
  Fled fearefull *Daphne* on th'*Ægæan* strond,
  As *Florimell* fled from that Monster yond,
  To reach the sea, ere she of him were raught:
  For in the sea to drowne her selfe she fond,
  Rather than of the tyrant to be caught:
Thereto feare gave her wings, and neede her courage taught.

27

It fortuned (high God did so ordaine)
  As she arrived on the roring shore,
  In minde to leape into the mighty maine,
  A little boate lay hoving her before,
  In which there slept a fisher old and pore,
  The whiles his nets were drying on the sand:
  Into the same she leapt, and with the ore
  Did thrust the shallop from the floting strand:
So safetie found at sea, which she found not at land.

28

The Monster ready on the pray to sease,
  Was of his forward hope deceived quight;
  Ne durst assay to wade the perlous seas,
  But greedily long gaping at the sight,
  At last in vaine was forst to turne his flight,
  And tell the idle tidings to his Dame:
  Yet to avenge his devilish despight,
  He set upon her Palfrey tired lame,
And slew him cruelly, ere any reskew came.

29

And after having him embowelled,
  To fill his hellish gorge, it chaunst a knight
  To passe that way, as forth he travelled;
  It was a goodly Swaine, and of great might,
  As ever man that bloudy field did fight;
  But in vaine sheows, that wont yong knights bewitch,
  And courtly services tooke no delight,
  But rather joyd to be, than seemen sich:
For both to be and seeme to him was labour lich.

30

It was to weete the good Sir *Satyrane*,
  That raungd abroad to seeke adventures wilde,
  As was his wont in forrest, and in plaine;
  He was all armd in rugged steele unfilde,
  As in the smoky forge it was compilde,
  And in his Scutchin bore a Satyres hed:
  He comming present, where the Monster vilde
  Upon that milke-white Palfreyes carkas fed,
Unto his reskew ran, and greedily him sped.

31

There well perceiv'd he, that it was the horse,
  Whereon faire *Florimell* was wont to ride,
  That of that feend was rent without remorse:
  Much feared he, least ought did ill betide
  To that faire Mayd, the flowre of womens pride;
  For her he dearely loved, and in all
  His famous conquests highly magnifide:
  Besides her golden girdle, which did fall
From her in flight, he found, that did him sore apall.

32

Full of sad feare, and doubtfull agony,
  Fiercely he flew upon that wicked feend,
  And with huge strokes, and cruell battery
  Him forst to leave his pray, for to attend
  Him selfe from deadly daunger to defend:
  Full many wounds in his corrupted flesh
  He did engrave, and muchell bloud did spend,
  Yet might not do him dye, but aye more fresh
And fierce he still appeard, the more he did him thresh.

33

He wist not, how him to despoile of life,
  Ne how to win the wished victory,
  Sith him he saw still stronger grow through strife,
  And him selfe weaker through infirmity;
  Greatly he grew enrag'd, and furiously
  Hurling his sword away, he lightly lept
  Upon the beast, that with great cruelty
  Rored, and raged to be under-kept:
Yet he perforce him held, and strokes upon him hept.

34

As he that strives to stop a suddein flood,
  And in strong banckes his violence enclose,
  Forceth it swell above his wonted mood,
  And largely overflow the fruitfull plaine,
  That all the countrey seemes to be a Maine,
  And the rich furrowes flote, all quite fordonne:
  The wofull husbandman doth lowd complaine,
  To see his whole yeares labour lost so soone,
For which to God he made so many an idle boone.

35

So him he held, and did through might amate:
  So long he held him, and him bet so long,
  That at the last his fiercenesse gan abate,
  And meekely stoup unto the victour strong:
  Who to avenge the implacable wrong,
  Which he supposed donne to *Florimell*,
  Sought by all meanes his dolour to prolong,
  Sith dint of steele his carcas could not quell:
His maker with her charmes had framed him so well.

36

The golden ribband, which that virgin wore
  About her sclender wast, he tooke in hand,
  And with it bound the beast, that lowd did rore
  For great despight of that unwonted band,
  Yet dared not his victour to withstand,
  But trembled like a lambe, fled from the pray,
  And all the way him followd on the strand,
  As he had long bene learned to obay;
Yet never learned he such service, till that day.

37

Thus as he led the Beast along the way,
  He spide far off a mighty Giauntesse,
  Fast flying on a Courser dapled gray,
  From a bold knight, that with great hardinesse
  Her hard pursewd, and sought for to suppresse;
  She bore before her lap a dolefull Squire,
  Lying athwart her horse in great distresse,
  Fast bounden hand and foote with cords of wire,
Whom she did meane to make the thrall of her desire.

38

Which whenas *Satyrane* beheld, in hast
  He left his captive Beast at liberty,
  And crost the nearest way, by which he cast
  Her to encounter, ere she passed by:
  But she the way shund nathemore for thy,
  But forward gallopt fast; which when he spyde,
  His mighty speare he couched warily,
  And at her ran: she having him descryde,
Her selfe to fight addrest, and threw her lode aside.

39

Like as a Goshauke, that in foote doth beare
  A trembling Culver, having spide on hight
  An Egle, that with plumy wings doth sheare
  The subtile ayre, stouping with all his might,
  The quarrey throwes to ground with fell despight,
  And to the battell doth her selfe prepare:
  So ran the Geauntesse unto the fight;
  Her firie eyes with furious sparkes did stare,
And with blasphemous bannes high God in peeces tare.

40

She caught in hand an huge great yron mace,
  Wherewith she many had of life deprived,
  But ere the stroke could seize his aymed place,
  His speare amids her sun-broad shield arrived;
  Yet nathemore the steele a sunder rived,
  All were the beame in bignesse like a mast,
  Ne her out of the stedfast sadle drived,
  But glauncing on the tempred mettall, brast
In thousand shivers, and so forth beside her past.

41

Her Steed did stagger with that puissaunt strooke;
  But she no more was moved with that might,
  Than it had lighted on an aged Oke;
  Or on the marble Pillour, that is pight
  Upon the top of Mount *Olympus* hight,
  For the brave youthly Champions to assay,
  With burning charet wheeles it nigh to smite:
  But who that smites it, mars his joyous play,
And is the spectacle of ruinous decay.

42

Yet therewith sore enrag'd, with sterne regard
  Her dreadfull weapon she to him addrest,
  Which on his helmet martelled so hard,
  That made him low incline his lofty crest,
  And bowd his battred visour to his brest:
  Wherewith he was so stund, that he n'ote ryde,
  But reeled to and fro from East to West:
  Which when his cruel enimy espyde,
She lightly unto him adjoyned side to syde;

43

And on his collar laying puissant hand,
  Out of his wavering seat him pluckt perforse,
  Perforse him pluckt, unable to withstand,
  Or helpe himselfe, and laying thwart her horse,
  In loathly wise like to a carion corse,
  She bore him fast away. Which when the knight,
  That her pursewed, saw, with great remorse
  He neare was touched in his noble spright,
And gan encrease his speed, as she encreast her flight.

44

Whom when as nigh approching she espyde,
  She threw away her burden angrily;
  For she list not the battell to abide,
  But made her selfe more light, away to fly:
  Yet her the hardy knight pursewd so nye,
  That almost in the backe he oft her strake:
  But still when him at hand she did espy,
  She turnd, and semblaunce of faire fight did make;
But when he stayd, to flight againe she did her take.

45

By this the good Sir *Satyrane* gan wake
  Out of his dreame, that did him long entraunce,
  And seeing none in place, he gan to make
  Exceeding mone, and curst that cruell chaunce,
  Which reft from him so faire a chevisaunce:
  At length he spide, whereas that wofull Squire,
  Whom he had reskewed from captivaunce
  Of his strong foe, lay tombled in the myre,
Unable to arise, or foot or hand to styre.

46

To whom approching, well he mote perceive
  In that foule plight a comely personage,
  And lovely face, made fit for to deceive
  Fraile Ladies hart with loves consuming rage,
  Now in the blossome of his freshest age:
  He reard him up, and loosd his yron bands,
  And after gan inquire his parentage,
  And how he fell into that Gyaunts hands,
And who that was, which chaced her along the lands.

47

Then trembling yet through feare, the Squire bespake,
  That Geauntesse *Argante* is behight,
  A daughter of the *Titans* which did make
  Warre against heaven, and heaped hils on hight,
  To scale the skyes, and put *Jove* from his right:
  Her sire *Typhæus* was, who mad through merth,
  And drunke with bloud of men, slaine by his might,
  Through incest, her of his owne mother Earth
Whilome begot, being but halfe twin of that berth.

48

For at that berth another Babe she bore,
  To weet the mighty *Ollyphant*, that wrought
  Great wreake to many errant knights of yore,
  And many hath to foule confusion brought.
  These twinnes, men say, (a thing far passing thought)
  Whiles in their mothers wombe enclosd they were,
  Ere they into the lightsome world were brought,
  In fleshly lust were mingled both yfere,
And in that monstrous wise did to the world appere.

49

So liv'd they ever after in like sin,
  Gainst natures law, and good behavioure:
  But greatest shame was to that maiden twin,
  Who not content so fowly to devoure
  Her native flesh, and staine her brothers bowre,
  Did wallow in all other fleshly myre,
  And suffred beasts her body to deflowre:
  So whot she burned in that lustfull fyre,
Yet all that might not slake her sensuall desyre.

50

But over all the countrey she did raunge,
  To seeke young men, to quench her flaming thrust,
  And feed her fancy with delightfull chaunge:
  Whom so she fittest finds to serve her lust,
  Through her maine strength, in which she most doth trust,
  She with her brings into a secret Ile,
  Where in eternall bondage, dye he must,
  Or be the vassall of her pleasures vile,
And in all shamefull sort him selfe with her defile.

51

Me seely wretch she so at vauntage caught,
  After she long in waite for me did lye,
  And meant unto her prison to have brought,
  Her lothsome pleasure there to satisfye;
  That thousand deathes me lever were to dye,
  Than breake the vow, that to faire *Columbell*
  I plighted have, and yet keepe stedfastly:
  As for my name, it mistreth not to tell;
Call me the *Squyre of Dames*, that me beseemeth well.

52

But that bold knight, whom ye pursuing saw
  That *Geauntesse*, is not such, as she seemed,
  But a faire virgin, that in martiall law,
  And deedes of armes above all Dames is deemed,
  And above many knights is eke esteemed,
  For her great worth; She *Palladine* is hight:
  She you from death, you me from dread redeemed.
  Ne any may that Monster match in fight,
But she, or such as she, that is so chaste a wight.

53

Her well beseemes that Quest (quoth *Satyrane*)
  But read, thou *Squyre of Dames*, what vow is this,
  Which thou upon thy selfe hast lately ta'ne?
  That shall I you recount (quoth he) ywis,
  So be ye pleasd to pardon all amis.
  That gentle Lady, whom I love and serve,
  After long suit and weary servicis,
  Did aske me, how I could her love deserve,
And how she might be sure, that I would never swerve.

54

I glad by any meanes her grace to gaine,
  Bad her commaund my life to save, or spill.
  Eftsoones she bad me, with incessaunt paine
  To wander through the world abroad at will,
  And every where, where with my power or skill
  I might do service unto gentle Dames,
  That I the same should faithfully fulfill,
  And at the twelve monethes end should bring their names
And pledges; as the spoiles of my victorious games.

55

So well I to faire Ladies service did,
  And found such favour in their loving hartes,
  That ere the yeare his course had compassid,
  Three hundred pledges for my good desartes,
  And thrise three hundred thanks for my good partes
  I with me brought, and did to her present:
  Which when she saw, more bent to eke my smartes,
  Than to reward my trusty true intent,
She gan for me devise a grievous punishment.

56

To weet, that I my travell should resume,
  And with like labour walke the world around,
  Ne ever to her presence should presume,
  Till I so many other Dames had found,
  The which, for all the suit I could propound,
  Would me refuse their pledges to afford,
  But did abide for ever chast and sound.
  Ah gentle Squire (quoth he) tell at one word,
How many foundst thou such to put in thy record?

57

In deed Sir knight (said he) one word may tell
  All, that I ever found so wisely stayd;
  For onely three they were disposd so well,
  And yet three yeares I now abroad have strayd,
  To find them out. Mote I (then laughing sayd
  The knight) inquire of thee, what were those three,
  The which thy proffred curtesie denayd?
  Or ill they seemed sure avizd to bee,
Or brutishly brought up, that nev'r did fashions see.

58

The first which then refused me (said hee)
  Certes was but a common Courtisane,
  Yet flat refusd to have a do with mee,
  Because I could not give her many a Jane.
  (Thereat full hartely laughed *Satyrane*)
  The second was an holy Nunne to chose,
  Which would not let me be her Chappellane,
  Because she knew, she said, I would disclose
Her counsell, if she should her trust in me repose.

59

The third a Damzell was of low degree,
  Whom I in countrey cottage found by chaunce;
  Full little weened I, that chastitee
  Had lodging in so meane a maintenaunce,
  Yet was she faire, and in her countenance
  Dwelt simple truth in seemely fashion.
  Long thus I woo'd her with dew observance,
  In hope unto my pleasure to have won;
But was as farre at last, as when I first begon.

60

Safe her, I never any woman found,
  That chastity did for it selfe embrace,
  But were for other causes firme and sound;
  Either for want of handsome time and place,
  Or else for feare of shame and fowle disgrace.
  Thus am I hopelesse ever to attaine
  My Ladies love, in such a desperate case,
  But all my dayes am like to wast in vaine,
Seeking to match the chaste with th'unchaste Ladies traine.

61

Perdy, (said *Satyrane*) thou *Squire of Dames*,
  Great labour fondly hast thou hent in hand,
  To get small thankes, and therewith many blames,
  That may emongst *Alcides* labours stand.
  Thence backe returning to the former land,
  Where late he left the Beast, he overcame,
  He found him not; for he had broke his band,
  And was return'd againe unto his Dame,
To tell what tydings of faire *Florimell* became.

CANT. VIII

The Witch creates a snowy Lady,
like to Florimell,
Who wrongd by Carle by Proteus sau'd,
is sought by Paridell.

I

SO oft as I this history record,
  My hart doth melt with meere compassion,
  To thinke, how causelesse of her owne accord
  This gentle Damzell, whom I write upon,
  Should plonged be in such affliction,
  Without all hope of comfort or reliefe,
  That sure I weene, the hardest hart of stone,
  Would hardly find to aggravate her griefe;
For misery craves rather mercie, than repriefe.

2

But that accursed Hag, her hostesse late,
  Had so enranckled her malitious hart,
  That she desyrd th'abridgement of her fate,
  Or long enlargement of her painefull smart.
  Now when the Beast, which by her wicked art
  Late forth she sent, she backe returning spyde,
  Tyde with her broken girdle, it a part
  Of her rich spoyles, whom he had earst destroyd,
She weend, and wondrous gladnesse to her hart applyde.

3

And with it running hast'ly to her sonne,
  Thought with that sight him much to have relived;
  Who thereby deeming sure the thing as donne,
  His former griefe with furie fresh revived,
  Much more than earst, and would have algates rived
  The hart out of his brest: for sith her ded
  He surely dempt, himselfe he thought deprived
  Quite of all hope, wherewith he long had fed
His foolish maladie, and long time had misled.

4

With thought whereof, exceeding mad he grew,
  And in his rage his mother would have slaine,
  Had she not fled into a secret mew,
  Where she was wont her Sprights to entertaine
  The maisters of her art: there was she faine
  To call them all in order to her ayde,
  And them conjure upon eternall paine,
  To counsell her so carefully dismayd,
How she might heale her sonne, whose senses were decayd.

5

By their advise, and her owne wicked wit,
  She there deviz'd a wondrous worke to frame,
  Whose like on earth was never framed yit,
  That even Nature selfe envide the same,
  And grudg'd to see the counterfet should shame
  The thing it selfe. In hand she boldly tooke
  To make another like the former Dame,
  Another *Florimell*, in shape and looke
So lively and so like, that many it mistooke.

6

The substance, whereof she the bodie made,
  Was purest snow in massie mould congeald,
  Which she had gathered in a shadie glade
  Of the *Riphæan* hils, to her reveald
  By errant Sprights, but from all men conceald:
  The same she tempred with fine Mercury,
  And virgin wex, that never yet was seald,
  And mingled them with perfect vermily,
That like a lively sanguine it seem'd to the eye.

7

In stead of eyes two burning lampes she set
  In silver sockets, shyning like the skyes,
  And a quicke moving Spirit did arret
  To stirre and roll them, like a womans eyes;
  In stead of yellow lockes she did devise,
  With golden wyre to weave her curled head;
  Yet golden wyre was not so yellow thrise
  As *Florimells* faire haire: and in the stead
Of life, she put a Spright to rule the carkasse dead.

8

A wicked Spright yfraught with fawning guile,
    And faire resemblance above all the rest,
    Which with the Prince of Darknesse fell somewhile,
    From heavens blisse and everlasting rest;
    Him needed not instruct, which way were best
    Himselfe to fashion likest *Florimell*,
    Ne how to speake, ne how to use his gest,
    For he in counterfeisance did excell,
And all the wyles of wemens wits knew passing well.

9

Him shaped thus, she deckt in garments gay,
    Which *Florimell* had left behind her late,
    That who so then her saw, would surely say,
    It was her selfe, whom it did imitate,
    Or fairer than her selfe, if ought algate
    Might fairer be. And then she forth her brought
    Unto her sonne, that lay in feeble state;
    Who seeing her gan streight upstart, and thought
She was the Lady selfe, whom he so long had sought.

10

Tho fast her clipping twixt his armes twaine,
    Extremely joyed in so happie sight,
    And soone forgot his former sickly paine;
    But she, the more to seeme such as she hight,
    Coyly rebutted his embracement light;
    Yet still with gentle countenaunce retained,
    Enough to hold a foole in vaine delight:
    Him long she so with shadowes entertained,
As her Creatresse had in charge to her ordained.

11

Till on a day, as he disposed was
    To walke the woods with that his Idole faire,
    Her to disport, and idle time to pas,
    In th'open freshnesse of the gentle aire,
    A knight that way there chaunced to repaire;
    Yet knight he was not, but a boastfull swaine,
    That deedes of armes had ever in despaire,
    Proud *Braggadocchio*, that in vaunting vaine
His glory did repose, and credit did maintaine.

12

He seeing with that Chorle so faire a wight,
 Decked with many a costly ornament,
 Much merveiled thereat, as well he might,
 And thought that match a fowle disparagement:
 His bloudie speare eftsoones he boldly bent
 Against the silly clowne, who dead through feare,
 Fell streight to ground in great astonishment;
 Villein (said he) this Ladie is my deare,
Dy, if thou it gainesay: I will away her beare.

13

The fearefull Chorle durst not gainesay, nor dooe,
 But trembling stood, and yielded him the pray;
 Who finding litle leasure her to wooe,
 On *Tromparts* steed her mounted without stay,
 And without reskew led her quite away.
 Proud man himselfe then *Braggadocchio* deemed,
 And next to none, after that happie day,
 Being possessed of that spoyle, which seemed
The fairest wight on ground, and most of men esteemed.

14

But when he saw himselfe free from poursute,
 He gan make gentle purpose to his Dame,
 With termes of love and lewdnesse dissolute;
 For he could well his glozing speaches frame
 To such vaine uses, that him best became:
 But she thereto would lend but light regard,
 As seeming sory, that she ever came
 Into his powre, that used her so hard,
To reave her honor, which she more than life prefard.

15

Thus as they two of kindnesse treated long,
 There them by chaunce encountred on the way
 An armed knight, upon a courser strong,
 Whose trampling feet upon the hollow lay
 Seemed to thunder, and did nigh affray
 That Capons courage: yet he looked grim,
 And fain'd to cheare his Ladie in dismay;
 Who seem'd for feare to quake in every lim,
And her to save from outrage, meekely prayed him.

16

Fiercely that stranger forward came, and nigh
    Approching, with bold words and bitter threat,
    Bad that same boaster, as he mote, on high
    To leave to him that Lady for excheat,
    Or bide him battell without further treat.
    That challenge did too peremptory seeme,
    And fild his senses with abashment great;
    Yet seeing nigh him jeopardy extreme,
He it dissembled well, and light seem'd to esteeme.

17

Saying, Thou foolish knight, that weenst with words
    To steale away, that I with blowes have wonne,
    And brought throgh points of many perilous swords:
    But if thee list to see thy Courser ronne,
    Or prove thy selfe, this sad encounter shonne,
    And seeke else without hazard of thy hed.
    At those proud words that other knight begonne
    To wexe exceeding wroth, and him ared
To turne his steede about, or sure he should be ded.

18

Sith then (said *Braggadocchio*) needes thou wilt
    Thy dayes abridge, through proofe of puissance,
    Turne we our steedes, that both in equall tilt
    May meet againe, and each take happie chance.
    This said, they both a furlongs mountenance
    Retyrd their steeds, to ronne in even race:
    But *Braggadocchio* with his bloudie lance
    Once having turnd, no more returnd his face,
But left his love to losse, and fled himselfe apace.

19

The knight him seeing fly, had no regard
    Him to poursew, but to the Ladie rode,
    And having her from *Trompart* lightly reard,
    Upon his Courser set the lovely lode,
    And with her fled away without abode.
    Well weened he, that fairest *Florimell*
    It was, with whom in company he yode,
    And so her selfe did alwaies to him tell;
So made him thinke him selfe in heaven, that was in hell.

20

But *Florimell* her selfe was farre away,
Driven to great distresse by Fortune straunge,
And taught the carefull Mariner to play,
Sith late mischaunce had her compeld to chaunge
The land for sea, at randon there to raunge:
Yet there that cruell Queene avengeresse,
Not satisfide so farre her to estraunge
From courtly blisse and wonted happinesse,
Did heape on her new waves of weary wretchednesse.

21

For being fled into the fishers bote,
For refuge from the Monsters crueltie,
Long so she on the mightie maine did flote,
And with the tide drove forward careleslie;
For th'aire was milde, and cleared was the skie,
And all his windes *Dan Aeolus* did keepe,
From stirring up their stormy enmitie,
As pittying to see her waile and weepe;
But all the while the fisher did securely sleepe.

22

At last when droncke with drowsinesse, he woke,
And saw his drover drive along the streame,
He was dismayd, and thrise his breast he stroke,
For marvell of that accident extreame;
But when he saw that blazing beauties beame,
Which with rare light his bote did beautifie,
He marveild more, and thought he yet did dreame
Not well awakt, or that some extasie
Assotted had his sense, or dazed was his eie.

23

But when her well auizing, he perceived
To be no vision, nor fantasticke sight,
Great comfort of her presence he conceived,
And felt in his old courage new delight
To gin awake, and stirre his frozen spright:
Tho rudely askt her, how she thither came.
Ah (said she) father, I note read aright,
What hard misfortune brought me to the same;
Yet am I glad that here I now in safety am.

24

But thou good man, sith farre in sea we bee,
  And the great waters gin apace to swell,
  That now no more we can the maine-land see,
  Have care, I pray, to guide the cock-bote well,
  Least worse on sea than us on land befell.
  Thereat th'old man did nought but fondly grin,
  And said, his boat the way could wisely tell:
  But his deceiptfull eyes did never lin,
To looke on her faire face, and marke her snowy skin.

25

The sight whereof in his congealed flesh,
  Infixt such secret sting of greedy lust,
  That the drie withered stocke it gan refresh,
  And kindled heat, that soone in flame forth brust:
  The driest wood is soonest burnt to dust.
  Rudely to her he lept, and his rough hand
  Where ill became him, rashly would have thrust,
  But she with angry scorne him did withstond,
And shamefully reproved for his rudenesse fond.

26

But he, that never good nor maners knew,
  Her sharpe rebuke full litle did esteeme;
  Hard is to teach an old horse amble trew.
  The inward smoke, that did before but steeme,
  Broke into open fire and rage extreme,
  And now he strength gan adde unto his will,
  Forcing to doe, that did him fowle misseeme:
  Beastly he threw her downe, ne car'd to spill
Her garments gay with scales of fish, that all did fill.

27

The silly virgin strove him to withstand,
  All that she might, and him in vaine revild:
  She struggled strongly both with foot and hand,
  To save her honor from that villaine vild,
  And cride to heaven, from humane helpe exild.
  O ye brave knights, that boast this Ladies love,
  Where be ye now, when she is nigh defild
  Of filthy wretch? well may shee you reprove
Of falshood or of slouth, when most it may behove.

Florimell and Proteus

28

But if that thou, Sir *Satyran*, didst weete,
  Or thou, Sir *Peridure*, her sorie state,
  How soone would yee assemble many a fleete,
  To fetch from sea, that ye at land lost late;
  Towres, Cities, Kingdomes ye would ruinate,
  In your avengement and dispiteous rage,
  Ne ought your burning fury mote abate;
  But if Sir *Calidore* could it presage,
No living creature could his cruelty asswage.

29

But sith that none of all her knights is nye,
  See how the heavens of voluntary grace,
  And soveraine favour towards chastity,
  Doe succour send to her distressed cace:
  So much high God doth innocence embrace.
  It fortuned, whilest thus she stifly strove,
  And the wide sea importuned long space
  With shrilling shriekes, *Proteus* abroad did rove,
Along the fomy waves driving his finny drove.

30

Proteus is Shepheard of the seas of yore,
  And hath the charge of *Neptunes* mightie heard;
  An aged sire with head all frory hore,
  And sprinckled frost upon his deawy beard:
  Who when those pittifull outcries he heard,
  Through all the seas so ruefully resound,
  His charet swift in haste he thither steard,
  Which with a teeme of scaly *Phocas* bound
Was drawne upon the waves, that fomed him around.

31

And comming to that Fishers wandring bote,
  That went at will, withouten carde or sayle,
  He therein saw that yrkesome sight, which smote
  Deepe indignation and compassion frayle
  Into his hart attonce: streight did he hayle
  The greedy villein from his hoped pray,
  Of which he now did very litle fayle,
  And with his staffe, that drives his Heard astray,
Him bet so sore, that life and sense did much dismay.

32

The whiles the pitteous Ladie up did ryse,
  Ruffled and fowly raid with filthy soyle,
  And blubbred face with teares of her faire eyes:
  Her heart nigh broken was with weary toyle,
  To save her selfe from that outrageous spoyle,
  But when she looked up, to weet, what wight
  Had her from so infamous fact assoyld,
  For shame, but more for feare of his grim sight,
Downe in her lap she hid her face, and loudly shright.

33

Her selfe not saved yet from daunger dred
  She thought, but chaung'd from one to other feare;
  Like as a fearefull Partridge, that is fled
  From the sharpe Hauke, which her attached neare,
  And fals to ground, to seeke for succour theare,
  Whereas the hungry Spaniels she does spy,
  With greedy jawes her readie for to teare;
  In such distresse and sad perplexity
Was *Florimell*, when *Proteus* she did see thereby.

34

But he endevoured with speeches milde
  Her to recomfort, and accourage bold,
  Bidding her feare no more her foeman vilde,
  Nor doubt himselfe; and who he was, her told.
  Yet all that could not from affright her hold,
  Ne to recomfort her at all prevayld;
  For her faint heart was with the frozen cold
  Benumbd so inly, that her wits nigh fayld,
And all her senses with abashment quite were quayld.

35

Her up betwixt his rugged hands he reard,
  And with his frory lips full softly kist,
  Whiles the cold ysickles from his rough beard,
  Dropped adowne upon her yvorie brest:
  Yet he himselfe so busily addrest,
  That her out of astonishment he wrought,
  And out of that same fishers filthy nest
  Removing her, into his charet brought,
And there with many gentle termes her faire besought.

36

But that old leachour, which with bold assault
 That beautie durst presume to violate,
 He cast to punish for his hainous fault;
 Then tooke he him yet trembling sith of late,
 And tyde behind his charet, to aggrate
 The virgin, whom he had abusde so sore:
 So drag'd him through the waves in scornefull state,
 And after cast him up, upon the shore;
But *Florimell* with him unto his bowre he bore.

37

His bowre is in the bottome of the maine,
 Under a mightie rocke, gainst which do rave
 The roaring billowes in their proud disdaine,
 That with the angry working of the wave,
 Therein is eaten out an hollow cave,
 That seemes rough Masons hand with engines keene
 Had long while laboured it to engrave:
 There was his wonne, ne living wight was seene,
Save one old *Nymph*, hight *Panope* to keepe it cleane.

38

Thither he brought the sory *Florimell*,
 And entertained her the best he might
 And *Panope* her entertaind eke well,
 As an immortall mote a mortall wight,
 To winne her liking unto his delight:
 With flattering words he sweetly wooed her,
 And offered faire gifts t'allure her sight,
 But she both offers and the offerer
Despysde, and all the fawning of the flatterer.

39

Daily he tempted her with this or that,
 And never suffred her to be at rest:
 But evermore she him refused flat,
 And all his fained kindnesse did detest,
 So firmely she had sealed up her brest.
 Sometimes he boasted, that a God he hight:
 But she a mortall creature loved best:
 Than he would make himselfe a mortall wight;
But then she said she lov'd none, but a Faerie knight.

40

Then like a Faerie knight himselfe he drest;
 For every shape on him he could endew:
 Then like a king he was to her exprest,
 And offred kingdomes unto her in vew,
 To be his Leman and his Ladie trew:
 But when all this he nothing saw prevaile,
 With harder meanes he cast her to subdew,
 And with sharpe threates her often did assaile,
So thinking for to make her stubborne courage quaile.

41

To dreadfull shapes he did himselfe transforme,
 Now like a Gyant, now like to a feend,
 Then like a Centaure, then like to a storme,
 Raging within the waves: thereby he weend
 Her will to win unto his wished end.
 But when with feare, nor favour, nor with all
 He else could doe, he saw himselfe esteemd,
 Downe in a Dongeon deepe he let her fall,
And threatned there to make her his eternall thrall.

42

Eternall thraldome was to her more liefe,
 Than losse of chastitie, or chaunge of love:
 Die had she rather in tormenting griefe,
 Than any should of falsenesse her reprove,
 Or loosenesse, that she lightly did remove.
 Most vertuous virgin, glory be thy meed,
 And crowne of heavenly praise with Saints above,
 Where most sweet hymmes of this thy famous deed
Are still emongst them song, that far my rymes exceed.

43

Fit song of Angels caroled to bee;
 But yet what so my feeble Muse can frame,
 Shall be t'advance thy goodly chastitee,
 And to enroll thy memorable name,
 In th'heart of every honourable Dame,
 That they thy vertuous deedes may imitate,
 And be partakers of thy endlesse fame.
 It yrkes me, leave thee in this wofull state,
To tell of *Satyrane*, where I him left of late.

44

Who having ended with that *Squire of Dames*
 A long discourse of his adventures vaine,
 The which himselfe, than Ladies more defames,
 And finding not th'*Hyena* to be slaine,
 With that same *Squire*, returned backe againe
 To his first way. And as they forward went,
 They spyde a knight faire pricking on the plaine,
 As if he were on some adventure bent,
And in his port appeared manly hardiment.

45

Sir *Satyrane* him towards did addresse,
 To weet, what wight he was, and what his quest:
 And comming nigh, eftsoones he gan to gesse
 Both by the burning hart, which on his brest
 He bare, and by the colours in his crest,
 That *Paridell* it was. Tho to him yode,
 And him saluting, as beseemed best,
 Gan first inquire of tydings farre abrode;
And afterwardes, on what adventure now he rode.

46

Who thereto answering, said; The tydings bad,
 Which now in Faerie court all men do tell,
 Which turned hath great mirth, to mourning sad,
 Is the late ruine of proud *Marinell*,
 And suddein parture of faire *Florimell*,
 To find him forth: and after her are gone
 All the brave knights, that doen in armes excell,
 To saveguard her, ywandred all alone;
Emongst the rest my lot (unworthy) is to be one.

47

Ah gentle knight (said then Sir *Satyrane*)
 Thy labour all is lost, I greatly dread,
 That hast a thanklesse service on thee ta'ne,
 And offrest sacrifice unto the dead:
 For dead, I surely doubt, thou maist aread
 Henceforth for ever *Florimell* to be,
 That all the noble knights of *Maydenhead*,
 Which her ador'd, may sore repent with me,
And all faire Ladies may for ever sory be.

48

Which words when *Paridell* had heard, his hew
　　Gan greatly chaunge, and seem'd dismayd to bee;
　　Then said, Faire Sir, how may I weene it trew,
　　That ye doe tell in such uncertaintee?
　　Or speake ye of report, or did ye see
　　Just cause of dread, that makes ye doubt so sore?
　　For perdie else how mote it ever bee,
　　That ever hand should dare for to engore
Her noble bloud? the heavens such crueltie abhore.

49

These eyes did see, that they will ever rew
　　T'have seene, (quoth he) when as a monstrous beast
　　The Palfrey, whereon she did travell, slew,
　　And of his bowels made his bloudie feast:
　　Which speaking token sheweth at the least
　　Her certaine losse, if not her sure decay:
　　Besides, that more suspition encreast,
　　I found her golden girdle cast astray,
Distaynd with durt and bloud, as relique of the pray.

50

Aye me, (said *Paridell*) the signes be sad,
　　And but God turne the same to good soothsay,
　　That Ladies safetie is sore to be drad:
　　Yet will I not forsake my forward way,
　　Till triall doe more certaine truth bewray.
　　Faire Sir (quoth he) well may it you succeed,
　　Ne long shall *Satyrane* behind you stay,
　　But to the rest, which in this Quest proceed
My labour adde, and be partaker of their speed.

51

Ye noble knights (said then the *Squire of Dames*)
　　Well may ye speed in so praiseworthy paine:
　　But sith the Sunne now ginnes to slake his beames,
　　In deawy vapours of the westerne maine,
　　And lose the teme out of his weary waine,
　　Mote not mislike you also to abate
　　Your zealous hast, till morrow next againe
　　Both light of heaven, and strength of men relate:
Which if ye please, to yonder castle turne your gate.

52

That counsell pleased well; so all yfere
  Forth marched to a Castle them before,
  Where soone arriving, they restrained were
  Of readie entrance, which ought evermore
  To errant knights be commun: wondrous sore
  Thereat displeasd they were, till that young Squire
  Gan them informe the cause, why that same dore
  Was shut to all, which lodging did desire:
The which to let you weet, will further time require.

CANT. IX

Malbecco will no straunge knights host,
  For peevish gealosie:
Paridell giusts with Britomart:
  Both shew their auncestrie.

1

REDOUBTED knights, and honorable Dames,
  To whom I levell all my labours end,
  Right sore I feare, least with unworthy blames
  This odious argument my rimes should shend,
  Or ought your goodly patience offend,
  Whiles of a wanton Lady I do write,
  Which with her loose incontinence doth blend
  The shyning glory of your soveraigne light,
And knighthood fowle defaced by a faithlesse knight.

2

But never let th'ensample of the bad
  Offend the good: for good by paragone
  Of evill, may more notably be rad,
  As white seemes fairer, macht with blacke attone;
  Ne all are shamed by the fault of one:
  For lo in heaven, whereas all goodnesse is,
  Emongst the Angels, a whole legione
  Of wicked Sprights did fall from happy blis;
What wonder then, if one of women all did mis?

3

Then listen Lordings, if ye list to weet
  The cause, why *Satyrane* and *Paridell*
  Mote not be entertaynd, as seemed meet,
  Into that Castle (as that Squire does tell.)
  Therein a cancred crabbed Carle does dwell,
  That has no skill of Court nor courtesie,
  Ne cares, what men say of him ill or well;
  For all his dayes he drownes in privitie,
Yet has full large to live, and spend at libertie.

4

But all his mind is set on mucky pelfe,
  To hoord up heapes of evill gotten masse,
  For which he others wrongs, and wreckes himselfe;
  Yet is he lincked to a lovely lasse,
  Whose beauty doth her bounty far surpasse,
  The which to him both far unequall yeares,
  And also far unlike conditions has;
  For she does joy to play emongst her peares,
And to be free from hard restraint and gealous feares.

5

But he is old, and withered like hay,
  Unfit faire Ladies service to supply;
  The privie guilt whereof makes him alway
  Suspect her truth, and keepe continuall spy
  Upon her with his other blincked eye;
  Ne suffreth he resort of living wight
  Approch to her, ne keepe her company,
  But in close bowre her mewes from all mens sight,
Depriv'd of kindly joy and naturall delight.

6

Malbecco he, and *Hellenore* she hight,
  Unfitly yokt together in one teeme,
  That is the cause, why never any knight
  Is suffred here to enter, but he seeme
  Such, as no doubt of him he neede misdeeme.
  Thereat Sir *Satyrane* gan smile, and say;
  Extremely mad the man I surely deeme,
  That weenes with watch and hard restraint to stay
A womans will, which is disposd to go astray.

7

In vaine he feares that, which he cannot shonne:
  For who wotes not, that womans subtiltyes
  Can guilen *Argus*, when she list misdonne?
  It is not yron bandes, nor hundred eyes,
  Nor brasen walls, nor many wakefull spyes,
  That can withhold her wilfull wandring feet;
  But fast good will with gentle curtesyes,
  And timely service to her pleasures meet
May her perhaps containe, that else would algates fleet.

8

Then is he not more mad (said *Paridell*)
  That hath himselfe unto such service sold,
  In dolefull thraldome all his dayes to dwell?
  For sure a foole I do him firmely hold,
  That loves his fetters, though they were of gold.
  But why do we devise of others ill,
  Whiles thus we suffer this same dotard old,
  To keepe us out, in scorne of his owne will,
And rather do not ransack all, and him selfe kill?

9

Nay let us first (said *Satyrane*) entreat
  The man by gentle meanes, to let us in,
  And afterwardes affray with cruell threat,
  Ere that we to efforce it do begin:
  Then if all fayle, we will by force it win,
  And eke reward the wretch for his mesprise,
  As may be worthy of his haynous sin.
  That counsell pleasd: then *Paridell* did rise,
And to the Castle gate approcht in quiet wise.

10

Whereat soft knocking, entrance he desyrd.
  The good man selfe, which then the Porter playd,
  Him answered, that all were now retyrd
  Unto their rest, and all the keyes convayd
  Unto their maister, who in bed was layd,
  That none him durst awake out of his dreme;
  And therefore them of patience gently prayd.
  Then *Paridell* began to chaunge his theme,
And threatned him with force and punishment extreme.

11

But all in vaine; for nought mote him relent,
And now so long before the wicket fast
They wayted, that the night was forward spent,
And the faire welkin fowly overcast,
Gan blowen up a bitter stormy blast,
With shoure and hayle so horrible and dred,
That this faire many were compeld at last,
To fly for succour to a little shed,
The which beside the gate for swine was ordered.

12

It fortuned, soone after they were gone,
Another knight, whom tempest thither brought,
Came to that Castle, and with earnest mone,
Like as the rest, late entrance deare besought;
But like so as the rest he prayd for nought,
For flatly he of entrance was refusd,
Sorely thereat he was displeasd, and thought
How to avenge himselfe so sore abusd,
And evermore the Carle of curtesie accusd.

13

But to avoyde th'intollerable stowre,
He was compeld to seeke some refuge neare,
And to that shed, to shrowd him from the showre,
He came, which full of guests he found whyleare,
So as he was not let to enter there:
Whereat he gan to wex exceeding wroth,
And swore, that he would lodge with them yfere,
Or them dislodge, all were they liefe or loth;
And so defide them each, and so defide them both.

14

Both were full loth to leave that needfull tent,
And both full loth in darkenesse to debate;
Yet both full liefe him lodging to have lent,
And both full liefe his boasting to abate;
But chiefly *Paridell* his hart did grate,
To heare him threaten so despightfully,
As if he did a dogge to kenell rate,
That durst not barke; and rather had he dy,
Than when he was defide, in coward corner ly.

15

Tho hastily remounting to his steed,
  He forth issew'd; like as a boistrous wind,
  Which in th'earthes hollow caves hath long bin hid,
  And shut up fast within her prisons blind,
  Makes the huge element against her kind
  To move, and tremble as it were agast,
  Untill that it an issew forth may find;
  Then forth it breakes, and with his furious blast
Confounds both land and seas, and skyes doth overcast.

16

Their steel-hed speares they strongly coucht, and met
  Together with impetuous rage and forse,
  That with the terrour of their fierce affret,
  They rudely drove to ground both man and horse,
  That each awhile lay like a sencelesse corse.
  But *Paridell* sore brused with the blow,
  Could not arise, the counterchaunge to scorse,
  Till that young Squire him reared from below;
Then drew he his bright sword, and gan about him throw.

17

But *Satyrane* forth stepping, did them stay
  And with faire treatie pacifide their ire,
  Then when they were accorded from the fray,
  Against that Castles Lord they gan conspire,
  To heape on him dew vengeaunce for his hire.
  They bene agreed, and to the gates they goe
  To burne the same with unquenchable fire,
  And that uncurteous Carle their commune foe
To do fowle death to dye, or wrap in grievous woe.

18

Malbecco seeing them resolv'd in deed
  To flame the gates, and hearing them to call
  For fire in earnest, ran with fearefull speed,
  And to them calling from the castle wall,
  Besought them humbly, him to beare with all,
  As ignoraunt of servants bad abuse,
  And slacke attendaunce unto straungers call.
  The knights were willing all things to excuse,
Though nought belev'd, and entraunce late did not refuse.

19

They bene ybrought into a comely bowre,
    And serv'd of all things that mote needfull bee;
    Yet secretly their hoste did on them lowre,
    And welcomde more for feare, than charitee;
    But they dissembled, what they did not see,
    And welcomed themselves. Each gan undight
    Their garments wet, and weary armour free,
    To dry them selves by *Vulcanes* flaming light,
And eke their lately bruzed parts to bring in plight.

20

And eke that straunger knight emongst the rest
    Was for like need enforst to disaray:
    Tho whenas vailed was her loftie crest,
    Her golden locks, that were in tramels gay
    Upbounden, did them selves adowne display,
    And raught unto her heeles; like sunny beames,
    That in a cloud their light did long time stay,
    Their vapour vaded, shew their golden gleames,
And through the persant aire shoote forth their azure streames.

21

She also dofte her heavy haberjeon,
    Which the faire feature of her limbs did hyde,
    And her well plighted frock, which she did won
    To tucke about her short, when she did ryde,
    She low let fall, that flowd from her lanck syde
    Downe to her foot, with carelesse modestee.
    Then of them all she plainly was espyde,
    To be a woman wight, unwist to bee,
The fairest woman wight, that ever eye did see.

22

Like as *Minerva*, being late returnd
    From slaughter of the Giaunts conquered;
    Where proud *Encelade*, whose wide nosethrils burnd
    With breathed flames, like to a furnace red,
    Transfixed with the speare, downe tombled ded
    From top of *Hemus*, by him heaped hye;
    Hath loosd her helmet from her lofty hed,
    And her *Gorgonian* shield gins to untye
From her left arme, to rest in glorious victorye.

23

Which whenas they beheld, they smitten were
  With great amazement of so wondrous sight.
  And each on other, and they all on her
  Stood gazing, as if suddein great affright
  Had them surprised. At last avizing right,
  Her goodly personage and glorious hew,
  Which they so much mistooke, they tooke delight
  In their first errour, and yet still anew
With wonder of her beauty fed their hungry vew.

24

Yet note their hungry vew be satisfide,
  But seeing still the more desir'd to see,
  And ever firmely fixed did abide
  In contemplation of divinitie:
  But most they mervaild at her chevalree,
  And noble prowesse, which they had approved,
  That much they faynd to know, who she mote bee;
  Yet none of all them her thereof amoved,
Yet every one her likte, and every one her loved.

25

And *Paridell* though partly discontent
  With his late fall, and fowle indignity,
  Yet was soone wonne his malice to relent,
  Through gracious regard of her faire eye,
  And knightly worth, which he too late did try,
  Yet tried did adore. Supper was dight;
  Then they *Malbecco* prayd of curtesy,
  That of his Lady they might have the sight,
And company at meat, to do them more delight.

26

But he to shift their curious request,
  Gan causen, why she could not come in place;
  Her crased health, her late recourse to rest,
  And humid evening ill for sicke folkes cace:
  But none of those excuses could take place;
  Ne would they eate, till she in presence came.
  She came in presence with right comely grace,
  And fairely them saluted, as became,
And shewd her selfe in all a gentle curteous Dame.

27

They sate to meat, and *Satyrane* his chaunce
 Was her before, and *Paridell* besyde;
 But he him selfe sate looking still askaunce,
 Gainst *Britomart*, and ever closely eyde
 Sir *Satyrane*, that glaunces might not glyde:
 But his blind eye, that syded *Paridell*,
 All his demeasnure from his sight did hyde:
 On her faire face so did he feede his fill,
And sent close messages of love to her at will.

28

And ever and anone, when none was ware,
 With speaking lookes, that close embassage bore,
 He rov'd at her, and told his secret care:
 For all that art he learned had of yore.
 Ne was she ignoraunt of that lewd lore,
 But in his eye his meaning wisely red,
 And with the like him answerd evermore:
 She sent at him one firie dart, whose hed
Empoisned was with privy lust, and gealous dred.

29

He from that deadly throw made no defence,
 But to the wound his weake hart opened wyde;
 The wicked engine through false influence,
 Past through his eyes, and secretly did glyde
 Into his hart, which it did sorely gryde.
 But nothing new to him was that same paine,
 Ne paine at all; for he so oft had tryde
 The powre thereof, and lov'd so oft in vaine,
That thing of course he counted, love to entertaine.

30

Thenceforth to her he sought to intimate
 His inward griefe, by meanes to him well knowne,
 Now *Bacchus* fruit out of the silver plate
 He on the table dasht, as overthrowne,
 Or of the fruitfull liquor overflowne,
 And by the dauncing bubbles did divine,
 Or therein write to let his love be showne;
 Which well she red out of the learned line,
A sacrament prophane in mistery of wine.

31

And when so of his hand the pledge she raught,
　The guilty cup she fained to mistake,
And in her lap did shed her idle draught,
　Shewing desire her inward flame to slake:
　By such close signes they secret way did make
Unto their wils, and one eyes watch escape;
　Two eyes him needeth, for to watch and wake,
Who lovers will deceive. Thus was the ape,
By their faire handling, put into *Malbeccoes* cape.

32

Now when of meats and drinks they had their fill,
　Purpose was moved by that gentle Dame,
Unto those knights adventurous, to tell
　Of deeds of armes, which unto them became,
　And every one his kindred, and his name.
Then *Paridell*, in whom a kindly pryde
　Of gracious speach, and skill his words to frame
Abounded, being glad of so fit tyde
Him to commend to her, thus spake, of all well eyde.

33

Troy, that art now nought, but an idle name,
　And in thine ashes buried low dost lie,
Though whilome far much greater than thy fame,
　Before that angry Gods, and cruell skye
　Upon thee heapt a direfull destinie,
What boots it boast thy glorious descent,
　And fetch from heaven thy great Genealogie,
Sith all thy worthy prayses being blent,
Their of-spring hath embaste, and later glory shent.

34

Most famous Worthy of the world, by whome
　That warre was kindled, which did *Troy* inflame,
And stately towres of *Ilion* whilome
　Brought unto balefull ruine, was by name
　Sir *Paris* far renowmd through noble fame,
Who through great prowesse and bold hardinesse,
　From *Lacedæmon* fetcht the fairest Dame,
That ever *Greece* did boast, or knight possesse,
Whom *Venus* to him gave for meed of worthinesse.

35

Faire *Helene*, flowre of beautie excellent,
  And girlond of the mighty Conquerours,
  That madest many Ladies deare lament
  The heavie losse of their brave Paramours,
  Which they far off beheld from *Trojan* toures,
  And saw the fieldes of faire *Scamander* strowne
  With carcases of noble warrioures,
  Whose fruitlesse lives were under furrow sowne,
And *Xanthus* sandy bankes with bloud all overflowne.

36

From him my linage I derive aright,
  Who long before the ten yeares siege of *Troy*,
  Whiles yet on *Ida* he a shepheard hight,
  On faire *Oenone* got a lovely boy,
  Whom for remembraunce of her passed joy,
  She of his Father *Parius* did name;
  Who, after *Greekes* did *Priams* realme destroy,
  Gathred the *Trojan* reliques sav'd from flame,
And with them sayling thence, to th'Isle of *Paros* came.

37

That was by him cald *Paros*, which before
  Hight *Nausa*, there he many yeares did raine,
  And built *Nausicle* by the *Pontick* shore,
  The which he dying left next in remaine
  To *Paridas* his sonne.
  From whom I *Paridell* by kin descend;
  But for faire Ladies love, and glories gaine,
  My native soile have left, my dayes to spend
In sewing deeds of armes, my lives and labours end.

38

Whenas the noble *Britomart* heard tell
  Of *Trojan* warres, and *Priams* Citie sackt,
  The ruefull story of Sir *Paridell*,
  She was empassiond at that piteous act,
  With zelous envy of Greekes cruell fact,
  Against that nation, from whose race of old
  She heard, that she was lineally extract:
  For noble *Britons* sprong from *Trojans* bold,
And *Troynovant* was built of old *Troyes* ashes cold,

39

Then sighing soft awhile, at last she thus:
  O lamentable fall of famous towne,
  Which raignd so many yeares victorious,
  And of all *Asie* bore the soveraigne crowne,
  In one sad night consumd, and throwen downe:
  What stony hart, that heares thy haplesse fate,
  Is not empierst with deepe compassiowne,
  And makes ensample of mans wretched state,
That floures so fresh at morne, and fades at evening late?

40

Behold, Sir, how your pitifull complaint
  Hath found another partner of your payne:
  For nothing may impresse so deare constraint,
  As countries cause, and commune foes disdayne.
  But if it should not grieve you, backe agayne
  To turne your course, I would to heare desyre,
  What to *Aeneas* fell; sith that men sayne
  He was not in the Cities wofull fyre
Consum'd, but did him selfe to safetie retyre.

41

Anchyses sonne begot of *Venus* faire,
  (Said he,) out of the flames for safegard fled,
  And with a remnant did to sea repaire,
  Where he through fatall errour long was led
  Full many yeares, and weetlesse wandered
  From shore to shore, emongst the Lybicke sands,
  Ere rest he found. Much there he suffered,
  And many perils past in forreine lands,
To save his people sad from victours vengefull hands.

42

At last in *Latium* he did arrive,
  Where he with cruell warre was entertaind
  Of th'inland folke, which sought him backe to drive,
  Till he with old *Latinus* was constraind,
  To contract wedlock: (so the fates ordaind.)
  Wedlock contract in bloud, and eke in blood
  Accomplished, that many deare complaind:
  The rivall slaine, the victour through the flood
Escaped hardly, hardly praisd his wedlock good.

43

Yet after all, he victour did survive,
　And with *Latinus* did the kingdome part.
　But after, when both nations gan to strive,
　Into their names the title to convart,
　His sonne *Iülus* did from thence depart,
　With all the warlike youth of *Trojans* bloud,
　And in long *Alba* plast his throne apart,
　Where faire it florished, and long time stoud,
Till *Romulus* renewing it, to *Rome* removd.

44

There there (said *Britomart*) a fresh appeard
　The glory of the later world to spring,
　And *Troy* againe out of her dust was reard,
　To sit in second seat of soveraigne king,
　Of all the world under her governing.
　But a third kingdome yet is to arise,
　Out of the *Trojans* scattered of-spring,
　That in all glory and great enterprise,
Both first and second *Troy* shall dare to equalise.

45

It *Troynovant* is hight, that with the waves
　Of wealthy *Thamis* washed is along,
　Upon whose stubborne neck, whereat he raves
　With roring rage, and sore him selfe does throng,
　That all men feare to tempt his billowes strong,
　She fastned hath her foot, which standes so hy,
　That it a wonder of the world is song
　In forreine landes, and all which passen by,
Beholding it from far, do thinke it threates the skye.

46

The *Trojan Brute* did first that Citie found,
　And Hygate made the meare thereof by West,
　And *Overt* gate by North: that is the bound
　Toward the land; two rivers bound the rest.
　So huge a scope at first him seemed best,
　To be the compasse of his kingdomes seat:
　So huge a mind could not in lesser rest,
　Ne in small meares containe his glory great,
That *Albion* had conquered first by warlike feat.

47

Ah fairest Lady knight, (said *Paridell*)
  Pardon I pray my heedlesse oversight,
  Who had forgot, that whilome I heard tell
  From aged *Mnemon*; for my wits bene light.
  Indeed he said (if I remember right,)
  That of the antique *Trojan* stocke, there grew
  Another plant, that raught to wondrous hight,
  And far abroad his mighty branches threw,
Into the utmost Angle of the world he knew.

48

For that same *Brute*, whom much he did advaunce
  In all his speach, was *Sylvius* his sonne,
  Whom having slaine, through luckles arrowes glaunce
  He fled for feare of that he had misdonne,
  Or else for shame, so fowle reproch to shonne,
  And with him led to sea an youthly trayne,
  Where wearie wandring they long time did wonne,
  And many fortunes prov'd in th'*Ocean* mayne,
And great adventures found, that now were long to sayne.

49

At last by fatall course they driven were
  Into an Island spatious and brode,
  The furthest North, that did to them appeare.
  Which after rest they seeking far abrode,
  Found it the fittest soyle for their abode,
  Fruitfull of all things fit for living foode,
  But wholy wast, and void of peoples trode,
  Save an huge nation of the Geaunts broode,
That fed on living flesh, and druncke mens vitall blood.

50

Whom he through wearie wars and labours long,
  Subdewd with losse of many *Britons* bold:
  In which the great *Goemagot* of strong
  Corineus, and *Coulin* of *Debon* old
  Were overthrowne, and layd on th'earth full cold,
  Which quaked under their so hideous masse,
  A famous history to be enrold
  In everlasting moniments of brasse,
That all the antique Worthies merits far did passe.

51

His worke great *Troynovant*, his worke is eke
　Faire *Lincolne*, both renowmed far away,
　That who from East to West will endlong seeke,
　Cannot two fairer Cities find this day,
　Except *Cleopolis:* so heard I say
　Old *Mnemon*. Therefore Sir, I greet you well
　Your countrey kin, and you entirely pray
　Of pardon for the strife, which late befell
Betwixt us both unknowne. So ended *Paridell*.

52

But all the while, that he these speaches spent,
　Upon his lips hong faire Dame *Hellenore*,
　With vigilant regard, and dew attent,
　Fashioning worlds of fancies evermore
　In her fraile wit, that now her quite forlore:
　The whiles unwares away her wondring eye,
　And greedy eares her weake hart from her bore:
　Which he perceiving, ever privily
In speaking, many false belgardes at her let fly.

53

So long these knights discoursed diversly,
　Of straunge affaires, and noble hardiment,
　Which they had past with mickle jeopardy,
　That now the humid night was farforth spent,
　And heavenly lampes were halfendeale ybrent:
　Which th'old man seeing well, who too long thought
　Every discourse and every argument,
　Which by the houres he measured, besought
Them go to rest. So all unto their bowres were brought.

CANT. X

Paridell rapeth Hellenore
Malbecco her pursewes:
Findes emongst Satyres, whence with him
To turne she doth refuse.

I

THE morow next, so soone as *Phœbus* Lamp
   Bewrayed had the world with early light,
   And fresh *Aurora* had the shady damp
   Out of the goodly heaven amoved quight,
   Faire *Britomart* and that same *Faerie* knight
   Uprose, forth on their journey for to wend:
   But *Paridell* complaynd, that his late fight
   With *Britomart*, so sore did him offend,
That ryde he could not, till his hurts he did amend.

2

So forth they far'd, but he behind them stayd,
   Maulgre his host, who grudged grievously,
   To house a guest, that would be needes obayd,
   And of his owne him left not liberty:
   Might wanting measure moveth surquedry.
   Two things he feared, but the third was death;
   That fierce youngmans unruly maistery;
   His money, which he lov'd as living breath;
And his faire wife, whom honest long he kept uneath.

3

But patience perforce he must abie,
   What fortune and his fate on him will lay,
   Fond is the feare, that findes no remedie;
   Yet warily he watcheth every way,
   By which he feareth evill happen may:
   So th'evill thinkes by watching to prevent;
   Ne doth he suffer her, nor night, nor day,
   Out of his sight her selfe once to absent.
So doth he punish her and eke himselfe torment.

4

But *Paridell* kept better watch, than hee,
  A fit occasion for his turne to find:
  False love, why do men say, thou canst not see,
  And in their foolish fancie feigne thee blind,
  That with thy charmes the sharpest sight doest bind,
  And to thy will abuse? Thou walkest free.
  And seest every secret of the mind;
  Thou seest all, yet none at all sees thee;
All that is by the working of thy Deitee.

5

So perfect in that art was *Paridell*,
  That he *Malbeccoes* halfen eye did wyle,
  His halfen eye he wiled wondrous well,
  And *Hellenors* both eyes did eke beguyle,
  Both eyes and hart attonce, during the whyle
  That he there sojourned his wounds to heale;
  That *Cupid* selfe it seeing, close did smyle,
  To weet how he her love away did steale,
And bad, that none their joyous treason should reveale.

6

The learned lover lost no time nor tyde,
  That least avantage mote to him afford,
  Yet bore so faire a saile, that none espyde
  His secret drift, till he her layd abord.
  When so in open place, and commune bord,
  He fortun'd her to meet, with commune speach
  He courted her, yet bayted every word,
  That his ungentle hoste n'ote him appeach
Of vile ungentlenesse, or hospitages breach.

7

But when apart (if ever her apart)
  He found, then his false engins fast he plyde,
  And all the sleights unbosomd in his hart;
  He sigh'd, he sobd, he swownd, he perdy dyde,
  And cast himselfe on ground her fast besyde:
  Tho when againe he him bethought to live,
  He wept, and wayld, and false laments belyde,
  Saying, but if she Mercie would him give
That he mote algates dye, yet did his death forgive.

8

And otherwhiles with amorous delights,
　And pleasing toyes he would her entertaine,
　Now singing sweetly, to surprise her sprights,
　Now making layes of love and lovers paine,
　Bransles, Ballads, virelayes, and verses vaine;
　Oft purposes, oft riddles he devysd,
　And thousands like, which flowed in his braine,
　With which he fed her fancie, and entysd
To take to his new love, and leave her old despysd.

9

And every where he might, and every while
　He did her service dewtifull, and sewed
　At hand with humble pride, and pleasing guile,
　So closely yet, that none but she it vewed,
　Who well perceived all, and all indewed.
　Thus finely did he his false nets dispred,
　With which he many weake harts had subdewed
　Of yore, and many had ylike misled:
What wonder then, if she were likewise carried?

10

No fort so fensible, no wals so strong,
　But that continuall battery will rive,
　Or daily siege through dispurvayance long,
　And lacke of reskewes will to parley drive;
　And Peece, that unto parley eare will give,
　Will shortly yeeld it selfe, and will be made
　The vassall of the victors will bylive:
　That stratageme had oftentimes assayd
This crafty Paramoure, and now it plaine displayd.

11

For through his traines he her intrapped hath,
　That she her love and hart hath wholy sold
　To him, without regard of gaine, or scath,
　Or care of credite, or of husband old,
　Whom she hath vow'd to dub a faire Cucquold.
　Nought wants but time and place, which shortly shee
　Devized hath, and to her lover told.
　It pleased well.　So well they both agree;
So readie rype to ill, ill wemens counsels bee.

12

Darke was the Evening, fit for lovers stealth,
    When chaunst *Malbecco* busie be elsewhere,
    She to his closet went, where all his wealth
    Lay hid: thereof she countlesse summes did reare,
    The which she meant away with her to beare;
    The rest she fyr'd for sport, or for despight;
    As *Hellene*, when she saw aloft appeare
    The *Trojane* flames, and reach to heavens hight
Did clap her hands, and joyed at that dolefull sight.

13

This second *Hellene*, faire Dame *Hellenore*,
    The whiles her husband ranne with sory haste,
    To quench the flames, which she had tyn'd before,
    Laught at his foolish labour spent in waste;
    And ranne into her lovers armes right fast;
    Where streight embraced, she to him did cry,
    And call aloud for helpe, ere helpe were past;
    For loe that Guest would beare her forcibly,
And meant to ravish her, that rather had to dy.

14

The wretched man hearing her call for ayd,
    And readie seeing him with her to fly,
    In his disquiet mind was much dismayd:
    But when againe he backward cast his eye,
    And saw the wicked fire so furiously
    Consume his hart, and scorch his Idoles face,
    He was therewith distressed diversly,
    Ne wist he how to turne, nor to what place;
Was never wretched man in such a wofull cace.

15

Ay when to him she cryde, to her he turnd,
    And left the fire; love money overcame;
    But when he marked, how his money burnd,
    He left his wife; money did love disclame:
    Both was he loth to loose his loved Dame,
    And loth to leave his liefest pelfe behind,
    Yet sith he n'ote save both, he sav'd that same,
    Which was the dearest to his donghill mind,
The God of his desire, the joy of misers blind.

16

Thus whilest all things in troublous uprore were,
  And all men busie to suppresse the flame,
  The loving couple need no reskew feare,
  But leasure had, and libertie to frame
  Their purpost flight, free from all mens reclame;
  And Night, the patronesse of love-stealth faire,
  Gave them safe conduct, till to end they came:
So bene they gone yfeare, a wanton paire
Of lovers loosely knit, where list them to repaire.

17

Soone as the cruell flames yslaked were,
  Malbecco seeing, how his losse did lye,
  Out of the flames, which he had quencht whylere
  Into huge waves of griefe and gealosye
  Full deepe emplonged was, and drowned nye,
  Twixt inward doole and felonous despight;
  He rav'd, he wept, he stampt, he lowd did cry,
  And all the passions, that in man may light,
Did him attonce oppresse, and vex his caytive spright.

18

Long thus he chawd the cud of inward griefe,
  And did consume his gall with anguish sore,
  Still when he mused on his late mischiefe,
  Then still the smart thereof increased more,
  And seem'd more grievous, than it was before:
  At last when sorrow he saw booted nought,
  Ne griefe might not his love to him restore,
  He gan devise, how her he reskew mought,
Ten thousand wayes he cast in his confused thought.

19

At last resolving, like a pilgrim pore,
  To search her forth, where so she might be fond,
  And bearing with him treasure in close store,
  The rest he leaves in ground: So takes in hond
  To seeke her endlong, both by sea and lond.
  Long he her sought, he sought her farre and nere,
  And every where that he mote understond,
  Of knights and ladies any meetings were,
And of eachone he met, he tydings did inquere.

20

But all in vaine, his woman was too wise,
  Ever to come into his clouch againe,
  And he too simple ever to surprise
  The jolly *Paridell*, for all his paine.
  One day, as he forpassed by the plaine
  With weary pace, he farre away espide
  A couple, seeming well to be his twaine,
  Which hoved close under a forrest side,
As if they lay in wait, or else themselves did hide.

21

Well weened he, that those the same mote bee,
  And as he better did their shape avize,
  Him seemed more their manner did agree;
  For th'one was armed all in warlike wize,
  Whom, to be *Paridell* he did devize;
  And th'other all yclad in garments light,
  Discolour'd like to womanish disguise,
  He did resemble to his Ladie bright;
And ever his faint hart much earned at the sight.

22

And ever faine he towards them would goe,
  But yet durst not for dread approchen nie,
  But stood aloofe, unweeting what to doe;
  Till that prickt forth with loves extremitie,
  That is the father of foule gealosy,
  He closely nearer crept, the truth to weet:
  But, as he nigher drew, he easily
  Might scerne, that it was not his sweetest sweet,
Ne yet her Belamour, the partner of his sheet.

23

But it was scornefull *Braggadocchio*,
  That with his servant *Trompart* hoverd there,
  Sith late he fled from his too earnest foe:
  Whom such when as *Malbecco* spyed clere,
  He turned backe, and would have fled arere;
  Till *Trompart* ronning hastily, him did stay,
  And bad before his soveraine Lord appere:
  That was him loth, yet durst he not gainesay,
And comming him before, low louted on the lay.

24

The Boaster at him sternely bent his browe,
  As if he could have kild him with his looke,
  That to the ground him meekely made to bowe,
  And awfull terror deepe into him strooke,
  That every member of his bodie quooke.
  Said he, Thou man of nought, what doest thou here,
  Unfitly furnisht with thy bag and booke,
  Where I expected one with shield and spere,
To prove some deedes of armes upon an equall pere.

25

The wretched man at his imperious speach,
  Was all abasht, and low prostrating, said;
  Good Sir, let not my rudenesse be no breach
  Unto your patience, ne be ill ypaid;
  For I unwares this way by fortune straid,
  A silly Pilgrim driven to distresse,
  That seeke a Lady, There he suddein staid,
  And did the rest with grievous sighes suppresse,
While teares stood in his eies, few drops of bitternesse.

26

What Ladie, man? (said *Trompart*) take good hart,
  And tell thy griefe, if any hidden lye;
  Was never better time to shew thy smart,
  Than now, that noble succour is thee by,
  That is the whole worlds commune remedy.
  That cheareful word his weake hart much did cheare,
  And with vaine hope his spirits faint supply,
  That bold he said; O most redoubted Pere,
Vouchsafe with mild regard a wretches cace to heare.

27

Then sighing sore, It is not long (said hee)
  Sith I enjoyd the gentlest Dame alive;
  Of whom a knight, no knight at all perdee,
  But shame of all, that doe for honor strive,
  By treacherous deceipt did me deprive;
  Through open outrage he her bore away,
  And with fowle force unto his will did drive,
  Which all good knights, that armes do beare this day,
Are bound for to revenge, and punish if they may.

28

And you most noble Lord, that can and dare
  Redresse the wrong of miserable wight,
Cannot employ your most victorious speare
  In better quarrell, than defence of right,
  And for a Ladie gainst a faithlesse knight;
So shall your glory be advaunced much,
  And all faire Ladies magnifie your might,
  And eke my selfe, albe I simple such,
Your worthy paine shall well reward with guerdon rich.

29

With that out of his bouget forth he drew
  Great store of treasure, therewith him to tempt;
But he on it lookt scornefully askew,
  As much disdeigning to be so misdempt,
  Or a war-monger to be basely nempt;
And said; Thy offers base I greatly loth,
  And eke thy words uncourteous and unkempt;
  I tread in dust thee and thy money both,
That, were it not for shame, So turned from him wroth.

30

But *Trompart*, that his maisters humor knew,
  In lofty lookes to hide an humble mind,
Was inly tickled with that golden vew,
  And in his eare him rounded close behind:
  Yet stoupt he not, but lay still in the wind,
Waiting advauntage on the pray to sease;
  Till *Trompart* lowly to the ground inclind,
  Besought him his great courage to appease,
And pardon simple man, that rash did him displease.

31

Bigge looking like a doughtie Doucepere,
  At last he thus; Thou clod of vilest clay,
I pardon yield, and with thy rudenesse beare;
  But weete henceforth, that all that golden pray,
  And all that else the vaine world vaunten may,
I loath as doung, ne deeme my dew reward:
  Fame is my meed, and glory vertues pray.
  But minds of mortall men are muchell mard,
And mov'd amisse with massie mucks unmeet regard.

32

And more, I graunt to thy great miserie
  Gratious respect, thy wife shall backe be sent,
  And that vile knight, who ever that he bee,
  Which hath thy Lady reft, and knighthood shent,
  By *Sanglamort* my sword, whose deadly dent
  The bloud hath of so many thousands shed,
  I sweare, ere long shall dearely it repent;
  Ne he twixt heaven and earth shall hide his hed,
But soone he shall be found, and shortly doen be ded.

33

The foolish man thereat woxe wondrous blith,
  As if the word so spoken, were halfe donne,
  And humbly thanked him a thousand sith,
  That had from death to life him newly wonne.
  Tho forth the Boaster marching, brave begonne
  His stolen steed to thunder furiously,
  As if he heaven and hell would overronn
  And all the world confound with cruelty,
That much *Malbecco* joyed in his jollity.

34

Thus long they three together traveiled,
  Through many a wood, and many an uncouth way,
  To seeke his wife, that was farre wandered:
  But those two sought nought, but the present pray,
  To weete the treasure, which he did bewray,
  On which their eies and harts were wholly set,
  With purpose, how they might it best betray;
  For sith the houre, that first he did them let
The same behold, therewith their keene desires were whet.

35

It fortuned as they together far'd,
  They spide, where *Paridell* came pricking fast
  Upon the plaine, the which himselfe prepar'd
  To giust with that brave straunger knight a cast,
  As on adventure by the way he past:
  Alone he rode without his Paragone;
  For having filcht her bels, her up he cast
  To the wide world, and let her fly alone,
He nould be clogd. So had he served many one.

36

The gentle Lady, loose at randon left,
  The greene-wood long did walke, and wander wide
  At wilde adventure, like a forlorne weft,
  Till on a day the *Satyres* her espide
  Straying alone withouten groome or guide;
  Her up they tooke, and with them home her led,
  With them as housewife ever to abide,
  To milk their gotes, and make them cheese and bred,
And every one as commune good her handeled.

37

That shortly she *Malbecco* has forgot,
  And eke Sir *Paridell*, all were he deare;
  Who from her went to seeke another lot,
  And now by fortune was arrived here,
  Where those two guilers with *Malbecco* were:
  Soone as the oldman saw Sir *Paridell*,
  He fainted, and was almost dead with feare,
  Ne word he had to speake, his griefe to tell,
But to him louted low, and greeted goodly well.

38

And after asked him for *Hellenore*,
  I take no keepe of her (said *Paridell*)
  She wonneth in the forrest there before.
  So forth he rode, as his adventure fell;
  The whiles the Boaster from his loftie sell
  Faynd to alight, something amisse to mend;
  But the fresh Swayne would not his leasure dwell,
  But went his way; whom when he passed kend,
He up remounted light, and after faind to wend.

39

Perdy nay (said *Malbecco*) shall ye not:
  But let him passe as lightly, as he came:
  For litle good of him is to be got,
  And mickle perill to be put to shame.
  But let us go to seeke my dearest Dame,
  Whom he hath left in yonder forrest wyld:
  For of her safety in great doubt I am,
  Least salvage beastes her person have despoyld:
Then all the world is lost, and we in vaine have toyld.

40

They all agree, and forward them addrest:
　Ah but (said craftie *Trompart*) weete ye well,
　That yonder in that wastefull wildernesse
　Huge monsters haunt, and many dangers dwell;
　Dragons, and Minotaures, and feendes of hell,
　And many wilde woodmen, which robbe and rend
　All travellers; therefore advise ye well,
　Before ye enterprise that way to wend:
One may his journey bring too soone to evill end.

41

Malbecco stopt in great astonishment,
　And with pale eyes fast fixed on the rest,
　Their counsell crav'd, in daunger imminent.
　Said *Trompart*, You that are the most opprest
　With burden of great treasure, I thinke best
　Here for to stay in safetie behind;
　My Lord and I will search the wide forrest.
　That counsell pleased not *Malbeccoes* mind;
For he was much affraid, himselfe alone to find.

42

Then is it best (said he) that ye doe leave
　Your treasure here in some securitie,
　Either fast closed in some hollow greave,
　Or buried in the ground from jeopardie,
　Till we returne againe in safetie:
　As for us two, least doubt of us ye have,
　Hence farre away we will blindfolded lie,
　Ne privie be unto your treasures grave.
It pleased: so he did. Then they march forward brave.

43

Now when amid the thickest woods they were,
　They heard a noyse of many bagpipes shrill,
　And shrieking Hububs them approching nere,
　Which all the forrest did with horror fill:
　That dreadfull sound the boasters hart did thrill,
　With such amazement, that in haste he fled,
　Ne ever looked backe for good or ill,
　And after him eke fearefull *Trompart* sped;
The old man could not fly, but fell to ground halfe ded.

44

Yet afterwards close creeping, as he might,
　　He in a bush did hide his fearefull hed,
　　The jolly *Satyres* full of fresh delight,
　　Came dauncing forth, and with them nimbly led
　　Faire *Hellenore*, with girlonds all bespred,
　　Whom their May-lady they had newly made:
　　She proud of that new honour, which they red,
　　And of their lovely fellowship full glade,
Daunst lively, and her face did with a Lawrell shade.

45

The silly man that in the thicket lay
　　Saw all this goodly sport, and grieved sore,
　　Yet durst he not against it doe or say,
　　But did his hart with bitter thoughts engore,
　　To see th'unkindnesse of his *Hellenore*.
　　All day they daunced with great lustihed,
　　And with their horned feet the greene grasse wore,
　　The whiles their Gotes upon the brouzes fed,
Till drouping *Phœbus* gan to hide his golden hed.

46

Tho up they gan their merry pypes to trusse,
　　And all their goodly heards did gather round,
　　But every *Satyre* first did give a busse
　　To *Hellenore*: so busses did abound.
　　Now gan the humid vapour shed the ground
　　With perly deaw, and th'Earthes gloomy shade
　　Did dim the brightnesse of the welkin round,
　　That every bird and beast awarned made,
To shrowd themselves, whiles sleepe their senses did invade.

47

Which when *Malbecco* saw, out of his bush
　　Upon his hands and feete he crept full light,
　　And like a Gote emongst the Gotes did rush,
　　That through the helpe of his faire hornes on hight,
　　And misty dampe of misconceiving night,
　　And eke through likenesse of his gotish beard,
　　He did the better counterfeite aright:
　　So home he marcht emongst the horned heard,
That none of all the *Satyres* him espyde or heard.

48

At night, when all they went to sleepe, he vewd,
  Whereas his lovely wife emongst them lay,
  Embraced of a *Satyre* rough and rude,
  Who all the night did minde his joyous play:
  Nine times he heard him come aloft ere day,
  That all his hart with gealosie did swell;
  But yet that nights ensample did bewray,
  That not for nought his wife them loved so well,
When one so oft a night did ring his matins bell.

49

So closely as he could, he to them crept,
  When wearie of their sport to sleepe they fell,
  And to his wife, that now full soundly slept,
  He whispered in her eare, and did her tell,
  That it was he, which by her side did dwell,
  And therefore prayd her wake, to heare him plaine.
  As one out of a dreame not waked well,
  She turned her, and returned backe againe:
Yet her for to awake he did the more constraine.

50

At last with irkesome trouble she abrayd;
  And then perceiving, that it was indeed
  Her old *Malbecco*, which did her upbrayd,
  With loosenesse of her love, and loathly deed,
  She was astonisht with exceeding dreed,
  And would have wakt the *Satyre* by her syde;
  But he her prayd, for mercy, or for meed,
  To save his life, ne let him be descryde,
But hearken to his lore, and all his counsell hyde.

51

Tho gan he her perswade, to leave that lewd
  And loathsome life, of God and man abhord,
  And home returne, where all should be renewd
  With perfect peace, and bandes of fresh accord,
  And she receiv'd againe to bed and bord,
  As if no trespasse ever had bene donne:
  But she it all refused at one word,
  And by no meanes would to his will be wonne,
But chose emongst the jolly *Satyres* still to wonne.

52

He wooed her, till day spring he espyde;
  But all in vaine: and then turnd to the heard,
  Who butted him with hornes on every syde,
  And trode downe in the durt, where his hore beard
  Was fowly dight, and he of death afeard.
  Early before the heavens fairest light
  Out of the ruddy East was fully reard,
  The heardes out of their foldes were loosed quight,
And he emongst the rest crept forth in sory plight.

53

So soone as he the Prison dore did pas,
  He ran as fast, as both his feete could beare,
  And never looked, who behind him was,
  Ne scarsely who before: like as a Beare
  That creeping close, amongst the hives to reare
  An hony combe, the wakefull dogs espy,
  And him assayling, sore his carkasse teare,
  That hardly he with life away does fly,
Ne stayes, till safe himselfe he see from jeopardy.

54

Ne stayd he, till he came unto the place,
  Where late his treasure he entombed had,
  Where when he found it not (for *Trompart* bace
  Had it purloyned for his maister bad:)
  With extreme fury he became quite mad,
  And ran away, ran with himselfe away:
  That who so straungely had him seene bestad,
  With upstart haire, and staring eyes dismay,
From Limbo lake him late escaped sure would say.

55

High over hilles and over dales he fled,
  As if the wind him on his winges had borne,
  Ne banck nor bush could stay him, when he sped
  His nimble feet, as treading still on thorne:
  Griefe, and despight, and gealosie, and scorne
  Did all the way him follow hard behind,
  And he himselfe himselfe loath'd so forlorne,
  So shamefully forlorne of womankind;
That as a Snake, still lurked in his wounded mind.

56

Still fled he forward, looking backward still,
　Ne stayd his flight, nor fearefull agony,
　Till that he came unto a rockie hill,
　Over the sea, suspended dreadfully,
　That living creature it would terrify,
　To looke adowne, or upward to the hight:
　From thence he threw himselfe dispiteously,
　All desperate of his fore-damned spright,
That seem'd no helpe for him was left in living sight.

57

But through long anguish, and selfe-murdring thought
　He was so wasted and forpined quight,
　That all his substance was consum'd to nought,
　And nothing left, but like an aery Spright,
　That on the rockes he fell so flit and light,
　That he thereby receiv'd no hurt at all,
　But chaunced on a craggy cliff to light;
　Whence he with crooked clawes so long did crall,
That at the last he found a cave with entrance small.

58

Into the same he creepes, and thenceforth there
　Resolv'd to build his balefull mansion,
　In drery darkenesse, and continuall feare
　Of that rockes fall, which ever and anon
　Threates with huge ruine him to fall upon,
　That he dare never sleepe, but that one eye
　Still ope he keepes for that occasion;
　Ne ever rests he in tranquillity,
The roring billowes beat his bowre so boystrously.

59

Ne ever is he wont on ought to feed,
　But toades and frogs, his pasture poysonous,
　Which in his cold complexion do breed
　A filthy bloud, or humour rancorous,
　Matter of doubt and dread suspitious,
　That doth with curelesse care consume the hart,
　Corrupts the stomacke with gall vitious,
　Croscuts the liver with internall smart,
And doth transfixe the soule with deathes eternall dart.

60

Yet can he never dye, but dying lives,
  And doth himselfe with sorrow new sustaine,
  That death and life attonce unto him gives.
  And painefull pleasure turnes to pleasing paine.
  There dwels he ever, miserable swaine,
  Hatefull both to him selfe, and every wight;
  Where he through privy griefe, and horrour vaine,
  Is woxen so deform'd, that he has quight
Forgot he was a man, and *Gealosie* is hight.

CANT. XI

Britomart chaceth Ollyphant,
findes Scudamour distrest:
Assayes the house of Busyrane,
where Loves spoyles are exprest.

I

O HATEFULL hellish Snake, what furie furst
  Brought thee from balefull house of *Proserpine*,
  Where in her bosome she thee long had nurst,
  And fostred up with bitter milke of tine,
  Fowle Gealosie, that turnest love divine
  To joylesse dread, and mak'st the loving hart
  With hatefull thoughts to languish and to pine,
  And feed it selfe with selfe-consuming smart?
Of all the passions in the mind thou vilest art.

2

O let him far be banished away,
  And in his stead let Love for ever dwell,
  Sweet Love, that doth his golden wings embay
  In blessed Nectar, and pure Pleasures well,
  Untroubled of vile feare, or bitter fell.
  And ye faire Ladies, that your kingdomes make
  In th'harts of men, them governe wisely well,
  And of faire *Britomart* ensample take,
That was as trew in love, as Turtle to her make.

Britomart rescues Amoret

3

Who with Sir *Satyrane*, as earst ye red,
  Forth ryding from *Malbeccoes* hostlesse hous,
  Far off aspyde a young man, the which fled
  From an huge Geaunt, that with hideous
  And hatefull outrage long him chaced thus;
  It was that *Ollyphant*, the brother deare
  Of that *Argante* vile and vitious,
  From whom the *Squire of Dames* was reft whylere;
This all as bad as she, and worse, if worse ought were.

4

For as the sister did in feminine
  And filthy lust exceede all woman kind,
  So he surpassed his sex masculine,
  In beastly use that I did ever find;
  Whom when as *Britomart* beheld behind
  The fearefull boy so greedily pursew,
  She was emmoved in her noble mind,
  T'employ her puissaunce to his reskew,
And pricked fiercely forward, where she him did vew.

5

Ne was Sir *Satyrane* her far behinde,
  But with like fiercenesse did ensew the chace:
  Whom when the Gyaunt saw, he soone resinde
  His former suit, and from them fled apace;
  They after both, and boldly bad him bace,
  And each did strive the other to out-goe,
  But he them both outran a wondrous space,
  For he was long, and swift as any Roe,
And now made better speed, t'escape his feared foe.

6

It was not *Satyrane*, whom he did feare,
  But *Britomart* the flowre of chastity;
  For he the powre of chast hands might not beare,
  But always did their dread encounter fly
  And now so fast his feet he did apply,
  That he has gotten to a forrest neare,
  Where he is shrowded in security.
  The wood they enter, and search every where,
They searched diversely, so both divided were.

7

Faire *Britomart* so long him followed,
  That she at last came to a fountaine sheare,
By which there lay a knight all wallowed
Upon the grassy ground, and by him neare
His haberjeon, his helmet, and his speare;
  A little off, his shield was rudely throwne,
  On which the winged boy in colours cleare
Depeincted was, full easie to be knowne,
And he thereby, where ever it in field was showne.

8

His face upon the ground did groveling ly,
  As if he had bene slombring in the shade,
That the brave Mayd would not for courtesy,
Out of his quiet slomber him abrade,
Nor seeme too suddeinly him to invade:
  Still as she stood, she heard with grievous throb
  Him grone, as if his hart were peeces made,
And with most painefull pangs to sigh and sob,
That pitty did the Virgins hart of patience rob.

9

At last forth breaking into bitter plaintes
  He said; O soveraigne Lord that sit'st on hye,
And raignst in blis emongst thy blessed Saintes,
How suffrest thou such shamefull cruelty,
So long unwreaked of thine enimy?
  Or hast thou, Lord, of good mens cause no heed?
  Or doth thy justice sleepe, and silent ly?
What booteth then the good and righteous deed,
If goodnesse find no grace, nor righteousnesse no meed?

10

If good find grace, and righteousnesse reward,
  Why then is *Amoret* in caytive band,
Sith that more bounteous creature never far'd
On foot, upon the face of living land?
Or if that heavenly justice may withstand
  The wrongfull outrage of unrighteous men,
  Why then is *Busirane* with wicked hand
Suffred, these seven monethes day in secret den
My Lady and my love so cruelly to pen?

11

My Lady and my love is cruelly pend
  In dolefull darkenesse from the vew of day,
  Whilest deadly torments do her chast brest rend,
  And the sharpe steele doth rive her hart in tway,
  All for she *Scudamore* will not denay.
  Yet thou vile man, vile *Scudamore* art sound,
  Ne canst her ayde, ne canst her foe dismay;
  Unworthy wretch to tread upon the ground,
For whom so faire a Lady feeles so sore a wound.

12

There an huge heape of singultes did oppresse
  His strugling soule, and swelling throbs empeach
  His foltring toung with pangs of drerinesse,
  Choking the remnant of his plaintife speach,
  As if his dayes were come to their last reach.
  Which when she heard, and saw the ghastly fit,
  Threatning into his life to make a breach,
  Both with great ruth and terrour she was smit,
Fearing least from her cage the wearie soule would flit.

13

Tho stooping downe she him amoved light;
  Who therewith somewhat starting, up gan looke,
  And seeing him behind a straunger knight,
  Whereas no living creature he mistooke,
  With great indignaunce he that sight forsooke,
  And downe againe himselfe disdainefully
  Abjecting, th'earth with his faire forhead strooke:
  Which the bold Virgin seeing, gan apply
Fit medcine to his griefe, and spake thus courtesly.

14

Ah gentle knight, whose deepe conceived griefe
  Well seemes t'exceede the powre of patience,
  Yet if that heavenly grace some good reliefe
  You send, submit you to high providence,
  And ever in your noble hart prepense,
  That all the sorrow in the world is lesse,
  Than vertues might, and values confidence,
  For who nill bide the burden of distresse,
Must not here thinke to live: for life is wretchednesse.

15

Therefore, faire Sir, do comfort to you take,
    And freely read, what wicked felon so
    Hath outrag'd you, and thrald your gentle make.
    Perhaps this hand may helpe to ease your woe,
    And wreake your sorrow on your cruell foe,
    At least it faire endevour will apply.
    Those feeling wordes so neare the quicke did goe,
    That up his head he reared easily,
And leaning on his elbow, these few wordes let fly.

16

What boots it plaine, that cannot be redrest,
    And sow vaine sorrow in a fruitlesse eare,
    Sith powre of hand, nor skill of learned brest,
    Ne worldly price cannot redeeme my deare,
    Out of her thraldome and continuall feare?
    For he the tyraunt, which her hath in ward
    By strong enchauntments and blacke Magicke leare,
    Hath in a dungeon deepe her close embard,
And many dreadfull feends hath pointed to her gard.

17

There he tormenteth her most terribly,
    And day and night afflicts with mortall paine,
    Because to yield him love she doth deny,
    Once to me yold, not to be yold againe:
    But yet by torture he would her constraine
    Love to conceive in her disdainfull brest;
    Till so she do, she must in doole remaine,
    Ne may by living meanes be thence relest:
What boots it then to plaine, that cannot be redrest?

18

With this sad hersall of his heavy stresse,
    The warlike Damzell was empassiond sore,
    And said; Sir knight, your cause is nothing lesse,
    Than is your sorrow, certes if not more;
    For nothing so much pitty doth implore,
    As gentle Ladies helplesse misery.
    But yet, if please ye listen to my lore,
    I will with proofe of last extremity,
Deliver her fro thence, or with her for you dy.

19

Ah gentlest knight alive, (said *Scudamore*)
   What huge heroicke magnanimity
   Dwels in thy bounteous brest? what couldst thou more,
   If she were thine, and thou as now am I?
   O spare thy happy dayes, and them apply
   To better boot, but let me dye, that ought;
   More is more losse: one is enough to dy.
   Life is not lost, (said she) for which is bought
Endlesse renowm, that more than death is to be sought.

20

Thus she at length perswaded him to rise,
   And with her wend, to see what new successe
   Mote him befall upon new enterprise;
   His armes, which he had vowed to disprofesse,
   She gathered up and did about him dresse,
   And his forwandred steed unto him got:
   So forth they both yfere make their progresse,
   And march not past the mountenaunce of a shot,
Till they arriv'd, whereas their purpose they did plot.

21

There they dismounting, drew their weapons bold
   And stoutly came unto the Castle gate;
   Whereas no gate they found, them to withhold,
   Nor ward to wait at morne and evening late,
   But in the Porch, that did them sore amate,
   A flaming fire, ymixt with smouldry smoke,
   And stinking Sulphure, that with griesly hate
   And dreadfull horrour did all entraunce choke,
Enforced them their forward footing to revoke.

22

Greatly thereat was *Britomart* dismayd,
   Ne in that stownd wist, how her selfe to beare;
   For daunger vaine it were, to have assayd
   That cruell element, which all things feare,
   Ne none can suffer to approchen neare:
   And turning backe to *Scudamour*, thus sayd;
   What monstrous enmity provoke we heare,
   Foolhardy as th'Earthes children, the which made
Battell against the Gods? so we a God invade.

23

Daunger without discretion to attempt,
　Inglorious and beastlike is: therefore Sir knight,
　Aread what course of you is safest dempt,
　And how we with our foe may come to fight.
　This is (quoth he) the dolorous despight,
　Which earst to you I playnd: for neither may
　This fire be quencht by any wit or might,
　Ne yet by any meanes remov'd away,
So mighty be th'enchauntments, which the same do stay.

24

What is there else, but cease these fruitlesse paines,
　And leave me to my former languishing?
　Faire *Amoret* must dwell in wicked chaines,
　And *Scudamore* here dye with sorrowing.
　Perdy not so; (said she) for shamefull thing
　It were t'abandon noble chevisaunce,
　For shew of perill, without venturing:
　Rather let try extremities of chaunce,
Than enterprised prayse for dread to disavaunce.

25

Therewith resolv'd to prove her utmost might,
　Her ample shield she threw before her face,
　And her swords point directing forward right,
　Assayld the flame, the which eftsoones gave place,
　And did it selfe divide with equall space,
　That through she passed; as a thunder bolt
　Perceth the yielding ayre, and doth displace
　The soring clouds into sad showres ymolt;
So to her yold the flames, and did their force revolt.

26

Whom whenas *Scudamour* saw past the fire,
　Safe and untoucht, he likewise gan assay,
　With greedy will, and envious desire,
　And bad the stubborne flames to yield him way:
　But cruell *Mulciber* would not obay
　His threatfull pride, but did the more augment
　His mighty rage, and with imperious sway
　Him forst (maulgre) his fiercenesse to relent,
And backe retire, all scorcht and pitifully brent.

27

With huge impatience he inly swelt,
　More for great sorrow, that he could not pas,
　Than for the burning torment, which he felt,
　That with fell woodnesse he effierced was,
　And wilfully him throwing on the gras,
　Did beat and bounse his head and brest full sore;
　The whiles the Championesse now entred has
　The utmost rowme, and past the formest dore,
The utmost rowme, abounding with all precious store.

28

For round about, the wals yclothed were
　With goodly arras of great majesty,
　Woven with gold and silke so close and nere,
　That the rich metall lurked privily,
　As faining to be hid from envious eye;
　Yet here, and there, and every where unwares
　It shewd it selfe, and shone unwillingly;
　Like a discolourd Snake, whose hidden snares
Through the greene gras his long bright burnisht backe declares.

29

And in those Tapets weren fashioned
　Many faire pourtraicts, and many a faire feate,
　And all of love, and all of lusty-hed,
　As seemed by their semblaunt did entreat;
　And eke all *Cupids* warres they did repeate,
　And cruell battels, which he whilome fought
　Gainst all the Gods, to make his empire great;
　Besides the huge massacres, which he wrought
On mighty kings and kesars, into thraldome brought.

30

Therein was writ, how often thundring *Jove*
　Had felt the point of his hart-percing dart,
　And leaving heavens kingdome, here did rove
　In straunge disguize, to slake his scalding smart;
　Now like a Ram, faire *Helle* to pervart,
　Now like a Bull, *Europa* to withdraw:
　Ah, how the fearefull Ladies tender hart
　Did lively seeme to tremble, when she saw
The huge seas under her t'obay her servaunts law.

31

Soone after that into a golden showre
　Him selfe he chaung'd faire *Danaë* to vew,
And through the roofe of her strong brasen towre
　Did raine into her lap an hony dew,
　The whiles her foolish garde, that little knew
Of such deceipt, kept th'yron dore fast bard,
　And watcht, that none should enter nor issew;
　Vaine was the watch, and bootlesse all the ward,
Whenas the God to golden hew him selfe transfard.

32

Then was he turnd into a snowy Swan,
　To win faire *Leda* to his lovely trade:
O wondrous skill, and sweet wit of the man,
　That her in daffadillies sleeping made,
　From scorching heat her daintie limbes to shade:
Whiles the proud Bird ruffing his fethers wyde,
　And brushing his faire brest, did her invade;
　She slept, yet twixt her eyelids closely spyde,
How towards her he rusht, and smiled at his pryde.

33

Then shewd it, how the *Thebane Semelee*
　Deceiv'd of gealous *Juno*, did require
To see him in his soveraigne majestee,
　Armd with his thunderbolts and lightning fire,
　Whence dearely she with death bought her desire.
But faire *Alcmena* better match did make,
　Joying his love in likenesse more entire;
　Three nights in one, they say, that for her sake
He then did put, her pleasures lenger to partake.

34

Twise was he seene in soaring Eagles shape,
　And with wide wings to beat the buxome ayre,
Once, when he with *Asterie* did scape,
　Againe, when as the *Trojane* boy so faire
　He snatcht from *Ida* hill, and with him bare:
Wondrous delight it was, there to behould,
　How the rude Shepheards after him did stare,
　Trembling through feare, least down he fallen should,
And often to him calling, to take surer hould.

35

In *Satyres* shape *Antiopa* he snatcht:
  And like a fire, when he *Aegin'* assayd:
  A shepheard, when *Mnemosyne* he catcht:
  And like a Serpent to the *Thracian* mayd.
  Whiles thus on earth great *Jove* these pageaunts playd,
  The winged boy did thrust into his throne,
  And scoffing, thus unto his mother sayd,
  Lo now the heavens obey to me alone,
And take me for their *Jove*, whiles *Jove* to earth is gone.

36

And thou, faire *Phœbus*, in thy colours bright
  Wast there enwoven, and the sad distresse,
  In which that boy thee plonged, for despight,
  That thou bewray'dst his mothers wantonnesse,
  When she with *Mars* was meynt in joyfulnesse:
  For thy he thrild thee with a leaden dart,
  To love faire *Daphne*, which thee loved lesse:
  Lesse she thee lov'd, than was thy just desart,
Yet was thy love her death, and her death was thy smart.

37

So lovedst thou the lusty *Hyacinct*,
  So lovedst thou the faire *Coronis* deare:
  Yet both are of thy haplesse hand extinct,
  Yet both in flowres do live, and love thee beare,
  The one a Paunce, the other a sweet breare:
  For griefe whereof, ye mote have lively seene
  The God himselfe rending his golden heare,
  And breaking quite his gyrlond ever greene,
With other signes of sorrow and impatient teene.

38

Both for those two, and for his owne deare sonne,
  The sonne of *Climene* he did repent,
  Who bold to guide the charet of the Sunne,
  Himselfe in thousand peeces fondly rent,
  And all the world with flashing fier brent;
  So like, that all the walles did seeme to flame.
  Yet cruell *Cupid*, not herewith content,
  Forst him eftsoones to follow other game,
And love a Shepheards daughter for his dearest Dame.

39

He loved *Isse* for his dearest Dame,
  And for her sake her cattell fed a while,
  And for her sake a cowheard vile became,
  The servant of *Admetus* cowheard vile,
  Whiles that from heaven he suffered exile.
  Long were to tell each other lovely fit,
  Now like a Lyon, hunting after spoile,
  Now like a Stag, now like a faulcon flit:
All which in that faire arras was most lively writ.

40

Next unto him was *Neptune* pictured,
  In his divine resemblance wondrous lyke:
  His face was rugged, and his hoarie hed
  Dropped with brackish deaw; his three-forkt Pyke
  He stearnly shooke, and therewith fierce did stryke
  The raging billowes, that on every syde
  They trembling stood, and made a long broad dyke,
  That his swift charet might have passage wyde,
Which foure great *Hippodames* did draw in temewise tyde.

41

His sea-horses did seeme to snort amayne,
  And from their nosethrilles blow the brynie streame,
  That made the sparckling waves to smoke agayne,
  And flame with gold, but the white fomy creame,
  Did shine with silver, and shoot forth his beame.
  The God himselfe did pensive seeme and sad,
  And hong adowne his head, as he did dreame:
  For privy love his brest empierced had,
Ne ought but deare *Bisaltis* ay could make him glad.

42

He loved eke *Iphimedia* deare,
  And *Aeolus* faire daughter *Arne* hight,
  For whom he turnd him selfe into a Steare,
  And fed on fodder, to beguile her sight.
  Also to win *Deucalions* daughter bright,
  He turnd him selfe into a Dolphin fayre;
  And like a winged horse he tooke his flight,
  To snaky-locke *Medusa* to repayre,
On whom he got faire *Pegasus*, that flitteth in the ayre.

43

Next *Saturne* was, (but who would ever weene,
  That sullein *Saturne* ever weend to love?
  Yet love is sullein, and *Saturnlike* seene,
  As he did for *Erigone* it prove,)
  That to a *Centaure* did him selfe transmove.
  So proov'd it eke that gracious God of wine,
  When for to compasse *Philliras* hard love,
  He turnd himselfe into a fruitfull vine,
And into her faire bosome made his grapes decline.

44

Long were to tell the amorous assayes,
  And gentle pangues, with which he maked meeke
  The mighty *Mars*, to learne his wanton playes:
  How oft for *Venus*, and how often eek
  For many other Nymphes he sore did shreek,
  With womanish teares, and with unwarlike smarts,
  Privily moystening his horrid cheek.
  There was he painted full of burning darts,
And many wide woundes launched through his inner parts.

45

Ne did he spare (so cruell was the Elfe)
  His owne deare mother, (ah why should he so?)
  Ne did he spare sometime to pricke himselfe,
  That he might tast the sweet consuming woe,
  Which he had wrought to many others moe.
  But to declare the mournfull Tragedyes,
  And spoiles, wherewith he all the ground did strow,
  More eath to number, with how many eyes
High heaven beholds sad lovers nightly theeveryes.

46

Kings Queenes, Lords Ladies, Knights and Damzels gent
  Were heap'd together with the vulgar sort,
  And mingled with the raskall rablement,
  Without respect of person or of port,
  To shew Dan *Cupids* powre and great effort:
  And round about a border was entrayld,
  Of broken bowes and arrowes shivered short,
  And a long bloudy river through them rayld,
So lively and so like, that living sence it fayld.

47

And at the upper end of that faire rowme,
  There was an Altar built of pretious stone,
  Of passing valew, and of great renowme,
  On which there stood an Image all alone,
  Of massy gold, which with his owne light shone;
  And wings it had with sundry colours dight,
  More sundry colours, than the proud *Pavone*
  Beares in his boasted fan, or *Iris* bright,
When her discolourd bow she spreds through heaven bright.

48

Blindfold he was, and in his cruell fist
  A mortall bow and arrowes keene did hold,
  With which he shot at randon, when him list,
  Some headed with sad lead, some with pure gold;
  (Ah man beware, how thou those darts behold)
  A wounded Dragon under him did ly,
  Whose hideous tayle his left foot did enfold,
  And with a shaft was shot through either eye,
That no man forth might draw, ne no man remedye.

49

And underneath his feet was written thus,
  Unto the Victor of the Gods this bee:
  And all the people in that ample hous
  Did to that image bow their humble knee,
  And oft committed fowle Idolatree.
  That wondrous sight faire *Britomart* amazed,
  Ne seeing could her wonder satisfie,
  But evermore and more upon it gazed,
The whiles the passing brightnes her fraile sences dazed.

50

Tho as she backward cast her busie eye,
  To search each secret of that goodly sted,
  Over the dore thus written she did spye
  Be bold: she oft and oft it over-red,
  Yet could not find what sence it figured:
  But what so were therein or writ or ment,
  She was no whit thereby discouraged
  From prosecuting of her first intent,
But forward with bold steps into the next roome went.

51

Much fairer, than the former, was that roome,
  And richlier by many partes arayd:
For not with arras made in painefull loome,
But with pure gold it all was overlayd,
Wrought with wilde Antickes, which their follies playd,
In the rich metall, as they living were:
A thousand monstrous formes therein were made,
Such as false love doth oft upon him weare,
For love in thousand monstrous formes doth oft appeare.

52

And all about, the glistring walles were hong
  With warlike spoiles, and with victorious prayes,
Of mighty Conquerours and Captaines strong,
Which were whilome captived in their dayes
To cruell love, and wrought their owne decayes:
Their swerds and speres were broke, and hauberques rent;
And their proud girlonds of tryumphant bayes
Troden in dust with fury insolent,
To shew the victors might and mercilesse intent.

53

The warlike Mayde beholding earnestly
  The goodly ordinance of this rich place,
Did greatly wonder, ne could satisfie
Her greedy eyes with gazing a long space,
But more she mervaild that no footings trace,
Nor wight appear'd, but wastefull emptinesse,
And solemne silence over all that place:
Straunge thing it seem'd, that none was to possesse
So rich purveyance, ne them keepe with carefulnesse.

54

And as she lookt about, she did behold,
  How over that same dore was likewise writ,
Be bold, be bold, and every where *Be bold,*
That much she muz'd, yet could not construe it
By any ridling skill, or commune wit.
At last she spyde at that roomes upper end,
Another yron dore, on which was writ,
Be not too bold; whereto though she did bend
Her earnest mind, yet wist not what it might intend.

55

Thus she there waited untill eventyde,
Yet living creature none she saw appeare:
And now sad shadowes gan the world to hyde,
From mortall vew, and wrap in darkenesse dreare;
Yet nould she d'off her weary armes, for feare
Of secret daunger, ne let sleepe oppresse
Her heavy eyes with natures burdein deare,
But drew her selfe aside in sickernesse,
And her welpointed weapons did about her dresse.

CANT. XII

The maske of Cupid, and th'enchaunted
Chamber are displayd.
Whence Britomart redeemes faire
Amoret, through charmes decayd.

I

THO when as chearelesse Night ycovered had
Faire heaven with an universall cloud,
That every wight dismayd with darknesse sad,
In silence and in sleepe themselves did shroud,
She heard a shrilling Trompet sound aloud,
Signe of nigh battell, or got victory;
Nought therewith daunted was her courage proud,
But rather stird to cruell enmity,
Expecting ever, when some foe she might descry.

2

With that, an hideous storme of winde arose,
With dreadfull thunder and lightning atwixt,
And an earth-quake, as if it streight would lose
The worlds foundations from his centre fixt;
A direfull stench of smoke and sulphure mixt
Ensewd, whose noyance fild the fearefull sted,
From the fourth houre of night untill the sixt;
Yet the bold *Britonesse* was nought ydred,
Though much emmov'd, but stedfast still persevered.

3

All suddenly a stormy whirlwind blew
   Throughout the house, that clapped every dore,
   With which that yron wicket open flew,
   As it with mightie levers had bene tore:
   And forth issewd, as on the ready flore
   Of some Theatre, a grave personage,
   That in his hand a branch of laurell bore,
   With comely haveour and count'nance sage,
Yclad in costly garments, fit for tragicke Stage.

4

Proceeding to the midst, he still did stand,
   As if in mind he somewhat had to say,
   And to the vulgar beckning with his hand,
   In signe of silence, as to heare a play,
   By lively actions he gan bewray
   Some argument of matter passioned;
   Which doen, he backe retyred soft away,
   And passing by, his name discovered,
Ease, on his robe in golden letters cyphered.

5

The noble Mayd, still standing all this vewd,
   And merveild at his strange intendiment;
   With that a joyous fellowship issewd
   Of Minstrals, making goodly meriment,
   With wanton Bardes, and Rymers impudent,
   All which together sung full chearefully
   A lay of loves delight, with sweet concent:
   After whom marcht a jolly company,
In manner of a maske, enranged orderly.

6

The whiles a most delitious harmony,
   In full straunge notes was sweetly heard to sound,
   That the rare sweetnesse of the melody
   The feeble senses wholly did confound,
   And the fraile soule in deepe delight nigh dround:
   And when it ceast, shrill trompets loud did bray,
   That their report did farre away rebound,
   And when they ceast, it gan againe to play,
The whiles the maskers marched forth in trim aray.

7

The first was *Fancy*, like a lovely boy,
　Of rare aspect, and beautie without peare;
　Matchable either to that ympe of *Troy*,
　Whom *Jove* did love, and chose his cup to beare,
　Or that same daintie lad, which was so deare
　To great *Alcides*, that when as he dyde,
　He wailed womanlike with many a teare,
　And every wood, and every valley wyde
He fild with *Hylas* name; the Nymphes eke *Hylas* cryde.

8

His garment neither was of silke nor say,
　But painted plumes, in goodly order dight,
　Like as the sunburnt *Indians* do aray
　Their tawney bodies, in their proudest plight:
　As those same plumes, so seemd he vaine and light,
　That by his gate might easily appeare;
　For still he far'd as dauncing in delight,
　And in his hand a windy fan did beare,
That in the idle aire he mov'd still here and there.

9

And him beside marcht amorous *Desyre*,
　Who seemd of riper yeares, than th'other Swaine,
　Yet was that other swayne this elders syre,
　And gave him being, commune to them twaine:
　His garment was disguised very vaine,
　And his embrodered Bonet sat awry;
　Twixt both his hands few sparkes he close did straine,
　Which still he blew, and kindled busily,
That soone they life conceiv'd, and forth in flames did fly.

10

Next after him went *Doubt*, who was yclad
　In a discolour'd cote, of straunge disguyse,
　That at his backe a brode Capuccio had,
　And sleeves dependant *Albanese*-wyse:
　He lookt askew with his mistrustfull eyes,
　And nicely trode, as thornes lay in his way,
　Or that the flore to shrinke he did avyse,
　And on a broken reed he still did stay
His feeble steps, which shrunke, when hard theron he lay.

11

With him went *Daunger*, cloth'd in ragged weed,
   Made of Beares skin, that him more dreadfull made,
   Yet his owne face was dreadfull, ne did need
   Straunge horrour, to deforme his griesly shade;
   A net in th'one hand, and a rustie blade
   In th'other was, this Mischiefe, that Mishap;
   With th'one his foes he threatned to invade,
   With th'other he his friends ment to enwrap:
For whom he could not kill, he practizd to entrap.

12

Next him was *Feare*, all arm'd from top to toe,
   Yet thought himselfe not safe enough thereby,
   But feard each shadow moving to and fro,
   And his owne armes when glittering he did spy,
   Or clashing heard, he fast away did fly,
   As ashes pale of hew, and wingyheeld;
   And evermore on daunger fixt his eye,
   Gainst whom he alwaies bent a brasen shield,
Which his right hand unarmed fearefully did wield.

13

With him went *Hope* in rancke, a handsome Mayd,
   Of chearefull looke and lovely to behold;
   In silken samite she was light arayd,
   And her faire lockes were woven up in gold;
   She alway smyld, and in her hand did hold
   An holy water Sprinckle, dipt in deowe,
   With which she sprinckled favours manifold,
   On whom she list, and did great liking sheowe,
Great liking unto many, but true love to feowe.

14

And after them *Dissemblance*, and *Suspect*
   Marcht in one rancke, yet an unequall paire:
   For she was gentle, and of milde aspect,
   Courteous to all, and seeming debonaire,
   Goodly adorned, and exceeding faire:
   Yet was that all but painted, and purloynd,
   And her bright browes were deckt with borrowed haire:
   Her deedes were forged, and her words false coynd,
And alwaies in her hand two clewes of silke she twynd.

15

But he was foule, ill favoured, and grim,
  Under his eyebrowes looking still askaunce;
  And ever as *Dissemblance* laught on him,
  He lowrd on her with daungerous eyeglaunce;
  Shewing his nature in his countenance;
  His rolling eyes did never rest in place,
  But walkt each where, for feare of hid mischaunce,
  Holding a lattice still before his face,
Through which he still did peepe, as forward he did pace.

16

Next him went *Griefe*, and *Fury* matcht yfere;
  Griefe all in sable sorrowfully clad,
  Downe hanging his dull head with heavy chere,
  Yet inly being more, than seeming sad:
  A paire of Pincers in his hand he had,
  With which he pinched people to the hart,
  That from thenceforth a wretched life they lad,
  In wilfull languor and consuming smart,
Dying each day with inward wounds of dolours dart.

17

But *Fury* was full ill appareiled
  In rags, that naked nigh she did appeare,
  With ghastly lookes and dreadfull drerihed;
  For from her backe her garments she did teare,
  And from her head oft rent her snarled heare:
  In her right hand a firebrand she did tosse
  About her head, still roming here and there;
  As a dismayed Deare in chace embost,
Forgetfull of his safety, hath his right way lost.

18

After them went *Displeasure* and *Pleasance*,
  He looking lompish and full sullein sad,
  And hanging downe his heavy countenance;
  She chearefull fresh and full of joyance glad,
  As if no sorrow she ne felt ne drad;
  That evill matched paire they seemd to bee:
  An angry Waspe th'one in a viall had
  Th'other in hers an hony-lady Bee;
Thus marched these six couples forth in faire degree.

19

After all these there marcht a most faire Dame,
  Led of two grysie villeins, th'one *Despight*,
  The other cleped *Cruelty* by name:
  She dolefull Lady, like a dreary Spright,
  Cald by strong charmes out of eternall night,
  Had deathes owne image figurd in her face,
  Full of sad signes, fearefull to living sight;
  Yet in that horror shewd a seemely grace,
And with her feeble feet did move a comely pace.

20

Her brest all naked, as net ivory,
  Without adorne of gold or silver bright,
  Wherewith the Craftesman wonts it beautify,
  Of her dew honour was despoyled quight,
  And a wide wound therein (O ruefull sight)
  Entrenched deepe with knife accursed keene,
  Yet freshly bleeding forth her fainting spright,
  (The worke of cruell hand) was to be seene,
That dyde in sanguine red her skin all snowy cleene.

21

At that wide orifice her trembling hart
  Was drawne forth, and in silver basin layd,
  Quite through transfixed with a deadly dart,
  And in her bloud yet steeming fresh embayd:
  And those two villeins, which her steps upstayd,
  When her weake feete could scarcely her sustaine,
  And fading vitall powers gan to fade,
  Her forward still with torture did constraine,
And evermore encreased her consuming paine.

22

Next after her the winged God himselfe
  Came riding on a Lion ravenous,
  Taught to obay the menage of that Elfe,
  That man and beast with powre imperious
  Subdeweth to his kingdome tyrannous:
  His blindfold eyes he bad a while unbind,
  That his proud spoyle of that same dolorous
  Faire Dame he might behold in perfect kind;
Which seene, he much rejoyced in his cruell mind.

23

Of which full proud, himselfe up rearing hye,
　He looked round about with sterne disdaine;
　And did survay his goodly company:
　And marshalling the evill ordered traine,
　With that the darts which his right hand did straine,
　Full dreadfully he shooke that all did quake,
　And clapt on hie his coulourd winges twaine,
　That all his many it affraide did make:
Tho blinding him againe, his way he forth did take.

24

Behinde him was *Reproch, Repentance, Shame*;
　Reproch the first, *Shame* next, *Repent* behind:
　Repentance feeble, sorrowfull, and lame:
　Reproch despightfull, carelesse, and unkind;
　Shame most ill favourd, bestiall, and blind:
　Shame lowrd, *Repentance* sigh'd, *Reproch* did scould;
　Reproch sharpe stings, *Repentance* whips entwind,
　Shame burning brond-yrons in her hand did hold:
All three to each unlike, yet all made in one mould.

25

And after them a rude confused rout
　Of persons flockt, whose names is hard to read:
　Emongst them was sterne *Strife*, and *Anger* stout,
　Unquiet *Care*, and fond *Unthriftihead*,
　Lewd *Losse of Time*, and *Sorrow* seeming dead,
　Inconstant *Chaunge*, and false *Disloyaltie*,
　Consuming *Riotise*, and guilty *Dread*
　Of heavenly vengeance, faint *Infirmitie*,
Vile *Povertie*, and lastly *Death* with infamie.

26

There were full many moe like maladies,
　Whose names and natures I note readen well;
　So many moe, as there be phantasies
　In wavering wemens wit, that none can tell,
　Or paines in love, or punishments in hell;
　All which disguized marcht in masking wise,
　About the chamber with that Damozell,
　And then returned, having marched thrise,
Into the inner roome, from whence they first did rise.

27

So soone as they were in, the dore streight way
   Fast locked, driven with that stormy blast,
   Which first it opened; and bore all away.
   Then the brave Maid, which all this while was plast
   In secret shade, and saw both first and last,
   Issewed forth, and went unto the dore,
   To enter in, but found it locked fast:
   It vaine she thought with rigorous uprore
For to efforce, when charmes had closed it afore.

28

Where force might not availe, there sleights and art
   She cast to use, both fit for hard emprize;
   For thy from that same roome not to depart
   Till morrow next, she did her selfe avize,
   When that same Maske againe should forth arize.
   The morrow next appeard with joyous cheare,
   Calling men to their daily exercize,
   Then she, as morrow fresh, her selfe did reare
Out of her secret stand, that day for to out weare.

29

All that day she outwore in wandering,
   And gazing on that Chambers ornament,
   Till that againe the second evening
   Her covered with her sable vestiment,
   Wherewith the worlds faire beautie she hath blent:
   Then when the second watch was almost past,
   That brasen dore flew open, and in went
   Bold *Britomart*, as she had late forecast,
Neither of idle shewes, nor of false charmes aghast.

30

So soone as she was entred, round about
   She cast her eies, to see what was become
   Of all those persons, which she saw without:
   But lo, they streight were vanisht all and some,
   Ne living wight she saw in all that roome,
   Save that same woefull Ladie, both whose hands
   Were bounden fast, that did her ill become,
   And her small wast girt round with yron bands,
Unto a brasen pillour, by the which she stands.

31

And her before the vile Enchaunter sate,
　Figuring straunge characters of his art,
　With living bloud he those characters wrate,
　Dreadfully dropping from her dying hart,
　Seeming transfixed with a cruell dart,
　And all perforce to make her him to love.
　Ah who can love the worker of her smart?
　A thousand charmes he formerly did prove;
Yet thousand charmes could not her stedfast heart remove.

32

Soone as that virgin knight he saw in place,
　His wicked bookes in hast he overthrew,
　Not caring his long labours to deface,
　And fiercely ronning to that Lady trew,
　A murdrous knife out of his pocket drew,
　The which he thought, for villeinous despight,
　In her tormented bodie to embrew:
　But the stout Damzell to him leaping light,
His cursed hand withheld, and maistered his might.

33

From her, to whom his fury first he ment,
　The wicked weapon rashly he did wrest,
　And turning to her selfe his fell intent,
　Unwares it strooke into her snowie chest,
　That little drops empurpled her faire brest.
　Exceeding wroth therewith the virgin grew,
　Albe the wound were nothing deepe imprest,
　And fiercely forth her mortall blade she drew,
To give him the reward for such vile outrage dew.

34

So mightily she smote him, that to ground
　He fell halfe dead; next stroke him should have slaine,
　Had not the Lady, which by him stood bound,
　Dernely unto her called to abstaine,
　From doing him to dy. For else her paine
　Should be remedilesse, sith none but hee,
　Which wrought it, could the same recure againe.
　Therewith she stayd her hand, loth stayd to bee;
For life she him envyde, and long'd revenge to see.

35

And to him said, Thou wicked man, whose meed
  For so huge mischiefe, and vile villany
  Is death, or if that ought do death exceed,
  Be sure, that nought may save thee from to dy,
  But if that thou this Dame doe presently
  Restore unto her health, and former state;
  This doe and live, else die undoubtedly.
  He glad of life, that lookt for death but late,
Did yield himselfe right willing to prolong his date.

36

And rising up, gan streight to overlooke
  Those cursed leaves, his charmes backe to reverse;
  Full dreadfull things out of that balefull booke
  He red, and measur'd many a sad verse,
  That horror gan the virgins hart to perse,
  And her faire locks up stared stiffe on end,
  Hearing him those same bloudy lines reherse;
  And all the while he red, she did extend
Her sword high over him, if ought he did offend.

37

Anon she gan perceive the house to quake,
  And all the dores to rattle round about;
  Yet all that did not her dismaied make,
  Nor slacke her threatfull hand for daungers dout,
  But still with stedfast eye and courage stout
  Abode, to weet what end would come of all.
  At last that mightie chaine, which round about
  Her tender waste was wound, adowne gan fall,
And that great brasen pillour broke in peeces small.

38

The cruell steele, which thrild her dying hart,
  Fell softly forth, as of his owne accord,
  And the wyde wound, which lately did dispart
  Her bleeding brest, and riven bowels gor'd,
  Was closed up, as it had not bene bor'd,
  And every part to safety full sound,
  As she were never hurt, was soone restor'd:
  Tho when she felt her selfe to be unbound,
And perfect hole, prostrate she fell unto the ground.

39

Before faire *Britomart*, she fell prostrate,
  Saying, Ah noble knight, what worthy meed
  Can wretched Lady, quit from wofull state,
  Yield you in liew of this your gratious deed?
  Your vertue selfe her owne reward shall breed,
  Even immortall praise, and glory wyde,
  Which I your vassall, by your prowesse freed,
  Shall through the world make to be notifyde,
And goodly well advance, that goodly well was tryde.

40

But *Britomart* uprearing her from ground,
  Said, Gentle Dame, reward enough I weene
  For many labours more, than I have found,
  This, that in safety now I have you seene,
  And meane of your deliverance have beene:
  Henceforth faire Lady comfort to you take,
  And put away remembrance of late teene;
  In stead thereof know, that your loving Make,
Hath no lesse griefe endured for your gentle sake.

41

She much was cheard to heare him mentiond,
  Whom of all living wights she loved best.
  Then laid the noble Championesse strong hond
  Upon th'enchaunter, which had her distrest
  So sore, and with foule outrages opprest:
  With that great chaine, wherewith not long ygo
  He bound that pitteous Lady prisoner, now relest,
  Himselfe she bound, more worthy to be so,
And captive with her led to wretchednesse and wo.

42

Returning backe, those goodly roomes, which erst
  She saw so rich and royally arayd,
  Now vanisht utterly, and cleane subverst
  She found, and all their glory quite decayd,
  That sight of such a chaunge her much dismayd.
  Thence forth descending to that perlous Porch,
  Those dreadfull flames she also found delayd,
  And quenched quite, like a consumed torch,
That erst all entrers wont so cruelly to scorch.

43

More easie issew now, than entrance late
  She found: for now that fained dreadfull flame,
  Which chokt the porch of that enchaunted gate,
  And passage bard to all, that thither came,
  Was vanisht quite, as it were not the same,
  And gave her leave at pleasure forth to passe.
  Th'Enchaunter selfe, which all that fraud did frame,
  To have efforst the love of that faire lasse,
Seeing his worke now wasted deepe engrieved was.

44

But when the victoresse arrived there,
  Where late she left the pensife *Scudamore*,
  With her owne trusty Squire, both full of feare,
  Neither of them she found where she them lore:
  Thereat her noble hart was stonisht sore;
  But most faire *Amoret*, whose gentle spright
  Now gan to feede on hope, which she before
  Conceived had, to see her owne deare knight,
Being thereof beguyld was fild with new affright.

45

But he sad man, when he had long in drede
  Awayted there for *Britomarts* returne,
  Yet saw her not nor signe of her good speed,
  His expectation to despaire did turne,
  Misdeeming sure that her those flames did burne;
  And therefore gan advize with her old Squire,
  Who her deare nourslings losse no lesse did mourne,
  Thence to depart for further aide t'enquire:
Where let them wend at will, whilest here I doe respire.

Britomart and Amoret

THE FOURTH BOOKE OF THE
FAERIE QUEENE
CONTAINING THE LEGEND OF CAMBEL
AND TELAMOND, OR OF FRIENDSHIP

1

HE rugged forhead that with grave foresight
Welds kingdomes causes, and affaires of state,
My looser rimes (I wote) doth sharply wite,
For praising love, as I have done of late,
And magnifying lovers deare debate;
By which fraile youth is oft to follie led,
Through false allurement of that pleasing baite,
That better were in vertues discipled,
Than with vaine poemes weeds to have their fancies fed.

2

Such ones ill judge of love, that cannot love,
Ne in their frosen hearts feele kindly flame:
For thy they ought not thing unknowne reprove,
Ne naturall affection faultlesse blame,
For fault of few that have abusd the same.
For it of honor and all vertue is
The roote, and brings forth glorious flowres of fame,
That crowne true lovers with immortall blis,
The meed of them that love, and do not live amisse.

3

Which who so list looke backe to former ages,
    And call to count the things that then were donne,
    Shall find, that all the workes of those wise sages,
    And brave exploits which great Heroes wonne,
    In love were either ended or begunne:
    Witnesse the father of Philosophie,
    Which to his *Critias*, shaded oft from sunne,
    Of love full manie lessons did apply,
The which these Stoicke censours cannot well deny.

4

To such therefore I do not sing at all,
    But to that sacred Saint my soveraigne Queene,
    In whose chast breast all bountie naturall,
    And treasures of true love enlocked beene,
    Bove all her sexe that ever yet was seene;
    To her I sing of love, that loveth best,
    And best is lov'd of all alive I weene:
    To her this song most fitly is addrest,
The Queene of love, and Prince of peace from heaven blest.

5

Which that she may the better deigne to heare,
    Do thou dred infant, *Venus* dearling dove,
    From her high spirit chase imperious feare,
    And use of awfull Majestie romove:
    In sted thereof with drops of melting love,
    Deawd with ambrosiall kisses, by thee gotten
    From thy sweete smyling mother from above,
    Sprinckle her heart, and haughtie courage soften,
That she may hearke to love, and reade this lesson often.

CANT. I

Fayre Britomart saves Amoret,
Duessa discord breedes
Twixt Scudamour and Blandamour:
Their fight and warlike deedes.

1

Of lovers sad calamities of old,
  Full many piteous stories doe remaine,
  But none more piteous ever was ytold,
  Than that of *Amorets* hart-binding chaine,
  And this of *Florimels* unworthie paine:
  The deare compassion of whose bitter fit
  My softened heart so sorely doth constraine,
  That I with teares full oft doe pittie it,
And oftentimes doe wish it never had bene writ.

2

For from the time that *Scudamour* her bought
  In perilous fight, she never joyed day,
  A perilous fight when he with force her brought
  From twentie Knights, that did him all assay:
  Yet fairely well he did them all dismay:
  And with great glorie both the shield of love,
  And eke the Ladie selfe he brought away,
  Whom having wedded as did him behove,
A new unknowen mischiefe did from him remove.

3

For that same vile Enchauntour *Busyran*,
  The very selfe same day that she was wedded,
  Amidst the bridale feast, whilest every man
  Surcharg'd with wine, were heedlesse and ill hedded,
  All bent to mirth before the bride was bedded,
  Brought in that mask of love which late was showen:
  And there the Ladie ill of friends bestedded,
  By way of sport, as oft in maskes is knowen,
Conveyed quite away to living wight unknowen.

4

Seven moneths he so her kept in bitter smart,
  Because his sinfull lust she would not serve,
  Untill such time as noble *Britomart*
  Released her, that else was like to sterve,
  Through cruell knife that her deare heart did kerve.
  And now she is with her upon the way,
  Marching in lovely wise, that could deserve
  No spot of blame, though spite did oft assay
To blot her with dishonor of so faire a pray.

5

Yet should it be a pleasant tale, to tell
  The diverse usage and demeanure daint,
  That each to other made, as oft befell.
  For *Amoret* right fearefull was and faint,
  Lest she with blame her honor should attaint,
  That everie word did tremble as she spake,
  And everie looke was coy, and wondrous quaint,
  And everie limbe that touched her did quake:
Yet could she not but curteous countenance to her make.

6

For well she wist, as true it was indeed,
  That her lives Lord and patrone of her health
  Right well deserved as his duefull meed,
  Her love, her service, and her utmost wealth.
  All is his justly, that all freely dealth:
  Nathlesse her honor dearer than her life,
  She sought to save, as thing reserv'd from stealth;
  Die had she lever with Enchanters knife,
Than to be false in love, profest a virgine wife.

7

Thereto her feare was made so much the greater
  Through fine abusion of that Briton mayd:
  Who for to hide her fained sex the better,
  And maske her wounded mind, both did and sayd
  Full many things so doubtfull to be wayd,
  That well she wist not what by them to gesse,
  For other whiles to her she purpos made
  Of love, and otherwhiles of lustfulnesse,
That much she feard his mind would grow to some excesse.

8

His will she feard; for him she surely thought
  To be a man, such as indeed he seemed,
  And much the more, by that he lately wrought,
  When her from deadly thraldome he redeemed,
  For which no service she too much esteemed,
  Yet dread of shame, and doubt of fowle dishonor
  Made her not yeeld so much, as due she deemed.
  Yet *Britomart* attended duly on her,
As well became a knight, and did to her all honor.

9

It so befell one evening, that they came
  Unto a Castell, lodged there to bee,
  Where many a knight, and many a lovely Dame
  Was then assembled, deeds of armes to see:
  Amongst all which was none more faire than shee,
  That many of them mov'd to eye her sore.
  The custome of that place was such, that hee
  Which had no love nor lemman there in store,
Should either winne him one, or lye without the dore.

10

Amongst the rest there was a jolly knight,
  Who being asked for his love, avow'd
  That fairest *Amoret* was his by right,
  And offred that to justifie alowd.
  The warlike virgine seeing his so prowd
  And boastfull chalenge, wexed inlie wroth,
  But for the present did her anger shrowd;
  And sayd, her love to lose she was full loth,
But either he should neither of them have, or both.

11

So foorth they went, and both together giusted;
  But that same younker soone was overthrowne,
  And made repent, that he had rashly lusted
  For thing unlawfull, that was not his owne:
  Yet since he seemed valiant, though unknowne,
  She that no lesse was courteous than stout,
  Cast how to salve, that both the custome showne
  Were kept, and yet that Knight not locked out,
That seem'd full hard t'accord two things so far in dout.

12

The Seneschall was cal'd to deeme the right,
  Whom she requir'd, that first fayre *Amoret*
  Might be to her allow'd, as to a Knight,
  That did her win and free from chalenge set:
  Which straight to her was yeelded without let.
  Then since that strange Knights love from him was quitted,
  She claim'd that to her selfe, as Ladies det,
  He as a Knight might justly be admitted;
So none should be out shut, sith all of loves were fitted.

13

With that her glistring helmet she unlaced;
  Which doft, her golden lockes, that were up bound
  Still in a knot, unto her heeles downe traced,
  And like a silken veile in compasse round
  About her backe and all her bodie wound:
  Like as the shining skie in summers night,
  What time the dayes with scorching heat abound,
  Is creasted all with lines of firie light,
That it prodigious seemes in common peoples sight.

14

Such when those Knights and Ladies all about
  Beheld her, all were with amazement smit,
  And every one gan grow in secret dout
  Of this and that, according to each wit:
  Some thought that some enchantment faygned it;
  Some, that *Bellona* in that warlike wise
  To them appear'd, with shield and armour fit;
  Some, that it was a maske of strange disguise:
So diversely each one did sundrie doubts devise.

15

But that young Knight, which through her gentle deed
  Was to that goodly fellowship restor'd,
  Ten thousand thankes did yeeld her for her meed,
  And doubly overcommen, her ador'd:
  So did they all their former strife accord;
  And eke fayre *Amoret* now freed from feare,
  More franke affection did to her afford,
  And to her bed, which she was wont forbeare,
Now freely drew, and found right safe assurance theare.

16

Where all that night they of their loves did treat,
    And hard adventures twixt themselves alone,
    That each the other gan with passion great,
    And griefull pittie privately bemone.
    The morow next so soone as *Titan* shone,
    They both uprose, and to their waies them dight:
    Long wandred they, yet never met with none,
    That to their willes could them direct aright,
Or to them tydings tell, that mote their harts delight.

17

Lo thus they rode, till at the last they spide
    Two armed Knights, that toward them did pace,
    And ech of them had ryding by his side
    A Ladie, seeming in so farre a space,
    But Ladies none they were, albee in face
    And outward shew faire semblance they did beare;
    For under maske of beautie and good grace,
    Vile treason and fowle falshood hidden were,
That mote to none but to the warie wise appeare.

18

The one of them the false *Duessa* hight,
    That now had chang'd her former wonted hew:
    For she could d'on so manie shapes in sight,
    As ever could Cameleon colours new;
    So could she forge all colours, save the trew.
    The other no whit better was than shee,
    But that such as she was, she plaine did shew;
    Yet otherwise much worse, if worse might bee,
And dayly more offensive unto each degree.

19

Her name was *Ate*, mother of debate,
    And all dissention, which doth dayly grow
    Amongst fraile men, that many a publike state
    And many a private oft doth overthrow.
    Her false *Duessa* who full well did know,
    To be most fit to trouble noble knights,
    Which hunt for honor, raised from below,
    Out of the dwellings of the damned sprights,
Where she in darknes wastes her cursed daies and nights.

20

Hard by the gates of hell her dwelling is,
   There whereas all the plagues and harmes abound,
   Which punish wicked men, that walke amisse:
   It is a darksome delve farre under ground,
   With thornes and barren brakes environd round,
   That none the same may easily out win;
   Yet many waies to enter may be found,
   But none to issue forth when one is in:
For discord harder is to end than to begin.

21

And all within the riven walls were hung
   With ragged monuments of times forepast,
   All which the sad effects of discord sung:
   There were rent robes, and broken scepters plast,
   Altars defyl'd, and holy things defast,
   Disshivered speares, and shields ytorne in twaine,
   Great cities ransackt, and strong castles rast,
   Nations captived, and huge armies slaine:
Of all which ruines there some relicks did remaine.

22

There was the signe of antique Babylon,
   Of fatall Thebes, of Rome that raigned long,
   Of sacred Salem, and sad Ilion,
   For memorie of which on high there hong
   The golden Apple, cause of all their wrong,
   For which the three faire Goddesses did strive:
   There also was the name of *Nimrod* strong,
   Of *Alexander*, and his Princes five,
Which shar'd to them the spoiles that he had got alive.

23

And there the relicks of the drunken fray,
   The which amongst the *Lapithees* befell,
   And of the bloodie feast, which sent away
   So many *Centaures* drunken soules to hell,
   That under great *Alcides* furie fell:
   And of the dreadfull discord, which did drive
   The noble *Argonauts* to outrage fell,
   That each of life sought others to deprive,
All mindlesse of the Golden fleece, which made them strive.

24

And eke of private persons many moe,
  That were too long a worke to count them all;
  Some of sworne friends, that did their faith forgoe;
  Some of borne brethren, prov'd unnaturall;
  Some of deare lovers, foes perpetuall:
  Witnesse their broken bandes there to be seene,
  Their girlonds rent, their bowres despoyled all;
  The moniments whereof there byding beene,
As plaine as at the first, when they were fresh and greene.

25

Such was her house within; but all without,
  The barren ground was full of wicked weedes,
  Which she her selfe had sowen all about,
  Now growen great, at first of little seedes,
  The seedes of evill wordes, and factious deedes;
  Which when to ripenesse due they growen arre,
  Bring foorth an infinite increase, that breedes
  Tumultuous trouble and contentious jarre,
The which most often end in bloudshed and in warre.

26

And those same cursed seedes doe also serve
  To her for bread, and yeeld her living food:
  For life it is to her, when others sterve
  Through mischievous debate, and deadly feood,
  That she may sucke their life, and drinke their blood,
  With which she from her childhood had bene fed.
  For she at first was borne of hellish brood,
  And by infernall furies nourished,
That by her monstrous shape might easily be red.

27

Her face most fowle and filthy was to see,
  With squinted eyes contrarie wayes intended,
  And loathly mouth, unmeete a mouth to bee,
  That nought but gall and venim comprehended,
  And wicked wordes that God and man offended:
  Her lying tongue was in two parts divided,
  And both the parts did speake, and both contended;
  And as her tongue, so was her hart discided,
That never thoght one thing, but doubly stil was guided.

28

Als as she double spake, so heard she double,
  With matchlesse eares deformed and distort,
  Fild with false rumors and seditious trouble,
  Bred in assemblies of the vulgar sort,
  That still are led with every light report.
  And as her eares so eke her feet were odde,
  And much unlike, th'one long, the other short,
  And both misplast; that when th'one forward yode,
The other backe retired, and contrarie trode.

29

Likewise unequall were her handes twaine,
  That one did reach, the other pusht away,
  That one did make, the other mard againe,
  And sought to bring all things unto decay;
  Whereby great riches gathered manie a day,
  She in short space did often bring to nought,
  And their possessours often did dismay.
  For all her studie was and all her thought,
How she might overthrow the things that Concord wrought.

30

So much her malice did her might surpas,
  That even th'Almightie selfe she did maligne,
  Because to man so mercifull he was,
  And unto all his creatures so benigne,
  Sith she her selfe was of his grace indigne:
  For all this worlds faire workmanship she tride,
  Unto his last confusion to bring,
  And that great golden chaine quite to divide,
With which it blessed Concord hath together tide.

31

Such was that hag, which with *Duessa* roade,
  And serving her in her malitious use,
  To hurt good knights, was as it were her baude,
  To sell her borrowed beautie to abuse.
  For though like withered tree, that wanteth juyce,
  She old and crooked were, yet now of late,
  As fresh and fragrant as the floure deluce
  She was become, by chaunge of her estate,
And made full goodly joyance to her new found mate.

32

Her mate he was a jollie youthfull knight,
That bore great sway in armes and chivalrie,
And was indeed a man of mickle might:
His name was *Blandamour*, that did descrie
His fickle mind full of inconstancie.
And now himselfe he fitted had right well,
With two companions of like qualitie,
Faithlesse *Duessa*, and false *Paridell*,
That whether were more false, full hard it is to tell.

33

Now when this gallant with his goodly crew,
From farre espide the famous *Britomart*,
Like knight adventurous in outward vew,
With his faire paragon, his conquests part,
Approching nigh, eftsoones his wanton hart
Was tickled with delight, and jesting sayd;
Lo there Sir *Paridel*, for your desart,
Good lucke presents you with yond lovely mayd,
For pitie that ye want a fellow for your ayd.

34

By that the lovely paire drew nigh to hond:
Whom when as *Paridel* more plaine beheld,
Albee in heart he like affection fond,
Yet mindfull how he late by one was feld,
That did those armes and that same scutchion weld,
He had small lust to buy his love so deare,
But answerd, Sir him wise I never held,
That having once escaped perill neare,
Would afterwards afresh the sleeping evill reare.

35

This knight too late his manhood and his might,
I did assay, that me right dearely cost,
Ne list I for revenge provoke new fight,
Ne for light Ladies love, that soone is lost.
The hot-spurre youth so scorning to be crost,
Take then to you this Dame of mine (quoth hee)
And I without your perill or your cost,
Will chalenge yond same other for my fee:
So forth he fiercely prickt, that one him scarce could see.

36

The warlike Britonesse her soone addrest,
And with such uncouth welcome did receave
Her fayned Paramour, her forced guest,
That being forst his saddle soone to leave,
Him selfe he did of his new love deceave:
And made him selfe thensample of his follie.
Which done, she passed forth not taking leave,
And left him now as sad, as whilome jollie,
Well warned to beware with whom he dar'd to dallie.

37

Which when his other companie beheld,
They to his succour ran with readie ayd:
And finding him unable once to weld,
They reared him on horsebacke, and upstayd,
Till on his way they had him forth convayd:
And all the way with wondrous griefe of mynd,
And shame, he shewd him selfe to be dismayd,
More for the love which he had left behynd,
Than that which he had to Sir *Paridel* resynd.

38

Nathlesse he forth did march well as he might,
And made good semblance to his companie,
Dissembling his disease and evill plight;
Till that ere long they chaunced to espie
Two other knights, that towards them did ply
With speedie course, as bent to charge them new.
Whom when as *Blandamour* approching nie,
Perceiv'd to be such as they seemd in vew,
He was full wo, and gan his former griefe renew.

39

For th'one of them he perfectly descride,
To be Sir *Scudamour*, by that he bore
The God of love, with wings displayed wide,
Whom mortally he hated evermore,
Both for his worth, that all men did adore,
And eke because his love he wonne by right:
Which when he thought, it grieved him full sore,
That through the bruses of his former fight,
He now unable was to wreake his old despight.

40

For thy he thus to *Paridel* bespake,
　　Faire Sir, of friendship let me now you pray,
　　That as I late adventured for your sake,
　　The hurts whereof me now from battell stay,
　　Ye will me now with like good turne repay,
　　And justifie my cause on yonder knight.
　　Ah Sir (said *Paridel*) do not dismay
　　Your selfe for this, my selfe will for you fight,
As ye have done for me: the left hand rubs the right.

41

With that he put his spurres unto his steed,
　　With speare in rest, and toward him did fare,
　　Like shaft out of a bow preventing speed.
　　But *Scudamour* was shortly well aware
　　Of his approch, and gan him selfe prepare
　　Him to receive with entertainment meete.
　　So furiously they met, that either bare
　　The other downe under their horses feete,
That what of them became, themselves did scarsly weete.

42

As when two billowes in the Irish sowndes,
　　Forcibly driven with contrarie tydes
　　Do meete together, each abacke rebowndes
　　With roaring rage; and dashing on all sides,
　　That filleth all the sea with fome, divydes
　　The doubtfull current into divers wayes:
　　So fell those two in spight of both their prydes,
　　But *Scudamour* himselfe did soone uprayse,
And mounting light his foe for lying long upbrayes.

43

Who rolled on an heape lay still in swound,
　　All carelesse of his taunt and bitter rayle
　　Till that the rest him seeing lie on ground,
　　Ran hastily, to weete what did him ayle.
　　Where finding that the breath gan him to fayle,
　　With busie care they strove him to awake,
　　And doft his helmet, and undid his mayle:
　　So much they did, that at the last they brake
His slomber, yet so mazed, that he nothing spake.

44

Which when as *Blandamour* beheld, he sayd,
  False faitour *Scudamour*, that hast by slight
  And foule advantage this good Knight dismayd,
  A Knight much better than thy selfe behight,
  Well falles it thee that I am not in plight
  This day, to wreake the dammage by thee donne:
  Such is thy wont, that still when any Knight
  Is weakned, then thou doest him overronne:
So hast thou to thy selfe false honour often wonne.

45

He little answer'd, but in manly heart
  His mightie indignation did forbeare,
  Which was not yet so secret, but some part
  Thereof did in his frouning face appeare:
  Like as a gloomie cloud, the which doth beare
  An hideous storme, is by the Northerne blast
  Quite overblowne, yet doth not passe so cleare,
  But that it all the skie doth overcast
With darknes dred, and threatens all the world to wast.

46

Ah gentle knight, then false *Duessa* sayd,
  Why do ye strive for Ladies love so sore,
  Whose chiefe desire is love and friendly aid
  Mongst gentle Knights to nourish evermore?
  Ne be ye wroth Sir *Scudamour* therefore,
  That she your love list love another knight,
  Ne do your selfe dislike a whit the more;
  For Love is free, and led with selfe delight,
Ne will enforced be with maisterdome or might.

47

So false *Duessa*, but vile *Ate* thus;
  Both foolish knights, I can but laugh at both,
  That strive and storme with stirre outrageous,
  For her that each of you alike doth loth,
  And loves another, with whom now she goth
  In lovely wise, and sleepes, and sports, and playes;
  Whilest both you here with many a cursed oth,
  Sweare she is yours, and stirre up bloudie frayes,
To win a willow bough, whilest other weares the bayes.

48

Vile hag (sayd *Scudamour*) why dost thou lye?
　And falsely seekst a vertuous wight to shame?
　Fond knight (sayd she) the thing that with this eye
　I saw, why should I doubt to tell the same?
　Then tell (quoth *Blandamour*) and feare no blame,
　Tell what thou saw'st, maulgre who so it heares.
　I saw (quoth she) a stranger knight, whose name
　I wote not well, but in his shield he beares
(That well I wote) the heads of many broken speares.

49

I saw him have your *Amoret* at will,
　I saw him kisse, I saw him her embrace,
　I saw him sleepe with her all night his fill,
　All manie nights, and manie by in place,
　That present were to testifie the case.
　Which when as *Scudamour* did heare, his heart
　Was thrild with inward griefe, as when in chace
　The Parthian strikes a stag with shivering dart,
The beast astonisht stands in middest of his smart.

50

So stood Sir *Scudamour*, when this he heard,
　Ne word he had to speake for great dismay,
　But lookt on *Glauce* grim, who woxe afeard
　Of outrage for the words, which she heard say,
　Albee untrue she wist them by assay.
　But *Blandamour*, whenas he did espie
　His chaunge of cheere, that anguish did bewray,
　He woxe full blithe, as he had got thereby,
And gan thereat to triumph without victorie.

51

Lo recreant (sayd he) the fruitlesse end
　Of thy vaine boast, and spoile of love misgotten,
　Whereby the name of knight-hood thou dost shend,
　And all true lovers with dishonor blotten,
　All things not rooted well, will soone be rotten.
　Fy fy false knight (then false *Duessa* cryde)
　Unworthy life that love with guile hast gotten,
　Be thou, where ever thou do go or ryde,
Loathed of ladies all, and of all knights defyde.

52

But *Scudamour* for passing great despight
　Staid not to answer, scarcely did refraine,
　But that in all those knights and ladies sight,
　He for revenge had guiltlesse *Glauce* slaine:
　But being past, he thus began amaine;
　False traitour squire, false squire, of falsest knight,
　Why doth mine hand from thine avenge abstaine,
　Whose Lord hath done my love this foule despight?
Why do I not it wreake, on thee now in my might?

53

Discourteous, disloyall *Britomart*,
　Untrue to God, and unto man unjust,
　What vengeance due can equall thy desart,
　That hast with shamefull spot of sinfull lust
　Defil'd the pledge committed to thy trust?
　Let ugly shame and endlesse infamy
　Colour thy name with foule reproaches rust.
　Yet thou false Squire his fault shalt deare aby,
And with thy punishment his penance shalt supply.

54

The aged Dame him seeing so enraged,
　Was dead with feare, nathlesse as neede required,
　His flaming furie sought to have assuaged
　With sober words, that sufferance desired,
　Till time the tryall of her truth expyred:
　And evermore sought *Britomart* to cleare.
　But he the more with furious rage was fyred,
　And thrise his hand to kill her did upreare,
And thrise he drew it backe: so did at last forbeare.

CANT. II

Blandamour winnes false Florimell,
Paridell for her strives,
They are accorded: Agape
doth lengthen her sonnes lives.

I

FIREBRAND of hell first tynd in Phlegeton,
By thousand furies, and from thence out throwen
Into this world, to worke confusion,
And set it all on fire by force unknowen,
Is wicked discord, whose small sparkes once blowen
None but a God or godlike man can slake;
Such as was *Orpheus*, that when strife was growen
Amongst those famous ympes of Greece, did take
His silver Harpe in hand, and shortly friends them make.

2

Or such as that celestiall Psalmist was,
That when the wicked feend his Lord tormented,
With heavenly notes, that did all other pas,
The outrage of his furious fit relented.
Such Musicke is wise words with time concented,
To moderate stiffe minds, disposd to strive:
Such as that prudent Romane well invented,
What time his people into partes did rive,
Them reconcyld againe, and to their homes did drive.

3

Such us'd wise *Glauce* to that wrathfull knight,
To calme the tempest of his troubled thought:
Yet *Blandamour* with termes of foule despight,
And *Paridell* her scornd, and set at nought,
As old and crooked and not good for ought.
Both they unwise, and warelesse of the evill,
That by themselves unto themselves is wrought,
Through that false witch, and that foule aged drevill,
The one a feend, the other an incarnate devill.

4

With whom as they thus rode accompanide,
  They were encountred of a lustie Knight,
  That had a goodly Ladie by his side,
  To whom he made great dalliance and delight.
  It was to weete the bold Sir *Ferraugh* hight,
  He that from *Braggadocchio* whilome reft
  The snowy *Florimell*, whose beautie bright
  Made him seeme happie for so glorious theft;
Yet was it in due triall but a wandring weft.

5

Which when as *Blandamour*, whose fancie light
  Was alwaies flitting as the wavering wind,
  After each beautie, that appeard in sight,
  Beheld, eftsoones it prickt his wanton mind
  With sting of lust, that reasons eye did blind,
  That to Sir *Paridell* these words he sent;
  Sir knight why ride ye dumpish thus behind,
  Since so good fortune doth to you present
So fayre a spoyle, to make you joyous meriment?

6

But *Paridell* that had too late a tryall
  Of the bad issue of his counsell vaine,
  List not to hearke, but made this faire denyall;
  Last turne was mine, well proved to my paine,
  This now be yours, God send you better gaine.
  Whose scoffed words he taking halfe in scorne,
  Fiercely forth prickt his steed as in disdaine,
  Against that Knight, ere he him well could torne:
By meanes whereof he hath him lightly overborne.

7

Who with the sudden stroke astonisht sore,
  Upon the ground a while in slomber lay;
  The whiles his love away the other bore,
  And shewing her, did *Paridell* upbray;
  Lo sluggish Knight the victors happie pray:
  So fortune friends the bold: whom *Paridell*
  Seeing so faire indeede, as he did say,
  His hart with secret envie gan to swell,
And inly grudge at him, that he had sped so well.

8

Nathlesse proud man himselfe the other deemed,
  Having so peerelesse paragon ygot:
  For sure the fayrest *Florimell* him seemed,
  To him was fallen for his happie lot,
  Whose like alive on earth he weened not:
  Therefore he her did court, did serve, did wooe,
  With humblest suit that he imagine mot,
  And all things did devise, and all things dooe,
That might her love prepare, and liking win theretoo.

9

She in regard thereof him recompenst
  With golden words, and goodly countenance,
  And such fond favours sparingly dispenst:
  Sometimes him blessing with a light eye-glance,
  And coy lookes tempring with loose dalliance;
  Sometimes estranging him in sterner wise,
  That having cast him in a foolish trance,
  He seemed brought to bed in Paradise,
And prov'd himselfe most foole, in what he seem'd most wise.

10

So great a mistresse of her art she was,
  And perfectly practiz'd in womans craft,
  That though therein himselfe he thought to pas,
  And by his false allurements wylie draft
  Had thousand women of their love beraft,
  Yet now he was surpriz'd: for that false spright,
  Which that same witch had in this forme engraft,
  Was so expert in every subtile slight,
That it could overreach the wisest earthly wight.

11

Yet he to her did dayly service more,
  And dayly more deceived was thereby;
  Yet *Paridell* him envied therefore,
  As seeming plast in sole felicity:
  So blind is lust, false colours to descry.
  But *Ate* soone discovering his desire,
  And finding now fit opportunity
  To stirre up strife, twixt love and spight and ire,
Did privily put coles unto his secret fire.

12

By sundry meanes thereto she prickt him forth,
　Now with remembrance of those spightfull speaches,
　Now with opinion of his owne more worth,
　Now with recounting of like former breaches
Made in their friendship, as that Hag him teaches:
　And ever when his passion is allayd,
　She it revives and new occasion reaches:
　That on a time as they together way'd,
He made him open chalenge, and thus boldly sayd.

13

Too boastfull *Blandamour*, too long I beare
　The open wrongs, thou doest me day by day;
　Well know'st thou, when we friendship first did sweare,
　The covenant was, that every spoyle or pray
Should equally be shard betwixt us tway:
　Where is my part then of this Ladie bright,
　Whom to thy selfe thou takest quite away?
　Render therefore therein to me my right,
Or answere for thy wrong, as shall fall out in fight.

14

Exceeding wroth thereat was *Blandamour*,
　And gan this bitter answere to him make;
　Too foolish *Paridell*, that fayrest floure
　Wouldst gather faine, and yet no paines wouldst take:
But not so easie will I her forsake;
　This hand her wonne, this hand shall her defend.
　With that they gan their shivering speares to shake,
　And deadly points at eithers breast to bend,
Forgetfull each to have bene ever others frend.

15

Their firie Steedes with so untamed forse
　Did beare them both to fell avenges end,
　That both their speares with pitilesse remorse,
　Through shield and mayle, and haberjeon did wend,
And in their flesh a griesly passage rend,
　That with the furie of their owne affret,
　Each other horse and man to ground did send;
　Where lying still a while, both did forget
The perilous present stownd, in which their lives were set.

16

As when two warlike Brigandines at sea,
　With murdrous weapons arm'd to cruell fight,
　Doe meete together on the watry lea,
　They stemme ech other with so fell despight,
　That with the shocke of their owne heedlesse might,
　Their wooden ribs are shaken nigh a sonder;
　They which from shore behold the dreadfull sight
　Of flashing fire, and heare the ordenance thonder,
Do greatly stand amaz'd at such unwonted wonder.

17

At length they both upstarted in amaze,
　As men awaked rashly out of dreme;
　And round about themselves a while did gaze,
　Till seeing her, that *Florimell* did seme,
　In doubt to whom she victorie should deeme,
　Therewith their dulled sprights they edgd anew,
　And drawing both their swords with rage extreme,
　Like two mad mastiffes each on other flew,
And shields did share, and mailes did rash, and helmes did hew.

18

So furiously each other did assayle
　As if their soules they would attonce have rent
　Out of their brests, that streames of bloud did rayle
　Adowne, as if their springs of life were spent;
　That all the ground with purple bloud was sprent,
　And all their armours staynd with bloudie gore,
　Yet scarcely once to breath would they relent,
　So mortall was their malice and so sore,
Become of fayned friendship which they vow'd afore.

19

And that which is for Ladies most besitting,
　To stint all strife, and foster friendly peace,
　Was from those Dames so farre and so unfitting,
　As that in stead of praying them surcease,
　They did much more their cruelty encrease;
　Bidding them fight for honour of their love,
　And rather die than Ladies cause release.
　With which vaine termes so much they did them move,
That both resolv'd the last extremities to prove.

20

There they I weene would fight untill this day,
  Had not a Squire, even he the Squire of Dames,
  By great adventure travelled that way;
  Who seeing both bent to so bloudy games,
  And both of old well knowing by their names,
  Drew nigh, to weete the cause of their debate:
  And first laide on those Ladies thousand blames,
  That did not seeke t'appease their deadly hate,
But gazed on their harmes, not pittying their estate.

21

And then those Knights he humbly did beseech,
  To stay their hands, till he a while had spoken:
  Who lookt a little up at that his speech,
  Yet would not let their battell so be broken,
  Both greedie fiers on other to be wroken.
  Yet he to them so earnestly did call,
  And them conjur'd by some well knowen token,
  That they at last their wrothfull hands let fall,
Content to heare him speake, and glad to rest withall.

22

First he desir'd their cause of strife to see:
  They said, it was for love of *Florimell*.
  Ah gentle knights (quoth he) how may that bee,
  And she so farre astray, as none can tell.
  Fond Squire, full angry then sayd *Paridell*,
  Seest not the Ladie there before thy face?
  He looked backe, and her advizing well,
  Weend as he said, by that her outward grace,
That fayrest *Florimell* was present there in place.

23

Glad man was he to see that joyous sight,
  For none alive but joy'd in *Florimell*,
  And lowly to her lowting thus behight;
  Fayrest of faire, that fairenesse doest excell,
  This happie day I have to greete you well,
  In which you safe I see, whom thousand late
  Misdoubted lost through mischiefe that befell;
  Long may you live in health and happie state.
She litle answer'd him, but lightly did aggrate.

24

Then turning to those Knights, he gan a new;
  And you Sir *Blandamour* and *Paridell*,
  That for this Ladie present in your vew,
  Have rays'd this cruell warre and outrage fell,
  Certes me seemes bene not advised well,
  But rather ought in friendship for her sake
  To joyne your force, their forces to repell,
  That seeke perforce her from you both to take,
And of your gotten spoyle their owne triumph to make.

25

Thereat Sir *Blandamour* with countenance sterne,
  All full of wrath, thus fiercely him bespake;
  A read thou Squire, that I the man may learne,
  That dare fro me thinke *Florimell* to take.
  Not one (quoth he) but many doe partake
  Herein, as thus. It lately so befell,
  That *Satyran* a girdle did uptake,
  Well knowne to appertaine to *Florimell*,
Which for her sake he wore, as him beseemed well.

26

But when as she her selfe was lost and gone,
  Full many knights, that loved her like deare,
  Thereat did greatly grudge, that he alone
  That lost faire Ladies ornament should weare,
  And gan therefore close spight to him to beare:
  Which he to shun, and stop vile envies sting,
  Hath lately caus'd to be proclaim'd each where
  A solemne feast, with publike turneying,
To which all knights with them their Ladies are to bring.

27

And of them all she that is fayrest found,
  Shall have that golden girdle for reward,
  And of those Knights who is most stout on ground,
  Shall to that fairest Ladie be prefard.
  Since therefore she her selfe is now your ward,
  To you that ornament of hers pertaines,
  Against all those, that chalenge it to gard,
  And save her honour with your ventrous paines;
That shall you win more glory, than ye here find gaines.

28

When they the reason of his words had hard,
　They gan abate the rancour of their rage,
　And with their honours and their loves regard,
　The furious flames of malice to asswage.
　Tho each to other did his faith engage,
　Like faithfull friends thenceforth to joyne in one
　With all their force, and battell strong to wage
　Gainst all those knights, as their professed fone,
That chaleng'd ought in *Florimell*, save they alone.

29

So well accorded forth they rode together
　In friendly sort, that lasted but a while;
　And of all old dislikes they made faire weather,
　Yet all was forg'd and spred with golden foyle,
　That under it hidde hate and hollow guyle.
　Ne certes can that friendship long endure,
　How ever gay and goodly be the style,
　That doth ill cause or evill end enure:
For vertue is the band, that bindeth harts most sure.

30

Thus as they marched all in close disguise
　Of fayned love, they chaunst to overtake
　Two knights, that lincked rode in lovely wise,
　As if they secret counsels did partake;
　And each not farre behinde him had his make,
　To weete, two Ladies of most goodly hew,
　That twixt themselves did gentle purpose make,
　Unmindfull both of that discordfull crew,
The which with speedie pace did after them pursew.

31

Who as they now approched nigh at hand,
　Deeming them doughtie as they did appeare,
　They sent that Squire afore, to understand,
　What mote they be: who viewing them more neare
　Returned readie newes, that those same weare
　Two of the prowest Knights in Faery lond;
　And those two Ladies their two lovers deare,
　Couragious *Cambell*, and stout *Triamond*,
With *Canacee* and *Cambine* linckt in lovely bond.

32

Whylome as antique stories tellen us,
  Those two were foes the fellonest on ground,
  And battell made the dreddest daungerous,
  That ever shrilling trumpet did resound;
  Though now their acts be no where to be found,
  As that renowmed Poet them compyled,
  With warlike numbers and Heroicke sound,
  Dan *Chaucer*, well of English undefyled,
On Fames eternall beadroll worthie to be fyled.

33

But wicked Time that all good thoughts doth waste,
  And workes of noblest wits to nought out weare,
  That famous moniment hath quite defaste,
  And robd the world of threasure endlesse deare,
  The which mote have enriched all us heare.
  O cursed Eld the cankerworme of writs,
  How may these rimes, so rude as doth appeare,
  Hope to endure, sith workes of heavenly wits
Are quite devourd, and brought to nought by little bits?

34

Then pardon, O most sacred happie spirit,
  That I thy labours lost may thus revive,
  And steale from thee the meede of thy due merit,
  That none durst ever whilest thou wast alive,
  And being dead in vaine yet many strive:
  Ne dare I like, but through infusion sweete
  Of thine owne spirit, which doth in me survive,
  I follow here the footing of thy feete,
That with thy meaning so I may the rather meete.

35

Cambelloes sister was fayre *Canacee*,
  That was the learnedst Ladie in her dayes,
  Well seene in everie science that mote bee,
  And every secret worke of natures wayes,
  In wittie riddles, and in wise soothsayes,
  In power of herbes, and tunes of beasts and burds;
  And, that augmented all her other prayse,
  She modest was in all her deedes and words,
And wondrous chast of life, yet lov'd of Knights and Lords.

36

Full many Lords, and many Knights her loved,
  Yet she to none of them her liking lent,
  Ne ever was with fond affection moved,
  But rul'd her thoughts with goodly governement,
  For dread of blame and honours blemishment;
  And eke unto her lookes a law she made,
  That none of them once out of order went,
  But like to warie Centonels well stayd,
Still watcht on every side, of secret foes affrayd.

37

So much the more as she refusd to love,
  So much the more she loved was and sought,
  That oftentimes unquiet strife did move
  Amongst her lovers, and great quarrels wrought,
  That oft for her in bloudie armes they fought.
  Which whenas *Cambell*, that was stout and wise,
  Perceiv'd would breede great mischiefe, he bethought
  How to prevent the perill that mote rise,
And turne both him and her to honour in this wise.

38

One day, when all that troupe of warlike wooers
  Assembled were, to weet whose she should bee,
  All mightie men and dreadfull derring dooers,
  (The harder it to make them well agree)
  Amongst them all this end he did decree;
  That of them all, which love to her did make,
  They by consent should chose the stoutest three,
  That with himselfe should combat for her sake,
And of them all the victour should his sister take.

39

Bold was the chalenge, as himselfe was bold,
  And courage full of haughtie hardiment,
  Approved oft in perils manifold,
  Which he atchiev'd to his great ornament:
  But yet his sisters skill unto him lent
  Most confidence and hope of happie speed,
  Conceived by a ring, which she him sent,
  That mongst the manie vertues, which we reed,
Had power to staunch al wounds, that mortally did bleed.

40

Well was that rings great vertue knowen to all,
　That dread thereof, and his redoubted might
　Did all that youthly rout so much appall,
　That none of them durst undertake the fight;
　More wise they weend to make of love delight,
　Than life to hazard for faire Ladies looke,
　And yet uncertaine by such outward sight,
　Though for her sake they all that perill tooke,
Whether she would them love, or in her liking brooke.

41

Amongst those knights there were three brethren bold,
　Three bolder brethren never were yborne,
　Borne of one mother in one happie mold,
　Borne at one burden in one happie morne,
　Thrise happie mother, and thrise happie morne,
　That bore three such, three such not to be fond;
　Her name was *Agape* whose children werne
　All three as one, the first hight *Priamond*,
The second *Dyamond*, the youngest *Triamond*.

42

Stout *Priamond*, but not so strong to strike,
　Strong *Diamond*, but not so stout a knight,
　But *Triamond* was stout and strong alike:
　On horsebacke used *Triamond* to fight,
　And *Priamond* on foote had more delight,
　But horse and foote knew *Diamond* to wield:
　With curtaxe used *Diamond* to smite,
　And *Triamond* to handle speare and shield,
But speare and curtaxe both usd *Priamond* in field.

43

These three did love each other dearely well,
　And with so firme affection were allyde,
　As if but one soule in them all did dwell,
　Which did her powre into three parts divyde;
　Like three faire branches budding farre and wide,
　That from one roote deriv'd their vitall sap:
　And like that roote that doth her life divide,
　Their mother was, and had full blessed hap,
These three so noble babes to bring forth at one clap.

44

Their mother was a Fay, and had the skill
  Of secret things, and all the powres of nature,
  Which she by art could use unto her will,
  And to her service bind each living creature,
  Through secret understanding of their feature.
  Thereto she was right faire, when so her face
  She list discover, and of goodly stature;
  But she as Fayes are wont, in privie place
Did spend her dayes, and lov'd in forests wyld to space.

45

There on a day a noble youthly knight
  Seeking adventures in the salvage wood,
  Did by great fortune get of her the sight,
  As she sate carelesse by a cristall flood,
  Combing her golden lockes, as seemd her good:
  And unawares upon her laying hold,
  That strove in vaine him long to have withstood,
  Oppressed her, and there (as it is told)
Got these three lovely babes, that prov'd three champions bold.

46

Which she with her long fostred in that wood,
  Till that to ripenesse of mans state they grew:
  Then shewing forth signes of their fathers blood,
  They loved armes, and knighthood did ensew,
  Seeking adventures, where they anie knew.
  Which when their mother saw, she gan to dout
  Their safetie, least by searching daungers new,
  And rash provoking perils all about,
Their days mote be abridged through their corage stout.

47

Therefore desirous th'end of all their dayes
  To know, and them t'enlarge with long extent,
  By wondrous skill, and many hidden wayes,
  To the three fatall sisters house she went.
  Farre under ground from tract of living went,
  Downe in the bottome of the deepe *Abysse*,
  Where *Demogorgon* in dull darkenesse pent,
  Farre from the view of Gods and heavens blis,
The hideous *Chaos* keepes, their dreadfull dwelling is.

48

There she them found, all sitting round about
  The direfull distaffe standing in the mid,
  And with unwearied fingers drawing out
  The lines of life, from living knowledge hid.
  Sad *Clotho* held the rocke, the whiles the thrid
  By griesly *Lachesis* was spun with paine,
  That cruell *Atropos* eftsoones undid,
  With cursed knife cutting the twist in twaine:
Most wretched men, whose dayes depend on thrids so vaine.

49

She them saluting, there by them sate still,
  Beholding how the thrids of life they span:
  And when at last she had beheld her fill,
  Trembling in heart, and looking pale and wan,
  Her cause of comming she to tell began.
  To whom fierce *Atropos*, Bold Fay, that durst
  Come see the secret of the life of man,
  Well worthie thou to be of *Jove* accurst,
And eke thy childrens thrids to be a sunder burst.

50

Whereat she sore affrayd, yet her besought
  To graunt her boone, and rigour to abate,
  That she might see her childrens thrids forth brought,
  And know the measure of their utmost date,
  To them ordained by eternall fate.
  Which *Clotho* graunting, shewed her the same:
  That when she saw, it did her much amate,
  To see their thrids so thin, as spiders frame,
And eke so short, that seemd their ends out shortly came.

51

She then began them humbly to intreate,
  To draw them longer out, and better twine,
  That so their lives might be prolonged late.
  But *Lachesis* thereat gan to repine,
  And sayd, Fond dame that deem'st of things divine
  As of humane, that they may altred bee,
  And chaung'd at pleasure for those impes of thine.
  Not so; for what the Fates do once decree,
Not all the gods can chaunge, nor *Jove* him self can free.

52

Then since (quoth she) the terme of each mans life
  For nought may lessened nor enlarged bee,
  Graunt this, that when ye shred with fatall knife
  His line, which is the eldest of the three,
  Which is of them the shortest, as I see,
  Eftsoones his life may passe into the next;
  And when the next shall likewise ended bee,
  That both their lives may likewise be annext
Unto the third, that his may so be trebly wext.

53

They graunted it; and then that carefull Fay
  Departed thence with full contented mynd;
  And comming home, in warlike fresh aray
  Them found all three according to their kynd:
  But unto them what destinie was assynd,
  Or how their lives were eekt, she did not tell;
  But evermore, when she fit time could fynd,
  She warned them to tend their safeties well,
And love each other deare, what ever them befell.

54

So did they surely during all their dayes,
  And never discord did amongst them fall;
  Which much augmented all their other praise.
  And now t'increase affection naturall,
  In love of *Canacee* they joyned all:
  Upon which ground this same great battell grew,
  Great matter growing of beginning small;
  The which for length I will not here pursew,
But rather will reserve it for a Canto new.

CANT. III

The battell twixt three brethren with
Cambell for Canacee:
Cambina with true friendships bond
doth their long strife agree.

1

O WHY doe wretched men so much desire,
  To draw their dayes unto the utmost date,
  And doe not rather wish them soone expire,
  Knowing the miserie of their estate,
  And thousand perills which them still awate,
  Tossing them like a boate amid the mayne,
  That every houre they knocke at deathes gate?
  And he that happie seemes and least in payne,
Yet is as nigh his end, as he that most doth playne.

2

Therefore this Fay I hold but fond and vaine,
  The which in seeking for her children three
  Long life, thereby did more prolong their paine.
  Yet whilest they lived none did ever see
  More happie creatures, than they seem'd to bee,
  Nor more ennobled for their courtesie,
  That made them dearely lov'd of each degree;
  Ne more renowmed for their chevalrie,
That made them dreaded much of all men farre and nie.

3

These three that hardie chalenge tooke in hand,
  For *Canacee* with *Cambell* for to fight:
  The day was set, that all might understand,
  And pledges pawnd the same to keepe a right,
  That day, the dreddest day that living wight
  Did ever see upon this world to shine,
  So soone as heavens window shewed light,
  These warlike Champions all in armour shine,
Assembled were in field, the chalenge to define.

4

The field with listes was all about enclos'd,
  To barre the prease of people farre away;
  And at th'one side sixe judges were dispos'd,
  To view and deeme the deedes of armes that day;
  And on the other side in fresh aray,
  Fayre *Canacee* upon a stately stage
  Was set, to see the fortune of that fray,
  And to be seene, as his most worthie wage,
That could her purchase with his lives adventur'd gage.

5

Then entred *Cambell* first into the list,
  With stately steps, and fearelesse countenance,
  As if the conquest his he surely wist.
  Soone after did the brethren three advance,
  In brave aray and goodly amenance,
  With scutchins gilt and banners broad displayd:
  And marching thrise in warlike ordinance,
  Thrise lowted lowly to the noble Mayd,
The whiles shril trompets and loud clarions sweetly playd.

6

Which doen the doughty chalenger came forth,
  All arm'd to point his chalenge to abet:
  Gainst whom Sir *Priamond* with equall worth,
  And equall armes himselfe did forward set.
  A trompet blew; they both together met,
  With dreadfull force, and furious intent,
  Carelesse of perill in their fiers affret,
  As if that life to losse they had forelent,
And cared not to spare, that should be shortly spent.

7

Right practicke was Sir *Priamond* in fight,
  And throughly skild in use of shield and speare;
  Ne lesse approved was *Cambelloes* might,
  Ne lesse his skill in weapons did appeare,
  That hard it was to weene which harder were.
  Full many mightie strokes on either side
  Were sent, that seemed death in them to beare,
  But they were both so watchfull and well eyde,
That they avoyded were, and vainely by did slyde.

Turneyment of Knights

8

Yet one of many was so strongly bent
  By *Priamond*, that with unluckie glaunce
  Through *Cambels* shoulder it unwarely went,
  That forced him his shield to disadvaunce:
  Much was he grieved with that gracelesse chaunce,
  Yet from the wound no drop of bloud there fell,
  But wondrous paine, that did the more enhaunce
  His haughtie courage to advengement fell:
Smart daunts not mighty harts, but makes them more to swell.

9   .

With that his poynant speare he fierce aventred,
  With doubled force close underneath his shield,
  That through the mayles into his thigh it entred,
  And there arresting, readie way did yield,
  For bloud to gush forth on the grassie field;
  That he for paine himselfe n'ote right upreare,
  But too and fro in great amazement reel'd,
  Like an old Oke whose pith and sap is seare,
At puffe of every storme doth stagger here and theare.

10

Whom so dismayd when *Cambell* had espide,
  Againe he drove at him with double might,
  That nought mote stay the steele, till in his side
  The mortall point most cruelly empight:
  Where fast infixed, whilest he sought by slight
  It forth to wrest, the staffe a sunder brake,
  And left the head behind: with which despight
  He all enrag'd, his shivering speare did shake,
And charging him a fresh thus felly him bespake.

11

Lo faitour there thy meede unto thee take,
  The meede of thy mischalenge and abet:
  Not for thine owne, but for thy sisters sake,
  Have I thus long thy life unto thee let:
  But to forbeare doth not forgive the det.
  The wicked weapon heard his wrathfull vow,
  And passing forth with furious affret,
  Pierst through his bever quite into his brow,
That with the force it backward forced him to bow.

12

Therewith a sunder in the midst it brast,
  And in his hand nought but the troncheon left,
  The other halfe behind yet sticking fast,
  Out of his headpeece *Cambell* fiercely reft,
  And with such furie backe at him it heft,
  That making way unto his dearest life,
  His weasand pipe it through his gorget cleft:
  Thence streames of purple bloud issuing rife,
Let forth his wearie ghost and made an end of strife.

13

His wearie ghost assoyld from fleshly band,
  Did not as others wont, directly fly
  Unto her rest in Plutoes griesly land,
  Ne into ayre did vanish presently,
  Ne chaunged was into a starre in sky:
  But through traduction was eftsoones derived,
  Like as his mother prayd the Destinie,
  Into his other brethren, that survived,
In whom he liv'd a new, of former life deprived.

14

Whom when on ground his brother next beheld,
  Though sad and sorie for so heavy sight,
  Yet leave unto his sorrow did not yeeld,
  But rather stird to vengeance and despight,
  Through secret feeling of his generous spright,
  Rusht fiercely forth, the battell to renew,
  As in reversion of his brothers right;
  And chalenging the Virgin as his dew.
His foe was soone addrest: the trompets freshly blew.

15

With that they both together fiercely met,
  As if that each ment other to devoure;
  And with their axes both so sorely bet,
  That neither plate nor mayle, whereas their powre
  They felt, could once sustaine the hideous stowre,
  But rived were like rotten wood a sunder,
  Whilest through their rifts the ruddie bloud did showre
  And fire did flash, like lightning after thunder,
That fild the lookers on attonce with ruth and wonder.

16

As when two Tygers prickt with hungers rage,
  Have by good fortune found some beasts fresh spoyle,
  On which they weene their famine to asswage,
  And gaine a feastfull guerdon of their toyle,
  Both falling out doe stirre up strifefull broyle,
  And cruell battell twixt themselves doe make,
  Whiles neither lets the other touch the soyle,
  But either sdeignes with other to partake:
So cruelly these Knights strove for that Ladies sake.

17

Full many strokes, that mortally were ment,
  The whiles were enterchaunged twixt them two;
  Yet they were all with so good wariment
  Or warded, or avoyded and let goe,
  That still the life stood fearelesse of her foe:
  Till *Diamond* disdeigning long delay
  Of doubtfull fortune wavering to and fro,
  Resolv'd to end it one or other way;
And heav'd his murdrous axe at him with mighty sway.

18

The dreadfull stroke in case it had arrived,
  Where it was ment, (so deadly it was ment)
  The soule had sure out of his bodie rived,
  And stinted all the strife incontinent.
  But *Cambels* fate that fortune did prevent:
  For seeing it at hand, he swarv'd asyde,
  And so gave way unto his fell intent:
  Who missing of the marke which he had eyde,
Was with the force nigh feld whilst his right foot did slyde.

19

As when a Vulture greedie of his pray,
  Through hunger long, that hart to him doth lend,
  Strikes at an Heron with all his bodies sway,
  That from his force seemes nought may it defend;
  The warie fowle that spies him toward bend
  His dreadfull souse, avoydes it shunning light,
  And maketh him his wing in vaine to spend;
  That with the weight of his owne weeldlesse might,
He falleth nigh to ground, and scarse recovereth flight.

20

Which faire adventure when *Cambello* spide,
  Full lightly, ere himselfe he could recower,
  From daungers dread to ward his naked side,
  He can let drive at him with all his power,
  And with his axe him smote in evill hower,
  That from his shoulders quite his head he reft:
  The headlesse tronke, as heedlesse of that stower,
  Stood still a while, and his fast footing kept,
Till feeling life to fayle, it fell, and deadly slept.

21

They which that piteous spectacle beheld,
  Were much amaz'd the headlesse tronke to see
  Stand up so long, and weapon vaine to weld,
  Unweeting of the Fates divine decree,
  For lifes succession in those brethren three.
  For notwithstanding that one soule was reft,
  Yet, had the bodie not dismembred bee,
  It would have lived, and revived eft;
But finding no fit seat, the lifelesse corse it left.

22

It left; but that same soule, which therein dwelt,
  Streight entring into *Triamond*, him fild
  With double life, and griefe, which when he felt,
  As one whose inner parts had bene ythrild
  With point of steele, that close his hartbloud spild,
  He lightly lept out of his place of rest,
  And rushing forth into the emptie field,
  Against *Cambello* fiercely him addrest;
Who him affronting soone to fight was readie prest.

23

Well mote ye wonder how that noble Knight,
  After he had so often wounded beene,
  Could stand on foot, now to renew the fight.
  But had ye then him forth advauncing seene,
  Some newborne wight ye would him surely weene:
  So fresh he seemed and so fierce in sight;
  Like as a Snake, whom wearie winters teene
  Hath worne to nought, now feeling sommers might,
Casts off his ragged skin and freshly doth him dight.

24

All was through vertue of the ring he wore,
  The which not onely did not from him let
  One drop of bloud to fall, but did restore
  His weakned powers, and dulled spirits whet,
  Through working of the stone therein yset.
  Else how could one of equall might with most,
  Against so many no lesse mightie met,
  Once thinke to match three such on equall cost,
Three such as able were to match a puissant host.

25

Yet nought thereof was *Triamond* adredde,
  Ne desperate of glorious victorie,
  But sharpely him assayld, and sore bestedde,
  With heapes of strokes, which he at him let flie,
  As thicke as hayle forth poured from the skie:
  He stroke, he soust, he foynd, he hewd, he lasht,
  And did his yron brond so fast applie,
  That from the same the fierie sparkles flasht,
As fast as water-sprinkles gainst a rocke are dasht.

26

Much was *Cambello* daunted with his blowes.
  So thicke they fell, and forcibly were sent,
  That he was forst from daunger of the throwes
  Backe to retire, and somewhat to relent,
  Till th'heat of his fierce furie he had spent:
  Which when for want of breath gan to abate,
  He then afresh with new encouragement
  Did him assayle, and mightily amate,
As fast as forward erst, now backward to retrate.

27

Like as the tide that comes fro th'Ocean mayne,
  Flowes up the Shenan with contrarie forse,
  And overruling him in his owne rayne,
  Drives backe the current of his kindly course,
  And makes it seeme to have some other sourse:
  But when the floud is spent, then backe againe
  His borrowed waters forst to redisbourse,
  He sends the sea his owne with double gaine,
And tribute eke withall, as to his Soveraine.

28

Thus did the battell varie to and fro,
  With diverse fortune doubtfull to be deemed:
  Now this the better had, now had his fo;
  Then he halfe vanquisht, then the other seemed,
  Yet victors both them selves alwayes esteemed.
  And all the while the disentrayled blood
  Adowne their sides like litle rivers stremed,
  That with the wasting of his vitall flood,
Sir *Triamond* at last full faint and feeble stood.

29

But *Cambell* still more strong and greater grew,
  Ne felt his blood to wast, ne powres emperisht,
  Through that rings vertue, that with vigour new,
  Still when as he enfeebled was, him cherisht,
  And all his wounds, and all his bruses guarisht,
  Like as a withered tree through husbands toyle
  Is often seene full freshly to have florisht,
  And fruitfull apples to have borne awhile,
As fresh as when it first was planted in the soyle.

30

Through which advantage, in his strength he rose,
  And smote the other with so wondrous might,
  That through the seame, which did his hauberk close,
  Into his throate and life it pierced quight,
  That downe he fell as dead in all mens sight:
  Yet dead he was not, yet he sure did die,
  As all men do, that lose the living spright:
  So did one soule out of his bodie flie
Unto her native home from mortall miserie.

31

But nathelesse whilst all the lookers on
  Him dead behight, as he to all appeard,
  All unawares he started up anon,
  As one that had out of a dreame bene reard,
  And fresh assayld his foe, who halfe affeard
  Of th'uncouth sight, as he some ghost had seene,
  Stood still amaz'd, holding his idle sweard;
  Till having often by him stricken beene,
He forced was to strike, and save him selfe from teene.

32

Yet from thenceforth more warily he fought,
  As one in feare the Stygian gods t'offend,
  Ne followd on so fast, but rather sought
  Him selfe to save, and daunger to defend,
  Than life and labour both in vaine to spend.
  Which *Triamond* perceiving, weened sure
  He gan to faint, toward the battels end,
  And that he should not long on foote endure,
A signe which did to him the victorie assure.

33

Whereof full blith, eftsoones his mightie hand
  He heav'd on high, in mind with that same blow
  To make an end of all that did withstand:
  Which *Cambell* seeing come, was nothing slow
  Him selfe to save from that so deadly throw;
  And at that instant reaching forth his sweard
  Close underneath his shield, that scarce did show,
  Stroke him, as he his hand to strike upreard,
In th'arm-pit full, that through both sides the wound appeard.

34

Yet still that direfull stroke kept on his way,
  And falling heavie on *Cambelloes* crest,
  Strooke him so hugely, that in swowne he lay,
  And in his head an hideous wound imprest:
  And sure had it not happily found rest
  Upon the brim of his brode plated shield,
  It would have cleft his braine downe to his brest.
  So both at once fell dead upon the field,
And each to other seemd the victorie to yield.

35

Which when as all the lookers on beheld,
  They weened sure the warre was at an end,
  And Judges rose, and Marshals of the field
  Broke up the listes, their armes away to rend;
  And *Canacee* gan wayle her dearest frend.
  All suddenly they both upstarted light,
  The one out of the swownd, which him did blend,
  The other breathing now another spright,
And fiercely each assayling, gan afresh to fight.

36

Long while they then continued in that wize,
　　As if but then the battell had begonne:
　　Strokes, wounds, wards, weapons, all they did despise,
　　Ne either car'd to ward, or perill shonne,
　　Desirous both to have the battell donne;
　　Ne either cared life to save or spill,
　　Ne which of them did winne, ne which were wonne.
　　So wearie both of fighting had their fill,
That life it selfe seemd loathsome, and long safetie ill.

37

Whilst thus the case in doubtfull ballance hong,
　　Unsure to whether side it would incline,
　　And all mens eyes and hearts, which there among
　　Stood gazing, filled were with rufull tine,
　　And secret feare, to see their fatall fine,
　　All suddenly they heard a troublous noyes,
　　That seemd some perilous tumult to desine,
　　Confusd with womens cries, and shouts of boyes,
Such as the troubled Theaters oftimes annoyes.

38

Thereat the Champions both stood still a space,
　　To weeten what that sudden clamour ment;
　　Lo where they spyde with speedie whirling pace,
　　One in a charet of straunge furniment,
　　Towards them driving like a storme out sent.
　　The charet decked was in wondrous wize,
　　With gold and many a gorgeous ornament,
　　After the Persian Monarks antique guize,
Such as the maker selfe could best by art devize.

39

And drawne it was (that wonder is to tell)
　　Of two grim lyons, taken from the wood,
　　In which their powre all others did excell;
　　Now made forget their former cruell mood,
　　T'obey their riders hest, as seemed good.
　　And therein sate a Ladie passing faire
　　And bright, that seemed borne of Angels brood,
　　And with her beautie bountie did compare,
Whether of them in her should have the greater share.

40

Thereto she learned was in Magicke leare,
And all the artes, that subtill wits discover,
Having therein bene trained many a yeare,
And well instructed by the Fay her mother,
That in the same she farre exceld all other.
Who understanding by her mightie art,
Of th'evill plight, in which her dearest brother
Now stood, came forth in hast to take his part,
And pacifie the strife, which causd so deadly smart.

41

And as she passed through th'unruly preace
Of people, thronging thicke her to behold,
Her angrie teame breaking their bonds of peace,
Great heapes of them, like sheepe in narrow fold,
For hast did over-runne, in dust enrould,
That thorough rude confusion of the rout,
Some fearing shriekt, some being harmed hould,
Some laught for sport, some did for wonder shout,
And some that would seeme wise, their wonder turnd to dout.

42

In her right hand a rod of peace shee bore,
About the which two Serpents weren wound,
Entrayled mutually in lovely lore,
And by the tailes together firmely bound,
And both were with one olive garland crownd,
Like to the rod which *Maias* sonne doth wield,
Wherewith the hellish fiends he doth confound.
And in her other hand a cup she hild,
The which was with Nepenthe to the brim upfild.

43

Nepenthe is a drinck of soverayne grace,
Devized by the Gods, for to asswage
Harts grief, and bitter gall away to chace,
Which stirs up anguish and contentious rage:
In stead thereof sweet peace and quiet age
It doth establish in the troubled mynd.
Few men, but such as sober are and sage,
Are by the Gods to drinck thereof assynd;
But such as drinck, eternall happinesse do fynd.

44

Such famous men, such worthies of the earth,
As *Jove* will have advaunced to the skie,
And there made gods, though borne of mortall berth,
For their high merits and great dignitie,
Are wont, before they may to heaven flie,
To drincke hereof, whereby all cares forepast
Are washt away quite from their memorie.
So did those olde Heroes hereof taste,
Before that they in blisse amongst the Gods were plaste.

45

Much more of price and of more gratious powre
Is this, than that same water of Ardenne,
The which *Rinaldo* drunck in happie howre,
Described by that famous Tuscan penne:
For that had might to change the hearts of men
Fro love to hate, a change of evill choise:
But this doth hatred make in love to brenne
And heavy heart with comfort doth rejoyce.
Who would not to this vertue rather yeeld his voice?

46

At last arriving by the listes side,
Shee with her rod did softly smite the raile,
Which straight flew ope, and gave her way to ride.
Eftsoones out of her Coch she gan availe,
And pacing fairely forth, did bid all haile,
First to her brother, whom she loved deare,
That so to see him made her heart to quaile:
And next to *Cambell*, whose sad ruefull cheare
Made her to change her hew, and hidden love t'appeare.

47

They lightly her requit (for small delight
They had as then her long to entertaine,)
And eft them turned both againe to fight,
Which when she saw, downe on the bloudy plaine
Herselfe she threw, and teares gan shed amaine;
Amongst her teares immixing prayers meeke,
And with her prayers reasons to restraine
From blouddy strife, and blessed peace to seeke,
By all that unto them was deare, did them beseeke.

48

But when as all might nought with them prevaile,
  Shee smote them lightly with her powrefull wand.
  Then suddenly as if their hearts did faile,
  Their wrathfull blades downe fell out of their hand,
  And they like men astonisht still did stand.
  Thus whilest their minds were doubtfully distraught,
  And mighty spirites bound with mightier band,
  Her golden cup to them for drinke she raught,
Whereof full glad for thirst, ech drunk an harty draught.

49

Of which so soone as they once tasted had,
  Wonder it is that sudden change to see:
  Instead of strokes, each other kissed glad,
  And lovely haulst from feare of treason free,
  And plighted hands for ever friends to be.
  When all men saw this sudden change of things,
  So mortall foes so friendly to agree,
  For passing joy, which so great marvaile brings,
They all gan shout aloud, that all the heaven rings.

50

All which, when gentle *Canacee* beheld,
  In hast she from her lofty chaire descended,
  To weet what sudden tidings was befeld:
  Where when she saw that cruell war so ended,
  And deadly foes so faithfully affrended,
  In lovely wise she gan that Lady greet,
  Which had so great dismay so well amended,
  And entertaining her with curt'sies meet,
Profest to her true friendship and affection sweet.

51

Thus when they all accorded goodly were,
  The trumpets sounded, and they all arose,
  Thence to depart with glee and gladsome chere.
  Those warlike champions both together chose,
  Homeward to march, themselves there to repose,
  And wise *Cambina* taking by her side
  Faire *Canacee*, as fresh as morning rose,
  Unto her Coch remounting, home did ride,
Admir'd of all the people, and much glorifide,

52

Where making joyous feast theire daies they spent
  In perfect love, devoide of hatefull strife,
  Allide with bands of mutuall couplement;
  For *Triamond* had *Canacee* to wife,
  With whom he ledd a long and happie life;
  And *Cambel* tooke *Cambina* to his fere,
  The which as life were each to other liefe.
  So all alike did love, and loved were,
That since their days such lovers were not found elswhere.

CANT. IIII

Satyrane makes a Turneyment
For love of Florimell:
Britomart winnes the prize from all,
And Artegall doth quell.

I

IT often fals, (as here it earst befell)
  That mortall foes doe turne to faithfull frends,
  And friends profest are chaungd to foemen fell:
  The cause of both, of both their minds depends,
  And th'end of both likewise of both their ends.
  For enmitie, that of no ill proceeds,
  But of occasion, with th'occasion ends;
  And friendship, which a faint affection breeds
Without regard of good, dyes like ill grounded seeds.

2

That well (me seemes) appeares, by that of late
  Twixt *Cambell* and Sir *Triamond* befell,
  As els by this, that now a new debate
  Stird up twixt *Scudamour* and *Paridell*,
  The which by course befals me here to tell:
  Who having those two other Knights espide
  Marching afore, as ye remember well,
  Sent forth their Squire to have them both descride,
And eke those masked Ladies riding them beside.

3

Who backe returning, told as he had seene,
　That they were doughtie knights of dreaded name;
　And those two Ladies, their two loves unseene;
　And therefore wisht them without blot or blame,
　To let them passe at will, for dread of shame.
　But *Blandamour* full of vainglorious spright,
　And rather stird by his discordfull Dame,
　Upon them gladly would have prov'd his might,
But that he yet was sore of his late lucklesse fight.

4

Yet nigh approching, he them fowle bespake,
　Disgracing them, him selfe thereby to grace,
　As was his wont, so weening way to make
　To Ladies love, where so he came in place,
　And with lewd termes their lovers to deface.
　Whose sharpe provokement them incenst so sore,
　That both were bent t'avenge his usage base,
　And gan their shields addresse them selves afore:
For evill deedes may better than bad words be bore.

5

But faire *Cambina* with perswasions myld,
　Did mitigate the fiercenesse of their mode,
　That for the present they were reconcyld,
　And gan to treate of deeds of armes abrode,
　And strange adventures, all the way they rode:
　Amongst the which they told, as then befell,
　Of that great turney, which was blazed brode,
　For that rich girdle of faire *Florimell*,
The prize of her, which did in beautie most excell.

6

To which folke-mote they all with one consent,
　Sith each of them his Ladie had him by,
　Whose beautie each of them thought excellent,
　Agreed to travell, and their fortunes try.
　So as they passed forth, they did espy
　One in bright armes, with ready speare in rest,
　That toward them his course seem'd to apply,
　Gainst whom Sir *Paridell* himselfe addrest,
Him weening, ere he nigh approcht to have represt.

7

Which th'other seeing, gan his course relent,
  And vaunted speare eftsoones to disadvaunce,
  As if he naught but peace and pleasure ment,
  Now falne into their fellowship by chance,
  Whereat they shewed curteous countenaunce.
  So as he rode with them accompanide,
  His roving eie did on the Lady glaunce,
  Which *Blandamour* had riding by his side
Whom sure he weend, that he some wher tofore had eide.

8

It was to weete that snowy *Florimell*,
  Which *Ferrau* late from *Braggadochio* wonne,
  Whom he now seeing, her remembred well,
  How having reft her from the witches sonne,
  He soone her lost: wherefore he now begunne
  To challenge her anew, as his owne prize,
  Whom formerly he had in battell wonne,
  And proffer made by force her to reprize,
Which scornefull offer, *Blandamour* gan soone despize.

9

And said, Sir Knight, sith ye this Lady clame,
  Whom he that hath, were loth to lose so light,
  (For so to lose a Lady, were great shame)
  Yee shall her winne, as I have done in fight:
  And lo shee shall be placed here in sight,
  Together with this Hag beside her set,
  That who so winnes her, may her have by right:
  But he shall have the Hag that is ybet,
And with her alwaies ride, till he another get.

10

That offer pleased all the company,
  So *Florimell* with *Ate* forth was brought,
  At which they all gan laugh full merrily:
  But *Braggadochio* said, he never thought
  For such an Hag, that seemed worse than nought,
  His person to emperill so in fight.
  But if to match that Lady they had sought
  Another like, that were like faire and bright,
His life he then would spend to justifie his right.

11

At which his vaine excuse they all gan smile,
  As scorning his unmanly cowardize:
And *Florimell* him fowly gan revile,
  That for her sake refus'd to enterprize
  The battell, offred in so knightly wize.
And *Ate* eke provokt him privily,
  With love of her, and shame of such mesprize.
  But naught he car'd for friend or enemy,
For in base mind nor friendship dwels nor enmity.

12

But *Cambell* thus did shut up all in jest,
  Brave Knights and Ladies, certes ye doe wrong
To stirre up strife, when most us needeth rest,
  That we may us reserve both fresh and strong,
  Against the Turneiment which is not long.
When who so list to fight, may fight his fill,
  Till then your challenges ye may prolong;
  And then it shall be tried, if ye will,
Whether shall have the Hag, or hold the Lady still.

13

They all agreed, so turning all to game,
  And pleasaunt bord, they past forth on their way,
And all that while, where so they rode or came,
  That masked Mock-knight was their sport and play.
  Till that at length upon th'appointed day,
Unto the place of turneyment they came;
  Where they before them found in fresh aray
  Manie a brave knight, and manie a daintie dame
Assembled, for to get the honour of that game.

14

There this faire crewe arriving, did divide
  Them selves asunder: *Blandamour* with those
Of his, on th'one; the rest on th'other side.
  But boastfull *Braggadocchio* rather chose,
  For glorie vaine their fellowship to lose,
That men on him the more might gaze alone.
  The rest them selves in troupes did else dispose,
  Like as it seemed best to every one;
The knights in couples marcht, with ladies linckt attone.

15

Then first of all forth came Sir *Satyrane*,
  Bearing that precious relicke in an arke
  Of gold, that bad eyes might it not prophane:
  Which drawing softly forth out of the darke,
  He open shewd, that all men it mote marke.
  A gorgeous girdle, curiously embost
  With pearle and precious stone, worth many a marke;
  Yet did the workmanship farre passe the cost:
It was the same, which lately *Florimel* had lost.

16

That same aloft he hong in open vew,
  To be the prize of beautie and of might;
  The which eftsoones discovered, to it drew
  The eyes of all, allur'd with close delight,
  And hearts quite robbed with so glorious sight,
  That all men threw out vowes and wishes vaine.
  Thrise happie Ladie, and thrise happie knight,
  Them seemd that could so goodly riches gaine,
So worthie of the perill, worthy of the paine.

17

Then tooke the bold Sir *Satyrane* in hand
  An huge great speare, such as he wont to wield,
  And vauncing forth from all the other band
  Of knights, addrest his maiden-headed shield,
  Shewing him selfe all ready for the field.
  Gainst whom there singled from the other side
  A Painim knight, that well in armes was skild,
  And had in many a battell oft bene tride,
Hight *Bruncheval* the bold, who fiersly forth did ride.

18

So furiously they both together met,
  That neither could the others force sustaine;
  As two fierce Buls, that strive the rule to get
  Of all the heard, meete with so hideous maine,
  That both rebutted, tumble on the plaine:
  So these two champions to the ground were feld,
  Where in a maze they both did long remaine,
  And in their hands their idle troncheons held,
Which neither able were to wag, or once to weld.

19

Which when the noble *Ferramont* espide,
  He pricked forth in ayd of *Satyran*;
And him against Sir *Blandamour* did ride
  With all the strength and stifnesse that he can.
  But the more strong and stiffely that he ran,
  So much more sorely to the ground he fell,
  That on an heape were tumbled horse and man.
  Unto whose rescue forth rode *Paridell*;
But him likewise with that same speare he eke did quell.

20

Which *Braggadocchio* seeing, had no will
  To hasten greatly to his parties ayd,
Albee his turne were next; but stood there still,
  As one that seemed doubtfull or dismayd.
  But *Triamond* halfe wroth to see him staid,
  Sternly stept forth, and raught away his speare,
  With which so sore he *Ferramont* assaid,
  That horse and man to ground he quite did beare,
That neither could in hast themselves againe upreare.

21

Which to avenge, Sir *Devon* him did dight,
  But with no better fortune than the rest:
For him likewise he quickly downe did smight,
  And after him Sir *Douglas* him addrest,
  And after him Sir *Paliumord* forth prest,
  But none of them against his strokes could stand,
  But all the more, the more his praise increst.
  For either they were left uppon the land,
Or went away sore wounded of his haplesse hand.

22

And now by this, Sir *Satyrane* abraid,
  Out of the swowne, in which too long he lay;
And looking round about, like one dismaid,
  When as he saw the mercilesse affray,
  Which doughty *Triamond* had wrought that day,
  Unto the noble Knights of Maidenhead,
  His mighty heart did almost rend in tway,
  For very gall, that rather wholly dead
Himselfe he wisht have beene, than in so bad a stead.

23

Eftsoones he gan to gather up around
　His weapons, which lay scattered all abrode,
　And as it fell, his steed he ready found.
　On whom remounting, fiercely forth he rode,
　Like sparke of fire that from the andvile glode,
　There where he saw the valiant *Triamond*
　Chasing, and laying on them heavy lode.
　That none his force were able to withstond,
So dreadfull were his strokes, so deadly was his hond.

24

With that at him his beamlike speare he aimed,
　And thereto all his power and might applide:
　The wicked steele for mischiefe first ordained,
　And having now misfortune got for guide,
　Staid not, till it arrived in his side,
　And therein made a very griesly wound,
　That streames of bloud his armour all bedide.
　Much was he daunted with that direfull stound,
That scarse he him upheld from falling in a sound.

25

Yet as he might, himselfe he soft withdrew
　Out of the field, that none perceiv'd it plaine,
　Then gan the part of Chalengers anew
　To range the field, and victorlike to raine,
　That none against them battell durst maintaine.
　By that the gloomy evening on them fell,
　That forced them from fighting to refraine,
　And trumpets sound to cease did them compell,
So *Satyrane* that day was judg'd to beare the bell.

26

The morrow next the Turney gan anew,
　And with the first the hardy *Satyrane*
　Appear'd in place, with all his noble crew,
　On th'other side, full many a warlike swaine,
　Assembled were, that glorious prize to gaine.
　But mongst them all, was not Sir *Triamond*,
　Unable he new battell to darraine,
　Through grievaunce of his late received wound,
That doubly did him grieve, when so himselfe he found.

27

Which *Cambell* seeing, though he could not salve,
　Ne done undoe, yet for to salve his name,
　And purchase honour in his friends behalve,
　This goodly counterfesaunce he did frame.
　The shield and armes well knowne to be the same,
　Which *Triamond* had worne, unwares to wight,
　And to his friend unwist, for doubt of blame,
　If he misdid, he on himselfe did dight,
That none could him discerne, and so went forth to fight.

28

There *Satyrane* Lord of the field he found,
　Triumphing in great joy and jolity;
　Gainst whom none able was to stand on ground;
　That much he gan his glorie to envy,
　And cast t'avenge his friends indignity.
　A mightie speare eftsoones at him he bent;
　Who seeing him come on so furiously,
　Met him mid-way with equall hardiment,
That forcibly to ground they both together went.

29

They up againe them selves can lightly reare,
　And to their tryed swords them selves betake;
　With which they wrought such wondrous marvels there,
　That all the rest it did amazed make,
　Ne any dar'd their perill to partake;
　Now cuffling close, now chacing to and fro,
　Now hurtling round advantage for to take:
　As two wild Boares together grapling go,
Chaufing and foming choler each against his fo.

30

So as they courst, and turneyd here and theare,
　It chaunst Sir *Satyrane* his steed at last,
　Whether through foundring or through sodein feare
　To stumble, that his rider nigh he cast;
　Which vauntage *Cambell* did pursue so fast,
　That ere him selfe he had recovered well,
　So sore he sowst him on the compast creast,
　That forced him to leave his loftie sell,
And rudely tumbling downe under his horse feete fell.

31

Lightly *Cambello* leapt downe from his steed,
  For to have rent his shield and armes away,
  That whylome wont to be the victors meed;
  When all unwares he felt an hideous sway
  Of many swords, that lode on him did lay.
  An hundred knights had him enclosed round,
  To rescue *Satyrane* out of his pray;
  All which at once huge strokes on him did pound,
In hope to take him prisoner, where he stood on ground.

32

He with their multitude was nought dismayd,
  But with stout courage turnd upon them all,
  And with his brondiron round about him layd;
  Of which he dealt large almes, as did befall:
  Like as a Lion that by chaunce doth fall
  Into the hunters toile, doth rage and rore,
  In royall heart disdaining to be thrall.
  But all in vaine: for what might one do more?
They have him taken captive, though it grieve him sore.

33

Whereof when newes to *Triamond* was brought,
  There as he lay, his wound he soone forgot,
  And starting up, streight for his armour sought:
  In vaine he sought; for there he found it not;
  Cambello it away before had got:
  Cambelloes armes therefore he on him threw,
  And lightly issewd forth to take his lot.
  There he in troupe found all that warlike crew,
Leading his friend away, full sorie to his vew.

34

Into the thickest of that knightly preasse
  He thrust, and smote downe all that was betweene,
  Caried with fervent zeale, ne did he ceasse,
  Till that he came, where he had *Cambell* seene,
  Like captive thral two other Knights atweene,
  There he amongst them cruell havocke makes,
  That they which lead him, soone enforced beene
  To let him loose, to save their proper stakes,
Who being freed, from one a weapon fiercely takes.

35

With that he drives at them with dreadfull might,
  Both in remembrance of his friends late harme,
  And in revengement of his owne despight,
  So both together give a new allarme,
  As if but now the battell wexed warme.
  As when two greedy Wolves doe breake by force
  Into an heard, farre from the husband farme,
  They spoile and ravine without all remorse,
So did these two through all the field their foes enforce.

36

Fiercely they followd on their bolde emprize,
  Till trumpets sound did warne them all to rest;
  Then all with one consent did yeeld the prize
  To *Triamond* and *Cambell* as the best.
  But *Triamond* to *Cambell* it relest.
  And *Cambell* it to *Triamond* transferd;
  Each labouring t'advance the others gest,
  And make his praise before his owne preferd:
So that the doome was to another day differd.

37

The last day came, when all those knightes againe
  Assembled were their deedes of armes to shew.
  Full many deedes that day were shewed plaine:
  But *Satyrane* bove all the other crew,
  His wondrous worth declared in all mens view.
  For from the first he to the last endured,
  And though some while Fortune from him withdrew,
  Yet evermore his honour he recured,
And with unwearied powre his party still assured.

38

Ne was there Knight that ever thought of armes,
  But that his utmost prowesse there made knowen,
  That by their many wounds, and carelesse harmes,
  By shivered speares, and swords all under strowen,
  By scattered shields was easie to be showen.
  There might ye see loose steeds at random ronne,
  Whose luckelesse riders late were overthrowen;
  And squiers make hast to helpe their Lords fordonne,
But still the Knights of Maidenhead the better wonne.

39

Till that there entred on the other side,
  A straunger knight, from whence no man could reed,
  In quyent disguise, full hard to be descride.
  For all his armour was like salvage weed,
  With woody mosse bedight, and all his steed
  With oaken leaves attrapt, that seemed fit
  For salvage wight, and thereto well agreed
  His word, which on his ragged shield was writ,
Salvagesse sans finesse, shewing secret wit.

40

He at his first incomming, charg'd his spere
  At him, that first appeared in his sight:
  That was to weet, the stout Sir *Sangliere*,
  Who well was knowen to be a valiant Knight,
  Approved oft in many a perlous fight.
  Him at the first encounter downe he smote,
  And overbore beyond his crouper quight,
  And after him another Knight, that hote
Sir *Brianor*, so sore, that none him life behote.

41

Then ere his hand he reard, he overthrew
  Seven Knights one after other as they came:
  And when his speare was brust, his sword he drew,
  The instrument of wrath, and with the same
  Far'd like a lyon in his bloodie game,
  Hewing, and slashing shields, and helmets bright,
  And beating downe, what ever nigh him came,
  That every one gan shun his dreadfull sight,
No lesse than death it selfe, in daungerous affright.

42

Much wondred all men, what, or whence he came,
  That did amongst the troupes so tyrannize;
  And each of other gan inquire his name.
  But when they could not learne it by no wize,
  Most answerable to his wyld disguize
  It seemed, him to terme the salvage knight.
  But certes his right name was otherwize,
  Though knowne to few, that *Arthegall* he hight,
The doughtiest knight that liv'd that day, and most of might.

43

Thus was Sir *Satyrane* with all his band
  By his sole manhood and atchievement stout
  Dismayd, that none of them in field durst stand,
  But beaten were, and chased all about.
  So he continued all that day throughout,
  Till evening, that the Sunne gan downward bend.
  Then rushed forth out of the thickest rout
  A stranger knight, that did his glorie shend:
So nought may be esteemed happie till the end.

44

He at his entrance charg'd his powrefull speare
  At *Artegall*, in middest of his pryde,
  And therewith smote him on his Umbriere
  So sore, that tombling backe he downe did slyde
  Over his horses taile above a stryde;
  Whence litle lust he had to rise againe.
  Which *Cambell* seeing, much the same envyde,
  And ran at him with all his might and maine;
But shortly was likewise seene lying on the plaine.

45

Whereat full inly wroth was *Triamond*,
  And cast t'avenge the shame doen to his freend:
  But by his friend himselfe eke soone he fond,
  In no lesse neede of helpe, than him he weend.
  All which when *Blandamour* from end to end
  Beheld, he woxe therewith displeased sore,
  And thought in mind it shortly to amend:
  His speare he feutred, and at him it bore;
But with no better fortune, than the rest afore.

46

Full many others at him likewise ran:
  But all of them likewise dismounted were,
  Ne certes wonder; for no powre of man
  Could bide the force of that enchaunted speare,
  The which this famous *Britomart* did beare;
  With which she wondrous deeds of arms atchieved,
  And overthrew, what ever came her neare,
  That all those stranger knights full sore agrieved,
And that late weaker band of chalengers relieved.

47

Like as in sommers day when raging heat
　Doth burne the earth, and boyled rivers drie,
　That all brute beasts forst to refraine fro meat,
　Doe hunt for shade, where shrowded they may lie,
　And missing it, faine from themselves to flie;
　All travellers tormented are with paine:
　A watry cloud doth overcast the skie,
　And poureth forth a sudden shoure of raine,
That all the wretched world recomforteth againe.

48

So did the warlike *Britomart* restore
　The prize, to knights of Maydenhead that day,
　Which else was like to have bene lost, and bore
　The prayse of prowesse from them all away.
　Then shrilling trompets loudly gan to bray,
　And bad them leave their labours and long toyle,
　To joyous feast and other gentle play,
　Where beauties prize shold win that pretious spoyle:
Where I with sound of trompe will also rest a whyle.

CANT. V

The Ladies for the girdle strive
of famous Florimell:
Scudamour comming to Cares house,
doth sleepe from him expell.

1

IT hath bene through all ages ever seene,
　That with the praise of armes and chevalrie,
　The prize of beautie still hath joyned beene;
　And that for reasons speciall privitie:
　For either doth on other much relie.
　For he me seemes most fit the faire to serve,
　That can her best defend from villenie;
　And she most fit his service doth deserve,
That fairest is and from her faith will never swerve.

2

So fitly now here commeth next in place,
  After the proofe of prowesse ended well,
  The controverse of beauties soveraine grace;
  In which to her that doth the most excell,
  Shall fall the girdle of faire *Florimell*:
  That many wish to win for glorie vaine,
  And not for vertuous use, which some doe tell
  That glorious belt did in it selfe containe,
Which Ladies ought to love, and seeke for to obtaine.

3

That girdle gave the vertue of chast love,
  And wivehood true, to all that did it beare;
  But whosoever contrarie doth prove,
  Might not the same about her middle weare,
  But it would loose, or else a sunder teare.
  Whilome it was (as Faeries wont report)
  Dame *Venus* girdle, by her steemed deare,
  What time she usd to live in wively sort;
But layd aside, when so she usd her looser sport.

4

Her husband *Vulcan* whylome for her sake,
  When first he loved her with heart entire,
  This pretious ornament they say did make,
  And wrought in *Lemno* with unquenched fire:
  And afterwards did for her loves first hire,
  Give it to her, for ever to remaine,
  Therewith to bind lascivious desire,
  And loose affections streightly to restraine;
Which vertue it for ever after did retaine.

5

The same one day, when she her selfe disposd
  To visite her beloved Paramoure,
  The God of warre, she from her middle loosd,
  And left behind her in her secret bowre,
  On *Acidalian* mount, where many an howre
  She with the pleasant *Graces* wont to play.
  There *Florimell* in her first ages flowre
  Was fostered by those *Graces*, (as they say)
And brought with her from thence that goodly belt away.

6

That goodly belt was *Cestus* hight by name,
  And as her life by her esteemed deare.
  No wonder then, if that to winne the same
  So many Ladies sought, as shall appeare;
  For pearelesse she was thought, that did it beare.
  And now by this their feast all being ended,
  The judges which thereto selected were,
  Into the Martian field adowne descended,
To deeme this doutfull case, for which they all contended.

7

But first was question made, which of those Knights
  That lately turneyd, had the wager wonne:
  There was it judged by those worthie wights,
  That *Satyrane* the first day best had donne:
  For he last ended, having first begonne.
  The second was to *Triamond* behight,
  For that he sav'd the victour from fordonne:
  For *Cambell* victour was in all mens sight,
Till by mishap he in his foemens hand did light.

8

The third dayes prize unto that straunger Knight,
  Whom all men term'd Knight of the Hebene speare,
  To *Britomart* was given by good right;
  For that with puissant stroke she downe did beare
  The *Salvage* Knight, that victour was whileare,
  And all the rest, which had the best afore,
  And to the last unconquer'd did appeare;
  For last is deemed best. To her therefore
The fayrest Ladie was adjudgd for Paramore.

9

But thereat greatly grudged *Arthegall*,
  And much repynd, that both of victors meede,
  And eke of honour she did him forestall.
  Yet mote he not withstand, what was decreede;
  But inly thought of that despightfull deede
  Fit time t'awaite avenged for to bee.
  This being ended thus, and all agreed,
  Then next ensew'd the Paragon to see
Of beauties praise, and yeeld the fayrest her due fee.

10

Then first *Cambello* brought unto their view
　His faire *Cambina*, covered with a veale;
　Which being once withdrawne, most perfect hew
　And passing beautie did eftsoones reveale,
　That able was weake harts away to steale.
　Next did Sir *Triamond* unto their sight
　The face of his deare *Canacee* unheale;
　Whose beauties beame eftsoones did shine so bright,
That daz'd the eyes of all, as with exceeding light.

11

And after her did *Paridell* produce
　His false *Duessa*, that she might be seene,
　Who with her forged beautie did seduce
　The hearts of some, that fairest her did weene;
　As diverse wits affected divers beene.
　Then did Sir *Ferramont* unto them shew
　His *Lucida*, that was full faire and sheene,
　And after these an hundred Ladies moe
Appear'd in place, the which each other did outgoe.

12

All which who so dare thinke for to enchace,
　Him needeth sure a golden pen I weene,
　To tell the feature of each goodly face.
　For since the day that they created beene,
　So many heavenly faces were not seene
　Assembled in one place: ne he that thought
　For *Chian* folke to pourtraict beauties Queene,
　By view of all the fairest to him brought,
So many faire did see, as here he might have sought.

13

At last the most redoubted *Britonesse*,
　Her lovely *Amoret* did open shew;
　Whose face discovered, plainely did expresse
　The heavenly pourtraict of bright Angels hew.
　Well weened all, which her that time did vew,
　That she should surely beare the bell away,
　Till *Blandamour*, who thought he had the trew
　And very *Florimell*, did her display:
The sight of whom once seene did all the rest dismay.

14

For all afore that seemed fayre and bright,
  Now base and contemptible did appeare,
  Compar'd to her, that shone as Phebes light,
  Amongst the lesser starres in evening cleare.
  All that her saw with wonder ravisht weare,
  And weend no mortall creature she should bee,
  But some celestiall shape, that flesh did beare:
  Yet all were glad there *Florimell* to see;
Yet thought that *Florimell* was not so faire as shee.

15

As guilefull Goldsmith that by secret skill,
  With golden foyle doth finely over spred
  Some baser metall, which commend he will
  Unto the vulgar for good gold insted,
  He much more goodly glosse thereon doth shed,
  To hide his falshood, than if it were trew:
  So hard, this Idole was to be ared,
  That *Florimell* her selfe in all mens vew
She seem'd to passe: so forged things do fairest shew.

16

Then was that golden belt by doome of all
  Graunted to her, as to the fayrest Dame.
  Which being brought, about her middle small
  They thought to gird, as best it her became;
  But by no meanes they could it thereto frame.
  For ever as they fastned it, it loos'd
  And fell away, as feeling secret blame.
  Full oft about her wast she it enclos'd;
And it as oft was from about her wast disclos'd.

17

That all men wondred at the uncouth sight,
  And each one thought, as to their fancies came.
  But she her selfe did thinke it doen for spight,
  And touched was with secret wrath and shame
  Therewith, as thing deviz'd her to defame.
  Then many other Ladies likewise tride,
  About their tender loynes to knit the same;
  But it would not on none of them abide,
But when they thought it fast, eftsoones it was untide.

18

Which when that scornefull *Squire of Dames* did vew,
    He lowdly gan to laugh, and thus to jest;
    Alas for pittie that so faire a crew,
    As like can not be seene from East to West,
    Cannot find one this girdle to invest.
    Fie on the man, that did it first invent,
    To shame us all with this, *Ungirt unblest*.
    Let never Ladie to his love assent,
That hath this day so many so unmanly shent.

19

Thereat all Knights gan laugh, and Ladies lowre:
    Till that at last the gentle *Amoret*
    Likewise assayd, to prove that girdles powre;
    And having it about her middle set,
    Did find it fit, withouten breach or let.
    Whereat the rest gan greatly to envie:
    But *Florimell* exceedingly did fret,
    And snatching from her hand halfe angrily
The belt againe, about her bodie gan it tie.

20

Yet nathemore would it her bodie fit;
    Yet nathelesse to her, as her dew right,
    It yeelded was by them, that judged it:
    And she her selfe adjudged to the Knight,
    That bore the Hebene speare, as wonne in fight.
    But *Britomart* would not thereto assent,
    Ne her owne *Amoret* forgoe so light
    For that strange Dame, whose beauties wonderment
She lesse esteem'd, than th'others vertuous government.

21

Whom when the rest did see her to refuse,
    They were full glad, in hope themselves to get her:
    Yet at her choice they all did greatly muse.
    But after that the Judges did arret her
    Unto the second best, that lov'd her better;
    That was the *Salvage* Knight: but he was gone
    In great displeasure, that he could not get her.
    Then was she judged *Triamond* his one;
But *Triamond* lov'd *Canacee*, and other none.

22

Tho unto *Satyran* she was adjudged,
  Who was right glad to gaine so goodly meed:
  But *Blandamour* thereat full greatly grudged,
  And litle prays'd his labours evill speed,
  That for to winne the saddle, lost the steed.
  Ne lesse thereat did *Paridell* complaine,
  And thought t'appeale from that, which was decreed,
  To single combat with Sir *Satyrane*.
Thereto him *Ate* stird, new discord to maintaine.

23

And eke with these, full many other Knights
  She through her wicked working did incense,
  Her to demaund, and chalenge as their rights,
  Deserved for their perils recompense.
  Amongst the rest with boastfull vaine pretense
  Stept *Braggadochio* forth, and as his thrall
  Her claym'd, by him in battell wonne long sens:
  Whereto her selfe he did to witnesse call;
Who being askt, accordingly confessed all.

24

Thereat exceeding wroth was *Satyran*;
  And wroth with *Satyran* was *Blandamour*;
  And wroth with *Blandamour* was *Erivan*;
  And at them both Sir *Paridell* did loure.
  So all together stird up strifull stoure,
  And readie were new battell to darraine.
  Each one profest to be her paramoure,
  And vow'd with speare and shield it to maintaine;
Ne Iudges powre, ne reasons rule mote them restraine.

25

Which troublous stirre when *Satyrane* aviz'd,
  He gan to cast how to appease the same,
  And to accord them all, this meanes deviz'd:
  First in the midst to set that fayrest Dame,
  To whom each one his chalenge should disclame,
  And he himselfe his right would eke releasse:
  Then looke to whom she voluntarie came,
  He should without disturbance her possesse:
Sweete is the love that comes alone with willingnesse.

26

They all agreed, and then that snowy Mayd
 Was in the middest plast among them all;
 All on her gazing wisht, and vowd, and prayd,
 And to the Queene of beautie close did call,
 That she unto their portion might befall.
 Then when she long had lookt upon each one,
 As though she wished to have pleasd them all,
 At last to *Braggadochio* selfe alone
She came of her accord, in spight of all his fone.

27

Which when they all beheld they chaft and rag'd,
 And woxe nigh mad for very harts despight,
 That from revenge their willes they scarse asswag'd:
 Some thought from him her to have reft by might;
 Some proffer made with him for her to fight.
 But he nought car'd for all that they could say:
 For he their words as wind esteemed light.
 Yet not fit place he thought it there to stay,
But secretly from thence that night her bore away.

28

They which remaynd, so soone as they perceiv'd,
 That she was gone, departed thence with speed,
 And follow'd them, in mind her to have reav'd
 From wight unworthie of so noble meed.
 In which poursuit how each one did succeede,
 Shall else be told in order, as it fell.
 But now of *Britomart* it here doth neede,
 The hard adventures and strange haps to tell;
Since with the rest she went not after *Florimell*.

29

For soone as she them saw to discord set,
 Her list no longer in that place abide;
 But taking with her lovely *Amoret*,
 Upon her first adventure forth did ride,
 To seeke her lov'd, making blind love her guide.
 Unluckie Mayd to seeke her enemie,
 Unluckie Mayd to seeke him farre and wide,
 Whom, when he was unto her selfe most nie,
She through his late disguizement could him not descrie.

30

So much the more her griefe, the more her toyle:
  Yet neither toyle nor griefe she once did spare,
  In seeking him, that should her paine assoyle;
  Whereto great comfort in her sad misfare
  Was *Amoret*, companion of her care:
  Who likewise sought her lover long miswent,
  The gentle *Scudamour*, whose hart whileare
  That stryfull hag with gealous discontent
Had fild, that he to fell reveng was fully bent.

31

Bent to revenge on blamelesse *Britomart*
  The crime, which cursed *Ate* kindled earst,
  The which like thornes did pricke his gealous hart,
  And through his soule like poysned arrow perst,
  That by no reason it might be reverst,
  For ought that *Glauce* could or doe or say.
  For aye the more that she the same reherst,
  The more it gauld, and griev'd him night and day,
That nought but dire revenge his anger mote defray.

32

So as they travelled, the drouping night
  Covered with cloudie storme and bitter showre,
  That dreadfull seem'd to every living wight,
  Upon them fell, before her timely howre;
  That forced them to seeke some covert bowre,
  Where they might hide their heads in quiet rest,
  And shrowd their persons from that stormie stowre.
  Not farre away, not meete for any guest
They spide a little cottage, like some poore mans nest.

33

Under a steepe hilles side it placed was,
  There where the mouldred earth had cav'd the banke;
  And fast beside a little brooke did pas
  Of muddie water, that like puddle stanke,
  By which few crooked sallowes grew in ranke:
  Whereto approaching nigh, they heard the sound
  Of many yron hammers beating ranke,
  And answering their wearie turnes around,
That seemed some blacksmith dwelt in that desert ground.

34

There entring in, they found the goodman selfe,
　Full busily unto his worke ybent;
　Who was to weet a wretched wearish elfe,
　With hollow eyes and rawbone cheekes forspent,
　As if he had in prison long bene pent:
　Full blacke and griesly did his face appeare,
　Besmeard with smoke that nigh his eye-sight blent;
　With rugged beard, and hoarie shagged heare,
The which he never wont to combe, or comely sheare.

35

Rude was his garment, and to rags all rent,
　Ne better had he, ne for better cared:
　With blistred hands emongst the cinders brent,
　And fingers filthie, with long nayles unpared,
　Right fit to rend the food, on which he fared.
　His name was *Care*; a blacksmith by his trade,
　That neither day nor night from working spared,
　But to small purpose yron wedges made:
Those be unquiet thoughts, that carefull minds invade.

36

In which his worke he had six servants prest,
　About the Andvile standing evermore,
　With huge great hammers, that did never rest
　From heaping stroakes, which thereon soused sore:
　All six strong groomes, but one than other more;
　For by degrees they all were disagreed;
　So likewise did the hammers which they bore,
　Like belles in greatnesse orderly succeed,
That he which was the last, the first did farre exceede.

37

He like a monstrous Gyant seem'd in sight,
　Farre passing *Bronteus*, or *Pyracmon* great,
　The which in *Lipari* doe day and night
　Frame thunderbolts for *Joves* avengefull threate.
　So dreadfully he did the andvile beat,
　That seem'd to dust he shortly would it drive:
　So huge his hammer and so fierce his heat,
　That seem'd a rocke of Diamond it could rive,
And rend a sunder quite, if he thereto list strive,

38

Sir *Scudamour* there entring, much admired
  The manner of their worke and wearie paine;
  And having long beheld, at last enquired
  The cause and end thereof: but all in vaine;
  For they for nought would from their worke refraine,
  Ne let his speeches come unto their eare.
  And eke the breathfull bellowes blew amaine,
  Like to the Northren winde, that none could heare:
Those *Pensifenesse* did move; and *Sighes* the bellowes weare.

39

Which when that warriour saw, he said no more,
  But in his armour layd him downe to rest:
  To rest he layd him downe upon the flore,
  (Whylome for ventrous Knights the bedding best)
  And thought his wearie limbs to have redrest.
  And that old aged Dame, his faithfull Squire,
  Her feeble joynts layd eke a downe to rest;
  That needed much her weake age to desire,
After so long a travell, which them both did tire.

40

There lay Sir *Scudamour* long while expecting,
  When gentle sleepe his heavie eyes would close;
  Oft chaunging sides, and oft new place electing,
  Where better seem'd he mote himselfe repose;
  And oft in wrath he thence againe uprose;
  And oft in wrath he layd him downe againe.
  But wheresoever he did himselfe dispose,
  He by no meanes could wished ease obtaine:
So every place seem'd painefull, and ech changing vaine.

41

And evermore, when he to sleepe did thinke,
  The hammers sound his senses did molest;
  And evermore, when he began to winke,
  The bellowes noyse disturb'd his quiet rest,
  Ne suffred sleepe to settle in his brest.
  And all the night the dogs did barke and howle
  About the house, at sent of stranger guest:
  And now the crowing Cocke, and now the Owle
Lowde shriking him afflicted to the very sowle.

42

And if by fortune any litle nap
  Upon his heavie eye-lids chaunst to fall,
  Eftsoones one of those villeins him did rap
  Upon his headpeece with his yron mall;
  That he was soone awaked therewithall,
  And lightly started up as one affrayd;
  Or as if one him suddenly did call.
  So oftentimes he out of sleepe abrayd,
And then lay musing long, on that him ill apayd.

43

So long he muzed, and so long he lay,
  That at the last his wearie sprite opprest
  With fleshly weaknesse, which no creature may
  Long time resist, gave place to kindly rest,
  That all his senses did full soone arrest:
  Yet in his soundest sleepe, his dayly feare
  His ydle braine gan busily molest,
  And made him dreame those two disloyall were:
The things that day most minds, at night doe most appeare.

44

With that, the wicked carle the maister Smith
  A paire of redwhot yron tongs did take
  Out of the burning cinders, and therewith
  Under his side him nipt, that forst to wake,
  He felt his hart for very paine to quake,
  And started up avenged for to be
  On him, the which his quiet slomber brake:
  Yet looking round about him none could see;
Yet did the smart remaine, though he himselfe did flee.

45

In such disquiet, and hartfretting payne,
  He all that night, that too long night did passe.
  And now the day out of the Ocean mayne
  Began to peepe above this earthly masse,
  With pearly dew sprinkling the morning grasse:
  Then up he rose like heavie lumpe of lead,
  That in his face, as in a looking glasse,
  The signes of anguish one mote plainely read,
And ghesse the man to be dismayd with gealous dread.

46

Unto his lofty steede he clombe anone,
  And forth upon his former voiage fared,
  And with him eke that aged Squire attone;
  Who whatsoever perill was prepared,
  Both equall paines and equall perill shared:
  The end whereof and daungerous event
  Shall for another canticle be spared.
  But here my wearie teeme nigh over spent
Shall breath it selfe awhile, after so long a went.

CANT. VI

Both Scudamour and Arthegall
Doe fight with Britomart,
He sees her face; doth fall in love,
and soone from her depart.

1

WHAT equall torment to the griefe of mind,
  And pyning anguish hid in gentle hart,
  That inly feeds it selfe with thoughts unkind,
  And nourisheth her owne consuming smart?
  What medicine can any Leaches art
  Yeeld such a sore, that doth her grievance hide,
  And will to none her maladie impart?
  Such was the wound that *Scudamour* did gride;
For which *Dan Phebus* selfe cannot a salve provide.

2

Who having left that restlesse house of *Care*,
  The next day, as he on his way did ride,
  Full of melancholie and sad misfare,
  Through misconceipt; all unawares espide
  An armed Knight under a forrest side,
  Sitting in shade beside his grazing steede;
  Who soone as them approaching he descride,
  Gan towards them to pricke with eger speede,
That seem'd he was full bent to some mischievous deede.

3

Which *Scudamour* perceiving, forth issewed
  To have rencountred him in equall race;
  But soone as th'other nigh approaching, vewed
  The armes he bore, his speare he gan abase,
  And voide his course: at which so suddain case
  He wondred much. But th'other thus can say;
  Ah gentle *Scudamour*, unto your grace
  I me submit, and you of pardon pray,
That almost had against you trespassed this day.

4

Whereto thus *Scudamour*, Small harme it were
  For any knight, upon a ventrous knight
  Without displeasance for to prove his spere.
  But reade you Sir, sith ye my name have hight,
  What is your owne, that I mote you requite.
  Certes (sayd he) ye mote as now excuse
  Me from discovering you my name aright:
  For time yet serves that I the same refuse,
But call ye me the *Salvage Knight*, as others use.

5

Then this, Sir *Salvage Knight* (quoth he) areede;
  Or doe you here within this forrest wonne,
  That seemeth well to answere to your weede?
  Or have ye it for some occasion donne?
  That rather seemes, sith knowen armes ye shonne.
  This other day (sayd he) a stranger knight
  Shame and dishonour hath unto me donne;
  On whom I waite to wreake that foule despight,
When ever he this way shall passe by day or night.

6

Shame be his meede (quoth he) that meaneth shame.
  But what is he, by whom ye shamed were?
  A stranger knight, sayd he, unknowne by name,
  But knowne by fame, and by an Hebene speare,
  With which he all that met him, downe did beare.
  He in an open Turney lately held,
  Fro me the honour of that game did reare;
  And having me all wearie earst, downe feld,
The fayrest Ladie reft, and ever since withheld.

7

When *Scudamour* heard mention of that speare,
  He wist right well, that it was *Britomart*,
  The which from him his fairest love did beare.
  Tho gan he swell in every inner part,
  For fell despight, and gnaw his gealous hart,
  That thus he sharply sayd; Now by my head,
  Yet is not this the first unknightly part,
  Which that same knight, whom by his launce I read,
Hath doen to noble knights, that many makes him dread.

8

For lately he my love hath fro me reft,
  And eke defiled with foule villanie
  The sacred pledge, which in his faith was left,
  In shame of knighthood and fidelitie;
  The which ere long full deare he shall abie.
  And if to that avenge by you decreed
  This hand may helpe, or succour ought supplie,
  It shall not fayle, when so ye shall it need.
So both to wreake their wrathes on *Britomart* agreed.

9

Whiles thus they communed, lo farre away
  A Knight soft ryding towards them they spyde,
  Attyr'd in forraine armes and straunge aray:
  Whom when they nigh approcht, they plaine descryde
  To be the same, for whom they did abyde.
  Sayd then Sir *Scudamour*, Sir *Salvage* knight
  Let me this crave, sith first I was defyde,
  That first I may that wrong to him requite:
And if I hap to fayle, you shall recure my right.

10

Which being yeelded, he his threatfull speare
  Gan fewter, and against her fiercely ran.
  Who soone as she him saw approaching neare
  With so fell rage, her selfe she lightly gan
  To dight, to welcome him, well as she can:
  But entertaind him in so rude a wise,
  That to the ground she smote both horse and man;
  Whence neither greatly hasted to arise,
But on their common harmes together did devise.

11

But *Artegall* beholding his mischaunce,
  New matter added to his former fire;
  And eft aventring his steeleheaded launce,
  Against her rode, full of despiteous ire,
  That nought but spoyle and vengeance did require.
  But to himselfe his felonous intent
  Returning, disappointed his desire,
  Whiles unawares his saddle he forwent,
And found himselfe on ground in great amazement.

12

Lightly he started up out of that stound,
  And snatching forth his direfull deadly blade,
  Did leape to her, as doth an eger hound
  Thrust to an Hynd within some covert glade,
  Whom without perill he cannot invade.
  With such fell greedines he her assayled,
  That though she mounted were, yet he her made
  To give him ground, (so much his force prevayled)
And shun his mightie strokes, gainst which no armes avayled.

13

So as they coursed here and there, it chaunst
  That in her wheeling round, behind her crest
  So sorely he her strooke, that thence it glaunst
  Adowne her backe, the which it fairely blest
  From foule mischance; ne did it ever rest,
  Till on her horses hinder parts it fell;
  Where byting deepe, so deadly it imprest,
  That quite it chynd his backe behind the sell,
And to alight on foote her algates did compell.

14

Like as the lightning brond from riven skie,
  Throwne out by angry *Jove* in his vengeance,
  With dreadfull force falles on some steeple hie;
  Which battring, downe it on the church doth glance,
  And teares it all with terrible mischance.
  Yet she no whit dismayd, her steed forsooke,
  And casting from her that enchaunted lance,
  Unto her sword and shield her soone betooke;
And therewithall at him right furiously she strooke.

15

So furiously she strooke in her first heat,
　Whiles with long fight on foot he breathlesse was,
　That she him forced backward to retreat,
　And yeeld unto her weapon way to pas:
　Whose raging rigour neither steele nor bras
　Could stay, but to the tender flesh it went,
　And pour'd the purple bloud forth on the gras;
　That all his mayle yriv'd, and plates yrent,
Shew'd all his bodie bare unto the cruell dent.

16

At length when as he saw her hastie heat
　Abate, and panting breath begin to fayle,
　He through long sufferance growing now more great,
　Rose in his strength, and gan her fresh assayle,
　Heaping huge strokes, as thicke as showre of hayle,
　And lashing dreadfully at every part,
　As if he thought her soule to disentrayle.
　Ah cruell hand, and thrise more cruell hart,
That workst such wrecke on her, to whom thou dearest art.

17

What yron courage ever could endure,
　To worke such outrage on so faire a creature?
　And in his madnesse thinke with hands impure
　To spoyle so goodly workmanship of nature,
　The maker selfe resembling in her feature?
　Certes some hellish furie, or some feend
　This mischiefe framd, for their first loves defeature,
　To bath their hands in bloud of dearest freend,
Thereby to make their loves beginning, their lives end.

18

Thus long they trac'd, and traverst to and fro,
　Sometimes pursewing, and sometimes pursewed,
　Still as advantage they espyde thereto:
　But toward th'end Sir *Arthegall* renewed
　His strength still more, but she still more decrewed.
　At last his lucklesse hand he heav'd on hie,
　Having his forces all in one accrewed,
　And therewith stroke at her so hideouslie,
That seemed nought but death mote be her destinie.

19

The wicked stroke upon her helmet chaunst,
 And with the force, which in it selfe it bore,
 Her ventayle shard away, and thence forth glaunst
 A downe in vaine, ne harm'd her any more.
 With that her angels face, unseene afore,
 Like to the ruddie morne appeard in sight,
 Deawed with silver drops, through sweating sore,
 But somewhat redder, than beseem'd aright,
Through toylesome heate and labour of her weary fight.

20

And round about the same, her yellow heare
 Having through stirring loosd their wonted band,
 Like to a golden border did appeare,
 Framed in goldsmithes forge with cunning hand:
 Yet goldsmithes cunning could not understand
 To frame such subtile wire, so shinie cleare.
 For it did glister like the golden sand,
 The which *Pactolus* with his waters shere,
Throwes forth upon the rivage round about him nere.

21

And as his hand he up againe did reare,
 Thinking to worke on her his utmost wracke,
 His powrelesse arme benumbd with secret feare
 From his revengefull purpose shronke abacke,
 And cruell sword out of his fingers slacke
 Fell downe to ground, as if the steele had sence,
 And felt some ruth, or sence his hand did lacke,
 Or both of them did thinke, obedience
To doe to so divine a beauties excellence.

22

And he himselfe long gazing thereupon,
 At last fell humbly downe upon his knee,
 And of his wonder made religion,
 Weening some heavenly goddesse he did see,
 Or else unweeting, what it else might bee;
 And pardon her besought his errour frayle,
 That had done outrage in so high degree:
 Whilest trembling horrour did his sense assayle,
And made ech member quake, and manly hart to quayle.

23

Nathelesse she full of wrath for that late stroke,
　All that long while upheld her wrathfull hand,
　With fell intent, on him to bene ywroke,
　And looking sterne, still over him did stand,
　Threatning to strike, unlesse he would withstand:
　And bad him rise, or surely he should die.
　But die or live for nought he would upstand
　But her of pardon prayd more earnestlie,
Or wreake on him her will for so great injurie.

24

Which when as *Scudamour*, who now abrayd,
　Beheld, whereas he stood not farre aside,
　He was therewith right wondrously dismayd,
　And drawing nigh, when as he plaine descride
　That peerelesse paterne of Dame natures pride,
　And heavenly image of perfection,
　He blest himselfe, as one sore terrifide,
　And turning his feare to faint devotion,
Did worship her as some celestiall vision.

25

But *Glauce*, seeing all that chaunced there,
　Well weeting how their errour to assoyle,
　Full glad of so good end, to them drew nere,
　And her salewd with seemely belaccoyle,
　Joyous to see her safe after long toyle.
　Then her besought, as she to her was deare,
　To graunt unto those warriours truce a whyle;
　Which yeelded, they their bevers up did reare,
And shew'd themselves to her, such as indeed they were.

26

When *Britomart* with sharpe avizefull eye
　Beheld the lovely face of *Artegall*,
　Tempred with sternesse and stout majestie,
　She gan eftsoones it to her mind to call,
　To be the same which in her fathers hall
　Long since in that enchaunted glasse she saw.
　Therewith her wrathfull courage gan appall,
　And haughtie spirits meekely to adaw,
That her enhaunced hand she downe can soft withdraw.

27

Yet she it forst to have againe upheld,
  As fayning choler, which was turn'd to cold:
  But ever when his visage she beheld,
  Her hand fell downe, and would no longer hold
  The wrathfull weapon gainst his countnance bold:
  But when in vaine to fight she oft assayd,
  She arm'd her tongue, and thought at him to scold;
  Nathlesse her tongue not to her will obayd,
But brought forth speeches myld, when she would have missayd.

28

But *Scudamour* now woxen inly glad,
  That all his gealous feare he false had found,
  And how that Hag his love abused had
  With breach of faith and loyaltie unsound,
  The which long time his grieved hart did wound,
  He thus bespake; Certes Sir *Artegall*,
  I joy to see you lout so low on ground,
  And now become to live a Ladies thrall,
That whylome in your minde wont to despise them all.

29

Soone as she heard the name of *Artegall*,
  Her hart did leape, and all her hart-strings tremble,
  For sudden joy, and secret feare withall,
  And all her vitall powres with motion nimble,
  To succour it, themselves gan there assemble,
  That by the swift recourse of flushing blood
  Right plaine appeard, though she it would dissemble,
  And fayned still her former angry mood,
Thinking to hide the depth by troubling of the flood.

30

When *Glauce* thus gan wisely all upknit;
  Ye gentle Knights, whom fortune here hath brought,
  To be spectators of this uncouth fit,
  Which secret fate hath in this Ladie wrought,
  Against the course of kind, ne mervaile nought,
  Ne thenceforth feare the thing that hethertoo
  Hath troubled both your mindes with idle thought,
  Fearing least she your loves away should woo,
Feared in vaine, sith meanes ye see there wants theretoo.

31

And you Sir *Artegall*, the salvage knight,
  Henceforth may not disdaine, that womans hand
  Hath conquered you anew in second fight:
  For whylome they have conquerd sea and land,
  And heaven it selfe, that nought may them withstand.
  Ne henceforth be rebellious unto love,
  That is the crowne of knighthood, and the band
  Of noble minds derived from above,
Which being knit with vertue, never will remove.

32

And you faire Ladie knight, my dearest Dame,
  Relent the rigour of your wrathfull will,
  Whose fire were better turn'd to other flame;
  And wiping out remembrance of all ill,
  Graunt him your grace, but so that he fulfill
  The penance, which ye shall to him empart:
  For lovers heaven must passe by sorrowes hell.
  Thereat full inly blushed *Britomart*;
But *Artegall* close smyling joy'd in secret hart.

33

Yet durst he not make love so suddenly,
  Ne thinke th'affection of her hart to draw
  From one to other so quite contrary:
  Besides her modest countenance he saw
  So goodly grave, and full of princely aw,
  That it his ranging fancie did refraine,
  And looser thoughts to lawfull bounds withdraw;
  Whereby the passion grew more fierce and faine,
Like to a stubborne steede whom strong hand would restraine.

34

But *Scudamour* whose hart twixt doubtfull feare
  And feeble hope hung all this while suspence,
  Desiring of his *Amoret* to heare
  Some gladfull newes and sure intelligence,
  Her thus bespake; But Sir without offence
  Mote I request you tydings of my love,
  My *Amoret*, sith you her freed fro thence,
  Where she captived long, great woes did prove;
That where ye left, I may her seeke, as doth behove.

35

To whom thus *Britomart*, Certes Sir knight,
  What is of her become, or whether reft,
  I can not unto you aread a right.
  For from that time I from enchaunters theft
  Her freed, in which ye her all hopelesse left,
  I her preserv'd from perill and from feare,
  And evermore from villenie her kept:
  Ne ever was there wight to me more deare
Than she, ne unto whom I more true love did beare.

36

Till on a day as through a desert wyld
  We travelled, both wearie of the way
  We did alight, and sate in shadow myld;
  Where fearelesse I to sleepe me downe did lay.
  But when as I did out of sleepe abray,
  I found her not, where I her left whyleare,
  But thought she wandred was, or gone astray.
  I cal'd her loud, I sought her farre and neare;
But no where could her find, nor tydings of her heare.

37

When *Scudamour* those heavie tydings heard,
  His hart was thrild with point of deadly feare;
  Ne in his face or bloud or life appeard,
  But senselesse stood, like to a mazed steare,
  That yet of mortall stroke the stound doth beare.
  Till *Glauce* thus; Faire Sir, be nought dismayd
  With needelesse dread, till certaintie ye heare:
  For yet she may be safe though somewhat strayd;
Its best to hope the best, though of the worst affrayd.

38

Nathlesse he hardly of her chearefull speech
  Did comfort take, or in his troubled sight
  Shew'd change of better cheare: so sore a breach
  That sudden newes had made into his spright;
  Till *Britomart* him fairely thus behight;
  Great cause of sorrow certes Sir ye have:
  But comfort take: for by this heavens light
  I vow, you dead or living not to leave,
Till I her find, and wreake on him that her did reave.

39

Therewith he rested, and well pleased was.
　So peace being confirm'd amongst them all,
　They tooke their steeds, and forward thence did pas
　Unto some resting place, which mote befall,
　All being guided by Sir *Artegall*.
　Where goodly solace was unto them made,
　And dayly feasting both in bowre and hall,
　Untill that they their wounds well healed had,
And wearie limmes recur'd after late usage bad.

40

In all which time, Sir *Artegall* made way
　Unto the love of noble *Britomart*,
　And with meeke service and much suit did lay
　Continuall siege unto her gentle hart,
　Which being whylome launcht with lovely dart,
　More eath was new impression to receive,
　How ever she her paynd with womanish art
　To hide her wound, that none might it perceive:
Vaine is the art that seekes it selfe for to deceive.

41

So well he woo'd her, and so well he wrought her,
　With faire entreatie and sweet blandishment,
　That at the length unto a bay he brought her,
　So as she to his speeches was content
　To lend an eare, and softly to relent.
　At last through many vowes which forth he pour'd,
　And many othes, she yeelded her consent
　To be his love, and take him for her Lord,
Till they with mariage meet might finish that accord.

42

Tho when they had long time there taken rest,
　Sir *Artegall*, who all this while was bound
　Upon an hard adventure yet in quest,
　Fit time for him thence to depart it found,
　To follow that, which he did long propound;
　And unto her his congee came to take.
　But her therewith full sore displeasd he found,
　And loth to leave her late betrothed make,
Her dearest love full loth so shortly to forsake.

43

Yet he with strong perswasions her asswaged,
  And wonne her will to suffer him depart;
  For which his faith with her he fast engaged,
  And thousand vowes from bottome of his hart,
  That all so soone as he by wit or art
  Could that atchieve, whereto he did aspire,
  He unto her would speedily revert:
  No longer space thereto he did desire,
But till the horned moone three courses did expire.

44

With which she for the present was appeased,
  And yeelded leave, how ever malcontent
  She inly were, and in her mind displeased.
  So early in the morrow next he went
  Forth on his way, to which he was ybent.
  Ne wight him to attend, or way to guide,
  As whylome was the custome ancient
  Mongst Knights, when on adventures they did ride,
Save that she algates him a while accompanide.

45

And by the way she sundry purpose found
  Of this or that, the time for to delay,
  And of the perils whereto he was bound,
  The feare whereof seem'd much her to affray:
  But all she did was but to weare out day.
  Full oftentimes she leave of him did take;
  And eft againe deviz'd some what to say,
  Which she forgot, whereby excuse to make:
So loth she was his companie for to forsake.

46

At last when all her speeches she had spent,
  And new occasion fayld her more to find,
  She left him to his fortunes government,
  And backe returned with right heavie mind,
  To *Scudamour*, who she had left behind,
  With whom she went to seeke faire *Amoret*,
  Her second care, though in another kind;
  For vertues onely sake, which doth beget
True love and faithfull friendship, she by her did set.

47

Backe to that desert forrest they retyred,
　Where sorie *Britomart* had lost her late;
　There they her sought, and every where inquired,
　Where they might tydings get of her estate;
　Yet found they none. But by what haplesse fate,
　Or hard misfortune she was thence convayd,
　And stolne away from her beloved mate,
　Were long to tell; therefore I here will stay
Untill another tyde, that I it finish may.

CANT. VII

Amoret rapt by greedie lust
　　Belphebe saves from dread,
The Squire her loves, and being blam'd
　　his dayes in dole doth lead.

I

GREAT God of love, that with thy cruell dart
　Doest conquer greatest conquerors on ground,
　And setst thy kingdome in the captive harts
　Of Kings and Keasars, to thy service bound,
　What glorie, or what guerdon hast thou found
　In feeble Ladies tyranning so sore;
　And adding anguish to the bitter wound,
　With which their lives thou lanchedst long afore,
By heaping stormes of trouble on them daily more?

2

So whylome didst thou to faire *Florimell*;
　And so and so to noble *Britomart*;
　So doest thou now to her, of whom I tell,
　The lovely *Amoret*, whose gentle hart
　Thou martyrest with sorow and with smart,
　In salvage forrests, and in deserts wide,
　With Beares and Tygers taking heavie part,
　Withouten comfort, and withouten guide,
That pittie is to heare the perils, which she tride.

3

So soone as she with that brave Britonesse
  Had left that Turneyment for beauties prise,
  They travel'd long, that now for wearinesse,
  Both of the way, and warlike exercise,
  Both through a forest ryding did devise
  T'alight, and rest their wearie limbs awhile.
  There heavie sleepe the eye-lids did surprise
  Of *Britomart* after long tedious toyle,
That did her passed paines in quiet rest assoyle.

4

The whiles faire *Amoret*, of nought affeard,
  Walkt through the wood, for pleasure, or for need;
  When suddenly behind her backe she heard
  One rushing forth out of the thickest weed,
  That ere she backe could turne to taken heed,
  Had unawares her snatched up from ground.
  Feebly she shriekt, but so feebly indeed,
  That *Britomart* heard not the shrilling sound,
There where through weary travel she lay sleeping sound.

5

It was to weet a wilde and salvage man,
  Yet was no man, but onely like in shape
  And eke in stature higher by a span,
  All overgrowne with haire, that could awhape
  An hardy hart, and his wide mouth did gape
  With huge great teeth, like to a tusked Bore:
  For he liv'd all on ravin and on rape
  Of men and beasts; and fed on fleshly gore,
The signe whereof yet stain'd his bloudy lips afore.

6

His neather lip was not like man nor beast,
  But like a wide deepe poke, downe hanging low,
  In which he wont the relickes of his feast,
  And cruell spoyle, which he had spard, to stow:
  And over it his huge great nose did grow,
  Full dreadfully empurpled all with bloud;
  And downe both sides two wide long eares did glow,
  And raught downe to his waste, when up he stood,
More great than th'eares of Elephants by *Indus* flood.

7

His wast was with a wreath of yvie greene
  Engirt about, ne other garment wore:
  For all his haire was like a garment seene;
  And in his hand a tall young oake he bore,
  Whose knottie snags were sharpned all afore,
  And beath'd in fire for steele to be in sted.
  But whence he was, or of what wombe ybore,
  Of beasts, or of the earth, I have not red:
But certes was with milke of Wolves and Tygres fed.

8

This ugly creature in his armes her snatcht,
  And through the forrest bore her quite away,
  With briers and bushes all to rent and scratcht;
  Ne care he had, ne pittie of the pray,
  Which many a knight had sought so many a day.
  He stayed not, but in his armes her bearing
  Ran, till he came to th'end of all his way,
  Unto his cave farre from all peoples hearing,
And there he threw her in, nought feeling, ne nought fearing.

9

For she deare Ladie all the way was dead,
  Whilest he in armes her bore; but when she felt
  Her selfe downe soust, she waked out of dread
  Streight into griefe, that her deare hart nigh swelt,
  And eft gan into tender teares to melt.
  Then when she lookt about, and nothing found
  But darknesse and dread horrour, where she dwelt,
  She almost fell againe into a swound,
Ne wist whether above she were, or under ground.

10

With that she heard some one close by her side
  Sighing and sobbing sore, as if the paine
  Her tender hart in peeces would divide:
  Which she long listning, softly askt againe
  What mister wight it was that so did plaine?
  To whom thus aunswer'd was: Ah wretched wight
  That seekes to know anothers griefe in vaine,
  Unweeting of thine owne like haplesse plight:
Selfe to forget to mind another, is oversight.

11

Aye me (said she) where am I, or with whom?
  Emong the living, or emong the dead?
  What shall of me unhappy maid become?
  Shall death be th'end, or ought else worse, aread.
  Unhappy mayd (then answerd she) whose dread
  Untride, is lesse than when thou shalt it try:
  Death is to him, that wretched life doth lead,
  Both grace and gaine; but he in hell doth lie,
That lives a loathed life, and wishing cannot die.

12

This dismall day hath thee a caytive made,
  And vassall to the vilest wretch alive,
  Whose cursed usage and ungodly trade
  The heavens abhorre, and into darkenesse drive.
  For on the spoile of women he doth live,
  Whose bodies chast, when ever in his powre
  He may them catch, unable to gainestrive,
  He with his shamefull lust doth first deflowre,
And afterwards themselves doth cruelly devoure.

13

Now twenty daies, by which the sonnes of men
  Divide their works, have past through heven sheene,
  Since I was brought into this dolefull den;
  During which space these sory eies have seen
  Seaven women by him slaine, and eaten clene.
  And now no more for him but I alone,
  And this old woman here remaining beene;
  Till thou cam'st hither to augment our mone,
And of us three to morrow he will sure eate one.

14

Ah dreadfull tidings which thou doest declare,
  (Quoth she) of all that ever hath bene knowen:
  Full many great calamities and rare
  This feeble brest endured hath, but none
  Equall to this, where ever I have gone.
  But what are you, whom like unlucky lot
  Hath linckt with me in the same chaine attone?
  To tell (quoth she) that which ye see, needs not;
A wofull wretched maid, of God and man forgot.

15

But what I was, it irkes me to reherse;
  Daughter unto a Lord of high degree;
  That joyd in happy peace, till fates perverse
  With guilefull love did secretly agree,
  To overthrow my state and dignitie.
  It was my lot to love a gentle swaine,
  Yet was he but a Squire of low degree;
  Yet was he meet, unlesse mine eye did faine,
By any Ladies side for Leman to have laine.

16

But for his meannesse and disparagement,
  My Sire, who me too dearely well did love,
  Unto my choise by no meanes would assent,
  But often did my folly fowle reprove.
  Yet nothing could my fixed mind remove,
  But whether willed or nilled friend or foe,
  I me resolv'd the utmost end to prove,
  And rather than my love abandon so,
Both sire, and friends, and all for ever to forgo.

17

Thenceforth I sought by secret meanes to worke
  Time to my will, and from his wrathfull sight
  To hide th'intent, which in my heart did lurke,
  Till I thereto had all things ready dight.
  So on a day unweeting unto wight,
  I with that Squire agreede away to flit,
  And in a privy place, betwixt us hight,
  Within a grove appointed him to meete;
To which I boldly came upon my feeble feete.

18

But ah unhappy houre me thither brought:
  For in that place where I him thought to find,
  There was I found, contrary to my thought,
  Of this accursed Carle of hellish kind,
  The shame of men, and plague of womankind,
  Who trussing me, as Eagle doth his pray,
  Me hether brought with him, as swift as wind,
  Where yet untouched till this present day,
I rest his wretched thrall, the sad *Æmylia*.

19

Ah sad *Æmylia* (then sayd *Amoret*,)
  Thy ruefull plight I pitty as mine owne.
  But read to me, by what devise or wit,
  Hast thou in all this time, from him unknowne
  Thine honor sav'd, though into thraldome throwne.
  Through helpe (quoth she) of this old woman here
  I have so done, as she to me hath showne.
  For ever when he burnt in lustfull fire,
She in my stead supplide his bestiall desire.

20

Thus of their evils as they did discourse,
  And each did other much bewaile and mone;
  Loe where the villaine selfe, their sorrowes sourse,
  Came to the cave, and rolling thence the stone,
  Which wont to stop the mouth thereof, that none
  Might issue forth, came rudely rushing in,
  And spredding over all the flore alone,
  Gan dight him selfe unto his wonted sinne:
Which ended, then his bloudy banket should beginne.

21

Which when as fearefull *Amoret* perceived,
  She staid not the utmost end thereof to try,
  But like a ghastly Gelt, whose wits are reaved,
  Ran forth in hast with hideous outcry,
  For horrour of his shamefull villany.
  But after her full lightly he uprose,
  And her pursu'd as fast as she did flie:
  Full fast she flies, and farre afore him goes,
Ne feeles the thorns and thickets pricke her tender toes.

22

Nor hedge, nor ditch, nor hill, nor dale she staies,
  But overleapes them all, like Robucke light,
  And through the thickest makes her nighest waies;
  And evermore when with regardfull sight
  She looking backe, espies that griesly wight
  Approching nigh, she gins to mend her pace,
  And makes her feare a spur to hast her flight:
  More swift than *Myrrh'* or *Daphne* in her race,
Or any of the Thracian Nimphes in salvage chase.

23

Long so she fled, and so he follow'd long;
  Ne living aide for her on earth appeares,
  But if the heavens helpe to redresse her wrong,
  Moved with pity of her plenteous teares.
  It fortuned *Belphebe* with her peares
  The woody Nimphs, and with that lovely boy,
  Was hunting then the Libbards and the Beares,
  In these wild woods, as was her wonted joy,
To banish sloth, that oft doth noble mindes annoy.

24

It so befell, as oft it fals in chace,
  That each of them from other sundred were,
  And that same gentle Squire arriv'd in place,
  Where this same cursed caytive did appeare,
  Pursuing that faire Lady full of feare,
  And now he her quite overtaken had;
  And now he her away with him did beare
  Under his arme, as seeming wondrous glad,
That by his grenning laughter mote farre off be rad.

25

Which drery sight the gentle Squire espying,
  Doth hast to crosse him by the nearest way,
  Led with that wofull Ladies piteous crying,
  And him assailes with all the might he may,
  Yet will not he the lovely spoile downe lay,
  But with his craggy club in his right hand,
  Defends him selfe, and saves his gotten pray.
  Yet had it bene right hard him to withstand,
But that he was full light and nimble on the land.

26

Thereto the villaine used craft in fight;
  For ever when the Squire his javelin shooke,
  He held the Lady forth before him right,
  And with her body, as a buckler, broke
  The puissance of his intended stroke.
  And if it chaunst, (as needs it must in fight)
  Whilest he on him was greedy to be wroke,
  That any little blow on her did light,
Then would he laugh aloud, and gather great delight.

27

Which subtill sleight did him encumber much,
   And made him oft, when he would strike, forbeare;
   For hardly could he come the carle to touch,
   But that he her must hurt, or hazard neare:
   Yet he his hand so carefully did beare,
   That at the last he did himselfe attaine,
   And therein left the pike head of his speare.
   A streame of coleblacke bloud thence gusht amaine,
That all her silken garments did with bloud bestaine.

28

With that he threw her rudely on the flore,
   And laying both his hands upon his glave,
   With dreadfull strokes let drive at him so sore,
   That forst him flie abacke, himselfe to save:
   Yet he therewith so felly still did rave,
   That scarse the Squire his hand could once upreare,
   But for advantage ground unto him gave,
   Tracing and traversing, now here, now there;
For bootlesse thing it was to think such blowes to beare.

29

Whilest thus in battell they embusied were,
   Belphebe raunging in that forrest wide,
   The hideous noise of their huge strokes did heare,
   And drew thereto, making her eare her guide.
   Whom when that theefe approching nigh espide,
   With bow in hand, and arrowes ready bent,
   He by his former combate would not bide,
   But fled away with ghastly dreriment,
Well knowing her to be his deaths sole instrument.

30

Whom seeing flie, she speedily poursewed
   With winged feete, as nimble as the winde,
   And ever in her bow she ready shewed
   The arrow, to his deadly marke desynde.
   As when *Latonaes* daughter cruell kynde,
   In vengement of her mothers great disgrace,
   With fell despight her cruell arrowes tynde
   Gainst wofull *Niobes* unhappy race,
That all the gods did mone her miserable case.

31

So well she sped her and so far she ventred,
  That ere unto his hellish den he raught,
  Even as he ready was there to have entred,
  She sent an arrow forth with mighty draught,
  That in the very dore him overcaught,
  And in his nape arriving, through it thrild
  His greedy throte, therewith in two distraught,
  That all his vitall spirites thereby spild,
And all his hairy brest with gory bloud was fild.

32

Whom when on ground she groveling saw to rowle,
  She ran in hast his life to have bereft:
  But ere she could him reach, the sinfull sowle
  Having his carrion corse quite sencelesse left,
  Was fled to hell, surcharg'd with spoile and theft.
  Yet over him she there long gazing stood,
  And oft admir'd his monstrous shape, and oft
  His mighty limbs, whilest all with filthy bloud
The place there overflowne, seemd like a sodaine flood.

33

Thence forth she past into his dreadfull den,
  Where nought but darkesome drerinesse she found,
  Ne creature saw, but hearkned now and then
  Some litle whispering, and soft groning sound.
  With that she askt, what ghosts there under ground
  Lay hid in horrour of eternall night?
  And bad them, if so be they were not bound,
  To come and shew themselves before light,
Now freed from feare and danger of that dismall wight.

34

Then forth the sad *Æmylia* issewed,
  Yet trembling every joynt through former feare;
  And after her the Hag, there with her mewed,
  A foule and lothsome creature did appeare;
  A leman fit for such a lover deare.
  That mov'd *Belphebe* her no lesse to hate,
  Than for to rue the others heavy cheare;
  Of whom she gan enquire of her estate.
Who all to her at large, as hapned, did relate.

35

Thence she them brought toward the place, where late
    She left the gentle Squire with *Amoret:*
    There she him found by that new lovely mate,
    Who lay the whiles in swoune, full sadly set,
    From her faire eyes wiping the deawy wet,
    Which softly stild, and kissing them atweene,
    And handling soft the hurts, which she did get.
    For of that Carle she sorely bruz'd had beene,
Als of his owne rash hand one wound was to be seene.

36

Which when she saw, with sodaine glauncing eye,
    Her noble heart with sight thereof was fild
    With deepe disdaine, and great indignity,
    That in her wrath she thought them both have thrild,
    With that selfe arrow, which the Carle had kild:
    Yet held her wrathfull hand from vengeance sore,
    But drawing nigh, ere he her well beheld;
    Is this the faith, she said, and said no more,
But turnd her face, and fled away for evermore.

37

He seeing her depart, arose up light,
    Right sore agrieved at her sharpe reproofe,
    And follow'd fast: but when he came in sight,
    He durst not nigh approch, but kept aloofe,
    For dread of her displeasures utmost proofe.
    And evermore, when he did grace entreat,
    And framed speaches fit for his behoofe,
    Her mortall arrowes she at him did threat,
And forst him backe with fowle dishonor to retreat.

38

At last when long he follow'd had in vaine,
    Yet found no ease of griefe, nor hope of grace,
    Unto those woods he turned backe againe,
    Full of sad anguish, and in heavy case:
    And finding there fit solitary place
    For wofull wight, chose out a gloomy glade,
    Where hardly eye mote see bright heavens face,
    For mossy trees, which covered all with shade
And sad melancholy: there he his cabin made.

39

His wonted warlike weapons all he broke,
  And threw away, with vow to use no more,
  Ne thenceforth ever strike in battell stroke,
  Ne ever word to speake to woman more;
  But in that wildernesse, of men forlore,
  And of the wicked world forgotten quight,
  His hard mishap in dolor to deplore,
  And wast his wretched daies in wofull plight;
So on him selfe to wreake his follies owne despight.

40

And eke his garment, to be thereto meet,
  He wilfully did cut and shape anew;
  And his faire lockes, that wont with ointment sweet
  To be embaulm'd, and sweat out dainty dew,
  He let to grow and griesly to concrew,
  Uncomb'd, uncurl'd, and carelesly unshed;
  That in short time his face they overgrew,
  And over all his shoulders did dispred,
That who he whilome was, uneath was to be red.

41

There he continued in this carefull plight,
  Wretchedly wearing out his youthly yeares,
  Through wilfull penury consumed quight,
  That like a pined ghost he soone appeares.
  For other food than that wilde forrest beares,
  Ne other drinke there did he ever tast,
  Than running water, tempred with his teares,
  The more his weakened body so to wast:
That out of all mens knowledge he was worne at last.

42

For on a day, by fortune as it fell,
  His owne deare Lord Prince *Arthure* came that way,
  Seeking adventures, where he mote heare tell;
  And as he through the wandring wood did stray,
  Having espide this Cabin far away,
  He to it drew, to weet who there did wonne;
  Weening therein some holy Hermit lay,
  That did resort of sinfull people shonne;
Or else some woodman shrowded there from scorching sunne.

43

Arriving there, he found this wretched man,
　Spending his daies in dolour and despaire,
　And through long fasting woxen pale and wan,
　All overgrowen with rude and rugged haire;
　That albeit his owne deare Squire he were,
　Yet he him knew not, ne aviz'd at all,
　But like strange wight, whom he had seene no where,
　Saluting him, gan into speach to fall,
And pitty much his plight, that liv'd like outcast thrall.

44

But to his speach he aunswered no whit,
　But stood still mute, as if he had beene dum,
　Ne signe of sence did shew, ne common wit,
　As one with griefe and anguishe overcum,
　And unto every thing did aunswere mum:
　And ever when the Prince unto him spake,
　He louted lowly, as did him becum,
　And humble homage did unto him make,
Midst sorrow shewing joyous semblance for his sake.

45

At which his uncouth guise and usage quaint
　The Prince did wonder much, yet could not ghesse
　The cause of that his sorrowfull constraint;
　Yet weend by secret signes of manlinesse,
　Which close appeard in that rude brutishnesse,
　That he whilome some gentle swaine had beene,
　Traind up in feats of armes and knightlinesse;
　Which he observ'd, by that he him had seene
To weld his naked sword, and try the edges keene.

46

And eke by that he saw on every tree,
　How he the name of one engraven had,
　Which likly was his liefest love to be,
　For whom he now so sorely was bestad;
　Which was by him *BELPHEBE* rightly rad.
　Yet who was that *Belphebe*, he ne wist;
　Yet saw he often how he wexed glad,
　When he it heard, and how the ground he kist,
Wherein it written was, and how himselfe he blist:

47

Tho when he long had marked his demeanor,
  And saw that all he said and did, was vaine,
  Ne ought mote make him change his wonted tenor,
  Ne ought mote ease or mitigate his paine,
  He left him there in languor to remaine,
  Till time for him should remedy provide,
  And him restore to former grace againe.
  Which for it is too long here to abide,
I will deferre the end untill another tide.

CANT. VIII

The gentle Squire recovers grace,
  Sclaunder her guests doth staine:
Corflambo chaseth Placidas,
  And is by Arthure slaine.

I

WELL said the wiseman, now prov'd true by this,
  Which to this gentle Squire did happen late,
  That the displeasure of the mighty is
  Than death it selfe more dread and desperate.
  For naught the same may calme ne mitigate,
  Till time the tempest doe thereof delay
  With sufferaunce soft, which rigour can abate,
  And have the sterne remembrance wypt away
Of bitter thoughts, which deepe therein infixed lay.

2

Like as it fell to this unhappy boy,
  Whose tender heart the faire *Belphebe* had
  With one sterne looke so daunted, that no joy
  In all his life, which afterwards he lad,
  He ever tasted, but with penaunce sad
  And pensive sorrow pind and wore away,
  Ne ever laught, ne once shew'd countenance glad;
  But alwaies wept and wailed night and day,
As blasted bloosme through heat doth languish and decay;

3

Till on a day, as in his wonted wise
  His doole he made, there chaunst a turtle Dove
  To come, where he his dolors did devise,
  That likewise late had lost her dearest love,
  Which losse her made like passion also prove.
  Who seeing his sad plight, her tender heart
  With deare compassion deeply did emmove,
  That she gan mone his undeserved smart,
And with her dolefull accent beare with him a part.

4

Shee sitting by him as on ground he lay,
  Her mournefull notes full piteously did frame,
  And thereof made a lamentable lay,
  So sensibly compyld, that in the same
  Him seemed oft he heard his owne right name.
  With that he forth would poure so plenteous teares,
  And beat his breast unworthy of such blame,
  And knocke his head, and rend his rugged heares,
That could have perst the hearts of Tigres and of Beares.

5

Thus long this gentle bird to him did use,
  Withouten dread of perill to repaire
  Unto his wonne, and with her mournefull muse
  Him to recomfort in his greatest care,
  That much did ease his mourning and misfare:
  And every day for guerdon of her song,
  He part of his small feast to her would share;
  That at the last of all his woe and wrong
Companion she became, and so continued long.

6

Upon a day as she him sate beside,
  By chance he certaine miniments forth drew,
  Which yet with him as relickes did abide
  Of all the bounty, which *Belphebe* threw
  On him, whilst goodly grace she did him shew:
  Amongst the rest a jewell rich he found,
  That was a Ruby of right perfect hew,
  Shap'd like a heart, yet bleeding of the wound,
And with a litle golden chaine about it bound.

7

The same he tooke, and with a riband new,
  In which his Ladies colours were, did bind
  About the turtles necke, that with the vew
  Did greatly solace his engrieved mind.
  All unawares the bird, when she did find
  Her selfe so deckt, her nimble wings displaid,
  And flew away, as lightly as the wind:
  Which sodaine accident him much dismaid,
And looking after long, did marke which way she straid.

8

But when as long he looked had in vaine,
  Yet saw her forward still to make her flight,
  His weary eie returnd to him againe,
  Full of discomfort and disquiet plight,
  That both his juell he had lost so light,
  And eke his deare companion of his care.
  But that sweet bird departing, flew forth right
  Through the wide region of the wastfull aire,
Untill she came where wonned his *Belphebe* faire.

9

There found she her (as then it did betide)
  Sitting in covert shade of arbors sweet,
  After late weary toile, which she had tride
  In salvage chase, to rest as seem'd her meet.
  There she alighting, fell before her feet,
  And gan to her her mournfull plaint to make,
  As was her wont, thinking to let her weet
  The great tormenting griefe, that for her sake
Her gentle Squire through her displeasure did pertake.

10

She her beholding with attentive eye,
  At length did marke about her purple brest
  That precious juell, which she formerly
  Had knowne right well with colourd ribbands drest:
  Therewith she rose in hast, and her addrest
  With ready hand it to have reft away.
  But the swift bird obayd not her behest,
  But swarv'd aside, and there againe did stay;
She follow'd her, and thought againe it to assay.

11

And ever when she nigh approcht, the Dove
    Would flit a litle forward, and then stay,
    Till she drew neare, and then againe remove;
    So tempting her still to pursue the pray,
    And still from her escaping soft away:
    Till that at length into that forrest wide,
    She drew her far, and led with slow delay.
    In th'end she her unto that place did guide,
Whereas that wofull man in languor did abide.

12

Eftsoones she flew unto his fearelesse hand,
    And there a piteous ditty new deviz'd,
    As if she would have made him understand,
    His sorrowes cause to be of her despis'd.
    Whom when she saw in wretched weedes disguiz'd,
    With heary glib deform'd, and meiger face,
    Like ghost late risen from his grave agryz'd,
    She knew him not, but pittied much his case,
And wisht it were in her to doe him any grace.

13

He her beholding, at her feet downe fell,
    And kist the ground on which her sole did tread,
    And washt the same with water, which did well
    From his moist eies, and like two streames procead,
    Yet spake no word, whereby she might aread
    What mister wight he was, or what he ment,
    But as one daunted with her presence dread,
    Onely few ruefull lookes unto her sent,
As messengers of his true meaning and intent.

14

Yet nathemore his meaning she ared,
    But wondred much at his so selcouth case,
    And by his persons secret seemlyhed
    Well weend, that he had beene some man of place,
    Before misfortune did his hew deface
    That being mov'd with ruth she thus bespake.
    Ah wofull man, what heavens hard disgrace,
    Or wrath of cruell wight on thee ywrake?
Or selfe disliked life doth thee thus wretched make?

15

If heaven, then none may it redresse or blame,
  Sith to his powre we all are subject borne:
  If wrathfull wight, then fowle rebuke and shame
  Be theirs, that have so cruell thee forlorne;
  But if through inward griefe or wilfull scorne
  Of life it be, then better doe advise.
  For he whose daies in wilfull woe are worne,
  The grace of his Creator doth despise,
That will not use his gifts for thanklesse nigardise.

16

When so he heard her say, eftsoones he brake
  His sodaine silence, which he long had pent,
  And sighing inly deepe, her thus bespake;
  Then have they all themselves against me bent:
  For heaven, first author of my languishment,
  Envying my too great felicity,
  Did closely with a cruell one consent,
  To cloud my daies in dolefull misery,
And make me loath this life, still longing for to die.

17

Ne any but your selfe, O dearest dred,
  Hath done this wrong, to wreake on worthlesse wight
  Your high displeasure, through misdeeming bred:
  That when your pleasure is to deeme aright,
  Ye may redresse, and me restore to light.
  Which sory words her mightie hart did mate
  With mild regard, to see his ruefull plight,
  That her inburning wrath she gan abate,
And him receiv'd againe to former favours state.

18

In which he long time afterwards did lead
  An happie life with grace and good accord,
  Fearlesse of fortunes chaunge or envies dread,
  And eke all mindlesse of his owne deare Lord
  The noble Prince, who never heard one word
  Of tydings, what did unto him betide,
  Or what good fortune did to him afford,
  But through the endlesse world did wander wide,
Him seeking evermore, yet no where him descride.

19

Till on a day as through that wood he rode,
  He chaunst to come where those two Ladies late,
  Æmylia and *Amoret* abode,
  Both in full sad and sorrowfull estate;
  The one right feeble through the evill rate
  Of food, which in her duresse she had found:
  The other almost dead and desperate
  Through her late hurts, and through that haplesse wound,
With which the Squire in her defence her sore astound.

20

Whom when the Prince beheld, he gan to rew
  The evill case in which those Ladies lay;
  But most was moved at the piteous vew
  Of *Amoret*, so neare unto decay,
  That her great daunger did him much dismay.
  Eftsoones that pretious liquour forth he drew,
  Which he in store about him kept alway,
  And with few drops thereof did softly dew
Her wounds, that unto strength restor'd her soone anew.

21

Tho when they both recovered were right well,
  He gan of them inquire, what evill guide
  Them thether brought, and how their harmes befell.
  To whom they told all, that did them betide,
  And how from thraldome vile they were untide
  Of that same wicked Carle, by Virgins hond;
  Whose bloudie corse they shew'd him there beside,
  And eke his cave, in which they both were bond:
At which he wondred much, when all those signes he fond.

22

And evermore he greatly did desire
  To know, what Virgin did them thence unbind;
  And oft of them did earnestly inquire,
  Where was her won, and how he mote her find.
  But when as nought according to his mind
  He could outlearne, he them from ground did reare:
  No service lothsome to a gentle kind;
  And on his warlike beast them both did beare,
Himselfe by them on foot, to succour them from feare.

23

So when that forrest they had passed well,
  A litle cotage farre away they spide,
  To which they drew, ere night upon them fell;
  And entring in, found none therein abide,
  But one old woman sitting there beside,
  Upon the ground in ragged rude attyre,
  With filthy lockes about her scattered wide,
  Gnawing her nayles for felnesse and for yre,
And there out sucking venime to her parts entyre.

24

A foule and loathly creature sure in sight,
  And in conditions to be loath'd no lesse:
  For she was stuft with rancour and despight
  Up to the throat, that oft with bitternesse
  It forth would breake, and gush in great excesse,
  Pouring out streames of poyson and of gall
  Gainst all, that truth or vertue doe professe,
  Whom she with leasings lewdly did miscall,
And wickedly backbite: Her name men *Sclaunder* call.

25

Her nature is all goodnesse to abuse,
  And causelesse crimes continually to frame,
  With which she guiltlesse persons may accuse,
  And steale away the crowne of their good name;
  Ne ever Knight so bold, ne ever Dame
  So chast and loyall liv'd, but she would strive
  With forged cause them falsely to defame;
  Ne ever thing so well was doen alive,
But she with blame would blot, and of due praise deprive.

26

Her words were not, as common words are ment,
  T'expresse the meaning of the inward mind,
  But noysome breath, and poysnous spirit sent
  From inward parts, with cancred malice lind,
  And breathed forth with blast of bitter wind;
  Which passing through the eares, would pierce the hart,
  And wound the soule it selfe with griefe unkind:
  For like the stings of Aspes, that kill with smart,
Her spightfull words did pricke, and wound the inner part.

27

Such was that Hag, unmeet to host such guests,
  Whom greatest Princes court would welcome fayne,
  But neede, that answers not to all requests,
  Bad them not looke for better entertayne;
  And eke that age despysed nicenesse vaine,
  Enur'd to hardnesse and to homely fare,
  Which them to warlike discipline did trayne,
  And manly limbs endur'd with litle care
Against all hard mishaps and fortunelesse misfare.

28

Then all that evening welcommed with cold,
  And chearelesse hunger, they together spent;
  Yet found no fault, but that the Hag did scold
  And rayle at them with grudgefull discontent,
  For lodging there without her owne consent:
  Yet they endured all with patience milde,
  And unto rest themselves all onely lent,
  Regardlesse of that queane so base and vilde,
To be unjustly blamd, and bitterly revilde.

29

Here well I weene, when as these rimes be red
  With misregard, that some rash witted wight,
  Whose looser thought will lightly be misled,
  These gentle Ladies will misdeeme too light,
  For thus conversing with this noble Knight;
  Sith now of dayes such temperance is rare
  And hard to finde, that heat of youthfull spright
  For ought will from his greedie pleasure spare,
More hard for hungry steed t'abstaine from pleasant lare.

30

But antique age yet in the infancie
  Of time, did live then like an innocent,
  In simple truth and blamelesse chastitie,
  Ne then of guile had made experiment,
  But voide of vile and treacherous intent,
  Held vertue for it selfe in soveraine awe:
  Then loyall love had royall regiment,
  And each unto his lust did make a lawe,
From all forbidden things his liking to withdraw.

31

The Lyon there did with the Lambe consort,
    And eke the Dove sate by the Faulcons side,
    Ne each of other feared fraud or tort,
    But did in safe securitie abide,
    Withouten perill of the stronger pride:
    But when the world woxe old, it woxe warre old
    (Whereof it hight) and having shortly tride
    The traines of wit, in wickednesse woxe bold,
And dared of all sinnes the secrets to unfold.

32

Then beautie, which was made to represent
    The great Creatours owne resemblance bright,
    Unto abuse of lawlesse lust was lent,
    And made the baite of bestiall delight:
    Then faire grew foule, and foule grew faire in sight,
    And that which wont to vanquish God and man,
    Was made the vassall of the victors might;
    Then did her glorious flowre wex dead and wan,
Despisd and troden downe of all that overran.

33

And now it is so utterly decayd,
    That any bud thereof doth scarse remaine,
    But if few plants preserv'd through heavenly ayd,
    In Princes Court doe hap to sprout againe,
    Dew'd with her drops of bountie Soveraine,
    Which from that goodly glorious flowre proceed,
    Sprung of the auncient stocke of Princes straine,
    Now th'onely remnant of that royall breed,
Whose noble kind at first was sure of heavenly seed.

34

Tho soone as day discovered heavens face
    To sinfull men with darknes overdight,
    This gentle crew gan from their eye-lids chace
    The drowzie humour of the dampish night,
    And did themselves unto their journey dight.
    So forth they yode, and forward softly paced,
    That them to view had bene an uncouth sight;
    How all the way the Prince on footpace traced,
The Ladies both on horse, together fast embraced.

35

Soone as they thence departed were afore,
  That shamefull Hag, the slaunder of her sexe,
  Them follow'd fast, and them reviled sore,
  Him calling theefe, them whores; that much did vexe
  His noble hart; thereto she did annexe
  False crimes and facts, such as they never ment,
  That those two Ladies much asham'd did wexe:
  The more did she pursue her lewd intent,
And rayl'd and rag'd, till she had all her poyson spent.

36

At last when they were passed out of sight,
  Yet she did not her spightfull speach forbeare,
  But after them did barke, and still backbite,
  Though there were none her hatefull words to heare:
  Like as a curre doth felly bite and teare
  The stone, which passed straunger at him threw;
  So she them seeing past the reach of eare,
  Against the stones and trees did rayle anew,
Till she had duld the sting, which in her tongs end grew.

37

They passing forth kept on their readie way,
  With easie steps so soft as foot could stryde,
  Both for great feeblesse, which did oft assay
  Faire *Amoret*, that scarcely she could ryde,
  And eke through heavie armes, which sore annoyd
  The Prince on foot, not wonted so to fare;
  Whose steadie hand was faine his steede to guyde,
  And all the way from trotting hard to spare,
So was his toyle the more, the more that was his care.

38

At length they spide, where towards them with speed
  A Squire came gallopping, as he would flie;
  Bearing a litle Dwarfe before his steed,
  That all the way full loud for aide did crie,
  That seem'd his shrikes would rend the brasen skie:
  Whom after did a mightie man pursew,
  Ryding upon a Dromedare on hie,
  Of stature huge, and horrible of hew,
That would have maz'd a man his dreadfull face to vew.

39

For from his fearefull eyes two fierie beames,
  More sharpe than points of needles did proceede,
  Shooting forth farre away two flaming streames,
  Full of sad powre, that poysonous bale did breede
  To all, that on him lookt without good heed,
  And secretly his enemies did slay:
  Like as the Basiliske of serpents seede,
  From powrefull eyes close venim doth convay
Into the lookers hart, and killeth farre away.

40

He all the way did rage at that same Squire,
  And after him full many threatnings threw,
  With curses vaine in his avengefull ire:
  But none of them (so fast away he flew)
  Him overtooke, before he came in vew.
  Where when he saw the Prince in armour bright,
  He cald to him aloud, his case to rew,
  And rescue him through succour of his might,
From that his cruell foe, that him pursewd in sight.

41

Eftsoones the Prince tooke downe those Ladies twaine
  From loftie steede, and mounting in their stead
  Came to that Squire, yet trembling every vaine:
  Of whom he gan enquire his cause of dread;
  Who as he gan the same to him aread,
  Loe hard behind his backe his foe was prest,
  With dreadfull weapon aymed at his head,
  That unto death had doen him unredrest,
Had not the noble Prince his readie stroke represt.

42

Who thrusting boldly twixt him and the blow,
  The burden of the deadly brunt did beare
  Upon his shield, which lightly he did throw
  Over his head, before the harme came neare.
  Nathlesse it fell with so despiteous dreare
  And heavie sway, that hard unto his crowne
  The shield it drove, and did the covering reare,
  Therewith both Squire and dwarfe did tomble downe
Unto the earth, and lay long while in senselesse swowne.

43

Whereat the Prince full wrath, his strong right hand
  In full avengement heaved up on hie,
  And stroke the Pagan with his steely brand
  So sore, that to his saddle bow thereby
  He bowed low, and so a while did lie:
  And sure had not his massie yron mace
  Betwixt him and his hurt bene happily,
  It would have cleft him to the girding place,
Yet as it was, it did astonish him long space.

44

But when he to himselfe returnd againe,
  All full of rage he gan to curse and sweare,
  And vow by *Mahoune* that he should be slaine.
  With that his murdrous mace he up did reare,
  That seemed nought the souse thereof could beare,
  And therewith smote at him with all his might.
  But ere that it to him approched neare,
  The royall child with readie quicke foresight,
Did shun the proofe thereof and it avoyded light.

45

But ere his hand he could recure againe,
  To ward his bodie from the balefull stound,
  He smote at him with all his might and maine,
  So furiously, that ere he wist, he found
  His head before him tombling on the ground.
  The whiles his babling tongue did yet blaspheme
  And curse his God, that did him so confound;
  The whiles his life ran foorth in bloudie streame,
His soule descended downe into the Stygian reame.

46

Which when that Squire beheld, he woxe full glad
  To see his foe breath out his spright in vaine:
  But that same dwarfe right sorie seem'd and sad,
  And howld aloud to see his Lord there slaine,
  And rent his haire and scratcht his face for paine.
  Then gan the Prince at leasure to inquire
  Of all the accident, there hapned plaine,
  And what he was, whose eyes did flame with fire;
All which was thus to him declared by that Squire.

47

This mightie man (quoth he) whom you have slaine,
  Of an huge Geauntesse whylome was bred;
  And by his strength rule to himselfe did gaine
  Of many Nations into thraldome led,
  And mightie kingdomes of his force adred;
  Whom yet he conquer'd not by bloudie fight,
  Ne hostes of men with banners brode dispred,
  But by the powre of his infectious sight,
With which he killed all, that came within his might.

48

Ne was he ever vanquished afore,
  But ever vanquisht all, with whom he fought;
  Ne was there man so strong, but he downe bore,
  Ne woman yet so faire, but he her brought
  Unto his bay, and captived her thought.
  For most of strength and beautie his desire
  Was spoyle to make, and wast them unto nought,
  By casting secret flakes of lustfull fire
From his false eyes, into their harts and parts entire.

49

Therefore *Corflambo* was he cald aright,
  Though namelesse there his bodie now doth lie,
  Yet hath he left one daughter that is hight
  The faire *Pæana*; who seemes outwardly
  So faire, as ever yet saw living eie:
  And were her vertue like her beautie bright,
  She were as faire as any under skie.
  But ah she given is to vaine delight,
And eke too loose of life, and eke of love too light.

50

So as it fell there was a gentle Squire,
  That lov'd a Ladie of high parentage,
  But for his meane degree might not aspire
  To match so high, her friends with counsell sage,
  Dissuaded her from such a disparage.
  But she, whose hart to love was wholly lent,
  Out of his hands could not redeeme her gage.
  But firmely following her first intent,
Resolv'd with him to wend, gainst all her friends consent.

51

So twixt themselves they pointed time and place,
    To which when he according did repaire,
    An hard mishap and disaventrous case
    Him chaunst; in stead of his *Æmylia* faire
    This Gyants sonne, that lies there on the laire
    An headlesse heape, him unawares there caught,
    And all dismayd through mercilesse despaire,
    Him wretched thrall unto his dongeon brought,
Where he remaines, of all unsuccour'd and unsought.

52

This Gyants daughter came upon a day
    Unto the prison in her joyous glee,
    To view the thrals, which there in bondage lay:
    Amongst the rest she chaunced there to see
    This lovely swaine the Squire of low degree;
    To whom she did her liking lightly cast,
    And wooed him her paramour to bee:
    From day to day she woo'd and prayd him fast,
And for his love him promist libertie at last.

53

He though affide unto a former love,
    To whom his faith he firmely ment to hold,
    Yet seeing not how thence he mote remove,
    But by that meanes, which fortune did unfold,
    Her graunted love, but with affection cold
    To win her grace his libertie to get.
    Yet she him still detaines in captive hold,
    Fearing least if she should him freely set,
He would her shortly leave, and former love forget.

54

Yet so much favour she to him hath hight,
    Above the rest, that he sometimes may space
    And walke about her gardens of delight,
    Having a keeper still with him in place,
    Which keeper is this Dwarfe, her dearling base,
    To whom the keyes of every prison dore
    By her committed be, of speciall grace,
    And at his will may whom he list restore,
And whom he list reserve, to be afflicted more.

55

Whereof when tydings came unto mine eare,
  Full inly sorie for the fervent zeale,
  Which I to him as to my soule did beare;
  I thether went where I did long conceale
  My selfe, till that the Dwarfe did me reveale,
  And told his Dame, her Squire of low degree
  Did secretly out of her prison steale;
  For me he did mistake that Squire to bee;
For never two so like did living creature see.

56

Then was I taken and before her brought,
  Who through the likenesse of my outward hew,
  Being likewise beguiled in her thought,
  Gan blame me much for being so untrew,
  To seeke by flight her fellowship t'eschew,
  That lov'd me deare, as dearest thing alive.
  Thence she commaunded me to prison new;
  Whereof I glad did not gainesay nor strive,
But suffred that same Dwarfe me to her dongeon drive.

57

There did I finde mine onely faithfull frend
  In heavy plight and sad perplexitie;
  Whereof I sorie, yet my selfe did bend,
  Him to recomfort with my companie.
  But him the more agreev'd I found thereby:
  For all his joy, he said, in that distresse
  Was mine and his *Æmylias* libertie.
  Æmylia well he lov'd, as I mote ghesse;
Yet greater love to me than her he did professe.

58

But I with better reason him aviz'd,
  And shew'd him how through error and mis-thought
  Of our like persons eath to be disguiz'd,
  Or his exchange, or freedome might be wrought.
  Whereto full loth was he, ne would for ought
  Consent, that I who stood all fearelesse free,
  Should wilfully be into thraldome brought,
  Till fortune did perforce it so decree.
Yet overrul'd at last, he did to me agree.

59

The morrow next about the wonted howre,
  The Dwarfe cald at the doore of *Amyas*,
  To come forthwith unto his Ladies bowre.
  In steed of whom forth came I *Placidas*,
  And undiscerned, forth with him did pas.
  There with great joyance and with gladsome glee,
  Of faire *Pæana* I received was,
  And oft imbrast, as if that I were hee,
And with kind words accoyd, vowing great love to mee.

60

Which I, that was not bent to former love,
  As was my friend, that had her long refusd,
  Did well accept, as well it did behove,
  And to the present neede it wisely usd.
  My former hardnesse first I faire excusd;
  And after promist large amends to make.
  With such smooth termes her error I abusd,
  To my friends good, more than for mine owne sake,
For whose sole libertie I love and life did stake.

61

Thenceforth I found more favour at her hand,
  That to her Dwarfe, which had me in his charge,
  She bad to lighten my too heavie band,
  And graunt more scope to me to walke at large.
  So on a day as by the flowrie marge
  Of a fresh streame I with that Elfe did play,
  Finding no meanes how I might us enlarge,
  But if that Dwarfe I could with me convay,
I lightly snatcht him up, and with me bore away.

62

Thereat he shriekt aloud, that with his cry
  The Tyrant selfe came forth with yelling bray,
  And me pursew'd; but nathemore would I
  Forgoe the purchase of my gotten pray,
  But have perforce him hether brought away.
  Thus as they talked, loe where nigh at hand
  Those Ladies two yet doubtfull through dismay
  In presence came, desirous t'understand
Tydings of all, which there had hapned on the land.

63

Where soone as sad *Æmylia* did espie
  Her captive lovers friend, young *Placidas*;
  All mindlesse of her wonted modestie,
  She to him ran, and him with streight embras
  Enfolding said, And lives yet *Amyas*?
  He lives (quoth he) and his *Æmylia* loves.
  Then lesse (said she) by all the woe I pas,
  With which my weaker patience fortune proves.
But what mishap thus long him fro my selfe removes?

64

Then gan he all this storie to renew,
  And tell the course of his captivitie;
  That her deare hart full deepely made to rew,
  And sigh full sore, to heare the miserie,
  In which so long he mercilesse did lie.
  Then after many teares and sorrowes spent,
  She deare besought the Prince of remedie:
  Who thereto did with readie will consent,
And well perform'd, as shall appeare by his event.

CANT. IX

The Squire of low degree releast
* Pæana takes to wife:*
Britomart fightes with many Knights,
* Prince Arthur stints their strife.*

I

HARD is the doubt, and difficult to deeme,
  When all three kinds of love together meet,
  And doe dispart the hart with powre extreme,
  Whether shall weigh the balance downe; to weet
  The deare affection unto kindred sweet,
  Or raging fire of love to woman kind,
  Or zeale of friends combynd with vertues meet.
  But of them all the band of vertuous mind
Me seemes the gentle hart should most assured bind.

2

For naturall affection soone doth cesse,
  And quenched is with *Cupids* greater flame:
  But faithfull friendship doth them both suppresse,
  And them with maystring discipline doth tame,
  Through thoughts aspyring to eternall fame.
  For as the soule doth rule the earthly masse,
  And all the service of the bodie frame,
  So love of soule doth love of bodie passe,
No lesse than perfect gold surmounts the meanest brasse.

3

All which who list by tryall to assay,
  Shall in this storie find approved plaine;
  In which these Squires true friendship more did sway,
  Than either care of parents could refraine,
  Or love of fairest Ladie could constraine.
  For though *Pœana* were as faire as morne,
  Yet did this trustie Squire with proud disdaine
  For his friends sake her offred favours scorne,
And she her selfe her syre, of whom she was yborne.

4

Now after that Prince *Arthur* graunted had,
  To yeeld strong succour to that gentle swayne,
  Who now long time had lyen in prison sad,
  He gan advise how best he mote darrayne
  That enterprize, for greatest glories gayne.
  That headlesse tyrants tronke he reard from ground,
  And having ympt the head to it agayne,
  Upon his usuall beast it firmely bound,
And made it so to ride, as it alive was found.

5

Then did he take that chaced Squire, and layd
  Before the ryder, as he captive were,
  And made his Dwarfe, though with unwilling ayd,
  To guide the beast, that did his maister beare,
  Till to his castle they approched neare.
  Whom when the watch, that kept continuall ward
  Saw comming home; all voide of doubtfull feare,
  He running downe, the gate to him unbard;
Whom straight the Prince ensuing, in together far'd.

6

There he did find in her delitious boure
  The faire *Pæana* playing on a Rote,
  Complayning of her cruell Paramoure,
  And singing all her sorrow to the note,
  As she had learned readily by rote.
  That with the sweetnesse of her rare delight,
  The Prince halfe rapt, began on her to dote:
  Till better him bethinking of the right,
He her unwares attacht, and captive held by might.

7

Whence being forth produc'd, when she perceived
  Her owne deare sire, she cald to him for aide.
  But when of him no aunswere she received,
  But saw him sencelesse by the Squire upstaide,
  She weened well, that then she was betraide:
  Then gan she loudly cry, and weepe, and waile,
  And that same Squire of treason to upbraide.
  But all in vaine, her plaints might not prevaile,
Ne none there was to reskue her, ne none to baile.

8

Then tooke he that same Dwarfe, and him compeld
  To open unto him the prison dore,
  And forth to bring those thrals, which there he held.
  Thence forth were brought to him above a score
  Of Knights and Squires to him unknowne afore:
  All which he did from bitter bondage free,
  And unto former liberty restore.
  Amongst the rest, that Squire of low degree
Came forth full weake and wan, not like him selfe to bee.

9

Whom soone as faire *Æmylia* beheld,
  And *Placidas*, they both unto him ran,
  And him embracing fast betwixt them held,
  Striving to comfort him all that they can,
  And kissing oft his visage pale and wan.
  That faire *Pæana* them beholding both,
  Gan both envy, and bitterly to ban;
  Through jealous passion weeping inly wroth,
To see the sight perforce, that both her eyes were loth.

10

But when a while they had together beene,
  And diversly conferred of their case,
  She, though full oft she both of them had seene
  A sunder, yet not ever in one place,
  Began to doubt, when she them saw embrace,
  Which was the captive Squire she lov'd so deare,
  Deceived through great likenesse of their face,
  For they so like in person did appeare,
That she uneath discerned, whether whether weare.

11

And eke the Prince, when as he them avized,
  Their like resemblaunce much admired there,
  And mazd how nature had so well disguized
  Her worke, and counterfet her selfe so nere,
  As if that by one patterne seene somewhere,
  She had them made a paragone to be,
  Or whether it through skill, or errour were.
  Thus gazing long, at them much wondred he,
So did the other knights and Squires, which him did see.

12

Then gan they ransacke that same Castle strong,
  In which he found great store of hoorded threasure,
  The which that tyrant gathered had by wrong
  And tortious powre, without respect or measure.
  Upon all which the Briton Prince made seasure,
  And afterwards continu'd there a while,
  To rest him selfe, and solace in soft pleasure
  Those weaker Ladies after weary toile;
To whom he did divide part of his purchast spoile.

13

And for more joy, that captive Lady faire
  The faire *Pæana* he enlarged free;
  And by the rest did set in sumptuous chaire,
  To feast and frollicke; nathemore would she
  Shew gladsome countenaunce nor pleasaunt glee:
  But grieved was for losse both of her sire,
  And eke of Lordship, with both land and fee:
  But most she touched was with griefe entire,
For losse of her new love, the hope of her desire.

14

But her the Prince through his well wonted grace,
  To better termes of myldnesse did entreat,
  From that fowle rudenesse, which did her deface;
  And that same bitter corsive, which did eat
  Her tender heart, and made refraine from meat,
  He with good thewes and speaches well applyde,
  Did mollifie, and calme her raging heat.
  For though she were most faire, and goodly dyde,
Yet she it all did mar with cruelty and pride.

15

And for to shut up all in friendly love,
  Sith love was first the ground of all her griefe,
  That trusty Squire he wisely well did move
  Not to despise that dame, which lov'd him liefe,
  Till he had made of her some better priefe,
  But to accept her to his wedded wife.
  Thereto he offred for to make him chiefe
  Of all her land and lordship during life:
He yeelded, and her tooke; so stinted all their strife.

16

From that day forth in peace and joyous blis,
  They liv'd together long without debate,
  Ne private jarre, ne spite of enemis
  Could shake the safe assuraunce of their state.
  And she whom Nature did so faire create,
  That she mote match the fairest of her daies,
  Yet with lewd loves and lust intemperate
  Had it defaste; thenceforth reformd her waies,
That all men much admyrde her change, and spake her praise.

17

Thus when the Prince had perfectly compylde
  These paires of friends in peace and setled rest,
  Him selfe, whose minde did travell as with chylde,
  Of his old love, conceav'd in secret brest,
  Resolved to pursue his former quest;
  And taking leave of all, with him did beare
  Faire *Amoret*, whom Fortune by bequest
  Had left in his protection whileare,
Exchanged out of one into an other feare.

18

Feare of her safety did her not constraine,
  For well she wist now in a mighty hond,
  Her person late in perill, did remaine,
  Who able was all daungers to withstond.
  But now in feare of shame she more did stond,
  Seeing her selfe all soly succourlesse,
  Left in the victors powre, like vassall bond;
  Whose will her weakenesse could no way represse,
In case his burning lust should breake into excesse.

19

But cause of feare sure had she none at all
  Of him, who goodly learned had of yore
  The course of loose affection to forstall,
  And lawlesse lust to rule with reasons lore
  That all the while he by his side her bore,
  She was as safe as in a Sanctuary;
  Thus many miles they two together wore,
  To seeke their loves dispersed diversly,
Yet neither shewed to other their hearts privity.

20

At length they came, whereas a troupe of Knights
  They saw together skirmishing, as seemed:
  Sixe they were all, all full of fell despight,
  But foure of them the battell best beseemed,
  That which of them was best, mote not be deemed.
  Those foure were they, from whom false *Florimell*
  By *Braggadochio* lately was redeemed.
  To weet, sterne *Druon*, and lewd *Claribell*,
Love-lavish *Blandamour*, and lustfull *Paridell*.

21

Druons delight was all in single life,
  And unto Ladies love would lend no leasure:
  The more was *Claribell* enraged rife
  With fervent flames, and loved out of measure:
  So eke lov'd *Blandamour*, but yet at pleasure
  Would change his liking, and new Lemans prove:
  But *Paridell* of love did make no threasure,
  But lusted after all, that him did move.
So diversly these foure disposed were to love.

22

But those two other which beside them stoode,
  Were *Britomart*, and gentle *Scudamour*,
  Who all the while beheld their wrathfull moode,
  And wondred at their impacable stoure,
  Whose like they never saw till that same houre:
  So dreadfull strokes each did at other drive,
  And laid on load with all their might and powre,
  As if that every dint the ghost would rive
Out of their wretched corses, and their lives deprive.

23

As when *Dan Æolus* in great displeasure,
  For losse of his deare love by *Neptune* hent,
  Sends forth the winds out of his hidden threasure,
  Upon the sea to wreake his fell intent;
  They breaking forth with rude unruliment,
  From all foure parts of heaven doe rage full sore,
  And tosse the deepes, and teare the firmament,
  And all the world confound with wide uprore,
As if in stead thereof they *Chaos* would restore.

24

Cause of their discord, and so fell debate,
  Was for the love of that same snowy maid,
  Whome they had lost in Turneyment of late,
  And seeking long, to weet which way she straid,
  Met here together, where through lewd upbraide
  Of *Ate* and *Duessa* they fell out,
  And each one taking part in others aide,
  This cruell conflict raised thereabout,
Whose dangerous successe depended yet in dout.

25

For sometimes *Paridell* and *Blandamour*
  The better had, and bet the others backe,
  Eftsoones the others did the field recoure,
  And on their foes did worke full cruell wracke:
  Yet neither would their fiendlike fury slacke,
  But evermore their malice did augment;
  Till that uneath they forced were for lacke
  Of breath, their raging rigour to relent,
And rest themselves for to recover spirits spent.

26

There gan they change their sides, and new parts take;
  For *Paridell* did take to *Druons* side,
  For old despight, which now forth newly brake
  Gainst *Blandamour*, whom alwaies he envide
  And *Blandamour* to *Claribell* relide.
  So all afresh gan former fight renew.
  As when two Barkes, this caried with the tide,
  That with the wind, contrary courses sew,
If wind and tide doe change, their courses change anew.

27

Thenceforth they much more furiously gan fare,
  As if but then the battell had begonne,
  Ne helmets bright, ne hawberks strong did spare,
  That through the clifts the vermeil bloud out sponne,
  And all adowne their riven sides did ronne.
  Such mortall malice, wonder was to see
  In friends profest, and so great outrage donne:
  But sooth is said, and tride in each degree,
Faint friends when they fall out, most cruell fomen bee.

28

Thus they long while continued in fight,
  Till *Scudamour*, and that same Briton maide,
  By fortune in that place did chance to light:
  Whom soone as they with wrathfull eie bewraide,
  They gan remember of the fowle upbraide,
  The which that Britonesse had to them donne,
  In that late Turney for the snowy maide;
  Where she had them both shamefully fordonne,
And eke the famous prize of beauty from them wonne.

29

Eftsoones all burning with a fresh desire
  Of fell revenge, in their malicious mood
  They from them selves gan turne their furious ire,
  And cruell blades yet steeming with whot bloud,
  Against those two let drive, as they were wood:
  Who wondring much at that so sodaine fit,
  Yet nought dismayd, them stoutly well withstood;
  Ne yeelded foote, ne once abacke did flit,
But being doubly smitten likewise doubly smit.

30

The warlike Dame was on her part assaid,
  Of *Claribell* and *Blandamour* attone;
And *Paridell* and *Druon* fiercely laid
  At *Scudamour*, both his professed fone.
Foure charged two, and two surcharged one;
  Yet did those two them selves so bravely beare,
That the other litle gained by the lone,
  But with their owne repayed duely weare,
And usury withall: such gaine was gotten deare.

31

Full oftentimes did *Britomart* assay
  To speake to them, and some emparlance move;
But they for nought their cruell hands would stay,
  Ne lend an eare to ought, that might behove,
As when an eager mastiffe once doth prove
  The tast of bloud of some engored beast,
No words may rate, nor rigour him remove
  From greedy hold of that his blouddy feast:
So litle did they hearken to her sweet beheast.

32

Whom when the Briton Prince a farre beheld
  With ods of so unequall match opprest,
His mighty heart with indignation sweld,
  And inward grudge fild his heroicke brest:
Eftsoones him selfe he to their aide addrest,
  And thrusting fierce into the thickest preace,
Divided them, how ever loth to rest,
  And would them faine from battell to surceasse,
With gentle words perswading them to friendly peace.

33

But they so farre from peace or patience were,
  That all at once at him gan fiercely flie,
And lay on load, as they him downe would beare;
  Like to a storme, which hovers under skie
Long here and there, and round about doth stie,
  At length breakes downe in raine, and haile, and sleet,
First from one coast, till nought thereof be drie;
  And then another, till that likewise fleet;
And so from side to side till all the world it weet.

34

But now their forces greatly were decayd,
  The Prince yet being fresh untoucht afore;
  Who them with speaches milde gan first disswade
  From such foule outrage, and them long forbore:
  Till seeing them through suffrance hartned more,
  Him selfe he bent their furies to abate,
  And layd at them so sharpely and so sore,
  That shortly them compelled to retrate,
And being brought in daunger, to relent too late.

35

But now his courage being throughly fired,
  He ment to make them know their follies prise,
  Had not those two him instantly desired
  T'asswage his wrath, and pardon their mesprise.
  At whose request he gan him selfe advise
  To stay his hand, and of a truce to treat
  In milder tearmes, as list them to devise:
  Mongst which the cause of their so cruell heat
He did them aske, who all that passed gan repeat.

36

And told at large how that same errant Knight,
  To weet faire *Britomart*, them late had foyled
  In open turney, and by wrongfull fight
  Both of their publicke praise had them despoyled,
  And also of their private loves beguyled,
  Of two full hard to read the harder theft.
  But she that wrongfull challenge soone assoyled,
  And shew'd that she had not that Lady reft,
(As they supposd) but her had to her liking left.

37

To whom the Prince thus goodly well replied;
  Certes sir Knight, ye seemen much to blame,
  To rip up wrong, that battell once hath tried;
  Wherein the honor both of Armes ye shame,
  And eke the love of Ladies foule defame;
  To whom the world this franchise ever yeelded,
  That of their loves choise they might freedom clame,
  And in that right should by all knights be shielded:
Gainst which me seemes this war ye wrongfully have wielded.

38

And yet (quoth she) a greater wrong remaines:
  For I thereby my former love have lost,
  Whom seeking ever since with endlesse paines,
  Hath me much sorrow and much travell cost;
  Aye me to see that gentle maide so tost.
  But *Scudamour* then sighing deepe, thus saide,
  Certes her losse ought me to sorrow most,
  Whose right she is, where ever she be straide,
Through many perils wonne, and many fortunes waide.

39

For from the first that I her love profest,
  Unto this houre, this present lucklesse howre,
  I never joyed happinesse nor rest,
  But thus turmoild from one to other stowre,
  I wast my life, and doe my daies devowre
  In wretched anguishe and incessant woe,
  Passing the measure of my feeble powre,
  That living thus, a wretch and loving so,
I neither can my love, ne yet my life forgo.

40

Then good sir *Claribell* him thus bespake,
  Now were it not sir *Scudamour* to you
  Dislikefull paine, so sad a taske to take,
  Mote we entreat you, sith this gentle crew
  Is now so well accorded all anew;
  That as we ride together on our way,
  Ye will recount to us in order dew
  All that adventure, which ye did assay
For that faire Ladies love: past perils well apay.

41

So gan the rest him likewise to require,
  But *Britomart* did him importune hard,
  To take on him that paine: whose great desire
  He glad to satisfie, him selfe prepar'd
  To tell through what misfortune he had far'd,
  In that atchievement, as to him befell.
  And all those daungers unto them declar'd,
  Which sith they cannot in this Canto well
Comprised be, I will them in another tell.

CANT. X

Scudamour doth his conquest tell,
Of vertuous Amoret:
Great Venus Temple is describ'd,
And lovers life forth set.

1

TRUE he it said, what ever man it sayd,
  That love with gall and hony doth abound,
  But if the one be with the other wayd,
  For every dram of hony therein found,
  A pound of gall doth over it redound.
  That I too true by triall have approved:
  For since the day that first with deadly wound
  My heart was launcht, and learned to have loved,
I never joyed howre, but still with care was moved.

2

And yet such grace is given them from above,
  That all the cares and evill which they meet,
  May nought at all their setled mindes remove,
  But seeme gainst common sence to them most sweet;
  As bosting in their martyrdome unmeet.
  So all that ever yet I have endured,
  I count as naught, and tread downe under feet,
  Since of my love at length I rest assured,
That to disloyalty she will not be allured.

3

Long were to tell the travell and long toile,
  Through which this shield of love I late have wonne,
  And purchased this peerelesse beauties spoile,
  That harder may be ended, than begonne.
  But since ye so desire, your will be donne.
  Then hearke ye gentle knights and Ladies free,
  My hard mishaps, that ye may learne to shonne;
  For though sweet love to conquer glorious bee,
Yet is the paine thereof much greater than the fee.

4

What time the fame of this renowmed prise
  Flew first abroad, and all mens eares possest,
  I having armes then taken, gan avise
  To winne me honour by some noble gest,
  And purchase me some place amongst the best.
  I boldly thought (so young mens thoughts are bold)
  That this same brave emprize for me did rest,
  And that both shield and she whom I behold,
Might be my lucky lot; sith all by lot we hold.

5

So on that hard adventure forth I went,
  And to the place of perill shortly came.
  That was a temple faire and auncient,
  Which of great mother *Venus* bare the name,
  And farre renowmed through exceeding fame;
  Much more than that, which was in *Paphos* built,
  Or that in *Cyprus*, both long since this same,
  Though all the pillours of the one were guilt,
And all the others pavement were with yvory spilt.

6

And it was seated in an Island strong,
  Abounding all with delices most rare,
  And wall'd by nature gainst invaders wrong,
  That none mote have accesse, nor inward fare,
  But by one way, that passage did prepare.
  It was a bridge ybuilt in goodly wize,
  With curious Corbes and pendants graven faire,
  And arched all with porches, did arize
On stately pillours, fram'd after the Doricke guize.

7

And for defence thereof, on th'other end
  There reared was a castle faire and strong,
  That warded all which in or out did wend,
  And flancked both the bridges sides along,
  Gainst all that would it faine to force or wrong.
  And therein wonned twenty valiant Knights;
  All twenty tride in warres experience long;
  Whose office was, against all manner wights
By all meanes to maintaine that castels ancient rights.

8

Before that Castle was an open plaine,
  And in the midst thereof a piller placed;
  On which this shield, of many sought in vaine,
  The shield of Love, whose guerdon me hath graced,
  Was hangd on high with golden ribbands laced;
  And in the marble stone was written this,
  With golden letters goodly well enchaced,
  Blessed the man that well can use his blis:
Whose ever be the shield, faire Amoret be his.

9

Which when I red, my heart did inly earne,
  And pant with hope of that adventures hap:
  Ne stayed further newes thereof to learne,
  But with my speare upon the shield did rap,
  That all the castle ringed with the clap.
  Streight forth issewd a Knight all arm'd to proofe,
  And bravely mounted to his most mishap
  Who staying nought to question from aloofe,
Ran fierce at me, that fire glaunst from his horses hoofe.

10

Whom boldly I encountred (as I could)
  And by good fortune shortly him unseated.
  Eftsoones out sprung two more of equall mould;
  But I them both with equall hap defeated:
  So all the twenty I likewise entreated,
  And left them groning there upon the plaine.
  Then preacing to the pillour I repeated
  The read thereof for guerdon of my paine,
And taking downe the shield, with me did it retaine.

11

So forth without impediment I past,
  Till to the Bridges utter gate I came:
  The which I found sure lockt and chained fast.
  I knockt, but no man aunswred me by name;
  I cald, but no man answerd to my clame.
  Yet I persever'd still to knocke and call,
  Till at the last I spide within the same,
  Where one stood peeping through a crevis small,
To whom I cald aloud, halfe angry therewithall.

12

That was to weet the Porter of the place,
   Unto whose trust the charge thereof was lent:
   His name was *Doubt*, that had a double face,
   Th'one forward looking, th'other backeward bent,
   Therein resembling *Janus* auncient,
   Which hath in charge the ingate of the yeare:
   And evermore his eyes about him went,
   As if some proved perill he did feare,
Or did misdoubt some ill, whose cause did not appeare.

13

On th'one side he, on th'other sate *Delay*,
   Behinde the gate, that none her might espy
   Whose manner was all passengers to stay,
   And entertaine with her occasions sly,
   Through which some lost great hope unheedily,
   Which never they recover might againe;
   And others quite excluded forth, did ly
   Long languishing there in unpittied paine,
And seeking often entraunce, afterwards in vaine.

14

Me when as he had privily espide,
   Bearing the shield which I had conquerd late,
   He kend it streight, and to me opened wide.
   So in I past, and streight he closd the gate.
   But being in, *Delay* in close awaite
   Caught hold on me, and thought my steps to stay,
   Feigning full many a fond excuse to prate,
   And time to steale, the threasure of mans day,
Whose smallest minute lost, no riches render may.

15

But by no meanes my way I would forslow,
   For ought that ever she could doe or say,
   But from my lofty steede dismounting low,
   Past forth on foote, beholding all the way
   The goodly workes, and stones of rich assay,
   Cast into sundry shapes by wondrous skill,
   That like on earth no where I recken may:
   And underneath, the river rolling still
With murmure soft, that seem'd to serve the workmans will.

16

Thence forth I passed to the second gate,
  The *Gate of good desert*, whose goodly pride
  And costly frame, were long here to relate.
  The same to all stoode alwaies open wide:
  But in the Porch did evermore abide
  An hideous Giant, dreadfull to behold,
  That stopt the entraunce with his spacious stride,
  And with the terrour of his countenance bold
Full many did affray, that else faine enter would.

17

His name was *Daunger* dreaded over all,
  Who day and night did watch and duely ward,
  From fearefull cowards, entrance to forstall,
  And faint-heart-fooles, whom shew of perill hard
  Could terrifie from Fortunes faire adward:
  For oftentimes faint hearts at first espiall
  Of his grim face, were from approaching scard;
  Unworthy they of grace, whom one deniall
Excludes from fairest hope, withouten further triall.

18

Yet many doughty warriours, often tride
  In greater perils to be stout and bold,
  Durst not the sternnesse of his looke abide,
  But soone as they his countenance did behold,
  Began to faint, and feele their corage cold.
  Againe some other, that in hard assaies
  Were cowards knowne, and litle count did hold,
  Either through gifts, or guile, or such like waies,
Crept in by stouping low, or stealing of the kaies.

19

But I though meanest man of many moe,
  Yet much disdaining unto him to lout,
  Or creepe betweene his legs, so in to goe,
  Resolv'd him to assault with manhood stout,
  And either beat him in, or drive him out.
  Eftsoones advauncing that enchaunted shield,
  With all my might I gan to lay about:
  Which when he saw, the glaive which he did wield
He gan forthwith t'avale, and way unto me yield.

20

So as I entred, I did backeward looke,
  For feare of harme, that might lie hidden there;
  And loe his hindparts, whereof heed I tooke,
  Much more deformed fearefull ugly were,
  Than all his former parts did earst appere.
  For hatred, murther, treason, and despight,
  With many moe lay in ambushment there,
  Awayting to entrap the warelesse wight,
Which did not them prevent with vigilant foresight.

21

Thus having past all perill, I was come
  Within the compasse of that Islands space;
  The which did seeme unto my simple doome
  The onely pleasant and delightfull place,
  That ever troden was of footings trace.
  For all that nature by her mother wit
  Could frame in earth, and forme of substance base,
  Was there, and all that nature did omit,
Art playing second natures part, supplyed it.

22

No tree, that is of count, in greenewood growes,
  From lowest Juniper to Ceder tall,
  No flowre in field, that daintie odour throwes,
  And deckes his branch with blossomes over all,
  But there was planted, or grew naturall:
  Nor sense of man so coy and curious nice,
  But there mote find to please it selfe withall;
  Nor hart could wish for any queint device,
But there it present was, and did fraile sense entice.

23

In such luxurious plentie of all pleasure,
  It seem'd a second paradise to ghesse,
  So lavishly enricht with natures threasure,
  That if the happie soules, which doe possesse
  Th'Elysian fields, and live in lasting blesse,
  Should happen this with living eye to see,
  They soone would loath their lesser happinesse,
  And wish to life return'd againe to bee,
That in this joyous place they mote have joyance free.

24

Fresh shadowes, fit to shroud from sunny ray;
    Faire lawnds, to take the sunne in season dew;
    Sweet springs, in which a thousand Nymphs did play;
    Soft rombling brookes, that gentle slomber drew;
    High reared mounts, the lands about to vew;
    Low looking dales, disloignd from common gaze;
    Delightfull bowres, to solace lovers trew;
    False Labyrinthes, fond runners eyes to daze;
All which by nature made did nature selfe amaze.

25

And all without were walkes and alleyes dight
    With divers trees, enrang'd in even rankes;
    And here and there were pleasant arbors pight,
    And shadie seates, and sundry flowring bankes,
    To sit and rest the walkers wearie shankes,
    And therein thousand payres of lovers walkt,
    Praysing their god, and yeelding him great thankes,
    Ne ever ought but of their true loves talkt,
Ne ever for rebuke or blame of any balkt.

26

All these together by themselves did sport
    Their spotlesse pleasures, and sweet loves content.
    But farre away from these, another sort
    Of lovers lincked in true harts consent;
    Which loved not as these, for like intent,
    But on chast vertue grounded their desire,
    Farre from all fraud, or fayned blandishment;
    Which in their spirits kindling zealous fire,
Brave thoughts and noble deedes did evermore aspire.

27

Such were great *Hercules*, and *Hylas* deare;
    Trew *Jonathan*, and *David* trustie tryde;
    Stout *Theseus*, and *Pirithous* his feare;
    Pylades and *Orestes* by his syde;
    Myld *Titus* and *Gesippus* without pryde;
    Damon and *Pythias* whom death could not sever:
    All these and all that ever had bene tyde
    In bands of friendship, there did live for ever,
Whose lives although decay'd, yet loves decayed never.

28

Which when as I, that never tasted blis,
    Nor happie howre, beheld with gazefull eye,
    I thought there was none other heaven than this;
    And gan their endlesse happinesse envye,
    That being free from feare and gealosye,
    Might frankely there their loves desire possesse;
    Whilest I through paines and perlous jeopardie,
    Was forst to seeke my lifes deare patronesse:
Much dearer be the things, which come through hard distresse.

29

Yet all those sights, and all that else I saw,
    Might not my steps withhold, but that forthright
    Unto that purposd place I did me draw,
    Where as my love was lodged day and night:
    The temple of great *Venus*, that is hight
    The Queene of beautie, and of love the mother,
    There worshipped of every living wight;
    Whose goodly workmanship farre past all other
That ever were on earth, all were they set together.

30

Not that same famous Temple of *Diane*,
    Whose hight all *Ephesus* did oversee,
    And which all *Asia* sought with vowes prophane,
    One of the worlds seven wonders sayd to bee,
    Might match with this by many a degree:
    Nor that, which that wise King of *Jurie* framed,
    With endlesse cost, to be th'Almighties see;
    Nor all that else through all the world is named
To all the heathen Gods, might like to this be clamed.

31

I much admyring that so goodly frame,
    Unto the porch approcht, which open stood;
    But therein sate an amiable Dame,
    That seem'd to be of very sober mood,
    And in her semblant shewed great womanhood:
    Strange was her tyre; for on her head a crowne
    She wore much like unto a Danisk hood,
    Poudred with pearle and stone, and all her gowne
Enwoven was with gold, that raught full low a downe.

32

On either side of her, two young men stood,
  Both strongly arm'd, as fearing one another;
  Yet were they brethren both of halfe the blood,
  Begotten by two fathers of one mother,
  Though of contrarie natures each to other:
  The one of them hight *Love*, the other *Hate*,
  Hate was the elder, *Love* the younger brother;
  Yet was the younger stronger in his state
Than th'elder, and him maystred still in all debate.

33

Nathlesse that Dame so well them tempred both,
  That she them forced hand to joyne in hand,
  Albe that *Hatred* was thereto full loth,
  And turn'd his face away, as he did stand,
  Unwilling to behold that lovely band.
  Yet she was of such grace and vertuous might,
  That her commaundment he could not withstand,
  But bit his lip for felonous despight,
And gnasht his yron tuskes at that displeasing sight.

34

Concord she cleeped was in common reed,
  Mother of blessed *Peace*, and *Friendship* trew;
  They both her twins, both borne of heavenly seed,
  And she her selfe likewise divinely grew;
  The which right well her workes divine did shew:
  For strength, and wealth, and happinesse she lends,
  And strife, and warre, and anger does subdew:
  Of litle much, of foes she maketh frends,
And to afflicted minds sweet rest and quiet sends.

35

By her the heaven is in his course contained,
  And all the world in state unmoved stands,
  As their Almightie maker first ordained,
  And bound them with inviolable bands;
  Else would the waters overflow the lands,
  And fire devoure the ayre, and hell them quight,
  But that she holds them with her blessed hands.
  She is the nourse of pleasure and delight,
And unto *Venus* grace the gate doth open right.

36

By her I entring halfe dismayed was,
  But she in gentle wise me entertayned,
  And twixt her selfe and *Love* did let me pas;
  But *Hatred* would my entrance have restrayned,
  And with his club me threatned to have brayned,
  Had not the Ladie with her powrefull speach
  Him from his wicked will uneath refrayned;
  And th'other eke his malice did empeach,
Till I was throughly past the perill of his reach.

37

Into the inmost Temple thus I came,
  Which fuming all with frankensence I found,
  And odours rising from the altars flame.
  Upon an hundred marble pillors round
  The roofe up high was reared from the ground,
  All deckt with crownes, and chaynes, and girlands gay,
  And thousand pretious gifts worth many a pound,
  The which sad lovers for their vowes did pay;
And all the ground was strow'd with flowres, as fresh as May.

38

An hundred Altars round about were set,
  All flaming with their sacrifices fire,
  That with the steme thereof the Temple swet,
  Which rould in clouds to heaven did aspire,
  And in them bore true lovers vowes entire:
  And eke an hundred brasen caudrons bright,
  To bath in joy and amorous desire,
  Every of which was to a damzell hight;
For all the Priests were damzels, in soft linnen dight.

39

Right in the midst the Goddesse selfe did stand
  Upon an altar of some costly masse,
  Whose substance was uneath to understand:
  For neither pretious stone, nor durefull brasse,
  Nor shining gold, nor mouldring clay it was;
  But much more rare and pretious to esteeme,
  Pure in aspect, and like to christall glasse,
  Yet glasse was not, if one did rightly deeme,
But being faire and brickle, likest glasse did seeme.

Florimell rescued by Cymodoce

40

But it in shape and beautie did excell
  All other Idoles, which the heathen adore,
  Farre passing that, which by surpassing skill
  Phidias did make in *Paphos* Isle of yore,
  With which that wretched Greeke, that life forlore,
  Did fall in love: yet this much fairer shined,
  But covered with a slender veile afore;
  And both her feete and legs together twyned
Were with a snake, whose head and tail were fast combyned.

41

The cause why she was covered with a vele,
  Was hard to know, for that her Priests the same
  From peoples knowledge labour'd to concele.
  But sooth it was not sure for womanish shame,
  Nor any blemish, which the worke mote blame;
  But for, they say, she hath both kinds in one,
  Both male and female, both under one name:
  She syre and mother is her selfe alone,
Begets and eke conceives, ne needeth other none.

42

And all about her necke and shoulders flew
  A flocke of litle loves, and sports, and joyes,
  With nimble wings of gold and purple hew;
  Whose shapes seem'd not like to terrestriall boyes,
  But like to Angels playing heavenly toyes;
  The whilest their eldest brother was away,
  Cupid their eldest brother; he enjoyes
  The wide kingdome of love with Lordly sway,
And to his law compels all creatures to obay.

43

And all about her altar scattered lay
  Great sorts of lovers piteously complayning,
  Some of their losse, some of their loves delay,
  Some of their pride, some paragons disdayning,
  Some fearing fraud, some fraudulently fayning,
  As every one had cause of good or ill.
  Amongst the rest some one through loves constrayning,
  Tormented sore, could not containe it still,
But thus brake forth, that all the temple it did fill.

44

Great *Venus*, Queene of beautie and of grace,
  The joy of Gods and men, that under skie
  Doest fayrest shine, and most adorne thy place,
  That with thy smyling looke doest pacifie
  The raging seas, and makst the stormes to flie;
  Thee goddesse, thee the winds, the clouds doe feare,
  And when thou spredst thy mantle forth on hie,
  The waters play and pleasant lands appeare,
And heavens laugh, and al the world shews joyous cheare.

45

Then doth the dædale earth throw forth to thee
  Out of her fruitfull lap aboundant flowres,
  And then all living wights, soone as they see
  The spring breake forth out of his lusty bowres,
  They all doe learne to play the Paramours;
  First doe the merry birds, thy prety pages
  Frivily pricked with thy lustfull powres,
  Chirpe loud to thee out of their leavy cages,
And thee their mother call to coole their kindly rages.

46

Then doe the salvage beasts begin to play
  Their pleasant friskes, and loath their wonted food;
  The Lyons rore, the Tygres loudly bray,
  The raging Buls rebellow through the wood,
  And breaking forth, dare tempt the deepest flood,
  To come where thou doest draw them with desire:
  So all things else, that nourish vitall blood,
  Soone as with fury thou doest them inspire,
In generation seeke to quench their inward fire.

47

So all the world by thee at first was made,
  And dayly yet thou doest the same repayre:
  Ne ought on earth that merry is and glad,
  Ne ought on earth that lovely is and fayre,
  But thou the same for pleasure didst prepayre.
  Thou art the root of all that joyous is,
  Great God of men and women, queene of th'ayre,
  Mother of laughter, and welspring of blisse,
O graunt that of my love at last I may not misse.

48

So did he say: but I with murmure soft,
　That none might heare the sorrow of my hart,
　Yet inly groning deepe and sighing oft,
　Besought her to graunt ease unto my smart,
　And to my wound her gratious help impart.
　Whilest thus I spake, behold with happy eye
　I spyde, where at the Idoles feet apart
　A bevie of fayre damzels close did lye,
Wayting when as the Antheme should be sung on hye.

49

The first of them did seeme of ryper yeares,
　And graver countenance than all the rest;
　Yet all the rest were eke her equall peares,
　Yet unto her obayed all the best.
　Her name was *Womanhood*, that she exprest
　By her sad semblant and demeanure wyse:
　For stedfast still her eyes did fixed rest,
　Ne rov'd at randon after gazers guyse,
Whose luring baytes oftimes doe heedlesse harts entyse.

50

And next to her sate goodly *Shamefastnesse*,
　Ne ever durst her eyes from ground upreare,
　Ne ever once did looke up from her desse,
　As if some blame of evill she did feare,
　That in her cheekes made roses oft appeare:
　And her against sweet *Cherefulnesse* was placed,
　Whose eyes like twinkling stars in evening cleare,
　Were deckt with smyles, that all sad humors chaced,
And darted forth delights, the which her goodly graced.

51

And next to her sate sober *Modestie*,
　Holding her hand upon her gentle hart;
　And her against sate comely *Curtesie*,
　That unto every person knew her part;
　And her before was seated overthwart
　Soft *Silence*, and submisse *Obedience*,
　Both linckt together never to dispart,
　Both gifts of God not gotten but from thence,
Both girlonds of his Saints against their foes offence.

52

Thus sate they all a round in seemely rate:
　And in the midst of them a goodly mayd,
　Even in the lap of *Womanhood* there sate,
　The which was all in lilly white arayd,
　With silver streames amongst the linnen stray'd;
　Like to the Morne, when first her shyning face
　Hath to the gloomy world it selfe bewray'd,
　That same was fayrest *Amoret* in place,
Shyning with beauties light, and heavenly vertues grace.

53

Whom soone as I beheld, my hart gan throb,
　And wade in doubt, what best were to be donne:
　For sacrilege me seem'd the Church to rob,
　And folly seem'd to leave the thing undonne,
　Which with so strong attempt I had begonne.
　Tho shaking off all doubt and shamefast feare,
　Which Ladies love I heard had never wonne
　Mongst men of worth, I to her stepped neare,
And by the lilly hand her labour'd up to reare.

54

Thereat that formost matrone me did blame,
　And sharpe rebuke, for being over bold;
　Saying it was to Knight unseemely shame,
　Upon a recluse Virgin to lay hold,
　That unto *Venus* services was sold.
　To whom I thus, Nay but it fitteth best,
　For *Cupids* man with *Venus* mayd to hold,
　For ill your goddesse services are drest
By virgins, and her sacrifices let to rest.

55

With that my shield I forth to her did show,
　Which all that while I closely had conceld;
　On which when *Cupid* with his killing bow
　And cruell shafts emblazond she beheld,
　At sight thereof she was with terror queld,
　And said no more: but I which all that while
　The pledge of faith, her hand engaged held,
　Like warie Hynd within the weedie soyle,
For no intreatie would forgoe so glorious spoyle.

56

And evermore upon the Goddesse face
  Mine eye was fixt, for feare of her offence,
  Whom when I saw with amiable grace
  To laugh at me, and favour my pretence,
  I was emboldned with more confidence,
  And nought for nicenesse nor for envy sparing,
  In presence of them all forth led her thence,
  All looking on, and like astonisht staring,
Yet to lay hand on her, not one of all them daring.

57

She often prayd, and often me besought,
  Sometime with tender teares to let her goe,
  Sometime with witching smyles: but yet for nought,
  That ever she to me could say or doe,
  Could she her wished freedome fro me wooe;
  But forth I led her through the Temple gate,
  By which I hardly past with much adoe:
  But that same Ladie which me friended late
In entrance, did me also friend in my retrate.

58

No lesse did *Daunger* threaten me with dread,
  When as he saw me, maugre all his powre,
  That glorious spoyle of beautie with me lead,
  Than *Cerberus*, when *Orpheus* did recoure
  His Leman from the Stygian Princes boure.
  But evermore my shield did me defend,
  Against the storme of every dreadfull stoure:
  Thus safely with my love I thence did wend.
So ended he his tale, where I this Canto end.

CANT. XI

Marinells former wound is heald,
he comes to Proteus hall,
Where Thames doth the Medway wedd,
and feasts the Sea-gods all.

1

BUT ah for pittie that I have thus long
　　Left a fayre Ladie languishing in payne:
　　Now well away, that I have doen such wrong,
　　To let faire *Florimell* in bands remayne,
　　In bands of love, and in sad thraldomes chayne;
　　From which unlesse some heavenly powre her free
　　By miracle, not yet appearing playne,
　　She lenger yet is like captiv'd to bee:
That even to thinke thereof, it inly pitties mee.

2

Here neede you to remember, how erewhile
　　Unlovely *Proteus*, missing to his mind
　　That Virgins love to win by wit or wile,
　　Her threw into a dongeon deepe and blind,
　　And there in chaynes her cruelly did bind,
　　In hope thereby her to his bent to draw:
　　For when as neither gifts nor graces kind
　　Her constant mind could move at all he saw,
He thought her to compell by crueltie and awe.

3

Deepe in the bottome of an huge great rocke
　　The dongeon was, in which her bound he left,
　　That neither yron barres, nor brasen locke
　　Did neede to gard from force, or secret theft
　　Of all her lovers, which would her have reft.
　　For wall'd it was with waves, which rag'd and ror'd
　　As they the cliffe in peeces would have cleft;
　　Besides ten thousand monsters foule abhor'd
Did waite about it, gaping griesly all begor'd.

4

And in the midst thereof did horror dwell,
  And darkenesse dredd, that never viewed day
  Like to the balefull house of lowest hell,
  In which old *Styx* her aged bones alway,
  Old *Styx* the Grandame of the Gods, doth lay.
  There did this lucklesse mayd seven months abide,
  Ne ever evening saw, ne mornings ray,
  Ne ever from the day the night descride,
But thought it all one night, that did no houres divide.

5

And all this was for love of *Marinell*,
  Who her despysd (ah who would her despyse?)
  And wemens love did from his hart expell,
  And all those joyes that weake mankind entyse.
  Nathlesse his pride full dearely he did pryse;
  For of a womans hand it was ywroke,
  That of the wound he yet in languor lyes,
  Ne can be cured of that cruell stroke
Which *Britomart* him gave, when he did her provoke.

6

Yet farre and neare the Nymph his mother sought,
  And many salves did to his sore applie,
  And many herbes did use. But when as nought
  She saw could ease his rankling maladie,
  At last to *Tryphon* she for helpe did hie,
  (This *Tryphon* is the seagods surgeon hight)
  Whom she besought to find some remedie:
  And for his paines a whistle him behight
That of a fishes shell was wrought with rare delight.

7

So well that Leach did hearke to her request,
  And did so well employ his carefull paine,
  That in short space his hurts he had redrest,
  And him restor'd to healthfull state againe:
  In which he long time after did remaine
  There with the Nymph his mother, like her thrall;
  Who sore against his will did him retaine,
  For feare of perill, which to him mote fall,
Through his too ventrous prowesse proved over all.

8

It fortun'd then, a solemne feast was there
　To all the Sea-gods and their fruitfull seede,
　In honour of the spousalls, which then were
　Betwixt the *Medway* and the *Thames* agreed.
　Long had the *Thames* (as we in records reed)
　Before that day her wooed to his bed;
　But the proud Nymph would for no worldly meed,
　Nor no entreatie to his love be led;
Till now at last relenting, she to him was wed.

9

So both agreed, that this their bridale feast
　Should for the Gods in *Proteus* house be made;
　To which they all repayr'd, both most and least,
　Aswell which in the mightie Ocean trade,
　As that in rivers swim, or brookes doe wade.
　All which not if an hundred tongues to tell,
　And hundred mouthes, and voice of brasse I had,
　And endlesse memorie, that mote excell,
In order as they came, could I recount them well.

10

Helpe therefore, O thou sacred imp of *Jove*,
　The noursling of Dame *Memorie* his deare,
　To whom those rolles, layd up in heaven above,
　And records of antiquitie appeare,
　To which no wit of man may comen neare;
　Helpe me to tell the names of all those floods,
　And all those Nymphes, which then assembled were
　To that great banquet of the watry Gods,
And all their sundry kinds, and all their hid abodes.

11

First came great *Neptune* with his threeforkt mace,
　That rules the Seas, and makes them rise or fall;
　His dewy lockes did drop with brine apace,
　Under his Diademe imperiall:
　And by his side his Queene with coronall,
　Faire *Amphitrite*, most divinely faire,
　Whose yvorie shoulders weren covered all,
　As with a robe, with her owne silver haire,
And deckt with pearles, which th'Indian seas for her prepaire.

12

These marched farre afore the other crew;
  And all the way before them as they went,
  Triton his trompet shrill before them blew,
  For goodly triumph and great jollyment,
  That made the rockes to roare, as they were rent.
  And after them the royall issue came,
  Which of them sprung by lineall descent:
  First the Sea-gods, which to themselves doe clame
The powre to rule the billowes, and the waves to tame.

13

Phorcys, the father of that fatall brood,
  By whom those old Heroes wonne such fame;
  And *Glaucus*, that wise southsayes understood;
  And tragicke *Inoes* sonne, the which became
  A God of seas through his mad mothers blame,
  Now hight *Palemon*, and is saylers frend;
  Great *Brontes*, and *Astræus*, that did shame
  Himselfe with incest of his kin unkend;
And huge *Orion*, that doth tempests still portend.

14

The rich *Cteatus*, and *Eurytus* long;
  Neleus and *Pelias* lovely brethren both;
  Mightie *Chrysaor*, and *Caïcus* strong;
  Eurypulus, that calmes the waters wroth;
  And faire *Euphœmus*, that upon them goth
  As on the ground, without dismay or dread:
  Fierce *Eryx*, and *Alebius* that know'th
  The waters depth, and doth their bottome tread;
And sad *Asopus*, comely with his hoarie head.

15

There also some most famous founders were
  Of puissant Nations, which the world possest;
  Yet sonnes of *Neptune*, now assembled here:
  Ancient *Ogyges*, even th'auncientest,
  And *Inachus* renowmd above the rest;
  Phœnix, and *Aon*, and *Pelasgus* old,
  Great *Belus*, *Phœax*, and *Agenor* best;
  And mightie *Albion*, father of the bold
And warlike people, which the *Britaine* Islands hold.

16

For *Albion* the sonne of *Neptune* was,
  Who for the proofe of his great puissance,
  Out of his *Albion* did on dry-foot pas
  Into old *Gall*, that now is cleeped *France*,
  To fight with *Hercules*, that did advance
  To vanquish all the world with matchlesse might,
  And there his mortall part by great mischance
  Was slaine: but that which is th'immortall spright
Lives still: and to this feast with *Neptunes* seed was hight.

17

But what doe I their names seeke to reherse,
  Which all the world have with their issue fild?
  How can they all in this so narrow verse
  Contayned be, and in small compasse hild?
  Let them record them, that are better skild,
  And know the moniments of passed times:
  Onely what needeth, shall be here fulfild,
  T'expresse some part of that great equipage,
Which from great *Neptune* do derive their parentage.

18

Next came the aged *Ocean*, and his Dame,
  Old *Tethys*, th'oldest two of all the rest,
  For all the rest of those two parents came,
  Which afterward both sea and land possest:
  Of all which *Nereus* th'eldest, and the best,
  Did first proceed, than which none more upright,
  Ne more sincere in word and deed profest;
  Most voide of guile, most free from fowle despight,
Doing him selfe, and teaching others to doe right.

19

Thereto he was expert in prophecies,
  And could the ledden of the Gods unfold,
  Through which, when *Paris* brought his famous prise
  The faire Tindarid lasse, he him fortold,
  That her all *Greece* with many a champion bold
  Should fetch againe, and finally destroy
  Proud *Priams* towne. So wise is *Nereus* old,
  And so well skild; nathlesse he takes great joy
Oft-times amongst the wanton Nymphs to sport and toy.

20

And after him the famous rivers came,
  Which doe the earth enrich and beautifie:
  The fertile Nile, which creatures new doth frame;
  Long Rhodanus, whose sourse springs from the skie;
  Fair Ister, flowing from the mountaines hie;
  Divine Scamander, purpled yet with blood
  Of Greekes and Trojans, which therein did die;
  Pactolus glistring with his golden flood,
And Tygris fierce, whose streames of none may be withstood.

21

Great Ganges, and immortall Euphrates,
  Deepe Indus, and Mæander intricate,
  Slow Peneus, and tempestuous Phasides,
  Swift Rhene, and Alpheus still immaculate:
  Ooraxes, feared for great *Cyrus* fate;
  Tybris, renowmed for the Romaines fame,
  Rich Oranochy, though but knowen late;
  And that huge River, which doth beare his name
Of warlike Amazons, which doe possesse the same.

22

Joy on those warlike women, which so long
  Can from all men so rich a kingdome hold;
  And shame on you, O men, which boast your strong
  And valiant hearts, in thoughts lesse hard and bold,
  Yet quaile in conquest of that land of gold.
  But this to you, O Britons, most pertaines,
  To whom the right hereof it selfe hath sold;
  The which for sparing litle cost or paines,
Loose so immortall glory, and so endlesse gaines.

23

Then was there heard a most celestiall sound,
  Of dainty musicke, which did next ensew
  Before the spouse: that was *Arion* crownd;
  Who playing on his harpe, unto him drew
  The eares and hearts of all that goodly crew,
  That even yet the Dolphin, which him bore
  Through the Ægæan seas from Pirates vew,
  Stood still by him astonisht at his lore,
And all the raging seas for joy forgot to rore.

24

So went he playing on the watery plaine.
  Soone after whom the lovely Bridegroome came,
  The noble Thamis, with all his goodly traine,
  But him before there went, as best became,
  His auncient parents, namely th'auncient Thame.
  But much more aged was his wife than he,
  The Ouze, whom men doe Isis rightly name;
  Full weake and crooked creature seemed shee,
And almost blind through eld, that scarce her way could see.

25

Therefore on either side she was sustained
  Of two smal grooms, which by their names were hight
  The *Churne*, and *Charwell*, two small streames, which pained
  Them selves her footing to direct aright,
  Which fayled oft through faint and feeble plight:
  But *Thame* was stronger, and of better stay;
  Yet seem'd full aged by his outward sight,
  With head all hoary, and his beard all gray,
Deawed with silver drops, that trickled downe alway.

26

And eke he somewhat seem'd to stoupe afore
  With bowed backe, by reason of the lode,
  And auncient heavy burden, which he bore
  Of that faire City, wherein make abode
  So many learned impes, that shoote abrode,
  And with their braunches spred all Britany,
  No lesse than do her elder sisters broode.
  Joy to you both, ye double noursery
Of Arts, but Oxford thine doth *Thame* most glorify.

27

But he their sonne full fresh and jolly was,
  All decked in a robe of watchet hew,
  On which the waves, glittering like Christall glas,
  So cunningly enwoven were, that few
  Could weenen, whether they were false or trew.
  And on his head like to a Coronet
  He wore, that seemed strange to common vew,
  In which were many towres and castels set,
That it encompast round as with a golden fret.

28

Like as the mother of the Gods, they say,
  In her great iron charet wonts to ride,
  When to *Joves* pallace she doth take her way:
  Old *Cybele*, arayd with pompous pride,
  Wearing a Diademe embattild wide
  With hundred turrets, like a Turribant.
  With such an one was Thamis beautifide;
  That was to weet the famous Troynovant,
In which her kingdomes throne is chiefly resiant.

29

And round about him many a pretty Page
  Attended duely, ready to obay;
  All little Rivers, which owe vassallage
  To him, as to their Lord, and tribute pay:
  The chaulky Kenet, and the Thetis gray,
  The morish Cole, and the soft sliding Breane,
  The wanton Lee, that oft doth loose his way,
  And the still Darent, in whose waters cleane
Ten thousand fishes play, and decke his pleasant streame.

30

Then came his neighbour flouds, which nigh him dwell,
  And water all the English soile throughout;
  They all on him this day attended well;
  And with meet service waited him about;
  Ne none disdained low to him to lout:
  No not the stately Severne grudg'd at all,
  Ne storming Humber, though he looked stout;
  But both him honor'd as their principall,
And let their swelling waters low before him fall.

31

There was the speedy Tamar, which devides
  The Cornish and the Devonish confines;
  Through both whose borders swiftly downe it glides,
  And meeting Plim, to Plimmouth thence declines:
  And Dart, nigh chockt with sands of tinny mines.
  But Avon marched in more stately path,
  Proud of his Adamants, with which he shines
  And glisters wide, as als' of wondrous Bath,
And Bristow faire, which on his waves he builded hath.

32

And there came Stoure with terrible aspect,
  Bearing his sixe deformed heads on hye,
  That doth his course through Blandford plains direct,
  And washeth Winborne meades in season drye.
  Next him went Wylibourne with passage slye,
  That of his wylinesse his name doth take,
  And of him selfe doth name the shire thereby:
  And Mole, that like a nousling Mole doth make
His way still under ground, till Thamis he overtake.

33

Then came the Rother, decked all with woods
  Like a wood God, and flowing fast to Rhy:
  And Sture, that parteth with his pleasant floods
  The Easterne Saxons from the Southerne ny,
  And Clare, and Harwitch both doth beautify:
  Him follow'd Yar, soft washing Norwitch wall,
  And with him brought a present joyfully
  Of his owne fish unto their festivall,
Whose like none else could shew, the which they Ruffins call.

34

Next these the plenteous Ouse came far from land,
  By many a city, and by many a towne,
  And many rivers taking under hand
  Into his waters, as he passeth downe,
  The Cle, the Were, the Grant, the Sture, the Rowne.
  Thence doth by Huntingdon and Cambridge flit,
  My mother Cambridge, whom as with a Crowne
  He doth adorne, and is adorn'd of it
With many a gentle Muse, and many a learned wit.

35

And after him the fatall Welland went,
  That if old sawes prove true (which God forbid)
  Shall drowne all Holland with his excrement,
  And shall see Stamford, though now homely hid,
  Then shine in learning, more than ever did
  Cambridge or Oxford, Englands goodly beames.
  And next to him the Nene downe softly slid;
  And bounteous Trent, that in himselfe enseames
Both thirty sorts of fish, and thirty sundry streames.

36

Next these came Tyne, along whose stony bancke
  That Romaine Monarch built a brasen wall,
  Which mote the feebled Britons strongly flancke
  Against the Picts, that swarmed over all,
  Which yet thereof Gualsever they doe call:
  And Twede the limit betwixt Logris land
  And Albany: And Eden though but small,
  Yet often stainde with bloud of many a band
Of Scots and English both, that tyned on his strand.

37

Then came those sixe sad brethren, like forlorne,
  That whilome were (as antique fathers tell)
  Sixe valiant Knights, of one faire Nymphe yborne,
  Which did in noble deedes of armes excell,
  And wonned there, where now Yorke people dwell;
  Still Ure, swift Werfe, and Oze the most of might,
  High Swale, unquiet Nide, and troublous Skell;
  All whom a Scythian king, that Humber hight,
Slew cruelly, and in the river drowned quight.

38

But past not long, ere *Brutus* warlicke sonne
  Locrinus them aveng'd, and the same date,
  Which the proud Humber unto them had donne,
  By equall dome repayd on his owne pate:
  For in the selfe same river, where he late
  Had drenched them, he drowned him againe;
  And named the river of his wretched fate;
  Whose bad condition yet it doth retaine,
Oft tossed with his stormes, which therein still remaine.

39

These after, came the stony shallow Lone,
  That to old Loncaster his name doth lend;
  And following Dee, which Britons long ygone
  Did call divine, that doth by Chester tend;
  And Conway which out of his streame doth send
  Plenty of pearles to decke his dames withall,
  And Lindus that his pikes doth most commend,
  Of which the auncient Lincolne men doe call;
All these together marched toward *Proteus* hall.

40

Ne thence the Irishe Rivers absent were,
   Sith no lesse famous than the rest they bee,
   And joyne in neighbourhood of kingdome nere,
   Why should they not likewise in love agree,
   And joy likewise this solemne day to see?
   They saw it all, and present were in place;
   Though I them all according their degree,
   Cannot recount, nor tell their hidden race,
Nor read the salvage cuntreis, thorough which they pace.

41

There was the Liffy rolling downe the lea,
   The sandy Slane, the stony Aubrian,
   The spacious Shenan spreading like a sea,
   The pleasant Boyne, the fishy fruitfull Ban,
   Swift Awniduff, which of the English man
   Is cal'de Blacke water, and the Liffar deep,
   Sad Trowis, that once his people overran,
   Strong Allo tombling from Slewlogher steep,
And Mulla mine, whose waves I whilom taught to weep.

42

And there the three renowmed brethren were,
   Which that great Gyant *Blomius* begot,
   Of the faire Nimph *Rheusa* wandring there.
   One day, as she to shunne the season whot,
   Under Slewbloome in shady grove was got,
   This Gyant found her, and by force deflowr'd,
   Whereof conceiving, she in time forth brought
   These three faire sons, which being thence forth powrd
In three great rivers ran, and many countreis scowrd.

43

The first, the gentle Shure that making way
   By sweet Clonmell, adornes rich Waterford;
   The next, the stubborne Newre, whose waters gray
   By faire Kilkenny and Rosseponte boord,
   The third, the goodly Barow, which doth hoord
   Great heapes of Salmons in his deepe bosome:
   All which long sundred, doe at last accord
   To joyne in one, ere to the sea they come,
So flowing all from one, all one at last become.

44

There also was the wide embayed Mayre,
  The pleasaunt Bandon crownd with many a wood,
  The spreading Lee, that like an Island fayre
  Encloseth Corke with his devided flood;
  And balefull Oure, late staind with English blood:
  With many more, whose names no tongue can tell.
  All which that day in order seemly good
  Did on the Thamis attend, and waited well
To doe their duefull service, as to them befell.

45

Then came the Bride, the lovely *Medua* came,
  Clad in a vesture of unknowen geare,
  And uncouth fashion, yet her well became;
  That seem'd like silver, sprinckled here and theare
  With glittering spangs, that did like starres appeare,
  And wav'd upon, like water Chamelot,
  To hide the metall, which yet every where
  Bewrayd it selfe, to let men plainely wot,
It was no mortall worke, that seem'd and yet was not.

46

Her goodly lockes adowne her backe did flow
  Unto her waste, with flowres bescattered,
  The which ambrosiall odours forth did throw
  To all about, and all her shoulders spred
  As a new spring; and likewise on her hed
  A Chapelet of sundry flowers she wore,
  From under which the deawy humour shed,
  Did tricle downe her haire, like to the hore
Congealed litle drops, which doe the morne adore.

47

On her two pretty handmaides did attend,
  One cald the *Theise*, the other cald the *Crane*;
  Which on her waited, things amisse to mend,
  And both behind upheld her spredding traine;
  Under the which, her feet appeared plaine,
  Her silver feet, faire washt against this day:
  And her before there paced Pages twaine,
  Both clad in colours like, and like array,
The *Doune* and eke the *Frith*, both which prepard her way.

48

And after these the Sea Nymphs marched all,
  All goodly damzels, deckt with long greene haire,
  Whom of their sire *Nereides* men call,
  All which the Oceans daughter to him bare
  The gray eyde *Doris*: all which fifty are;
  All which she there on her attending had.
  Swift *Proto*, milde *Eucrate*, *Thetis* faire,
  Soft *Spio*, sweete *Eudore*, *Sao* sad,
Light *Doto*, wanton *Glauce*, and *Galene* glad.

49

White hand *Eunica*, proud *Dynamene*,
  Joyous *Thalia*, goodly *Amphitrite*,
  Lovely *Pasithee*, kinde *Eulimene*,
  Light foote *Cymothoe*, and sweete *Melite*,
  Fairest *Pherusa*, *Phao* lilly white,
  Wondred *Agave*, *Poris*, and *Nesæa*,
  With *Erato* that doth in love delite,
  And *Panopæ*, and wise *Protomedæa*,
And snowy neckd *Doris*, and milkewhite *Galathæa*.

50

Speedy *Hippothoe*, and chaste *Actea*,
  Large *Lisianassa*, and *Pronæa* sage,
  Evagore, and light *Pontoporea*,
  And she, that with her least word can asswage
  The surging seas, when they do sorest rage,
  Cymodoce, and stout *Autonoe*,
  And *Neso*, and *Eione* well in age,
  And seeming still to smile, *Glauconome*,
And she that hight of many heastes *Polynome*.

51

Fresh *Alimeda*, deckt with girlond greene;
  Hyponeo, with salt bedewed wrests:
  Laomedia, like the christall sheene;
  Liagore, much praisd for wise behests;
  And *Psamathe*, for her brode snowy brests;
  Cymo, *Eupompe*, and *Themiste* just;
  And she that vertue loves and vice detests
  Evarna, and *Menippe* true in trust,
And *Nemertea* learned well to rule her lust.

52

All these the daughters of old *Nereus* were,
  Which have the sea in charge to them assinde,
  To rule his tides, and surges to uprere,
  To bring forth stormes, or fast them to upbinde,
  And sailers save from wreckes of wrathfull winde.
  And yet besides three thousand more there were
  Of th'Oceans seede, but *Joves* and *Phœbus* kinde;
  The which in floods and fountaines doe appere,
And all mankinde do nourish with their waters clere.

53

The which, more eath it were for mortall wight,
  To tell the sands, or count the starres on hye,
  Or ought more hard, than thinke to reckon right.
  But well I wote, that these which I descry,
  Were present at this great solemnity:
  And there amongst the rest, the mother was
  Of luckelesse *Marinell Cymodoce*.
  Which, for my Muse her selfe now tyred has,
Unto an other Canto I will overpas.

CANT. XII

Marin for love of Florimell,
In languor wastes his life:
The Nymph his mother getteth her,
And gives to him for wife.

I

O WHAT an endlesse worke have I in hand,
  To count the seas abundant progeny,
  Whose fruitfull seede farre passeth those in land,
  And also those which wonne in th'azure sky?
  For much more eath to tell the starres on hy,
  Albe they endlesse seeme in estimation,
  Than to recount the Seas posterity:
  So fertile be the flouds in generation,
So huge their numbers, and so numberlesse their nation.

2

Therefore the antique wisards well invented,
  That *Venus* of the fomy sea was bred;
  For that the seas by her are most augmented.
  Witnesse th'exceeding fry, which there are fed,
  And wondrous sholes, which may of none be red.
  Then blame me not, if I have err'd in count
  Of Gods, of Nymphs, of rivers yet unred:
  For though their numbers do much more surmount,
Yet all those same were there, which erst I did recount.

3

All those were there, and many other more,
  Whose names and nations were too long to tell,
  That *Proteus* house they fild even to the dore;
  Yet were they all in order, as befell,
  According their degrees disposed well.
  Amongst the rest, was faire *Cymodoce*,
  The mother of unlucky *Marinell*,
  Who thither with her came, to learne and see
The manner of the Gods when they at banquet be.

4

But for he was halfe mortall, being bred
  Of mortall sire, though of immortall wombe,
  He might not with immortall food be fed,
  Ne with th'eternall Gods to bancket come;
  But walkt abrode, and round about did rome,
  To view the building of that uncouth place,
  That seem'd unlike unto his earthly home:
  Where, as he to and fro by chaunce did trace,
There unto him betid a disaventrous case.

5

Under the hanging of an hideous clieffe,
  He heard the lamentable voice of one,
  That piteously complaind her carefull grieffe,
  Which never she before disclosd to none,
  But to her selfe her sorrow did bemone.
  So feelingly her case she did complaine,
  That ruth it moved in the rocky stone,
  And made it seeme to feele her grievous paine,
And oft to grone with billowes beating from the maine.

6

Though vaine I see my sorrowes to unfold,
  And count my cares, when none is nigh to heare,
  Yet hoping griefe may lessen being told,
  I will them tell though unto no man neare:
  For heaven that unto all lends equall eare,
  Is farre from hearing of my heavy plight;
  And lowest hell, to which I lie most neare,
  Cares not what evils hap to wretched wight;
And greedy seas doe in the spoile of life delight.

7

Yet loe the seas I see by often beating,
  Doe pearce the rockes, and hardest marble weares;
  But his hard rocky hart for no entreating
  Will yeeld, but when my piteous plaints he heares,
  Is hardned more with my aboundant teares.
  Yet though he never list to me relent,
  But let me waste in woe my wretched yeares,
  Yet will I never of my love repent,
But joy that for his sake I suffer prisonment.

8

And when my weary ghost with griefe outworne,
  By timely death shall winne her wished rest,
  Let then this plaint unto his eares be borne,
  That blame it is to him, that armes profest,
  To let her die, whom he might have redrest.
  There did she pause, inforced to give place
  Unto the passion, that her heart opprest,
  And after she had wept and wail'd a space,
She gan afresh thus to renew her wretched case.

9

Ye Gods of seas, if any Gods at all
  Have care of right, or ruth of wretches wrong,
  By one or other way me woefull thrall,
  Deliver hence out of this dungeon strong,
  In which I daily dying am too long.
  And if ye deeme me death for loving one,
  That loves not me, then doe it not prolong,
  But let me die and end my daies attone,
And let him live unlov'd, or love him selfe alone.

10

But if that life ye unto me decree,
    Then let mee live, as lovers ought to do,
    And of my lifes deare love beloved be:
    And if he shall through pride your doome undo,
    Do you by duresse him compell thereto,
    And in this prison put him here with me:
    One prison fittest is to hold us two:
    So had I rather to be thrall, than free;
Such thraldome or such freedome let it surely be.

11

But O vaine judgement, and conditions vaine,
    The which the prisoner points unto the free,
    The whiles I him condemne, and deeme his paine,
    He where he list goes loose, and laughes at me.
    So ever loose, so ever happy be.
    But where so loose or happy that thou art,
    Know *Marinell* that all this is for thee.
    With that she wept and wail'd, as if her hart
Would quite have burst through great abundance of her smart.

12

All which complaint when *Marinell* had heard,
    And understood the cause of all her care
    To come of him, for using her so hard,
    His stubborne heart, that never felt misfare
    Was toucht with soft remorse and pitty rare;
    That even for griefe of minde he oft did grone,
    And inly wish, that in his powre it weare
    Her to redresse: but since he meanes found none
He could no more but her great misery bemone.

13

Thus whilst his stony heart with tender ruth
    Was toucht, and mighty courage mollifide,
    Dame *Venus* sonne that tameth stubborne youth
    With iron bit, and maketh him abide,
    Till like a victor on his backe he ride,
    Into his mouth his maystring bridle threw,
    That made him stoupe, till he did him bestride:
    Then gan he make him tread his steps anew,
And learne to love, by learning lovers paines to rew.

14

Now gan he in his grieved minde devise,
 How from that dungeon he might her enlarge:
 Some while he thought, by faire and humble wise
 To *Proteus* selfe to sue for her discharge:
 But then he fear'd his mothers former charge
 Gainst womens love, long given him in vaine.
 Then gan he thinke, perforce with sword and targe
 Her forth to fetch, and *Proteus* to constraine:
But soone he gan such folly to forthinke againe.

15

Then did he cast to steale her thence away,
 And with him beare, where none of her might know.
 But all in vaine: for why he found no way
 To enter in, or issue forth below:
 For all about that rocke the sea did flow.
 And though unto his will she given were,
 Yet without ship or bote her thence to row,
 He wist not how her thence away to bere;
And daunger well he wist long to continue there.

16

At last when as no meanes he could invent,
 Backe to him selfe he gan returne the blame,
 That was the author of her punishment;
 And with vile curses, and reprochfull shame
 To damne him selfe by every evill name;
 And deeme unworthy or of love or life
 That had despisde so chast and faire a dame,
 Which him had sought through trouble and long strife;
Yet had refusde a God that her had sought to wife.

17

In this sad plight he walked here and there,
 And romed round about the rocke in vaine,
 As he had lost him selfe, he wist not where;
 Oft listening if he mote her heare againe;
 And still bemoning her unworthy paine.
 Like as an Hynde whose calfe is falne unwares
 Into some pit, where she him heares complaine,
 An hundred times about the pit side fares,
Right sorrowfully mourning her bereaved cares.

18

And now by this the feast was throughly ended,
　　And every one gan homeward to resort.
　　Which seeing *Marinell*, was sore offended,
　　That his departure thence should be so short,
　　And leave his love in that sea-walled fort.
　　Yet durst he not his mother disobay,
　　But her attending in full seemly sort,
　　Did march amongst the many all the way:
And all the way did inly mourne, like one astray.

19

Being returned to his mothers bowre,
　　In solitary silence far from wight,
　　He gan record the lamentable stowre,
　　In which his wretched love lay day and night,
　　For his deare sake, that ill deserv'd that plight:
　　The thought whereof empierst his hart so deepe,
　　That of no worldly thing he tooke delight;
　　Ne dayly food did take, ne nightly sleepe,
But pyn'd, and mourn'd, and languisht, and alone did weepe.

20

That in short space his wonted chearefull hew
　　Gan fade, and lively spirits deaded quight:
　　His cheeke bones raw, and eie-pits hollow grew,
　　And brawney armes had lost their knowen might,
　　That nothing like himselfe he seem'd in sight.
　　Ere long so weake of limbe, and sicke of love
　　He woxe, that lenger he note stand upright,
　　But to his bed was brought, and layd above,
Like ruefull ghost, unable once to stirre or move.

21

Which when his mother saw, she in her mind
　　Was troubled sore, ne wist well what to weene,
　　Ne could by search nor any meanes out find
　　The secret cause and nature of his teene,
　　Whereby she might apply some medicine;
　　But weeping day and night, did him attend,
　　And mourn'd to see her losse before her eyne,
　　Which griev'd her more, that she it could not mend:
To see an helpelesse evill, double griefe doth lend.

22

Nought could she read the roote of his disease,
  Ne weene what mister maladie it is,
  Whereby to seeke some meanes it to appease.
  Most did she thinke, but most she thought amis,
  That that same former fatall wound of his
  Whyleare by *Tryphon* was not throughly healed,
  But closely rankled under th'orifis:
  Least did she thinke, that which he most concealed,
That love it was, which in his hart lay unrevealed.

23

Therefore to *Tryphon* she againe doth hast,
  And him doth chyde as false and fraudulent,
  That fayld the trust, which she in him had plast,
  To cure her sonne, as he his faith had lent:
  Who now was falne into new languishment
  Of his old hurt, which was not throughly cured.
  So backe he came unto her patient,
  Where searching every part, her well assured,
That it was no old sore, which his new paine procured.

24

But that it was some other maladie,
  Or griefe unknowne, which he could not discerne:
  So left he her withouten remedie.
  Then gan her heart to faint, and quake, and earne,
  And inly troubled was, the truth to learne.
  Unto himselfe she came, and him besought,
  Now with faire speches, now with threatnings sterne,
  If ought lay hidden in his grieved thought,
It to reveale: who still her answered, there was nought.

25

Nathlesse she rested not so satisfide,
  But leaving watry gods, as booting nought,
  Unto the shinie heaven in haste she hide,
  And thence *Apollo* King of Leaches brought.
  Apollo came; who soone as he had sought
  Through his disease, did by and by out find,
  That he did languish of some inward thought,
  The which afflicted his engrieved mind;
Which love he red to be, that leads each living kind.

26

Which when he had unto his mother told,
  She gan thereat to fret, and greatly grieve.
  And comming to her sonne, gan first to scold,
  And chyde at him, that made her misbelieve:
  But afterwards she gan him soft to shrieve,
  And wooe with faire intreatie, to disclose,
  Which of the Nymphes his heart so sore did mieve.
  For sure she weend it was some one of those,
Which he had lately seene, that for his love he chose.

27

Now lesse she feared that same fatall read,
  That warned him of womens love beware:
  Which being ment of mortall creatures sead,
  For love of Nymphes she thought she need not care,
  But promist him, what ever wight she weare,
  That she her love to him would shortly gaine:
  So he her told: but soone as she did heare
  That *Florimell* it was, which wrought his paine,
She gan a fresh to chafe, and grieve in every vaine.

28

Yet since she saw the streight extremitie,
  In which his life unluckily was layd,
  It was no time to scan the prophecie,
  Whether old *Proteus* true or false had sayd,
  That his decay should happen by a mayd.
  It's late in death of daunger to advize,
  Or love forbid him, that is life denayd:
  But rather gan in troubled mind devize,
How she that Ladies libertie might enterprize.

29

To *Proteus* selfe to sew she thought it vaine,
  Who was the root and worker of her woe:
  Nor unto any meaner to complaine,
  But unto great king *Neptune* selfe did goe,
  And on her knee before him falling lowe,
  Made humble suit unto his Majestie,
  To graunt to her, her sonnes life, which his foe
  A cruell Tyrant had presumpteouslie
By wicked doome condemn'd, a wretched death to die.

30

To whom God *Neptune* softly smyling, thus;
　　Daughter me seemes of double wrong ye plaine,
　　Gainst one that hath both wronged you, and us:
　　For death t'adward I ween'd did appertaine
　　To none, but to the seas sole Soveraine.
　　Read therefore who it is, which this hath wrought,
　　And for what cause; the truth discover plaine.
　　For never wight so evill did or thought,
But would some rightfull cause pretend, though rightly nought.

31

To whom she answerd, Then it is by name
　　Proteus, that hath ordayn'd my sonne to die;
　　For that a waift, the which by fortune came
　　Upon your seas, he claym'd as propertie:
　　And yet nor his, nor his in equitie,
　　But yours the waift by high prerogative.
　　Therefore I humbly crave your Majestie,
　　It to replevie, and my sonne reprive:
So shall you by one gift save all us three alive.

32

He graunted it: and streight his warrant made,
　　Under the Sea-gods seale autenticall,
　　Commaunding *Proteus* straight t'enlarge the mayd,
　　Which wandring on his seas imperiall,
　　He lately tooke, and sithence kept as thrall.
　　Which she receiving with meete thankefulnesse,
　　Departed straight to *Proteus* therewithall:
　　Who reading it with inward loathfulnesse,
Was grieved to restore the pledge, he did possesse.

33

Yet durst he not the warrant to withstand,
　　But unto her delivered *Florimell*.
　　Whom she receiving by the lilly hand,
　　Admyr'd her beautie much, as she mote well:
　　For she all living creatures did excell;
　　And was right joyous, that she gotten had
　　So faire a wife for her sonne *Marinell*.
　　So home with her she streight the virgin lad,
And shewed her to him, then being sore bestad.

34

Who soone as he beheld that angels face,
  Adorn'd with all divine perfection,
  His cheared heart eftsoones away gan chace
Sad death, revived with her sweet inspection,
And feeble spirit inly felt refection;
  As withered weed through cruell winters tine,
  That feeles the warmth of sunny beames reflection,
  Liftes up his head, that did before decline
And gins to spread his leafe before the faire sunshine.

35

Right so himselfe did *Marinell* upreare,
  When he in place his dearest love did spy;
  And though his limbs could not his bodie beare,
Ne former strength returne so suddenly,
Yet chearefull signes he shewed outwardly.
  Ne lesse was she in secret hart affected,
  But that she masked it with modestie,
  For feare she should of lightnesse be detected:
Which to another place I leave to be perfected.

THE FIFTH BOOKE OF THE
FAERIE QUEENE
CONTAYNING THE LEGEND OF ARTEGALL
OR OF JUSTICE

I

S O oft as I with state of present time,
The image of the antique world compare,
When as mans age was in his freshest prime,
And the first blossome of faire vertue bare,
Such oddes I find twixt those, and these which are,
As that, through long continuance of his course,
Me seemes the world is runne quite out of square,
From the first point of his appointed sourse,
And being once amisse growes daily wourse and wourse.

2

For from the golden age, that first was named,
It's now at earst become a stonie one;
And men themselves, the which at first were framed
Of earthly mould, and form'd of flesh and bone,
Are now transformed into hardest stone:
Such as behind their backs (so backward bred)
Were throwne by *Pyrrha* and *Deucalione*:
And if then those may any worse be red,
They into that ere long will be degendered.

3

Let none then blame me, if in discipline
    Of vertue and of civill uses lore,
I doe not forme them to the common line
    Of present dayes, which are corrupted sore,
    But to the antique use, which was of yore,
    When good was onely for it selfe desyred,
    And all men sought their owne, and none no more;
    When Justice was not for most meed outhyred,
But simple Truth did rayne, and was of all admyred.

4

For that which all men then did vertue call,
    Is now cald vice; and that which vice was hight,
Is now hight vertue, and so us'd of all:
    Right now is wrong, and wrong that was is right,
    As all things else in time are chaunged quight.
    Ne wonder; for the heavens revolution
    Is wandred farre from where it first was pight,
    And so doe make contrarie constitution
Of all this lower world, toward his dissolution.

5

For who so list into the heavens looke,
    And search the courses of the rowling spheares,
Shall find that from the point, where they first tooke
    Their setting forth, in these few thousand yeares
    They all are wandred much; that plaine appeares.
    For that same golden fleecy Ram, which bore
    Phrixus and *Helle* from their stepdames feares,
    Hath now forgot, where he was plast of yore,
And shouldred hath the Bull, which fayre *Europa* bore.

6

And eke the Bull hath with his bow-bent horne
    So hardly butted those two twinnes of *Jove*,
That they have crusht the Crab, and quite him borne
    Into the great *Nemæan* lions grove.
    So now all range, and doe at randon rove
    Out of their proper places farre away,
    And all this world with them amisse doe move,
    And all his creatures from their course astray,
Till they arrive at their last ruinous decay.

7

Ne is that same great glorious lampe of light,
  That doth enlumine all these lesser fyres,
  In better case, ne keepes his course more right,
  But is miscaried with the other Spheres.
  For since the terme of fourteene hundred yeres,
  That learned *Ptolomæe* his hight did take,
  He is declyned from that marke of theirs,
  Nigh thirtie minutes to the Southerne lake;
That makes me feare in time he will us quite forsake.

8

And if to those Ægyptian wisards old,
  Which in Star-read were wont have best insight,
  Faith may be given, it is by them told,
  That since the time they first tooke the Sunnes hight,
  Foure times his place he shifted hath in sight,
  And twice hath risen, where he now doth West,
  And wested twice, where he ought rise aright.
  But most is *Mars* amisse of all the rest,
And next to him old *Saturne*, that was wont be best.

9

For during *Saturnes* ancient raigne it's sayd,
  That all the world with goodnesse did abound:
  All loved vertue, no man was affrayd
  Of force, ne fraud in wight was to be found:
  No warre was knowne, no dreadfull trompets sound,
  Peace universall rayn'd mongst men and beasts,
  And all things freely grew out of the ground:
  Justice sate high ador'd with solemne feasts,
And to all people did divide her dred beheasts.

10

Most sacred vertue she of all the rest,
  Resembling God in his imperiall might;
  Whose soveraine powre is herein most exprest,
  That both to good and bad he dealeth right,
  And all his workes with Justice hath bedight.
  That powre he also doth to Princes lend,
  And makes them like himselfe in glorious sight,
  To sit in his owne seate, his cause to end,
And rule his people right, as he doth recommend.

11

Dread Soverayne Goddesse, that doest highest sit
　In seate of judgement, in th'Almighties stead,
　And with magnificke might and wondrous wit
Doest to thy people righteous doome aread,
That furthest Nations filles with awfull dread,
Pardon the boldnesse of thy basest thrall,
That dare discourse of so divine a read,
As thy great justice praysed over all:
The instrument whereof loe here thy *Artegall*.

CANT. I

Artegall trayn'd in Justice lore
Irenaes quest pursewed,
He doeth avenge on Sanglier
　his Ladies bloud embrewed.

1

THOUGH vertue then were held in highest price,
　In those old times, of which I doe intreat,
　Yet then likewise the wicked seede of vice
Began to spring which shortly grew full great,
And with their boughes the gentle plants did beat.
But evermore some of the vertuous race
Rose up, inspired with heroicke heat,
That cropt the branches of the sient base,
And with strong hand their fruitfull rancknes did deface.

2

Such first was *Bacchus*, that with furious might
　All th'East before untam'd did overronne,
　And wrong repressed, and establisht right,
Which lawlesse men had formerly fordonne.
There Justice first her princely rule begonne.
Next *Hercules* his like ensample shewed,
Who all the West with equall conquest wonne,
And monstrous tyrants with his club subdewed;
The club of Justice dread, with kingly powre endewed.

Artegall and Talus

3

And such was he, of whom I have to tell,
The Champion of true Justice *Artegall*,
Whom (as ye lately mote remember well)
An hard adventure, which did then befall,
Into redoubted perill forth did call;
That was to succour a distressed Dame,
Whom a strong tyrant did unjustly thrall,
And from the heritage, which she did clame,
Did with strong hand withhold: *Grantorto* was his name.

4

Wherefore the Lady, which *Irena* hight,
Did to the Faery Queene her way addresse,
To whom complayning her afflicted plight,
She her besought of gratious redresse.
That soveraine Queene, that mightie Emperesse,
Whose glorie is to aide all suppliants pore,
And of weake Princes to be Patronesse,
Chose *Artegall* to right her to restore;
For that to her he seem'd best skild in righteous lore.

5

For *Artegall* in justice was upbrought
Even from the cradle of his infancie,
And all the depth of rightfull doome was taught
By faire *Astræa*, with great industrie,
Whilest here on earth she lived mortallie.
For till the world from his perfection fell
Into all filth and foule iniquitie,
Astræa here mongst earthly men did dwell,
And in the rules of justice them instructed well.

6

Whiles through the world she walked in this sort,
Upon a day she found this gentle childe,
Amongst his peres playing his childish sport:
Whom seeing fit, and with no crime defilde,
She did allure with gifts and speaches milde,
To wend with her. So thence him farre she brought
Into a cave from companie exilde,
In which she noursled him, till yeares he raught,
And all the discipline of justice there him taught.

7

There she him taught to weigh both right and wrong
  In equall ballance with due recompence,
  And equitie to measure out along,
  According to the line of conscience,
  When so it needs with rigour to dispence.
  Of all the which, for want there of mankind,
  She caused him to make experience
  Upon wyld beasts, which she in woods did find,
With wrongfull powre oppressing others of their kind.

8

Thus she him trayned, and thus she him taught
  In all the skill of deeming wrong and right,
  Untill the ripenesse of mans yeares he raught;
  That even wilde beasts did feare his awfull sight,
  And men admyr'd his overruling might;
  Ne any liv'd on ground, that durst withstand
  His dreadfull heast, much lesse him match in fight,
  Or bide the horror of his wreakfull hand,
When so he list in wrath lift up his steely brand.

9

Which steely brand, to make him dreaded more,
  She gave unto him, gotten by her slight
  And earnest search, where it was kept in store
  In *Joves* eternall house, unwist of wight,
  Since he himselfe it us'd in that great fight
  Against the *Titans*, that whylome rebelled
  Gainst highest heaven; *Chrysaor* it was hight;
  Chrysaor that all other swords excelled,
Well prov'd in that same day, when *Jove* those Gyants quelled.

10

For of most perfect metall it was made,
  Tempred with Adamant amongst the same,
  And garnisht all with gold upon the blade
  In goodly wise, whereof it tooke his name,
  And was of no lesse vertue, than of fame.
  For there no substance was so firme and hard,
  But it would pierce or cleave, where so it came;
  Ne any armour could his dint out ward,
But wheresoever it did light, it throughly shard.

11

Now when the world with sinne gan to abound,
  Astræa loathing lenger here to space
  Mongst wicked men, in whom no truth she found,
  Return'd to heaven, whence she deriv'd her race;
  Where she hath now an everlasting place,
  Mongst those twelve signes, which nightly we doe see
  The heavens bright-shining baudricke to enchace;
  And is the *Virgin*, sixt in her degree,
And next her selfe her righteous ballance hanging bee.

12

But when she parted hence, she left her groome
  An yron man, which did on her attend
  Alwayes, to execute her stedfast doome,
  And willed him with *Artegall* to wend,
  And doe what ever thing he did intend.
  His name was *Talus*, made of yron mould,
  Immoveable, resistlesse, without end.
  Who in his hand an yron flale did hould,
With which he thresht out falshood, and did truth unfould.

13

He now went with him in this new inquest,
  Him for to aide, if aide he chaunst to neede,
  Against that cruell Tyrant, which opprest
  The faire *Irena* with his foule misdeede,
  And kept the crowne in which she should succeed.
  And now together on their way they bin,
  When as they saw a Squire in squallid weed,
  Lamenting sore his sorowfull sad tyne,
With many bitter teares shed from his blubbred eyne.

14

To whom as they approched, they espide
  A sorie sight, as ever seene with eye;
  An headlesse Ladie lying him beside,
  In her owne blood all wallow'd wofully,
  That her gay clothes did in discolour die.
  Much was he moved at that ruefull sight;
  And flam'd with zeale of vengeance inwardly,
  He askt, who had that Dame so fouly dight;
Or whether his owne hand, or whether other wight?

15

Ah woe is me, and well away (quoth hee)
  Bursting forth teares, like springs out of a banke,
  That ever I this dismall day did see:
  Full farre was I from thinking such a pranke;
  Yet litle losse it were, and mickle thanke,
  If I should graunt that I have doen the same,
  That I mote drinke the cup, whereof she dranke:
  But that I should die guiltie of the blame,
The which another did, who now is fled with shame.

16

Who was it then (sayd *Artegall*) that wrought?
  And why? doe it declare unto me trew.
  A knight (said he) if knight he may be thought,
  That did his hand in Ladies bloud embrew,
  And for no cause, but as I shall you shew.
  This day as I in solace sate hereby
  With a fayre love, whose losse I now do rew,
  There came this knight, having in companie
This lucklesse Ladie, which now here doth headlesse lie.

17

He, whether mine seem'd fayrer in his eye,
  Or that he wexed weary of his owne,
  Would change with me; but I did it denye;
  So did the Ladies both, as may be knowne,
  But he, whose spirit was with pride upblowne,
  Would not so rest contented with his right,
  But having from his courser her downe throwne,
  Fro me reft mine away by lawlesse might,
And on his steed her set, to beare her out of sight.

18

Which when his Ladie saw, she follow'd fast,
  And on him catching hold, gan loud to crie
  Not so to leave her, nor away to cast,
  But rather of his hand besought to die.
  With that his sword he drew all wrathfully,
  And at one stroke cropt off her head with scorne,
  In that same place, whereas it now doth lie.
  So he my love away with him hath borne,
And left me here, both his and mine own love to morne.

19

Aread (sayd he) which way then did he make?
  And by what markes may he be knowne againe?
  To hope (quoth he) him soone to overtake,
  That hence so long departed, is but vaine:
  But yet he pricked over yonder plaine,
  And as I marked, bore upon his shield,
  By which it's easie him to know againe,
  A broken sword within a bloodie field;
Expressing well his nature, which the same did wield.

20

No sooner sayd, but streight he after sent
  His yron page, who him pursew'd so light,
  As that it seem'd above the ground he went:
  For he was swift as swallow in her flight,
  And strong as Lyon in his Lordly might.
  It was not long, before he overtooke
  Sir *Sanglier*; (so cleeped was that Knight)
  Whom at the first he ghessed by his looke,
And by the other markes, which of his shield he tooke.

21

He bad him stay, and backe with him retire;
  Who full of scorne to be commaunded so,
  The Lady to alight did eft require,
  Whilest he reformed that uncivill fo:
  And streight at him with all his force did go.
  Who mov'd no more therewith, than when a rocke
  Is lightly stricken with some stones throw;
  But to him leaping, lent him such a knocke,
That on the ground he layd him like a sencelesse blocke.

22

But ere he could him selfe recure againe,
  Him in his iron paw he seized had;
  That when he wak't out of his warelesse paine,
  He found him selfe, unwist, so ill bestad,
  That lim he could not wag. Thence he him lad,
  Bound like a beast appointed to the stall:
  The sight whereof the Lady sore adrad,
  And fain'd to fly for feare of being thrall;
But he her quickly stayd, and forst to wend withall.

23

When to the place they came, where *Artegall*
  By that same carefull Squire did then abide,
  He gently gan him to demaund of all,
  That did betwixt him and that Squire betide.
  Who with sterne countenance and indignant pride
  Did aunswere, that of all he guiltlesse stood,
  And his accuser thereuppon defide:
  For neither he did shed that Ladies bloud,
Nor tooke away his love, but his owne proper good.

24

Well did the Squire perceive him selfe too weake,
  To aunswere his defiaunce in the field,
  And rather chose his challenge off to breake,
  Than to approve his right with speare and shield.
  And rather guilty chose him selfe to yield.
  But *Artegall* by signes perceiving plaine,
  That he it was not, which that Lady kild,
  But that strange Knight, the fairer love to gaine,
Did cast about by sleight the truth thereout to straine.

25

And sayd, Now sure this doubtfull causes right
  Can hardly but by Sacrament be tride,
  Or else by ordele, or by blooddy fight;
  That ill perhaps mote fall to either side.
  But if ye please, that I your cause decide,
  Perhaps I may all further quarrell end,
  So ye will sweare my judgement to abide.
  Thereto they both did franckly condiscend,
And to his doome with listfull eares did both attend.

26

Sith then (sayd he) ye both the dead deny,
  And both the living Lady claime your right,
  Let both the dead and living equally
  Devided be betwixt you here in sight,
  And each of either take his share aright.
  But looke who does dissent from this my read,
  He for a twelve moneths day shall in despight
  Beare for his penaunce that same Ladies head;
To witnesse to the world, that she by him is dead.

27

Well pleased with that doome was *Sangliere*,
  And offred streight the Lady to be slaine.
  But that same Squire, to whom she was more dere,
  When as he saw she should be cut in twaine,
  Did yield, she rather should with him remaine
  Alive, than to him selfe be shared dead;
  And rather than his love should suffer paine,
  He chose with shame to beare that Ladies head.
True love despiseth shame, when life is cald in dread.

28

Whom when so willing *Artegall* perceaved;
  Not so thou Squire, (he sayd) but thine I deeme
  The living Lady, which from thee he reaved:
  For worthy thou of her doest rightly seeme.
  And you, Sir Knight, that love so light esteeme,
  As that ye would for little leave the same,
  Take here your owne, that doth you best beseeme,
  And with it beare the burden of defame;
Your owne dead Ladies head, to tell abrode your shame.

29

But *Sangliere* disdained much his doome,
  And sternly gan repine at his beheast;
  Ne would for ought obay, as did become,
  To beare that Ladies head before his breast.
  Untill that *Talus* had his pride represt,
  And forced him, maulgre, it up to reare.
  Who when he saw it bootelesse to resist,
  He tooke it up, and thence with him did beare,
As rated Spaniell takes his burden up for feare.

30

Much did that Squire Sir *Artegall* adore,
  For his great justice, held in high regard;
  And as his Squire him offred evermore
  To serve, for want of other meete reward,
  And wend with him on his adventure hard.
  But he thereto would by no meanes consent;
  But leaving him forth on his journey far'd:
  Ne wight with him but onely *Talus* went.
They two enough t'encounter an whole Regiment.

CANT. II

Artegall heares of Florimell,
Does with the Pagan fight:
Him slaies, drownes Lady Munera,
Does race her castle quight.

I

NOUGHT is more honorable to a knight,
  Ne better doth beseeme brave chevalry,
  Than to defend the feeble in their right,
  And wrong redresse in such as wend awry.
  Whilome those great Heroes got thereby
  Their greatest glory, for their rightfull deedes,
  And place deserved with the Gods on hy.
  Herein the noblesse of this knight exceedes,
Who now to perils great for justice sake proceedes.

2

To which as he now was uppon the way,
  He chaunst to meet a Dwarfe in hasty course;
  Whom he requir'd his forward hast to stay,
  Till he of tidings mote with him discourse.
  Loth was the Dwarfe, yet did he stay perforse,
  And gan of sundry newes his store to tell,
  As to his memory they had recourse:
  But chiefely of the fairest *Florimell*,
How she was found againe, and spousde to *Marinell*.

3

For this was *Dony*, *Florimels* owne Dwarfe,
  Whom having lost (as ye have heard whyleare)
  And finding in the way the scattred scarfe,
  The fortune of her life long time did feare.
  But of her health when *Artegall* did heare,
  And safe returne, he was full inly glad,
  And askt him where, and when her bridale cheare
  Should be solemniz'd: for if time he had,
He would be there, and honor to her spousall ad.

4

Within three daies (quoth hee) as I do here,
  It will be at the Castle of the strond;
  What time if naught me let, I will be there
  To doe her service, so as I am bond.
  But in my way a little here beyond
  A cursed cruell Sarazin doth wonne,
  That keepes a Bridges passage by strong hond,
  And many errant Knights hath there fordonne;
That makes all men for feare that passage for to shonne.

5

What mister wight (quoth he) and how far hence
  Is he, that doth to travellers such harmes?
  He is (said he) a man of great defence;
  Expert in battell and in deedes of armes;
  And more emboldned by the wicked charmes,
  With which his daughter doth him still support;
  Having great Lordships got and goodly farmes,
  Through strong oppression of his powre extort;
By which he stil them holds, and keepes with strong effort.

6

And dayly he his wrongs encreaseth more,
  For never wight he lets to passe that way,
  Over his Bridge, albee he rich or poore,
  But he him makes his passage-penny pay:
  Else he doth hold him backe or beat away.
  Thereto he hath a groome of evill guize,
  Whose scalp is bare, that bondage doth bewray,
  Which pols and pils the poore in piteous wize;
But he him selfe uppon the rich doth tyrannize.

7

His name is hight *Pollente*, rightly so
  For that he is so puissant and strong,
  That with his powre he all doth overgo,
  And makes them subject to his mighty wrong;
  And some by sleight he eke doth underfong.
  For on a Bridge he custometh to fight,
  Which is but narrow, but exceeding long;
  And in the same are many trap fals pight,
Through which the rider downe doth fall through oversight.

8

And underneath the same a river flowes,
  That is both swift and dangerous deepe withall;
  Into the which whom so he overthrowes,
  All destitute of helpe doth headlong fall,
  But he him selfe, through practise usuall,
  Leapes forth into the floud, and there assaies
  His foe confused through his sodaine fall,
  That horse and man he equally dismaies,
And either both them drownes, or trayterously slaies.

9

Then doth he take the spoile of them at will,
  And to his daughter brings, that dwels thereby:
  Who all that comes doth take, and therewith fill
  The coffers of her wicked threasury;
  Which she with wrongs hath heaped up so hy,
  That many Princes she in wealth exceedes,
  And purchast all the countrey lying ny
  With the revenue of her plenteous meedes,
Her name is *Munera*, agreeing with her deedes.

10

Thereto she is full faire, and rich attired,
  With golden hands and silver feete beside,
  That many Lords have her to wife desired:
  But she them all despiseth for great pride.
  Now by my life (sayd he) and God to guide,
  None other way will I this day betake,
  But by that Bridge, whereas he doth abide:
  Therefore me thither lead. No more he spake,
But thitherward forthright his ready way did make.

11

Unto the place he came within a while,
  Where on the Bridge he ready armed saw
  The Sarazin, awayting for some spoile.
  Who as they to the passage gan to draw,
  A villaine to them came with scull all raw,
  That passage money did of them require,
  According to the custome of their law.
  To whom he aunswerd wroth, Loe there thy hire;
And with that word him strooke, that streight he did expire.

12

Which when the Pagan saw, he wexed wroth,
　And streight him selfe unto the fight addrest,
　Ne was Sir *Artegall* behinde: so both
　Together ran with ready speares in rest.
　Right in the midst, whereas they brest to brest
　Should meete, a trap was letten downe to fall
　Into the floud: streight leapt the Carle unblest,
　Well weening that his foe was falne withall:
But he was well aware, and leapt before his fall.

13

There being both together in the floud,
　They each at other tyrannously flew;
　Ne ought the water cooled their whot bloud,
　But rather in them kindled choler new.
　But there the Paynim, who that use well knew
　To fight in water, great advantage had,
　That oftentimes him nigh he overthrew:
　And eke the courser, whereuppon he rad,
Could swim like to a fish, whiles he his backe bestrad.

14

Which oddes when as Sir *Artegall* espide,
　He saw no way, but close with him in hast;
　And to him driving strongly downe the tide,
　Uppon his iron coller griped fast,
　That with the straint his wesand nigh he brast.
　There they together strove and struggled long,
　Either the other from his steede to cast;
　Ne ever *Artegall* his griple strong
For any thing wold slacke, but still uppon him hong.

15

As when a Dolphin and a Sele are met,
　In the wide champian of the Ocean plaine:
　With cruell chaufe their courages they whet,
　The maysterdome of each by force to gaine,
　And dreadfull battaile twixt them do darraine:
　They snuf, they snort, they bounce, they rage, they rore,
　That all the sea disturbed with their traine,
　Doth frie with fome above the surges hore.
Such was betwixt these two the troublesome uprore.

16

So *Artegall* at length him forst forsake
His horses backe, for dread of being drownd,
And to his handy swimming him betake.
Eftsoones him selfe he from his hold unbownd,
And then no ods at all in him he fownd:
For *Artegall* in swimming skilfull was,
And durst the depth of any water sownd.
So ought each Knight, that use of perill has,
In swimming be expert through waters force to pas.

17

Then very doubtfull was the warres event,
Uncertaine whether had the better side:
For both were skild in that experiment,
And both in armes well traind and throughly tride.
But *Artegall* was better breath'd beside,
And towards th'end, grew greater in his might,
That his faint foe no longer could abide
His puissance, ne beare him selfe upright,
But from the water to the land betooke his flight.

18

But *Artegall* pursewd him still so neare,
With bright Chrysaor in his cruell hand,
That as his head he gan a litle reare
Above the brincke, to tread upon the land,
He smote it off, that tumbling on the strand
It bit the earth for very fell despight,
And gnashed with his teeth, as if he band
High God, whose goodnesse he despaired quight,
Or curst the hand, which did that vengeance on him dight.

19

His corps was carried downe along the Lee,
Whose waters with his filthy bloud it stayned:
But his blasphemous head, that all might see,
He pitcht upon a pole on high ordayned;
Where many years it afterwards remayned,
To be a mirrour to all mighty men,
In whose right hands great power is contayned,
That none of them the feeble overren,
But alwaies doe their powre within just compasse pen.

20

That done, unto the Castle he did wend,
 In which the Paynims daughter did abide,
 Guarded of many which did her defend:
 Of whom he entrance sought, but was denide,
 And with reprochfull blasphemy defide,
 Beaten with stones downe from the battilment,
 That he was forced to withdraw aside;
 And bad his servant *Talus* to invent
Which way he enter might, without endangerment.

21

Eftsoones his Page drew to the Castle gate,
 And with his iron flale at it let flie,
 That all the warders it did sore amate,
 The which erewhile spake so reprochfully,
 And made them stoupe, that looked earst so hie.
 Yet still he bet, and bounst uppon the dore,
 And thundred strokes thereon so hideouslie,
 That all the peece he shaked from the flore,
And filled all the house with feare and great uprore.

22

With noise whereof the Lady forth appeared
 Uppon the Castle wall, and when she saw
 The daungerous state, in which she stood, she feared
 The sad effect of her neare overthrow;
 And gan entreat that iron man below,
 To cease his outrage, and him faire besought,
 Sith neither force of stones which they did throw,
 Nor powr of charms, which she against him wrought,
Might otherwise prevaile, or make him cease for ought.

23

But when as yet she saw him to proceede,
 Unmov'd with praiers, or with piteous thought,
 She ment him to corrupt with goodly meede;
 And causde great sackes with endlesse riches fraught,
 Unto the battilment to be upbrought,
 And powred forth over the Castle wall,
 That she might win some time, though dearly bought
Whilest he to gathering of the gold did fall.
But he was nothing mov'd, nor tempted therewithall.

24

But still continu'd his assault the more,
And layd on load with his huge yron flaile,
That at the length he has yrent the dore,
And made way for his maister to assaile.
Who being entred, nought did then availe
For wight, against his powre them selves to reare:
Each one did flie; their hearts began to faile,
And hid them selves in corners here and there;
And eke their dame halfe dead did hide her self for feare.

25

Long they her sought, yet no where could they finde her,
That sure they ween'd she was escapt away:
But *Talus*, that could like a limehound winde her,
And all things secrete wisely could bewray,
At length found out, whereas she hidden lay
Under an heape of gold. Thence he her drew
By the faire lockes, and fowly did array,
Withouten pitty of her goodly hew,
That *Artegall* him selfe her seemelesse plight did rew.

26

Yet for no pitty would he change the course
Of Justice, which in *Talus* hand did lye;
Who rudely hayld her forth without remorse,
Still holding up her suppliant hands on hye,
And kneeling at his feete submissively.
But he her suppliant hands, those hands of gold,
And eke her feete, those feete of silver trye,
Which sought unrighteousnesse, and justice sold,
Chopt off, and nayld on high, that all might them behold.

27

Her selfe then tooke he by the sclender wast,
In vaine loud crying, and into the flood
Over the Castle wall adowne her cast,
And there her drowned in the durty mud:
But the streame washt away her guilty blood.
Thereafter all that mucky pelfe he tooke,
The spoile of peoples evill gotten good,
The which her sire had scrap't by hooke and crooke,
And burning all to ashes, powr'd it downe the brooke.

28

And lastly all that Castle quite he raced,
　Even from the sole of his foundation,
　And all the hewen stones thereof defaced,
　That there mote be no hope of reparation,
　Nor memory thereof to any nation.
　All which when *Talus* throughly had perfourmed,
　Sir *Artegall* undid the evill fashion,
　And wicked customes of that Bridge refourmed.
Which done, unto his former journey he retourned.

29

In which they measur'd mickle weary way,
　Till that at length nigh to the sea they drew;
　By which as they did travell on a day,
　They saw before them, far as they could vew,
　Full many people gathered in a crew;
　Whose great assembly they did much admire.
　For never there the like resort they knew.
　So towardes them they coasted, to enquire
What thing so many nations met, did there desire.

30

There they beheld a mighty Gyant stand
　Upon a rocke, and holding forth on hie
　An huge great paire of ballance in his hand,
　With which he boasted in his surquedrie,
　That all the world he would weigh equallie,
　If ought he had the same to counterpoys.
　For want whereof he weighed vanity,
　And fild his ballaunce full of idle toys:
Yet was admired much of fooles, women, and boys.

31

He sayd that he would all the earth uptake,
　And all the sea, devided each from either:
　So would he of the fire one ballaunce make,
　And one of th'ayre, without or wind, or wether:
　Then would he ballaunce heaven and hell together,
　And all that did within them all containe;
　Of all whose weight, he would not misse a fether.
　And looke what surplus did of each remaine,
He would to his owne part restore the same againe.

32

For why, he sayd they all unequall were,
    And had encroched uppon others share,
    Like as the sea (which plaine he shewed there)
    Had worne the earth, so did the fire the aire,
    So all the rest did others parts empaire.
    And so were realmes and nations run awry.
    All which he undertooke for to repaire,
    In sort as they were formed aunciently;
And all things would reduce unto equality.

33

Therefore the vulgar did about him flocke,
    And cluster thicke unto his leasings vaine,
    Like foolish flies about an hony crocke,
    In hope by him great benefite to gaine,
    And uncontrolled freedome to obtaine.
    All which when *Artegall* did see, and heare,
    How he mis-led the simple peoples traine,
    In sdeignfull wize he drew unto him neare,
And thus unto him spake, without regard or feare.

34

Thou that presum'st to weigh the world anew,
    And all things to an equall to restore,
    In stead of right me seemes great wrong dost shew,
    And far above thy forces pitch to sore.
    For ere thou limit what is lesse or more
    In every thing, thou oughtest first to know,
    What was the poyse of every part of yore:
    And looke then how much it doth overflow,
Or faile thereof, so much is more than just to trow.

35

For at the first they all created were
    In goodly measure, by their Makers might,
    And weighed out in ballaunces so nere,
    That not a dram was missing of their right,
    The earth was in the middle centre pight,
    In which it doth immoveable abide,
    Hemd in with waters like a wall in sight;
    And they with aire, that not a drop can slide:
Al which the heavens containe, and in their courses guide.

36

Such heavenly justice doth among them raine,
  That every one doe know their certaine bound,
  In which they doe these many yeares remaine,
  And mongst them al no change hath yet beene found.
  But if thou now shouldst weigh them new in pound,
  We are not sure they would so long remaine:
  All change is perillous, and all chaunce unsound.
  Therefore leave off to weigh them all againe,
Till we may be assur'd they shall their course retaine.

37

Thou foolishe Elfe (said then the Gyant wroth)
  Seest not, how badly all things present bee,
  And each estate quite out of order goth?
  The sea it selfe doest thou not plainely see
  Encroch uppon the land there under thee;
  And th'earth it selfe how daily its increast,
  By all that dying to it turned be?
  Were it not good that wrong were then surceast,
And from the most, that some were given to the least?

38

Therefore I will throw downe these mountaines hie,
  And make them levell with the lowly plaine:
  These towring rocks, which reach unto the skie,
  I will thrust downe into the deepest maine,
  And as they were, them equalize againe.
  Tyrants that make men subject to their law,
  I will suppresse, that they no more may raine;
  And Lordings curbe, that commons over-aw;
And all the wealth of rich men to the poore will draw.

39

Of things unseene how canst thou deeme aright,
  Then answered the righteous *Artegall*,
  Sith thou misdeem'st so much of things in sight?
  What though the sea with waves continuall
  Doe eate the earth, it is no more at all:
  Ne is the earth the lesse, or loseth ought,
  For whatsoever from one place doth fall,
  Is with the tide unto an other brought:
For there is nothing lost, that may be found, **if sought**

40

Likewise the earth is not augmented more,
  By all that dying into it doe fade.
  For of the earth they formed were of yore,
  How ever gay their blossome or their blade
  Doe flourish now, they into dust shall vade.
  What wrong then is it, if that when they die,
  They turne to that, whereof they first were made?
  All in the powre of their great Maker lie:
All creatures must obey the voice of the most hie.

41

They live, they die, like as he doth ordaine,
  Ne ever any asketh reason why.
  The hils doe not the lowly dales disdaine;
  The dales doe not the lofty hills envy.
  He maketh Kings to sit in soverainty;
  He maketh subjects to their powre obay;
  He pulleth downe, he setteth up on hy;
  He gives to this, from that he takes away.
For all we have is his: what he list doe, he may.

42

What ever thing is done, by him is donne,
  Ne any may his mighty will withstand;
  Ne any may his soveraine power shonne,
  Ne loose that he hath bound with stedfast band.
  In vaine therefore doest thou now take in hand,
  To call to count, or weigh his workes anew,
  Whose counsels depth thou canst not understand,
  Sith of things subject to thy daily vew
Thou doest not know the causes, nor their courses dew.

43

For take thy ballaunce, if thou be so wise,
  And weigh the winde, that under heaven doth blow;
  Or weigh the light, that in the East doth rise;
  Or weigh the thought, that from mans mind doth flow.
  But if the weight of these thou canst not show,
  Weigh but one word which from thy lips doth fall.
  For how canst thou those greater secrets know,
  That doest not know the least thing of them all?
Ill can he rule the great, that cannot reach the small.

44

Therewith the Gyant much abashed sayd;
  That he of little things made reckoning light,
  Yet the least word that ever could be layd
  Within his ballaunce, he could way aright.
  Which is (sayd he) more heavy then in weight,
  The right or wrong, the false or else the trew?
  He answered, that he would try it streight,
  So he the words into his ballaunce threw,
But streight the winged words out of his ballaunce flew.

45

Wroth wext he then, and sayd, that words were light,
  Ne would within his ballaunce well abide.
  But he could justly weigh the wrong or right.
  Well then, sayd *Artegall*, let it be tride.
  First in one ballance set the true aside.
  He did so first; and then the false he layd
  In th'other scale; but still it downe did slide,
  And by no meane could in the weight be stayd.
For by no meanes the false will with the truth be wayd.

46

Now take the right likewise, sayd *Artegale*,
  And counterpeise the same with so much wrong.
  So first the right he put into one scale;
  And then the Gyant strove with puissance strong
  To fill the other scale with so much wrong.
  But all the wrongs that he therein could lay,
  Might not it peise; yet did he labour long,
  And swat, and chauf'd, and proved every way:
Yet all the wrongs could not a little right downe way.

47

Which when he saw, he greatly grew in rage,
  And almost would his balances have broken:
  But *Artegall* him fairely gan asswage,
  And said; Be not upon thy balance wroken:
  For they doe nought but right or wrong betoken;
  But in the mind the doome of right must bee;
  And so likewise of words, the which be spoken,
  The eare must be the ballance, to decree
And judge, whether with truth or falshood they agree.

48

But set the truth and set the right aside,
　For they with wrong or falshood will not fare;
And put two wrongs together to be tride,
　Or else two falses, of each equall share;
　And then together doe them both compare.
For truth is one, and right is ever one:
　So did he, and then plaine it did appeare,
　Whether of them the greater were attone.
But right sate in the middest of the beame alone.

49

But he the right from thence did thrust away,
　For it was not the right, which he did seeke;
But rather strove extremities to way,
　Th'one to diminish, th'other for to eeke:
　For of the meane he greatly did misleeke.
Whom when so lewdly minded *Talus* found,
　Approching nigh unto him cheeke by cheeke,
　He shouldered him from off the higher ground,
And down the rock him throwing, in the sea him dround.

50

Like as a ship, whom cruell tempest drives
　Upon a rocke with horrible dismay,
Her shattered ribs in thousand peeces rives,
　And spoyling all her geares and goodly ray,
　Does make her selfe misfortunes piteous pray.
So downe the cliffe the wretched Gyant tumbled;
　His battred ballances in peeces lay,
　His timbered bones all broken rudely rumbled,
So was the high aspyring with huge ruine humbled.

51

That when the people, which had there about
　Long wayted, saw his sudden desolation,
They gan to gather in tumultuous rout,
　And mutining, to stirre up civill faction,
　For certaine losse of so great expectation.
For well they hoped to have got great good,
　And wondrous riches by his innovation.
　Therefore resolving to revenge his blood,
They rose in armes, and all in battell order stood.

52

Which lawlesse multitude him comming too
  In warlike wise, when *Artegall* did vew,
  He much was troubled, ne wist what to doo.
  For loth he was his noble hands t'embrew
  In the base blood of such a rascall crew;
  And otherwise, if that he should retire,
  He fear'd least they with shame would him pursew.
  Therefore he *Talus* to them sent, t'inquire
The cause of their array, and truce for to desire.

53

But soone as they him nigh approching spide,
  They gan with all their weapons him assay,
  And rudely stroke at him on every side:
  Yet nought they could him hurt, ne ought dismay.
  But when at them he with his flaile gan lay,
  He like a swarme of flyes them overthrew;
  Ne any of them durst come in his way,
  But here and there before his presence flew,
And hid themselves in holes and bushes from his vew.

54

As when a Faulcon hath with nimble flight
  Flowne at a flush of Ducks, foreby the brooke,
  The trembling foule dismayd with dreadfull sight
  Of death, the which them almost overtooke,
  Doe hide themselves from her astonying looke,
  Amongst the flags and covert round about.
  When *Talus* saw they all the field forsooke
  And none appear'd of all that raskall rout,
To *Artegall* he turn'd, and went with him throughout.

CANT. III

The spousals of faire Florimell,
where turney many knights:
There Braggadochio is uncas'd
in all the Ladies sights.

I

AFTER long stormes and tempests overblowne,
　The sunne at length his joyous face doth cleare:
　So when as fortune all her spight hath showne,
　Some blisfull houres at last must needes appeare;
　Else should afflicted wights oftimes despeire.
　So comes it now to *Florimell* by tourne,
　After long sorrowes suffered whyleare,
　In which captiv'd she many moneths did mourne,
To tast of joy, and to wont pleasures to retourne.

2

Who being freed from *Proteus* cruell band
　By *Marinell*, was unto him affide,
　And by him brought againe to Faerie land;
　Where he her spous'd, and made his joyous bride.
　The time and place was blazed farre and wide;
　And solemne feasts and giusts ordain'd therefore.
　To which there did resort from every side
　Of Lords and Ladies infinite great store;
Ne any Knight was absent, that brave courage bore.

3

To tell the glorie of the feast that day,
　The goodly service, the devicefull sights,
　The bridegromes state, the brides most rich aray,
　The pride of Ladies, and the worth of knights,
　The royall banquets, and the rare delights
　Were worke fit for an Herauld, not for me:
　But for so much as to my lot here lights,
　That with this present treatise doth agree,
True vertue to advance, shall here recounted bee.

4

When all men had with full satietie
  Of meates and drinkes their appetites suffiz'd,
  To deedes of armes and proofe of chevalrie
  They gan themselves addresse, full rich aguiz'd,
  As each one had his furnitures deviz'd.
  And first of all issu'd Sir *Marinell*,
  And with him sixe knights more, which enterpriz'd
  To chalenge all in right of *Florimell*,
And to maintaine, that she all others did excell.

5

The first of them was hight Sir *Orimont*,
  A noble Knight, and tride in hard assayes:
  The second had to name Sir *Bellisont*,
  But second unto none in prowesse prayse;
  The third was *Brunell*, famous in his dayes;
  The fourth *Ecastor*, of exceeding might;
  The fift *Armeddan*, skild in lovely layes;
  The sixt was *Lansack*, a redoubted Knight:
All sixe well seene in armes, and prov'd in many a fight.

6

And them against came all that list to giust,
  From every coast and countrie under sunne:
  None was debard, but all had leave that lust.
  The trompets sound; then all together ronne.
  Full many deedes of armes that day were donne,
  And many knights unhorst, and many wounded,
  As fortune fell; yet litle lost or wonne:
  But all that day the greatest prayse redounded
To *Marinell*, whose name the Heralds loud resounded.

7

The second day, so soone as morrow light
  Appear'd in heaven, into the field they came,
  And there all day continew'd cruell fight,
  With divers fortune fit for such a game,
  In which all strove with perill to winne fame.
  Yet whether side was victor, note be ghest:
  But at the last the trompets did proclame
  That *Marinell* that day deserved best.
So they disparted were, and all men went to rest.

8

The third day came, that should due tryall lend
  Of all the rest, and then this warlike crew
  Together met, of all to make an end.
  There *Marinell* great deeds of armes did shew;
  And through the thickest like a Lyon flew,
  Rashing off helmes, and ryving plates a sonder,
  That every one his daunger did eschew.
  So terribly his dreadfull strokes did thonder,
That all men stood amaz'd, and at his might did wonder.

9

But what on earth can alwayes happie stand?
  The greater prowesse greater perils find.
  So farre he past amongst his enemies band,
  That they have him enclosed so behind,
  As by no meanes he can himselfe outwind.
  And now perforce they have him prisoner taken;
  And now they doe with captive bands him bind;
  And now they lead him thence, of all forsaken,
Unlesse some succour had in time him overtaken.

10

It fortun'd whylest they were thus ill beset,
  Sir *Artegall* into the Tilt-yard came,
  With *Braggadochio*, whom he late met
  Upon the way, with that his snowy Dame.
  Where when he understood by common fame,
  What evill hap to *Marinell* betid,
  He much was mov'd at so unworthie shame,
  And streight that boaster prayd, with whom he rid,
To change his shield with him, to be the better hid.

11

So forth he went, and soone them over hent,
  Where they were leading *Marinell* away,
  Whom he assayld with dreadlesse hardiment,
  And forst the burden of their prize to stay.
  They were an hundred knights of that array;
  Of which th'one halfe upon himselfe did set,
  The other stayd behind to gard the pray.
  But he ere long the former fiftie bet;
And from the other fiftie soone the prisoner fet.

12

So backe he brought Sir *Marinell* againe;
  Whom having quickly arm'd againe anew,
  They both together joyned might and maine,
  To set afresh on all the other crew.
  Whom with sore havocke soone they overthrew,
  And chaced quite out of the field, that none
  Against them durst his head to perill shew.
  So were they left Lords of the field alone:
So *Marinell* by him was rescu'd from his fone.

13

Which when he had perform'd, then backe againe
  To *Braggadochio* did his shield restore:
  Who all this while behind him did remaine,
  Keeping there close with him in pretious store
  That his false Ladie, as ye heard afore.
  Then did the trompets sound, and Judges rose,
  And all these knights, which that day armour bore,
  Came to the open hall, to listen whose
The honour of the prize should be adjudg'd by those.

14

And thether also came in open sight
  Fayre *Florimell*, into the common hall,
  To greet his guerdon unto every knight,
  And best to him, to whom the best should fall.
  Then for that stranger knight they loud did call,
  To whom that day they should the girlond yield
  Who came not forth, but for Sir *Artegall*
  Came *Braggadochio*, and did shew his shield,
Which bore the Sunne brode blazed in a golden field.

15

The sight whereof did all with gladnesse fill:
  So unto him they did addeeme the prise
  Of all that Tryumph. Then the trompets shrill
  Don *Braggadochios* name resounded thrise:
  So courage lent a cloke to cowardise.
  And then to him came fayrest *Florimell*,
  And goodly gan to greet his brave emprise,
  And thousand thankes him yeeld, that had so well
Approv'd that day, that she all others did excell.

16

To whom the boaster, that all knights did blot,
　With proud disdaine did scornefull answere make;
　That what he did that day, he did it not
　For her, but for his owne deare Ladies sake,
　Whom on his perill he did undertake,
　Both her and eke all others to excell:
　And further did uncomely speaches crake.
　Much did his words the gentle Ladie quell,
And turn'd aside for shame to heare, what he did tell.

17

Then forth he brought his snowy *Florimele*,
　Whom *Trompart* had in keeping there beside,
　Covered from peoples gazement with a vele.
　Whom when discovered they had throughly eide,
　With great amazement they were stupefide;
　And said, that surely *Florimell* it was,
　Or if it were not *Florimell* so tride,
　That *Florimell* her selfe she then did pas.
So feeble skill of perfect things the vulgar has.

18

Which when as *Marinell* beheld likewise,
　He was therewith exceedingly dismayd;
　Ne wist he what to thinke, or to devise,
　But like as one, whom feends had made affrayd,
　He long astonisht stood, ne ought he sayd,
　Ne ought he did, but with fast fixed eies
　He gazed still upon that snowy mayd;
　Whom ever as he did the more avize,
The more to be true *Florimell* he did surmize.

19

As when two sunnes appeare in the azure skye,
　Mounted in *Phœbus* charet fierie bright,
　Both darting forth faire beames to each mans eye,
　And both adorn'd with lampes of flaming light,
　All that behold so strange prodigious sight,
　Not knowing natures worke, nor what to weene,
　Are rapt with wonder, and with rare affright.
　So stood Sir *Marinell*, when he had seene
The semblant of this false by his faire beauties Queene.

20

All which when *Artegall*, who all this while
   Stood in the preasse close covered, well advewed,
   And saw that boasters pride and gracelesse guile,
   He could no longer beare, but forth issewed,
   And unto all himselfe there open shewed,
   And to the boaster said; Thou losell base,
   That hast with borrowed plumes thy selfe endewed,
   And others worth with leasings doest deface,
When they are all restor'd, thou shalt rest in disgrace.

21

That shield, which thou doest beare, was it indeed,
   Which this dayes honour sav'd to *Marinell*;
   But not that arme, nor thou the man I reed,
   Which didst that service unto *Florimell*.
   For proofe shew forth thy sword, and let it tell,
   What strokes, what dreadfull stoure it stird this day:
   Or shew the wounds, which unto thee befell;
   Or shew the sweat, with which thou diddest sway
So sharpe a battell, that so many did dismay.

22

But this the sword, which wrought those cruell stounds,
   And this the arme, the which that shield did beare,
   And these the signes, (so shewed forth his wounds)
   By which that glorie gotten doth appeare.
   As for this Ladie, which he sheweth here,
   Is not (I wager) *Florimell* at all;
   But some fayre Franion, fit for such a fere,
   That by misfortune in his hand did fall.
For proofe whereof, he bad them *Florimell* forth call.

23

So forth the noble Ladie was ybrought,
   Adorn'd with honor and all comely grace:
   Whereto her bashfull shamefastnesse ywrought
   A great increase in her faire blushing face;
   As roses did with lillies interlace.
   For of those words, the which that boaster threw,
   She inly yet conceived great disgrace.
   Whom when as all the people such did vew,
They shouted loud, and signes of gladnesse all did shew.

24

Then did he set her by that snowy one
  Like the true saint beside the image set,
  Of both their beauties to make paragone,
  And triall, whether should the honor get.
  Streight way so soone as both together met,
  Th'enchaunted Damzell vanisht into nought:
  Her snowy substance melted as with heat,
  Ne of that goodly hew remayned ought,
But th'emptie girdle, which about her wast was wrought.

25

As when the daughter of *Thaumantes* faire,
  Hath in a watry cloud displayed wide
  Her goodly bow, which paints the liquid ayre;
  That all men wonder at her colours pride;
  All suddenly, ere one can looke aside,
  The glorious picture vanisheth away,
  Ne any token doth thereof abide:
  So did this Ladies goodly forme decay,
And into nothing goe, ere one could it bewray.

26

Which when as all that present were, beheld,
  They stricken were with great astonishment,
  And their faint harts with senselesse horrour queld,
  To see the thing, that seem'd so excellent,
  So stolen from their fancies wonderment;
  That what of it became, none understood.
  And *Braggadochio* selfe with dreriment
  So daunted was in his despeyring mood,
That like a lifelesse corse immoveable he stood.

27

But *Artegall* that golden belt uptooke,
  The which of all her spoyle was onely left;
  Which was not hers, as many it mistooke,
  But *Florimells* owne girdle, from her reft,
  While she was flying, like a weary weft,
  From that foule monster, which did her compell
  To perils great; which he unbuckling eft,
  Presented to the fayrest *Florimell*;
Who round about her tender wast it fitted well.

28

Full many Ladies often had assayd,
  About their middles that faire belt to knit;
  And many a one suppos'd to be a mayd:
  Yet it to none of all their loynes would fit,
  Till *Florimell* about her fastned it.
  Such power it had, that to no womans wast
  By any skill or labour it would sit,
  Unlesse that she were continent and chast,
But it would lose or breake, that many had disgrast.

29

Whilest thus they busied were bout *Florimell*,
  And boastfull *Braggadochio* to defame,
  Sir *Guyon* as by fortune then befell,
  Forth from the thickest preasse of people came,
  His owne good steed, which he had stolne, to clame;
  And th'one hand seizing on his golden bit,
  With th'other drew his sword: for with the same
  He ment the thiefe there deadly to have smit:
And had he not bene held, he nought had fayld of it.

30

Thereof great hurly burly moved was
  Throughout the hall, for that same warlike horse.
  For *Braggadochio* would not let him pas;
  And *Guyon* would him algates have perforse,
  Or it approve upon his carrion corse.
  Which troublous stirre when *Artegall* perceived,
  He nigh them drew to stay th'avengers forse,
  And gan inquire, how was that steed bereaved,
Whether by might extort, or else by slight deceaved.

31

Who all that piteous storie, which befell
  About that wofull couple, which were slaine,
  And their young bloodie babe to him gan tell;
  With whom whiles he did in the wood remaine,
  His horse purloyned was by subtill traine:
  For which he chalenged the thiefe to fight.
  But he for nought could him thereto constraine.
  For as the death he hated such despight,
And rather had to lose, than trie in armes his right.

32

Which *Artegall* well hearing, though no more
By law of armes there neede ones right to trie,
As was the wont of warlike knights of yore,
Than that his foe should him the field denie,
Yet further right by tokens to descrie,
He askt, what privie tokens he did beare.
If that (said *Guyon*) may you satisfie,
Within his mouth a blacke spot doth appeare,
Shapt like a horses shoe, who list to seeke it there.

33

Whereof to make due tryall, one did take
The horse in hand, within his mouth to looke:
But with his heeles so sorely he him strake,
That all his ribs he quite in peeces broke,
That never word from that day forth he spoke.
Another that would seeme to have more wit,
Him by the bright embrodered hedstall tooke:
But by the shoulder him so sore he bit,
That he him maymed quite, and all his shoulder split.

34

Ne he his mouth would open unto wight,
Untill that *Guyon* selfe unto him spake,
And called *Brigadore* (so was he hight)
Whose voice so soone as he did undertake,
Eftsoones he stood as still as any stake,
And suffred all his secret marke to see:
And when as he him nam'd, for joy he brake
His bands, and follow'd him with gladfull glee,
And friskt, and flong aloft, and louted low on knee.

35

Thereby Sir *Artegall* did plaine areed,
That unto him the horse belong'd, and sayd;
Lo there Sir *Guyon*, take to you the steed,
As he with golden saddle is arayd;
And let that losell, plainely now displayd,
Hence fare on foot, till he an horse have gayned.
But the proud boaster gan his doome upbrayd,
And him revil'd, and rated, and disdayned,
That judgement so unjust against him had ordayned.

36

Much was the knight incenst with his lewd word,
  To have revenged that his villeny;
  And thrise did lay his hand upon his sword,
  To have him slaine, or dearely doen aby.
  But *Guyon* did his choler pacify,
  Saying, Sir knight, it would dishonour bee
  To you, that are our judge of equity,
  To wreake your wrath on such a carle as hee:
It's punishment enough, that all his shame doe see.

37

So did he mitigate Sir *Artegall*,
  But *Talus* by the backe the boaster hent,
  And drawing him out of the open hall,
  Upon him did inflict this punishment.
  First he his beard did shave, and fowly shent:
  Then from him reft his shield, and it renverst,
  And blotted out his armes with falshood blent,
  And himselfe baffuld, and his armes unherst,
And broke his sword in twaine, and all his armour sperst.

38

The whiles his guilefull groome was fled away:
  But vaine it was to thinke from him to flie.
  Who overtaking him did disaray,
  And all his face deform'd with infamie,
  And out of court him scourged openly.
  So ought all faytours, that true knighthood shame,
  And armes dishonour with base villanie,
  From all brave knights be banisht with defame:
For oft their lewdnes blotteth good deserts with blame.

39

Now when these counterfeits were thus uncased
  Out of the foreside of their forgerie,
  And in the sight of all men cleane disgraced,
  All gan to jest and gibe full merilie
  At the remembrance of their knaverie.
  Ladies can laugh at Ladies, Knights at Knights,
  To thinke with how great vaunt of braverie
  He them abused, through his subtill slights,
And what a glorious shew he made in all their sights.

40

There leave we them in pleasure and repast,
　Spending their joyous dayes and gladfull nights,
　And taking usurie of time forepast,
　With all deare delices and rare delights,
　Fit for such Ladies and such lovely knights:
　And turne we here to this faire furrowes end
　Our wearie yokes, to gather fresher sprights,
　That when as time to *Artegall* shall tend,
We on his first adventure may him forward send.

CANT. IIII

Artegall dealeth right betwixt
two brethren that doe strive,
Saves Terpine from the gallow tree,
and doth from death reprive.

1

WHO so upon him selfe will take the skill
　True Justice unto people to divide,
　Had neede have mightie hands, for to fulfill
　That, which he doth with righteous doome decide,
　And for to maister wrong and puissant pride.
　For vaine it is to deeme of things aright,
　And makes wrong doers justice to deride,
　Unlesse it be perform'd with dreadlesse might.
For powre is the right hand of Justice truely hight.

2

Therefore whylome to knights of great emprise
　The charge of Justice given was in trust,
　That they might execute her judgements wise,
　And with their might beat downe licentious lust,
　Which proudly did impugne her sentence just.
　Whereof no braver president this day
　Remaines on earth, preserv'd from yron rust
　Of rude oblivion, and long times decay,
Than this of *Artegall*, which here we have to say.

3

Who having lately left that lovely payre,
  Enlincked fast in wedlockes loyall bond,
  Bold *Marinell* with *Florimell* the fayre,
  With whom great feast and goodly glee he fond,
  Departed from the Castle of the strond,
  To follow his adventures first intent,
  Which long agoe he taken had in hond:
  Ne wight with him for his assistance went,
But that great yron groome, his gard and government.

4

With whom as he did passe by the sea shore,
  He chaunst to come, whereas two comely Squires,
  Both brethren, whom one wombe together bore,
  But stirred up with different desires,
  Together strove, and kindled wrathfull fires:
  And them beside two seemely damzels stood,
  By all meanes seeking to asswage their ires,
  Now with faire words; but words did little good,
Now with sharpe threats; but threats the more increast their mood.

5

And there before them stood a Coffer strong,
  Fast bound on every side with iron bands,
  But seeming to have suffred mickle wrong,
  Either by being wreckt uppon the sands,
  Or being carried farre from forraine lands.
  Seem'd that for it these Squires at ods did fall,
  And bent against them selves their cruell hands.
  But evermore, those Damzels did forestall
Their furious encounter, and their fiercenesse pall.

6

But firmely fixt they were, with dint of sword,
  And battailes doubtfull proofe their rights to try,
  Ne other end their fury would afford,
  But what to them Fortune would justify.
  So stood they both in readinesse thereby,
  To joyne the combate with cruell intent;
  When *Artegall* arriving happily,
  Did stay a while their greedy bickerment,
Till he had questioned the cause of their dissent.

7

To whom the elder did this aunswere frame;
  Then weete ye Sir, that we two brethren be,
  To whom our sire, *Milesio* by name,
  Did equally bequeath his lands in fee,
  Two Ilands, which ye there before you see
  Not farre in sea; of which the one appeares
  But like a little Mount of small degree;
  Yet was as great and wide ere many yeares,
As that same other Isle, that greater bredth now beares.

8

But tract of time, that all things doth decay,
  And this devouring Sea, that naught doth spare,
  The most part of my land hath washt away,
  And throwne it up unto my brothers share:
  So his encreased, but mine did empaire.
  Before which time I lov'd, as was my lot,
  That further mayd, hight *Philtera* the faire,
  With whom a goodly doure I should have got,
And should have joyned bene to her in wedlocks knot.

9

Then did my younger brother *Amidas*
  Love that same other Damzell, *Lucy* bright,
  To whom but little dowre allotted was;
  Her vertue was the dowre, that did delight.
  What better dowre can to a dame be hight?
  But now when *Philtra* saw my lands decay,
  And former livelod fayle, she left me quight,
  And to my brother did ellope streight way:
Who taking her from me, his owne love left astray.

10

She seeing then her selfe forsaken so,
  Through dolorous despaire, which she conceyved,
  Into the Sea her selfe did headlong throw,
  Thinking to have her griefe by death bereaved.
  But see how much her purpose was deceaved.
  Whilest thus amidst the billowes beating of her
  Twixt life and death, long to and fro she weaved,
  She chaunst unwares to light uppon this coffer,
Which to her in that daunger hope of life did offer.

11

The wretched mayd that earst desir'd to die,
  When as the paine of death she tasted had,
  And but halfe seene his ugly visnomie,
  Gan to repent, that she had beene so mad,
  For any death to chaunge life though most bad:
  And catching hold of this Sea-beaten chest,
  The lucky Pylot of her passage sad,
  After long tossing in the seas distrest,
Her weary barke at last uppon mine Isle did rest.

12

Where I by chaunce then wandring on the shore,
  Did her espy, and through my good endevour
  From dreadfull mouth of death, which threatned sore
  Her to have swallow'd up, did helpe to save her.
  She then in recompence of that great favour,
  Which I on her bestowed, bestowed on me
  The portion of that good, which Fortune gave her,
  Together with her selfe in dowry free;
Both goodly portions, but of both the better she.

13

Yet in this coffer, which she with her brought,
  Great threasure sithence we did finde contained;
  Which as our owne we tooke, and so it thought.
  But this same other Damzell since hath fained,
  That to her selfe that threasure appertained;
  And that she did transport the same by sea,
  To bring it to her husband new ordained,
  But suffred cruell shipwracke by the way.
But whether it be so or no, I can not say.

14

But whether it indeede be so or no,
  This doe I say, that what so good or ill
  Or God or Fortune unto me did throw,
  Not wronging any other by my will,
  I hold mine owne, and so will hold it still.
  And though my land he first did winne away,
  And then my love (though now it little skill,)
  Yet my good lucke he shall not likewise pray;
But I will it defend, whilst ever that I may.

15

So having sayd, the younger did ensew;
  Full true it is, what so about our land
  My brother here declared hath to you:
  But not for it this ods twixt us doth stand,
  But for this threasure throwne uppon his strand;
  Which well I prove, as shall appeare by triall,
  To be this maides, with whom I fastned hand,
  Known by good markes, and perfect good espiall,
Therefore it ought be rendred her without deniall.

16

When they thus ended had, the Knight began;
  Certes your strife were easie to accord,
  Would ye remit it to some righteous man.
  Unto your selfe, said they, we give our word,
  To bide what judgement ye shall us afford.
  Then for assuraunce to my doome to stand,
  Under my foote let each lay downe his sword,
  And then you shall my sentence understand.
So each of them layd downe his sword out of his hand.

17

Then *Artegall* thus to the younger sayd;
  Now tell me *Amidas*, if that ye may,
  Your brothers land the which the sea hath layd
  Unto your part, and pluckt from his away,
  By what good right doe you withhold this day?
  What other right (quoth he) should you esteeme,
  But that the sea it to my share did lay?
  Your right is good (sayd he) and so I deeme,
That what the sea unto you sent, your own should seeme.

18

Then turning to the elder thus he sayd;
  Now *Bracidas* let this likewise be showne.
  Your brothers threasure, which from him is strayd,
  Being the dowry of his wife well knowne,
  By what right doe you claime to be your owne?
  What other right (quoth he) should you esteeme,
  But that the sea hath it unto me throwne?
  Your right is good (sayd he) and so I deeme,
That what the sea unto you sent, your own should seeme.

19

For equall right in equall things doth stand,
  For what the mighty Sea hath once possest,
  And plucked quite from all possessors hand,
  Whether by rage of waves, that never rest,
  Or else by wracke, that wretches hath distrest,
  He may dispose by his imperiall might,
  As thing at randon left, to whom he list.
So *Amidas*, the land was yours first hight,
And so the threasure yours is *Bracidas* by right.

20

When he his sentence thus pronounced had,
  Both *Amidas* and *Philtra* were displeased:
  But *Bracidas* and *Lucy* were right glad,
  And on the threasure by that judgement seased.
  So was their discord by this doome appeased,
  And each one had his right. Then *Artegall*
  When as their sharpe contention he had ceased,
  Departed on his way, as did befall,
To follow his old quest, the which him forth did call.

21

So as he travelled uppon the way,
  He chaunst to come, where happily he spide
  A rout of many people farre away;
  To whom his course he hastily applide,
  To weete the cause of their assemblaunce wide.
  To whom when he approched neare in sight,
  (An uncouth sight) he plainely then describe
  To be a troupe of women warlike dight,
With weapons in their hands, as ready for to fight.

22

And in the midst of them he saw a Knight,
  With both his hands behinde him pinnoed hard,
  And round about his necke an halter tight,
  As ready for the gallow tree prepard:
  His face was covered, and his head was bar'd,
  That who he was, uneath was to descry;
  And with full heavy heart with them he far'd,
  Griev'd to the soule, and groning inwardly,
That he of womens hands so base a death should dy.

23

But they like tyrants, mercilesse the more,
  Rejoyced at his miserable case,
  And him reviled, and reproched sore
  With bitter taunts, and termes of vile disgrace.
  Now when as *Artegall* arriv'd in place,
  Did aske, what cause brought that man to decay,
  They round about him gan to swarme apace,
  Meaning on him their cruell hands to lay,
And to have wrought unwares some villanous assay.

24

But he was soone aware of their ill minde,
  And drawing backe deceived their intent;
  Yet though him selfe did shame on womankinde
  His mighty hand to shend, he *Talus* sent
  To wrecke on them their follies hardyment:
  Who with few sowces of his yron flale,
  Dispersed all their troupe incontinent,
  And sent them home to tell a piteous tale,
Of their vaine prowesse, turned to their proper bale.

25

But that same wretched man, ordayned to die,
  They left behind them, glad to be so quit:
  Him *Talus* tooke out of perplexitie,
  And horrour of fowle death for Knight unfit,
  Who more than losse of life ydreaded it;
  And him restoring unto living light,
  So brought unto his Lord, where he did sit,
  Beholding all that womanish weake fight;
Whom soone as he beheld, he knew, and thus behight.

26

Sir *Terpine*, haplesse man, what make you here?
  Or have you lost your selfe, and your discretion,
  That ever in this wretched case ye were?
  Or have ye yeelded you to proude oppression
  Of womens powre, that boast of mens subjection?
  Or else what other deadly dismall day
  Is falne on you, by heavens hard direction,
  That ye were runne so fondly far astray,
As for to lead your selfe unto your owne decay?

27

Much was the man confounded in his mind,
    Partly with shame, and partly with dismay,
    That all astonisht he him selfe did find,
    And little had for his excuse to say,
    But onely thus; Most haplesse well ye may
    Me justly terme, that to this shame am brought,
    And made the scorne of Knighthod this same day.
    But who can scape, what his owne fate hath wrought?
The worke of heavens will surpasseth humaine thought.

28

Right true: but faulty men use oftentimes
    To attribute their folly unto fate,
    And lay on heaven the guilt of their owne crimes.
    But tell, Sir *Terpin*, ne let you amate
    Your misery, how fell ye in this state.
    Then sith ye needs (quoth he) will know my shame,
    And all the ill, which chaunst to me of late,
    I shortly will to you rehearse the same,
In hope ye will not turne misfortune to my blame.

29

Being desirous (as all Knights are woont)
    Through hard adventures deedes of armes to try,
    And after fame and honour for to hunt,
    I heard report that farre abrode did fly,
    That a proud Amazon did late defy
    All the brave Knights, that hold of Maidenhead,
    And unto them wrought all the villany,
    That she could forge in her malicious head,
Which some hath put to shame, and many done be dead.

30

The cause, they say, of this her cruell hate,
    Is for the sake of *Bellodant* the bold,
    To whom she bore most fervent love of late,
    And wooed him by all the waies she could:
    But when she saw at last, that he ne would
    For ought or nought be wonne unto her will,
    She turn'd her love to hatred manifold,
    And for his sake vow'd to doe all the ill
Which she could doe to Knights, which now she doth fulfill.

31

For all those Knights, the which by force or guile
  She doth subdue, she fowly doth entreate.
  First she doth them of warlike armes despoile,
  And cloth in womens weedes: And then with threat
  Doth them compell to worke, to earne their meat,
  To spin, to card, to sew, to wash, to wring;
  Ne doth she give them other thing to eat,
  But bread and water, or like feeble thing,
Them to disable from revenge adventuring.

32

But if through stout disdaine of manly mind,
  Any her proud observaunce will withstand,
  Upon that gibbet, which is there behind,
  She causeth them be hang'd up out of hand;
  In which condition I right now did stand.
  For being overcome by her in fight,
  And put to that base service of her band,
  I rather chose to die in lives despight,
Than lead that shamefull life, unworthy of a Knight.

33

How hight that Amazon (sayd *Artegall*)?
  And where, and how far hence does she abide?
  Her name (quoth he) they *Radigund* doe call,
  A Princesse of great powre, and greater pride,
  And Queene of Amazons, in armes well tride,
  And sundry battels, which she hath atchieved
  With great successe, that her hath glorifide,
  And made her famous, more than is believed;
Ne would I it have ween'd, had I not late it prieved.

34

Now sure (said he) and by the faith that I
  To Maydenhead and noble knighthood owe,
  I will not rest, till I her might doe trie,
  And venge the shame, that she to Knights doth show.
  Therefore Sir *Terpin* from you lightly throw
  This squalid weede, the patterne of dispaire,
  And wend with me, that ye may see and know,
  How Fortune will your ruin'd name repaire,
And knights of Maidenhead, whose praise she would empaire.

35

With that, like one that hopelesse was repryv'd
From deathes dore, at which he lately lay,
Those yron fetters, wherewith he was gyv'd,
The badges of reproch, he threw away,
And nimbly did him dight to guide the way
Unto the dwelling of that Amazone.
Which was from thence not past a mile or tway:
A goodly citty and a mighty one,
The which of her owne name she called *Radegone*.

36

Where they arriving, by the watchmen were
Descried streight, who all the citty warned,
How that three warlike persons did appeare,
Of which the one him seem'd a Knight all armed,
And th'other two well likely to have harmed.
Eftsoones the people all to harnesse ran,
And like a sort of Bees in clusters swarmed:
Ere long their Queene her selfe, halfe like a man
Came forth into the rout, and them t'array began.

37

And now the Knights being arrived neare,
Did beat upon the gates to enter in,
And at the Porter, skorning them so few,
Threw many threats, if they the towne did win,
To teare his flesh in peeces for his sin.
Which when as *Radigund* there comming heard,
Her heart for rage did grate, and teeth did grin:
She bad that streight the gates should be unbard,
And to them way to make, with weapons well prepard.

38

Soone as the gates were open to them set,
They pressed forward, entraunce to have made.
But in the middle way they were ymet
With a sharpe showre of arrowes, which them staid,
And better bad advise, ere they assaid
Unknowen perill of bold womens pride.
Then all that rout uppon them rudely laid,
And heaped strokes so fast on every side,
And arrowes haild so thicke, that they could not abide.

39

But *Radigund* her selfe, when she espide
  Sir *Terpin*, from her direfull doome acquit,
So cruell doale amongst her maides divide,
  T'avenge that shame, they did on him commit,
  All sodainely enflam'd with furious fit,
Like a fell Lionesse at him she flew,
  And on his head-peece him so fiercely smit,
  That to the ground him quite she overthrew,
Dismayd so with the stroke, that he no colours knew.

40

Soone as she saw him on the ground to grovell,
  She lightly to him leapt, and in his necke
Her proud foote setting, at his head did levell,
  Weening at once her wrath on him to wreake,
  And his contempt, that did her judg'ment breake.
As when a Beare hath seiz'd her cruell clawes
  Uppon the carkasse of some beast too weake,
  Proudly stands over, and a while doth pause,
To heare the piteous beast pleading her plaintiffe cause.

41

Whom when as *Artegall* in that distresse
  By chaunce beheld, he left the bloudy slaughter,
In which he swam, and ranne to his redresse.
  There her assayling fiercely fresh, he raught her
  Such an huge stroke, that it of sence distraught her:
And had she not it warded warily,
  It had depriv'd her mother of a daughter.
  Nathlesse for all the powre she did apply,
It made her stagger oft, and stare with ghastly eye.

42

Like to an Eagle in his kingly pride,
  Soring through his wide Empire of the aire,
To weather his brode sailes, by chaunce hath spide
  A Goshauke, which hath seized for her share
  Uppon some fowle, that should her feast prepare;
With dreadfull force he flies at her bylive,
  That with his souce, which none enduren dare,
  Her from the quarrey he away doth drive,
And from her griping pounce the greedy prey doth rive.

43

But soone as she her sence recover'd had,
   She fiercely towards him her selfe gan dight,
   Through vengeful wrath and sdeignfull pride half mad:
   For never had she suffred such despight.
   But ere she could joyne hand with him to fight,
   Her warlike maides about her flockt so fast,
   That they disparted them, maugre their might,
   And with their troupes did far a sunder cast:
But mongst the rest the fight did untill evening last.

44

And every while that mighty yron man,
   With his strange weapon, never wont in warre,
   Them sorely vext, and courst, and overran,
   And broke their bowes, and did their shooting marre,
   That none of all the many once did darre
   Him to assault, nor once approach him nie,
   But like a sort of sheepe dispersed farre
   For dread of their devouring enemie,
Through all the fields and vallies did before him flie.

45

But when as daies faire shinie-beame, yclowded
   With fearefull shadowes of deformed night,
   Warn'd man and beast in quiet rest be shrowded,
   Bold *Radigund* with sound of trumpe on hight,
   Causd all her people to surcease from fight,
   And gathering them unto her citties gate,
   Made them all enter in before her sight,
   And all the wounded, and the weake in state,
To be convayed in, ere she would once retrate.

46

When thus the field was voided all away,
   And all things quieted, the Elfin Knight
   Weary of toile and travell of that day,
   Causd his pavilion to be richly pight
   Before the city gate, in open sight;
   Where he him selfe did rest in safety,
   Together with sir *Terpin* all that night:
   But *Talus* usde in times of jeopardy
To keepe a nightly watch, for dread of treachery.

47

But *Radigund* full of heart-gnawing griefe,
  For the rebuke, which she sustain'd that day,
  Could take no rest, ne would receive reliefe,
  But tossed in her troublous minde, what way
  She mote revenge that blot, which on her lay.
  There she resolv'd her selfe in single fight
  To try her Fortune, and his force assay,
  Rather than see her people spoiled quight,
As she had seene that day a disaventerous sight.

48

She called forth to her a trusty mayd,
  Whom she thought fittest for that businesse,
  Her name was *Clarin*, and thus to her sayd;
  Goe damzell quickly, doe thy selfe addresse,
  To doe the message, which I shall expresse.
  Goe thou unto that stranger Faery Knight,
  Who yesterday drove us to such distresse,
  Tell, that to morrow I with him wil fight,
And try in equall field, whether hath greater might.

49

But these conditions doe to him propound.
  That if I vanquishe him, he shall obay
  My law, and ever to my lore be bound,
  And so will I, if me he vanquish may;
  What ever he shall like to doe or say:
  Goe streight, and take with thee, to witnesse it,
  Sixe of thy fellowes of the best array,
  And beare with you both wine and juncates fit,
And bid him eate, henceforth he oft shall hungry sit.

50

The Damzell streight obayd, and putting all
  In readinesse, forth to the Towne-gate went,
  Where sounding loud a Trumpet from the wall,
  Unto those warlike Knights she warning sent.
  Then *Talus* forth issuing from the tent,
  Unto the wall his way did fearelesse take,
  To weeten what that trumpets sounding ment:
  Where that same Damzell lowdly him bespake,
And shew'd, that with his Lord she would emparlaunce make.

51

So he them streight conducted to his Lord,
  Who, as he could, them goodly well did greete,
  Till they had told their message word by word:
  Which he accepting well, as he could weete,
  Them fairely entertaynd with curt'sies meete,
  And gave them gifts and things of deare delight.
  So backe againe they homeward turnd their feete.
  But *Artegall* him selfe to rest did dight,
That he mote fresher be against the next daies fight.

CANT. V

Artegall fights with Radigund
  And is subdewd by guile:
He is by her emprisoned,
  But wrought by Clarins wile.

1

SO soone as day forth dawning from the East,
  Nights humid curtaine from the heavens withdrew,
  And earely calling forth both man and beast,
  Comaunded them their daily workes renew,
  These noble warriors, mindefull to pursew
  The last daies purpose of their vowed fight,
  Them selves thereto preparde in order dew;
  The Knight, as best was seeming for a Knight,
And th'Amazon, as best it likt her selfe to dight.

2

All in a Camis light of purple silke
  Woven uppon with silver, subtly wrought,
  And quilted uppon sattin white as milke,
  Trayled with ribbands diversly distraught
  Like as the workeman had their courses taught;
  Which was short tucked for light motion
  Up to her ham, but when she list, it raught
  Downe to her lowest heele, and thereuppon
She wore for her defence a mayled habergeon.

3

And on her legs she painted buskins wore,
  Basted with bends of gold on every side,
  And mailes betweene, and laced close afore:
  Uppon her thigh her Cemitare was tide,
  With an embrodered belt of mickell pride;
  And on her shoulder hung her shield, bedeckt
  Uppon the bosse with stones, that shined wide,
  As the faire Moone in her most full aspect,
That to the Moone it mote be like in each respect.

4

So forth she came out of the citty gate,
  With stately port and proud magnificence,
  Guarded with many damzels, that did waite
  Uppon her person for her sure defence,
  Playing on shaumes and trumpets, that from hence
  Their sound did reach unto the heavens hight.
  So forth into the field she marched thence,
  Where was a rich Pavilion ready pight,
Her to receive, till time they should begin the fight.

5

Then forth came *Artegall* out of his tent,
  All arm'd to point, and first the Lists did enter:
  Soone after eke came she, with fell intent,
  And countenaunce fierce, as having fully bent her,
  That battels utmost triall to adventer.
  The Lists were closed fast, to barre the rout
  From rudely pressing to the middle center;
  Which in great heapes them circled all about,
Wayting, how Fortune would resolve that daungerous dout.

6

The Trumpets sounded, and the field began;
  With bitter strokes it both began, and ended.
  She at the first encounter on him ran
  With furious rage, as if she had intended
  Out of his breast the very heart have rended:
  But he that had like tempests often tride,
  From that first flaw him selfe right well defended.
  The more she rag'd, the more he did abide;
She hewd, she foynd, she lasht, she laid on every side.

7

Yet still her blowes he bore, and her forbore,
  Weening at last to win advantage new;
  Yet still her crueltie increased more,
  And though powre faild, her courage did accrew,
  Which fayling he gan fiercely her pursew.
  Like as a Smith that to his cunning feat
  The stubborne mettall seeketh to subdew,
  Soone as he feeles it mollifide with heat,
With his great yron sledge doth strongly on it beat.

8

So did Sir *Artegall* upon her lay,
  As if she had an yron andvile beene,
  That flakes of fire, bright as the sunny ray,
  Out of her steely armes were flashing seene,
  That all on fire ye would her surely weene.
  But with her shield so well her selfe she warded,
  From the dread daunger of his weapon keene,
  That all that while her life she safely garded:
But he that helpe from her against her will discarded.

9

For with his trenchant blade at the next blow
  Halfe of her shield he shared quite away,
  That halfe her side it selfe did naked show,
  And thenceforth unto daunger opened way.
  Much was she moved with the mightie sway
  Of that sad stroke, that halfe enrag'd she grew,
  And like a greedie Beare unto her pray,
  With her sharpe Cemitare at him she flew,
That glauncing downe his thigh, the purple bloud forth drew.

10

Thereat she gan to triumph with great boast,
  And to upbrayd that chaunce, which him misfell,
  As if the prize she gotten had almost,
  With spightfull speaches, fitting with her well;
  That his great hart gan inwardly to swell
  With indignation, at her vaunting vaine,
  And at her strooke with puissance fearefull fell;
  Yet with her shield she warded it againe,
That shattered all to peeces round about the plaine.

11

Having her thus disarmed of her shield,
  Upon her helmet he againe her strooke,
  That downe she fell upon the grassie field,
  In sencelesse swoune, as if her life forsooke,
  And pangs of death her spirit overtooke.
  Whom when he saw before his foote prostrated,
  He to her lept with deadly dreadfull looke,
  And her sunshynie helmet soone unlaced,
Thinking at once both head and helmet to have raced.

12

But when as he discovered had her face,
  He saw his senses straunge astonishment,
  A miracle of natures goodly grace,
  In her faire visage voide of ornament,
  But bath'd in bloud and sweat together ment;
  Which in the rudenesse of that evill plight,
  Bewrayd the signes of feature excellent:
  Like as the Moone in foggie winters night,
Doth seeme to be her selfe, though darkned be her light.

13

At sight thereof his cruell minded hart
  Empierced was with pittifull regard,
  That his sharpe sword he threw from him apart,
  Cursing his hand that had that visage mard:
  No hand so cruell, nor no hart so hard,
  But ruth of beautie will it mollifie.
  By this upstarting from her swoune, she star'd
  A while about her with confused eye;
Like one that from his dreame is waked suddenlye.

14

Soone as the knight she there by her did spy,
  Standing with emptie hands all weaponlesse,
  With fresh assault upon him she did fly,
  And gan renew her former cruelnesse:
  And though he still retyr'd, yet nathelesse
  With huge redoubled strokes she on him layd;
  And more increast her outrage mercilesse,
  The more that he with meeke intreatie prayd,
Her wrathful hand from greedy vengeance to have stayd.

15

Like as a Puttocke having spyde in sight
　A gentle Faulcon sitting on an hill,
　Whose other wing, now made unmeete for flight,
　Was lately broken by some fortune ill;
　The foolish Kyte, led with licentious will,
　Doth beat upon the gentle bird in vaine,
　With many idle stoups her troubling still:
　Even so did *Radigund* with bootlesse paine
Annoy this noble Knight, and sorely him constraine.

16

Nought could he do, but shun the dred despight
　Of her fierce wrath, and backward still retyre,
　And with his single shield, well as he might,
　Beare off the burden of her raging yre;
　And evermore he gently did desyre,
　To stay her stroks, and he himselfe would yield:
　Yet nould she hearke, ne let him once respyre,
　Till he to her delivered had his shield,
And to her mercie him submitted in plaine field.

17

So was he overcome, not overcome,
　But to her yeelded of his owne accord;
　Yet was he justly damned by the doome
　Of his owne mouth, that spake so warelesse word,
　To be her thrall, and service her afford.
　For though that he first victorie obtayned,
　Yet after by abandoning his sword,
　He wilfull lost, that he before attayned.
No fayrer conquest, than that with goodwill is gayned.

18

Tho with her sword on him she flatling strooke,
　In signe of true subjection to her powre,
　And as her vassall him to thraldome tooke.
　But *Terpine* borne to'a more unhappy howre,
　As he, on whom the lucklesse starres did lowre,
　She causd to be attacht, and forthwith led
　Unto the crooke t'abide the balefull stowre,
　From which he lately had through reskew fled:
Where he full shamefully was hanged by the hed.

19

But when they thought on *Talus* hands to lay,
  He with his yron flaile amongst them thondred,
  That they were fayne to let him scape away,
  Glad from his companie to be so sondred;
  Whose presence all their troups so much encombred
  That th'heapes of those, which he did wound and slay,
  Besides the rest dismayd, might not be nombred:
  Yet all that while he would not once assay,
To reskew his owne Lord, but thought it just t'obay.

20

Then tooke the Amazon this noble knight,
  Left to her will by his owne wilfull blame,
  And caused him to be disarmed quight,
  Of all the ornaments of knightly name,
  With which whylome he gotten had great fame:
  In stead whereof she made him to be dight
  In womans weedes, that is to manhood shame,
  And put before his lap a napron white,
In stead of Curiets and bases fit for fight.

21

So being clad, she brought him from the field,
  In which he had bene trayned many a day,
  Into a long large chamber, which was sield
  With moniments of many knights decay,
  By her subdewed in victorious fray:
  Amongst the which she causd his warlike armes
  Be hang'd on high, that mote his shame bewray;
  And broke his sword, for feare of further harmes,
With which he wont to stirre up battailous alarmes.

22

There entred in, he round about him saw
  Many brave knights, whose names right well he knew,
  There bound t'obay that Amazons proud law,
  Spinning and carding all in comely rew,
  That his bigge hart loth'd so uncomely vew.
  But they were forst through penurie and pyne,
  To doe those workes, to them appointed dew:
  For nought was given them to sup or dyne,
But what their hands could earne by twisting linnen twyne.

23

Amongst them all she placed him most low,
  And in his hand a distaffe to him gave,
  That he thereon should spin both flax and tow;
  A sordid office for a mind so brave.
  So hard it is to be a womans slave.
  Yet he it tooke in his owne selfes despight,
  And thereto did himselfe right well behave,
  Her to obay, sith he his faith had plight,
Her vassall to become, if she him wonne in fight.

24

Who had him seene, imagine mote thereby,
  That whylome hath of *Hercules* bene told,
  How for *Iolas* sake he did apply
  His mightie hands, the distaffe vile to hold,
  For his huge club, which had subdew'd of old
  So many monsters, which the world annoyed;
  His Lyons skin chaungd to a pall of gold,
  In which forgetting warres, he onely joyed
In combats of sweet love, and with his mistresse toyed.

25

Such is the crueltie of womenkynd,
  When they have shaken off the shamefast band,
  With which wise Nature did them strongly bynd,
  T'obay the heasts of mans well ruling hand,
  That then all rule and reason they withstand,
  To purchase a licentious libertie.
  But vertuous women wisely understand,
  That they were borne to base humilitie,
Unlesse the heavens them lift to lawfull soveraintie.

26

Thus there long while continu'd *Artegall*,
  Serving proud *Radigund* with true subjection;
  How ever it his noble heart did gall,
  T'obay a womans tyrannous direction,
  That might have had of life or death election:
  But having chosen, now he might not chaunge.
  During which time, the warlike Amazon,
  Whose wandring fancie after lust did raunge,
Gan cast a secret liking to this captive straunge.

27

Which long concealing in her covert brest,
  She chaw'd the cud of lovers carefull plight;
  Yet could it not so thoroughly digest,
  Being fast fixed in her wounded spright,
  But it tormented her both day and night:
  Yet would she not thereto yeeld free accord,
  To serve the lowly vassall of her might,
  And of her servant make her soverayne Lord:
So great her pride, that she such basenesse much abhord.

28

So much the greater still her anguish grew,
  Through stubborne handling of her love-sicke hart;
  And still the more she strove it to subdew,
  The more she still augmented her owne smart,
  And wyder made the wound of th'hidden dart.
  At last when long she struggled had in vaine,
  She gan to stoupe, and her proud mind convert
  To meeke obeysance of loves mightie raine,
And him entreat for grace, that had procur'd her paine.

29

Unto her selfe in secret she did call
  Her nearest handmayd, whom she most did trust,
  And to her said; *Clarinda* whom of all
  I trust a live, sith I thee fostred first;
  Now is the time, that I untimely must
  Thereof make tryall, in my greatest need:
  It is so hapned, that the heavens unjust,
  Spighting my happie freedome, have agreed,
To thrall my looser life, or my last bale to breed.

30

With that she turn'd her head, as halfe abashed,
  To hide the blush which in her visage rose,
  And through her eyes like sudden lightning flashed,
  Decking her cheeke with a vermilion rose:
  But soone she did her countenance compose,
  And to her turning, thus began againe;
  This griefes deepe wound I would to thee disclose,
  Thereto compelled through hart-murdring paine,
But dread of shame my doubtfull lips doth still restraine.

31

Ah my deare dread (said then the faithfull Mayd)
    Can dread of ought your dreadlesse hart withhold,
    That many hath with dread of death dismayd,
    And dare even deathes most dreadfull face behold?
    Say on my soverayne Ladie, and be bold;
    Doth not your handmayds life at your foot lie?
    Therewith much comforted, she gan unfold
    The cause of her conceived maladie,
As one that would confesse, yet faine would it denie.

32

Clarin (sayd she) thou seest yond Fayry Knight,
    Whom not my valour, but his owne brave mind
    Subjected hath to my unequall might;
    What right is it, that he should thraldome find,
    For lending life to me a wretch unkind;
    That for such good him recompence with ill?
    Therefore I cast, how I may him unbind,
    And by his freedome get his free goodwill;
Yet so, as bound to me he may continue still.

33

Bound unto me, but not with such hard bands
    Of strong compulsion, and streight violence,
    As now in miserable state he stands;
    But with sweet love and sure benevolence,
    Voide of malitious mind, or foule offence.
    To which if thou canst win him any way,
    Without discoverie of my thoughts pretence,
    Both goodly meede of him it purchase may,
And eke with gratefull service me right well apay.

34

Which that thou mayst the better bring to pas,
    Loe here this ring, which shall thy warrant bee,
    And token true to old *Eumenias*,
    From time to time, when thou it best shalt see,
    That in and out thou mayst have passage free.
    Goe now, *Clarinda*, well thy wits advise,
    And all thy forces gather unto thee;
    Armies of lovely lookes, and speeches wise,
With which thou canst even *Jove* himselfe to love entise.

35

The trustie Mayd, conceiving her intent,
  Did with sure promise of her good indevour,
  Give her great comfort, and some harts content.
So from her parting, she thenceforth did labour
By all the meanes she might, to curry favour
With th'Elfin Knight, her Ladies best beloved;
  With daily shew of courteous kind behaviour,
  Even at the markewhite of his hart she roved,
And with wide glauncing words, one day she thus him proved.

36

Unhappie Knight, upon whose hopelesse state
  Fortune envying good, hath felly frowned,
  And cruell heavens have heapt an heavy fate;
I rew that thus thy better dayes are drowned
In sad despaire, and all thy senses swowned
In stupid sorow, sith thy juster merit
  Might else have with felicitie bene crowned:
  Looke up at last, and wake thy dulled spirit,
To thinke how this long death thou mightest disinhe rit.

37

Much did he marvell at her uncouth speach,
  Whose hidden drift he could not well perceive;
  And gan to doubt, least she him sought t'appeach
Of treason, or some guilefull traine did weave,
Through which she might his wretched life bereave.
Both which to barre, he with this answere met her;
  Faire Damzell, that with ruth (as I perceave)
  Of my mishaps, art mov'd to wish me better,
For such your kind regard, I can but rest your detter.

38

Yet weet ye well, that to a courage great
  It is no lesse beseeming well, to beare
  The storme of fortunes frowne, or heavens threat,
Than in the sunshine of her countenance cleare
Timely to joy, and carrie comely cheare.
For though this cloud have now me overcast,
  Yet doe I not of better times despeyre;
  And, though (unlike) they should for ever last,
Yet in my truthes assurance I rest fixed fast.

39

But what so stonie mind (she then replyde)
  But if in his owne powre occasion lay,
  Would to his hope a windowe open wyde,
  And to his fortunes helpe make readie way?
  Unworthy sure (quoth he) of better day,
  That will not take the offer of good hope,
  And eke pursew, if he attaine it may.
  Which speaches she applying to the scope
Of her intent, this further purpose to him shope.

40

Then why doest not, thou ill advized man,
  Make meanes to win thy libertie forlorne,
  And try if thou by faire entreatie, can
  Move *Radigund*? who though she still have worne
  Her dayes in warre, yet (weet thou) was not borne
  Of Beares and Tygres, nor so salvage mynded,
  As that, albe all love of men she scorne,
  She yet forgets, that she of men was kynded:
And sooth oft seene, that proudest harts base love hath blynded.

41

Certes *Clarinda*, not of cancred will,
  (Sayd he) nor obstinate disdainefull mind,
  I have forbore this duetie to fulfill:
  For well I may this weene, by that I fynd,
  That she a Queene, and come of Princely kynd,
  Both worthie is for to be sewd unto,
  Chiefely by him, whose life her law doth bynd,
  And eke of powre her owne doome to undo,
And als' of princely grace to be inclyn'd thereto.

42

But want of meanes hath bene mine onely let,
  From seeking favour, where it doth abound;
  Which if I might by your good office get,
  I to your selfe should rest for ever bound,
  And readie to deserve, what grace I found.
  She feeling him thus bite upon the bayt,
  Yet doubting least his hold was but unsound,
  And not well fastened, would not strike him strayt,
But drew him on with hope, fit leasure to awayt.

43

But foolish Mayd, whyles heedlesse of the hooke,
　　She thus oft times was beating off and on,
　　Through slipperie footing, fell into the brooke,
　　And there was caught to her confusion.
　　For seeking thus to salve the Amazon,
　　She wounded was with her deceipts owne dart,
　　And gan thenceforth to cast affection,
　　Conceived close in her beguiled hart,
To *Artegall*, through pittie of his causelesse smart.

44

Yet durst she not disclose her fancies wound,
　　Ne to himselfe, for doubt of being sdayned,
　　Ne yet to any other wight on ground,
　　For feare her mistresse shold have knowledge gayned,
　　But to her selfe it secretly retayned,
　　Within the closet of her covert brest:
　　The more thereby her tender hart was payned.
　　Yet to awayt fit time she weened best,
And fairely did dissemble her sad thoughts unrest.

45

One day her Ladie, calling her apart,
　　Gan to demaund of her some tydings good,
　　Touching her loves successe, her lingring smart.
　　Therewith she gan at first to change her mood,
　　As one adaw'd, and halfe confused stood;
　　But quickly she it overpast, so soone
　　As she her face had wypt, to fresh her blood:
　　Tho gan she tell her all, that she had donne,
And all the wayes she sought, his love for to have wonne.

46

But sayd, that he was obstinate and sterne,
　　Scorning her offers and conditions vaine;
　　Ne would be taught with any termes, to lerne
　　So fond a lesson, as to love againe.
　　Die rather would he in penurious paine,
　　And his abridged dayes in dolour wast,
　　Than his foes love or liking entertaine:
　　His resolution was both first and last,
His bodie was her thrall, his hart was freely plast.

47

Which when the cruell Amazon perceived,
  She gan to storme, and rage, and rend her gall,
  For very fell despight, which she conceived,
  To be so scorned of a base borne thrall,
  Whose life did lie in her least eye-lids fall;
  Of which she vow'd with many a cursed threat,
  That she therefore would him ere long forstall.
  Nathlesse when calmed was her furious heat,
She chang'd that threatfull mood, and mildly gan entreat.

48

What now is left *Clarinda?* what remaines,
  That we may compasse this our enterprize?
  Great shame to lose so long employed paines,
  And greater shame t'abide so great misprize,
  With which he dares our offers thus despize.
  Yet that his guilt the greater may appeare,
  And more my gratious mercie by this wize,
  I will a while with his first folly beare,
Till thou have tride againe, and tempted him more neare.

49

Say, and do all, that may thereto prevaile;
  Leave nought unpromist, that may him perswade,
  Life, freedome, grace, and gifts of great availe,
  With which the Gods themselves are mylder made:
  Thereto adde art, even womens witty trade,
  The art of mightie words, that men can charme;
  With which in case thou canst him not invade,
  Let him feele hardnesse of thy heavie arme:
Who will not stoupe with good, shall be made stoupe with harme.

50

Some of his diet doe from him withdraw;
  For I him find to be too proudly fed.
  Give him more labour, and with streighter law,
  That he with worke may be forwearied.
  Let him lodge hard, and lie in strawen bed,
  That may pull downe the courage of his pride;
  And lay upon him, for his greater dread,
  Cold yron chaines, with which let him be tide;
And let, what ever he desires, be him denide.

51

When thou hast all this doen, then bring me newes
  Of his demeane: thenceforth not like a lover,
  But like a rebell stout I will him use.
  For I resolve this siege not to give over,
  Till I the conquest of my will recover.
  So she departed, full of griefe and sdaine,
  Which inly did to great impatience move her.
  But the false mayden shortly turn'd againe
Unto the prison, where her hart did thrall remaine.

52

There all her subtill nets she did unfold,
  And all the engins of her wit display;
  In which she meant him warelesse to enfold,
  And of his innocence to make her pray.
  So cunningly she wrought her crafts assay,
  That both her Ladie, and her selfe withall,
  And eke the knight attonce she did betray:
  But most the knight, whom she with guilefull call
Did cast for to allure, into her trap to fall.

53

As a bad Nurse, which fayning to receive
  In her owne mouth the food, ment for her chyld,
  Withholdes it to her selfe, and doeth deceive
  The infant, so for want of nourture spoyld:
  Even so *Clarinda* her owne Dame beguyld,
  And turn'd the trust, which was in her affyde,
  To feeding of her private fire, which boyld
  Her inward brest, and in her entrayles fryde,
The more that she it sought to cover and to hyde.

54

For comming to this knight, she purpose fayned,
  How earnest suit she earst for him had made
  Unto her Queene, his freedome to have gayned;
  But by no meanes could her thereto perswade:
  But that in stead thereof, she sternely bade
  His miserie to be augmented more,
  And many yron bands on him to lade.
  All which nathlesse she for his love forbore:
So praying him t'accept her service evermore.

55

And more than that, she promist that she would,
  In case she might finde favour in his eye,
  Devize how to enlarge him out of hould.
  The Fayrie glad to gaine his libertie,
  Can yeeld great thankes for such her curtesie,
  And with faire words, fit for the time and place,
  To feede the humour of her maladie,
  Promist, if she would free him from that case,
He wold by all good means he might, deserve such grace.

56

So daily he faire semblant did her shew,
  Yet never meant he in his noble mind,
  To his owne absent love to be untrew:
  Ne ever did deceiptfull *Clarin* find
  In her false hart, his bondage to unbind;
  But rather how she mote him faster tye.
  Therefore unto her mistresse most unkind
  She daily told, her love he did defye,
And him she told, her Dame his freedome did denye.

57

Yet thus much friendship she to him did show,
  That his scarse diet somewhat was amended,
  And his worke lessened, that his love mote grow:
  Yet to her Dame him still she discommended,
  That she with him mote be the more offended.
  Thus he long while in thraldome there remayned,
  Of both beloved well, but litle frended;
  Untill his owne true love his freedome gayned,
Which in an other Canto will be best contayned.

CANT. VI

Talus brings newes to Britomart,
of Artegals mishap,
She goes to seeke him, Dolon meetes,
who seekes her to entrap.

I

SOME men, I wote, will deeme in *Artegall*
  Great weaknesse, and report of him much ill,
  For yeelding so himselfe a wretched thrall,
  To th'insolent commaund of womens will;
  That all his former praise doth fowly spill.
  But he the man, that say or doe so dare,
  Be well adviz'd, that he stand stedfast still:
  For never yet was wight so well aware,
But he at first or last was trapt in womens snare.

2

Yet in the streightnesse of that captive state,
  This gentle knight himselfe so well behaved,
  That notwithstanding all the subtill bait,
  With which those Amazons his love still craved,
  To his owne love his loialtie he saved:
  Whose character in th'Adamantine mould
  Of his true hart so firmely was engraved,
  That no new loves impression ever could
Bereave it thence: such blot his honour blemish should.

3

Yet his owne love, the noble *Britomart*,
  Scarse so conceived in her jealous thought,
  What time sad tydings of his balefull smart
  In womans bondage, *Talus* to her brought;
  Brought in untimely houre, ere it was sought.
  For after that the utmost date, assynde
  For his returne, she waited had for nought,
  She gan to cast in her misdoubtfull mynde
A thousand feares, that love-sicke fancies faine to fynde.

4

Sometime she feared, least some hard mishap
  Had him misfalne in his adventurous quest;
  Sometime least his false foe did him entrap
  In traytrous traine, or had unwares opprest:
  But most she did her troubled mynd molest,
  And secretly afflict with jealous feare,
  Least some new love had him from her possest;
  Yet loth she was, since she no ill did heare,
To thinke of him so ill: yet could she not forbeare.

5

One while she blam'd her selfe; another whyle
  She him condemn'd, as trustlesse and untrew:
  And then, her griefe with errour to beguyle,
  She fayn'd to count the time againe anew,
  As if before she had not counted trew.
  For houres but dayes; for weekes, that passed were,
  She told but moneths, to make them seeme more few:
  Yet when she reckned them, still drawing neare,
Each hour did seeme a moneth, and every moneth a yeare.

6

But when as yet she saw him not returne,
  She thought to send some one to seeke him out;
  But none she found so fit to serve that turne,
  As her owne selfe, to ease her selfe of dout.
  Now she deviz'd amongst the warlike rout
  Of errant Knights, to seeke her errant Knight;
  And then againe resolv'd to hunt him out
  Amongst loose Ladies, lapped in delight:
And then both Knights envide, and Ladies eke did spight.

7

One day, when as she long had sought for ease
  In every place, and every place thought best,
  Yet found no place, that could her liking please,
  She to a window came, that opened West,
  Towards which coast her love his way addrest.
  There looking forth, shee in her heart did find
  Many vaine fancies, working her unrest;
  And sent her winged thoughts, more swift than wind,
To beare unto her love the message of her mind.

8

There as she looked long, at last she spide
One comming towards her with hasty speede:
Well weend she then, ere him she plaine describe,
That it was one sent from her love indeede.
Who when he nigh approcht, shee mote arede
That it was *Talus*, *Artegall* his groome;
Whereat her heart was fild with hope and drede;
Ne would she stay, till he in place could come,
But ran to meete him forth, to know his tidings somme.

9

Even in the dore him meeting, she begun;
And where is he thy Lord, and how far hence?
Declare at once; and hath he lost or wun?
The yron man, albe he wanted sence
And sorrowes feeling, yet with conscience
Of his ill newes, did inly chill and quake,
And stood still mute, as one in great suspence,
As if that by his silence he would make
Her rather reade his meaning, than him selfe it spake.

10

Till she againe thus sayd; *Talus* be bold,
And tell what ever it be, good or bad,
That from thy tongue thy hearts intent doth hold.
To whom he thus at length. The tidings sad,
That I would hide, will needs, I see, be rad.
My Lord, your love, by hard mishap doth lie
In wretched bondage, wofully bestad.
Ay me (quoth she) what wicked destinie?
And is he vanquisht by his tyrant enemy?

11

Not by that Tyrant, his intended foe;
But by a Tyrannesse (he then replide,)
That him captived hath in haplesse woe.
Cease thou bad newes-man, badly doest thou hide
Thy maisters shame, in harlots bondage tide.
The rest my selfe too readily can spell.
With that in rage she turn'd from him aside,
Forcing in vaine the rest to her to tell,
And to her chamber went like solitary cell.

12

There she began to make her monefull plaint
  Against her Knight, for being so untrew;
And him to touch with falshoods fowle attaint,
  That all his other honour overthrew.
  Oft did she blame her selfe, and often rew,
For yeelding to a straungers love so light,
  Whose life and manners straunge she never knew;
  And evermore she did him sharpely twight
For breach of faith to her, which he had firmely plight.

13

And then she in her wrathfull will did cast,
  How to revenge that blot of honour blent;
To fight with him, and goodly die her last:
  And then againe she did her selfe torment,
  Inflicting on her selfe his punishment.
A while she walkt, and chauft; a while she threw
  Her selfe uppon her bed, and did lament:
  Yet did she not lament with loude alew,
As women wont, but with deepe sighes, and singults few.

14

Like as a wayward childe, whose sounder sleepe
  Is broken with some fearefull dreames affright,
With froward will doth set him selfe to weepe;
  Ne can be stild for all his nurses might,
  But kicks, and squals, and shriekes for fell despight:
Now scratching her, and her loose locks misusing;
  Now seeking darkenesse, and now seeking light;
  Then craving sucke, and then the sucke refusing.
Such was this Ladies fit, in her loves fond accusing.

15

But when she had with such unquiet fits
  Her selfe there close afflicted long in vaine,
Yet found no easement in her troubled wits,
  She unto *Talus* forth return'd againe,
  By change of place seeking to ease her paine;
And gan enquire of him, with mylder mood,
  The certaine cause of *Artegals* detaine;
  And what he did, and in what state he stood,
And whether he did woo, or whether he were woo'd.

16

Ah wellaway (sayd then the yron man,)
　That he is not the while in state to woo;
　But lies in wretched thraldome, weake and wan,
　Not by strong hand compelled thereunto,
　But his owne doome, that none can now undoo.
　Sayd I not then (quoth shee) erwhile aright,
　That this is things compacte betwixt you two,
　Me to deceive of faith unto me plight,
Since that he was not forst, nor overcome in fight?

17

With that he gan at large to her dilate
　The whole discourse of his captivance sad,
　In sort as ye have heard the same of late.
　All which when she with hard enduraunce had
　Heard to the end, she was right sore bestad,
　With sodaine stounds of wrath and griefe attone:
　Ne would abide, till she had aunswere made,
　But streight her selfe did dight, and armor don;
And mounting to her steede, bad *Talus* guide her on.

18

So forth she rode uppon her ready way,
　To seeke her Knight, as *Talus* her did guide:
　Sadly she rode, and never word did say,
　Nor good nor bad, ne ever lookt aside,
　But still right downe, and in her thought did hide
　The felnesse of her heart, right fully bent
　To fierce avengement of that womans pride,
　Which had her Lord in her base prison pent,
And so great honour with so fowle reproch had blent.

19

So as she thus melancholicke did ride,
　Chawing the cud of griefe and inward paine,
　She chaunst to meete toward the even-tide
　A Knight, that softly paced on the plaine,
　As if him selfe to solace he were faine.
　Well shot in yeares he seem'd, and rather bent
　To peace, than needlesse trouble to constraine.
　As well by view of that his vestiment,
As by his modest semblant, that no evill ment.

Britomart on the Perillous Bridge

20

He comming neare, gan gently her salute,
  With curteous words, in the most comely wize;
  Who though desirous rather to rest mute,
  Than termes to entertaine of common guize,
  Yet rather than she kindnesse would despize,
  She would her selfe displease, so him requite.
  Then gan the other further to devize
  Of things abrode, as next to hand did light,
And many things demaund, to which she answer'd light.

21

For little lust had she to talke of ought,
  Or ought to heare, that mote delightfull bee;
  Her minde was whole possessed of one thought,
  That gave none other place. Which when as hee
  By outward signes, (as well he might) did see,
  He list no lenger to use lothfull speach,
  But her besought to take it well in gree,
  Sith shady dampe had dimd the heavens reach,
To lodge with him that night, unles good cause empeach.

22

The Championesse, now seeing night at dore,
  Was glad to yeeld unto his good request:
  And with him went without gaine-saying more.
  Not farre away, but little wide by West,
  His dwelling was, to which he him addrest;
  Where soone arriving they received were
  In seemely wise, as them beseemed best:
  For he their host them goodly well did cheare,
And talk't of pleasant things, the night away to weare.

23

Thus passing th'evening well, till time of rest,
  Then *Britomart* unto a bowre was brought;
  Where groomes awayted her to have undrest.
  But she ne would undressed be for ought,
  Ne doffe her armes, though he her much besought.
  For she had vow'd, she sayd, not to forgo
  Those warlike weedes, till she revenge had wrought
  Of a late wrong uppon a mortall foe;
Which she would sure performe, betide her wele or wo.

24

Which when their Host perceiv'd, right discontent
  In minde he grew, for feare least by that art
  He should his purpose misse, which close he ment:
  Yet taking leave of her, he did depart.
  There all that night remained *Britomart*,
  Restlesse, recomfortlesse, with heart deepe grieved,
  Not suffering the least twinckling sleepe to start
  Into her eye, which th'heart mote have relieved,
But if the least appear'd, her eyes she streight reprieved.

25

Ye guilty eyes (sayd she) the which with guyle
  My heart at first betrayd, will ye betray
  My life now to, for which a little whyle
  Ye will not watch? false watches, wellaway,
  I wote when ye did watch both night and day
  Unto your losse: and now needes will ye sleepe?
  Now ye have made my heart to wake alway,
  Now will ye sleepe? ah wake, and rather weepe,
To thinke of your nights want, that should yee waking keepe.

26

Thus did she watch, and weare the weary night
  In waylfull plaints, that none was to appease;
  Now walking soft, now sitting still upright,
  As sundry chaunge her seemed best to ease.
  Ne lesse did *Talus* suffer sleepe to seaze
  His eye-lids sad, but watcht continually,
  Lying without her dore in great disease;
  Like to a Spaniell wayting carefully
Least any should betray his Lady treacherously.

27

What time the native Belman of the night,
  The bird, that warned *Peter* of his fall,
  First rings his silver Bell t'each sleepy wight,
  That should their mindes up to devotion call,
  She heard a wondrous noise below the hall.
  All sodainely the bed, where she should lie,
  By a false trap was let adowne to fall
  Into a lower roome, and by and by
The loft was raysd againe, that no man could it spie.

28

With sight whereof she was dismayd right sore,
  Perceiving well the treason, which was ment:
  Yet stirred not at all for doubt of more,
  But kept her place with courage confident,
  Wayting what would ensue of that event.
  It was not long, before she heard the sound
  Of armed men, comming with close intent
  Towards her chamber; at which dreadfull stound
She quickly caught her sword, and shield about her bound.

29

With that there came unto her chamber dore
  Two Knights, all armed ready for to fight,
  And after them full many other more,
  A raskall rout, with weapons rudely dight.
  Whom soone as *Talus* spide by glims of night,
  He started up, there where on ground he lay,
  And in his hand his thresher ready keight.
  They seeing that, let drive at him streight way,
And round about him preace in riotous aray.

30

But soone as he began to lay about
  With his rude yron flaile, they gan to flie,
  Both armed Knights, and eke unarmed rout:
  Yet *Talus* after them apace did plie,
  Where ever in the darke he could them spie;
  That here and there like scattred sheepe they lay.
  Then backe returning, where his Dame did lie,
  He to her told the story of that fray,
And all that treason there intended did bewray.

31

Wherewith though wondrous wroth, and inly burning,
  To be avenged for so fowle a deede,
  Yet being forst to abide the daies returning,
  She there remain'd, but with right wary heede,
  Least any more such practise should proceede.
  Now mote ye know (that which to *Britomart*
  Unknowen was) whence all this did proceede,
  And for what cause so great mischievous smart
Was ment to her, that never evill ment in hart.

32

The goodman of this house was *Dolon* hight,
  A man of subtill wit and wicked minde,
  That whilome in his youth had bene a Knight,
  And armes had borne, but little good could finde,
  And much lesse honour by that warlike kinde
  Of life: for he was nothing valorous,
  But with slie shiftes and wiles did underminde
  All noble Knights, which were adventurous,
And many brought to shame by treason treacherous.

33

He had three sonnes, all three like fathers sonnes,
  Like treacherous, like full of fraud and guile,
  Of all that on this earthly compasse wonnes:
  The eldest of the which was slaine erewhile
  By *Artegall*, through his owne guilty wile;
  His name was *Guizor*, whose untimely fate
  For to avenge, full many treasons vile
  His father *Dolon* had deviz'd of late
With these his wicked sons, and shewd his cankred hate.

34

For sure he weend, that this his present guest
  Was *Artegall*, by many tokens plaine;
  But chiefly by that yron page he ghest,
  Which still was wont with *Artegall* remaine;
  And therefore ment him surely to have slaine.
  But by Gods grace, and her good heedinesse,
  She was preserved from their traytrous traine.
  Thus she all night wore out in watchfulnesse,
Ne suffred slothfull sleepe her eyelids to oppresse.

35

The morrow next, so soone as dawning houre
  Discovered had the light to living eye,
  She forth yssew'd out of her loathed bowre,
  With full intent t'avenge that villany,
  On that vilde man, and all his family.
  And comming down to seeke them, where they wond,
  Nor sire, nor sonnes, nor any could she spie:
  Each rowme she sought, but them all empty fond:
They all were fled for feare, but whether, nether kond.

36

She saw it vaine to make there lenger stay,
  But tooke her steede, and thereon mounting light,
  Gan her addresse unto her former way.
  She had not rid the mountenance of a flight,
  But that she saw there present in her sight,
  Those two false brethren, on that perillous Bridge,
  On which *Pollente* with *Artegall* did fight.
  Streight was the passage like a ploughed ridge,
That if two met, the one mote needes fall over the lidge.

37

There they did thinke them selves on her to wreake:
  Who as she nigh unto them drew, the one
  These vile reproches gan unto her speake;
  Thou recreant false traytor, that with lone
  Of armes hast knighthood stolne, yet Knight art none,
  No more shall now the darkenesse of the night
  Defend thee from the vengeance of thy fone,
  But with thy bloud thou shalt appease the spright
Of *Guizor*, by thee slaine, and murdred by thy slight.

38

Strange were the words in *Britomartis* eare;
  Yet stayd she not for them, but forward fared,
  Till to the perillous Bridge she came, and there
  Talus desir'd, that he might have prepared
  The way to her, and those two losels scared.
  But she thereat was wroth, that for despight
  The glauncing sparkles through her bever glared,
  And from her eies did flash out fiery light,
Like coles, that through a silver Censer sparkle bright.

39

She stayd not to advise which way to take;
  But putting spurres unto her fiery beast,
  Thorough the midst of them she way did make.
  The one of them, which most her wrath increast,
  Uppon her speare she bore before her breast,
  Till to the Bridges further end she past,
  Where falling downe, his challenge he releast:
  The other over side the Bridge she cast
Into the river, where he drunke his deadly last.

40

As when the flashing Levin haps to light
  Uppon two stubborne oakes, which stand so neare,
  That way betwixt them none appeares in sight;
  The Engin fiercely flying forth, doth teare
  Th'one from the earth, and through the aire doth beare;
  The other it with force doth overthrow,
  Uppon one side, and from his rootes doth reare.
So did the Championesse those two there strow,
And to their sire their carcasses left to bestow.

CANT. VII

Britomart comes to Isis Church,
  Where shee strange visions sees:
  She fights with Radigund, her slaies,
  And Artegall thence frees.

1

NOUGHT is on earth more sacred or divine,
  That Gods and men doe equally adore,
  Than this same vertue, that doth right define:
  For th'hevens themselves, whence mortal men implore
  Right in their wrongs, are rul'd by righteous lore
  Of highest Jove, who doth true justice deale
  To his inferiour Gods, and evermore
  Therewith containes his heavenly Commonweale:
The skill whereof to Princes hearts he doth reveale.

2

Well therefore did the antique world invent,
  That Justice was a God of soveraine grace,
  And altars unto him, and temples lent,
  And heavenly honours in the highest place;
  Calling him great *Osyris*, of the race
  Of th'old Ægyptian Kings, that whylome were;
  With fayned colours shading a true case:
  For that *Osyris*, whilest he lived here,
The justest man alive, and truest did appeare.

3

His wife was *Isis*, whom they likewise made
    A Goddesse of great powre and soverainty,
    And in her person cunningly did shade
    That part of Justice, which is Equity,
    Whereof I have to treat here presently.
    Unto whose temple when as *Britomart*
    Arrived, shee with great humility
    Did enter in, ne would that night depart;
But *Talus* mote not be admitted to her part.

4

There she received was in goodly wize
    Of many Priests, which duely did attend
    Uppon the rites and daily sacrifize,
    All clad in linnen robes with silver hemd;
    And on their heads with long locks comely kemd,
    They wore rich Mitres shaped like the Moone,
    To shew that *Isis* doth the Moone portend;
    Like as *Osyris* signifies the Sunne.
For that they both like race in equall justice runne.

5

The Championesse them greeting, as she could,
    Was thence by them into the Temple led;
    Whose goodly building when she did behould,
    Borne uppon stately pillours, all dispred
    With shining gold, and arched over hed,
    She wondred at the workemans passing skill,
    Whose like before she never saw nor red;
    And thereuppon long while stood gazing still,
But thought, that she thereon could never gaze her fill.

6

Thence forth unto the Idoll they her brought,
    The which was framed all of silver fine,
    So well as could with cunning hand be wrought,
    And clothed all in garments made of line,
    Hemd all about with fringe of silver twine.
    Uppon her head she wore a Crowne of gold,
    To shew that she had powre in things divine;
    And at her feete a Crocodile was rold,
That with her wreathed taile her middle did enfold.

7

One foote was set uppon the Crocodile,
  And on the ground the other fast did stand,
  So meaning to suppresse both forged guile,
  And open force: and in her other hand
  She stretched forth a long white sclender wand.
  Such was the Goddesse; whom when *Britomart*
  Had long beheld, her selfe uppon the land
  She did prostrate, and with right humble hart,
Unto her selfe her silent prayers did impart.

8

To which the Idoll as it were inclining,
  Her wand did move with amiable looke,
  By outward shew her inward sence desining.
  Who well perceiving, how her wand she shooke,
  It as a token of good fortune tooke.
  By this the day with dampe was overcast,
  And joyous light the house of *Jove* forsooke:
  Which when she saw, her helmet she unlaste,
And by the altars side her selfe to slumber plaste.

9

For other beds the Priests there used none,
  But on their mother Earths deare lap did lie,
  And bake their sides uppon the cold hard stone,
  T'enure them selves to sufferaunce thereby
  And proud rebellious flesh to mortify.
  For by the vow of their religion
  They tied were to stedfast chastity,
  And continence of life, that all forgon,
They mote the better tend to their devotion.

10

Therefore they mote not taste of fleshly food,
  Ne feed on ought, the which doth bloud containe,
  Ne drinke of wine, for wine they say is blood,
  Even the bloud of Gyants, which were slaine,
  By thundring Jove in the Phlegrean plaine.
  For which the earth (as they the story tell)
  Wroth with the Gods, which to perpetuall paine
  Had damn'd her sonnes, which gainst them did rebell,
With inward griefe and malice did against them swell.

11

And of their vitall bloud, the which was shed
　Into her pregnant bosome, forth she brought
　The fruitfull vine, whose liquor blouddy red
　Having the mindes of men with fury fraught,
　Mote in them stirre up old rebellious thought,
　To make new warre against the Gods againe:
　Such is the powre of that same fruit, that nought
　The fell contagion may thereof restraine,
Ne within reasons rule, her madding mood containe.

12

There did the warlike Maide her selfe repose,
　Under the wings of *Isis* all that night,
　And with sweete rest her heavy eyes did close,
　After that long daies toile and weary plight.
　Where whilest her earthly parts with soft delight
　Of sencelesse sleepe did deeply drowned lie,
　There did appeare unto her heavenly spright
　A wondrous vision, which did close implie
The course of all her fortune and posteritie.

13

Her seem'd, as she was doing sacrifize
　To *Isis*, deckt with Mitre on her hed,
　And linnen stole after those Priestes guize,
　All sodainely she saw transfigured
　Her linnen stole to robe of scarlet red,
　And Moone-like Mitre to a Crowne of gold,
　That even she her selfe much wondered
　At such a chaunge, and joyed to behold
Her selfe, adorn'd with gems and jewels manifold.

14

And in the midst of her felicity,
　An hideous tempest seemed from below,
　To rise through all the Temple sodainely,
　That from the Altar all about did blow
　The holy fire, and all the embers strow
　Uppon the ground, which kindled privily,
　Into outragious flames unwares did grow,
　That all the Temple put in jeopardy
Of flaming, and her selfe in great perplexity.

15

With that the Crocodile, which sleeping lay
  Under the Idols feete in fearelesse bowre,
  Seem'd to awake in horrible dismay,
  As being troubled with that stormy stowre;
  And gaping greedy wide, did streight devoure
  Both flames and tempest: with which growen great,
  And swolne with pride of his owne peerelesse powre,
  He gan to threaten her likewise to eat;
But that the Goddesse with her rod him backe did beat.

16

Tho turning all his pride to humblesse meeke,
  Him selfe before her feete he lowly threw,
  And gan for grace and love of her to seeke:
  Which she accepting, he so neare her drew,
  That of his game she soone enwombed grew,
  And forth did bring a Lion of great might;
  That shortly did all other beasts subdew.
  With that she waked, full of fearefull fright,
And doubtfully dismayd through that so uncouth sight.

17

So thereuppon long while she musing lay,
  With thousand thoughts feeding her fantasie,
  Untill she spide the lampe of lightsome day,
  Up-lifted in the porch of heaven hie.
  Then up she rose fraught with melancholy,
  And forth into the lower parts did pas;
  Whereas the Priestes she found full busily
  About their holy things for morrow Mas:
Whom she saluting faire, faire resaluted was.

18

But by the change of her unchearefull looke,
  They might perceive, she was not well in plight;
  Or that some pensivenesse to heart she tooke.
  Therefore thus one of them, who seem'd in sight
  To be the greatest, and the gravest wight,
  To her bespake; Sir Knight it seemes to me,
  That thorough evill rest of this last night,
  Or ill apayd, or much dismayd ye be,
That by your change of cheare is easie for to see.

19

Certes (sayd she) sith ye so well have spide
The troublous passion of my pensive mind,
I will not seeke the same from you to hide,
But will my cares unfolde, in hope to find
Your aide, to guide me out of errour blind.
Say on (quoth he) the secret of your hart:
For by the holy vow, which me doth bind,
I am adjur'd, best counsell to impart
To all, that shall require my comfort in their smart.

20

Then gan she to declare the whole discourse
Of all that vision, which to her appeard,
As well as to her minde it had recourse.
All which when he unto the end had heard,
Like to a weake faint-hearted man he fared,
Through great astonishment of that strange sight;
And with long locks up-standing, stifly stared
Like one adawed with some dreadfull spright.
So fild with heavenly fury, thus he her behight.

21

Magnificke Virgin, that in queint disguise
Of British armes doest maske thy royall blood,
So to pursue a perillous emprize,
How couldst thou weene, through that disguized hood,
To hide thy state from being understood?
Can from th'immortall Gods ought hidden bee?
They doe thy linage, and thy Lordly brood;
They doe thy sire, lamenting sore for thee;
They doe thy love, forlorne in womens thraldome see.

22

The end whereof, and all the long event,
They doe to thee in this same dreame discover.
For that same Crocodile doth represent
The righteous Knight, that is thy faithfull lover,
Like to *Osyris* in all just endever.
For that same Crocodile *Osyris* is,
That under *Isis* feete doth sleepe for ever:
To shew that clemence oft in things amis,
Restraines those sterne behests, and cruell doomes of his.

23

That Knight shall all the troublous stormes asswage,
  And raging flames, that many foes shall reare,
  To hinder thee from the just heritage
  Of thy sires Crowne, and from thy countrey deare.
  Then shalt thou take him to thy loved fere,
  And joyne in equall portion of thy realme.
  And afterwards a sonne to him shalt beare,
  That Lion-like shall shew his powre extreame:
So blesse thee God, and give thee joyance of thy dreame.

24

All which when she unto the end had heard,
  She much was eased in her troublous thought,
  And on those Priests bestowed rich reward:
  And royall gifts of gold and silver wrought,
  She for a present to their Goddesse brought.
  Then taking leave of them, she forward went,
  To seeke her love, where he was to be sought;
  Ne rested till she came without relent
Unto the land of Amazons, as she was bent.

25

Whereof when newes to *Radigund* was brought,
  Not with amaze, as women wonted bee,
  She was confused in her troublous thought,
  But fild with courage and with joyous glee,
  As glad to heare of armes, the which now she
  Had long surceast, she bad to open bold,
  That she the face of her new foe might see.
  But when they of that yron man had told,
Which late her folke had slaine, she bad them forth to hold.

26

So there without the gate (as seemed best)
  She caused her Pavilion be pight;
  In which stout *Britomart* her selfe did rest,
  Whiles *Talus* watched at the dore all night.
  All night likewise, they of the towne in fright,
  Uppon their wall good watch and ward did keepe.
  The morrow next, so soone as dawning light
  Bad doe away the dampe of drouzie sleepe,
The warlike Amazon out of her bowre did peepe.

27

And caused streight a Trumpet loud to shrill,
  To warne her foe to battell soone be prest:
  Who long before awoke (for she ful ill
  Could sleepe all night, that in unquiet brest
  Did closely harbour such a jealous guest)
  Was to the battell whilome ready dight.
  Eftsoones that warriouresse with haughty crest
  Did forth issue, all ready for the fight:
On th'other side her foe appeared soone in sight.

28

But ere they reared hand, the Amazone
  Began the streight conditions to propound,
  With which she used still to tye her fone;
  To serve her so, as she the rest had bound.
  Which when the other heard, she sternly frownd
  For high disdaine of such indignity,
  And would no lenger treat, but bad them sound.
  For her no other termes should ever tie
Than what prescribed were by lawes of chevalrie.

29

The Trumpets sound, and they together run
  With greedy rage, and with their faulchins smot;
  Ne either sought the others strokes to shun,
  But through great fury both their skill forgot,
  And practicke use in armes: ne spared not
  Their dainty parts, which nature had created
  So faire and tender, without staine or spot,
  For other uses, than they them translated;
Which they now hackt and hewd, as if such use they hated,

30

As when a Tygre and a Lionesse
  Are met at spoyling of some hungry pray,
  Both challenge it with equall greedinesse:
  But first the Tygre clawes thereon did lay;
  And therefore loth to loose her right away,
  Doth in defence thereof full stoutly stond:
  To which the Lion strongly doth gainesay,
  That she to hunt the beast first tooke in hond;
And therefore ought it have, where ever she it fond.

31

Full fiercely layde the Amazon about,
  And dealt her blowes unmercifully sore:
  Which *Britomart* withstood with courage stout,
  And them repaide againe with double more.
  So long they fought, that all the grassie flore
  Was fild with bloud, which from their sides did flow,
  And gushed through their armes, that all in gore
  They trode, and on the ground their lives did strow,
Like fruitles seede, of which untimely death should grow.

32

At last proud *Radigund* with fell despight,
  Having by chaunce espide advantage neare,
  Let drive at her with all her dreadfull might,
  And thus upbrayding said; This token beare
  Unto the man, whom thou doest love so deare;
  And tell him for his sake thy life thou gavest.
  Which spitefull words she sore engriev'd to heare,
  Thus answer'd; Lewdly thou my love depravest,
Who shortly must repent that now so vainely bravest.

33

Nath'lesse that stroke so cruell passage found,
  That glauncing on her shoulder plate, it bit
  Unto the bone, and made a griesly wound,
  That she her shield through raging smart of it
  Could scarse uphold; yet soone she it requit.
  For having force increast through furious paine,
  She her so rudely on the helmet smit,
  That it empierced to the very braine,
And her proud person low prostrated on the plaine.

34

Where being layd, the wrothfull Britonesse
  Stayd not, till she came to her selfe againe,
  But in revenge both of her loves distresse,
  And her late vile reproch, though vaunted vaine,
  And also of her wound, which sore did paine,
  She with one stroke both head and helmet cleft.
  Which dreadfull sight, when all her warlike traine
  There present saw, each one of sence bereft,
Fled fast into the towne, and her sole victor left.

35

But yet so fast they could not home retrate,
  But that swift *Talus* did the formost win;
  And pressing through the preace unto the gate,
  Pelmell with them attonce did enter in.
  There then a piteous slaughter did begin:
  For all that ever came within his reach,
  He with his yron flale did thresh so thin,
  That he no worke at all left for the leach:
Like to an hideous storme, which nothing may empeach.

36

And now by this the noble Conqueresse
  Her selfe came in, her glory to partake;
  Where though revengefull vow she did professe,
  Yet when she saw the heapes, which he did make,
  Of slaughtred carkasses, her heart did quake
  For very ruth, which did it almost rive,
  That she his fury willed him to slake:
  For else he sure had left not one alive,
But all in his revenge of spirite would deprive.

37

Tho when she had his execution stayd,
  She for that yron prison did enquire,
  In which her wretched love was captive layd:
  Which breaking open with indignant ire,
  She entred into all the partes entire.
  Where when she saw that lothly uncouth sight,
  Of men disguiz'd in womanishe attire,
  Her heart gan grudge, for very deepe despight
Of so unmanly maske, in misery misdight.

38

At last when as to her owne Love she came,
  Whom like disguize no lesse deformed had,
  At sight thereof abasht with secrete shame,
  She turnd her head aside, as nothing glad,
  To have beheld a spectacle so bad:
  And then too well beleev'd, that which tofore
  Jealous suspect as true untruely drad,
  Which vaine conceipt now nourishing no more,
She sought with ruth to salve his sad misfortunes sore.

39

Not so great wonder and astonishment,
　　Did the most chast *Penelope* possesse,
　　To see her Lord, that was reported drent,
　　And dead long since in dolorous distresse,
　　Come home to her in piteous wretchednesse,
　　After long travell of full twenty yeares,
　　That she knew not his favours likelynesse,
　　For many scarres and many hoary heares,
But stood long staring on him, mongst uncertaine feares.

40

Ah my deare Lord, what sight is this (quoth she)
　　What May-game hath misfortune made of you?
　　Where is that dreadfull manly looke? where be
　　Those mighty palmes, the which ye wont t'embrew
　　In bloud of Kings, and great hoastes to subdew?
　　Could ought on earth so wondrous change have wrought,
　　As to have robde you of that manly hew?
　　Could so great courage stouped have to ought?
Then farewell fleshly force; I see thy pride is nought.

41

Thenceforth she streight into a bowre him brought,
　　And causd him those uncomely weedes undight;
　　And in their steede for other rayment sought,
　　Whereof there was great store, and armors bright,
　　Which had bene reft from many a noble Knight;
　　Whom that proud Amazon subdewed had,
　　Whilest Fortune favourd her successe in fight,
　　In which when as she him anew had clad,
She was reviv'd, and joyd much in his semblance glad.

42

So there a while they afterwards remained,
　　Him to refresh, and her late wounds to heale:
　　During which space she there as Princess rained,
　　And changing all that forme of common weale,
　　The liberty of women did repeale,
　　Which they had long usurpt; and them restoring
　　To mens subjection, did true Justice deale:
　　That all they as a Goddesse her adoring,
Her wisedome did admire, and hearkned to her loring.

43

For all those Knights, which long in captive shade
  Had shrowded bene, she did from thraldome free;
  And magistrates of all that city made,
  And gave to them great living and large fee:
  And that they should for ever faithfull bee,
  Made them sweare fealty to *Artegall*.
  Who when him selfe now well recur'd did see,
  He purposd to proceed, what so be fall,
Uppon his first adventure, which him forth did call.

44

Full sad and sorrowfull was *Britomart*
  For his departure, her new cause of griefe;
  Yet wisely moderated her owne smart,
  Seeing his honor, which she tendred chiefe,
  Consisted much in that adventures priefe.
  The care whereof, and hope of his successe
  Gave unto her great comfort and reliefe,
  That womanish complaints she did represse,
And tempred for the time her present heavinesse.

45

There she continu'd for a certaine space,
  Till through his want her woe did more increase:
  Then hoping that the change of aire and place
  Would change her paine, and sorrow somewhat ease,
  She parted thence, her anguish to appease.
  Meane while her noble Lord sir *Artegall*
  Went on his way, ne ever howre did cease,
  Till he redeemed had that Lady thrall:
That for another Canto will more fitly fall.

CANT. VIII

Prince Arthure and Sir Artegall,
  Free Samient from feare:
They slay the Souldan, drive his wife,
  Adicia to despaire.

1

NOUGHT under heaven so strongly doth allure
  The sence of man, and all his minde possesse,
  As beauties lovely baite, that doth procure
  Great warriours oft their rigour to represse,
  And mighty hands forget their manlinesse;
  Drawne with the powre of an heart-robbing eye,
  And wrapt in fetters of a golden tresse,
  That can with melting pleasaunce mollifye
Their hardned hearts, enur'd to bloud and cruelty.

2

So whylome learnd that mighty Jewish swaine,
  Each of whose lockes did match a man in might,
  To lay his spoiles before his lemans traine:
  So also did that great Oetean Knight
  For his loves sake his Lions skin undight:
  And so did warlike *Antony* neglect
  The worlds whole rule for *Cleopatras* sight.
  Such wondrous powre hath wemens faire aspect,
To captive men, and make them all the world reject.

3

Yet could it not sterne *Artegall* retaine,
  Nor hold from suite of his avowed quest,
  Which he had undertane to *Gloriane*;
  But left his love, albe her strong request,
  Faire *Britomart* in languor and unrest,
  And rode him selfe uppon his first intent:
  Ne day nor night did ever idly rest;
  Ne wight but onely *Talus* with him went,
The true guide of his way and vertuous government.

4

So travelling, he chaunst far off to heed
  A Damzell, flying on a palfrey fast
  Before two Knights, that after her did speed
  With all their powre, and her full fiercely chast
  In hope to have her overhent at last:
  Yet fled she fast, and both them farre outwent,
  Carried with wings of feare, like fowle aghast,
  With locks all loose, and rayment all to rent;
And ever as she rode, her eye was backeward bent.

5

Soone after these he saw another Knight,
  That after those two former rode apace,
  With speare in rest, and prickt with all his might:
  So ran they all, as they had bene at bace,
  They being chased, that did others chase.
  At length he saw the hindmost overtake
  One of those two, and force him turne his face;
  How ever loth he were his way to slake,
Yet mote he algates now abide, and answere make.

6

But th'other still pursu'd the fearefull Mayd;
  Who still from him as fast away did flie,
  Ne once for ought her speedy passage stayd,
  Till that at length she did before her spie
  Sir *Artegall*, to whom she streight did hie
  With gladfull hast, in hope of him to get
  Succour against her greedy enimy:
  Who seeing her approch gan forward set,
To save her from her feare, and him from force to let.

7

But he like hound full greedy of his pray,
  Being impatient of impediment,
  Continu'd still his course, and by the way
  Thought with his speare him quight have overwent.
  So both together ylike felly bent,
  Like fiercely met. But *Artegall* was stronger,
  And better skild in Tilt and Turnament,
  And bore him quite out of his saddle, longer
Than two speares length; So mischiefe overmatcht the wronger.

8

And in his fall misfortune him mistooke;
  For on his head unhappily he pight,
  That his owne waight his necke asunder broke,
  And left there dead. Meane while the other Knight
  Defeated had the other faytour quight,
  And all his bowels in his body brast:
  Whom leaving there in that dispiteous plight,
  He ran still on, thinking to follow fast
His other fellow Pagan, which before him past.

9

In stead of whom finding there ready prest
  Sir *Artegall*, without discretion
  He at him ran, with ready speare in rest:
  Who seeing him come still so fiercely on,
  Against him made againe. So both anon
  Together met, and strongly either strooke
  And broke their speares; yet neither has forgon
  His horses backe, yet to and fro long shooke,
And tottred like two towres, which through a tempest quooke.

10

But when againe they had recovered sence,
  They drew their swords, in mind to make amends
  For what their speares had fayld of their pretence.
  Which when the Damzell, who those deadly ends
  Of both her foes had seene, and now her frends
  For her beginning a more fearefull fray,
  She to them runnes in hast, and her haire rends,
  Crying to them their cruell hands to stay,
Until they both doe heare, what she to them will say.

11

They stayd their hands, when she thus gan to speake;
  Ah gentle Knights, what meane ye thus unwise
  Upon your selves anothers wrong to wreake?
  I am the wrong'd, whom ye did enterprise
  Both to redresse, and both redrest likewise:
  Witnesse the Paynims both, whom ye may see
  There dead on ground. What doe ye then devise
  Of more revenge? if more, then I am shee,
Which was the roote of all, end your revenge on mee.

12

Whom when they heard so say, they lookt about,
    To weete if it were true, as she had told;
    Where when they saw their foes dead out of doubt,
    Eftsoones they gan their wrothfull hands to hold,
    And Ventailes reare, each other to behold.
    Tho when as *Artegall* did *Arthure* vew,
    So faire a creature, and so wondrous bold,
    He much admired both his heart and hew,
And touched with intire affection, nigh him drew.

13

Saying, Sir Knight, of pardon I you pray,
    That all unweeting have you wrong'd thus sore,
    Suffring my hand against my heart to stray:
    Which if ye please forgive, I will therefore
    Yeeld for amends my selfe yours evermore,
    Or what so penaunce shall by you be red.
    To whom the Prince; Certes me needeth more
    To crave the same, whom errour so misled,
As that I did mistake the living for the ded.

14

But sith ye please, that both our blames shall die,
    Amends may for the trespasse soone be made,
    Since neither is endamadg'd much thereby.
    So can they both them selves full eath perswade
    To faire accordaunce, and both faults to shade,
    Either embracing other lovingly,
    And swearing faith to either on his blade,
    Never thenceforth to nourish enmity,
But either others cause to maintaine mutually.

15

Then *Artegall* gan of the Prince enquire,
    What were those knights, which there on ground were layd,
    And had receiv'd their follies worthy hire,
    And for what cause they chased so that Mayd.
    Certes I wote not well (the Prince then sayd)
    But by adventure found them faring so,
    As by the way unweetingly I strayd,
    And lo the Damzell selfe, whence all did grow,
Of whom we may at will the whole occasion know.

16

Then they that Damzell called to them nie,
　　And asked her, what were those two her fone,
　　From whom she earst so fast away did flie;
　　And what was she her selfe so woe begone,
　　And for what cause pursu'd of them attone.
　　To whom she thus; Then wote ye well, that I
　　Doe serve a Queene, that not far hence doth wone,
　　A Princesse of great powre and majestie,
Famous through all the world, and honor'd far and nie.

17

Her name *Mercilla* most men use to call;
　　That is a mayden Queene of high renowne,
　　For her great bounty knowen over all,
　　And soveraine grace, with which her royall crowne
　　She doth support, and strongly beateth downe
　　The malice of her foes, which her envy,
　　And at her happinesse do fret and frowne:
　　Yet she her selfe the more doth magnify,
And even to her foes her mercies multiply.

18

Mongst many which maligne her happy state,
　　There is a mighty man, which wonnes here by
　　That with most fell despight and deadly hate,
　　Seekes to subvert her Crowne and dignity,
　　And all his powre doth thereunto apply:
　　And her good Knights, of which so brave a band
　　Serves her, as any Princesse under sky,
　　He either spoiles, if they against him stand,
Or to his part allures, and bribeth under hand.

19

Ne him sufficeth all the wrong and ill,
　　Which he unto her people does each day,
　　But that he seekes by traytrous traines to spill
　　Her person, and her sacred selfe to slay:
　　That O ye heavens defend, and turne away
　　From her, unto the miscreant him selfe,
　　That neither hath religion nor fay,
　　But makes his God of his ungodly pelfe,
And Idols serves; so let his Idols serve the Elfe.

20

To all which cruell tyranny they say,
   He is provokt, and stird up day and night
   By his bad wife, that hight *Adicia*,
   Who counsels him through confidence of might,
   To breake all bonds of law, and rules of right.
   For she her selfe professeth mortall foe
   To Justice, and against her still doth fight,
   Working to all, that love her, deadly woe,
And making all her Knights and people to doe so.

21

Which my liege Lady seeing, thought it best,
   With that his wife in friendly wise to deale,
   For stint of strife, and stablishment of rest
   Both to her selfe, and to her common weale,
   And all forepast displeasures to repeale.
   So me in message unto her she sent,
   To treat with her by way of enterdeale,
   Of finall peace and faire attonement,
Which might concluded be by mutuall consent.

22

All times have wont safe passage to afford
   To messengers, that come for causes just:
   But this proude Dame disdayning all accord,
   Not onely into bitter termes forth brust,
   Reviling me, and rayling as she lust,
   But lastly to make proofe of utmost shame,
   Me like a dog she out of dores did thrust,
   Miscalling me by many a bitter name,
That never did her ill, ne once deserved blame.

23

And lastly, that no shame might wanting be,
   When I was gone, soone after me she sent
   These two false Knights, whom there ye lying see,
   To be by them dishonoured and shent:
   But thankt be God, and your good hardiment,
   They have the price of their owne folly payd.
   So said this Damzell, that hight *Samient*,
   And to those knights, for their so noble ayd,
Her selfe most gratefull shew'd, and heaped thanks repayd.

24

But they now having throughly heard, and seene
　　Al those great wrongs, the which that mayd complained
　　To have bene done against her Lady Queene,
　　By that proud dame, which her so much disdained,
　　Were moved much thereat, and twixt them fained,
　　With all their force to worke avengement strong
　　Uppon the Souldan selfe, which it mayntained,
　　And on his Lady, th'author of that wrong,
And uppon all those Knights, that did to her belong.

25

But thinking best by counterfet disguise
　　To their deseigne to make the easier way,
　　They did this complot twixt them selves devise,
　　First, that sir *Artegall* should him array,
　　Like one of those two Knights, which dead there lay.
　　And then that Damzell, the sad *Samient*,
　　Should as his purchast prize with him convay
　　Unto the Souldans court, her to present
Unto his scornefull Lady, that for her had sent.

26

So as they had deviz'd, sir *Artegall*
　　Him clad in th'armour of a Pagan knight,
　　And taking with him, as his vanquisht thrall,
　　That Damzell, led her to the Souldans right.
　　Where soone as his proud wife of her had sight,
　　Forth of her window as she looking lay,
　　She weened streight, it was her Paynim Knight,
　　Which brought that Damzell, as his purchast pray;
And sent to him a Page, that mote direct his way.

27

Who bringing them to their appointed place,
　　Offred his service to disarme the Knight;
　　But he refusing him to let unlace,
　　For doubt to be discovered by his sight,
　　Kept himselfe still in his straunge armour dight.
　　Soone after whom the Prince arrived there,
　　And sending to the Souldan in despight
　　A bold defyance, did of him requere
That Damzell, whom he held as wrongfull prisonere.

28

Wherewith the Souldan all with furie fraught,
  Swearing, and banning most blasphemously,
  Commaunded straight his armour to be brought,
  And mounting straight upon a charret hye,
  With yron wheeles and hookes arm'd dreadfully,
  And drawne of cruell steedes, which he had fed
  With flesh of men, whom through fell tyranny
  He slaughtred had, and ere they were halfe ded,
Their bodies to his beasts for provender did spred.

29

So forth he came all in a cote of plate,
  Burnisht with bloudie rust, whiles on the greene
  The Briton Prince him readie did awayte,
  In glistering armes right goodly well beseene,
  That shone as bright, as doth the heaven sheene;
  And by his stirrup *Talus* did attend,
  Playing his pages part, as he had beene
  Before directed by his Lord; to th'end
He should his flale to finall execution bend.

30

Thus goe they both together to their geare,
  With like fierce minds, but meanings different:
  For the proud Souldan with presumpteous cheare,
  And countenance sublime and insolent,
  Sought onely slaughter and avengement:
  But the brave Prince for honour and for right,
  Gainst tortious powre and lawlesse regiment,
  In the behalfe of wronged weake did fight:
More in his causes truth he trusted than in might.

31

Like to the *Thracian* Tyrant, who they say
  Unto his horses gave his guests for meat,
  Till he himselfe was made their greedie pray,
  And torne in peeces by *Alcides* great.
  So thought the Souldan in his follies threat,
  Either the Prince in peeces to have torne
  With his sharpe wheeles, in his first rages heat,
  Or under his fierce horses feet have borne
And trampled downe in dust his thoughts disdained scorne.

32

But the bold child that perill well espying,
  If he too rashly to his charet drew,
  Gave way unto his horses speedie flying,
  And their resistlesse rigour did eschew.
  Yet as he passed by, the Pagan threw
  A shivering dart with so impetuous force,
  That had he not it shun'd with heedfull vew,
  It had himselfe transfixed, or his horse,
Or made them both one masse withouten more remorse.

33

Oft drew the Prince unto his charret nigh,
  In hope some stroke to fasten on him neare;
  But he was mounted in his seat so high,
  And his wingfooted coursers him did beare
  So fast away, that ere his readie speare
  He could advance, he farre was gone and past.
  Yet still he him did follow every where,
  And followed was of him likewise full fast;
So long as in his steedes the flaming breath did last.

34

Againe the Pagan threw another dart,
  Of which he had with him abundant store,
  On every side of his embatteld cart,
  And of all other weapons lesse or more,
  Which warlike uses had deviz'd of yore.
  The wicked shaft guyded through th'ayrie wyde,
  By some bad spirit, that it to mischiefe bore,
  Stayd not, till through his curat it did glyde,
And made a griesly wound in his enriven side.

35

Much was he grieved with that haplesse throe,
  That opened had the welspring of his blood;
  But much the more that to his hatefull foe
  He mote not come, to wreake his wrathfull mood.
  That made him rave, like to a Lyon wood,
  Which being wounded of the huntsmans hand
  Can not come neare him in the covert wood,
  Where he with boughes hath built his shady stand,
And fenst himselfe about with many a flaming brand.

36

Still when he sought t'approch unto him ny,
　His charret wheeles about him whirled round,
　And made him backe againe as fast to fly;
　And eke his steedes like to an hungry hound,
　That hunting after game hath carrion found,
　So cruelly did him pursew and chace,
　That his good steed, all were he much renound
　For noble courage, and for hardie race,
Durst not endure their sight, but fled from place to place.

37

Thus long they trast, and traverst to and fro,
　Seeking by every way to make some breach,
　Yet could the Prince not nigh unto him goe,
　That one sure stroke he might unto him reach,
　Whereby his strengthes assay he might him teach.
　At last from his victorious shield he drew
　The vaile, which did his powrefull light empeach;
　And comming full before his horses vew,
As they upon him prest, it plaine to them did shew.

38

Like lightening flash, that hath the gazer burned,
　So did the sight thereof their sense dismay,
　That backe againe upon themselves they turned,
　And with their ryder ranne perforce away:
　Ne could the Souldan them from flying stay,
　With raynes, or wonted rule, as well he knew.
　Nought feared they, what he could do, or say,
　But th'onely feare, that was before their vew;
From which like mazed deare, dismayfully they flew.

39

Fast did they fly, as them their feete could beare,
　High over hilles, and lowly over dales,
　As they were follow'd of their former feare.
　In vaine the Pagan bannes, and sweares, and rayles,
　And backe with both his hands unto him hayles
　The resty raynes, regarded now no more:
　He to them calles and speakes, yet nought avayles;
　They heare him not, they have forgot his lore,
But go, which way they list, their guide they have forlore.

40

As when the firie-mouthed steeds, which drew
　The Sunnes bright wayne to *Phaetons* decay,
　Soone as they did the monstrous Scorpion vew,
　With ugly craples crawling in their way,
　The dreadfull sight did them so sore affray,
　That their well knowen courses they forwent,
　And leading th'ever-burning lampe astray,
　This lower world nigh all to ashes brent,
And left their scorched path yet in the firmament.

41

Such was the furie of these head-strong steeds,
　Soone as the infants sunlike shield they saw,
　That all obedience both to words and deeds
　They quite forgot, and scornd all former law;
　Through woods, and rocks, and mountaines they did draw
　The yron charet, and the wheeles did teare,
　And tost the Paynim, without feare or awe;
　From side to side they tost him here and there,
Crying to them in vaine, that nould his crying heare.

42

Yet still the Prince pursew'd him close behind,
　Oft making offer him to smite, but found
　No easie meanes according to his mind.
　At last they have all overthrowne to ground
　Quite topside turvey, and the pagan hound
　Amongst the yron hookes and graples keene,
　Torne all to rags, and rent with many a wound,
　That no whole peece of him was to be seene,
But scattred all about, and strow'd upon the greene.

43

Like as the cursed sonne of *Theseus*,
　That following his chace in dewy morne,
　To fly his stepdames loves outrageous,
　Of his owne steedes was all to peeces torne,
　And his faire limbs left in the woods forlorne;
　That for his sake *Diana* did lament,
　And all the wooddy Nymphes did wayle and mourne.
　So was this Souldan rapt and all to rent,
That of his shape appear'd no litle moniment.

44

Onely his shield and armour, which there lay,
　Though nothing whole, but all to brusd and broken,
He up did take, and with him brought away,
　That mote remaine for an eternall token
To all, mongst whom this storie should be spoken,
　How worthily, by heavens high decree,
　Justice that day of wrong her selfe had wroken,
　That all men which that spectacle did see,
By like ensample mote for ever warned bee.

45

So on a tree, before the Tyrants dore,
　He caused them be hung in all mens sight,
To be a moniment for evermore.
　Which when his Ladie from the castles hight
Beheld, it much appald her troubled spright:
　Yet not, as women wont in dolefull fit,
　She was dismayd, or faynted through affright,
　But gathered unto her her troubled wit,
And gan eftsoones devize to be aveng'd for it.

46

Streight downe she ranne, like an enraged cow,
　That is berobbed of her youngling dere,
With knife in hand, and fatally did vow,
　To wreake her on that mayden messengere,
Whom she had causd be kept as prisonere,
　By *Artegall*, misween'd for her owne Knight,
　That brought her backe. And comming present there,
　She at her ran with all her force and might,
All flaming with revenge and furious despight.

47

Like raging *Ino*, when with knife in hand
　She threw her husbands murdred infant out,
Or fell *Medea*, when on *Colchicke* strand
　Her brothers bones she scattered all about;
Or as that madding mother, mongst the rout
　Of *Bacchus* Priests her owne deare flesh did teare.
　Yet neither *Ino*, nor *Medea* stout,
　Nor all the *Mænades* so furious were,
As this bold woman, when she saw that Damzell there.

48

But *Artegall* being thereof aware,
　Did stay her cruell hand, ere she her raught,
　And as she did her selfe to strike prepare,
　Out of her fist the wicked weapon caught:
　With that like one enfelon'd or distraught,
　She forth did rome, whether her rage her bore,
　With franticke passion, and with furie fraught;
　And breaking forth out at a posterne dore,
Unto the wyld wood ranne, her dolours to deplore.

49

As a mad bytch, when as the franticke fit
　Her burning tongue with rage inflamed hath,
　Doth runne at randon, and with furious bit
　Snatching at every thing, doth wreake her wrath
　On man and beast, that commeth in her path.
　There they doe say, that she transformed was
　Into a Tygre, and that Tygres scath
　In crueltie and outrage she did pas,
To prove her surname true, that she imposed has.

50

Then *Artegall* himselfe discovering plaine,
　Did issue forth gainst all that warlike rout
　Of knights and armed men, which did maintaine
　That Ladies part, and to the Souldan lout:
　All which he did assault with courage stout,
　All were they nigh an hundred knights of name,
　And like wyld Goates them chaced all about,
　Flying from place to place with cowheard shame,
So that with finall force them all he overcame.

51

Then caused he the gates be opened wyde,
　And there the Prince, as victour of that day,
　With tryumph entertayn'd and glorifyde,
　Presenting him with all the rich array,
　And roiall pompe, which there long hidden lay,
　Purchast through lawlesse powre and tortious wrong
　Of that proud Souldan, whom he earst did slay.
　So both for rest there having stayd not long,
Marcht with that mayd, fit matter for another song.

CANT. IX

Arthur and Artegall catch Guyle
whom Talus doth dismay,
They to Mercillaes pallace come,
and see her rich array.

1

WHAT Tygre, or what other salvage wight
  Is so exceeding furious and fell,
  As wrong, when it hath arm'd it selfe with might?
  Not fit mongst men, that doe with reason mell,
  But mongst wyld beasts and salvage woods to dwell;
  Where still the stronger doth the weake devoure,
  And they that most in boldnesse doe excell,
  Are dreadded most, and feared for their powre:
Fit for *Adicia*, there to build her wicked bowre.

2

There let her wonne farre from resort of men,
  Where righteous *Artegall* her late exyled;
  There let her ever keepe her damned den,
  Where none may be with her lewd parts defyled,
  Nor none but beasts may be of her despoyled:
  And turne we to the noble Prince, where late
  We did him leave, after that he had foyled
  The cruell Souldan, and with dreadfull fate
Had utterly subverted his unrighteous state.

3

Where having with Sir *Artegall* a space
  Well solast in that Souldans late delight,
  They both resolving now to leave the place,
  Both it and all the wealth therein behight
  Unto that Damzell in her Ladies right,
  And so would have departed on their way.
  But she them woo'd by all the meanes she might,
  And earnestly besought, to wend that day
With her, to see her Ladie thence not farre away.

4

By whose entreatie both they overcommen,
  Agree to goe with her, and by the way,
  (As often falles) of sundry things did commen.
  Mongst which that Damzell did to them bewray
  A straunge adventure, which not farre thence lay;
  To weet a wicked villaine, bold and stout,
  Which wonned in a rocke not farre away,
  That robbed all the countrie there about,
And brought the pillage home, whence none could get it out.

5

Thereto both his owne wylie wit, (she sayd)
  And eke the fastnesse of his dwelling place,
  Both unassaylable, gave him great ayde:
  For he so crafty was to forge and face,
  So light of hand, and nymble of his pace,
  So smooth of tongue, and subtile in his tale,
  That could deceive one looking in his face;
  Therefore by name *Malengin* they him call,
Well knowen by his feates, and famous over all.

6

Through these his slights he many doth confound,
  And eke the rocke, in which he wonts to dwell,
  Is wondrous strong, and hewen farre under ground
  A dreadfull depth, how deepe no man can tell;
  But some doe say, it goeth downe to hell.
  And all within, it full of wyndings is,
  And hidden wayes, that scarse an hound by smell
  Can follow out those false footsteps of his,
Ne none can backe returne, that once are gone amis.

7

Which when those knights had heard, their harts gan earne,
  To understand that villeins dwelling place,
  And greatly it desir'd of her to learne,
  And by which way they towards it should trace.
  Were not (sayd she) that it should let your pace
  Towards my Ladies presence by you ment,
  I would you guyde directly to the place.
  Then let not that (said they) stay your intent;
For neither will one foot, till we that carle have hent.

8

So forth they past, till they approched ny
  Unto the rocke, where was the villains won,
  Which when the Damzell neare at hand did spy,
  She warn'd the knights thereof: who thereupon
  Gan to advize, what best were to be done.
  So both agreed, to send that mayd afore,
  Where she might sit nigh to the den alone,
  Wayling, and raysing pittifull uprore,
As if she did some great calamitie deplore.

9

With noyse whereof when as the caytive carle
  Should issue forth, in hope to find some spoyle,
  They in awayt would closely him ensnarle,
  Ere to his den he backward could recoyle,
  And so would hope him easily to foyle.
  The Damzell straight went, as she was directed,
  Unto the rocke, and there upon the soyle
  Having her selfe in wretched wize abjected,
Gan weepe and wayle, as if great griefe had her affected.

10

The cry whereof entring the hollow cave,
  Eftsoones brought forth the villaine, as they ment,
  With hope of her some wishfull boot to have.
  Full dreadfull wight he was, as ever went
  Upon the earth, with hollow eyes deepe pent,
  And long curld locks, that downe his shoulders shagged,
  And on his backe an uncouth vestiment
  Made of straunge stuffe, but all to worne and ragged,
And underneath his breech was all to torne and jagged.

11

And in his hand an huge long staffe he held,
  Whose top was arm'd with many an yron hooke,
  Fit to catch hold of all that he could weld,
  Or in the compasse of his clouches tooke;
  And ever round about he cast his looke.
  Als at his backe a great wyde net he bore,
  With which he seldome fished at the brooke,
  But usd to fish for fooles on the dry shore,
Of which he in faire weather wont to take great store.

12

Him when the damzell saw fast by her side,
  So ugly creature, she was nigh dismayd,
  And now for helpe aloud in earnest cride.
  But when the villaine saw her so affrayd,
  He gan with guilefull words her to perswade,
  To banish feare, and with *Sardonian* smyle
  Laughing on her, his false intent to shade,
  Gan forth to lay his bayte her to beguyle,
That from her self unwares he might her steale the whyle.

13

Like as the fouler on his guilefull pype
  Charmes to the birds full many a pleasant lay,
  That they the whiles may take lesse heedie keepe,
  How he his nets doth for their ruine lay:
  So did the villaine to her prate and play,
  And many pleasant trickes before her show,
  To turne her eyes from his intent away:
  For he in slights and jugling feates did flow,
And of legierdemayne the mysteries did know.

14

To which whilest she lent her intentive mind,
  He suddenly his net upon her threw,
  That oversprad her like a puffe of wind;
  And snatching her soone up, ere well she knew,
  Ran with her fast away unto his mew,
  Crying for helpe aloud. But when as ny
  He came unto his cave, and there did vew
  The armed knights stopping his passage by,
He threw his burden downe, and fast away did fly.

15

But *Artegall* him after did pursew,
  The whiles the Prince there kept the entrance still:
  Up to the rocke he ran, and thereon flew
  Like a wyld Gote, leaping from hill to hill,
  And dauncing on the craggy cliffes at will;
  That deadly daunger seem'd in all mens sight,
  To tempt such steps, where footing was so ill:
  Ne ought avayled for the armed knight,
To thinke to follow him, that was so swift and light.

16

Which when he saw, his yron man he sent,
  To follow him; for he was swift in chace.
He him pursewd, where ever that he went,
  Both over rockes, and hilles, and every place,
  Where so he fled, he followd him apace:
So that he shortly forst him to forsake
  The hight, and downe descend unto the base.
There he him courst a fresh, and soone did make
To leave his proper forme, and other shape to take.

17

Into a Foxe himselfe he first did tourne;
  But he him hunted like a Foxe full fast:
Then to a bush himselfe he did transforme,
  But he the bush did beat, till that at last
  Into a bird it chaung'd, and from him past,
Flying from tree to tree, from wand to wand:
  But he then stones at it so long did cast,
That like a stone it fell upon the land,
But he then tooke it up, and held fast in his hand.

18

So he it brought with him unto the knights,
  And to his Lord Sir *Artegall* it lent,
Warning him hold it fast, for feare of slights.
  Who whilest in hand it gryping hard he hent,
  Into a Hedgehogge all unwares it went,
And prickt him so, that he away it threw.
  Then gan it runne away incontinent,
Being returned to his former hew:
But *Talus* soone him overtooke, and backward drew.

19

But when as he would to a snake againe
  Have turn'd himselfe, he with his yron flayle
Gan drive at him, with so huge might and maine,
  That all his bones, as small as sandy grayle
  He broke, and did his bowels disentrayle;
Crying in vaine for helpe, when helpe was past.
  So did deceipt the selfe deceiver fayle,
There they him left a carrion outcast;
For beasts and foules to feede upon for their repast.

20

Thence forth they passed with that gentle Mayd,
  To see her Ladie, as they did agree.
  To which when she approched, thus she sayd;
  Loe now, right noble knights, arriv'd ye bee
  Nigh to the place, which ye desir'd to see:
  There shall ye see my soverayne Lady Queene
  Most sacred wight, most debonayre and free,
  That ever yet upon this earth was seene,
Or that with Diademe hath ever crowned beene.

21

The gentle knights rejoyced much to heare
  The prayses of that Prince so manifold,
  And passing litle further, commen were,
  Where they a stately pallace did behold,
  Of pompous show, much more than she had told;
  With many towres, and tarras mounted hye,
  And all their tops bright glistering with gold,
  That seemed to outshine the dimmed skye,
And with their brightnesse daz'd the straunge beholders eye.

22

There they alighting, by that Damzell were
  Directed in, and shewed all the sight:
  Whose porch, that most magnificke did appeare,
  Stood open wyde to all men day and night;
  Yet warded well by one of mickle might,
  That sate thereby, with gyantlike resemblance,
  To keepe out guyle, and malice, and despight,
  That under shew oftimes of fayned semblance,
Are wont in Princes courts to worke great scath and hindrance.

23

His name was *Awe*; by whom they passing in
  Went up the hall, that was a large wyde roome,
  All full of people making troublous din,
  And wondrous noyse, as if that there were some,
  Which unto them was dealing righteous doome.
  By whom they passing, through the thickest preasse,
  The marshall of the hall to them did come;
  His name hight *Order*, who commaunding peace,
Them guyded through the throng, that did their clamors ceasse.

24

They ceast their clamors upon them to gaze;
  Whom seeing all in armour bright as day,
  Straunge there to see, it did them much amaze,
  And with unwonted terror halfe affray.
  For never saw they there the like array,
  Ne ever was the name of warre there spoken,
  But joyous peace and quietnesse alway,
  Dealing just judgements, that mote not be broken
For any brybes, or threates of any to be wroken.

25

There as they entred at the Scriene, they saw
  Some one, whose tongue was for his trespasse vyle
  Nayld to a post, adjudged so by law:
  For that therewith he falsely did revyle,
  And foule blaspheme that Queene for forged guyle,
  Both with bold speaches, which he blazed had,
  And with lewd poems, which he did compyle;
  For the bold title of a Poet bad
He on himselfe had ta'en, and rayling rymes had sprad.

26

Thus there he stood, whylest high over his head,
  There written was the purport of his sin,
  In cyphers strange, that few could rightly read,
  BONFONT: but *bon* that once had written bin,
  Was raced out, and *Mal* was now put in.
  So now *Malfont* was plainely to be red;
  Eyther for th'evill, which he did therein,
  Or that he likened was to a welhed
Of evill words, and wicked sclaunders by him shed.

27

They passing by, were guyded by degree
  Unto the presence of that gratious Queene:
  Who sate on high, that she might all men see,
  And might of all men royally be seene,
  Upon a throne of gold full bright and sheene,
  Adorned all with gemmes of endlesse price,
  As either might for wealth have gotten bene,
  Or could be fram'd by workmans rare device;
And all embost with Lyons and with Flourdelice.

28

All over her a cloth of state was spred,
　Not of rich tissew, nor of cloth of gold,
　Nor of ought else, that may be richest red,
　But like a cloud, as likest may be told,
　That her brode spreading wings did wyde unfold;
　Whose skirts were bordred with bright sunny beams,
　Glistring like gold, amongst the plights enrold,
　And here and there shooting forth silver streames,
Mongst which crept litle Angels through the glittering gleames.

29

Seemed those litle Angels did uphold
　The cloth of state, and on their purpled wings
　Did beare the pendants, through their nimblesse bold:
　Besides a thousand more of such, as sings
　Hymnes to high God, and carols heavenly things,
　Encompassed the throne, on which she sate:
　She Angel-like, the heyre of ancient kings
　And mightie Conquerors, in royall state,
Whylest kings and kesars at her feet did them prostrate.

30

Thus she did sit in soverayne Majestie,
　Holding a Scepter in her royall hand,
　The sacred pledge of peace and clemencie,
　With which high God had blest her happie land,
　Maugre so many foes, which did withstand.
　But at her feet her sword was likewise layde,
　Whose long rest rusted the bright steely brand;
　Yet when as foes enforst, or friends sought ayde,
She could it sternely draw, that all the world dismayde.

31

And round about, before her feet there sate
　A bevie of faire Virgins clad in white,
　That goodly seem'd t'adorne her royall state,
　All lovely daughters of high *Jove*, that hight
　Litæ, by him begot in loves delight,
　Upon the righteous *Themis*: those they say
　Upon *Joves* judgement seat wayt day and night,
　And when in wrath he threats the worlds decay,
They doe his anger calme, and cruell vengeance stay.

32

They also doe by his divine permission
  Upon the thrones of mortall Princes tend,
  And often treat for pardon and remission
  To suppliants, through frayltie which offend.
  Those did upon *Mercillaes* throne attend:
  Just *Dice*, wise *Eunomie*, myld *Eirene*,
  And them amongst, her glorie to commend,
  Sate goodly *Temperance* in garments clene,
And sacred *Reverence*, yborne of heavenly strene.

33

Thus did she sit in royall rich estate,
  Admyr'd of many, honoured of all,
  Whylest underneath her feete, thereas she sate,
  An huge great Lyon lay, that mote appall
  An hardie courage, like captived thrall,
  With a strong yron chaine and coller bound,
  That once he could not move, nor quich at all;
  Yet did he murmure with rebellious sound,
And softly royne, when salvage choler gan redound.

34

So sitting high in dreaded soverayntie,
  Those two strange knights were to her presence brought;
  Who bowing low before her Majestie,
  Did to her mylde obeysance, as they ought,
  And meekest boone, that they imagine mought.
  To whom she eke inclyning her withall,
  As a faire stoupe of her high soaring thought,
  A chearefull countenance on them let fall,
Yet tempred with some majestie imperiall.

35

As the bright sunne, what time his fierie teme
  Towards the westerne brim begins to draw,
  Gins to abate the brightnesse of his beme,
  And fervour of his flames somewhat adaw:
  So did this mightie Ladie, when she saw
  Those two strange knights such homage to her make,
  Bate somewhat of that Majestie and awe,
  That whylome wont to doe so many quake,
And with more myld aspect those two to entertake.

36

Now at that instant, as occasion fell,
  When these two stranger knights arriv'd in place,
  She was about affaires of common wele,
  Dealing of Justice with indifferent grace,
  And hearing pleas of people meane and base.
  Mongst which as then, there was for to be heard
  The tryall of a great and weightie case,
  Which on both sides was then debating hard:
But at the sight of these, those were a while debard.

37

But after all her princely entertayne,
  To th'hearing of that former cause in hand,
  Her selfe eftsoones she gan convert againe;
  Which that those knights likewise mote understand,
  And witnesse forth aright in forrain land,
  Taking them up unto her stately throne,
  Where they mote heare the matter throughly scand
  On either part, she placed th'one on th'one,
The other on the other side, and neare them none.

38

Then was there brought, as prisoner to the barre,
  A Ladie of great countenance and place,
  But that she it with foule abuse did marre;
  Yet did appeare rare beautie in her face,
  But blotted with condition vile and base,
  That all her other honour did obscure,
  And titles of nobilitie deface:
  Yet in that wretched semblant, she did sure
The peoples great compassion unto her allure.

39

Then up arose a person of deepe reach,
  And rare in-sight, hard matters to revele;
  That well could charme his tongue, and time his speach
  To all assayes; his name was called *Zele*:
  He gan that Ladie strongly to appele
  Of many haynous crymes, by her enured,
  And with sharpe reasons rang her such a pele,
  That those, whom she to pitie had allured,
He now t'abhorre and loath her person had procured.

40

First gan he tell, how this that seem'd so faire
   And royally arayd, *Duessa* hight
   That false *Duessa*, which had wrought great care,
   And mickle mischiefe unto many a knight,
   By her beguyled, and confounded quight:
   But not for those she now in question came,
   Though also those mote question'd be aright,
   But for vyld treasons, and outrageous shame,
Which she against the dred *Mercilla* oft did frame.

41

For she whylome (as ye mote yet right well
   Remember) had her counsels false conspyred,
   With faithlesse *Blandamour* and *Paridell*,
   (Both two her paramours, both by her hyred,
   And both with hope of shadowes vaine inspyred,)
   And with them practiz'd, how for to depryve
   Mercilla of her crowne, by her aspyred,
   That she might it unto her selfe deryve,
And tryumph in their blood, whom she to death did dryve.

42

But through high heavens grace, which favour not
   The wicked driftes of trayterous desynes,
   Gainst loiall Princes, all this cursed plot,
   Ere proofe it tooke, discovered was betymes,
   And th'actours won the meede meet for their crymes.
   Such be the meede of all, that by such mene
   Unto the type of kingdomes title clymes.
   But false *Duessa* now untitled Queene,
Was brought to her sad doome, as here was to be seene.

43

Strongly did *Zele* her haynous fact enforce,
   And many other crimes of foule defame
   Against her brought, to banish all remorse,
   And aggravate the horror of her blame.
   And with him to make part against her, came
   Many grave persons, that against her pled;
   First was a sage old Syre, that had to name
   The *Kingdomes care*, with a white silver hed,
That many high regards and reasons gainst her red.

44

Then gan *Authority* her to appose
  With peremptorie powre, that made all mute;
  And then the law of *Nations* gainst her rose,
  And reasons brought, that no man could refute;
  Next gan *Religion* gainst her to impute
  High Gods beheast, and powre of holy lawes;
  Then gan the Peoples cry and Commons sute,
  Importune care of their owne publicke cause;
And lastly *Justice* charged her with breach of lawes.

45

But then for her, on the contrarie part,
  Rose many advocates for her to plead:
  First there came *Pittie*, with full tender hart,
  And with her joyn'd *Regard* of womanhead;
  And then came *Daunger* threatning hidden dread,
  And high alliance unto forren powre;
  Then came *Nobilitie* of birth, that bread
  Great ruth through her misfortunes tragicke stowre;
And lastly *Griefe* did plead, and many teares forth powre.

46

With the neare touch whereof in tender hart
  The Briton Prince was sore empassionate,
  And woxe inclined much unto her part,
  Through the sad terror of so dreadfull fate,
  And wretched ruine of so high estate,
  That for great ruth his courage gan relent.
  Which when as *Zele* perceived to abate,
  He gan his earnest fervour to augment,
And many fearefull objects to them to present.

47

He gan t'efforce the evidence anew,
  And new accusements to produce in place:
  He brought forth that old hag of hellish hew,
  The cursed *Ate*, brought her face to face,
  Who privie was, and partie in the case:
  She, glad of spoyle and ruinous decay,
  Did her appeach, and to her more disgrace,
  The plot of all her practise did display,
And all her traynes, and all her treasons forth did lay.

48

Then brought he forth, with griesly grim aspect,
　Abhorred *Murder*, who with bloudie knyfe
　Yet dropping fresh in hand did her detect,
　And there with guiltie bloudshed charged ryfe:
　Then brought he forth *Sedition*, breeding stryfe
　In troublous wits, and mutinous uprore:
　Then brought he forth *Incontinence* of lyfe,
　Even foule *Adulterie* her face before,
And lewd *Impietie*, that her accused sore.

49

All which when as the Prince had heard and seene,
　His former fancies ruth he gan repent,
　And from her partie eftsoones was drawen cleene.
　But *Artegall* with constant firme intent,
　For zeale of Justice was against her bent.
　So was she guiltie deemed of them all.
　Then *Zele* began to urge her punishment,
　And to their Queene for judgement loudly call,
Unto *Mercilla* myld for Justice gainst the thrall.

50

But she, whose Princely breast was touched nere
　With piteous ruth of her so wretched plight,
　Though plaine she saw by all, that she did heare,
　That she of death was guiltie found by right,
　Yet would not let just vengeance on her light;
　But rather let in stead thereof to fall
　Few perling drops from her faire lampes of light;
　The which she covering with her purple pall
Would have the passion hid, and up arose withall.

CANT. X

Prince Arthur takes the enterprize
for Belge for to fight.
Gerioneos Seneschall
he slayes in Belges right.

I

SOME Clarkes doe doubt in their devicefull art,
　　Whether this heavenly thing, whereof I treat,
　　To weeten *Mercie*, be of Justice part,
　　Or drawne forth from her by divine extreate.
　　This well I wote, that sure she is as great,
　　And meriteth to have as high a place,
　　Sith in th'Almighties everlasting seat
　　She first was bred, and borne of heavenly race;
From thence pour'd down on men, by influence of grace.

2

For if that Vertue be of so great might,
　　Which from just verdict will for nothing start,
　　But to preserve inviolated right,
　　Oft spilles the principall, to save the part;
　　So much more then is that of powre and art,
　　That seekes to save the subject of her skill,
　　Yet never doth from doome of right depart:
　　As it is greater prayse to save, than spill,
And better to reforme, than to cut off the ill.

3

Who then can thee, *Mercilla*, throughly prayse,
　　That herein doest all earthly Princes pas?
　　What heavenly Muse shall thy great honour rayse
　　Up to the skies, whence first deriv'd it was,
　　And now on earth it selfe enlarged has,
　　From th'utmost brinke of the *Armericke* shore,
　　Unto the margent of the *Molucas*?
　　Those Nations farre thy justice doe adore:
But thine owne people do thy mercy prayse much more.

4

Much more it praysed was of those two knights;
   The noble Prince, and righteous *Artegall*,
   When they had seene and heard her doome a rights
   Against *Duessa*, damned by them all;
   But by her tempred without griefe or gall,
   Till strong constraint did her thereto enforce.
   And yet even then ruing her wilfull fall,
   With more than needfull naturall remorse,
And yeelding the last honour to her wretched corse.

5

During all which, those knights continu'd there,
   Both doing and receiving curtesies,
   Of that great Ladie, who with goodly chere
   Them entertayn'd, fit for their dignities,
   Approving dayly to their noble eyes
   Royall examples of her mercies rare,
   And worthie paterns of her clemencies;
   Which till this day mongst many living are,
Who them to their posterities doe still declare.

6

Amongst the rest, which in that space befell,
   There came two Springals of full tender yeares,
   Farre thence from forrein land, where they did dwell,
   To seeke for succour of her and of her Peares,
   With humble prayers and intreatfull teares;
   Sent by their mother, who a widow was,
   Wrapt in great dolours and in deadly feares,
   By a strong Tyrant, who invaded has
Her land, and slaine her children ruefully alas.

7

Her name was *Belge*, who in former age
   A Ladie of great worth and wealth had beene,
   And mother of a frutefull heritage,
   Even seventeene goodly sonnes; which who had seene
   In their first flowre, before this fatall teene
   Them overtooke, and their faire blossomes blasted,
   More happie mother would her surely weene,
   Than famous *Niobe*, before she tasted
Latonaes childrens wrath, that all her issue wasted.

8

But this fell Tyrant, through his tortious powre,
　Had left her now but five of all that brood:
　For twelve of them he did by times devoure,
　And to his Idols sacrifice their blood,
　Whylest he of none was stopped, nor withstood.
　For soothly he was one of matchlesse might,
　Of horrible aspect, and dreadfull mood,
　And had three bodies in one wast empight,
And th'armes and legs of three, to succour him in fight.

9

And sooth they say, that he was borne and bred
　Of Gyants race, the sonne of *Geryon*,
　He that whylome in Spaine so sore was dred,
　For his huge powre and great oppression,
　Which brought that land to his subjection,
　Through his three bodies powre, in one combynd;
　And eke all strangers in that region
　Arryving, to his kyne for food assynd;
The fayrest kyne alive, but of the fiercest kynd.

10

For they were all, they say, of purple hew,
　Kept by a cowheard, hight *Eurytion*,
　A cruell carle, the which all strangers slew,
　Ne day nor night did sleepe, t'attend them on,
　But walkt about them ever and anone,
　With his two headed dogge, that *Orthrus* hight;
　Orthrus begotten by great *Typhaon*,
　And foule *Echidna*, in the house of night;
But *Hercules* them all did overcome in fight.

11

His sonne was this, *Geryoneo* hight,
　Who after that his monstrous father fell
　Under *Alcides* club, streight tooke his flight
　From that sad land, where he his syre did quell,
　And came to this, where *Belge* then did dwell,
　And flourish in all wealth and happinesse,
　Being then new made widow (as befell)
　After her Noble husbands late decesse;
Which gave beginning to her woe and wretchednesse.

12

Then this bold Tyrant, of her widowhed
  Taking advantage, and her yet fresh woes,
  Himselfe and service to her offered,
  Her to defend against all forrein foes,
  That should their powre against her right oppose.
  Whereof she glad, now needing strong defence,
  Him entertayn'd, and did her champion chose:
  Which long he usd with carefull diligence,
The better to confirme her fearelesse confidence.

13

By meanes whereof, she did at last commit
  All to his hands, and gave him soveraine powre
  To doe, what ever he thought good or fit.
  Which having got, he gan forth from that howre
  To stirre up strife, and many a Tragicke stowre,
  Giving her dearest children one by one
  Unto a dreadfull Monster to devoure,
  And setting up an Idole of his owne,
The image of his monstrous parent *Geryone*.

14

So tyrannizing, and oppressing all,
  The woefull widow had no meanes now left,
  But unto gratious great *Mercilla* call
  For ayde, against that cruell Tyrants theft,
  Ere all her children he from her had reft.
  Therefore these two, her eldest sonnes she sent,
  To seeke for succour of this Ladies gieft:
  To whom their sute they humbly did present,
In th'hearing of full many Knights and Ladies gent.

15

Amongst the which then fortuned to bee
  The noble Briton Prince, with his brave Peare;
  Who when he none of all those knights did see
  Hastily bent, that enterprise to heare,
  Nor undertake the same, for cowheard feare,
  He stepped forth with courage bold and great,
  Admyr'd of all the rest in presence there,
  And humbly gan that mightie Queene entreat,
To graunt him that adventure for his former feat.

16

She gladly graunted it: then he straight way
    Himselfe unto his journey gan prepare,
    And all his armours readie dight that day,
    That nought the morrow next mote stay his fare.
    The morrow next appear'd, with purple hayre
    Yet dropping fresh out of the *Indian* fount,
    And bringing light into the heavens fayre,
    When he was readie to his steede to mount,
Unto his way, which now was all his care and count.

17

Then taking humble leave of that great Queene,
    Who gave him roiall giftes and riches rare,
    As tokens of her thankefull mind beseene,
    And leaving *Artegall* to his owne care,
    Upon his voyage forth he gan to fare,
    With those two gentle youthes, which him did guide,
    And all his way before him still prepare.
    Ne after him did *Artegall* abide,
But on his first adventure forward forth did ride.

18

It was not long, till that the Prince arrived
    Within the land, where dwelt that Ladie sad,
    Whereof that Tyrant had her now deprived,
    And into moores and marshes banisht had,
    Out of the pleasant soyle, and citties glad,
    In which she wont to harbour happily:
    But now his cruelty so sore she drad,
    That to those fennes for fastnesse she did fly,
And there her selfe did hyde from his hard tyranny.

19

There he her found in sorrow and dismay,
    All solitarie without living wight;
    For all her other children, through affray,
    Had hid themselves, or taken further flight:
    And eke her selfe through sudden strange affright,
    When one in armes she saw, began to fly;
    But when her owne two sonnes she had in sight,
    She gan take hart, and looke up joyfully:
For well she wist this knight came, succour to supply.

20

And running unto them with greedy joyes,
  Fell straight about their neckes, as they did kneele,
  And bursting forth in teares; Ah my sweet boyes,
  (Sayd she) yet now I gin new life to feele,
  And feeble spirits, that gan faint and reele,
  Now rise againe, at this your joyous sight.
  Alreadie seemes that fortunes headlong wheele
  Begins to turne, and sunne to shine more bright,
Than it was wont, through comfort of this noble knight.

21

Then turning unto him; And you Sir knight
  (Said she) that taken have this toylesome paine
  For wretched woman, miserable wight,
  May you in heaven immortall guerdon gaine
  For so great travell, as you doe sustaine:
  For other meede may hope for none of mee,
  To whom nought else, but bare life doth remaine,
  And that so wretched one, as ye do see
Is liker lingring death, than loathed life to bee.

22

Much was he moved with her piteous plight,
  And low dismounting from his loftie steede,
  Gan to recomfort her all that he might,
  Seeking to drive away deepe rooted dreede,
  With hope of helpe in that her greatest neede.
  So thence he wished her with him to wend,
  Unto some place, where they mote rest and feede,
  And she take comfort, which God now did send:
Good hart in evils doth the evils much amend.

23

Ay me (sayd she) and whether shall I goe?
  Are not all places full of forraine powres?
  My pallaces possessed of my foe,
  My cities sackt, and their sky-threating towres
  Raced, and made smooth fields now full of flowres?
  Onely these marishes, and myrie bogs,
  In which the fearefull ewftes do build their bowres,
  Yeeld me an hostry mongst the croking frogs,
And harbour here in safety from those ravenous dogs.

24

Nathlesse (said he) deare Ladie with me goe,
  Some place shall us receive, and harbour yield;
  If not, we will it force, maugre your foe,
  And purchase it to us with speare and shield:
  And if all fayle, yet farewell open field:
  The earth to all her creatures lodging lends.
  With such his chearefull speaches he doth wield
  Her mind so well, that to his will she bends
And bynding up her locks and weeds, forth with him wends.

25

They came unto a Citie farre up land,
  The which whylome that Ladies owne had bene;
  But now by force extort out of her hand,
  By her strong foe, who had defaced cleene
  Her stately towres, and buildings sunny sheene;
  Shut up her haven, mard her marchants trade,
  Robbed her people, that full rich had beene,
  And in her necke a Castle huge had made,
The which did her commaund, without needing perswade.

26

That Castle was the strength of all that state,
  Untill that state by strength was pulled downe,
  And that same citie, so now ruinate,
  Had bene the keye of all that kingdomes crowne;
  Both goodly Castle, and both goodly Towne,
  Till that th'offended heavens list to lowre
  Upon their blisse, and balefull fortune frowne.
  When those gainst states and kingdomes do conjure,
Who then can thinke their hedlong ruine to recure.

27

But he had brought it now in servile bond,
  And made it beare the yoke of inquisition,
  Stryving long time in vaine it to withstond;
  Yet glad at last to make most base submission,
  And life enjoy for any composition.
  So now he hath new lawes and orders new
  Imposd on it, with many a hard condition,
  And forced it, the honour that is dew
To God, to doe unto his Idole most untrew.

28

To him he hath, before this Castle greene,
  Built a faire Chappell, and an Altar framed
  Of costly Ivory, full rich beseene,
  On which that cursed Idole farre proclamed,
  He hath set up, and him his God hath named,
  Offring to him in sinfull sacrifice
  The flesh of men, to Gods owne likenesse framed,
  And powring forth their bloud in brutishe wize,
That any yron eyes to see it would agrize.

29

And for more horror and more crueltie,
  Under that cursed Idols altar stone
  An hideous monster doth in darknesse lie,
  Whose dreadfull shape was never seene of none
  That lives on earth; but unto those alone
  The which unto him sacrificed bee.
  Those he devoures, they say, both flesh and bone:
  What else they have, is all the Tyrants fee;
So that no whit of them remayning one may see.

30

There eke he placed a strong garrisone,
  And set a Seneschall of dreaded might,
  That by his powre oppressed every one,
  And vanquished all ventrous knights in fight;
  To whom he wont shew all the shame he might,
  After that them in battell he had wonne.
  To which when now they gan approch in sight,
  The Ladie counseld him the place to shonne,
Whereas so many knights had fouly bene fordonne.

31

Her fearefull speaches nought he did regard,
  But ryding streight under the Castle wall,
  Called aloud unto the watchfull ward,
  Which there did wayte, willing them forth to call
  Into the field their Tyrants Seneschall.
  To whom when tydings thereof came, he streight
  Cals for his armes, and arming him withall,
  Eftsoones forth pricked proudly in his might,
And gan with courage fierce addresse him to the fight.

32

They both encounter in the middle plaine,
  And their sharpe speares doe both together smite
  Amid their shields, with so huge might and maine,
  That seem'd their soules they wold have ryven quight
  Out of their breasts, with furious despight.
  Yet could the Seneschals no entrance find
  Into the Princes shield, where it empight;
  So pure the mettall was, and well refynd,
But shivered all about, and scattered in the wynd.

33

Not so the Princes, but with restlesse force,
  Into his shield it readie passage found,
  Both through his haberjeon, and eke his corse:
  Which tombling downe upon the senselesse ground,
  Gave leave unto his ghost from thraldome bound,
  To wander in the griesly shades of night.
  There did the Prince him leave in deadly swound,
  And thence unto the castle marched right,
To see if entrance there as yet obtaine he might.

34

But as he nigher drew, three knights he spyde,
  All arm'd to point, issuing forth a pace,
  Which towards him with all their powre did ryde,
  And meeting him right in the middle race,
  Did all their speares attonce on him enchace.
  As three great Culverings for battrie bent,
  And leveld all against one certaine place,
  Doe all attonce their thunders rage forth rent,
That makes the wals to stagger with astonishment.

35

So all attonce they on the Prince did thonder;
  Who from his saddle swarved nought asyde,
  Ne to their force gave way, that was great wonder,
  But like a bulwarke, firmely did abyde,
  Rebutting him, which in the midst did ryde,
  With so huge rigour, that his mortall speare
  Past through his shield, and pierst through either syde,
  That downe he fell upon his mother deare,
And powred forth his wretched life in deadly dreare.

36

Whom when his other fellowes saw, they fled
  As fast as feete could carry them away;
  And after them the Prince as swiftly sped,
  To be aveng'd of their unknightly play.
  There whilest they entring, th'one did th'other stay,
  The hindmost in the gate he overhent,
  And as he pressed in, him there did slay:
  His carkasse tumbling on the threshold, sent
His groning soule unto her place of punishment.

37

The other which was entred, laboured fast
  To sperre the gate; but that same lumpe of clay,
  Whose grudging ghost was thereout fled and past,
  Right in the middest of the threshold lay,
  That it the Posterne did from closing stay:
  The whiles the Prince hard preased in betweene,
  And entraunce wonne. Streight th'other fled away,
  And ran into the Hall, where he did weene
Him selfe to save: but he there slew him at the skreene.

38

Then all the rest which in that Castle were,
  Seeing that sad ensample them before,
  Durst not abide, but fled away for feare,
  And them convayd out at a Posterne dore.
  Long sought the Prince, but when he found no more
  T'oppose against his powre, he forth issued
  Unto that Lady, where he her had lore,
  And her gan cheare, with what she there had vewed,
And what she had not seene, within unto her shewed.

39

Who with right humble thankes him goodly greeting,
  For so great prowesse, as he there had proved,
  Much greater than was ever in her weeting,
  With great admiraunce inwardly was moved,
  And honourd him, with all that her behoved.
  Thenceforth into that Castle he her led,
  With her two sonnes, right deare of her beloved,
  Where all that night them selves they cherished,
And from her balefull minde all care he banished.

CANT. XI

Prince Arthure overcomes the great
Gerioneo in fight:
Doth slay the Monster, and restore
Belge unto her right.

1

IT often fals in course of common life,
   That right long time is overborne of wrong,
   Through avarice, or powre, or guile, or strife,
   That weakens her, and makes her party strong:
   But Justice, though her dome she doe prolong,
   Yet at the last she will her owne cause right.
   As by sad *Belge* seemes, whose wrongs though long
   She suffred, yet at length she did requight,
And sent redresse thereof by this brave Briton Knight.

2

Whereof when newes was to that Tyrant brought,
   How that the Lady *Belge* now had found
   A Champion, that had with his Champion fought,
   And laid his Seneschall low on the ground,
   And eke him selfe did threaten to confound,
   He gan to burne in rage, and friese in feare,
   Doubting sad end of principle unsound:
   Yet sith he heard but one, that did appeare,
He did him selfe encourage, and take better cheare.

3

Nathelesse him selfe he armed all in hast,
   And forth he far'd with all his many bad,
   Ne stayed step, till that he came at last
   Unto the Castle, which they conquerd had.
   There with huge terrour, to be more ydrad,
   He sternely marcht before the Castle gate,
   And with bold vaunts, and ydle threatning bad
   Deliver him his owne, ere yet too late,
To which they had no right, nor any wrongfull state.

4

The Prince staid not his aunswere to devize,
  But opening streight the Sparre, forth to him came,
  Full nobly mounted in right warlike wize;
  And asked him, if that he were the same,
  Who all that wrong unto that wofull Dame
  So long had done, and from her native land
  Exiled her, that all the world spake shame.
  He boldly aunswerd him, he there did stand
That would his doings justifie with his owne hand.

5

With that so furiously at him he flew,
  As if he would have overrun him streight,
  And with his huge great yron axe gan hew
  So hideously uppon his armour bright,
  As he to peeces would have chopt it quight:
  That the bold Prince was forced foote to give
  To his first rage, and yeeld to his despight;
  The whilest at him so dreadfully he drive,
That seem'd a marble rocke asunder could have rive.

6

Thereto a great advauntage eke he has
  Through his three double hands thrise multiplyde,
  Besides the double strength, which in them was:
  For stil when fit occasion did betyde,
  He could his weapon shift from side to syde,
  From hand to hand, and with such nimblesse sly
  Could wield about, that ere it were espide,
  The wicked stroke did wound his enemy,
Behinde, beside, before, as he it list apply.

7

Which uncouth use when as the Prince perceived,
  He gan to watch the wielding of his hand,
  Least by such slight he were unwares deceived;
  And ever ere he saw the stroke to land,
  He would it meete, and warily withstand.
  One time, when he his weapon faynd to shift,
  As he was wont, and chang'd from hand to hand,
  He met him with a counterstroke so swift,
That quite smit off his arme, as he it up did lift.

8

Therewith, all fraught with fury and disdaine,
　He brayd aloud for very fell despight,
　And sodainely t'avenge him selfe againe,
　Gan into one assemble all the might
　Of all his hands, and heaved them on hight,
　Thinking to pay him with that one for all:
　But the sad steele seizd not, where it was hight,
　Uppon the childe, but somewhat short did fall,
And lighting on his horses head, him quite did mall.

9

Downe streight to ground fell his astonisht steed,
　And eke to th'earth his burden with him bare:
　But he him selfe full lightly from him freed,
　And gan him selfe to fight on foote prepare.
　Whereof when as the Gyant was aware,
　He wox right blyth, as he had got thereby,
　And laught so loud, that all his teeth wide bare
　One might have seene enraung'd disorderly,
Like to a rancke of piles, that pitched are awry.

10

Eftsoones againe his axe he raught on hie,
　Ere he were throughly buckled to his geare,
　And can let drive at him so dreadfullie,
　That had he chaunced not his shield to reare,
　Ere that huge stroke arrived on him neare,
　He had him surely cloven quite in twaine.
　But th'Adamantine shield, which he did beare,
　So well was tempred, that for all his maine,
It would no passage yeeld unto his purpose vaine.

11

Yet was the stroke so forcibly applide,
　That made him stagger with uncertaine sway,
　As if he would have tottered to one side.
　Wherewith full wroth, he fiercely gan assay,
　That curt'sie with like kindnesse to repay;
　And smote at him with so importune might,
　That two more of his armes did fall away,
　Like fruitlesse braunches, which the hatchets slight
Hath pruned from the native tree, and cropped quight.

12

With that all mad and furious he grew,
Like a fell mastiffe through enraging heat,
And curst, and band, and blasphemies forth threw,
Against his Gods, and fire to them did threat,
And hell unto him selfe with horrour great.
Thenceforth he car'd no more, which way he strooke,
Nor where it light, but gan to chaufe and sweat,
And gnasht his teeth, and his head at him shooke,
And sternely him beheld with grim and ghastly looke.

13

Nought fear'd the childe his lookes, ne yet his threats,
But onely wexed now the more aware,
To save him selfe from those his furious heats,
And watch advauntage, how to worke his care:
The which good Fortune to him offred faire.
For as he in his rage him overstrooke,
He ere he could his weapon backe repaire,
His side all bare and naked overtooke,
And with his mortal steel quite throgh the body strooke.

14

Through all three bodies he him strooke attonce;
That all the three attonce fell on the plaine:
Else should he thrise have needed, for the nonce
Them to have stricken, and thrise to have slaine.
So now all three one sencelesse lumpe remaine,
Enwallow'd in his owne blacke bloudy gore,
And byting th'earth for very deaths disdaine;
Who with a cloud of night him covering, bore
Downe to the house of dole, his daies there to deplore.

15

Which when the Lady from the Castle saw,
Where she with her two sonnes did looking stand,
She towards him in hast her selfe did draw,
To greet him the good fortune of his hand:
And all the people both of towne and land,
Which there stood gazing from the Citties wall
Uppon these warriours, greedy t'understand,
To whether should the victory befall,
Now when they saw it falne, they eke him greeted all.

16

But *Belge* with her sonnes prostrated low
  Before his feete, in all that peoples sight,
  Mongst joyes mixing some tears, mongst wele, some wo
  Him thus bespake; O most redoubted Knight,
  The which hast me, of all most wretched wight,
  That earst was dead, restor'd to life againe,
  And these weake impes replanted by thy might;
  What guerdon can I give thee for thy paine,
But even that which thou savedst, thine still to remaine?

17

He tooke her up forby the lilly hand,
  And her recomforted the best he might,
  Saying; Deare Lady, deedes ought not be scand
  By th'authors manhood, nor the doers might,
  But by their trueth and by the causes right:
  That same is it, which fought for you this day.
  What other meed then need me to requight,
  But that which yeeldeth vertues meed alway?
That is the vertue selfe, which her reward doth pay.

18

She humbly thankt him for that wondrous grace,
  And further sayd; Ah Sir, but mote ye please,
  Sith ye thus farre have tendred my poore case,
  As from my chiefest foe me to release,
  That your victorious arme will not yet cease,
  Till ye have rooted all the relickes out
  Of that vilde race, and stablished my peace.
  What is there else (sayd he) left of their rout?
Declare it boldly Dame, and doe not stand in dout.

19

Then wote you, Sir, that in this Church hereby,
  There stands an Idole of great note and name,
  The which this Gyant reared first on hie,
  And of his owne vaine fancies thought did frame:
  To whom for endlesse horrour of his shame,
  He offred up for daily sacrifize
  My children and my people, burnt in flame;
  With all the tortures, that he could devize,
The more t'aggrate his God with such his blouddy guize.

20

And underneath this Idoll there doth lie
  An hideous monster, that doth it defend,
  And feedes on all the carkasses, that die
  In sacrifize unto that cursed feend:
  Whose ugly shape none ever saw, nor kend,
  That ever scap'd: for of a man they say
  It has the voice, that speaches forth doth send,
  Even blasphemous words, which she doth bray
Out of her poysnous entrails, fraught with dire decay.

21

Which when the Prince heard tell, his heart gan earne
  For great desire, that Monster to assay,
  And prayd the place of her abode to learne.
  Which being shew'd, he gan him selfe streight way
  Thereto addresse, and his bright shield display.
  So to the Church he came, where it was told,
  The Monster underneath the Altar lay;
  There he that Idoll saw of massy gold
Most richly made, but there no Monster did behold.

22

Upon the Image with his naked blade
  Three times, as in defiance, there he strooke;
  And the third time out of an hidden shade,
  There forth issewd, from under th'Altars smooke,
  A dreadfull feend, with fowle deformed looke,
  That stretcht it selfe, as it had long lyen still;
  And her long taile and fethers strongly shooke,
  That all the Temple did with terrour fill;
Yet him nought terrifide, that feared nothing ill.

23

An huge great Beast it was, when it in length
  Was stretched forth, that nigh fild all the place,
  And seem'd to be of infinite great strength;
  Horrible, hideous, and of hellish race,
  Borne of the brooding of *Echidna* base,
  Or other like infernall furies kinde:
  For of a Mayd she had the outward face,
  To hide the horrour, which did lurke behinde,
The better to beguile, whom she so fond did finde.

24

Thereto the body of a dog she had,
　　Full of fell ravin and fierce greedinesse;
　　A Lions clawes, with powre and rigour clad,
　　To rend and teare, what so she can oppresse;
　　A Dragons taile, whose sting without redresse
　　Full deadly wounds, where so it is empight;
　　And Eagles wings, for scope and speedinesse,
　　That nothing may escape her reaching might,
Whereto she ever list to make her hardy flight.

25

Much like in foulnesse and deformity
　　Unto that Monster, whom the Theban Knight,
　　The father of that fatall progeny,
　　Made kill her selfe for very hearts despight,
　　That he had red her Riddle, which no wight
　　Could ever loose, but suffred deadly doole.
　　So also did this Monster use like slight
　　To many a one, which came unto her schoole,
Whom she did put to death, deceived like a foole.

26

She comming forth, when as she first beheld
　　The armed Prince, with shield so blazing bright,
　　Her ready to assaile, was greatly queld,
　　And much dismayd with that dismayfull sight,
　　That backe she would have turnd for great affright.
　　But he gan her with courage fierce assay,
　　That forst her turne againe in her despight,
　　To save her selfe, least that he did her slay:
And sure he had her slaine, had she not turnd her way.

27

Tho when she saw, that she was forst to fight,
　　She flew at him, like to an hellish feend,
　　And on his shield tooke hold with all her might,
　　As if that it she would in peeces rend,
　　Or reave out of the hand, that did it hend.
　　Strongly he strove out of her greedy gripe
　　To loose his shield, and long while did contend:
　　But when he could not quite it, with one stripe
Her Lions clawes he from her feete away did wipe.

28

With that aloude she gan to bray and yell,
  And fowle blasphemous speaches forth did cast,
  And bitter curses, horrible to tell,
  That even the Temple, wherein she was plast,
  Did quake to heare, and nigh asunder brast.
  Tho with her huge long taile she at him strooke,
  That made him stagger, and stand halfe agast
  With trembling joynts, as he for terrour shooke;
Who nought was terrifide, but greater courage tooke.

29

As when the Mast of some well timbred hulke
  Is with the blast of some outragious storme
  Blowne downe, it shakes the bottome of the bulke,
  And makes her ribs to cracke, as they were torne,
  Whilest still she stands as stonisht and forlorne:
  So was he stound with stroke of her huge taile.
  But ere that it she backe againe had borne,
  He with his sword it strooke, that without faile
He joynted it, and mard the swinging of her flaile.

30

Then gan she cry much louder than afore,
  That all the people there without it heard,
  And *Belge* selfe was therewith stonied sore,
  As if the onely sound thereof she feard.
  But then the feend her selfe more fiercely reard
  Uppon her wide great wings, and strongly flew
  With all her body at his head and beard,
  That had he not foreseene with heedfull vew,
And thrown his shield atween, she had him done to rew.

31

But as she prest on him with heavy sway,
  Under her wombe his fatall sword he thrust,
  And for her entrailes made an open way,
  To issue forth; the which once being brust,
  Like to a great Mill damb forth fiercely gusht,
  And powred out of her infernall sinke
  Most ugly filth, and poyson therewith rusht,
  That him nigh choked with the deadly stinke:
Such loathly matter were small lust to speake, or thinke.

32

Then downe to ground fell that deformed Masse,
  Breathing out clouds of sulphure fowle and blacke,
  In which a puddle of contagion was,
  More loathd than *Lerna,* or than *Stygian* lake,
  That any man would nigh awhaped make.
  Whom when he saw on ground, he was full glad,
  And streight went forth his gladnesse to partake
  With *Belge,* who watcht all this while full sad,
Wayting what end would be of that same daunger drad.

33

Whom when she saw so joyously come forth,
  She gan rejoyce, and shew triumphant chere,
  Lauding and praysing his renowmed worth,
  By all the names that honorable were.
  Then in he brought her, and her shewed there
  The present of his paines, that Monsters spoyle,
  And eke that Idoll deem'd so costly dere;
  Whom he did all to peeces breake and foyle
In filthy durt, and left so in the loathely soyle.

34

Then all the people, which beheld that day,
  Gan shout aloud, that unto heaven it rong;
  And all the damzels of that towne in ray,
  Came dauncing forth, and joyous carrols song:
  So him they led through all their streetes along,
  Crowned with girlonds of immortall baies,
  And all the vulgar did about them throng,
  To see the man, whose everlasting praise
They all were bound to all posterities to raise.

35

There he with *Belge* did a while remaine,
  Making great feast and joyous merriment,
  Untill he had her settled in her raine,
  With safe assuraunce and establishment.
  Then to his first emprize his mind he lent,
  Full loath to *Belge,* and to all the rest:
  Of whom yet taking leave, thenceforth he went
  And to his former journey him addrest,
On which long way he rode, ne ever day did rest.

36

But turne we now to noble *Artegall*;
  Who having left *Mercilla*, streight way went
  On his first quest, the which him forth did call,
  To weet to worke *Irenaes* franchisement,
  And eke *Grantortoes* worthy punishment.
  So forth he fared as his manner was,
  With onely *Talus* wayting diligent,
  Through many perils and much way did pas,
Till nigh unto the place at length approcht he has.

37

There as he traveld by the way, he met
  An aged wight, wayfaring all alone,
  Who through his yeares long since aside had set
  The use of armes, and battell quite forgone:
  To whom as he approcht, he knew anone,
  That it was he which whilome did attend
  On faire *Irene* in her affliction,
  When first to Faery court he saw her wend,
Unto his soveraine Queene her suite for to commend.

38

Whom by his name saluting, thus he gan;
  Haile good Sir *Sergis*, truest Knight alive,
  Well tride in all thy Ladies troubles than,
  When her that Tyrant did of Crowne deprive;
  What new occasion doth thee hither drive,
  Whiles she alone is left, and thou here found?
  Or is she thrall, or doth she not survive?
  To whom he thus; She liveth sure and sound;
But by that Tyrant is in wretched thraldome bound.

39

For she presuming on th'appointed tyde,
  In which ye promist, as ye were a Knight,
  To meete her at the salvage Ilands syde,
  And then and there for triall of her right
  With her unrighteous enemy to fight,
  Did thither come, where she afrayd of nought,
  By guilefull treason and by subtill slight
  Surprized was, and to *Grantorto* brought,
Who her imprisond hath, and her life often sought.

40

And now he hath to her prefixt a day,
  By which if that no champion doe appeare,
  Which will her cause in battailous array
  Against him justifie, and prove her cleare
  Of all those crimes, that he gainst her doth reare,
  She death shall by. Those tidings sad
  Did much abash Sir *Artegall* to heare,
  And grieved sore, that through his fault she had
Fallen into that Tyrants hand and usage bad.

41

Then thus replide; Now sure and by my life,
  Too much am I to blame for that faire Maide,
  That have her drawne to all this troublous strife,
  Through promise to afford her timely aide,
  Which by default I have not yet defraide.
  But witnesse unto me, ye heavens, that know
  How cleare I am from blame of this upbraide:
  For ye into like thraldome me did throw,
And kept from complishing the faith, which I did owe.

42

But now aread, Sir *Sergis*, how long space,
  Hath he her lent, a Champion to provide?
  Ten daies (quoth he) he graunted hath of grace,
  For that he weeneth well, before that tide
  None can have tidings to assist her side.
  For all the shores, which to the sea accoste,
  He day and night doth ward both far and wide,
  That none can there arrive without an hoste:
So her he deemes already but a damned ghoste.

43

Now turne againe (Sir *Artegall* then sayd)
  For if I live till those ten daies have end,
  Assure your selfe, Sir Knight, she shall have ayd,
  Though I this dearest life for her doe spend:
  So backeward he attone with him did wend.
  Tho as they rode together on their way,
  A rout of people they before them kend,
  Flocking together in confusde array,
As if that there were some tumultuous affray.

Artegall and Grantorto

44

To which as they approcht, the cause to know,
  They saw a Knight in daungerous distresse
Of a rude rout him chasing to and fro,
That sought with lawlesse powre him to oppresse,
And bring in bondage of their brutishnesse:
And farre away, amid their rakehell bands,
  They spide a Lady left all succourlesse,
  Crying, and holding up her wretched hands
To him for aide, who long in vaine their rage withstands.

45

Yet still he strives, ne any perill spares,
  To reskue her from their rude violence,
And like a Lion wood amongst them fares,
Dealing his dreadfull blowes with large dispence,
Gainst which the pallid death findes no defence.
But all in vaine, their numbers are so great,
  That naught may boot to banishe them from thence:
  For soone as he their outrage backe doth beat,
They turne afresh, and oft renew their former threat.

46

And now they doe so sharpely him assay,
  That they his shield in peeces battred have,
And forced him to throw it quite away,
Fro dangers dread his doubtfull life to save;
Albe that it most safety to him gave,
And much did magnifie his noble name.
  For from the day that he thus did it leave,
  Amongst all Knights he blotted was with blame,
And counted but a recreant Knight, with endles shame.

47

Whom when they thus distressed did behold,
  They drew unto his aide; but that rude rout
Them also gan assaile with outrage bold,
And forced them, how ever strong and stout
They were, as well approv'd in many a doubt,
Backe to recule; untill that yron man
  With his huge flaile began to lay about,
  From whose sterne presence they diffused ran,
Like scattred chaffe, the which the wind away doth fan.

48

So when that Knight from perill cleare was freed,
  He drawing neare, began to greete them faire,
  And yeeld great thankes for their so goodly deed,
  In saving him from daungerous despaire
  Of those, which sought his life for to empaire.
  Of whom Sir *Artegall* gan then enquire
  The whole occasion of his late misfare,
  And who he was, and what those villaines were,
The which with mortall malice him pursu'd so nere.

49

To whom he thus; My name is *Burbon* hight,
  Well knowne, and far renowmed heretofore,
  Untill late mischiefe did uppon me light,
  That all my former praise hath blemisht sore;
  And that faire Lady, which in that uprore
  Ye with those caytives saw, *Flourdelis* hight,
  Is mine owne love, though me she have forlore,
  Whether withheld from me by wrongfull might,
Or with her owne good will, I cannot read aright.

50

But sure to me her faith she first did plight,
  To be my love, and take me for her Lord,
  Till that a Tyrant, which *Grandtorto* hight,
  With golden giftes and many a guilefull word
  Entyced her, to him for to accord.
  O who may not with gifts and words be tempted?
  Sith which she hath me ever since abhord,
  And to my foe hath guilefully consented:
Ay me, that ever guyle in wemen was invented.

51

And now he hath this troupe of villains sent,
  By open force to fetch her quite away:
  Gainst whom my selfe I long in vaine have bent,
  To rescue her, and daily meanes assay,
  Yet rescue her thence by no meanes I may:
  For they doe me with multitude oppresse,
  And with unequall might doe overlay,
  That oft I driven am to great distresse,
And forced to forgoe th'attempt remedilesse.

52

But why have ye (said *Artegall*) forborne
　Your owne good shield in daungerous dismay?
　That is the greatest shame and foulest scorne,
　Which unto any knight behappen may
　To loose the badge, that should his deedes display.
　To whom Sir *Burbon*, blushing halfe for shame,
　That shall I unto you (quoth he) bewray;
　Least ye therefore mote happily me blame,
And deeme it doen of will, that through inforcement came.

53

True is, that I at first was dubbed knight
　By a good knight, the knight of the *Redcrosse*;
　Who when he gave me armes, in field to fight,
　Gave me a shield, in which he did endosse
　His deare Redeemers badge upon the bosse:
　The same longwhile I bore, and therewithall
　Fought many battels without wound or losse;
　Therewith *Grandtorto* selfe I did appall,
And made him oftentimes in field before me fall.

54

But for that many did that shield envie,
　And cruell enemies increased more;
　To stint all strife and troublous enmitie,
　That bloudie scutchin being battered sore,
　I layd aside, and have of late forbore,
　Hoping thereby to have my love obtayned:
　Yet can I not my love have nathemore;
　For she by force is still fro me detayned,
And with corruptfull brybes is to untruth mis-trayned.

55

To whom thus *Artegall*; Certes Sir knight,
　Hard is the case, the which ye doe complaine;
　Yet not so hard (for nought so hard may light,
　That it to such a streight mote you constraine)
　As to abandon, that which doth containe
　Your honours stile, that is your warlike shield.
　All perill ought be lesse, and lesse all paine
　Than losse of fame in disaventrous field;
Dye rather, than doe ought, that mote dishonour yield.

56

Not so; (quoth he) for yet when time doth serve,
　My former shield I may resume againe:
　To temporize is not from truth to swerve,
　Ne for advantage terme to entertaine,
　When as necessitie doth it constraine.
　Fie on such forgerie (said *Artegall*)
　Under one hood to shadow faces twaine.
　Knights ought be true, and truth is one in all:
Of all things to dissemble fouly may befall.

57

Yet let me you of courtesie request,
　(Said *Burbon*) to assist me now at need
　Against these pesants, which have me opprest,
　And forced me to so infamous deed,
　That yet my love may from their hands be freed.
　Sir *Artegall*, albe he earst did wyte
　His wavering mind, yet to his aide agreed,
　And buckling him eftsoones unto the fight,
Did set upon those troupes with all his powre and might.

58

Who flocking round about them, as a swarme
　Of flyes upon a birchen bough doth cluster,
　Did them assault with terrible allarme,
　And over all the fields themselves did muster,
　With bils and glayves making a dreadfull luster;
　That forst at first those knights backe to retyre:
　As when the wrathfull *Boreas* doth bluster,
　Nought may abide the tempest of his yre,
Both man and beast doe fly, and succour doe inquyre.

59

But when as overblowen was that brunt,
　Those knights began a fresh them to assayle,
　And all about the fields like Squirrels hunt;
　But chiefly *Talus* with his yron flayle,
　Gainst which no flight nor rescue mote avayle,
　Made cruell havocke of the baser crew,
　And chaced them both over hill and dale:
　The raskall manie soone they overthrew,
But the two knights themselves their captains did subdew.

60

At last they came whereas that Ladie bode,
  Whom now her keepers had forsaken quight,
  To save themselves, and sçattered were abrode:
  Her halfe dismayd they found in doubtfull plight,
  As neither glad nor sorie for their sight;
  Yet wondrous faire she was, and richly clad
  In roiall robes, and many Jewels dight,
  But that those villens through their usage bad
Them fouly rent, and shamefully defaced had.

61

But *Burbon* streight dismounting from his steed,
  Unto her ran with greedie great desyre,
  And catching her fast by her ragged weed,
  Would have embraced her with hart entyre.
  But she backstarting with disdainefull yre,
  Bad him avaunt, ne would unto his lore
  Allured be, for prayer nor for meed.
  Whom when those knights so froward and forlore
Beheld, they her rebuked and upbrayded sore.

62

Sayd *Artegall*; What foule disgrace is this,
  To so faire Ladie, as ye seeme in sight,
  To blot your beautie, that unblemisht is,
  With so foule blame, as breach of faith once plight,
  Or change of love for any worlds delight?
  Is ought on earth so pretious or deare,
  As prayse and honour? Or is ought so bright
  And beautifull, as glories beames appeare,
Whose goodly light than *Phebus* lampe doth shine more cleare?

63

Why then will ye, fond Dame, attempted bee
  Unto a strangers love so lightly placed,
  For guiftes of gold, or any worldly glee
  To leave the love, that ye before embraced,
  And let your fame with falshood be defaced?
  Fie on the pelfe, for which good name is sold,
  And honour with indignitie debased:
  Dearer is love than life, and fame than gold;
But dearer than them both, your faith once plighted hold.

64

Much was the Ladie in her gentle mind
  Abasht at his rebuke, that bit her neare,
Ne ought to answere thereunto did find;
  But hanging downe her head with heavie cheare,
  Stood long amaz'd, as she amated weare.
Which *Burbon* seeing, her againe assayd,
  And clasping twixt his armes, her up did reare
Upon his steede, whiles she no whit gainesayd,
So bore her quite away, nor well nor ill apayd.

65

Nathlesse the yron man did still pursew
  That raskall many with unpittied spoyle,
Ne ceassed not, till all their scattred crew
  Into the sea he drove quite from that soyle,
  The which they troubled had with great turmoyle.
But *Artegall* seeing his cruell deed,
  Commaunded him from slaughter to recoyle,
And to his voyage gan againe proceed:
For that the terme approching fast, required speed.

CANT. XII

Artegall doth Sir Burbon aide,
* And blames for changing shield:*
He with the great Grantorto fights,
* And slaieth him in field.*

I

O SACRED hunger of ambitious mindes,
  And impotent desire of men to raine,
Whom neither dread of God, that devils bindes,
  Nor lawes of men, that common weales containe,
  Nor bands of nature, that wilde beastes restraine,
Can keepe from outrage, and from doing wrong,
  Where they may hope a kingdome to obtaine.
No faith so firme, no trust can be so strong,
No love so lasting then, that may enduren long.

2

Witnesse may *Burbon* be, whom all the bands,
  Which may a Knight assure, had surely bound,
  Untill the love of Lordship and of lands
  Made him become most faithlesse and unsound:
  And witnesse be *Gerioneo* found,
  Who for like cause faire *Belge* did oppresse,
  And right and wrong most cruelly confound:
  And so be now *Grantorto*, who no lesse
Than all the rest burst out to all outragiousnesse.

3

Gainst whom Sir *Artegall*, long having since
  Taken in hand th'exploit, being theretoo
  Appointed by that mightie Faerie Prince,
  Great *Gloriane*, that Tyrant to fordoo,
  Through other great adventures hethertoo
  Had it forslackt. But now time drawing ny,
  To him assynd, her high beheast to doo,
  To the sea shore he gan his way apply,
To weete if shipping readie he mote there descry.

4

Tho when they came to the sea coast, they found
  A ship all readie (as good fortune fell)
  To put to sea, with whom they did compound,
  To passe them over, where them list to tell:
  The winde and weather served them so well,
  That in one day they with the coast did fall;
  Whereas they readie found them to repell,
  Great hostes of men in order martiall,
Which them forbad to land, and footing did forstall.

5

But nathemore would they from land refraine,
  But when as nigh unto the shore they drew,
  That foot of man might sound the bottome plaine,
  Talus into the sea did forth issew,
  Though darts from shore and stones they at him threw;
  And wading through the waves with stedfast sway,
  Maugre the might of all those troupes in vew,
  Did win the shore, whence he them chast away,
And made to fly, like doves, whom the Eagle doth affray.

6

The whyles Sir *Artegall*, with that old knight
  Did forth descend, there being none them neare,
  And forward marched to a towne in sight.
  By this came tydings to the Tyrants eare,
  By those, which earst did fly away for feare
  Of their arrivall: wherewith troubled sore,
  He all his forces streight to him did reare,
  And forth issuing with his scouts afore,
Meant them to have incountred, ere they left the shore.

7

But ere he marched farre, he with them met,
  And fiercely charged them with all his force;
  But *Talus* sternely did upon them set,
  And brusht, and battred them without remorse,
  That on the ground he left full many a corse;
  Ne any able was him to withstand,
  But he them overthrew both man and horse,
  That they lay scattred over all the land,
As thicke as doth the seede after the sowers hand.

8

Till *Artegall* him seeing so to rage,
  Willd him to stay, and signe of truce did make:
  To which all harkning, did a while asswage
  Their forces furie, and their terror slake;
  Till he an Herauld cald, and to him spake,
  Willing him wend unto the Tyrant streight,
  And tell him that not for such slaughters sake
  He thether came, but for to trie the right
Of fayre *Irenaes* cause with him in single fight.

9

And willed him for to reclayme with speed
  His scattred people, ere they all were slaine,
  And time and place convenient to areed,
  In which they two the combat might darraine.
  Which message when *Grantorto* heard, full fayne
  And glad he was the slaughter so to stay,
  And pointed for the combat twixt them twayne
  The morrow next, ne gave him longer day.
So sounded the retraite, and drew his folke away.

10

That night Sir *Artegall* did cause his tent
  There to be pitched on the open plaine;
  For he had given streight commaundement,
  That none should dare him once to entertaine:
  Which none durst breake, though many would right faine
  For fayre *Irena*, whom they loved deare.
  But yet old *Sergis* did so well him paine,
  That from close friends, that dar'd not to appeare,
He all things did purvay, which for them needfull weare.

11

The morrow next, that was the dismall day,
  Appointed for *Irenas* death before,
  So soone as it did to the world display
  His chearefull face, and light to men restore,
  The heavy Mayd, to whom none tydings bore
  Of *Artegalls* arryvall, her to free,
  Lookt up with eyes full sad and hart full sore;
  Weening her lifes last howre then neare to bee,
Sith no redemption nigh she did nor heare nor see.

12

Then up she rose, and on her selfe did dight
  Most squalid garments, fit for such a day,
  And with dull countenance, and with doleful spright,
  She forth was brought in sorrowfull dismay,
  For to receive the doome of her decay.
  But comming to the place, and finding there
  Sir *Artegall*, in battailous array
  Wayting his foe, it did her dead hart cheare,
And new life to her lent, in midst of deadly feare.

13

Like as a tender Rose in open plaine,
  That with untimely drought nigh withered was,
  And hung the head, soone as few drops of raine
  Thereon distill, and deaw her daintie face,
  Gins to looke up, and with fresh wonted grace
  Dispreds the glorie of her leaves gay;
  Such was *Irenas* countenance, such her case,
  When *Artegall* she saw in that array,
There wayting for the Tyrant, till it was farre day.

14

Who came at length, with proud presumpteous gate,
  Into the field, as if he fearelesse were,
  All armed in a cote of yron plate,
  Of great defence to ward the deadly feare,
  And on his head a steele cap he did weare
  Of colour rustie browne, but sure and strong;
  And in his hand an huge Polaxe did beare,
  Whose steale was yron studded, but not long,
With which he wont to fight, to justifie his wrong.

15

Of stature huge and hideous he was,
  Like to a Giant for his monstrous hight,
  And did in strength most sorts of men surpas,
  Ne ever any found his match in might;
  Thereto he had great skill in single fight:
  His face was ugly, and his countenance sterne,
  That could have frayd one with the very sight,
  And gaped like a gulfe, when he did gerne,
That whether man or monster one could scarse discerne.

16

Soone as he did within the listes appeare,
  With dreadfull looke he *Artegall* beheld,
  As if he would have daunted him with feare,
  And grinning griesly, did against him weld
  His deadly weapon, which in hand he held.
  But th'Elfin swayne, that oft had seene like sight,
  Was with his ghastly count'nance nothing queld,
  But gan him streight to buckle to the fight,
And cast his shield about, to be in readie plight.

17

The trompets sound, and they together goe,
  With dreadfull terror, and with fell intent;
  And their huge strokes full daungerously bestow,
  To doe most dammage, where as most they meni.
  But with such force and furie violent,
  The tyrant thundred his thicke blowes so fast,
  That through the yron walles their way they rent,
  And even to the vitall parts they past,
Ne ought could them endure, but all they cleft or brast.

18

Which cruell outrage when as *Artegall*
    Did well avize, thenceforth with warie heed
He shund his strokes, where ever they did fall,
    And way did give unto their gracelesse speed:
    As when a skilfull Marriner doth reed
A storme approching, that doth perill threat,
    He will not bide the daunger of such dread,
    But strikes his sayles, and vereth his mainsheat,
And lends unto it leave the emptie ayre to beat.

19

So did the Faerie knight himselfe abeare,
    And stouped oft his head from shame to shield;
No shame to stoupe, ones head more high to reare,
    And much to gaine, a litle for to yield;
    So stoutest knights doen oftentimes in field.
But still the tyrant sternely at him layd,
    And did his yron axe so nimbly wield,
    That many wounds into his flesh it made,
And with his burdenous blowes him sore did overlade.

20

Yet when as fit advantage he did spy,
    The whiles the cursed felon high did reare
His cruell hand, to smite him mortally,
    Under his stroke he to him stepping neare,
    Right in the flanke him strooke with deadly dreare,
That the gore bloud thence gushing grievously,
    Did underneath him like a pond appeare,
    And all his armour did with purple dye;
Thereat he brayed loud, and yelled dreadfully.

21

Yet the huge stroke, which he before intended,
    Kept on his course, as he did it direct,
And with such monstrous poise adowne descended,
    That seemed nought could him from death protect:
    But he it well did ward with wise respect,
And twixt him and the blow his shield did cast,
    Which thereon seizing, tooke no great effect,
    But byting deepe therein did sticke so fast,
That by no meanes it backe againe he forth could wrast.

22

Long while he tug'd and strove, to get it out,
  And all his powre applyed thereunto,
  That he therewith the knight drew all about:
  Nathlesse, for all that ever he could doe,
  His axe he could not from his shield undoe.
  Which *Artegall* perceiving, strooke no more,
  But loosing soone his shield, did it forgoe,
  And whiles he combred was therewith so sore,
He gan at him let drive more fiercely than afore.

23

So well he him pursew'd, that at the last,
  He stroke him with *Chrysaor* on the hed,
  That with the souse thereof full sore aghast,
  He staggered to and fro in doubtfull sted.
  Againe whiles he him saw so ill bested,
  He did him smite with all his might and maine,
  That falling on his mother earth he fed:
  Whom when he saw prostrated on the plaine,
He lightly reft his head, to ease him of his paine.

24

Which when the people round about him saw,
  They shouted all for joy of his successe,
  Glad to be quit from that proud Tyrants awe,
  Which with strong powre did them long time oppresse;
  And running all with greedie joyfulnesse
  To faire *Irena*, at her feet did fall,
  And her adored with due humblenesse,
  As their true Liege and Princesse naturall;
And eke her champions glorie sounded over all.

25

Who streight her leading with meete majestie
  Unto the pallace, where their kings did rayne,
  Did her therein establish peaceablie,
  And to her kingdomes seat restore agayne;
  And all such persons, as did late maintayne
  That Tyrants part, with close or open ayde,
  He sorely punished with heavie payne;
  That in short space, whiles there with her he stayd,
Not one was left, that durst her once have disobayd.

26

During which time, that he did there remaine,
  His studie was true Justice how to deale,
  And day and night employ'd his busie paine
  How to reforme that ragged common-weale:
  And that same yron man which could reveale
  All hidden crimes, through all that realme he sent,
  To search out those, that usd to rob and steale,
  Or did rebell gainst lawfull government;
On whom he did inflict most grievous punishment.

27

But ere he could reforme it thoroughly,
  He through occasion called was away,
  To Faerie Court, that of necessity
  His course of Justice he was forst to stay,
  And *Talus* to revoke from the right way,
  In which he was that Realme for to redresse.
  But envies cloud still dimmeth vertues ray.
  So having freed *Irena* from distresse,
He tooke his leave of her, there left in heavinesse.

28

Tho as he backe returned from that land,
  And there arriv'd againe, whence forth he set,
  He had not passed farre upon the strand,
  When as two old ill favour'd Hags he met,
  By the way side being together set,
  Two griesly creatures; and, to that their faces
  Most foule and filthie were, their garments yet
  Being all rag'd and tatter'd, their disgraces
Did much the more augment, and made most ugly cases.

29

The one of them, that elder did appeare,
  With her dull eyes did seeme to looke askew,
  That her mis-shape much helpt; and her foule heare
  Hung loose and loathsomely: Thereto her hew
  Was wan and leane, that all her teeth arew,
  And all her bones might through her cheekes be red;
  Her lips were like raw lether, pale and blew,
  And as she spake, therewith she slavered;
Yet spake she seldom, but thought more, the lesse she sed.

30

Her hands were foule and durtie, never washt
  In all her life, with long nayles over raught,
  Like puttocks clawes: with th'one of which she scracht
  Her cursed head, although it itched naught;
  The other held a snake with venime fraught,
  On which she fed, and gnawed hungrily,
  As if that long she had not eaten ought;
  That round about her jawes one might descry
The bloudie gore and poyson dropping lothsomely.

31

Her name was *Envie*, knowen well thereby;
  Whose nature is to grieve, and grudge at all,
  That ever she sees doen prays-worthily,
  Whose sight to her is greatest crosse, may fall,
  And vexeth so, that makes her eat her gall.
  For when she wanteth other thing to eat,
  She feedes on her owne maw unnaturall,
  And of her owne foule entrayles makes her meat;
Meat fit for such a monsters monsterous dyeat.

32

And if she hapt of any good to heare,
  That had to any happily betid,
  Then would she inly fret, and grieve, and teare
  Her flesh for felnesse, which she inward hid:
  But if she heard of ill, that any did,
  Or harme, that any had, then would she make
  Great cheare, like one unto a banquet bid;
  And in anothers losse great pleasure take,
As she had got thereby, and gayned a great stake.

33

The other nothing better was, than shee;
  Agreeing in bad will and cancred kynd,
  But in bad maner they did disagree:
  For what so *Envie* good or bad did fynd,
  She did conceale, and murder her owne mynd;
  But this, what ever evill she conceived,
  Did spred abroad, and throw in th'open wynd.
  Yet this in all her words might be perceived,
That all she sought, was mens good name to have bereaved.

34

For what soever good by any sayd,
  Or doen she heard, she would streightwayes invent,
  How to deprave, or slaunderously upbrayd,
  Or to misconstrue of a mans intent,
  And turne to ill the thing, that well was ment.
  Therefore she used often to resort,
  To common haunts, and companies frequent,
  To hearke what any one did good report,
To blot the same with blame, or wrest in wicked sort.

35

And if that any ill she heard of any,
  She would it eeke, and make much worse by telling,
  And take great joy to publish it to many,
  That every matter worse was for her melling.
  Her name was hight *Detraction*, and her dwelling
  Was neare to *Envie*, even her neighbour next;
  A wicked hag, and *Envy* selfe excelling
  In mischiefe: for her selfe she onely vext;
But this same both her selfe, and others eke perplext.

36

Her face was ugly, and her mouth distort,
  Foming with poyson round about her gils,
  In which her cursed tongue full sharpe and short
  Appear'd like Aspis sting, that closely kils,
  Or cruelly does wound, whom so she wils:
  A distaffe in her other hand she had,
  Upon the which she litle spinnes, but spils,
  And faynes to weave false tales and leasings bad,
To throw amongst the good, which others had disprad.

37

These two now had themselves combynd in one,
  And linckt together gainst Sir *Artegall*,
  For whom they wayted as his mortall fone,
  How they might make him into mischiefe fall,
  For freeing from their snares *Irena* thrall,
  Besides unto themselves they gotten had
  A monster, which the *Blatant beast* men call,
  A dreadfull feend of gods and men ydrad,
Whom they by slights allur'd, and to their purpose lad.

38

Such were these Hags, and so unhandsome drest:
  Who when they nigh approching, had espyde
  Sir *Artegall* return'd from his late quest,
  They both arose, and at him loudly cryde,
  As it had bene two shepheards curres, had scryde
  A ravenous Wolfe amongst the scattered flockes.
  And *Envie* first, as she that first him eyde,
  Towardes him runs, and with rude flaring lockes
About her eares, does beat her brest, and forhead knockes.

39

Then from her mouth the gobbet she does take,
  The which whyleare she was so greedily
  Devouring, even that halfe-gnawen snake,
  And at him throwes it most despightfully.
  The cursed Serpent, though she hungrily
  Earst chawd thereon, yet was not all so dead,
  But that some life remayned secretly,
  And as he past afore withouten dread,
Bit him behind, that long the marke was to be read.

40

Then th'other comming neare, gan him revile,
  And fouly rayle, with all she could invent;
  Saying, that he had with unmanly guile,
  And foule abusion both his honour blent,
  And that bright sword, the sword of Justice lent,
  Had stayned with reprochfull crueltie,
  In guiltlesse blood of many an innocent:
  As for *Grandtorto*, him with treacherie
And traynes having surpriz'd, he fouly did to die.

41

Thereto the Blatant beast by them set on
  At him began aloud to barke and bay,
  With bitter rage and fell contention,
  That all the woods and rockes nigh to that way,
  Began to quake and tremble with dismay;
  And all the aire rebellowed againe.
  So dreadfully his hundred tongues did bray,
  And evermore those hags them selves did paine,
To sharpen him, and their owne cursed tongs did straine.

42

And still among most bitter wordes they spake,
  Most shamefull, most unrighteous, most untrew,
  That they the mildest man alive would make
  Forget his patience, and yeeld vengeaunce dew
  To her, that so false sclaunders at him threw.
  And more to make them pierce and wound more deepe,
  She with the sting, which in her vile tongue grew,
  Did sharpen them, and in fresh poyson steepe:
Yet he past on, and seem'd of them to take no keepe.

43

But *Talus* hearing her so lewdly raile,
  And speake so ill of him, that well deserved,
  Would her have chastiz'd with his yron flaile,
  If her Sir *Artegall* had not preserved,
  And him forbidden, who his heast observed.
  So much the more at him still did she scold,
  And stones did cast, yet he for nought would swerve
  From his right course, but still the way did hold
To Faery Court, where what him fell shall else be told.

THE SIXTE BOOKE OF THE

FAERIE QUEENE

CONTAYNING THE LEGEND
OF S. CALIDORE OR OF COURTESIE

1

THE waies, through which my weary steps I guyde,
 In this delightfull land of Faery,
 Are so exceeding spacious and wyde,
 And sprinckled with such sweet variety,
 Of all that pleasant is to eare or eye,
 That I nigh ravisht with rare thoughts delight,
 My tedious travell doe forget thereby;
 And when I gin to feele decay of might,
It strength to me supplies, and chears my dulled spright.

2

Such secret comfort, and such heavenly pleasures,
 Ye sacred imps, that on *Parnasso* dwell,
 And there the keeping have of learnings threasures,
 Which doe all worldly riches farre excell,
 Into the mindes of mortall men doe well,
 And goodly fury into them infuse;
 Guyde ye my footing, and conduct me well
 In these strange waies, where never foote did use,
Ne none can find, but who was taught them by the Muse.

3

Revele to me the sacred noursery
  Of vertue, which with you doth there remaine,
  Where it in silver bowre does hidden ly
  From view of men, and wicked worlds disdaine.
  Since it at first was by the Gods with paine
  Planted in earth, being deriv'd at furst
  From heavenly seedes of bounty soveraine,
  And by them long with carefull labour nurst,
Till it to ripenesse grew, and forth to honour burst.

4

Amongst them all growes not a fayrer flowre,
  Than is the bloosme of comely courtesie,
  Which though it on a lowly stalke doe bowre,
  Yet brancheth forth in brave nobilitie,
  And spreds it selfe through all civilitie:
  Of which though present age doe plenteous seeme,
  Yet being matcht with plaine Antiquitie,
  Ye will them all but fayned showes esteeme,
Which carry colours faire, that feeble eies misdeeme.

5

But in the triall of true curtesie,
  Its now so farre from that, which then it was,
  That it indeed is nought but forgerie,
  Fashion'd to please the eies of them, that pas,
  Which see not perfect things but in a glas:
  Yet is that glasse so gay, that it can blynd
  The wisest sight, to thinke gold that is bras.
  But vertues seat is deepe within the mynd,
And not in outward shows, but inward thoughts defynd.

6

But where shall I in all Antiquity
  So faire a patterne finde, where may be seene
  The goodly praise of Princely curtesie,
  As in your selfe, O soveraine Lady Queene,
  In whose pure minde, as in a mirrour sheene,
  It showes, and with her brightnesse doth inflame
  The eyes of all, which thereon fixed beene;
  But meriteth indeede an higher name:
Yet so from low to high uplifted is your name.

7

Then pardon me, most dreaded Soveraine,
  That from your selfe I doe this vertue bring,
  And to your selfe doe it returne againe:
So from the Ocean all rivers spring,
  And tribute backe repay as to their King.
Right so from you all goodly vertues well
  Into the rest, which round about you ring,
Faire Lords and Ladies, which about you dwell,
And doe adorne your Court, where courtesies excell.

CANT. I

Calidore saves from Maleffort,
  A Damzell used vylde:
Doth vanquish Crudor, and doth make
  Briana wexe more mylde.

I

OF Court it seemes, men Courtesie doe call,
  For that it there most useth to abound;
  And well beseemeth that in Princes hall
That vertue should be plentifully found,
Which of all goodly manners is the ground,
  And roote of civill conversation.
Right so in Faery court it did redound,
  Where curteous Knights and Ladies most did won
Of all on earth, and made a matchlesse paragon.

2

But mongst them all was none more courteous Knight,
  Than *Calidore*, beloved over all,
  In whom it seemes, that gentlenesse of spright
And manners mylde were planted naturall;
To which he adding comely guize withall,
  And gracious speach, did steale mens hearts away.
Nathlesse thereto he was full stout and tall,
  And well approv'd in batteilous affray,
That him did much renowme, and far his fame display.

3

Ne was there Knight, ne was there Lady found
  In Faery court, but him did deare embrace,
  For his faire usage and conditions sound,
  The which in all mens liking gayned place,
  And with the greatest purchast greatest grace:
  Which he could wisely use, and well apply,
  To please the best, and th'evill to embase.
  For he loathd leasing, and base flattery,
And loved simple truth and stedfast honesty.

4

And now he was in travell on his way,
  Uppon an hard adventure sore bestad,
  Whenas by chaunce he met uppon a day
  With *Artegall*, returning yet halfe sad
  From his late conquest, which he gotten had.
  Who whenas each of other had a sight,
  They knew them selves, and both their persons rad:
  When *Calidore* thus first; Haile noblest Knight
Of all this day on ground, that breathen living spright.

5

Now tell, if please you, of the good successe,
  Which ye have had in your late enterprize.
  To whom Sir *Artegall* gan to expresse
  His whole exploite, and valorous emprize,
  In order as it did to him arize.
  Now happy man (sayd then Sir *Calidore*)
  Which have so goodly, as ye can devize,
  Atchiev'd so hard a quest, as few before;
That shall you most renowmed make for evermore.

6

But where ye ended have, now I begin
  To tread an endlesse trace, withouten guyde,
  Or good direction, how to enter in,
  Or how to issue forth in waies untryde,
  In perils strange, in labours long and wide,
  In which although good Fortune me befall,
  Yet shall it not by none be testifyde.
  What is that quest (quoth then Sir *Artegall*)
That you into such perils presently doth call?

7

The Blattant Beast (quoth he) I doe pursew,
  And through the world incessantly doe chase,
  Till I him overtake, or else subdew:
  Yet know I not or how, or in what place
  To find him out, yet still I forward trace.
  What is that Blattant Beast? (then he replide.)
  It is a Monster bred of hellishe race,
  (Then answerd he) which often hath annoyd
Good Knights and Ladies true, and many else destroyd.

8

Of *Cerberus* whilome he was begot,
  And fell *Chimæra* in her darkesome den,
  Through fowle commixture of his filthy blot;
  Where he was fostred long in *Stygian* fen,
  Till he to perfect ripenesse grew, and then
  Into this wicked world he forth was sent,
  To be the plague and scourge of wretched men:
  Whom with vile tongue and venemous intent
He sore doth wound, and bite, and cruelly torment.

9

Then since the salvage Island I did leave,
  Sayd *Artegall*, I such a Beast did see,
  The which did seeme a thousand tongues to have,
  That all in spight and malice did agree,
  With which he bayd and loudly barkt at mee,
  As if that he attonce would me devoure.
  But I that knew my selfe from perill free,
  Did nought regard his malice nor his powre,
But he the more his wicked poyson forth did poure.

10

That surely is that Beast (saide *Calidore*)
  Which I pursue, of whom I am right glad
  To heare these tidings, which of none afore
  Through all my weary travell I have had:
  Yet now some hope your words unto me add.
  Now God you speed (quoth then Sir *Artegall*)
  And keepe your body from the daunger drad:
  For ye have much adoe to deale withall.
So both tooke goodly leave, and parted severall.

11

Sir *Calidore* thence travelled not long,
　When as by chaunce a comely Squire he found,
　That thorough some more mighty enemies wrong,
　Both hand and foote unto a tree was bound:
　Who seeing him from farre, with piteous sound
　Of his shrill cries him called to his aide.
　To whom approching, in that painefull stound
　When he him saw, for no demaunds he staide,
But first him losde, and afterwards thus to him saide.

12

Unhappy Squire, what hard mishap thee brought
　Into this bay of perill and disgrace?
　What cruell hand thy wretched thraldome wrought,
　And thee captyved in this shamefull place?
　To whom he answerd thus; My haplesse case
　Is not occasiond through my misdesert,
　But through misfortune, which did me abase
　Unto this shame, and my young hope subvert,
Ere that I in her guilefull traines was well expert.

13

Not farre from hence, uppon yond rocky hill,
　Hard by a streight there stands a castle strong,
　Which doth observe a custome lewd and ill,
　And it hath long mayntaind with mighty wrong:
　For may no Knight nor Lady passe along
　That way, (and yet they needs must passe that way,)
　By reason of the streight, and rocks among,
　But they that Ladies lockes doe shave away,
And that knights berd for toll, which they for passage pay.

14

A shamefull use as ever I did heare,
　Sayd *Calidore*, and to be overthrowne.
　But by what meanes did they at first it reare,
　And for what cause, tell if thou have it knowne.
　Sayd then that Squire: The Lady which doth owne
　This Castle, is by name *Briana* hight.
　Than which a prouder Lady liveth none:
　She long time hath deare lov'd a doughty Knight,
And sought to win his love by all the meanes she might.

15

His name is *Crudor*, who through high disdaine
  And proud despight of his selfe pleasing mynd,
  Refused hath to yeeld her love againe,
  Untill a Mantle she for him doe fynd,
  With beards of Knights and locks of Ladies lynd.
  Which to provide, she hath this Castle dight,
  And therein hath a Seneschall assynd,
  Cald *Maleffort*, a man of mickle might,
Who executes her wicked will, with worse despight.

16

He this same day, as I that way did come
  With a faire Damzell, my beloved deare,
  In execution of her lawlesse doome,
  Did set uppon us flying both for feare:
  For little bootes against him hand to reare.
  Me first he tooke, unhable to withstond;
  And whiles he her pursued every where,
  Till his returne unto this tree he bond:
Ne wote I surely, whether her he yet have fond.

17

Thus whiles they spake, they heard a ruefull shrieke
  Of one loud crying, which they streight way ghest,
  That it was she, the which for helpe did seeke.
  Tho looking up unto the cry to lest,
  They saw that Carle from farre, with hand unblest
  Hayling that mayden by the yellow heare,
  That all her garments from her snowy brest,
  And from her head her lockes he nigh did teare,
Ne would he spare for pitty, nor refraine for feare.

18

Which haynous sight when *Calidore* beheld,
  Eftsoones he loosd that Squire, and so him left,
  With hearts dismay and inward dolour queld,
  For to pursue that villaine, which had reft
  That piteous spoile by so injurious theft.
  Whom overtaking, loude to him he cryde;
  Leave faytor quickely that misgotten weft
  To him, that hath it better justifyde,
And turne thee soone to him, of whom thou art defyde.

19

Who hearkning to that voice, him selfe upreard,
    And seeing him so fiercely towardes make,
    Against him stoutly ran, as nought afeard,
    But rather more enrag'd for those words sake;
    And with sterne count'naunce thus unto him spake.
    Art thou the caytive, that defyest me,
    And for this Mayd, whose party thou doest take,
    Wilt give thy beard, though it but little bee?
Yet shall it not her lockes for raunsome fro me free.

20

With that he fiercely at him flew, and layd
    On hideous strokes with most importune might,
    That oft he made him stagger as unstayd,
    And oft recuile to shunne his sharpe despight.
    But *Calidore*, that was well skild in fight,
    Him long forbore, and still his spirite spar'd,
    Lying in waite, how him he damadge might.
    But when he felt him shrinke, and come to ward,
He greater grew, and gan to drive at him more hard.

21

Like as a water streame, whose swelling sourse
    Shall drive a Mill, within strong bancks is pent,
    And long restrayned of his ready course;
    So soone as passage is unto him lent,
    Breakes forth, and makes his way more violent.
    Such was the fury of Sir *Calidore*,
    When once he felt his foeman to relent;
    He fiercely him pursu'd, and pressed sore,
Who as he still decayd, so he encreased more.

22

The heavy burden of whose dreadfull might
    When as the Carle no longer could sustaine,
    His heart gan faint, and streight he tooke his flight
    Toward the Castle, where if need constraine,
    His hope of refuge used to remaine.
    Whom *Calidore* perceiving fast to flie,
    He him pursu'd and chaced through the plaine,
    That he for dread of death gan loude to crie
Unto the ward, to open to him hastilie.

23

They from the wall him seeing so aghast,
  The gate soone opened to receive him in,
  But *Calidore* did follow him so fast,
  That even in the Porch he him did win,
  And cleft his head asunder to his chin.
  The carkasse tumbling downe within the dore,
  Did choke the entraunce with a lumpe of sin,
  That it could not be shut, whilest *Calidore*
Did enter in, and slew the Porter on the flore.

24

With that the rest, the which the Castle kept,
  About him flockt, and hard at him did lay;
  But he them all from him full lightly swept,
  As doth a Steare, in heat of sommers day,
  With his long taile the bryzes brush away.
  Thence passing forth, into the hall he came,
  Where of the Lady selfe in sad dismay
  He was ymett, who with uncomely shame
Gan him salute, and fowle upbrayd with faulty blame.

25

False traytor Knight, (sayd she) no Knight at all,
  But scorne of armes that hast with guilty hand
  Murdred my men, and slaine my Seneschall;
  Now comest thou to rob my house unmand,
  And spoile my selfe, that can not thee withstand?
  Yet doubt thou not, but that some better Knight
  Than thou, that shall thy treason understand,
  Will it avenge, and pay thee with thy right:
And if none do, yet shame shal thee with shame requight.

26

Much was the Knight abashed at that word;
  Yet answerd thus; Not unto me the shame,
  But to the shamefull doer it afford.
  Bloud is no blemish; for it is no blame
  To punish those, that doe deserve the same;
  But they that breake bands of civilitie,
  And wicked customes make, those doe defame
  Both noble armes and gentle curtesie.
No greater shame to man than inhumanitie.

27

Then doe your selfe, for dread of shame, forgoe
  This evill manner, which ye here maintaine,
  And doe in stead thereof mild curt'sie showe
  To all, that passe. That shall you glory gaine
  More than his love, which thus ye seeke t'obtaine.
  Wherewith all full of wrath, she thus replyde;
  Vile recreant, know that I doe much disdaine
  Thy courteous lore, that doest my love deride,
Who scornes thy ydle scoffe, and bids thee be defyde.

28

To take defiaunce at a Ladies word
  (Quoth he) I hold it no indignity;
  But were he here, that would it with his sword
  Abett, perhaps he mote it deare aby.
  Cowherd (quoth she) were not, that thou wouldst fly,
  Ere he doe come, he should be soone in place.
  If I doe so, (sayd he) then liberty
  I leave to you, for aye me to disgrace
With all those shames, that erst ye spake me to deface.

29

With that a Dwarfe she cald to her in hast,
  And taking from her hand a ring of gould,
  A privy token, which betweene them past,
  Bad him to flie with all the speed he could,
  To *Crudor*, and desire him that he would
  Vouchsafe to reskue her against a Knight,
  Who through strong powre had now her self in hould,
  Having late slaine her Seneschall in fight,
And all her people murdred with outragious might.

30

The Dwarfe his way did hast, and went all night;
  But *Calidore* did with her there abyde
  The comming of that so much threatned Knight,
  Where that discourteous Dame with scornfull pryde,
  And fowle entreaty him indignifyde,
  That yron heart it hardly could sustaine:
  Yet he, that could his wrath full wisely guyde
  Did well endure her womanish disdaine,
And did him selfe from fraile impatience refraine.

31

The morrow next, before the lampe of light
  Above the earth upreard his flaming head,
  The Dwarfe, which bore that message to her knight,
  Brought aunswere backe, that ere he tasted bread,
  He would her succour, and alive or dead
  Her foe deliver up into her hand:
  Therefore he wild her doe away all dread;
  And that of him she mote assured stand,
He sent to her his basenet, as a faithfull band.

32

Thereof full blyth the Lady streight became,
  And gan t'augment her bitternesse much more:
  Yet no whit more appalled for the same,
  Ne ought dismayed was Sir *Calidore*,
  But rather did more chearefull seeme therefore.
  And having soone his armes about him dight,
  Did issue forth, to meete his foe afore;
  Where long he stayed not, when as a Knight
He spide come pricking on with al his powre and might.

33

Well weend he streight, that he should be the same,
  Which tooke in hand her quarrell to maintaine;
  Ne stayd to aske if it were he by name,
  But coucht his speare, and ran at him amaine.
  They bene ymett in middest of the plaine,
  With so fell fury, and dispiteous forse,
  That neither could the others stroke sustaine,
  But rudely rowld to ground both man and horse,
Neither of other taking pitty nor remorse.

34

But *Calidore* uprose againe full light,
  Whiles yet his foe lay fast in sencelesse sound,
  Yet would he not him hurt, although he might:
  For shame he weend a sleeping wight to wound.
  But when *Briana* saw that drery stound,
  There where she stood uppon the Castle wall,
  She deem'd him sure to have bene dead on ground,
  And made such piteous mourning therewithall,
That from the battlements she ready seem'd to fall.

35

Nathlesse at length him selfe he did upreare
  In lustlesse wise, as if against his will,
  Ere he had slept his fill, he wakened were,
  And gan to stretch his limbs; which feeling ill
  Of his late fall, a while he rested still:
  But when he saw his foe before in vew,
  He shooke off luskishnesse, and courage chill
  Kindling a fresh, gan battell to renew,
To prove if better foote than horsebacke would ensew.

36

There then began a fearefull cruell fray
  Betwixt them two, for maystery of might.
  For both were wondrous practicke in that play,
  And passing well expert in single fight,
  And both inflam'd with furious despight:
  Which as it still encreast, so still increast
  Their cruell strokes and terrible affright;
  Ne once for ruth their rigour they release,
Ne once to breath a while their angers tempest ceast.

37

Thus long they trac'd and traverst to and fro,
  And tryde all waies, how each mote entrance make
  Into the life of his malignant foe;
  They hew'd their helmes, and plates asunder brake,
  As they had potshares bene; for nought mote slake
  Their greedy vengeaunces, but goary blood,
  That at the last like to a purple lake
  Of bloudy gore congeal'd about them stood,
Which from their riven sides forth gushed like a flood.

38

At length it chaunst, that both their hands on hie
  At once did heave, with all their powre and might,
  Thinking the utmost of their force to trie,
  And prove the finall fortune of the fight:
  But *Calidore*, that was more quicke of sight,
  And nimbler handed, than his enemie,
  Prevented him before his stroke could light,
  And on the helmet smote him formerlie,
That made him stoupe to ground with meeke humilitie.

39

And ere he could recover foot againe,
    He following that faire advantage fast,
    His stroke redoubled with such might and maine,
    That him upon the ground he groveling cast;
    And leaping to him light, would have unlast
    His Helme, to make unto his vengeance way.
    Who seeing, in what daunger he was plast,
    Cryde out, Ah mercie Sir, doe me not slay,
But save my life, which lot before your foot doth lay.

40

With that his mortall hand a while he stayd,
    And having somewhat calm'd his wrathfull heat
    With goodly patience, thus he to him sayd;
    And is the boast of that proud Ladies threat,
    That menaced me from the field to beat,
    Now brought to this? By this now may ye learne,
    Strangers no more so rudely to intreat,
    But put away proud looke, and usage sterne,
The which shal nought to you but foule dishonor yearne.

41

For nothing is more blamefull to a knight,
    That court'sie doth as well as armes professe,
    How ever strong and fortunate in fight,
    Than the reproch of pride and cruelnesse.
    In vaine he seeketh others to suppresse,
    Who hath not learnd him selfe first to subdew:
    All flesh is frayle, and full of ficklenesse,
    Subject to fortunes chance, still chaunging new;
What haps to day to me, to morrow may to you.

42

Who will not mercie unto others shew,
    How can he mercy ever hope to have?
    To pay each with his owne is right and dew.
    Yet since ye mercie now doe need to crave,
    I will it graunt, your hopelesse life to save;
    With these conditions, which I will propound:
    First, that ye better shall your selfe behave
    Unto all errant knights, whereso on ground;
Next that ye Ladies ayde in every stead and stound.

43

The wretched man, that all this while did dwell
  In dread of death, his heasts did gladly heare,
  And promist to performe his precept well,
  And whatsoever else he would requere.
  So suffring him to rise, he made him sweare
  By his owne sword, and by the crosse thereon,
  To take *Briana* for his loving fere,
  Withouten dowre or composition;
But to release his former foule condition.

44

All which accepting, and with faithfull oth
  Bynding himselfe most firmely to obay,
  He up arose, how ever liefe or loth,
  And swore to him true fealtie for aye.
  Then forth he cald from sorrowfull dismay
  The sad *Briana*, which all this beheld:
  Who comming forth yet full of late affray,
  Sir *Calidore* upcheard, and to her teld
All this accord, to which he *Crudor* had compeld.

45

Whereof she now more glad, than sory earst,
  All overcome with infinite affect,
  For his exceeding courtesie, that pearst
  Her stubborne hart with inward deepe effect,
  Before his feet her selfe she did project,
  And him adoring as her lives deare Lord,
  With all due thankes, and dutifull respect,
  Her selfe acknowledg'd bound for that accord,
By which he had to her both life and love restord.

46

So all returning to the Castle glad,
  Most joyfully she them did entertaine,
  Where goodly glee and feast to them she made,
  To shew her thankefull mind and meaning faine,
  By all the meanes she mote it best explaine:
  And after all, unto Sir *Calidore*
  She freely gave that Castle for his paine,
  And her selfe bound to him for evermore;
So wondrously now chaung'd, from that she was afore.

47

But *Calidore* himselfe would not retaine
  Nor land nor fee, for hyre of his good deede,
  But gave them streight unto that Squire againe,
  Whom from her Seneschall he lately freed,
  And to his damzell as their rightfull meed,
  For recompence of all their former wrong:
  There he remaind with them right well agreed,
  Till of his wounds he wexed hole and strong,
And then to his first quest he passed forth along.

CANT. II

Calidore sees young Tristram slay
A proud discourteous knight,
He makes him Squire, and of him learnes
his state and present plight.

I

WHAT vertue is so fitting for a knight,
  Or for a Ladie, whom a knight should love,
  As Curtesie, to beare themselves aright
  To all of each degree, as doth behove?
  For whether they be placed high above,
  Or low beneath, yet ought they well to know
  Their good, that none them rightly may reprove
  Of rudenesse, for not yeelding what they owe:
Great skill it is such duties timely to bestow.

2

Thereto great helpe dame Nature selfe doth lend:
  For some so goodly gratious are by kind,
  That every action doth them much commend,
  And in the eyes of men great liking find;
  Which others, that have greater skill in mind,
  Though they enforce themselves, cannot attaine.
  For everie thing, to which one is inclin'd,
  Doth best become, and greatest grace doth gaine:
Yet praise likewise deserve good thewes, enforst with paine.

Calidore

3

That well in courteous *Calidore* appeares,
 Whose every deed and word, that he did say,
 Was like enchantment, that through both the eyes,
 And both the eares did steale the hart away.
 He now againe is on his former way,
 To follow his first quest, when as he spyde
 A tall young man from thence not farre away,
 Fighting on foot, as well he him descryde,
Against an armed knight, that did on horsebacke ryde.

4

And them beside a Ladie faire he saw,
 Standing alone on foot, in foule array:
 To whom himselfe he hastily did draw,
 To weet the cause of so uncomely fray,
 And to depart them, if so be he may.
 But ere he came in place, that youth had kild
 That armed knight, that low on ground he lay;
 Which when he saw, his hart was inly child
With great amazement, and his thought with wonder fild.

5

Him stedfastly he markt, and saw to bee
 A goodly youth of amiable grace,
 Yet but a slender slip, that scarse did see
 Yet seventeene yeares, but tall and faire of face
 That sure he deem'd him borne of noble race.
 All in a woodmans jacket he was clad
 Of Lincolne greene, belayd with silver lace;
 And on his head an hood with aglets sprad,
And by his side his hunters horne he hanging had.

6

Buskins he wore of costliest cordwayne,
 Pinckt upon gold, and paled part per part,
 As then the guize was for each gentle swayne;
 In his right hand he held a trembling dart,
 Whose fellow he before had sent apart;
 And in his left he held a sharpe borespeare,
 With which he wont to launch the salvage hart
 Of many a Lyon, and of many a Beare
That first unto his hand in chase did happen neare.

7

Whom *Calidore* a while well having vewed,
  At length bespake; What meanes this, gentle swaine?
  Why hath thy hand too bold it selfe embrewed
  In blood of knight, the which by thee is slaine,
  By thee no knight; which armes impugneth plaine?
  Certes (said he) loth were I to have broken
  The law of armes; yet breake it should againe,
  Rather than let my selfe of wight be stroken,
So long as these two armes were able to be wroken.

8

For not I him, as this his Ladie here
  May witnesse well, did offer first to wrong,
  Ne surely thus unarm'd I likely were;
  But he me first, through pride and puissance strong
  Assayld, not knowing what to armes doth long.
  Perdie great blame, (then said Sir *Calidore*)
  For armed knight a wight unarm'd to wrong.
  But then aread, thou gentle chyld, wherefore
Betwixt you two began this strife and sterne uprore.

9

That shall I sooth (saith he) to you declare.
  I whose unryper yeares are yet unfit
  For thing of weight, or worke of greater care,
  Doe spend my dayes, and bend my carelesse wit
  To salvage chace, where I thereon may hit
  In all this forrest, and wyld wooddie raine:
  Where, as this day I was enraunging it,
  I chaunst to meete this knight, who there lyes slaine,
Together with this Ladie, passing on the plaine.

10

The knight, as ye did see, on horsebacke was,
  And this his Ladie, (that him ill became,)
  On her faire feet by his horse side did pas
  Through thicke and thin, unfit for any Dame,
  Yet not content, more to increase his shame,
  When so she lagged, as she needs mote so,
  He with his speare, that was to him great blame,
  Would thumpe her forward, and inforce to goe,
Weeping to him in vaine, and making piteous woe.

11

Which when I saw, as they me passed by,
　Much was I moved in indignant mind,
　And gan to blame him for such cruelty
　Towards a Ladie, whom with usage kind
　He rather should have taken up behind.
　Wherewith he wroth, and full of proud disdaine,
　Tooke in foule scorne, that I such fault did find,
　And me in lieu thereof revil'd againe,
Threatning to chastize me, as doth t'a chyld pertaine.

12

Which I no lesse disdayning, backe returned
　His scornefull taunts unto his teeth againe,
　That he streight way with haughtie choler burned,
　And with his speare strooke me one stroke or twaine;
　Which I enforst to beare though to my paine,
　Cast to requite, and with a slender dart,
　Fellow of this I beare, throwne not in vaine,
　Strooke him, as seemeth, underneath the hart,
That through the wound his spirit shortly did depart.

13

Much did Sir *Calidore* admyre his speach
　Tempred so well, but more admyr'd the stroke
　That through the mayles had made so strong a breach
　Into his hart, and had so sternely wroke
　His wrath on him, that first occasion broke.
　Yet rested not, but further gan inquire
　Of that same Ladie, whether what he spoke,
　Were soothly so, and that th'unrighteous ire
Of her owne knight, had given him his owne due hire.

14

Of all which, when as she could nought deny,
　But cleard that stripling of th'imputed blame,
　Sayd then Sir *Calidore*; Neither will I
　Him charge with guilt, but rather doe quite clame:
　For what he spake, for you he spake it, Dame:
　And what he did, he did him selfe to save:
　Against both which that knight wrought knightlesse shame.
　For knights and all men this by nature have,
Towards all womenkind them kindly to behave.

15

But sith that he is gone irrevocable,
  Please it you Ladie, to us to aread,
  What cause could make him so dishonourable,
  To drive you so on foot unfit to tread,
  And lackey by him, gainst all womanhead?
  Certes Sir knight (sayd she) full loth I were
  To rayse a lyving blame against the dead:
  But since it me concernes, my selfe to clere,
I will the truth discover, as it chaunst whylere.

16

This day, as he and I together roade
  Upon our way, to which we weren bent,
  We chaunst to come foreby a covert glade
  Within a wood, whereas a Ladie gent
  Sate with a knight in joyous jolliment
  Of their franke loves, free from all gealous spyes:
  Faire was the Ladie sure, that mote content
  An hart, not carried with too curious eyes,
And unto him did shew all lovely courtesyes.

17

Whom when my knight did see so lovely faire,
  He inly gan her lover to envy,
  And wish, that he part of his spoyle might share.
  Whereto when as my presence he did spy
  To be a let, he bad me by and by
  For to alight: but when as I was loth,
  My loves owne part to leave so suddenly,
  He with strong hand down from his steed me throw'th,
And with presumpteous powre against that knight streight go'th.

18

Unarm'd all was the knight, as then more meete
  For Ladies service, and for loves delight,
  Than fearing any foeman there to meete:
  Whereof he taking oddes, streight bids him dight
  Himselfe to yeeld his love, or else to fight.
  Whereat the other starting up dismayd,
  Yet boldly answer'd, as he rightly might;
  To leave his love he should be ill apayd,
In which he had good right gaynst all, that it gainesayd.

19

Yet since he was not presently in plight
　Her to defend, or his to justifie,
　He him requested, as he was a knight,
　To lend him day his better right to trie,
　Or stay till he his armes, which were thereby,
　Might lightly fetch. But he was fierce and whot,
　Ne time would give, nor any termes aby,
　But at him flew, and with his speare him smot;
From which to thinke to save himselfe, it booted not.

20

Meane while his Ladie, which this outrage saw,
　Whilest they together for the quarrey strove,
　Into the covert did her selfe withdraw,
　And closely hid her selfe within the grove.
　My knight hers soone, as seemes, to daunger drove
　And left sore wounded: but when her he mist,
　He woxe halfe mad, and in that rage gan rove
　And range through all the wood, where so he wist
She hidden was, and sought her so long, as him list.

21

But when as her he by no meanes could find,
　After long search and chauff, he turned backe
　Unto the place, where me he left behind:
　There gan he me to curse and ban, for lacke
　Of that faire bootie, and with bitter wracke
　To wreake on me the guilt of his owne wrong.
　Of all which I yet glad to beare the packe,
　Strove to appease him, and perswaded long:
But still his passion grew more violent and strong.

22

Then as it were t'avenge his wrath on mee,
　When forward we should fare, he flat refused
　To take me up (as this young man did see)
　Upon his steed, for no just cause accused,
　But forst to trot on foot, and foule misused,
　Pounching me with the butt end of his speare,
　In vaine complayning, to be so abused.
　For he regarded neither playnt nor teare,
But more enforst my paine, the more my plaints to heare.

23

So passed we, till this young man us met,
　And being moov'd with pittie of my plight,
　Spake, as was meet, for ease of my regret:
　Whereof befell, what now is in your sight.
　Now sure (then said Sir *Calidore*) and right
　Me seemes, that him befell by his owne fault:
　Who ever thinkes through confidence of might,
　Or through support of count'nance proud and hault
To wrong the weaker, oft falles in his owne assault.

24

Then turning backe unto that gentle boy,
　Which had himselfe so stoutly well acquit;
　Seeing his face so lovely sterne and coy,
　And hearing th'answeres of his pregnant wit,
　He praysd it much, and much admyred it;
　That sure he weend him borne of noble blood,
　With whom those graces did so goodly fit:
　And when he long had him beholding stood,
He burst into these words, as to him seemed good.

25

Faire gentle swayne, and yet as stout as fayre,
　That in these woods amongst the Nymphs dost wonne,
　Which daily may to thy sweete lookes repayre,
　As they are wont unto *Latonaes* sonne,
　After his chace on woodie *Cynthus* donne:
　Well may I certes such an one thee read,
　As by thy worth thou worthily hast wonne,
　Or surely borne of some Heroicke sead,
That in thy face appeares and gratious goodlyhead.

26

But should it not displease thee it to tell;
　(Unlesse thou in these woods thy selfe conceale,
　For love amongst the woodie Gods to dwell;)
　I would thy selfe require thee to reveale,
　For deare affection and unfayned zeale,
　Which to thy noble personage I beare,
　And wish thee grow in worship and great weale.
　For since the day that armes I first did reare,
I never saw in any greater hope appeare.

27

To whom then thus the noble youth; May be
  Sir knight, that by discovering my estate,
  Harme may arise unweeting unto me;
  Nathelesse, sith ye so courteous seemed late,
  To you I will not feare it to relate.
  Then wote ye that I am a Briton borne,
  Sonne of a King, how ever thorough fate
  Or fortune I my countrie have forlorne,
And lost the crowne, which should my head by right adorne.

28

And *Tristram* is my name, the onely heire
  Of good king *Meliogras* which did rayne
  In Cornewale, till that he through lives despeire
  Untimely dyde, before I did attaine
  Ripe yeares of reason, my right to maintaine.
  After whose death, his brother seeing mee
  An infant, weake a kingdome to sustaine,
  Upon him tooke the roiall high degree,
And sent me, where him list, instructed for to bee.

29

The widow Queene my mother, which then hight
  Faire *Emiline*, conceiving then great feare
  Of my fraile safetie, resting in the might
  Of him, that did the kingly Scepter beare,
  Whose gealous dread induring not a peare,
  Is wont to cut off all, that doubt may breed,
  Thought best away me to remove somewhere
  Into some forrein land, where as no need
Of dreaded daunger might his doubtfull humor feed.

30

So taking counsell of a wise man red,
  She was by him adviz'd, to send me quight
  Out of the countrie, wherein I was bred,
  The which the fertile *Lionesse* is hight,
  Into the land of *Faerie*, where no wight
  Should weet of me, nor worke me any wrong.
  To whose wise read she hearkning, sent me streight
  Into this land, where I have wond thus long,
Since I was ten yeares old, now growen to stature strong.

31

All which my daies I have not lewdly spent,
  Nor spilt the blossome of my tender yeares
  In ydlesse, but as was convenient,
  Have trayned bene with many noble feres
  In gentle thewes, and such like seemely leres.
  Mongst which my most delight hath alwaies been,
  To hunt the salvage chace amongst my peres,
  Of all that raungeth in the forrest greene;
Of which none is to me unknowne, that ev'r was seene.

32

Ne is there hauke, which mantleth her on pearch,
  Whether high towring, or accoasting low,
  But I the measure of her flight doe search,
  And all her pray, and all her diet know.
  Such be our joyes, which in these forrests grow:
  Onely the use of armes, which most I joy,
  And fitteth most for noble swayne to know,
  I have not tasted yet, yet past a boy,
And being now high time these strong joynts to imploy.

33

Therefore, good Sir, sith now occasion fit
  Doth fall, whose like hereafter seldome may,
  Let me this crave, unworthy though of it,
  That ye will make me Squire without delay,
  That from henceforth in batteilous array
  I may beare armes, and learne to use them right;
  The rather since that fortune hath this day
  Given to me the spoile of this dead knight,
These goodly gilden armes, which I have won in fight.

34

All which when well Sir *Calidore* had heard,
  Him much more now, than earst he gan admire,
  For the rare hope which in his yeares appear'd,
  And thus replide; Faire chyld, the high desire
  To love of armes, which in you doth aspire,
  I may not certes without blame denie;
  But rather wish, that some more noble hire,
  (Though none more noble than is chevalrie,)
I had, you to reward with greater dignitie.

35

There him he causd to kneele, and made to sweare
　Faith to his knight, and truth to Ladies all,
　And never to be recreant, for feare
　Of perill, or of ought that might befall:
　So he him dubbed, and his Squire did call.
　Full glad and joyous then young *Tristram* grew,
　Like as a flowre, whose silken leaves small,
　Long shut up in the bud from heavens vew,
At length breakes forth, and brode displayes his smyling hew.

36

Thus when they long had treated to and fro,
　And *Calidore* betooke him to depart,
　Chyld *Tristram* prayd, that he with him might goe
　On his adventure, vowing not to start,
　But wayt on him in every place and part.
　Whereat Sir *Calidore* did much delight,
　And greatly joy'd at his so noble hart,
　In hope he sure would prove a doughtie knight
Yet for the time this answere he to him behight.

37

Glad would I surely be, thou courteous Squire
　To have thy presence in my present quest,
　That mote thy kindled courage set on fire,
　And flame forth honour in thy noble brest:
　But I am bound by vow, which I profest
　To my dread Soveraine, when I it assayd,
　That in atchievement of her high behest,
　I should no creature joyne unto mine ayde,
For thy I may not graunt, that ye so greatly prayde.

38

But since this Ladie is all desolate,
　And needeth safegard now upon her way,
　Ye may doe well in this her needfull state
　To succour her, from daunger of dismay;
　That thankfull guerdon may to you repay.
　The noble ympe of such new service fayne,
　It gladly did accept, as he did say.
　So taking courteous leave, they parted twayne,
And *Calidore* forth passed to his former payne.

39

But *Tristram* then despoyling that dead knight
  Of all those goodly implements of prayse,
  Long fed his greedie eyes with the faire sight
  Of the bright mettall, shyning like Sunne rayes;
  Handling and turning them a thousand wayes.
  And after having them upon him dight,
  He tooke that Ladie, and her up did rayse
  Upon the steed of her owne late dead knight,
So with her marched forth, as she did him behight.

40

There to their fortune leave we them awhile,
  And turne we backe to good Sir *Calidore*;
  Who ere he thence had traveild many a mile,
  Came to the place, whereas ye heard afore
  This knight, whom *Tristram* slew, had wounded sore
  Another knight in his despiteous pryde;
  There he that knight found lying on the flore,
  With many wounds full perilous and wyde,
That all his garments, and the grasse in vermeill dyde.

41

And there beside him sate upon the ground
  His wofull Ladie, piteously complayning
  With loud laments that most unluckie stound,
  And her sad selfe with carefull hand constrayning
  To wype his wounds, and ease their bitter payning.
  Which sorie sight when *Calidore* did vew
  With heavie eyne, from teares uneath refrayning,
  His mightie hart their mournefull case can rew,
And for their better comfort to them nigher drew.

42

Then speaking to the Ladie, thus he sayd:
  Ye dolefull Dame, let not your griefe empeach
  To tell, what cruell hand hath thus arayd
  This knight unarm'd, with so unknightly breach
  Of armes, that if I yet him nigh may reach,
  I may avenge him of so foule despight.
  The Ladie hearing his so courteous speach,
  Gan reare her eyes as to the chearefull light,
And from her sory hart few heavie words forth sight.

43

In which she shew'd, how that discourteous knight
  (Whom *Tristram* slew) them in that shadow found,
  Joying together in unblam'd delight,
  And him unarm'd, as now he lay on ground,
  Charg'd with his speare and mortally did wound,
  Withouten cause, but onely her to reave
  From him, to whom she was for ever bound:
  Yet when she fled into that covert greave,
He her not finding, both them thus nigh dead did leave.

44

When *Calidore* this ruefull storie had
  Well understood, he gan of her demand,
  What manner wight he was, and how yclad,
  Which had this outrage wrought with wicked hand.
  She then, like as she best could understand,
  Him thus describ'd, to be of stature large,
  Clad all in gilden armes, with azure band
  Quartred athwart, and bearing in his targe
A Ladie on rough waves, row'd in a sommer barge.

45

Then gan Sir *Calidore* to ghesse streight way
  By many signes, which she described had,
  That this was he, whom *Tristram* earst did slay,
  And to her said; Dame be no longer sad:
  For he, that hath your Knight so ill bestad,
  Is now him selfe in much more wretched plight;
  These eyes him saw upon the cold earth sprad,
  The meede of his desert for that despight,
Which to your selfe he wrought, and to your loved knight.

46

Therefore faire Lady lay aside this griefe,
  Which ye have gathered to your gentle hart,
  For that displeasure; and thinke what reliefe
  Were best devise for this your lovers smart,
  And how ye may him hence, and to what part
  Convay to be recur'd. She thankt him deare,
  Both for that newes he did to her impart,
  And for the courteous care, which he did beare
Both to her love, and to her selfe in that sad dreare.

47

Yet could she not devise by any wit,
　How thence she might convay him to some place.
　For him to trouble she it thought unfit,
　That was a straunger to her wretched case;
　And him to beare, she thought it thing too base.
　Which when as he perceiv'd, he thus bespake;
　Faire Lady let it not you seeme disgrace,
　To beare this burden on your dainty backe;
My selfe will beare a part, coportion of your packe.

48

So off he did his shield, and downeward layd
　Upon the ground, like to an hollow beare;
　And powring balme, which he had long purvayd,
　Into his wounds, him up thereon did reare,
　And twixt them both with parted paines did beare,
　Twixt life and death, not knowing what was donne.
　Thence they him carried to a Castle neare,
　In which a worthy auncient Knight did wonne:
Where what ensu'd, shall in next Canto be begonne.

CANT. III

Calidore brings Priscilla home,
Pursues the Blatant Beast:
Saves Serena whilest Calepine
By Turpine is opprest.

I

TRUE is, that whilome that good Poet sayd,
　The gentle minde by gentle deeds is knowne.
　For a man by nothing is so well bewrayd,
　As by his manners, in which plaine is showne
　Of what degree and what race he is growne.
　For seldome seene, a trotting Stalion get
　An ambling Colt, that is his proper owne:
　So seldome seene, that one in basenesse set
Doth noble courage shew, with curteous manners met.

2

But evermore contrary hath bene tryde,
 That gentle bloud will gentle manners breed;
 As well may be in *Calidore* descryde,
 By late ensample of that courteous deed,
 Done to that wounded Knight in his great need,
 Whom on his backe he bore, till he him brought
 Unto the Castle where they had decreed.
 There of the Knight, the which that Castle ought,
To make abode that night he greatly was besought.

3

He was to weete a man of full ripe yeares,
 That in his youth had beene of mickle might,
 And borne great sway in armes amongst his peares:
 But now weake age had dimd his candle light.
 Yet was he courteous still to every wight,
 And loved all that did to armes incline,
 And was the father of that wounded Knight,
 Whom *Calidore* thus carried on his chine,
And *Aldus* was his name, and his sonnes *Aladine*.

4

Who when he saw his sonne so ill bedight,
 With bleeding wounds, brought home upon a Beare,
 By a faire Lady, and a straunger Knight,
 Was inly touched with compassion deare,
 And deare affection of so dolefull dreare,
 That he these words burst forth; Ah sory boy,
 Is this the hope that to my hoary heare
 Thou brings? aie me, is this the timely joy,
Which I expected long, now turnd to sad annoy?

5

Such is the weakenesse of all mortall hope;
 So tickle is the state of earthly things,
 That ere they come unto their aymed scope,
 They fall too short of our fraile reckonings,
 And bring us bale and bitter sorrowings,
 In stead of comfort, which we should embrace:
 This is the state of Keasars and of Kings.
 Let none therefore, that is in meaner place,
Too greatly grieve at any his unlucky case.

6

So well and wisely did that good old Knight
　Temper his griefe, and turned it to cheare,
　To cheare his guests, whom he had stayd that night,
　And make their welcome to them well appeare:
　That to Sir *Calidore* was easie geare;
　But that faire Lady would be cheard for nought,
　But sigh'd and sorrow'd for her lover deare,
　And inly did afflict her pensive thought,
With thinking to what case her name should now be brought.

7

For she was daughter to a noble Lord,
　Which dwelt thereby, who sought her to affy
　To a great pere; but she did disaccord,
　Ne could her liking to his love apply,
　But lov'd this fresh young Knight, who dwelt her ny,
　The lusty *Aladine*, though meaner borne,
　And of lesse livelood and hability,
　Yet full of valour, the which did adorne
His meanesse much, and make her th'others riches scorne.

8

So having both found fit occasion,
　They met together in that luckelesse glade;
　Where that proud Knight in his presumption
　The gentle *Aladine* did earst invade,
　Being unarm'd, and set in secret shade.
　Whereof she now bethinking, gan t'advize,
　How great a hazard she at earst had made
　Of her good fame, and further gan devize,
How she the blame might salve with coloured disguize.

9

But *Calidore* with all good courtesie
　Fain'd her to frolicke, and to put away
　The pensive fit of her melancholie;
　And that old Knight by all meanes did assay,
　To make them both as merry as he may.
　So they the evening past, till time of rest,
　When *Calidore* in seemly good array
　Unto his bowre was brought, and there undrest,
Did sleepe all night through weary travell of his quest.

10

But faire *Priscilla* (so that Lady hight)
   Would to no bed, nor take no kindely sleepe,
   But by her wounded love did watch all night,
   And all the night for bitter anguish weepe,
   And with her teares his wounds did wash and steepe.
   So well she washt them, and so well she wacht him,
   That of the deadly swound, in which full deepe
   He drenched was, she at the length dispacht him,
And drove away the stound, which mortally attacht him.

11

The morrow next, when day gan to uplooke,
   He also gan uplooke with drery eye,
   Like one that out of deadly dreame awooke:
   Where when he saw his faire *Priscilla* by,
   He deepely sigh'd, and groaned inwardly,
   To thinke of this ill state, in which she stood,
   To which she for his sake had weetingly
   Now brought her selfe, and blam'd her noble blood:
For first, next after life, he tendered her good.

12

Which she perceiving, did with plenteous teares
   His care more than her owne compassionate,
   Forgetfull of her owne, to minde his feares:
   So both conspiring, gan to intimate
   Each others griefe with zeale affectionate,
   And twixt them twaine with equall care to cast,
   How to save whole her hazarded estate;
   For which the onely helpe now left them last
Seem'd to be *Calidore*: all other helpes were past.

13

Him they did deeme, as sure to them he seemed,
   A courteous Knight, and full of faithfull trust:
   Therefore to him their cause they best esteemed
   Whole to commit, and to his dealing just.
   Earely, so soone as *Titans* beames forth brust
   Through the thicke clouds, in which they steeped lay
   All night in darkenesse, duld with yron rust,
   Calidore rising up as fresh as day,
Gan freshly him addresse unto his former way.

14

But first him seemed fit, that wounded Knight
  To visite, after this nights perillous passe,
  And to salute him, if he were in plight,
  And eke that Lady his faire lovely lasse.
  There he him found much better than he was,
  And moved speach to him of things of course,
  The anguish of his paine to overpasse:
  Mongst which he namely did to him discourse,
Of former daies mishap, his sorrowes wicked sourse.

15

Of which occasion *Aldine* taking hold,
  Gan breake to him the fortunes of his love,
  And all his disadventures to unfold;
  That *Calidore* it dearly deepe did move.
  In th'end his kyndly courtesie to prove,
  He him by all the bands of love besought,
  And as it mote a faithfull friend behove,
  To safeconduct his love, and not for ought
To leave, till to her fathers house he had her brought.

16

Sir *Calidore* his faith thereto did plight,
  It to performe: so after little stay,
  That she her selfe had to the journey dight,
  He passed forth with her in faire array,
  Fearelesse, who ought did thinke, or ought did say,
  Sith his own thought he knew most cleare from wite.
  So as they past together on their way,
  He can devize this counter-cast of slight,
To give faire colour to that Ladies cause in sight.

17

Streight to the carkasse of that Knight he went,
  The cause of all this evill, who was slaine
  The day before by just avengement
  Of noble *Tristram*, where it did remaine:
  There he the necke thereof did cut in twaine,
  And tooke with him the head, the signe of shame.
  So forth he passed thorough that daies paine,
  Till to that Ladies fathers house he came,
Most pensive man, through feare, what of his childe became.

18

There he arriving boldly, did present
　The fearefull Lady to her father deare,
　Most perfect pure, and guiltlesse innocent
　Of blame, as he did on his Knighthood sweare,
　Since first he saw her, and did free from feare
　Of a discourteous Knight, who her had reft,
　And by outragious force away did beare:
　Witnesse thereof he shew'd his head there left,
And wretched life forlorne for vengement of his theft.

19

Most joyfull man her sire was her to see,
　And heare th'adventure of her late mischaunce;
　And thousand thankes to *Calidore* for fee
　Of his large paines in her deliveraunce
　Did yeeld; Ne lesse the Lady did advaunce.
　Thus having her restored trustily,
　As he had vow'd, some small continuaunce
　He there did make, and then most carefully
Unto his first exploite he did him selfe apply.

20

So as he was pursuing of his quest
　He chaunst to come whereas a jolly Knight,
　In covert shade him selfe did safely rest,
　To solace with his Lady in delight:
　His warlike armes he had from him undight:
　For that him selfe he thought from daunger free,
　And far from envious eyes that mote him spight.
　And eke the Lady was full faire to see,
And courteous withall, becomming her degree.

21

To whom Sir *Calidore* approaching nye,
　Ere they were well aware of living wight
　Them much abasht, but more him selfe thereby,
　That he so rudely did uppon them light,
　And troubled had their quiet loves delight.
　Yet since it was his fortune, not his fault,
　Him selfe thereof he labour'd to acquite,
　And pardon crav'd for his so rash default,
That he gainst courtesie so fowly did default.

22

With which his gentle words and goodly wit
  He soone allayd that Knights conceiv'd displeasure,
  That he besought him downe by him to sit,
  That they mote treat of things abrode at leasure;
  And of adventures, which had in his measure
  Of so long waies to him befallen late.
  So downe he sate, and with delightfull pleasure
  His long adventures gan to him relate,
Which he endured had through daungerous debate.

23

Of which whilest they discoursed both together,
  The faire *Serena* (so his Lady hight)
  Allur'd with myldnesse of the gentle wether,
  And pleasaunce of the place, the which was dight
  With divers flowres distinct with rare delight,
  Wandred about the fields, as liking led
  Her wavering lust after her wandring sight,
  To make a garland to adorne her hed,
Without suspect of ill or daungers hidden dred.

24

All sodainely out of the forrest nere
  The Blatant Beast forth rushing unaware,
  Caught her thus loosely wandring here and there,
  And in his wide great mouth away her bare,
  Crying aloud in vaine, to shew her sad misfare
  Unto the Knights, and calling oft for ayde,
  Who with the horrour of her haplesse care
  Hastily starting up, like men dismayde,
Ran after fast to reskue the distressed mayde.

25

The Beast with their pursuit incited more,
  Into the wood was bearing her apace
  For to have spoyled her, when *Calidore*
  Who was more light of foote and swift in chace,
  Him overtooke in middest of his race:
  And fiercely charging him with all his might,
  Forst to forgoe his pray there in the place,
  And to betake him selfe to fearefull flight;
For he durst not abide with *Calidore* to fight.

26

Who nathelesse, when he the Lady saw
　There left on ground, though in full evill plight,
　Yet knowing that her Knight now neare did draw,
　Staide not to succour her in that affright,
　But follow'd fast the Monster in his flight:
　Through woods and hils he follow'd him so fast,
　That he nould let him breath nor gather spright,
　But forst him gape and gaspe, with dread aghast,
As if his lungs and lites were nigh a sunder brast.

27

And now by this Sir *Calepine*, so hight,
　Came to the place, where he his Lady found
　In dolorous dismay and deadly plight,
　All in gore bloud there tumbled on the ground,
　Having both sides through grypt with griesly wound.
　His weapons soone from him he threw away,
　And stouping downe to her in drery swound,
　Uprear'd her from the ground whereon she lay,
And in his tender armes her forced up to stay.

28

So well he did his busie paines apply,
　That the faint sprite he did revoke againe,
　To her fraile mansion of mortality.
　Then up he tooke her twixt his armes twaine,
　And setting on his steede, her did sustaine
　With carefull hands soft footing her beside,
　Till to some place of rest they mote attaine,
　Where she in safe assuraunce mote abide,
Till she recured were of those her woundes wide.

29

Now when as *Phœbus* with his fiery waine
　Unto his Inne began to draw apace;
　Tho wexing weary of that toylesome paine,
　In travelling on foote so long a space,
　Not wont on foote with heavy armes to trace,
　Downe in a dale forby a rivers syde,
　He chaunst to spie a faire and stately place,
　To which he meant his weary steps to guyde,
In hope there for his love some succour to provyde

30

But comming to the rivers side, he found
  That hardly passable on foote it was:
  Therefore there still he stood as in a stound,
  Ne wist which way he through the foord mote pas.
  Thus whilest he was in this distressed case,
  Devising what to doe, he nigh espyde
  An armed Knight approaching to the place,
  With a faire Lady lincked by his syde,
The which themselves prepard thorough the foord to ride.

31

Whom *Calepine* saluting (as became)
  Besought of courtesie in that his neede,
  For safe conducting of his sickely Dame,
  Through that same perillous foord with better heede,
  To take him up behinde upon his steed.
  To whom that other did this taunt returne.
  Perdy thou peasant Knight, mightst rightly reed
  Me then to be full base and evill borne,
If I would beare behinde a burden of such scorne.

32

But as thou hast thy steed forlorne with shame,
  So fare on foote till thou another gayne,
  And let thy Lady likewise doe the same.
  Or beare her on thy backe with pleasing payne,
  And prove thy manhood on the billowes vayne.
  With which rude speach his Lady much displeased,
  Did him reprove, yet could him not restrayne,
  And would on her owne Palfrey him have eased,
For pitty of his Dame, whom she saw so diseased.

33

Sir *Calepine* her thanckt, yet inly wroth
  Against her Knight, her gentlenesse refused,
  And carelesly into the river goth,
  As in despight to be so fowle abused
  Of a rude churle, whom often he accused
  Of fowle discourtesie, unfit for Knight;
  And strongly wading through the waves unused,
  With speare in th'one hand, stayd him selfe upright,
With th'other staide his Lady up with steddy might.

34

And all the while, that same discourteous Knight,
  Stood on the further bancke beholding him,
  At whose calamity, for more despight
  He laught, and mockt to see him like to swim.
  But when as *Calepine* came to the brim,
  And saw his carriage past that perill well,
  Looking at that same Carle with count'nance grim,
  His heart with vengeaunce inwardly did swell,
And forth at last did breake in speaches sharpe and fell.

35

Unknightly Knight, the blemish of that name,
  And blot of all that armes uppon them take,
  Which is the badge of honour and of fame,
  Loe I defie thee, and here challenge make,
  That thou for ever doe those armes forsake,
  And be for ever held a recreant Knight,
  Unlesse thou dare for thy deare Ladies sake,
  And for thine owne defence on foote alight,
To justifie thy fault gainst me in equall fight.

36

The dastard, that did heare him selfe defyde,
  Seem'd not to weigh his threatfull words at all,
  But laught them out, as if his greater pryde
  Did scorne the challenge of so base a thrall:
  Or had no courage, or else had no gall.
  So much the more was *Calepine* offended,
  That him to no revenge he forth could call,
  But both his challenge and him selfe contemned,
Ne cared as a coward so to be condemned.

37

But he nought weighing what he sayd or did,
  Turned his steede about another way,
  And with his Lady to the Castle rid,
  Where was his won; ne did the other stay,
  But after went directly as he may,
  For his sicke charge some harbour there to seeke,
  Where he arriving with the fall of day,
  Drew to the gate, and there with prayers meeke,
And myld entreaty lodging did for her beseeke.

38

But the rude Porter that no manners had,
　Did shut the gate against him in his face,
　And entraunce boldly unto him forbad.
　Nathelesse the Knight now in so needy case,
　Gan him entreat even with submission base,
　And humbly praid to let them in that night:
　Who to him aunswer'd, that there was no place
　Of lodging fit for any errant Knight,
Unlesse that with his Lord he formerly did fight.

39

Full loth am I (quoth he) as now at earst,
　When day is spent, and rest us needeth most,
　And that this Lady, both whose sides are pearst
　With wounds, is ready to forgo the ghost:
　Ne would I gladly combate with mine host,
　That should to me such curtesie afford,
　Unlesse that I were thereunto enforst.
　But yet aread to me, how hight thy Lord,
That doth thus strongly ward the Castle of the ford.

40

His name (quoth he) if that thou list to learne,
　Is hight Sir *Turpine*, one of mickle might,
　And manhood rare, but terrible and stearne
　In all assaies to every errant Knight,
　Because of one, that wrought him fowle despight.
　Ill seemes (sayd he) if he so valiaunt be,
　That he should be so sterne to stranger wight:
　For seldome yet did living creature see,
That curtesie and manhood ever disagree.

41

But go thy waies to him, and fro me say,
　That here is at his gate an errant Knight,
　That house-rome craves, yet would be loth t'assay
　The proofe of battell, now in doubtfull night,
　Or curtesie with rudenesse to requite:
　Yet if he needes will fight, crave leave till morne,
　And tell withall, the lamentable plight,
　In which this Lady languisheth forlorne,
That pitty craves, as he of woman was yborne.

42

The groome went streight way in, and to his Lord
 Declar'd the message, which that Knight did move;
 Who sitting with his Lady then at bord,
 Not onely did not his demaund approve,
 But both himselfe revil'd, and eke his love;
 Albe his Lady, that *Blandina* hight,
 Him of ungentle usage did reprove
 And earnestly entreated that they might
Finde favour to be lodged there for that same night.

43

Yet would he not perswaded be for ought,
 Ne from his currish will awhit reclame.
 Which answer when the groome returning, brought
 To *Calepine*, his heart did inly flame
 With wrathfull fury for so foule a shame,
 That he could not thereof avenged bee:
 But most for pitty of his dearest Dame,
 Whom now in deadly daunger he did see;
Yet had no meanes to comfort, nor procure her glee.

44

But all in vaine; for why, no remedy
 He saw, the present mischiefe to redresse,
 But th'utmost end perforce for to aby,
 Which that nights fortune would for him addresse.
 So downe he tooke his Lady in distresse,
 And layd her underneath a bush to sleepe,
 Cover'd with cold, and wrapt in wretchednesse,
 Whiles he him selfe all night did nought but weepe,
And wary watch about her for her safegard keepe.

45

The morrow next, so soone as joyous day
 Did shew it selfe in sunny beames bedight,
 Serena full of dolorous dismay,
 Twixt darkenesse dread, and hope of living light,
 Uprear'd her head to see that chearefull sight.
 Then *Calepine*, how ever inly wroth,
 And greedy to avenge that vile despight,
 Yet for the feeble Ladies sake, full loth
To make there lenger stay, forth on his journey goth.

46

He goth on foote all armed by her side,
  Upstaying still her selfe uppon her steede,
  Being unhable else alone to ride;
  So sore her sides, so much her wounds did bleede:
  Till that at length, in his extreamest neede,
  He chaunst far off an armed Knight to spy,
  Pursuing him apace with greedy speede,
  Whom well he wist to be some enemy,
That meant to make advantage of his misery.

47

Wherefore he stayd, till that he nearer drew
  To weet what issue would thereof betyde,
  Tho whenas he approched nigh in vew,
  By certaine signes he plainely him descryde,
  To be the man, that with such scornefull pryde
  Had him abusde, and shamed yesterday;
  Therefore misdoubting, least he should misguyde
  His former malice to some new assay,
He cast to keepe him selfe so safely as he may.

48

By this the other came in place likewise,
  And couching close his speare and all his powre,
  As bent to some malicious enterprise,
  He bad him stand, t'abide the bitter stoure
  Of his sore vengeaunce, or to make avoure
  Of the lewd words and deedes, which he had done:
  With that ran at him, as he would devoure
  His life attonce; who nought could do, but shun
The perill of his pride, or else be overrun.

49

Yet he him still pursew'd from place to place,
  With full intent him cruelly to kill,
  And like a wilde goate round about did chace,
  Flying the fury of his bloudy will.
  But his best succour and refuge was still
  Behinde his Ladies backe, who to him cryde,
  And called oft with prayers loud and shrill,
  As ever he to Lady was affyde,
To spare her Knight, and rest with reason pacifyde.

50

But he the more thereby enraged was,
　And with more eager felnesse him pursew'd,
　So that at length, after long weary chace,
　Having by chaunce a close advantage vew'd,
　He over raught him, having long eschew'd
　His violence in vaine, and with his spere
　Strooke through his shoulder, that the blood ensew'd
　In great aboundance, as a well it were,
That forth out of an hill fresh gushing did appere.

51

Yet ceast he not for all that cruell wound,
　But chaste him still, for all his Ladies cry,
　Not satisfyde till on the fatall ground
　He saw his life powrd forth dispiteously:
　The which was certes in great jeopardy,
　Had not a wondrous chaunce his reskue wrought,
　And saved from his cruell villany.
　Such chaunces oft exceed all humaine thought:
That in another Canto shall to end be brought.

CANT. IIII

*Calepine by a salvage man
　from Turpine reskewed is,
And whylest an Infant from a Beare
　he saves, his love doth misse.*

I

LIKE as a ship with dreadfull storme long tost,
　Having spent all her mastes and her groundhold,
　Now farre from harbour likely to be lost,
　At last some fisher barke doth neare behold,
　That giveth comfort to her courage cold.
　Such was the state of this most courteous knight
　Being oppressed by that faytour bold,
　That he remayned in most perilous plight,
And his sad Ladie left in pitifull affright.

2

Till that by fortune, passing all foresight,
  A salvage man, which in those woods did wonne,
  Drawne with that Ladies loud and piteous shright,
  Toward the same incessantly did ronne,
  To understand what there was to be donne.
  There he this most discourteous craven found,
  As fiercely yet, as when he first begonne,
  Chasing the gentle *Calepine* around,
Ne sparing him the more for all his grievous wound.

3

The salvage man, that never till this houre
  Did taste of pittie, neither gentlesse knew,
  Seeing his sharpe assault and cruell stoure
  Was much emmoved at his perils vew,
  That even his ruder hart began to rew,
  And feele compassion of his evill plight,
  Against his foe that did him so pursew:
  From whom he meant to free him, if he might,
And him avenge of that so villenous despight.

4

Yet armes or weapon had he none to fight,
  Ne knew the use of warlike instruments,
  Save such as sudden rage him lent to smite,
  But naked without needfull vestiments,
  To clad his corpse with meete habiliments,
  He cared not for dint of sword nor speere,
  No more than for the stroke of strawes or bents:
  For from his mothers wombe, which him did beare,
He was invulnerable made by Magicke leare.

5

He stayed not t'advize, which way were best
  His foe t'assayle, or how himselfe to gard,
  But with fierce fury and with force infest
  Upon him ran; who being well prepard,
  His first assault full warily did ward,
  And with the push of his sharp-pointed speare
  Full on the breast him strooke, so strong and hard,
  That forst him backe recoyle, and reele areare;
Yet in his bodie made no wound nor bloud appeare.

6

With that the wyld man more enraged grew,
  Like to a Tygre that hath mist his pray,
  And with mad mood againe upon him flew,
  Regarding neither speare, that mote him slay,
  Nor his fierce steed, that mote him much dismay,
  The salvage nation doth all dread despize:
  Tho on his shield he griple hold did lay,
  And held the same so hard, that by no wize
He could him force to loose, or leave his enterprize.

7

Long did he wrest and wring it to and fro,
  And every way did try, but all in vaine:
  For he would not his greedie grype forgoe,
  But hayld and puld with all his might and maine,
  That from his steed him nigh he drew againe.
  Who having now no use of his long speare,
  So nigh at hand, nor force his shield to straine,
  Both speare and shield, as things that needlesse were,
He quite forsooke, and fled himselfe away for feare.

8

But after him the wyld man ran apace,
  And him pursewed with importune speed
  (For he was swift as any Bucke in chace)
  And had he not in his extreamest need,
  Bene helped through the swiftnesse of his steed,
  He had him overtaken in his flight.
  Who ever, as he saw him nigh succeed,
  Gan cry aloud with horrible affright,
And shrieked out, a thing uncomely for a knight.

9

But when the Salvage saw his labour vaine,
  In following of him, that fled so fast,
  He wearie woxe, and backe return'd againe
  With speede unto the place, whereas he last
  Had left that couple, nere their utmost cast.
  There he that knight full sorely bleeding found,
  And eke the Ladie fearefully aghast,
  Both for the perill of the present stound,
And also for the sharpnesse of her rankling wound.

10

For though she were right glad, so rid to bee
  From that vile lozell, which her late offended,
  Yet now no lesse encombrance she did see,
  And perill by this salvage man pretended;
  Gainst whom she saw no meanes to be defended,
  By reason that her knight was wounded sore.
  Therefore her selfe she wholy recommended
  To Gods sole grace, whom she did oft implore,
To send her succour, being of all hope forlore.

11

But the wyld man, contrarie to her feare,
  Came to her creeping like a fawning hound,
  And by rude tokens made to her appeare
  His deepe compassion of her dolefull stound,
  Kissing his hands, and crouching to the ground;
  For other language had he none nor speach,
  But a soft murmure, and confused sound
  Of senselesse words, which nature did him teach,
T'expresse his passions, which his reason did empeach.

12

And comming likewise to the wounded knight,
  When he beheld the streames of purple blood
  Yet flowing fresh, as moved with the sight,
  He made great mone after his salvage mood,
  And running streight into the thickest wood,
  A certaine herbe from thence unto him brought,
  Whose vertue he by use well understood:
  The juyce whereof into his wound he wrought,
And stopt the bleeding straight, ere he it staunched thought.

13

Then taking up that Recreants shield and speare,
  Which earst he left, he signes unto them made,
  With him to wend unto his wonning neare:
  To which he easily did them perswade.
  Farre in the forrest by a hollow glade,
  Covered with mossie shrubs, which spredding brode
  Did underneath them make a gloomy shade;
  Where foot of living creature never trode,
Ne scarse wyld beasts durst come, there was this wights abode.

14

Thether he brought these unacquainted guests;
  To whom faire semblance, as he could, he shewed
  By signes, by lookes, and all his other gests.
  But the bare ground, with hoarie mosse bestrowed,
  Must be their bed, their pillow was unsowed,
  And the frutes of the forrest was their feast:
  For their bad Stuard neither plough'd nor sowed,
  Ne fed on flesh, ne ever of wyld beast
Did taste the bloud, obaying natures first beheast.

15

Yet howsoever base and meane it were,
  They tooke it well, and thanked God for all,
  Which had them freed from that deadly feare,
  And sav'd from being to that caytive thrall.
  Here they of force (as fortune now did fall)
  Compelled were themselves a while to rest,
  Glad of that easement, though it were but small;
  That having there their wounds awhile redrest,
They mote the abler be to passe unto the rest.

16

During which time, that wyld man did apply
  His best endevour, and his daily paine,
  In seeking all the woods both farre and nye
  For herbes to dresse their wounds; still seeming faine,
  When ought he did, that did their lyking gaine.
  So as ere long he had that knightes wound
  Recured well, and made him whole againe:
  But that same Ladies hurts no herbe he found,
Which could redresse, for it was inwardly unsound.

17

Now when as *Calepine* was woxen strong,
  Upon a day he cast abrode to wend,
  To take the ayre, and heare the thrushes song,
  Unarm'd, as fearing neither foe nor frend,
  And without sword his person to defend.
  There him befell, unlooked for before,
  An hard adventure with unhappie end,
  A cruell Beare, the which an infant bore
Betwixt his bloodie jawes, besprinckled all with gore.

18

The litle babe did loudly scrike and squall,
 And all the woods with piteous plaints did fill,
 As if his cry did meane for helpe to call
 To *Calepine*, whose eares those shrieches shrill
 Percing his hart with pities point did thrill;
 That after him he ran with zealous haste,
 To rescue th'infant, ere he did him kill:
 Whom though he saw now somewhat overpast,
Yet by the cry he follow'd, and pursewed fast.

19

Well then him chaunst his heavy armes to want,
 Whose burden mote empeach his needfull speed,
 And hinder him from libertie to pant:
 For having long time, as his daily weed,
 Them wont to weare, and wend on foot for need,
 Now wanting them he felt himselfe so light,
 That like an Hauke, which feeling her selfe freed
 From bels and jesses, which did let her flight,
Him seem'd his feet did fly, and in their speed delight.

20

So well he sped him, that the wearie Beare
 Ere long he overtooke, and forst to stay,
 And without weapon him assayling neare,
 Compeld him soone the spoyle adowne to lay.
 Wherewith the beast enrag'd to loose his pray,
 Upon him turned, and with greedie force
 And furie, to be crossed in his way,
 Gaping full wyde, did thinke without remorse
To be aveng'd on him, and to devoure his corse.

21

But the bold knight no whit thereat dismayd,
 But catching up in hand a ragged stone,
 Which lay thereby (so fortune him did ayde)
 Upon him ran, and thrust it all attone
 Into his gaping throte, that made him grone
 And gaspe for breath, that he nigh choked was,
 Being unable to digest that bone;
 Ne could it upward come, nor downward passe,
Ne could he brooke the coldnesse of the stony masse.

22

Whom when as he thus combred did behold,
  Stryving in vaine that nigh his bowels brast,
  He with him closd, and laying mightie hold
  Upon his throte, did gripe his gorge so fast,
  That wanting breath, him downe to ground he cast;
  And then oppressing him with urgent paine,
  Ere long enforst to breath his utmost blast,
  Gnashing his cruell teeth at him in vaine,
And threatning his sharpe clawes, now wanting powre to straine.

23

Then tooke he up betwixt his armes twaine
  The litle babe, sweet relickes of his pray;
  Whom pitying to heare so sore complaine,
  From his soft eyes the teares he wypt away,
  And from his face the filth that did it ray,
  And every litle limbe he searcht around,
  And every part, that under sweathbands lay,
  Least that the beasts sharpe teeth had any wound
Made in his tender flesh, but whole them all he found.

24

So having all his bands againe uptyde,
  He with him thought backe to returne againe:
  But when he lookt about on every syde,
  To weet which way were best to entertaine,
  To bring him to the place, where he would faine,
  He could no path nor tract of foot descry,
  Ne by inquirie learne, nor ghesse by ayme.
  For nought but woods and forrests farre and nye,
That all about did close the compasse of his eye.

25

Much was he then encombred, ne could tell
  Which way to take: now West he went a while,
  Then North; then neither, but as fortune fell.
  So up and downe he wandred many a mile,
  With wearie travell and uncertaine toile,
  Yet nought the nearer to his journeys end;
  And evermore his lovely litle spoile
  Crying for food, did greatly him offend.
So all that day in wandring vainely he did spend.

26

At last about the setting of the Sunne,
 Him selfe out of the forest he did wynd,
 And by good fortune the plaine champion wonne:
 Where looking all about, where he mote fynd
 Some place of succour to content his mynd,
 At length he heard under the forrests syde
 A voice, that seemed of some woman kynd,
 Which to her selfe lamenting loudly cryde,
And oft complayn'd of fate, and fortune oft defyde.

27

To whom approching, when as she perceived
 A stranger wight in place, her plaint she stayd,
 As if she doubted to have bene deceived,
 Or loth to let her sorrowes be bewrayd.
 Whom when as *Calepine* saw so dismayd,
 He to her drew, and with faire blandishment
 Her chearing up, thus gently to her sayd;
 What be you wofull Dame, which thus lament,
And for what cause declare, so mote ye not repent.

28

To whom she thus, What need me Sir to tell,
 That which your selfe have earst ared so right?
 A wofull dame ye have me termed well;
 So much more wofull, as my wofull plight
 Cannot redressed be by living wight.
 Nathlesse (quoth he) if need doe not you bynd,
 Doe it disclose, to ease your grieved spright:
 Oftimes it haps, that sorrowes of the mynd
Find remedie unsought, which seeking cannot fynd.

29

Then thus began the lamentable Dame;
 Sith then ye needs will know the griefe I hoord,
 I am th'unfortunate *Matilde* by name,
 The wife of bold Sir *Bruin*, who is Lord
 Of all this land, late conquer'd by his sword
 From a great Gyant, called *Cormoraunt*;
 Whom he did overthrow by yonder foord,
 And in three battailes did so deadly daunt,
That he dare not returne for all his daily vaunt.

30

So is my Lord now seiz'd of all the land,
  As in his fee, with peaceable estate,
  And quietly doth hold it in his hand,
  Ne any dares with him for it debate.
  But to these happie fortunes, cruell fate
  Hath joyn'd one evill, which doth overthrow
  All these our joyes, and all our blisse abate;
  And like in time to further ill to grow,
And all this land with endlesse losse to overflow.

31

For th'heavens envying our prosperitie,
  Have not vouchsaft to graunt unto us twaine
  The gladfull blessing of posteritie,
  Which we might see after our selves remaine
  In th'heritage of our unhappie paine:
  So that for want of heires it to defend,
  All is in time like to returne againe
  To that foule feend, who dayly doth attend
To leape into the same after our lives end.

32

But most my Lord is grieved herewithall,
  And makes exceeding mone, when he does thinke
  That all this land unto his foe shall fall,
  For which he long in vaine did sweat and swinke,
  That now the same he greatly doth forthinke.
  Yet was it sayd, there should to him a sonne
  Be gotten, not begotten, which should drinke
  And dry up all the water, which doth ronne
In the next brooke, by whom that feend shold be fordonne.

33

Well hop't he then, when this was propheside,
  That from his sides some noble chyld should rize,
  The which through fame should farre be magnifide,
  And this proud gyant should with brave emprize
  Quite overthrow, who now ginnes to despize
  The good Sir *Bruin*, growing farre in yeares;
  Who thinkes from me his sorrow all doth rize.
  Lo this my cause of griefe to you appeares;
For which I thus doe mourne, and poure forth ceaselesse teares.

34

Which when he heard, he inly touched was
  With tender ruth for her unworthy griefe,
  And when he had devized of her case,
  He gan in mind conceive a fit reliefe
  For all her paine, if please her make the priefe.
  And having cheared her, thus said; Faire Dame,
  In evils counsell is the comfort chiefe,
  Which though I be not wise enough to frame,
Yet as I well it meane, vouchsafe it without blame.

35

If that the cause of this your languishment
  Be lacke of children, to supply your place,
  Lo how good fortune doth to you present
  This litle babe, of sweete and lovely face,
  And spotlesse spirit, in which ye may enchace
  What ever formes ye list thereto apply,
  Being now soft and fit them to embrace;
  Whether ye list him traine in chevalry,
Or noursle up in lore of learn'd Philosophy.

36

And certes it hath oftentimes bene seene,
  That of the like, whose linage was unknowne,
  More brave and noble knights have raysed beene,
  As their victorious deedes have often showen,
  Being with fame through many Nations blowen,
  Than those, which have bene dandled in the lap.
  Therefore some thought, that those brave imps were sowen
  Here by the Gods, and fed with heavenly sap,
That made them grow so high t'all honorable hap.

37

The Ladie hearkning to his sensefull speach,
  Found nothing that he said, unmeet nor geason,
  Having oft seene it tryde, as he did teach.
  Therefore inclyning to his goodly reason,
  Agreeing well both with the place and season,
  She gladly did of that same babe accept,
  As of her owne by liverey and seisin,
  And having over it a litle wept,
She bore it thence, and ever as her owne it kept.

38

Right glad was *Calepine* to be so rid
  Of his young charge, whereof he skilled nought:
  Ne she lesse glad; for she so wisely did,
  And with her husband under hand so wrought,
  That when that infant unto him she brought,
  She made him thinke it surely was his owne,
  And it in goodly thewes so well upbrought,
  That it became a famous knight well knowne
And did right noble deedes, the which elswhere are showne.

39

But *Calepine*, now being left alone
  Under the greenewoods side in sorie plight,
  Withouten armes or steede to ride upon,
  Or house to hide his head from heavens spight,
  Albe that Dame by all the meanes she might,
  Him oft desired home with her to wend,
  And offred him, his courtesie to requite,
  Both horse and armes, and what so else to lend,
Yet he them all refusd, though thankt her as a frend.

40

And for exceeding griefe which inly grew,
  That he his love so lucklesse now had lost,
  On the cold ground, maugre himselfe he threw,
  For fell despight, to be so sorely crost;
  And there all night himselfe in anguish tost,
  Vowing, that never he in bed againe
  His limbes would rest, ne lig in ease embost,
  Till that his Ladies sight he mote attaine,
Or understand, that she in safetie did remaine.

CANT. V

The salvage serves Matilda well
till she Prince Arthure fynd,
Who her together with his Squyre
with th'Hermit leaves behynd.

1

O WHAT an easie thing is to descry
 The gentle bloud, how ever it be wrapt
In sad misfortunes foule deformity,
 And wretched sorrowes, which have often hapt?
For howsoever it may grow mis-shapt,
 Like this wyld man, being undisciplynd,
That to all vertue it may seeme unapt,
 Yet will it shew some sparkes of gentle mynd,
And at the last breake forth in his owne proper kynd.

2

That plainely may in this wyld man be red,
 Who though he were still in this desert wood,
Mongst salvage beasts, both rudely borne and bred,
 Ne ever saw faire guize, ne learned good,
Yet shewd some token of his gentle blood,
 By gentle usage of that wretched Dame.
For certes he was borne of noble blood,
 How ever by hard hap he hether came;
As ye may know, when time shall be to tell the same.

3

Who when as now long time he lacked had
 The good Sir *Calepine*, that farre was strayd,
Did wexe exceeding sorrowfull and sad,
 As he of some misfortune were afrayd:
And leaving there this Ladie all dismayd,
 Went forth streightway into the forrest wyde,
To seeke, if he perchance a sleepe were layd,
 Or what so else were unto him betyde:
He sought him farre and neare, yet him no where he spyde.

4

Tho backe returning to that sorie Dame,
  He shewed semblant of exceeding mone,
  By speaking signes, as he them best could frame;
  Now wringing both his wretched hands in one,
  Now beating his hard head upon a stone,
  That ruth it was to see him so lament.
  By which she well perceiving, what was done,
  Gan teare her hayre, and all her garments rent,
And beat her breast, and piteously her selfe torment.

5

Upon the ground her selfe she fiercely threw,
  Regardlesse of her wounds, yet bleeding rife,
  That with their bloud did all the flore imbrew,
  As if her breast new launcht with murdrous knife,
  Would streight dislodge the wretched wearie life.
  There she long groveling, and deepe groning lay,
  As if her vitall powers were at strife
  With stronger death, and feared their decay,
Such were this Ladies pangs and dolorous assay.

6

Whom when the Salvage saw so sore distrest,
  He reared her up from the bloudie ground,
  And sought by all the meanes, that he could best
  Her to recure out of that stony swound,
  And staunch the bleeding of her dreary wound.
  Yet nould she be recomforted for nought,
  Ne cease her sorrow and impatient stound,
  But day and night did vexe her carefull thought,
And ever more and more her owne affliction wrought.

7

At length, when as no hope of his retourne
  She saw now left, she cast to leave the place,
  And wend abrode, though feeble and forlorne,
  To seeke some comfort in that sorie case.
  His steede now strong through rest so long a space,
  Well as she could, she got, and did bedight,
  And being thereon mounted, forth did pace,
  Withouten guide, her to conduct aright,
Or gard her to defend from bold oppressors might.

8

Whom when her Host saw readie to depart,
  He would not suffer her alone to fare,
  But gan himselfe addresse to take her part.
  Those warlike armes, which *Calepine* whyleare
  Had left behind, he gan eftsoones prepare,
  And put them all about himselfe unfit,
  His shield, his helmet, and his curats bare.
  But without sword upon his thigh to sit:
Sir *Calepine* himselfe away had hidden it.

9

So forth they traveld an uneven payre,
  That mote to all men seeme an uncouth sight;
  A salvage man matcht with a Ladie fayre,
  That rather seem'd the conquest of his might,
  Gotten by spoyle, than purchaced aright.
  But he did her attend most carefully,
  And faithfully did serve both day and night,
  Withouten thought of shame or villeny,
Ne ever shewed signe of foule disloyalty.

10

Upon a day as on their way they went,
  It chaunst some furniture about her steed
  To be disordred by some accident:
  Which to redresse, she did th'assistance need
  Of this her groome, which he by signes did reede,
  And streight his combrous armes aside did lay
  Upon the ground, withouten doubt or dreed,
  And in his homely wize began to assay
T'amend what was amisse, and put in right aray.

11

Bout which whilest he was busied thus hard,
  Lo where a knight together with his squire,
  All arm'd to point came ryding thetherward,
  Which seemed by their portance and attire,
  To be two errant knights, that did inquire
  After adventures, where they mote them get.
  Those were to weet (if that ye it require)
  Prince *Arthur* and young *Timias*, which met
By straunge occasion, that here needs forth be set.

12

After that *Timias* had againe recured
  The favour of *Belphebe*, (as ye heard)
  And of her grace did stand againe assured,
  To happie blisse he was full high uprear'd,
  Nether of envy, nor of chaunge afeard,
  Though many foes did him maligne therefore,
  And with unjust detraction him did beard;
  Yet he himselfe so well and wisely bore,
That in her soveraine lyking he dwelt evermore.

13

But of them all, which did his ruine seeke
  Three mightie enemies did him most despight,
  Three mightie ones, and cruell minded eeke,
  That him not onely sought by open might
  To overthrow, but to supplant by slight.
  The first of them by name was cald *Despetto*,
  Exceeding all the rest in powre and hight;
  The second not so strong but wise, *Decetto*;
The third nor strong nor wise, but spightfullest *Defetto*.

14

Oftimes their sundry powres they did employ,
  And severall deceipts, but all in vaine:
  For neither they by force could him destroy,
  Ne yet entrap in treasons subtill traine.
  Therefore conspiring all together plaine,
  They did their counsels now in one compound;
  Where singled forces faile, conjoynd may gaine.
  The *Blatant Beast* the fittest meanes they found,
To worke his utter shame, and throughly him confound.

15

Upon a day as they the time did waite,
  When he did raunge the wood for salvage game,
  They sent that *Blatant Beast* to be a baite,
  To draw him from his deare beloved dame,
  Unwares into the daunger of defame.
  For well they wist, that Squire to be so bold,
  That no one beast in forrest wylde or tame,
  Met him in chase, but he it challenge would,
And plucke the pray oftimes out of their greedy hould.

16

The hardy boy, as they devised had,
    Seeing the ugly Monster passing by,
    Upon him set, of perill nought adrad,
    Ne skilfull of the uncouth jeopardy;
    And charged him so fierce and furiously,
    That his great force unable to endure,
    He forced was to turne from him and fly:
    Yet ere he fled, he with his tooth impure
Him heedlesse bit, the whiles he was thereof secure.

17

Securely he did after him pursew,
    Thinking by speed to overtake his flight;
    Who through thicke woods and brakes and briers him drew,
    To weary him the more, and waste his spight,
    So that he now has almost spent his spright.
    Till that at length unto a woody glade
    He came, whose covert stopt his further sight,
    There his three foes shrowded in guilefull shade,
Out of their ambush broke, and gan him to invade.

18

Sharpely they all attonce did him assaile,
    Burning with inward rancour and despight,
    And heaped strokes did round about him haile
    With so huge force, that seemed nothing might
    Beare off their blowes, from percing thorough quite.
    Yet he them all so warily did ward,
    That none of them in his soft flesh did bite,
    And all the while his backe for best safegard,
He lent against a tree, that backeward onset bard.

19

Like a wylde Bull, that being at a bay,
    Is bayted of a mastiffe, and a hound,
    And a curre-dog; that doe him sharpe assay
    On every side, and beat about him round;
    But most that curre barking with bitter sownd,
    And creeping still behinde, doth him incomber,
    That in his chauffe he digs the trampled ground,
    And threats his horns, and bellowes like the thonder,
So did that Squire his foes disperse, and drive asonder.

20

Him well behoved so; for his three foes
    Sought to encompasse him on every side,
    And dangerously did round about enclose.
    But most of all *Defetto* him annoyde,
    Creeping behinde him still to have destroyde:
    So did *Decetto* eke him circumvent,
    But stout *Despetto* in his greater pryde,
    Did front him face to face against him bent,
Yet he them all withstood, and often made relent.

21

Till that at length nigh tyrd with former chace,
    And weary now with carefull keeping ward,
    He gan to shrinke, and somewhat to give place,
    Full like ere long to have escaped hard;
    When as unwares he in the forrest heard
    A trampling steede, that with his neighing fast
    Did warne his rider be uppon his gard;
    With noise whereof the Squire now nigh aghast,
Revived was, and sad dispaire away did cast.

22

Eftsoones he spide a Knight approching nye,
    Who seeing one in so great daunger set
    Mongst many foes, him selfe did faster hye;
    To reskue him, and his weake part abet,
    For pitty so to see him overset.
    Whom soone as his three enemies did vew,
    They fled, and fast into the wood did get:
    Him booted not to thinke them to pursew,
The covert was so thicke, that did no passage shew.

23

Then turning to that swaine, him well he knew
    To be his *Timias*, his owne true Squire,
    Whereof exceeding glad, he to him drew,
    And him embracing twixt his armes entire,
    Him thus bespake; My liefe, my lifes desire,
    Why have ye me alone thus long yleft?
    Tell me what worlds despight, or heavens yre
    Hath you thus long away from me bereft?
Where have ye all this while bin wandring, where bene weft?

24

With that he sighed deepe for inward tyne:
  To whom the Squire nought aunswered againe,
  But shedding few soft teares from tender eyne,
  His deare affect with silence did restraine,
  And shut up all his plaint in privy paine.
  There they awhile some gracious speaches spent,
  As to them seemed fit time to entertaine.
  After all which up to their steedes they went,
And forth together rode a comely couplement.

25

So now they be arrived both in sight
  Of this wyld man, whom they full busie found
  About the sad *Serena* things to dight,
  With those brave armours lying on the ground,
  That seem'd the spoile of some right well renownd.
  Which when that Squire beheld, he to them stept,
  Thinking to take them from that hylding hound:
  But he it seeing, lightly to him lept,
And sternely with strong hand it from his handling kept.

26

Gnashing his grinded teeth with griesly looke,
  And sparkling fire out of his furious eyne,
  Him with his fist unwares on th'head he strooke,
  That made him downe unto the earth encline;
  Whence soone upstarting much he gan repine,
  And laying hand upon his wrathfull blade,
  Thought therewithall forthwith him to have slaine,
  Who it perceiving, hand upon him layd,
And greedily him griping, his avengement stayd.

27

With that aloude the faire *Serena* cryde
  Unto the Knight, them to dispart in twaine:
  Who to them stepping did them soone divide,
  And did from further violence restraine,
  Albe the wyld-man hardly would refraine.
  Then gan the Prince, of her for to demand,
  What and from whence she was, and by what traine
  She fell into that salvage villaines hand,
And whether free with him she now were, or in band.

28

To whom she thus; I am, as now ye see,
The wretchedst Dame, that live this day on ground,
Who both in minde, the which most grieveth me,
And body have receiv'd a mortall wound,
That hath me driven to this drery stound.
I was erewhile, the love of *Calepine*,
Who whether he alive be to be found,
Or by some deadly chaunce be done to pine,
Since I him lately lost, uneath is to define.

29

In salvage forrest I him lost of late,
Where I had surely long ere this bene dead,
Or else remained in most wretched state,
Had not this wylde man in that wofull stead
Kept, and delivered me from deadly dread.
In such a salvage wight, of brutish kynd,
Amongst wilde beastes in desert forrests bred,
It is most straunge and wonderfull to fynd
So milde humanity, and perfect gentle mynd.

30

Let me therefore this favour for him finde,
That ye will not your wrath upon him wreake,
Sith he cannot expresse his simple minde,
Ne yours conceive, ne but by tokens speake:
Small praise to prove your powre on wight so weake.
With such faire words she did their heate asswage,
And the strong course of their displeasure breake,
That they to pitty turnd their former rage,
And each sought to supply the office of her page.

31

So having all things well about her dight,
She on her way cast forward to proceede,
And they her forth conducted, where they might
Finde harbour fit to comfort her great neede.
For now her wounds corruption gan to breed;
And eke this Squire, who likewise wounded was
Of that same Monster late, for lacke of heed,
Now gan to faint, and further could not pas
Through feeblenesse, which all his limbes oppressed has.

32

So forth they rode together all in troupe,
　To seeke some place, the which mote yeeld some ease
　To these sicke twaine, that now began to droupe,
　And all the way the Prince sought to appease
　The bitter anguish of their sharpe disease,
　By all the courteous meanes he could invent,
　Somewhile with merry purpose fit to please,
　And otherwhile with good encouragement,
To make them to endure the pains, did them torment.

33

Mongst which, *Serena* did to him relate
　The foule discourt'sies and unknightly parts,
　Which *Turpine* had unto her shewed late,
　Without compassion of her cruell smarts,
　Although *Blandina* did with all her arts
　Him otherwise perswade, all that she might;
　Yet he of malice, without her desarts,
　Not onely her excluded late at night,
But also trayterously did wound her weary Knight.

34

Wherewith the Prince sore moved, there avoud,
　That soone as he returned backe againe,
　He would avenge th'abuses of that proud
　And shamefull Knight, of whom she did complaine.
　This wize did they each other entertaine,
　To passe the tedious travell of the way;
　Till towards night they came unto a plaine,
　By which a little Hermitage there lay,
Far from all neighbourhood, the which annoy it may.

35

And nigh thereto a little Chappell stoode,
　Which being all with Yvy overspred,
　Deckt all the roofe, and shadowing the roode,
　Seem'd like a grove faire braunched over hed:
　Therein the Hermite, which his life here led
　In streight observaunce of religious vow,
　Was wont his howres and holy things to bed;
　And therein he likewise was praying now,
Whenas these Knights arriv'd, they wist not where nor how.

36

They stayd not there, but streight way in did pas.
  Whom when the Hermite present saw in place,
  From his devotion streight he troubled was;
  Which breaking off he toward them did pace,
  With stayed steps, and grave beseeming grace:
  For well it seem'd, that whilome he had beene
  Some goodly person, and of gentle race,
  That could his good to all, and well did weene,
How each to entertaine with curt'sie well beseene.

37

And soothly it was sayd by common fame,
  So long as age enabled him thereto,
  That he had bene a man of mickle name,
  Renowmed much in armes and derring doe:
  But being aged now and weary to
  Of warres delight, and worlds contentious toyle,
  The name of knighthood he did disavow,
  And hanging up his armes and warlike spoyle,
From all this worlds incombraunce did himselfe assoyle.

38

He thence them led into his Hermitage,
  Letting their steedes to graze upon the greene:
  Small was his house, and like a little cage,
  For his owne turne, yet inly neate and clene,
  Deckt with greene boughes, and flowers gay beseene.
  Therein he them full faire did entertaine
  Not with such forged showes, as fitter beene
  For courting fooles, that curtesies would faine,
But with entire affection and appearaunce plaine.

39

Yet was their fare but homely, such as hee
  Did use, his feeble body to sustaine;
  The which full gladly they did take in glee,
  Such as it was, ne did of want complaine,
  But being well suffiz'd, them rested faine.
  But faire *Serene* all night could take no rest,
  Ne yet that gentle Squire, for grievous paine
  Of their late woundes, the which the *Blatant Beast*
Had given them, whose griefe through suffraunce sore increast.

40

So all that night they past in great disease,
　Till that the morning, bringing earely light
　To guide mens labours, brought them also ease,
　And some asswagement of their painefull plight.
　Then up they rose, and gan them selves to dight
　Unto their journey; but that Squire and Dame
　So faint and feeble were, that they ne might
　Endure to travell, nor one foote to frame:
Their hearts were sicke, their sides were sore, their feete were lame.

41

Therefore the Prince, whom great affaires in mynd
　Would not permit, to make there lenger stay,
　Was forced there to leave them both behynd,
　In that good Hermits charge, whom he did pray
　To tend them well. So forth he went his way,
　And with him eke the salvage, that whyleare
　Seeing his royall usage and array,
　Was greatly growne in love of that brave pere,
Would needes depart, as shall declared be elsewhere.

CANT. VI

The Hermite heales both Squire and dame
Of their sore maladies:
He Turpine doth defeate, and shame
For his late villanies.

I

NO wound, which warlike hand of enemy
　Inflicts with dint of sword, so sore doth light,
　As doth the poysnous sting, which infamy
　Infixeth in the name of noble wight:
　For by no art, nor any leaches might
　It ever can recured be againe;
　Ne all the skill, which that immortall spright
　Of *Podalyrius* did in it retaine,
Can remedy such hurts; such hurts are hellish paine.

2

Such were the wounds, the which that *Blatant Beast*
  Made in the bodies of that Squire and Dame;
  And being such, were now much more increast,
  For want of taking heede unto the same,
  That now corrupt and curelesse they became.
  Howbe that carefull Hermite did his best,
  With many kindes of medicines meete, to tame
  The poysnous humour, which did most infest
Their ranckling wounds, and every day them duely drest.

3

For he right well in Leaches craft was seene,
  And through the long experience of his dayes,
  Which had in many fortunes tossed beene,
  And past through many perillous assayes,
  He knew the diverse went of mortall wayes,
  And in the mindes of men had great insight;
  Which with sage counsell, when they went astray,
  He could enforme, and them reduce aright,
And al the passions heale, which wound the weaker spright.

4

For whylome he had bene a doughty Knight,
  As any one, that lived in his daies,
  And proved oft in many perillous fight,
  Of which he grace and glory wonne alwaies,
  And in all battels bore away the baies.
  But being now attacht with timely age,
  And weary of this worlds unquiet waies,
  He tooke him selfe unto this Hermitage,
In which he liv'd alone, like carelesse bird in cage.

5

One day, as he was searching of their wounds,
  He found that they had festred privily,
  And ranckling inward with unruly stounds,
  The inner parts now gan to putrify,
  That quite they seem'd past helpe of surgery,
  And rather needed to be disciplinde
  With holesome reede of sad sobriety,
  To rule the stubborne rage of passion blinde:
Give salves to every sore, but counsell to the minde.

6

So taking them apart into his cell,
  He to that point fit speaches gan to frame,
  As he the art of words knew wondrous well,
  And eke could doe, as well as say the same,
  And thus he to them sayd; Faire daughter Dame,
  And you faire sonne, which here thus long now lie
  In piteous languor, since ye hither came,
  In vaine of me ye hope for remedie,
And I likewise in vaine doe salves to you applie.

7

For in your selfe your onely helpe doth lie,
  To heale your selves, and must proceed alone
  From your owne will, to cure your maladie.
  Who can him cure, that will be cur'd of none?
  If therefore health ye seeke, observe this one.
  First learne your outward sences to refraine
  From things, that stirre up fraile affection;
  Your eies, your eares, your tongue, your talk restraine
From that they most affect, and in due termes containe.

8

For from those outward sences ill affected,
  The seede of all this evill first doth spring,
  Which at the first before it had infected,
  Mote easie be supprest with little thing:
  But being growen strong, it forth doth bring
  Sorrow, and anguish, and impatient paine
  In th'inner parts, and lastly scattering
  Contagious poyson close through every vaine,
It never rests, till it have wrought his finall bane.

9

For that beastes teeth, which wounded you tofore,
  Are so exceeding venemous and keene,
  Made all of rusty yron, ranckling sore,
  That where they bite, it booteth not to weene
  With salve, or antidote, or other mene
  It ever to amend: ne marvaile ought;
  For that same beast was bred of hellish strene,
  And long in darksome *Stygian* den upbrought,
Begot of foule *Echidna*, as in bookes is taught.

10

Echidna is a Monster direfull dred,
  Whom Gods doe hate, and heavens abhor to see;
  So hideous is her shape, so huge her hed,
  That even the hellish fiends affrighted bee
  At sight thereof, and from her presence flee:
  Yet did her face and former parts professe
  A faire young Mayden, full of comely glee;
  But all her hinder parts did plaine expresse
A monstrous Dragon, full of fearefull uglinesse.

11

To her the Gods, for her so dreadfull face,
  In fearefull darkenesse, furthest from the skie,
  And from the earth, appointed have her place,
  Mongst rocks and caves, where she enrold doth lie
  In hideous horrour and obscurity,
  Wasting the strength of her immortall age.
  There did *Typhaon* with her company,
  Cruell *Typhaon*, whose tempestuous rage
Make th'heavens tremble oft, and him with vowes asswage.

12

Of that commixtion they did then beget
  This hellish Dog, that hight the *Blatant Beast*;
  A wicked Monster, that his tongue doth whet
  Gainst all, both good and bad, both most and least,
  And poures his poysnous gall forth to infest
  The noblest wights with notable defame:
  Ne ever Knight, that bore so lofty creast,
  Ne ever Lady of so honest name,
But he them spotted with reproch, or secrete shame.

13

In vaine therefore it were, with medicine
  To goe about to salve such kynd of sore,
  That rather needes wise read and discipline,
  Than outward salves, that may augment it more.
  Aye me (sayd then *Serena* sighing sore)
  What hope of helpe doth then for us remaine,
  If that no salves may us to health restore?
  But sith we need good counsel (sayd the swainel)
Aread good sire, some counsell, that may us sustaine.

14

The best (sayd he) that I can you advize,
  Is to avoide the occasion of the ill:
  For when the cause, whence evill doth arize,
  Removed is, th'effect surceaseth still.
  Abstaine from pleasure, and restraine your will,
  Subdue desire, and bridle loose delight,
  Use scanted diet, and forbeare your fill,
  Shun secresie, and talke in open sight:
So shall you soone repaire your present evill plight.

15

Thus having sayd, his sickely patients
  Did gladly hearken to his grave beheast,
  And kept so well his wise commaundements,
  That in short space their malady was ceast,
  And eke the biting of that harmefull Beast
  Was throughly heal'd. Tho when they did perceave
  Their wounds recur'd, and forces reincreast,
  Of that good Hermite both they tooke their leave,
And went both on their way, ne ech would other leave.

16

But each the other vow'd t'accompany,
  The Lady, for that she was much in dred,
  Now left alone in great extremity,
  The Squire, for that he courteous was indeed,
  Would not her leave alone in her great need.
  So both together traveld, till they met
  With a faire Mayden clad in mourning weed,
  Upon a mangy jade unmeetely set,
And a lewd foole her leading thorough dry and wet.

17

But by what meanes that shame to her befell,
  And how thereof her selfe she did acquite,
  I must a while forbeare to you to tell;
  Till that, as comes by course, I doe recite,
  What fortune to the Briton Prince did lite,
  Pursuing that proud Knight, the which whileare
  Wrought to Sir *Calidore* so foule despight;
  And eke his Lady, though she sickely were,
So lewdly had abusde, as ye did lately heare.

18

The Prince according to the former token,
　Which faire *Serene* to him delivered had,
　Pursu'd him streight, in mynd to bene ywroken
　Of all the vile demeane, and usage bad,
　With which he had those two so ill bestad:
　Ne wight with him on that adventure went,
　But that wylde man, whom though he oft forbad,
　Yet for no bidding, nor for being shent,
Would he restrayned be from his attendement.

19

Arriving there, as did by chaunce befall,
　He found the gate wyde ope, and in he rode,
　Ne stayd, till that he came into the hall:
　Where soft dismounting like a weary lode,
　Upon the ground with feeble feete he trode,
　As he unable were for very neede
　To move one foote, but there must make abode;
　The whiles the salvage man did take his steede,
And in some stable neare did set him up to feede.

20

Ere long to him a homely groome there came,
　That in rude wise him asked, what he was,
　That durst so boldly, without let or shame,
　Into his Lords forbidden hall to passe.
　To whom the Prince, him fayning to embase,
　Mylde answer made; he was an errant Knight,
　The which was fall'n into this feeble case,
　Through many wounds, which lately he in fight
Received had, and prayd to pitty his ill plight.

21

But he, the more outrageous and bold,
　Sternely did bid him quickely thence avaunt,
　Or deare aby, for why his Lord of old
　Did hate all errant Knights, which there did haunt,
　Ne lodging would to any of them graunt,
　And therefore lightly bad him packe away,
　Not sparing him with bitter words to taunt,
　And therewithall rude hand on him did lay,
To thrust him out of dore, doing his worst assay.

22

Which when the Salvage comming now in place,
  Beheld, eftsoones he all enraged grew,
  And running streight upon that villaine base,
  Like a fell Lion at him fiercely flew,
  And with his teeth and nailes, in present vew,
  Him rudely rent, and all to peeces tore:
  So miserably him all helpelesse slew,
  That with the noise, whilest he did loudly rore,
The people of the house rose forth in great uprore.

23

Who when on ground they saw their fellow slaine,
  And that same Knight and Salvage standing by,
  Upon them two they fell with might and maine,
  And on them layd so huge and horribly,
  As if they would have slaine them presently.
  But the bold Prince defended him so well,
  And their assault withstood so mightily,
  That maugre all their might, he did repell,
And beat them back, whilest many underneath him fell.

24

Yet he them still so sharpely did pursew,
  That few of them he left alive, which fled,
  Those evill tidings to their Lord to shew.
  Who hearing how his people badly sped,
  Came forth in hast: where when as with the dead
  He saw the ground all strow'd, and that same Knight
  And salvage with their bloud fresh steeming red,
  He woxe nigh mad with wrath and fell despight,
And with reprochfull words him thus bespake on hight.

25

Art thou he, traytor, that with treason vile,
  Hast slaine my men in this unmanly maner,
  And now triumphest in the piteous spoile
  Of these poore folk, whose soules with black dishonor
  And foule defame doe decke thy bloudy baner?
  The meede whereof shall shortly be thy shame,
  And wretched end, which still attendeth on her.
  With that him selfe to battell he did frame;
So did his forty yeomen, which there with him came.

26

With dreadfull force they all did him assaile,
  And round about with boystrous strokes oppresse,
  That on his shield did rattle like to haile
  In a great tempest; that in such distresse,
  He wist not to which side him to addresse.
  And evermore that craven cowherd Knight
  Was at his backe with heartlesse heedinesse,
  Wayting if he unwares him murther might:
For cowardize doth still in villany delight.

27

Whereof whenas the Prince was well aware,
  He to him turnd with furious intent,
  And him against his powre gan to prepare;
  Like a fierce Bull, that being busie bent
  To fight with many foes about him ment,
  Feeling some curre behinde his heeles to bite,
  Turnes him about with fell avengement;
  So likewise turnde the Prince upon the Knight,
And layd at him amaine with all his will and might.

28

Who when he once his dreadfull strokes had tasted,
  Durst not the furie of his force abyde,
  But turn'd abacke, and to retyre him hasted
  Through the thick prease, there thinking him to hyde.
  But when the Prince had once him plainely eyde,
  He foot by foot him followed alway,
  Ne would him suffer once to shrinke asyde
  But joyning close, huge lode at him did lay:
Who flying still did ward, and warding fly away.

29

But when his foe he still so eger saw,
  Unto his heeles himselfe he did betake,
  Hoping unto some refuge to withdraw:
  Ne would the Prince him ever foot forsake,
  Where so he went, but after him did make.
  He fled from roome to roome, from place to place,
  Whylest every joynt for dread of death did quake,
  Still looking after him, that did him chace;
That made him evermore increase his speedie pace.

30

At last he up into the chamber came,
　Whereas his love was sitting all alone,
　Wayting what tydings of her folke became.
　There did the Prince him overtake anone,
　Crying in vaine to her, him to bemone;
　And with his sword him on the head did smyte,
　That to the ground he fell in senselesse swone:
　Yet whether thwart or flatly it did lyte,
The tempred steele did not into his braynepan byte.

31

Which when the Ladie saw, with great affright
　She starting up, began to shrieke aloud,
　And with her garment covering him from sight,
　Seem'd under her protection him to shroud;
　And falling lowly at his feet, her bowd
　Upon her knee, intreating him for grace,
　And often him besought, and prayd, and vowd;
　That with the ruth of her so wretched case,
He stayd his second strooke, and did his hand abase.

32

Her weed she then withdrawing, did him discover,
　Who now come to himselfe, yet would not rize,
　But still did lie as dead, and quake, and quiver,
　That even the Prince his basenesse did despize,
　And eke his Dame him seeing in such guize,
　Gan him recomfort, and from ground to reare.
　Who rising up at last in ghastly wize,
　Like troubled ghost did dreadfully appeare,
As one that had no life him left through former feare.

33

Whom when the Prince so deadly saw dismayd,
　He for such basenesse shamefully him shent,
　And with sharpe words did bitterly upbrayd;
　Vile cowheard dogge, now doe I much repent,
　That ever I this life unto thee lent,
　Whereof thou caytive so unworthie art;
　That both thy love, for lacke of hardiment,
　And eke thy selfe, for want of manly hart,
And eke all knights hast shamed with this knightlesse part.

34

Yet further hast thou heaped shame to shame,
  And crime to crime, by this thy cowheard feare.
  For first it was to thee reprochfull blame,
  To erect this wicked custome, which I heare,
  Gainst errant Knights and Ladies thou dost reare;
  Whom when thou mayst, thou dost of arms despoile,
  Or of their upper garment, which they weare:
  Yet doest thou not with manhood, but with guile
Maintaine this evill use, thy foes thereby to foile.

35

And lastly in approvance of thy wrong,
  To shew such faintnesse and foule cowardize,
  Is greatest shame: for oft it falles, that strong
  And valiant knights doe rashly enterprize,
  Either for fame, or else for exercize,
  A wrongfull quarrell to maintaine by fight;
  Yet have, through prowesse and their brave emprize,
  Gotten great worship in this worldes sight.
For greater force there needs to maintaine wrong, than right.

36

Yet since thy life unto this Ladie fayre
  I given have, live in reproch and scorne;
  Ne ever armes, ne ever knighthood dare
  Hence to professe: for shame is to adorne
  With so brave badges one so basely borne;
  But onely breath sith that I did forgive.
  So having from his craven bodie torne
  Those goodly armes, he them away did give
And onely suffred him this wretched life to live.

37

There whilest he thus was setling things above,
  Atwene that Ladie myld and recreant knight,
  To whom his life he graunted for her love,
  He gan bethinke him, in what perilous plight
  He had behynd him left that salvage wight,
  Amongst so many foes, whom sure he thought
  By this quite slaine in so unequall fight:
  Therefore descending backe in haste, he sought
If yet he were alive, or to destruction brought.

38

There he him found environed about
  With slaughtred bodies, which his hand had slaine,
  And laying yet a fresh with courage stout
  Upon the rest, that did alive remaine;
  Whom he likewise right sorely did constraine,
  Like scattred sheepe, to seeke for safetie,
  After he gotten had with busie paine
  Some of their weapons, which thereby did lie,
With which he layd about, and made them fast to flie.

39

Whom when the Prince so felly saw to rage,
  Approching to him neare, his hand he stayd,
  And sought, by making signes, him to asswage:
  Who them perceiving, streight to him obayd,
  As to his Lord, and downe his weapons layd,
  As if he long had to his heasts bene trayned.
  Thence he him brought away, and up convayd
  Into the chamber, where that Dame remayned
With her unworthy knight, who ill him entertayned.

40

Whom when the Salvage saw from daunger free,
  Sitting beside his Ladie there at ease,
  He well remembred, that the same was hee,
  Which lately sought his Lord for to displease:
  Tho all in rage, he on him streight did seaze,
  As if he would in peeces him have rent;
  And were not, that the Prince did him appeaze,
  He had not left one limbe of him unrent:
But streight he held his hand at his commaundement.

41

Thus having all things well in peace ordayned,
  The Prince himselfe there all that night did rest,
  Where him *Blandina* fayrely entertayned,
  With all the courteous glee and goodly feast,
  The which for him she could imagine best.
  For well she knew the wayes to win good will
  Of every wight, that were not too infest,
  And how to please the minds of good and ill,
Through tempering of her words and lookes by wondrous skill.

42

Yet were her words and lookes but false and fayned,
　To some hid end to make more easie way,
　Or to allure such fondlings, whom she trayned
　Into her trap unto their owne decay:
　Thereto, when needed, she could weepe and pray,
　And when her listed, she could fawne and flatter;
　Now smyling smoothly, like to sommers day,
　Now glooming sadly, so to cloke her matter;
Yet were her words but wynd, and all her teares but water.

43

Whether such grace were given her by kynd,
　As women wont their guilefull wits to guyde;
　Or learn'd the art to please, I doe not fynd.
　This well I wote, that she so well applyde
　Her pleasing tongue, that soone she pacifyde
　The wrathfull Prince, and wrought her husbands peace.
　Who nathelesse not therewith satisfyde,
　His rancorous despight did not releasse,
Ne secretly from thought of fell revenge surceasse.

44

For all that night, the whyles the Prince did rest
　In carelesse couch, not weeting what was ment,
　He watcht in close awayt with weapons prest,
　Willing to worke his villenous intent
　On him, that had so shamefully him shent:
　Yet durst he not for very cowardize
　Effect the same, whylest all the night was spent.
　The morrow next the Prince did early rize,
And passed forth, to follow his first enterprize.

CANT. VII

Turpine is baffuld, his two knights
doe gaine their treasons meed,
Fayre Mirabellaes punishment
for loves disdaine decreed.

1

LIKE as the gentle hart it selfe bewrayes,
  In doing gentle deedes with franke delight,
  Even so the baser mind it selfe displayes,
  In cancred malice and revengefull spight.
  For to maligne, t'envie, t'use shifting slight,
  Be arguments of a vile donghill mind,
  Which what it dare not doe by open might,
  To worke by wicked treason wayes doth find,
By such discourteous deeds discovering his base kind.

2

That well appeares in this discourteous knight,
  The coward *Turpine*, whereof now I treat;
  Who notwithstanding that in former fight
  He of the Prince his life received late,
  Yet in his mind malitious and ingrate
  He gan devize, to be aveng'd anew
  For all that shame, which kindled inward hate.
  Therefore so soone as he was out of vew,
Himselfe in hast he arm'd, and did him fast pursew.

3

Well did he tract his steps, as he did ryde,
  Yet would not neare approch in daungers eye,
  But kept aloofe for dread to be descryde,
  Untill fit time and place he mote espy,
  Where he mote worke him scath and villeny.
  At last he met two knights to him unknowne,
  The which were armed both agreeably,
  And both combynd, what ever chaunce were blowne,
Betwixt them to divide, and each to make his owne.

4

To whom false *Turpine* comming courteously,
  To cloke the mischiefe, which he inly ment,
  Gan to complaine of great discourtesie,
  Which a straunge knight, that neare afore him went,
  Had doen to him, and his deare Ladie shent:
  Which if they would afford him ayde at need
  For to avenge, in time convenient,
  They should accomplish both a knightly deed,
And for their paines obtaine of him a goodly meed.

5

The knights beleev'd, that all he sayd, was trew,
  And being fresh and full of youthly spright,
  Were glad to heare of that adventure new,
  In which they mote make triall of their might,
  Which never yet they had approv'd in fight;
  And eke desirous of the offred meed,
  Said then the one of them; Where is that wight,
  The which hath doen to thee this wrongfull deed,
That we may it avenge, and punish him with speed?

6

He rides (said *Turpine*) there not farre afore,
  With a wyld man soft footing by his syde,
  That if ye list to haste a litle more,
  Ye may him overtake in timely tyde.
  Eftsoones they pricked forth with forward pryde,
  And ere that litle while they ridden had,
  The gentle Prince not farre away they spyde,
  Ryding a softly pace with portance sad,
Devizing of his love more, than of daunger drad.

7

Then one of them aloud unto him cryde,
  Bidding him turne againe, false traytour knight,
  Foule womanwronger, for he him defyde.
  With that they both at once with equall spight
  Did bend their speares, and both with equall might
  Against him ran; but th'one did misse his marke,
  And being carried with his force forthright,
  Glaunst swiftly by; like to that heavenly sparke,
Which glyding through the ayre lights all the heavens darke.

8

But th'other ayming better, did him smite
  Full in the shield, with so impetuous powre,
  That all his launce in peeces shivered quite,
  And scattered all about, fell on the flowre.
  But the stout Prince, with much more steddy stowre
  Full on his bever did him strike so sore,
  That the cold steele through piercing, did devowre
  His vitall breath, and to the ground him bore,
Where still he bathed lay in his owne bloody gore.

9

As when a cast of Faulcons make their flight
  At an Herneshaw, that lyes aloft on wing,
  The whyles they strike at him with heedlesse might,
  The warie foule his bill doth backward wring;
  On which the first, whose force her first doth bring,
  Her selfe quite through the bodie doth engore,
  And falleth downe to ground like senselesse thing,
  But th'other not so swift, as she before,
Fayles of her souse, and passing by doth hurt no more.

10

By this the other, which was passed by,
  Himselfe recovering, was return'd to fight;
  Where when he saw his fellow lifelesse ly,
  He much was daunted with so dismall sight;
  Yet nought abating of his former spight,
  Let drive at him with so malitious mynd,
  As if he would have passed through him quight:
  But the steele-head no stedfast hold could fynd,
But glauncing by, deceiv'd him of that he desynd.

11

Not so the Prince: for his well learned speare
  Tooke surer hould, and from his horses backe
  Above a launces length him forth did beare,
  And gainst the cold hard earth so sore him strake,
  That all his bones in peeces nigh he brake.
  Where seeing him so lie, he left his steed,
  And to him leaping, vengeance thought to take
  Of him, for all his former follies meed,
With flaming sword in hand his terror more to breed.

12

The fearefull swayne beholding death so nie,
  Cryde out aloud for mercie him to save;
  In lieu whereof he would to him descrie,
  Great treason to him meant, his life to reave.
  The Prince soone hearkned, and his life forgave.
  Then thus said he, There is a straunger knight,
  The which for promise of great meed, us drave
  To this attempt, to wreake his hid despight,
For that himselfe thereto did want sufficient might.

13

The Prince much mused at such villenie,
  And sayd; Now sure ye well have earn'd your meed,
  For th'one is dead, and th'other soone shall die,
  Unlesse to me thou hether bring with speed
  The wretch, that hyr'd you to this wicked deed.
  He glad of life, and willing eke to wreake
  The guilt on him, which did this mischiefe breed,
  Swore by his sword, that neither day nor weeke
He would surceasse, but him, where so he were, would seeke.

14

So up he rose, and forth streight way he went
  Backe to the place, where *Turpine* late he lore;
  There he him found in great astonishment,
  To see him so bedight with bloodie gore,
  And griesly wounds that him appalled sore.
  Yet thus at length he said, How now Sir knight?
  What meaneth this, which here I see before?
  How fortuneth this foule uncomely plight,
So different from that, which earst ye seem'd in sight?

15

Perdie (said he) in evill houre it fell,
  That ever I for meed did undertake
  So hard a taske, as life for hyre to sell;
  The which I earst adventur'd for your sake.
  Witnesse the wounds, and this wyde bloodie lake,
  Which ye may see yet all about me steeme.
  Therefore now yeeld, as ye did promise make,
  My due reward, the which right well I deeme
I yearned have, that life so dearely did redeeme.

16

But where then is (quoth he halfe wrothfully)
  Where is the bootie, which therefore I bought,
  That cursed caytive, my strong enemy,
  That recreant knight, whose hated life I sought?
  And where is eke your friend, which halfe it ought?
  He lyes (said he) upon the cold bare ground,
  Slayne of that errant knight, with whom he fought;
  Whom afterwards my selfe with many a wound
Did slay againe, as ye may see there in the stound.

17

Thereof false *Turpin* was full glad and faine,
  And needs with him streight to the place would ryde,
  Where he himselfe might see his foeman slaine;
  For else his feare could not be satisfyde.
  So as they rode, he saw the way all dyde
  With streames of bloud; which tracting by the traile,
  Ere long they came, whereas in evill tyde
  That other swayne, like ashes deadly pale,
Lay in the lap of death, rewing his wretched bale.

18

Much did the Craven seeme to mone his case,
  That for his sake his deare life had forgone;
  And him bewayling with affection base,
  Did counterfeit kind pittie, where was none:
  For wheres no courage, theres no ruth nor mone.
  Thence passing forth, not farre away he found,
  Whereas the Prince himselfe lay all alone,
  Loosely displayd upon the grassie ground,
Possessed of sweete sleepe, that luld him soft in swound.

19

Wearie of travell in his former fight,
  He there in shade himselfe had layd to rest,
  Having his armes and warlike things undight,
  Fearelesse of foes that mote his peace molest;
  The whyles his salvage page, that wont be prest,
  Was wandred in the wood another way,
  To doe some thing, that seemed to him best,
  The whyles his Lord in silver slomber lay,
Like to the Evening starre adorn'd with deawy ray.

20

Whom when as *Turpin* saw so loosely layd,
　He weened well, that he in deed was dead,
　Like as that other knight to him had sayd:
　But when he nigh approcht, he mote aread
　Plaine signes in him of life and livelihead.
　Whereat much griev'd against that straunger knight,
　That him too light of credence did mislead,
　He would have backe retyred from that sight,
That was to him on earth the deadliest despight.

21

But that same knight would not once let him start,
　But plainely gan to him declare the case
　Of all his mischiefe, and late lucklesse smart;
　How both he and his fellow there in place
　Were vanquished, and put to foule disgrace,
　And how that he in lieu of life him lent,
　Had vow'd unto the victor, him to trace
　And follow through the world, where so he went,
Till that he him delivered to his punishment.

22

He therewith much abashed and affrayd,
　Began to tremble every limbe and vaine;
　And softly whispering him, entyrely prayd,
　T'advize him better, than by such a traine
　Him to betray unto a straunger swaine:
　Yet rather counseld him contrarywize,
　Sith he likewise did wrong by him sustaine,
　To joyne with him and vengeance to devize,
Whylest time did offer meanes him sleeping to surprize.

23

Nathelesse for all his speach, the gentle knight
　Would not be tempted to such villenie,
　Regarding more his faith, which he did plight,
　All were it to his mortall enemie,
　Than to entrap him by false treacherie:
　Great shame in lieges blood to be embrew'd.
　Thus whylest they were debating diverslie,
　The Salvage forth out of the wood issew'd
Backe to the place, whereas his Lord he sleeping vew'd.

24

There when he saw those two so neare him stand,
  He doubted much what mote their meaning bee,
  And throwing downe his load out of his hand,
  To weet great store of forrest frute, which hee
  Had for his food late gathered from the tree,
  Himselfe unto his weapon he betooke,
  That was an oaken plant, which lately hee
  Rent by the root; which he so sternely shooke,
That like an hazell wand, it quivered and quooke.

25

Whereat the Prince awaking, when he spyde
  The traytour *Turpin* with that other knight,
  He started up, and snatching neare his syde
  His trustie sword, the servant of his might,
  Like a fell Lyon leaped to him light,
  And his left hand upon his collar layd.
  Therewith the cowheard deaded with affright,
  Fell flat to ground, ne word unto him sayd,
But holding up his hands, with silence mercie prayd.

26

But he so full of indignation was,
  That to his prayer nought he would incline,
  But as he lay upon the humbled gras,
  His foot he set on his vile necke, in signe
  Of servile yoke, that nobler harts repine.
  Then letting him arise like abject thrall,
  He gan to him object his haynous crime,
  And to revile, and rate, and recreant call,
And lastly to despoyle of knightly bannerall.

27

And after all, for greater infamie,
  He by the heeles him hung upon a tree,
  And baffuld so, that all which passed by,
  The picture of his punishment might see,
  And by the like ensample warned bee,
  How ever they through treason doe trespasse.
  But turne we now backe to that Ladie free,
  Whom late we left ryding upon an Asse,
Led by a Carle and foole, which by her side did passe.

28

She was a Ladie of great dignitie
  And lifted up to honorable place,
  Famous through all the land of Faerie,
  Though of meane parentage and kindred base,
  Yet deckt with wondrous giftes of natures grace,
  That all men did her person much admire,
  And praise the feature of her goodly face,
  The beames whereof did kindle lovely fire
In th'harts of many a knight, and many a gentle squire.

29

But she thereof grew proud and insolent,
  That none she worthie thought to be her fere,
  But scornd them all, that love unto her ment,
  Yet was she lov'd of many a worthy pere,
  Unworthy she to be belov'd so dere,
  That could not weigh of worthinesse aright.
  For beautie is more glorious bright and clere,
  The more it is admir'd of many a wight,
And noblest she, that served is of noblest knight.

30

But this coy Damzell thought contrariwize,
  That such proud looks would make her praysed more;
  And that the more she did all love despize,
  The more would wretched lovers her adore.
  What cared she, who sighed for her sore,
  Or who did wayle or watch the wearie night?
  Let them that list, their lucklesse lot deplore;
  She was borne free, not bound to any wight,
And so would ever live, and love her owne delight.

31

Through such her stubborne stifnesse, and hard hart,
  Many a wretch, for want of remedie,
  Did languish long in lifeconsuming smart,
  And at the last through dreary dolour die:
  Whylest she, the Ladie of her libertie,
  Did boast her beautie had such soveraine might,
  That with the onely twinckle of her eye,
  She could or save, or spill, whom she would hight.
What could the Gods doe more, but doe it more aright?

32

But loe the Gods, that mortall follies vew,
  Did worthily revenge this maydens pride;
  And nought regarding her so goodly hew,
  Did laugh at her, that many did deride,
  Whilest she did weepe, of no man mercifide.
  For on a day, when *Cupid* kept his court,
  As he is wont at each Saint Valentide,
  Unto the which all lovers doe resort,
That of their loves successe they there may make report;

33

It fortun'd then, that when the roules were red,
  In which the names of all loves folke were fyled,
  That many there were missing, which were ded,
  Or kept in bands, or from their loves exyled,
  Or by some other violence despoyled.
  Which when as *Cupid* heard, he wexed wroth,
  And doubting to be wronged, or beguyled,
  He bad his eyes to be unblindfold both,
That he might see his men, and muster them by oth.

34

Then found he many missing of his crew,
  Which wont doe suit and service to his might;
  Of whom what was becomen, no man knew.
  Therefore a Jurie was impaneld streight,
  T'enquire of them, whether by force, or sleight,
  Or their owne guilt, they were away convayd.
  To whom foule *Infamie*, and fell *Despight*
  Gave evidence, that they were all betrayd,
And murdred cruelly by a rebellious Mayd.

35

Fayre *Mirabella* was her name, whereby
  Of all those crymes she there indited was:
  All which when *Cupid* heard, he by and by
  In great displeasure, wild a *Capias*
  Should issue forth, t'attach that scornefull lasse.
  The warrant straight was made, and therewithall
  A Baylieffe errant forth in post did passe,
  Whom they by name there *Portamore* did call;
He which doth summon lovers to loves judgement hall.

36

The damzell was attacht, and shortly brought
  Unto the barre, whereas she was arrayned:
  But she thereto nould plead, nor answere ought
  Even for stubborne pride, which her restrayned.
  So judgement past, as is by law ordayned
  In cases like, which when at last she saw,
  Her stubborne hart, which love before disdayned,
  Gan stoupe, and falling downe with humble awe,
Cryde mercie, to abate the extremitie of law.

37

The sonne of *Venus* who is myld by kynd,
  But where he is provokt with peevishnesse,
  Unto her prayers piteously enclynd,
  And did the rigour of his doome represse;
  Yet not so freely, but that nathelesse
  He unto her a penance did impose,
  Which was, that through this worlds wyde wildernes
  She wander should in companie of those,
Till she had sav'd so many loves, as she did lose.

38

So now she had bene wandring two whole yeares
  Throughout the world, in this uncomely case,
  Wasting her goodly hew in heavie teares,
  And her good dayes in dolorous disgrace:
  Yet had she not in all these two yeares space,
  Saved but two, yet in two yeares before,
  Through her dispiteous pride, whilest love lackt place,
  She had destroyed two and twenty more.
Aie me, how could her love make half amends therefore?

39

And now she was uppon the weary way,
  When as the gentle Squire, with faire *Serene*,
  Met her in such misseeming foule array;
  The whiles that mighty man did her demeane
  With all the evill termes and cruell meane,
  That he could make: And eeke that angry foole
  Which follow'd her, with cursed hands uncleane
  Whipping her horse, did with his smarting toole
Oft whip her dainty selfe, and much augment her doole.

40

Ne ought it mote availe her to entreat
  The one or th'other, better her to use:
  For both so wilfull were and obstinate,
  That all her piteous plaint they did refuse,
  And rather did the more her beate and bruse.
  But most the former villaine, which did lead
  Her tyreling jade, was bent her to abuse;
  Who though she were with wearinesse nigh dead,
Yet would not let her lite, nor rest a little stead.

41

For he was sterne, and terrible by nature,
  And eeke of person huge and hideous,
  Exceeding much the measure of mans stature,
  And rather like a Gyant monstruous.
  For sooth he was descended of the hous
  Of those old Gyants, which did warres darraine
  Against the heaven in order battailous,
  And sib to great *Orgolio*, which was slaine
By *Arthure*, when as *Unas* Knight he did maintaine.

42

His lookes were dreadfull, and his fiery eies
  Like two great Beacons, glared bright and wyde,
  Glauncing askew, as if his enemies
  He scorned in his overweening pryde;
  And stalking stately like a Crane, did stryde
  At every step uppon the tiptoes hie,
  And all the way he went, on every syde
  He gaz'd about, and stared horriblie,
As if he with his lookes would all men terrifie.

43

He wore no armour, ne for none did care,
  As no whit dreading any living wight;
  But in a Jacket quilted richly rare
  Upon checklaton he was straungely dight,
  And on his head a roll of linnen plight,
  Like to the Mores of Malaber he wore;
  With which his locks, as blacke as pitchy night,
  Were bound about, and voyded from before,
And in his hand a mighty yron club he bore.

44

This was *Disdaine*, who led that Ladies horse
  Through thick and thin, through mountains and through plains,
  Compelling her, wher she would not, by force,
  Haling her palfrey by the hempen raines.
  But that same foole, which most increast her paines,
  Was *Scorne*, who having in his hand a whip,
  Her therewith yirks, and still when she complaines,
  The more he laughes, and does her closely quip,
To see her sore lament, and bite her tender lip.

45

Whose cruell handling when that Squire beheld,
  And saw those villaines her so vildely use,
  His gentle heart with indignation sweld,
  And could no lenger beare so great abuse,
  As such a Lady so to beate and bruse;
  But to him stepping, such a stroke him lent,
  That forst him th'halter from his hand to loose,
  And maugre all his might, backe to relent:
Else had he surely there bene slaine, or fowly shent.

46

The villaine, wroth for greeting him so sore,
  Gathered him selfe together soone againe,
  And with his yron batton, which he bore,
  Let drive at him so dreadfully amaine,
  That for his safety he did him constraine
  To give him ground, and shift to every side,
  Rather than once his burden to sustaine:
  For bootelesse thing him seemed, to abide
So mighty blowes, or prove the puissaunce of his pride.

47

Like as a Mastiffe having at a bay
  A salvage Bull, whose cruell hornes doe threat
  Desperate daunger, if he them assay,
  Traceth his ground, and round about doth beat,
  To spy where he may some advauntage get;
  The whiles the beast doth rage and loudly rore:
  So did the Squire, the whiles the Carle did fret,
  And fume in his disdainefull mynd the more,
And oftentimes by Turmagant and Mahound swore.

48

Nathelesse so sharpely still he him pursewd,
That at advantage him at last he tooke,
When his foote slipt (that slip he dearely rewd,)
And with his yron club to ground him strooke;
Where still he lay, ne out of swoune awooke,
Till heavy hand the Carle upon him layd,
And bound him fast: Tho when he up did looke,
And saw him selfe captiv'd, he was dismayd,
Ne powre had to withstand, ne hope of any ayd.

49

Then up he made him rise, and forward fare,
Led in a rope, which both his hands did bynd;
Ne ought that foole for pitty did him spare,
But with his whip him following behynd,
Him often scourg'd, and forst his feete to fynd;
And other whiles with bitter mockes and mowes
He would him scorne, that to his gentle mynd
Was much more grievous, than the others blowes:
Words sharpely wound, but greatest griefe of scorning growes.

50

The faire *Serena*, when she saw him fall
Under that villaines club, then surely thought
That slaine he was, or made a wretched thrall,
And fled away with all the speede she mought,
To seeke for safety, which long time she sought:
And past through many perils by the way,
Ere she againe to *Calepine* was brought;
The which discourse as now I must delay,
Till *Mirabellaes* fortunes I doe further say.

CANT. VIII

Prince Arthure overcomes Disdaine,
Quites Mirabell from dreed:
Serena found of Salvages,
By Calepine is freed.

I

YE gentle Ladies, in whose soveraine powre
  Love hath the glory of his kingdome left,
  And th'hearts of men, as your eternall dowre,
  In yron chaines, of liberty bereft,
  Delivered hath into your hands by gift;
  Be well aware, how ye the same doe use,
  That pride doe not to tyranny you lift;
  Least if men you of cruelty accuse,
He from you take that chiefedome, which ye doe abuse.

2

And as ye soft and tender are by kynde,
  Adornd with goodly gifts of beauties grace,
  So be ye soft and tender eeke in mynde;
  But cruelty and hardnesse from you chace,
  That all your other praises will deface,
  And from you turne the love of men to hate.
  Ensample take of *Mirabellaes* case,
  Who from the high degree of happy state,
Fell into wretched woes, which she repented late.

3

Who after thraldome of the gentle Squire,
  Which she beheld with lamentable eye,
  Was touched with compassion entire,
  And much lamented his calamity,
  That for her sake fell into misery:
  Which booted nought for prayers, nor for threat
  To hope for to release or mollify;
  For aye the more, that she did them entreat,
The more they him misust, and cruelly did beat.

4

So as they forward on their way did pas,
  Him still reviling and afflicting sore,
  They met Prince *Arthure* with Sir *Enias*,
  (That was that courteous Knight, whom he before
  Having subdew'd, yet did to life restore,)
  To whom as they approcht, they gan augment
  Their cruelty, and him to punish more,
  Scourging and haling him more vehement;
As if it them should grieve to see his punishment.

5

The Squire him selfe when as he saw his Lord,
  The witnesse of his wretchednesse, in place,
  Was much asham'd, that with an hempen cord
  He like a dog was led in captive case,
  And did his head for bashfulnesse abase,
  As loth to see, or to be seene at all:
  Shame would be hid. But whenas *Enias*
  Beheld two such, of two such villaines thrall,
His manly mynde was much emmoved therewithall.

6

And to the Prince thus sayd; See you Sir Knight,
  The greatest shame that ever eye yet saw?
  Yond Lady and her Squire with foule despight
  Abusde, against all reason and all law,
  Without regard of pitty or of awe.
  See how they doe that Squire beat and revile;
  See how they doe the Lady hale and draw.
  But if ye please to lend me leave a while,
I will them soone acquite, and both of blame assoile.

7

The Prince assented, and then he streight way
  Dismounting light, his shield about him threw,
  With which approching, thus he gan to say;
  Abide ye caytive treachetours untrew,
  That have with treason thralled unto you
  These two, unworthy of your wretched bands;
  And now your crime with cruelty pursew.
  Abide, and from them lay your loathly hands;
Or else abide the death, that hard before you stands.

8

The villaine stayd not aunswer to invent,
  But with his yron club preparing way,
  His mindes sad message backe unto him sent;
  The which descended with such dreadfull sway,
  That seemed nought the course thereof could stay:
  No more than lightening from the lofty sky.
  Ne list the Knight the powre thereof assay,
  Whose doome was death, but lightly slipping by,
Unwares defrauded his intended destiny.

9

And to requite him with the like againe,
  With his sharpe sword he fiercely at him flew,
  And strooke so strongly, that the Carle with paine
  Saved him selfe, but that he there him slew:
  Yet sav'd not so, but that the bloud it drew,
  And gave his foe good hope of victory.
  Who therewith flesht, upon him set anew,
  And with the second stroke, thought certainely
To have supplyde the first, and paide the usury.

10

But Fortune aunswerd not unto his call;
  For as his hand was heaved up on hight,
  The villaine met him in the middle fall,
  And with his club bet backe his brondyron bright
  So forcibly, that with his owne hands might
  Rebeaten backe upon him selfe againe,
  He driven was to ground in selfe despight;
  From whence ere he recovery could gaine,
He in his necke had set his foote with fell disdaine.

11

With that the foole, which did that end awayte,
  Came running in, and whilest on ground he lay,
  Laide heavy hands on him, and held so strayte,
  That downe he kept him with his scornefull sway,
  So as he could not weld him any way.
  The whiles that other villaine went about
  Him to have bound, and thrald without delay;
  The whiles the foole did him revile and flout,
Threatning to yoke them two and tame their corage stout.

12

As when a sturdy ploughman with his hynde
　　By strength have overthrowne a stubborne steare,
　　They downe him hold, and fast with cords do bynde,
　　Till they him force the buxome yoke to beare:
　　So did these two this Knight oft tug and teare.
　　Which when the Prince beheld, there standing by,
　　He left his lofty steede to aide him neare,
　　And buckling soone him selfe, gan fiercely fly
Uppon that Carle, to save his friend from jeopardy.

13

The villaine leaving him unto his mate
　　To be captiv'd, and handled as he list,
　　Himselfe addrest unto this new debate,
　　And with his club him all about so blist,
　　That he which way to turne him scarcely wist:
　　Sometimes aloft he layd, sometimes alow;
　　Now here, now there, and oft him neare he mist;
　　So doubtfully, that hardly one could know
Whether more wary were to give or ward the blow.

14

But yet the Prince so well enured was
　　With such huge strokes, approved oft in fight,
　　That way to them he gave forth right to pas.
　　Ne would endure the daunger of their might,
　　But wayt advantage, when they downe did light.
　　At last the caytive after long discourse,
　　When all his strokes he saw avoyded quite,
　　Resolved in one t'assemble all his force,
And make one end of him without ruth or remorse.

15

His dreadfull hand he heaved up aloft,
　　And with his dreadfull instrument of yre,
　　Thought sure have pownded him to powder soft,
　　Or deepe emboweld in the earth entyre:
　　But Fortune did not with his will conspire.
　　For ere his stroke attayned his intent,
　　The noble childe preventing his desire,
　　Under his club with wary boldnesse went,
And smote him on the knee, that never yet was bent.

16

It never yet was bent, ne bent it now,
　　Albe the stroke so strong and puissant were,
　　That seem'd a marble pillour it could bow,
　　But all that leg, which did his body beare,
　　It crackt throughout, yet did no bloud appeare;
　　So as it was unable to support
　　So huge a burden on such broken geare,
But fell to ground, like to a lumpe of durt,
Whence he assayd to rise, but could not for his hurt.

17

Eftsoones the Prince to him full nimbly stept,
　　And least he should recover foote againe,
　　His head meant from his shoulders to have swept.
　　Which when the Lady saw, she cryde amaine;
　　Stay stay, Sir Knight, for love of God abstaine,
　　From that unwares ye weetlesse doe intend;
　　Slay not that Carle, though worthy to be slaine:
　　For more on him doth than him selfe depend;
My life will by his death have lamentable end.

18

He staide his hand according her desire,
　　Yet nathemore him suffred to arize;
　　But still suppressing gan of her inquire,
　　What meaning mote those uncouth words comprize,
　　That in that villaines health her safety lies:
　　That, were no might in man, nor heart in Knights,
　　Which durst her dreaded reskue enterprize,
　　Yet heavens them selves, that favour feeble rights,
Would for it selfe redresse, and punish such despights.

19

Then bursting forth in teares, which gushed fast
　　Like many water streames, a while she stayd;
　　Till the sharpe passion being overpast,
　　Her tongue to her restord, then thus she sayd;
　　Nor heavens, nor men can me most wretched mayd
　　Deliver from the doome of my desart,
　　The which the God of love hath on me layd,
　　And damned to endure this direfull smart,
For penaunce of my proud and hard rebellious hart.

20

In prime of youthly yeares, when first the flowre
    Of beauty gan to bud, and bloosme delight,
    And nature me endu'd with plenteous dowre,
    Of all her gifts, that pleasde each living sight,
    I was belov'd of many a gentle Knight,
    And sude and sought with all the service dew:
    Full many a one for me deepe groand and sight,
    And to the dore of death for sorrow drew,
Complayning out on me, that would not on them rew.

21

But let them love that list, or live or die;
    Me list not die for any lovers doole:
    Ne list me leave my loved libertie,
    To pitty him that list to play the foole:
    To love my selfe I learned had in schoole.
    Thus I triumphed long in lovers paine,
    And sitting carelesse on the scorners stoole,
    Did laugh at those that did lament and plaine:
But all is now repayd with interest againe.

22

For loe the winged God, that woundeth harts,
    Causde me be called to accompt therefore,
    And for revengement of those wrongfull smarts,
    Which I to others did inflict afore,
    Addeem'd me to endure this penaunce sore;
    That in this wize, and this unmeete array,
    With these two lewd companions, and no more,
    Disdaine and *Scorne*, I through the world should stray,
Till I have sav'd so many, as I earst did slay.

23

Certes (sayd then the Prince) the God is just,
    That taketh vengeaunce of his peoples spoile.
    For were no law in love, but all that lust,
    Might them oppresse, and painefully turmoile,
    His kingdome would continue but a while.
    But tell me Lady, wherefore doe you beare
    This bottle thus before you with such toile,
    And eeke this wallet at your backe arreare,
That for these Carles to carry much more comely were?

24

Here in this bottle (sayd the sory Mayd)
  I put the teares of my contrition,
  Till to the brim I have it full defrayd:
  And in this bag which I behinde me don,
  I put repentaunce for things past and gon.
  Yet is the bottle leake, and bag so torne,
  That all which I put in, fals out anon;
  And is behinde me trodden downe of *Scorne*,
Who mocketh all my paine, and laughs the more I mourn.

25

The Infant hearkned wisely to her tale,
  And wondred much at *Cupids* judg'ment wise,
  That could so meekly make proud hearts avale,
  And wreake him selfe on them, that him despise.
  Then suffred he *Disdaine* up to arise,
  Who was not able up him selfe to reare,
  By meanes his leg through his late luckelesse prise,
  Was crackt in twaine, but by his foolish feare
Was holpen up, who him supported standing neare.

26

But being up, he lookt againe aloft,
  As if he never had received fall;
  And with sterne eye-browes stared at him oft,
  As if he would have daunted him withall:
  And standing on his tiptoes, to seeme tall,
  Downe on his golden feete he often gazed,
  As if such pride the other could apall;
  Who was so far from being ought amazed,
That he his lookes despised, and his boast dispraized.

27

Then turning backe unto that captive thrall,
  Who all this while stood there beside them bound,
  Unwilling to be knowne, or seene at all,
  He from those bands weend him to have unwound.
  But when approching neare, he plainely found,
  It was his owne true groome, the gentle Squire,
  He thereat wext exceedingly astound,
  And him did oft embrace, and oft admire,
Ne could with seeing satisfie his great desire.

28

Meane while the Salvage man, when he beheld
 That huge great foole oppressing th'other Knight,
 Whom with his weight unweldy downe he held,
 He flew upon him, like a greedy kight
 Unto some carrion offered to his sight,
 And downe him plucking, with his nayles and teeth
 Gan him to hale, and teare, and scratch, and bite;
 And from him taking his owne whip, therewith
So sore him scourgeth, that the bloud downe followeth.

29

And sure I weene, had not the Ladies cry
 Procur'd the Prince his cruell hand to stay,
 He would with whipping, him have done to dye:
 But being checkt, he did abstaine streight way,
 And let him rise. Then thus the Prince gan say;
 Now Lady sith your fortunes thus dispose,
 That if ye list have liberty, ye may,
 Unto your selfe I freely leave to chose,
Whether I shall you leave, or from these villaines lose.

30

Ah nay Sir Knight (sayd she) it may not be,
 But that I needes must by all meanes fulfill
 This penaunce, which enjoyned is to me,
 Least unto me betide a greater ill;
 Yet no lesse thankes to you for your good will.
 So humbly taking leave, she turnd aside,
 But *Arthure* with the rest, went onward still
 On his first quest, in which did him betide
A great adventure, which did him from them devide.

31

But first it falleth me by course to tell
 Of faire *Serena*, who as earst you heard,
 When first the gentle Squire at variaunce fell
 With those two Carles, fled fast away, afeard
 Of villany to be to her inferd:
 So fresh the image of her former dread,
 Yet dwelling in her eye, to her appeard,
 That every foote did tremble, which did tread,
And every body two, and two she foure did read.

32

Through hils and dales, through bushes and through breres
  Long thus she fled, till that at last she thought
  Her selfe now past the perill of her feares.
  Then looking round about, and seeing nought,
  Which doubt of daunger to her offer mought,
  She from her palfrey lighted on the plaine,
  And sitting downe, her selfe a while bethought
  Of her long travell and turmoyling paine;
And often did of love, and oft of lucke complaine.

33

And evermore she blamed *Calepine*,
  The good Sir *Calepine*, her owne true Knight,
  As th'onely author of her wofull tine:
  For being of his love to her so light,
  As her to leave in such a piteous plight.
  Yet never Turtle truer to his make,
  Than he was tride unto his Lady bright
  Who all this while endured for her sake,
Great perill of his life, and restlesse paines did take.

34

Tho when as all her plaints she had displayd,
  And well disburdened her engrieved brest,
  Upon the grasse her selfe adowne she layd;
  Where being tyrde with travell, and opprest
  With sorrow, she betooke her selfe to rest.
  There whilest in *Morpheus* bosome safe she lay,
  Fearelesse of ought, that mote her peace molest,
  False Fortune did her safety betray,
Unto a straunge mischaunce, that menac'd her decay.

35

In these wylde deserts, where she now abode,
  There dwelt a salvage nation, which did live
  Of stealth and spoile, and making nightly rode
  Into their neighbours borders; ne did give
  Them selves to any trade, as for to drive
  The painefull plough, or cattell for to breed,
  Or by adventrous marchandize to thrive;
  But on the labours of poore men to feed,
And serve their owne necessities with others need.

36

Thereto they usde one most accursed order,
  To eate the flesh of men, whom they mote fynde,
  And straungers to devoure, which on their border
  Were brought by errour, or by wreckfull wynde.
  A monstrous cruelty gainst course of kynde.
  They towards evening wandring every way,
  To seeke for booty, came by fortune blynde,
  Whereas this Lady, like a sheepe astray,
Now drowned in the depth of sleepe all fearelesse lay.

37

Soone as they spide her, Lord what gladfull glee
  They made amongst them selves; but when her face
  Like the faire yvory shining they did see,
  Each gan his fellow solace and embrace,
  For joy of such good hap by heavenly grace.
  Then gan they to devize what course to take:
  Whether to slay her there upon the place,
  Or suffer her out of her sleepe to wake,
And then her eate attonce; or many meales to make.

38

The best advizement was of bad, to let her
  Sleepe out her fill, without encomberment:
  For sleepe they sayd would make her battill better.
  Then when she wakt, they all gave one consent,
  That since by grace of God she there was sent,
  Unto their God they would her sacrifize,
  Whose share, her guiltlesse bloud they would present,
  But of her dainty flesh they did devize
To make a common feast, and feed with gurmandize.

39

So round about her they them selves did place
  Upon the grasse, and diversely dispose,
  As each thought best to spend the lingring space.
  Some with their eyes the daintest morsels chose;
  Some praise her paps, some praise her lips and nose;
  Some whet their knives, and strip their elboes bare:
  The Priest him selfe a garland doth compose
  Of finest flowres, and with full busie care
His bloudy vessels wash, and holy fire prepare.

40

The Damzell wakes, then all attonce upstart,
    And round about her flocke, like many flies,
    Whooping, and hallowing on every part,
    As if they would have rent the brasen skies.
    Which when she sees with ghastly griefull eies,
    Her heart does quake, and deadly pallid hew
    Benumbes her cheekes: Then out aloud she cries,
    Where none is nigh to heare, that will her rew,
And rends her golden locks, and snowy brests embrew.

41

But all bootes not: they hands upon her lay;
    And first they spoile her of her jewels deare,
    And afterwards of all her rich array;
    The which amongst them they in peeces teare,
    And of the pray each one a part doth beare.
    Now being naked, to their sordid eyes
    The goodly threasures of nature appeare:
    Which as they view with lustfull fantasyes,
Each wisheth to him selfe, and to the rest envyes.

42

Her yvorie necke, her alablaster brest,
    Her paps, which like white silken pillowes were,
    For love in soft delight thereon to rest;
    Her tender sides, her bellie white and clere,
    Which like an Altar did it selfe uprere,
    To offer sacrifice divine thereon;
    Her goodly thighes, whose glorie did appeare
    Like a triumphall Arch, and thereupon
The spoiles of Princes hang'd, which were in battel won.

43

Those daintie parts, the dearlings of delight,
    Which mote not be prophan'd of common eyes,
    Those villeins vew'd with loose lascivious sight,
    And closely tempted with their craftie spyes;
    And some of them gan mongst themselves devize.
    Thereof by force to take their beastly pleasure.
    But them the Priest rebuking, did advize
    To dare not to pollute so sacred threasure,
Vow'd to the gods: religion held even theeves in measure.

44

So being stayd, they her from thence directed
  Unto a litle grove not farre asyde,
In which an altar shortly they erected,
To slay her on. And now the Eventyde
His brode black wings had through the heavens wyde
By this dispred, that was the tyme ordayned
For such a dismall deed, their guilt to hyde:
Of few greene turfes an altar soone they fayned,
And deckt it all with flowres, which they nigh hand obtayned.

45

Tho when as all things readie were aright,
  The Damzell was before the altar set,
Being alreadie dead with fearefull fright.
To whom the Priest with naked armes full net
Approching nigh, and murdrous knife well whet,
Gan mutter close a certaine secret charme,
With other divelish ceremonies met:
Which doen he gan aloft t'advance his arme,
Whereat they shouted all, and made a loud alarme.

46

Then gan the bagpypes and the hornes to shrill,
  And shrieke aloud, that with the peoples voyce
Confused, did the ayre with terror fill,
And made the wood to tremble at the noyce:
The whyles she wayld, the more they did rejoyce.
Now mote ye understand that to this grove
Sir *Calepine* by chaunce, more than by choyce,
The selfe same evening fortune hether drove,
As he to seeke *Serena* through the woods did rove.

47

Long had he sought her, and through many a soyle
  Had traveld still on foot in heavie armes,
Ne ought was tyred with his endlesse toyles,
Ne ought was feared of his certaine harmes:
And now all weetlesse of the wretched stormes,
In which his love was lost, he slept full fast,
Till being waked with these loud alarmes,
He lightly started up like one aghast,
And catching up his arms streight to the noise forth past.

48

There by th'uncertaine glims of starry night,
  And by the twinkling of their sacred fire,
  He mote perceive a litle dawning sight
  Of all, which there was doing in that quire:
  Mongst whom a woman spoyld of all attire
  He spyde, lamenting her unluckie strife,
  And groning sore from grieved hart entire,
  Eftsoones he saw one with a naked knife
Readie to launch her brest, and let out loved life.

49

With that he thrusts into the thickest throng,
  And even as his right hand adowne descends,
  He him preventing, layes on earth along,
  And sacrifizeth to th'infernall feends.
  Then to the rest his wrathfull hand he bends,
  Of whom he makes such havocke and such hew,
  That swarmes of damned soules to hell he sends:
  The rest that scape his sword and death eschew,
Fly like a flocke of doves before a Faulcons vew.

50

From them returning to that Ladie backe,
  Whom by the Altar he doth sitting find,
  Yet fearing death, and next to death the lacke
  Of clothes to cover, what they ought by kind,
  He first her hands beginneth to unbind;
  And then to question of her present woe;
  And afterwards to cheare with speaches kind.
  But she for nought that he could say or doe,
One word durst speake, or answere him a whit thereto.

51

So inward shame of her uncomely case
  She did conceive, through care of womanhood,
  That though the night did cover her disgrace,
  Yet she in so unwomanly a mood,
  Would not bewray the state in which she stood.
  So all that night to him unknowen she past.
  But day, that doth discover bad and good,
  Ensewing, made her knowen to him at last:
The end whereof Ile keepe untill another cast.

CANT. IX

Calidore hostes with Melibæ
and loves fayre Pastorell;
Coridon envies him, yet he
for ill rewards him well.

1

NOW turne againe my teme thou jolly swayne,
  Backe to the furrow which I lately left;
  I lately left a furrow, one or twayne
  Unplough'd, the which my coulter hath not cleft:
  Yet seem'd the soyle both fayre and frutefull eft,
  As I it past, that were too great a shame,
  That so rich frute should be from us bereft;
  Besides the great dishonour and defame,
Which should befall to *Calidores* immortall name.

2

Great travell hath the gentle *Calidore*
  And toyle endured, sith I left him last
  Sewing the *Blatant beast*, which I forbore
  To finish then, for other present hast.
  Full many pathes and perils he hath past,
  Through hils, through dales, throgh forests, and throgh plaines
  In that same quest which fortune on him cast,
  Which he atchieved to his owne great gaines,
Reaping eternall glorie of his restlesse paines.

3

So sharply he the Monster did pursew,
  That day nor night he suffred him to rest,
  Ne rested he himselfe but natures dew,
  For dread of daunger, not to be redrest,
  If he for slouth forslackt so famous quest.
  Him first from court he to the citties coursed,
  And from the citties to the townes him prest,
  And from the townes into the countrie forsed,
And from the country back to private farmes he scorsed.

4

From thence into the open fields he fled,
    Whereas the Heardes were keeping of their neat,
    And shepheards singing to their flockes, that fed,
    Layes of sweete love and youthes delightfull heat:
    Him thether eke for all his fearefull threat
    He followed fast, and chaced him so nie,
    That to the folds, where sheepe at night doe seat,
    And to the litle cots, where shepherds lie
In winters wrathfull time, he forced him to flie.

5

There on a day as he pursew'd the chace,
    He chaunst to spy a sort of shepheard groomes,
    Playing on pypes, and caroling apace,
    The whyles their beasts there in the budded broomes
    Beside them fed, and nipt the tender bloomes:
    For other worldly wealth they cared nought.
    To whom Sir *Calidore* yet sweating comes,
    And them to tell him courteously besought,
If such a beast they saw, which he had thether brought.

6

They answer'd him, that no such beast they saw,
    Nor any wicked feend, that mote offend
    Their happie flockes, nor daunger to them draw:
    But if that such there were (as none they kend)
    They prayd high God him farre from them to send.
    Then one of them him seeing so to sweat,
    After his rusticke wise, that well he weend,
    Offred him drinke, to quench his thirstie heat,
And if he hungry were, him offred eke to eat.

7

The knight was nothing nice, where was no need,
    And tooke their gentle offer: so adowne
    They prayd him sit, and gave him for to feed
    Such homely what, as serves the simple clowne,
    That doth despise the dainties of the towne.
    Tho having fed his fill, he there besyde
    Saw a faire damzell, which did weare a crowne
    Of sundry flowres, with silken ribbands tyde,
Yclad in home-made greene that her owne hands had dyde.

8

Upon a litle hillocke she was placed
  Higher than all the rest, and round about
  Environ'd with a girland, goodly graced,
  Of lovely lasses, and them all without
  The lustie shepheard swaynes sate in a rout,
  The which did pype and sing her prayses dew,
  And oft rejoyce, and oft for wonder shout,
  As if some miracle of heavenly hew
Were downe to them descended in that earthly vew.

9

And soothly sure she was full fayre of face,
  And perfectly well shapt in every lim,
  Which she did more augment with modest grace,
  And comely carriage of her count'nance trim,
  That all the rest like lesser lamps did dim:
  Who her admiring as some heavenly wight,
  Did for their soveraine goddesse her esteeme,
  And caroling her name both day and night,
The fayrest *Pastorella* her by name did hight.

10

Ne was there heard, ne was there shepheards swayne
  But her did honour, and eke many a one
  Burnt in her love, and with sweet pleasing payne
  Full many a night for her did sigh and grone:
  But most of all the shepheard *Coridon*
  For her did languish, and his deare life spend;
  Yet neither she for him, nor other none
  Did care a whit, ne any liking lend:
Though meane her lot, yet higher did her mind ascend.

11

Her whyles Sir *Calidore* there vewed well,
  And markt her rare demeanure, which him seemed
  So farre the meane of shepheards to excell,
  As that he in his mind her worthy deemed,
  To be a Princes Paragone esteemed,
  He was unwares surprisd in subtile bands
  Of the blynd boy, ne thence could be redeemed
  By any skill out of his cruell hands,
Caught like the bird, which gazing still on others stands.

12

So stood he still long gazing thereupon,
　Ne any will had thence to move away,
　Although his quest were farre afore him gon;
　But after he had fed, yet did he stay,
　And sate there still, untill the flying day
　Was farre forth spent, discoursing diversly
　Of sundry things, as fell, to worke delay;
　And evermore his speach he did apply
To th'heards, but meant them to the damzels fantazy.

13

By this the moystie night approching fast,
　Her deawy humour gan on th'earth to shed,
　That warn'd the shepheards to their homes to hast
　Their tender flocks, now being fully fed,
　For feare of wetting them before their bed;
　Then came to them a good old aged syre,
　Whose silver lockes bedeckt his beard and hed,
　With shepheards hooke in hand, and fit attyre,
That wild the damzell rise; the day did now expyre.

14

He was to weet by common voice esteemed
　The father of the fayrest *Pastorell*,
　And of her selfe in very deede so deemed;
　Yet was not so, but as old stories tell
　Found her by fortune, which to him befell,
　In th'open fields an Infant left alone,
　And taking up brought home, and noursed well
　As his owne chyld; for other he had none,
That she in tract of time accompted was his owne.

15

She at his bidding meekely did arise,
　And streight unto her litle flocke did fare:
　Then all the rest about her rose likewise,
　And each his sundrie sheepe with severall care
　Gathered together, and them homeward bare:
　Whylest everie one with helping hands did strive
　Amongst themselves, and did their labours share,
　To helpe faire *Pastorella*, home to drive
Her fleecie flocke; but *Coridon* most helpe did give.

16

But *Melibæe* (so hight that good old man)
  Now seeing *Calidore* left all alone,
  And night arrived hard at hand, began
  Him to invite unto his simple home;
  Which though it were a cottage clad with lome,
  And all things therein meane, yet better so
  To lodge, than in the salvage fields to rome.
  The knight full gladly soone agreed thereto,
Being his harts owne wish, and home with him did go.

17

There he was welcom'd of that honest syre,
  And of his aged Beldame homely well;
  Who him besought himselfe to disattyre,
  And rest himselfe, till supper time befell.
  By which home came the fayrest *Pastorell*,
  After her flocke she in their fold had tyde,
  And supper readie dight, they to it fell
  With small adoe, and nature satisfyde,
The which doth litle crave contented to abyde.

18

Tho when they had their hunger slaked well,
  And the fayre mayd the table ta'ne away,
  The gentle knight, as he that did excell
  In courtesie, and well could doe and say,
  For so great kindnesse as he found that day,
  Gan greatly thanke his host and his good wife;
  And drawing thence his speach another way,
  Gan highly to commend the happie life,
Which Shepheards lead, without debate or bitter strife.

19

How much (sayd he) more happie is the state,
  In which ye father here doe dwell at ease,
  Leading a life so free and fortunate,
  From all the tempests of these worldly seas,
  Which tosse the rest in daungerous disease;
  Where warres, and wreckes, and wicked enmitie
  Doe them afflict, which no man can appease,
  That certes I your happinesse envie,
And wish my lot were plast in such felicitie.

20

Surely my sonne (then answer'd he againe)
  If happie, then it is in this intent,
  That having small, yet doe I not complaine
  Of want, ne wish for more it to augment,
  But doe my selfe, with that I have, content;
  So taught of nature, which doth litle need
  Of forreine helpes to lifes due nourishment:
  The fields my food, my flocke my rayment breed;
No better doe I weare, no better doe I feed.

21

Therefore I doe not any one envy,
  Nor am envyde of any one therefore;
  They that have much, feare much to loose thereby,
  And store of cares doth follow riches store.
  The litle that I have, growes dayly more
  Without my care, but onely to attend it;
  My lambes doe every yeare increase their score,
  And my flockes father daily doth amend it.
What have I, but to praise th'Almighty, that doth send it?

22

To them, that list, the worlds gay showes I leave,
  And to great ones such follies doe forgive,
  Which oft through pride do their owne perill weave,
  And through ambition downe themselves doe drive
  To sad decay, that might contented live.
  Me no such cares nor combrous thoughts offend,
  Ne once my minds unmoved quiet grieve,
  But all the night in silver sleepe I spend,
And all the day, to what I list, I doe attend.

23

Sometimes I hunt the Fox, the vowed foe
  Unto my Lambes, and him dislodge away;
  Sometime the fawne I practise from the Doe,
  Or from the Goat her kidde how to convay;
  Another while I baytes and nets display,
  The birds to catch, or fishes to beguyle:
  And when I wearie am, I downe doe lay
  My limbes in every shade, to rest from toyle,
And drinke of every brooke, when thirst my throte doth boyle.

24

The time was once, in my first prime of yeares,
  When pride of youth forth pricked my desire,
  That I disdain'd amongst mine equall peares
  To follow sheepe, and shepheards base attire:
  For further fortune then I would inquire.
  And leaving home, to roiall court I sought;
  Where I did sell my selfe for yearely hire,
  And in the Princes gardin daily wrought:
There I beheld such vainenesse, as I never thought.

25

With sight whereof soone cloyd, and long deluded
  With idle hopes, which them doe entertaine,
  After I had ten yeares my selfe excluded
  From native home, and spent my youth in vaine,
  I gan my follies to my selfe to plaine,
  And this sweet peace, whose lacke did then appeare.
  Tho backe returning to my sheepe againe,
  I from thenceforth have learn'd to love more deare
This lowly quiet life, which I inherite here.

26

Whylest thus he talkt, the knight with greedy eare
  Hong still upon his melting mouth attent;
  Whose sensefull words empierst his hart so neare,
  That he was rapt with double ravishment,
  Both of his speach that wrought him great content,
  And also of the object of his vew,
  On which his hungry eye was alwayes bent;
  That twixt his pleasing tongue, and her faire hew,
He lost himselfe, and like one halfe entraunced grew.

27

Yet to occasion meanes, to worke his mind,
  And to insinuate his harts desire,
  He thus replyde; Now surely syre, I find,
  That all this worlds gay showes, which we admire,
  Be but vaine shadowes to this safe retyre
  Of life, which here in lowlinesse ye lead,
  Fearelesse of foes, or fortunes wrackfull yre,
  Which tosseth states, and under foot doth tread
The mightie ones, affrayd of every chaunges dread.

28

That even I which daily doe behold
   The glorie of the great, mongst whom I won,
   And now have prov'd, what happinesse ye hold
   In this small plot of your dominion,
   Now loath great Lordship and ambition;
   And wish the heavens so much had graced mee,
   As graunt me live in like condition;
   Or that my fortunes might transposed bee
From pitch of higher place, unto this low degree.

29

In vaine (said then old *Melibæ*) doe men
   The heavens of their fortunes fault accuse,
   Sith they know best, what is the best for them:
   For they to each such fortune doe diffuse,
   As they doe know each can most aptly use.
   For not that, which men covet most, is best,
   Nor that thing worst, which men do most refuse;
   But fittest is, that all contented rest
With that they hold: each hath his fortune in his brest.

30

It is the mynd, that maketh good or ill,
   That maketh wretch or happie, rich or poore:
   For some, that hath abundance at his will,
   Hath not enough, but wants in greatest store;
   And other, that hath litle, askes no more,
   But in that litle is both rich and wise.
   For wisedome is most riches; fooles therefore
   They are, which fortunes doe by vowes devize,
Sith each unto himselfe his life may fortunize.

31

Since then in each mans self (said *Calidore*)
   It is, to fashion his owne lyfes estate,
   Give leave awhyle, good father, in this shore
   To rest my barcke, which hath bene beaten late
   With stormes of fortune and tempestuous fate,
   In seas of troubles and of toylesome paine,
   That whether quite from them for to retrate
   I shall resolve, or backe to turne againe,
I may here with your selfe some small repose obtaine.

32

Not that the burden of so bold a guest
　Shall chargefull be, or chaunge to you at all;
For your meane food shall be my daily feast,
And this your cabin both my bowre and hall.
Besides for recompence hereof, I shall
　You well reward, and golden guerdon give,
That may perhaps you better much withall,
　And in this quiet make you safer live.
So forth he drew much gold, and toward him it drive.

33

But the good man, nought tempted with the offer
　Of his rich mould, did thrust it farre away,
And thus bespake; Sir knight, your bounteous proffer
Be farre fro me, to whom ye ill display
That mucky masse, the cause of mens decay,
　That mote empaire my peace with daungers dread.
But if ye algates covet to assay
　This simple sort of life, that shepheards lead,
Be it your owne: our rudenesse to your selfe aread.

34

So there that night Sir *Calidore* did dwell,
　And long while after, whilest him list remaine,
Dayly beholding the faire *Pastorell*,
And feeding on the bayt of his owne bane.
During which time he did her entertaine
　With all kind courtesies, he could invent;
And every day, her companie to gaine,
　When to the field she went, he with her went:
So for to quench his fire, he did it more augment.

35

But she that never had acquainted beene
　With such queint usage, fit for Queenes and Kings,
Ne ever had such knightly service seene,
But being bred under base shepheards wings,
Had ever learn'd to love the lowly things,
　Did litle whit regard his courteous guize,
But cared more for *Colins* carolings
　Than all that he could doe, or ever devize:
His layes, his loves, his lookes she did them all despize.

36

Which *Calidore* perceiving, thought it best
　To chaunge the manner of his loftie looke;
　And doffing his bright armes, himselfe addrest
　In shepheards weed, and in his hand he tooke,
　In stead of steelehead speare, a shepheards hooke,
　That who had seene him then, would have bethought
　On *Phrygian Paris* by *Plexippus* brooke,
　When he the love of fayre *Oenone* sought,
What time the golden apple was unto him brought.

37

So being clad, unto the fields he went
　With the faire *Pastorella* every day,
　And kept her sheepe with diligent attent,
　Watching to drive the ravenous Wolfe away,
　The whylest at pleasure she mote sport and play;
　And every evening helping them to fold:
　And otherwhiles for need, he did assay
　In his strong hand their rugged teats to hold,
And out of them to presse the milke: love so much could.

38

Which seeing *Coridon*, who her likewise
　Long time had lov'd, and hop'd her love to gaine,
　He much was troubled at that straungers guize,
　And many gealous thoughts conceiv'd in vaine,
　That this of all his labour and long paine
　Should reap the harvest, ere it ripened were,
　That made him scoule, and pout, and oft complaine
　Of *Pastorell* to all the shepheards there,
That she did love a stranger swayne than him more dere.

39

And ever when he came in companie,
　Where *Calidore* was present, he would loure,
　And byte his lip, and even for gealousie
　Was readie oft his owne hart to devoure,
　Impatient of any paramoure:
　Who on the other side did seeme so farre
　From malicing, or grudging his good houre,
　That all he could, he graced him with her,
Ne ever shewed signe of rancour or of jarre.

40

And oft, when *Coridon* unto her brought
  Or litle sparrowes, stolen from their nest,
  Or wanton squirrels, in the woods farre sought,
  Or other daintie thing for her addrest,
  He would commend his guift, and make the best.
  Yet she no whit his presents did regard,
  Ne him could find to fancie in her brest:
  This newcome shepheard had his market mard.
Old love is litle worth when new is more prefard.

41

One day when as the shepheard swaynes together
  Were met, to make their sports and merrie glee,
  As they are wont in faire sunshynie weather,
  The whiles their flockes in shadowes shrouded bee,
  They fell to daunce: then did they all agree,
  That *Colin Clout* should pipe as one most fit;
  And *Calidore* should lead the ring, as hee
  That most in *Pastorellaes* grace did sit.
Thereat frown'd *Coridon*, and his lip closely bit.

42

But *Calidore* of courteous inclination
  Tooke *Coridon*, and set him in his place,
  That he should lead the daunce, as was his fashion;
  For *Coridon* could daunce, and trimly trace.
  And when as *Pastorella*, him to grace,
  Her flowry garlond tooke from her owne head,
  And plast on his, he did it soone displace,
  And did it put on *Coridons* in stead:
Then *Coridon* woxe frollicke, that earst seemed dead.

43

Another time, when as they did dispose
  To practise games, and maisteries to try,
  They for their Judge did *Pastorella* chose;
  A garland was the meed of victory.
  There *Coridon* forth stepping openly,
  Did chalenge *Calidore* to wrestling game:
  For he through long and perfect industry,
  Therein well practisd was, and in the same
Thought sure t'avenge his grudge, and worke his foe great shame.

44

But *Calidore* he greatly did mistake;
  For he was strong and mightily stiffe pight,
  That with one fall his necke he almost brake,
  And had he not upon him fallen light,
  His dearest joynt he sure had broken quight.
  Then was the oaken crowne by *Pastorell*
  Given to *Calidore*, as his due right;
  But he, that did in courtesie excell,
Gave it to *Coridon*, and said he wonne it well.

45

Thus did the gentle knight himselfe abeare
  Amongst that rusticke rout in all his deeds,
  That even they, the which his rivals were,
  Could not maligne him, but commend him needs:
  For courtesie amongst the rudest breeds
  Good will and favour. So it surely wrought
  With this faire Mayd, and in her mynde the seeds
  Of perfect love did sow, that last forth brought
The fruite of joy and blisse, though long time dearely bought.

46

Thus *Calidore* continu'd there long time,
  To winne the love of the faire *Pastorell*;
  Which having got, he used without crime
  Or blamefull blot, but menaged so well,
  That he of all the rest, which there did dwell,
  Was favoured, and to her grace commended.
  But what straunge fortunes unto him befell,
  Ere he attain'd the point by him intended,
Shall more conveniently in other place be ended.

CANT. X

Calidore sees the Graces daunce,
To Colins melody:
The whiles his Pastorell is led,
Into captivity.

1

WHO now does follow the foule *Blatant Beast*,
   Whilest *Calidore* does follow that faire Mayd,
   Unmyndfull of his vow and high beheast,
   Which by the Faery Queene was on him layd,
   That he should never leave, nor be delayd
   From chacing him, till he had it attchieved?
   But now entrapt of love, which him betrayd,
   He mindeth more, how he may be relieved
With grace from her, whose love his heart hath sore engrieved.

2

That from henceforth he meanes no more to sew
   His former quest, so full of toile and paine;
   Another quest, another game in vew
   He hath, the guerdon of his love to gaine:
   With whom he myndes for ever to remaine,
   And set his rest amongst the rusticke sort,
   Rather than hunt still after shadowes vaine
   Of courtly favour, fed with light report
Of every blaste, and sayling alwaies in the port.

3

Ne certes mote he greatly blamed be,
   From so high step to stoupe unto so low,
   For who had tasted once (as oft did he)
   The happy peace, which there doth overflow,
   And prov'd the perfect pleasures, which doe grow
   Amongst poore hyndes, in hils, in woods, in dales,
   Would never more delight in painted show
   Of such false blisse, as there is set for stales,
T'entrap unwary fooles in their eternall bales.

Calidore with Shepheards

4

For what hath all that goodly glorious gaze
  Like to one sight, which *Calidore* did vew?
  The glaunce whereof their dimmed eies would daze,
  That never more they should endure the shew
  Of that sunne-shine, that makes them looke askew.
  Ne ought in all that world of beauties rare,
  (Save onely *Glorianaes* heavenly hew
  To which what can compare?) can it compare;
The which as commeth now, by course I will declare.

5

One day as he did raunge the fields abroad,
  Whilest his faire *Pastorella* was elsewhere,
  He chaunst to come, far from all peoples troad,
  Unto a place, whose pleasaunce did appere
  To passe all others, on the earth which were:
  For all that ever was by natures skill
  Devized to worke delight, was gathered there,
  And there by her were poured forth at fill,
As if this to adorne, she all the rest did pill.

6

It was an hill plaste in an open plaine,
  That round about was bordered with a wood
  Of matchlesse hight, that seem'd th'earth to disdaine,
  In which all trees of honour stately stood,
  And did all winter as in sommer bud,
  Spredding pavilions for the birds to bowre,
  Which in their lower braunches sung aloud;
  And in their tops the soring hauke did towre,
Sitting like King of fowles in majesty and powre.

7

And at the foote thereof, a gentle flud
  His silver waves did softly tumble downe,
  Unmard with ragged mosse or filthy mud,
  Ne mote wylde beastes, ne mote the ruder clowne
  Thereto approch, ne filth mote therein drowne:
  But Nymphes and Faeries by the bancks did sit,
  In the woods shade, which did the waters crowne,
  Keeping all noysome things away from it,
And to the waters fall tuning their accents fit.

8

And on the top thereof a spacious plaine
  Did spred it selfe, to serve to all delight,
  Either to daunce, when they to daunce would faine,
  Or else to course about their bases light;
  Ne ought there wanted, which for pleasure might
  Desired be, or thence to banish bale:
  So pleasauntly the hill with equall hight,
  Did seeme to overlooke the lowly vale;
Therefore it rightly cleeped was mount *Acidale*.

9

They say that *Venus*, when she did dispose
  Her selfe to pleasaunce, used to resort
  Unto this place, and therein to repose
  And rest her selfe, as in a gladsome port,
  Or with the Graces there to play and sport;
  That even her owne Cytheron, though in it
  She used most to keepe her royall court,
  And in her soveraine Majesty to sit,
She in regard hereof refusde and thought unfit.

10

Unto this place when as the Elfin Knight
  Approcht, him seemed that the merry sound
  Of a shrill pipe he playing heard on hight,
  And many feete fast thumping th'hollow ground,
  That through the woods their Eccho did rebound.
  He nigher drew, to weete what mote it be;
  There he a troupe of Ladies dauncing found
  Full merrily, and making gladfull glee,
And in the midst a Shepheard piping he did see.

11

He durst not enter into th'open greene,
  For dread of them unwares to be descryde,
  For breaking of their daunce, if he were seene;
  But in the covert of the wood did byde,
  Beholding all, yet of them unespyde.
  There he did see, that pleased much his sight,
  That even he him selfe his eyes envyde,
  An hundred naked maidens lilly white,
All raunged in a ring, and dauncing in delight.

12

All they without were raunged in a ring,
  And daunced round; but in the midst of them
  Three other Ladies did both daunce and sing,
  The whilest the rest them round about did hemme,
  And like a girlond did in compasse stemme:
  And in the middest of those same three, was placed
  Another Damzell, as a precious gemme,
  Amidst a ring most richly well enchaced,
That with her goodly presence all the rest much graced.

13

Looke how the Crowne, which *Ariadne* wore
  Upon her yvory forehead that same day,
  That *Theseus* her unto his bridale bore,
  When the bold *Centaures* made that bloudy fray,
  With the fierce *Lapithes*, which did them dismay;
  Being now placed in the firmament,
  Through the bright heaven doth her beams display,
  And is unto the starres an ornament,
Which round about her move in order excellent.

14

Such was the beauty of this goodly band,
  Whose sundry parts were here too long to tell:
  But she that in the midst of them did stand,
  Seem'd all the rest in beauty to excell,
  Crownd with a rosie girlond, that right well
  Did her beseeme. And ever, as the crew
  About her daunst, sweet flowres, that far did smell,
  And fragrant odours they uppon her threw;
But most of all, those three did her with gifts endew.

15

Those were the Graces, daughters of delight,
  Handmaides of *Venus*, which are wont to haunt
  Uppon this hill, and daunce there day and night:
  Those three to men all gifts of grace do graunt,
  And all, that *Venus* in her selfe doth vaunt,
  Is borrowed of them. But that faire one,
  That in the midst was placed paravaunt,
  Was she to whom that shepheard pypt alone,
That made him pipe so merrily, as never none.

16

She was to weete that jolly Shepheards lasse,
  Which piped there unto that merry rout,
  That jolly shepheard, which there piped, was
  Poore *Colin Clout* (who knowes not *Colin Clout?*)
  He pypt apace, whilest they him daunst about.
  Pype jolly shepheard, pype thou now apace
  Unto thy love, that made thee low to lout:
  Thy love is present there with thee in place,
Thy love is there advaunst to be another Grace.

17

Much wondred *Calidore* at this straunge sight,
  Whose like before his eye had never seene,
  And standing long astonished in spright,
  And rapt with pleasaunce, wist not what to weene;
  Whether it were the traine of beauties Queene,
  Or Nymphes, or Faeries, or enchaunted show,
  With which his eyes mote have deluded beene.
  Therefore resolving, what it was, to know,
Out of the wood he rose, and toward them did go.

18

But soone as he appeared to their vew,
  They vanisht all away out of his sight,
  And cleane were gone, which way he never knew;
  All save the shepheard, who for fell despight
  Of that displeasure, broke his bag-pipe quight,
  And made great mone for that unhappy turne.
  But *Calidore*, though no lesse sory wight,
  For that mishap, yet seeing him to mourne,
Drew neare, that he the truth of all by him mote learne.

19

And first him greeting, thus unto him spake,
  Haile jolly shepheard, which thy joyous dayes
  Here leadest in this goodly merry make,
  Frequented of these gentle Nymphes alwayes,
  Which to thee flocke, to heare thy lovely layes;
  Tell me, what mote these dainty Damzels be,
  Which here with thee doe make their pleasant playes?
  Right happy thou, that mayst them freely see:
But why when I them saw, fled they away from me?

20

Not I so happy, answerd then that swaine,
  As thou unhappy, which them thence didst chace,
  Whom by no meanes thou canst recall againe,
  For being gone, none can them bring in place,
  But whom they of them selves list so to grace.
  Right sory I, (said then Sir *Calidore*,)
  That my ill fortune did them hence displace.
  But since things passed none may now restore,
Tell me, what were they all, whose lacke thee grieves so sore.

21

Tho gan that shepheard thus for to dilate;
  Then wote thou shepheard, whatsoever thou bee,
  That all those Ladies, which thou sawest late,
  Are *Venus* Damzels, all within her fee,
  But differing in honour and degree:
  They all are Graces, which on her depend,
  Besides a thousand more, which ready bee
  Her to adorne, when so she forth doth wend:
But those three in the midst, doe chiefe on her attend.

22

They are the daughters of sky-ruling Jove,
  By him begot of faire *Eurynome*,
  The Oceans daughter, in this pleasant grove,
  As he this way comming from feastfull glee,
  Of *Thetis* wedding with *Æacidee*,
  In sommers shade him selfe here rested weary.
  The first of them hight mylde *Euphrosyne*,
  Next faire *Aglaia*, last *Thalia* merry:
Sweete Goddesses all three which me in mirth do cherry.

23

These three on men all gracious gifts bestow,
  Which decke the body or adorne the mynde,
  To make them lovely or well favoured show,
  As comely carriage, entertainement kynde,
  Sweete semblaunt, friendly offices that bynde,
  And all the complements of curtesie:
  They teach us, how to each degree and kynde
  We should our selves demeane, to low, to hie;
To friends, to foes, which skill men call Civility.

24

Therefore they alwaies smoothly seeme to smile,
  That we likewise should mylde and gentle be,
  And also naked are, that without guile
  Or false dissemblaunce all them plaine may see,
  Simple and true from covert malice free:
  And eeke them selves so in their daunce they bore,
  That two of them still froward seem'd to bee,
  But one still towards shew'd her selfe afore;
That good should from us goe, then come in greater store.

25

Such were those Goddesses, which ye did see;
  But that fourth Mayd, which there amidst them traced,
  Who can aread, what creature mote she bee,
  Whether a creature, or a goddesse graced
  With heavenly gifts from heven first enraced?
  But what so sure she was, she worthy was,
  To be the fourth with those three other placed:
  Yet was she certes but a countrey lasse,
Yet she all other countrey lasses farre did passe.

26

So farre as doth the daughter of the day,
  All other lesser lights in light excell,
  So farre doth she in beautyfull array,
  Above all other lasses beare the bell,
  Ne lesse in vertue that beseemes her well,
  Doth she exceede the rest of all her race,
  For which the Graces that here wont to dwell,
  Have for more honor brought her to this place,
And graced her so much to be another Grace.

27

Another Grace she well deserves to be,
  In whom so many Graces gathered are,
  Excelling much the meane of her degree;
  Divine resemblaunce, beauty soveraine rare,
  Firme Chastity, that spight ne blemish dare;
  All which she with such courtesie doth grace,
  That all her peres cannot with her compare,
  But quite are dimmed, when she is in place.
She made me often pipe and now to pipe apace.

28

Sunne of the world, great glory of the sky,
  That all the earth doest lighten with thy rayes,
  Great *Gloriana*, greatest Majesty,
  Pardon thy shepheard, mongst so many layes,
  As he hath sung of thee in all his dayes,
  To make one minime of thy poore handmayd,
  And underneath thy feete to place her prayse,
  That when thy glory shall be farre displayd
To future age of her this mention may be made.

29

When thus that shepherd ended had his speach,
  Sayd *Calidore*; Now sure it yrketh mee,
  That to thy blisse I made this luckelesse breach,
  As now the author of thy bale to be,
  Thus to bereave thy loves deare sight from thee:
  But gentle Shepheard pardon thou my shame,
  Who rashly sought that, which I mote not see.
  Thus did the courteous Knight excuse his blame,
And to recomfort him, all comely meanes did frame.

30

In such discourses they together spent
  Long time, as fit occasion forth them led;
  With which the Knight him selfe did much content,
  And with delight his greedy fancy fed,
  Both of his words, which he with reason red;
  And also of the place, whose pleasures rare
  With such regard his sences ravished,
  That thence, he had no will away to fare,
But wisht, that with that shepheard he mote dwelling share.

31

But that envenimd sting, the which of yore,
  His poysnous point deepe fixed in his hart
  Had left, now gan afresh to rancle sore,
  And to renue the rigour of his smart:
  Which to recure, no skill of Leaches art
  Mote him availe, but to returne againe
  To his wounds worker, that with lovely dart
  Dinting his brest, had bred his restlesse paine.
Like as the wounded Whale to shore flies from the maine.

32

So taking leave of that same gentle swaine,
  He backe returned to his rusticke wonne,
  Where his faire *Pastorella* did remaine:
  To whome in sort, as he at first begonne,
  He daily did apply him selfe to donne
  All dewfull service voide of thoughts impure:
  Ne any paines ne perill did he shonne,
  By which he might her to his love allure,
And liking in her yet untamed heart procure.

33

And evermore the shepheard *Coridon*,
  What ever thing he did her to aggrate,
  Did strive to match with strong contention,
  And all his paines did closely emulate;
  Whether it were to caroll, as they sate
  Keeping their sheepe, or games to exercize,
  Or to present her with their labours late;
  Through which if any grace chaunst to arize
To him, the Shepheard streight with jealousie did frize.

34

One day as they all three together went
  To the greene wood, to gather strawberies,
  There chaunst to them a dangerous accident;
  A Tigre forth out of the wood did rise,
  That with fell clawes full of fierce gourmandize,
  And greedy mouth, wide gaping like hell gate,
  Did runne at *Pastorell* her to surprize:
  Whom she beholding, now all desolate
Gan cry to them aloud, to helpe her all too late.

35

Which *Coridon* first hearing, ran in hast
  To reskue her, but when he saw the feend,
  Through cowherd feare he fled away as fast,
  Ne durst abide the daunger of the end;
  His life he steemed dearer than his frend.
  But *Calidore* soone comming to her ayde,
  When he the beast saw ready now to rend
  His loves deare spoile, in which his heart was prayde,
He ran at him enraged in stead of being frayde.

36

He had no weapon, but his shepheards hooke,
  To serve the vengeaunce of his wrathfull will,
  With which so sternely he the monster strooke,
  That to the ground astonished he fell;
  Whence ere he could recou'r, he did him quell,
  And hewing off his head, ⟨he⟩ it presented
  Before the feete of the faire *Pastorell*;
  Who scarcely yet from former feare exempted,
A thousand times him thankt, that had her death prevented.

37

From that day forth she gan him to affect,
  And daily more her favour to augment;
  But *Coridon* for cowherdize reject,
  Fit to keepe sheepe, unfit for loves content:
  The gentle heart scornes base disparagement.
  Yet *Calidore* did not despise him quight,
  But usde him friendly for further intent,
  That by his fellowship, he colour might
Both his estate, and love from skill of any wight.

38

So well he wood her, and so well he wrought her,
  With humble service, and with daily sute,
  That at the last unto his will he brought her;
  Which he so wisely well did prosecute,
  That of his love he reapt the timely frute,
  And joyed long in close felicity:
  Till fortune fraught with malice, blinde, and brute,
  That envies lovers long prosperity,
Blew up a bitter storme of foule adversity.

39

It fortuned one day, when *Calidore*
  Was hunting in the woods (as was his trade)
  A lawlesse people, *Brigants* hight of yore,
  That never usde to live by plough nor spade,
  But fed on spoile and booty, which they made
  Upon their neighbours, which did nigh them border,
  The dwelling of these shepheards did invade,
  And spoyld their houses, and them selves did murder;
And drove away their flocks, with other much disorder.

40

Amongst the rest, the which they then did pray,
  They spoyld old *Melibee* of all he had,
  And all his people captive led away,
  Mongst which this lucklesse mayd away was lad,
  Faire *Pastorella*, sorrowfull and sad,
  Most sorrowfull, most sad, that ever sight,
  Now made the spoile of theeves and *Brigants* bad,
  Which was the conquest of the gentlest Knight,
That ever liv'd, and th'onely glory of his might.

41

With them also was taken *Coridon*,
  And carried captive by those theeves away;
  Who in the covert of the night, that none
  Mote them descry, nor reskue from their pray,
  Unto their dwelling did them close convay.
  Their dwelling in a little Island was,
  Covered with shrubby woods, in which no way
  Appeard for people in nor out to pas,
Nor any footing fynde for overgrowen gras.

42

For underneath the ground their way was made,
  Through hollow caves, that no man mote discover
  For the thicke shrubs, which did them alwaies shade
  From view of living wight, and covered over:
  But darkenesse dred and daily night did hover
  Through all the inner parts, wherein they dwelt,
  Ne lightned was with window, nor with lover,
  But with continuall candlelight, which delt
A doubtfull sense of things, not so well seene, as felt.

43

Hither those *Brigants* brought their present pray,
  And kept them with continuall watch and ward,
  Meaning so soone, as they convenient may,
  For slaves to sell them, for no small reward,
  To merchants, which them kept in bondage hard,
  Or sold againe. Now when faire *Pastorell*
  Into this place was brought, and kept with gard
  Of griesly theeves, she thought her self in hell,
Where with such damned fiends she should in darknesse dwell.

44

But for to tell the dolefull dreriment,
　And pittifull complaints, which there she made,
　Where day and night she nought did but lament
　Her wretched life, shut up in deadly shade,
　And waste her goodly beauty, which did fade
　Like to a flowre, that feeles no heate of sunne,
　Which may her feeble leaves with comfort glade.
　But what befell her in that theevish wonne,
Will in an other Canto better be begonne.

CANT. XI

The theeves fall out for Pastorell,
Whilest Melibee is slaine:
Her Calidore from them redeemes,
And bringeth backe againe.

1

THE joyes of love, if they should ever last,
　Without affliction or disquietnesse,
　That worldly chaunces doe amongst them cast,
　Would be on earth too great a blessednesse,
　Liker to heaven, than mortall wretchednesse.
　Therefore the winged God, to let men weet,
　That here on earth is no sure happinesse,
　A thousand sowres hath tempred with one sweet,
To make it seeme more deare and dainty, as is meet.

2

Like as is now befalne to this faire Mayd,
　Faire *Pastorell,* of whom is now my song,
　Who being now in dreadfull darknesse layd,
　Amongst those theeves, which her in bondage strong
　Detaynd, yet Fortune not with all this wrong
　Contented, greater mischiefe on her threw,
　And sorrowes heapt on her in greater throng;
　That who so heares her heavinesse, would rew
And pitty her sad plight, so chang'd from pleasaunt hew.

3

Whylest thus she in these hellish dens remayned,
　　Wrapped in wretched cares and hearts unrest,
　　It so befell (as Fortune had ordayned)
　　That he, which was their Capitaine profest,
　　And had the chiefe commaund of all the rest,
　　One day as he did all his prisoners vew,
　　With lustfull eyes, beheld that lovely guest,
　　Faire *Pastorella*, whose sad mournefull hew
Like the faire Morning clad in misty fog did shew.

4

At sight whereof his barbarous heart was fired,
　　And inly burnt with flames most raging whot,
　　That her alone he for his part desired
　　Of all the other pray, which they had got,
　　And her in mynde did to him selfe allot.
　　From that day forth he kyndnesse to her showed,
　　And sought her love, by all the meanes he mote;
　　With looks, with words, with gifts he oft her wowed;
And mixed threats among, and much unto her vowed.

5

But all that ever he could doe or say,
　　Her constant mynd could not a whit remove,
　　Nor draw unto the lure of his lewd lay,
　　To graunt him favour, or afford him love.
　　Yet ceast he not to sew and all waies prove,
　　By which he mote accomplish his request,
　　Saying and doing all that mote behove;
　　Ne day nor night he suffred her to rest,
But her all night did watch, and all the day molest.

6

At last when him she so importune saw,
　　Fearing least he at length the raines would lend
　　Unto his lust, and make his will his law,
　　Sith in his powre she was to foe or frend,
　　She thought it best, for shadow to pretend
　　Some shew of favour, by him gracing small,
　　That she thereby mote either freely wend,
　　Or at more ease continue there his thrall:
A little well is lent, that gaineth more withall.

7

So from thenceforth, when love he to her made,
　With better tearmes she did him entertaine,
　Which gave him hope, and did him halfe perswade,
　That he in time her joyaunce should obtaine.
　But when she saw, through that small favours gaine,
　That further, than she willing was, he prest,
　She found no meanes to barre him, but to faine
　A sodaine sickenesse, which her sore opprest,
And made unfit to serve his lawlesse mindes behest.

8

By meanes whereof she would not him permit
　Once to approch to her in privity,
　But onely mongst the rest by her to sit,
　Mourning the rigour of her malady,
　And seeking all things meete for remedy.
　But she resolv'd no remedy to fynde,
　Nor better cheare to shew in misery,
　Till Fortune would her captive bonds unbynde,
Her sickenesse was not of the body but the mynde.

9

During which space that she thus sicke did lie,
　It chaunst a sort of merchants, which were wount
　To skim those coastes, for bondmen there to buy,
　And by such trafficke after gaines to hunt,
　Arrived in this Isle though bare and blunt,
　T'inquire for slaves; where being readie met
　By some of these same theeves at the instant brunt,
　Were brought unto their Captaine, who was set
By his faire patients side with sorrowfull regret.

10

To whom they shewed, how those marchants were
　Arriv'd in place, their bondslaves for to buy,
　And therefore prayd, that those same captives there
　Mote to them for their most commodity
　Be sold, and mongst them shared equally.
　This their request the Captaine much appalled;
　Yet could he not their just demaund deny,
　And willed streight the slaves should forth be called,
And sold for most advantage not to be forstalled.

11

Then forth the good old *Melibœ* was brought,
　And *Coridon*, with many other moe,
　Whom they before in diverse spoyles had caught:
　All which he to the marchants sale did showe.
　Till some, which did the sundry prisoners knowe,
　Gan to inquire for that faire shepherdesse,
　Which with the rest they tooke not long agoe,
　And gan her forme and feature to expresse,
The more t'augment her price, through praise of comlinesse.

12

To whom the Captaine in full angry wize
　Made answere, that the Mayd of whom they spake,
　Was his owne purchase and his onely prize,
　With which none had to doe, ne ought partake,
　But he himselfe, which did that conquest make;
　Litle for him to have one silly lasse:
　Besides through sicknesse now so wan and weake,
　That nothing meet in marchandise to passe.
So shew'd them her, to prove how pale and weake she was.

13

The sight of whom, though now decayd and mard,
　And eke but hardly seene by candle-light,
　Yet like a Diamond of rich regard,
　In doubtfull shadow of the darkesome night,
　With starrie beames about her shining bright,
　These marchants fixed eyes did so amaze,
　That what through wonder, and what through delight,
　A while on her they greedily did gaze,
And did her greatly like, and did her greatly praize.

14

At last when all the rest them offred were,
　And prises to them placed at their pleasure,
　They all refused in regard of her,
　Ne ought would buy, how ever prisd with measure,
　Withouten her, whose worth above all threasure
　They did esteeme, and offred store of gold.
　But then the Captaine fraught with more displeasure,
　Bad them be still, his love should not be sold:
The rest take if they would, he her to him would hold.

15

Therewith some other of the chiefest theeves
 Boldly him bad such injurie forbeare;
 For that same mayd, how ever it him greeves,
 Should with the rest be sold before him theare,
 To make the prises of the rest more deare.
 That with great rage he stoutly doth denay;
 And fiercely drawing forth his blade, doth sweare,
 That who so hardie hand on her doth lay,
It dearely shall aby, and death for handsell pay.

16

Thus as they words amongst them multiply,
 They fall to strokes, the frute of too much talke,
 And the mad steele about doth fiercely fly,
 Not sparing wight, ne leaving any balke,
 But making way for death at large to walke:
 Who in the horror of the griesly night,
 In thousand dreadful shapes doth mongst them stalke,
 And makes huge havocke, whiles the candlelight
Out quenched, leaves no skill nor difference of wight.

17

Like as a sort of hungry dogs ymet
 About some carcase by the common way,
 Doe fall together, stryving each to get
 The greatest portion of the greedie pray;
 All on confused heapes themselves assay,
 And snatch, and byte, and rend, and tug, and teare;
 That who them sees, would wonder at their fray,
 And who sees not, would be affrayd to heare.
Such was the conflict of those cruell *Brigants* there.

18

But first of all, their captives they doe kill,
 Least they should joyne against the weaker side,
 Or rise against the remnant at their will;
 Old *Meliboe* is slaine, and him beside
 His aged wife, with many others wide,
 But *Coridon* escaping craftily,
 Creepes forth of dores, whilst darknes him doth hide,
 And flyes away as fast as he can hye,
Ne stayeth leave to take, before his friends doe dye.

19

But *Pastorella*, wofull wretched Elfe,
  Was by the Captaine all this while defended,
  Who minding more her safety than himselfe,
  His target alwayes over her pretended;
  By meanes whereof, that mote not be amended,
  He at the length was slaine, and layd on ground,
  Yet holding fast twixt both his armes extended
  Fayre *Pastorell*, who with the selfe same wound
Launcht through the arme, fell down with him in drerie swound.

20

There lay she covered with confused preasse
  Of carcases, which dying on her fell.
  Tho when as he was dead, the fray gan ceasse,
  And each to other calling, did compell
  To stay their cruell hands from slaughter fell,
  Sith they that were the cause of all, were gone.
  Thereto they all attonce agreed well,
  And lighting candles new, gan search anone,
How many of their friends were slaine, how many fone.

21

Their Captaine there they cruelly found kild,
  And in his armes the dreary dying mayd,
  Like a sweet Angell twixt two clouds uphild:
  Her lovely light was dimmed and decayd,
  With cloud of death upon her eyes displayd;
  Yet did the cloud make even that dimmed light
  Seeme much more lovely in that darknesse layd,
  And twixt the twinckling of her eye-lids bright,
To sparke out litle beames, like starres in foggie night.

22

But when they mov'd the carcases aside,
  They found that life did yet in her remaine:
  Then all their helpes they busily applyde,
  To call the soule backe to her home againe;
  And wrought so well with labour and long paine,
  That they to life recovered her at last.
  Who sighing sore, as if her hart in twaine
  Had riven bene, and all her hart strings brast,
With drearie drouping eyne lookt up like one aghast.

23

There she beheld, that sore her griev'd to see,
  Her father and her friends about her lying,
  Her selfe sole left, a second spoyle to bee
  Of those, that having saved her from dying,
  Renew'd her death by timely death denying:
  What now is left her, but to wayle and weepe,
  Wringing her hands, and ruefully loud crying?
  Ne cared she her wound in teares to steepe,
Albe with all their might those *Brigants* her did keepe.

24

But when they saw her now reliv'd againe,
  They left her so, in charge of one the best
  Of many worst, who with unkind disdaine
  And cruell rigour her did much molest;
  Scarse yeelding her due food, or timely rest,
  And scarsely suffring her infestred wound,
  That sore her payn'd, by any to be drest.
  So leave we her in wretched thraldome bound,
And turne we backe to *Calidore*, where we him found.

25

Who when he backe returned from the wood,
  And saw his shepheards cottage spoyled quight,
  And his love reft away, he wexed wood,
  And halfe enraged at that ruefull sight,
  That even his hart for very fell despight,
  And his owne flesh he readie was to teare,
  He chauft, he griev'd he fretted, and he sight,
  And fared like a furious wyld Beare,
Whose whelpes are stolne away, she being otherwhere.

26

Ne wight he found, to whom he might complaine,
  Ne wight he found, of whom he might inquire;
  That more increast the anguish of his paine.
  He sought the woods; but no man could see there:
  He sought the plaines; but could no tydings heare.
  The woods did nought but ecchoes vaine rebound;
  The playnes all waste and emptie did appeare:
  Where wont the shepheards oft their pypes resound,
And feed an hundred flocks, there now not one he found.

27

At last as there he romed up and downe,
  He chaunst one comming towards him to spy,
  That seem'd to be some sorie simple clowne,
  With ragged weedes, and lockes upstaring hye,
  As if he did from some late daunger fly,
  And yet his feare did follow him behynd:
  Who as he unto him approched nye,
  He mote perceive by signes, which he did fynd,
That *Coridon* it was, the silly shepherds hynd.

28

Tho to him running fast, he did not stay
  To greet him first, but askt where were the rest;
  Where *Pastorell*? who full of fresh dismay,
  And gushing forth in teares, was so opprest,
  That he no word could speake, but smit his brest,
  And up to heaven his eyes fast streming threw.
  Whereat the knight amaz'd, yet did not rest,
  But askt againe, what ment that rufull hew;
Where was his *Pastorell*? where all the other crew?

29

Ah well away (sayd he then sighing sore)
  That ever I did live, this day to see,
  This dismall day, and was not dead before,
  Before I saw faire *Pastorella* dye.
  Die? out alas! then *Calidore* did cry:
  How could the death dare ever her to quell?
  But read thou shepheard, read what destiny,
  Or other dyrefull hap from heaven or hell
Hath wrought this wicked deed, doe feare away, and tell.

30

Tho when the shepheard breathed had a whyle,
  He thus began: Where shall I then commence
  This wofull tale? or how those *Brigants* vyle,
  With cruell rage and dreadfull violence
  Spoyld all our cots, and caried us from hence?
  Or how faire *Pastorell* should have bene sold
  To marchants, but was sav'd with strong defence?
  Or how those theeves, whilest one sought her to hold,
Fell all at ods, and fought through fury fierce and bold.

31

In that same conflict (woe is me) befell
  This fatall chaunce, this dolefull accident,
  Whose heavy tydings now I have to tell.
  First all the captives, which they here had hent,
  Were by them slaine by generall consent;
  Old *Meliboe* and his good wife withall
  These eyes saw die, and dearely did lament:
  But when the lot to *Pastorell* did fall,
Their Captaine long withstood, and did her death forstall.

32

But what could he gainst all them doe alone?
  It could not boot, needs mote she die at last:
  I onely scapt through great confusione
  Of cryes and clamors, which amongst them past,
  In dreadfull darknesse dreadfully aghast;
  That better were with them to have bene dead,
  Than here to see all desolate and wast,
  Despoyled of those joyes and jollyhead,
Which with those gentle shepherds here I wont to lead.

33

When *Calidore* these ruefull newes had raught,
  His hart quite deaded was with anguish great,
  And all his wits with doole were nigh distraught,
  That he his face, his head, his brest did beat,
  And death it selfe unto himselfe did threat;
  Oft cursing th'heavens, that so cruell were
  To her, whose name he often did repeat;
  And wishing oft, that he were present there,
When she was slaine, or had bene to her succour nere.

34

But after griefe awhile had had his course,
  And spent it selfe in mourning, he at last
  Began to mitigate his swelling sourse,
  And in his mind with better reason cast,
  How he might save her life, if life did last;
  Or if that dead, how he her death might wreake,
  Sith otherwise he could not mend thing past;
  Or if it to revenge he were too weake,
Then for to die with her, and his lives threed to breake.

35

Tho *Coridon* he prayd, sith he well knew
　The readie way unto that theevish wonne,
　To wend with him, and be his conduct trew
　Unto the place, to see what should be donne.
　But he, whose hart through feare was late fordonne,
　Would not for ought be drawne to former drede,
　But by all meanes the daunger knowne did shonne:
　Yet *Calidore* so well him wrought with meed,
And faire bespoke with words, that he at last agreed.

36

So forth they goe together (God before)
　Both clad in shepheards weeds agreeably,
　And both with shepheards hookes: But *Calidore*
　Had underneath, him armed privily.
　Tho to the place when they approched nye,
　They chaunst, upon an hill not farre away,
　Some flockes of sheepe and shepheards to espy;
　To whom they both agreed to take their way,
In hope there newes to learne, how they mote best assay.

37

There did they find, that which they did not feare,
　The selfe same flocks, the which those theeves had reft
　From *Melibæ* and from themselves whyleare,
　And certaine of the theeves there by them left,
　The which for want of heards themselves then kept.
　Right well knew *Coridon* his owne late sheepe,
　And seeing them, for tender pittie wept:
　But when he saw the theeves, which did them keepe,
His hart gan fayle, albe he saw them all asleepe.

38

But *Calidore* recomforting his griefe,
　Though not his feare; for nought may feare disswade;
　Him hardly forward drew, whereas the thiefe
　Lay sleeping soundly in the bushes shade,
　Whom *Coridon* him counseld to invade
　Now all unwares, and take the spoyle away;
　But he, that in his mind had closely made
　A further purpose, would not so them slay,
But gently waking them, gave them the time of day.

39

Tho sitting downe by them upon the greene,
  Of sundrie things he purpose gan to faine;
  That he by them might certaine tydings weene
  Of *Pastorell*, were she alive or slaine.
  Mongst which the theeves them questioned againe,
  What mister men, and eke from whence they were.
  To whom they answer'd, as did appertaine,
  That they were poore heardgroomes, the which whylere
Had from their maisters fled, and now sought hyre elswhere.

40

Whereof right glad they seem'd, and offer made
  To hyre them well, if they their flockes would keepe:
  For they themselves were evill groomes, they sayd,
  Unwont with heards to watch, or pasture sheepe,
  But to forray the land, or scoure the deepe.
  Thereto they soone agreed, and earnest tooke,
  To keepe their flockes for litle hyre and chepe:
  For they for better hyre did shortly looke,
So there all day they bode, till light the sky forsooke.

41

Tho when as towards darksome night it drew,
  Unto their hellish dens those theeves them brought,
  Where shortly they in great acquaintance grew,
  And all the secrets of their entrayles sought.
  There did they find, contrarie to their thought,
  That *Pastorell* yet liv'd, but all the rest
  Were dead, right so as *Coridon* had taught:
  Whereof they both full glad and blyth did rest,
But chiefly *Calidore*, whom griefe had most possest.

42

At length when they occasion fittest found,
  In dead of night, when all the theeves did rest
  After a late forray, and slept full sound,
  Sir *Calidore* him arm'd, as he thought best,
  Having of late by diligent inquest,
  Provided him a sword of meanest sort:
  With which he streight went to the Captaines nest.
  But *Coridon* durst not with him consort,
Ne durst abide behind, for dread of worse effort.

43

When to the Cave they came, they found it fast:
But *Calidore* with huge resistlesse might,
The dores assayled, and the locks upbrast.
With noyse whereof the theefe awaking light,
Unto the entrance ran: where the bold knight
Encountring him with small resistance slew;
The whiles faire *Pastorell* through great affright
Was almost dead, misdoubting least of new
Some uprore were like that, which lately she did vew.

44

But when as *Calidore* was comen in,
And gan aloud for *Pastorell* to call,
Knowing his voice although not heard long sin,
She sudden was revived therewithall,
And wondrous joy felt in her spirits thrall:
Like him that being long in tempest tost,
Looking each houre into deathes mouth to fall,
At length espyes at hand the happie cost,
On which he safety hopes, that earst feard to be lost.

45

Her gentle hart, that now long season past
Had never joyance felt, nor chearefull thought,
Began some smacke of comfort new to tast,
Like lyfull heat to nummed senses brought,
And life to feele, that long for death had sought;
Ne lesse in hart rejoyced *Calidore*,
When he her found, but like to one distraught
And robd of reason, towards her him bore,
A thousand times embrast, and kist a thousand more.

46

But now by this, with noyse of late uprore,
The hue and cry was raysed all about;
And all the *Brigants* flocking in great store,
Unto the cave gan preasse, nought having dout
Of that was doen, and entred in a rout.
But *Calidore* in th'entry close did stand,
And entertayning them with courage stout,
Still slew the formost, that came first to hand,
So long till all the entry was with bodies mand.

47

Tho when no more could nigh to him approch,
  He breath'd his sword, and rested him till day,
  Which when he spyde upon the earth t'encroch,
  Through the dead carcases he made his way,
  Mongst which he found a sword of better say,
  With which he forth went into th'open light:
  Where all the rest for him did readie stay,
  And fierce assayling him, with all their might
Gan all upon him lay: there gan a dreadfull fight.

48

How many flyes in whottest sommers day
  Do seize upon some beast, whose flesh is bare,
  That all the place with swarmes do overlay,
  And with their litle stings right felly fare,
  So many theeves about him swarming are,
  All which do him assayle on every side,
  And sore oppresse, ne any him doth spare:
  But he doth with his raging brond divide
Their thickest troups, and round about him scattreth wide.

49

Like as a Lion mongst an heard of dere,
  Disperseth them to catch his choysest pray,
  So did he fly amongst them here and there,
  And all that nere him came, did hew and slay,
  Till he had strowd with bodies all the way;
  That none his daunger daring to abide,
  Fled from his wrath, and did themselves convay
  Into their caves, their heads from death to hide,
Ne any left, that victorie to him envide.

50

Then backe returning to his dearest deare,
  He her gan to recomfort, all he might,
  With gladfull speaches, and with lovely cheare,
  And forth her bringing to the joyous light,
  Whereof she long had lackt the wishfull sight,
  Deviz'd all goodly meanes, from her to drive
  The sad remembrance of her wretched plight.
  So her uneath at last he did revive,
That long had lyen dead, and made againe alive.

51

This doen, into those theevish dens he went,
  And thence did all the spoyles and threasures take,
  Which they from many long had robd and rent,
  But fortune now the victors meed did make;
  Of which the best he did his love betake;
  And also all those flockes, which they before
  Had reft from *Melibæ* and from his make,
  He did them all to *Coridon* restore.
So drove them all away, and his love with him bore.

CANT. XII

Fayre Pastorella by great hap
her parents understands,
Calidore doth the Blatant beast
subdew, and bynd in bands.

1

LIKE as a ship, that through the Ocean wyde
  Directs her course unto one certaine cost,
  Is met of many a counter winde and tyde,
  With which her winged speed is let and crost,
  And she her selfe in stormie surges tost;
  Yet making many a borde, and many a bay,
  Still winneth way, ne hath her compasse lost:
  Right so it fares with me in this long way,
Whose course is often stayd, yet never is astray.

2

For all that hetherto hath long delayd
  This gentle knight, from sewing his first quest,
  Though out of course, yet hath not bene missayd,
  To shew the courtesie by him profest,
  Even unto the lowest and the least.
  But now I come into my course againe,
  To his atchievement of the *Blatant beast*;
  Who all this while at will did range and raine,
Whilst none was him to stop, nor none him to restraine.

3

Sir *Calidore* when thus he now had raught
  Faire *Pastorella* from those *Brigants* powre,
  Unto the Castle of *Belgard* her brought,
  Whereof was Lord the good Sir *Bellamoure*;
  Who whylome was in his youthes freshest flowre
  A lustie knight, as ever wielded speare,
  And had endured many a dreadfull stoure
  In bloudy battell for a Ladie deare,
The fayrest Ladie then of all that living were.

4

Her name was *Claribell*, whose father hight
  The Lord of *Many Ilands*, farre renound
  For his great riches and his greater might.
  He through the wealth, wherein he did abound,
  This daughter thought in wedlocke to have bound
  Unto the Prince of *Picteland* bordering nere,
  But she whose sides before with secret wound
  Of love to *Bellamoure* empierced were,
By all meanes shund to match with any forrein fere.

5

And *Bellamour* againe so well her pleased,
  With dayly service and attendance dew,
  That of her love he was entyrely seized,
  And closely did her wed, but knowne to few.
  Which when her father understood, he grew
  In so great rage, that them in dongeon deepe
  Without compassion cruelly he threw;
  Yet did so streightly them a sunder keepe,
That neither could to company of th'other creepe.

6

Nathlesse Sir *Bellamour*, whether through grace
  Or secret guifts so with his keepers wrought,
  That to his love sometimes he came in place,
  Whereof her wombe unwist to wight was fraught,
  And in dew time a mayden child forth brought.
  Which she streight way for dread least, if her syre
  Should know thereof, to slay he would have sought,
  Delivered to her handmayd, that for hyre
She should it cause be fostred under straunge attyre.

7

The trustie damzell bearing it abrode
　Into the emptie fields, where living wight
Mote not bewray the secret of her lode,
　She forth gan lay unto the open light
　The litle babe, to take thereof a sight.
　Whom whylest she did with watrie eyne behold,
　Upon the litle brest like christall bright,
　She mote perceive a litle purple mold,
That like a rose her silken leaves did faire unfold.

8

Well she it markt, and pittied the more,
　Yet could not remedie her wretched case,
But closing it againe like as before,
　Bedeaw'd with teares there left it in the place:
　Yet left not quite, but drew a litle space
　Behind the bushes, where she her did hyde,
　To weet what mortall hand, or heavens grace
　Would for the wretched infants helpe provyde,
For which it loudly cald, and pittifully cryde.

9

At length a Shepheard, which there by did keepe
　His fleecie flocke upon the playnes around,
Led with the infants cry, that loud did weepe,
　Came to the place, where when he wrapped found
　Th'abandond spoyle, he softly it unbound;
　And seeing there, that did him pittie sore,
　He tooke it up, and in his mantle wound;
　So home unto his honest wife it bore,
Who as her owne it nurst, and named evermore.

10

Thus long continu'd *Claribell* a thrall,
　And *Bellamour* in bands, till that her syre
Departed life, and left unto them all.
　Then all the stormes of fortunes former yre
　Were turnd, and they to freedome did retyre,
　Thenceforth they joy'd in happinesse together,
　And lived long in peace and love entyre,
　Without disquiet or dislike of ether,
Till time that *Calidore* brought *Pastorella* thether.

11

Both whom they goodly well did entertaine;
  For *Bellamour* knew *Calidore* right well,
  And loved for his prowesse, sith they twaine
  Long since had fought in field. Als *Claribell*
  No lesse did tender the faire *Pastorell*,
    Seeing her weake and wan, through durance long.
  There they a while together thus did dwell
  In much delight, and many joyes among,
Untill the damzell gan to wex more sound and strong.

12

Tho gan Sir *Calidore* him to advize
  Of his first quest, which he had long forlore,
  Asham'd to thinke, how he that enterprize,
  The which the Faery Queene had long afore
  Bequeath'd to him, forslacked had so sore;
    That much he feared, least reprochfull blame
  With foule dishonour him mote blot therefore;
  Besides the losse of so much loos and fame,
As through the world thereby should glorifie his name.

13

Therefore resolving to returne in hast
  Unto so great atchievement, he bethought
  To leave his love, now perill being past,
  With *Claribell*, whylest he that monster sought
  Throughout the world, and to destruction brought.
    So taking leave of his faire *Pastorell*,
  Whom to recomfort, all the meanes he wrought,
  With thanks to *Bellamour* and *Claribell*,
He went forth on his quest, and did, that him befell.

14

But first, ere I doe his adventures tell,
  In this exploite, me needeth to declare,
  What did betide to the faire *Pastorell*,
  During his absence left in heavy care,
  Through daily mourning, and nightly misfare:
    Yet did that auncient matrone all she might,
  To cherish her with all things choice and rare:
  And her owne handmayd, that *Melissa* hight,
Appointed to attend her dewly day and night.

15

Who in a morning, when this Mayden faire
 Was dighting her, having her snowy brest
 As yet not laced, nor her golden haire
 Into their comely tresses dewly drest,
 Chaunst to espy upon her yvory chest
 The rosie marke, which she remembred well
 That litle Infant had, which forth she kest,
 The daughter of her Lady *Claribell*,
The which she bore, the whiles in prison she did dwell.

16

Which well avizing, streight she gan to cast
 In her conceiptfull mynd, that this faire Mayd
 Was that same infant, which so long sith past
 She in the open fields had loosely layd
 To fortunes spoile, unable it to ayd.
 So full of joy, streight forth she ran in hast
 Unto her mistresse, being halfe dismayd,
 To tell her, how the heavens had her graste,
To save her chylde, which in misfortunes mouth was plaste.

17

The sober mother seeing such her mood,
 Yet knowing not, what meant that sodaine thro,
 Askt her, how mote her words be understood,
 And what the matter was, that mov'd her so.
 My liefe (sayd she) ye know, that long ygo,
 Whilest ye in durance dwelt, ye to me gave
 A little mayde, the which ye chylded tho;
 The same againe if now ye list to have,
The same is yonder Lady, whom high God did save.

18

Much was the Lady troubled at that speach,
 And gan to question streight how she it knew.
 Most certaine markes, (sayd she) do me it teach,
 For on her brest I with these eyes did vew
 The litle purple rose, which thereon grew,
 Whereof her name ye then to her did give.
 Besides her countenaunce, and her likely hew,
 Matched with equall yeares, do surely prieve
That yond same is your daughter sure, which yet doth live.

19

The matrone stayd no lenger to enquire,
    But forth in hast ran to the straunger Mayd;
    Whom catching greedily for great desire,
    Rent up her brest, and bosome open layd,
    In which that rose she plainely saw displayd.
    Then her embracing twixt her armes twaine,
    She long so held, and softly weeping sayd;
    And livest thou my daughter now againe?
And art thou yet alive, whom dead I long did faine?

20

Tho further asking her of sundry things,
    And times comparing with their accidents,
    She found at last by very certaine signes,
    And speaking markes of passed monuments,
    That this young Mayd, whom chance to her presents
    Is her owne daughter, her owne infant deare.
    Tho wondring long at those so straunge events,
    A thousand times she her embraced nere,
With many a joyfull kisse, and many a melting teare.

21

Who ever is the mother of one chylde,
    Which having thought long dead, she fyndes alive,
    Let her by proofe of that, which she hath fylde
    In her owne breast, this mothers joy descrive:
    For other none such passion can contrive
    In perfect forme, as this good Lady felt,
    When she so faire a daughter saw survive,
    As *Pastorella* was, that nigh she swelt
For passing joy, which did all into pitty melt.

22

Thence running forth unto her loved Lord,
    She unto him recounted, all that fell:
    Who joyning joy with her in one accord,
    Acknowledg'd for his owne faire *Pastorell*.
    There leave we them in joy, and let us tell
    Of *Calidore*, who seeking all this while
    That monstrous Beast by finall force to quell,
    Through every place, with restlesse paine and toile
Him follow'd, by the tract of his outragious spoile.

23

Through all estates he found that he had past,
  In which he many massacres had left,
  And to the Clergy now was come at last;
  In which such spoile, such havocke, and such theft
  He wrought, that thence all goodnesse he bereft,
  That endlesse were to tell. The Elfin Knight,
  Who now no place besides unsought had left,
  At length into a Monastere did light,
Where he him found despoyling all with maine and might.

24

Into their cloysters now he broken had,
  Through which the Monckes he chaced here and there,
  And them pursu'd into their dortours sad,
  And searched all their cels and secrets neare;
  In which what filth and ordure did appeare,
  Were yrkesome to report; yet that foule Beast
  Nought sparing them, the more did tosse and teare,
  And ransacke all their dennes from most to least,
Regarding nought religion, nor their holy heast.

25

From thence into the sacred Church he broke,
  And robd the Chancell, and the deskes downe threw,
  And Altars fouled, and blasphemy spoke,
  And th'Images for all their goodly hew,
  Did cast to ground, whilest none was them to rew;
  So all confounded and disordered there.
  But seeing *Calidore*, away he flew,
  Knowing his fatall hand by former feare;
But he him fast pursuing, soone approched neare.

26

Him in a narrow place he overtooke,
  And fierce assailing forst him turne againe:
  Sternely he turnd againe, when he him strooke
  With his sharpe steele, and ran at him amaine
  With open mouth, that seemed to containe
  A full good pecke within the utmost brim,
  All set with yron teeth in raunges twaine,
  That terrifide his foes, and armed him,
Appearing like the mouth of *Orcus* griesly grim.

27

And therein were a thousand tongs empight,
  Of sundry kindes, and sundry quality,
  Some were of dogs, that barked day and night,
  And some of cats, that wrawling still did cry,
  And some of Beares, that groynd continually,
  And some of Tygres, that did seeme to gren,
  And snar at all, that ever passed by:
  But most of them were tongues of mortall men,
Which spake reprochfully, not caring where nor when.

28

And them amongst were mingled here and there,
  The tongues of Serpents with three forked stings,
  That spat out poyson and gore bloudy gere
  At all, that came within his ravenings,
  And spake licentious words, and hatefull things
  Of good and bad alike, of low and hie;
  Ne Kesars spared he a whit, nor Kings,
  But either blotted them with infamie,
Or bit them with his banefull teeth of injury.

29

But *Calidore* thereof no whit afrayd,
  Rencountred him with so impetuous might,
  That th'outrage of his violence he stayd,
  And bet abacke, threatning in vaine to bite,
  And spitting forth the poyson of his spight,
  That fomed all about his bloody jawes.
  Tho rearing up his former feete on hight,
  He rampt upon him with his ravenous pawes,
As if he would have rent him with his cruell clawes.

30

But he right well aware, his rage to ward,
  Did cast his shield atweene, and therewithall
  Putting his puissaunce forth, pursu'd so hard,
  That backeward he enforced him to fall,
  And being downe, ere he new helpe could call,
  His shield he on him threw, and fast downe held,
  Like as a bullocke, that in bloudy stall
  Of butchers balefull hand to ground is feld,
Is forcibly kept downe, till he be throughly queld.

31

Full cruelly the Beast did rage and rore,
   To be downe held, and maystred so with might,
   That he gan fret and fome out bloudy gore,
   Striving in vaine to rere him selfe upright.
   For still the more he strove, the more the Knight
   Did him suppresse, and forcibly subdew;
   That made him almost mad for fell despight.
   He grind, hee bit, he scratcht, he venim threw,
And fared like a feend, right horrible in hew.

32

Or like the hell-borne *Hydra*, which they faine
   That great *Alcides* whilome overthrew,
   After that he had labourd long in vaine,
   To crop his thousand heads, the which still new
   Forth budded, and in greater number grew.
   Such was the fury of this hellish Beast,
   Whilest *Calidore* him under him downe threw;
   Who nathemore his heavy load releast,
But aye the more he rag'd, the more his powre increast.

33

Tho when the Beast saw, he mote nought availe,
   By force, he gan his hundred tongues apply,
   And sharpely at him to revile and raile,
   With bitter termes of shamefull infamy;
   Oft interlacing many a forged lie,
   Whose like he never once did speake, nor heare,
   Nor ever thought thing so unworthily:
   Yet did he nought for all that him forbeare,
But strained him so streightly, that he chokt him neare.

34

At last when as he found his force to shrincke,
   And rage to quaile, he tooke a muzzell strong
   Of surest yron, made with many a lincke;
   Therewith he mured up his mouth along,
   And therein shut up his blasphemous tong,
   For never more defaming gentle Knight,
   Or unto lovely Lady doing wrong:
   And thereunto a great long chaine he tight,
With which he drew him forth, even in his own despight.

Calidore subdews Blatant Beast

35

Like as whylome that strong *Tirynthian* swaine,
　Brought forth with him the dreadfull dog of hell,
　Against his will fast bound in yron chaine,
　And roring horribly, did him compell
　To see the hatefull sunne, that he might tell
　To griesly *Pluto*, what on earth was donne,
　And to the other damned ghosts, which dwell
　For aye in darkenesse, which day light doth shonne.
So led this Knight his captyve with like conquest wonne.

36

Yet greatly did the Beast repine at those
　Straunge bands, whose like till then he never bore,
　Ne ever any durst till then impose,
　And chauffed inly, seeing now no more
　Him liberty was left aloud to rore:
　Yet durst he not draw backe; nor once withstand
　The proved powre of noble *Calidore*,
　But trembled underneath his mighty hand,
And like a fearefull dog him followed through the land.

37

Him through all Faery land he follow'd so,
　As if he learned had obedience long,
　That all the people where so he did go,
　Out of their townes did round about him throng,
　To see him leade that Beast in bondage strong,
　And seeing it, much wondred at the sight;
　And all such persons, as he earst did wrong,
　Rejoyced much to see his captive plight,
And much admyr'd the Beast, but more admyr'd the Knight.

38

Thus was this Monster by the maystring might
　Of doughty *Calidore*, supprest and tamed,
　That never more he mote endammadge wight
　With his vile tongue, which many had defamed,
　And many causelesse caused to be blamed:
　So did he eeke long after this remaine,
　Untill that, whether wicked fate so framed,
　Or fault of men, he broke his yron chaine,
And got into the world at liberty againe.

39

Thenceforth more mischiefe and more scath he wrought
    To mortall men, than he had done before;
    Ne ever could by any more be brought
    Into like bands, ne maystred any more:
    Albe that long time after *Calidore*,
    The good Sir *Pelleas* him tooke in hand,
    And after him Sir *Lamoracke* of yore,
    And all his brethren borne in Britaine land;
Yet none of them could ever bring him into band.

40

So now he raungeth through the world againe,
    And rageth sore in each degree and state;
    Ne any is, that may him now restraine,
    He growen is so great and strong of late,
    Barking and biting all that him doe bate,
    Albe they worthy blame, or cleare of crime:
    Ne spareth he most learned wits to rate,
    Ne spareth he the gentle Poets rime,
But rends without regard of person or of time.

41

Ne may this homely verse, of many meanest,
    Hope to escape his venemous despite,
    More than my former writs, all were they clearest
    From blamefull blot, and free from all that wite,
    With which some wicked tongues did it backebite,
    And bring into a mighty Peres displeasure,
    That never so deserved to endite.
    Therfore do you my rimes keep better measure,
And seeke to please, that now is counted wisemens threasure.

FINIS

TWO CANTOS OF *MUTABILITIE:*

WHICH, BOTH FOR FORME AND MATTER, APPEARE TO BE PARCELL OF SOME FOLLOWING BOOKE OF THE *FAERIE QUEENE*, UNDER THE LEGEND OF *CONSTANCIE*

Never before imprinted

CANTO VI

Proud Change (*not pleasd, in mortall things,*
beneath the Moone, to raigne)
Pretends, as well of Gods, as Men,
to be the Soveraine.

1

HAT man that sees the ever-whirling wheele
Of *Change*, the which all mortall things doth sway,
But that therby doth find, and plainly feele,
How *MUTABILITY* in them doth play
Her cruell sports, to many mens decay?
Which that to all may better yet appeare,
I will rehearse that whylome I heard say,
How she at first her selfe began to reare,
Gainst all the Gods, and th'empire sought from them
    to beare.

2

But first, here falleth fittest to unfold
Her antique race and linage ancient,
As I have found it registred of old,
In *Faery* Land mongst records permanent:
She was, to weet, a daughter by descent
Of those old *Titans*, that did whylome strive
With *Saturnes* sonne for heavens regiment.
Whom, though high *Jove* of kingdome did deprive,
Yet many of their stemme long after did survive.

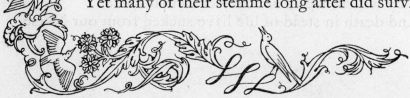

3

And many of them, afterwards obtain'd
  Great power of *Jove*, and high authority;
  As *Hecaté*, in whose almighty hand,
  He plac't all rule and principality,
  To be by her disposed diversly,
  To Gods, and men, as she them list divide:
  And drad *Bellona*, that doth sound on hie
  Warres and allarums unto Nations wide,
That makes both heaven and earth to tremble at her pride.

4

So likewise did this *Titanesse* aspire,
  Rule and dominion to her selfe to gaine;
  That as a Goddesse, men might her admire,
  And heavenly honours yield, as to them twaine.
  At first, on earth she sought it to obtaine;
  Where she such proofe and sad examples shewed
  Of her great power, to many ones great paine,
  That not men onely (whom she soone subdewed)
But eke all other creatures, her bad dooings rewed.

5

For, she the face of earthly things so changed,
  That all which Nature had establisht first
  In good estate, and in meet order ranged,
  She did pervert, and all their statutes burst:
  And all the worlds faire frame (which none yet durst
  Of Gods or men to alter or misguide)
  She alter'd quite, and made them all accurst
  That God had blest; and did at first provide
In that still happy state for ever to abide.

6

Ne shee the lawes of Nature onely brake,
  But eke of Justice, and of Policie;
  And wrong of right, and bad of good did make,
  And death for life exchanged foolishlie:
  Since which, all living wights have learn'd to die,
  And all this world is woxen daily worse.
  O pittious worke of *MUTABILITIE*!
  By which, we all are subject to that curse,
And death in stead of life have sucked from our Nurse.

7

And now, when all the earth she thus had brought
   To her behest, and thralled to her might,
   She gan to cast in her ambitious thought,
   T'attempt the empire of the heavens hight,
   And *Jove* himselfe to shoulder from his right.
   And first, she past the region of the ayre,
   And of the fire, whose substance thin and slight,
   Made no resistance, ne could her contraire,
But ready passage to her pleasure did prepaire.

8

Thence, to the Circle of the Moone she clambe,
   Where *Cynthia* raignes in everlasting glory,
   To whose bright shining palace straight she came,
   All fairely deckt with heavens goodly story;
   Whose silver gates (by which there sate an hory
   Old aged Sire, with hower-glasse in hand,
   Hight *Tyme*) she entred, were he liefe or sory:
   Ne staide till she the highest stage had scand,
Where *Cynthia* did sit, that never still did stand.

9

Her sitting on an Ivory throne shee found,
   Drawne of two steeds, th'one black, the other white,
   Environd with tenne thousand starres around,
   That duly her attended day and night;
   And by her side, there ran her Page, that hight
   Vesper, whom we the Evening-starre intend:
   That with his Torche, still twinkling like twylight,
   Her lightened all the way where she should wend,
And joy to weary wandring travailers did lend:

10

That when the hardy *Titanesse* beheld
   The goodly building of her Palace bright,
   Made of the heavens substance, and up-held
   With thousand Crystall pillors of huge hight,
   Shee gan to burne in her ambitious spright,
   And t'envie her that in such glorie raigned.
   Eftsoones she cast by force and tortious might,
   Her to displace; and to her selfe to have gained
The kingdome of the Night, and waters by her wained.

11

Boldly she bid the Goddesse downe descend,
  And let her selfe into that Ivory throne;
For, shee her selfe more worthy thereof wend,
  And better able it to guide alone:
  Whether to men, whose fall she did bemone,
  Or unto Gods, whose state she did maligne,
  Or to th'infernall Powers, her need give lone
  Of her faire light, and bounty most benigne,
Her selfe of all that rule shee deemed most condigne.

12

But shee that had to her that soveraigne seat
  By highest *Jove* assign'd, therein to beare
Nights burning lamp, regarded not her threat,
  Ne yielded ought for favour or for feare;
  But with sterne countenaunce and disdainfull cheare,
  Bending her horned browes, did put her back:
  And boldly blaming her for comming there,
  Bade her attonce from heavens coast to pack,
Or at her perill bide the wrathfull Thunders wrack.

13

Yet nathemore the *Giantesse* forbare:
  But boldly preacing-on, raught forth her hand
To pluck her downe perforce from off her chaire;
  And there-with lifting up her golden wand,
  Threatned to strike her if she did with-stand.
  Where-at the starres, which round about her blazed,
  And eke the Moones bright wagon, still did stand,
  All beeing with so bold attempt amazed,
And on her uncouth habit and sterne looke still gazed.

14

Meane-while, the lower World, which nothing knew
  Of all that chaunced here, was darkned quite;
And eke the heavens, and all the heavenly crew
  Of happy wights, now unpurvaide of light,
  Were much afraid, and wondred at that sight;
  Fearing least *Chaos* broken had his chaine,
  And brought againe on them eternall night:
  But chiefely *Mercury*, that next doth raigne,
Ran forth in haste, unto the king of Gods to plaine.

15

All ran together with a great out-cry,
  To *Joves* faire Palace, fixt in heavens hight;
And beating at his gates full earnestly,
Gan call to him aloud with all their might,
To know what meant that suddaine lack of light.
The father of the Gods when this he heard,
Was troubled much at their so strange affright,
Doubting least *Typhon* were againe uprear'd,
Or other his old foes, that once him sorely fear'd.

16

Eftsoones the sonne of *Maia* forth he sent
  Downe to the Circle of the Moone, to knowe
The cause of this so strange astonishment,
And why shee did her wonted course forslowe;
And if that any were on earth belowe
That did with charmes or Magick her molest,
Him to attache, and downe to hell to throwe:
  But, if from heaven it were, then to arrest
The Author, and him bring before his presence prest.

17

The wingd-foot God, so fast his plumes did beat,
  That soone he came where-as the *Titanesse*
Was striving with faire *Cynthia* for her seat:
At whose strange sight, and haughty hardinesse,
He wondred much, and feared her no lesse.
Yet laying feare aside to doe his charge,
At last, he bade her (with bold stedfastnesse)
  Ceasse to molest the Moone to walke at large,
Or come before high *Jove*, her dooings to discharge.

18

And there-with-all, he on her shoulder laid
  His snaky-wreathed Mace, whose awfull power
Doth make both Gods and hellish fiends affraid:
Where-at the *Titanesse* did sternely lower,
And stoutly answer'd, that in evill hower
He from his *Jove* such message to her brought,
To bid her leave faire *Cynthias* silver bower;
  Sith shee his *Jove* and him esteemed nought,
No more than *Cynthia's* selfe; but all their kingdoms sought.

19

The Heavens Herald staid not to reply,
  But past away, his doings to relate
  Unto his Lord; who now in th'highest sky,
  Was placed in his principall Estate,
  With all the Gods about him congregate:
  To whom when *Hermes* had his message told,
  It did them all exceedingly amate,
  Save *Jove*; who, changing nought his count'nance bold,
Did unto them at length these speeches wise unfold;

20

Harken to mee awhile yee heavenly Powers;
  Ye may remember since th'Earths cursed seed
  Sought to assaile the heavens eternall towers,
  And to us all exceeding feare did breed:
  But how we then defeated all their deed,
  Yee all doe knowe, and them destroied quite;
  Yet not so quite, but that there did succeed
  An off-spring of their bloud, which did alite
Upon the fruitfull earth, which doth us yet despite.

21

Of that bad seed is this bold woman bred,
  That now with bold presumption doth aspire
  To thrust faire *Phœbe* from her silver bed,
  And eke our selves from heavens high Empire,
  If that her might were match to her desire:
  Wherefore, it now behoves us to advise
  What way is best to drive her to retire;
  Whether by open force, or counsell wise,
Areed ye sonnes of God, as best ye can devise.

22

So having said, he ceast; and with his brow
  (His black eye-brow, whose doomefull dreaded beck
  Is wont to wield the world unto his vow,
  And even the highest Powers of heaven to check)
  Made signe to them in their degrees to speake:
  Who straight gan cast their counsell grave and wise.
  Meane-while, th'Earths daughter, thogh she nought did reck
  Of *Hermes* message; yet gan now advise,
What course were best to take in this hot bold emprize.

23

Eftsoones she thus resolv'd; that whil'st the Gods
  (After returne of *Hermes* Embassie)
  Were troubled, and amongst themselves at ods,
  Before they could new counsels re-allie,
  To set upon them in that extasie;
  And take what fortune time and place would lend:
  So, forth she rose, and through the purest sky
  To *Joves* high Palace straight cast to ascend,
To prosecute her plot: Good on-set boads good end.

24

Shee there arriving, boldly in did pass;
  Where all the Gods she found in counsell close,
  All quite unarm'd, as then their manner was.
  At sight of her they suddaine all arose,
  In great amaze, ne wist what way to chose.
  But *Jove*, all fearelesse, forc't them to aby;
  And in his soveraine throne, gan straight dispose
  Himselfe more full of grace and Majestie,
That mote encheare his friends, and foes mote terrifie.

25

That, when the haughty *Titanesse* beheld,
  All were she fraught with pride and impudence,
  Yet with the sight thereof was almost queld;
  And inly quaking, seem'd as reft of sense,
  And voyd of speech in that drad audience;
  Untill that *Jove* himselfe, her selfe bespake:
  Speake thou fraile woman, speake with confidence,
  Whence art thou, and what doost thou here now make?
What idle errand hast thou, earths mansion to forsake?

26

Shee, halfe confused with his great commaund,
  Yet gathering spirit of her natures pride,
  Him boldly answer'd thus to his demaund:
  I am a daughter, by the mothers side,
  Of her that is Grand-mother magnifide
  Of all the Gods, great *Earth*, great *Chaos* child:
  But by the fathers (be it not envide)
  I greater am in bloud (whereon I build)
Than all the Gods, though wrongfully from heaven exil'd.

27

For, *Titan* (as ye all acknowledge must)
  Was *Saturnes* elder brother by birth-right;
  Both, sonnes of *Uranus*: but by unjust
  And guilefull meanes, through *Corybantes* slight,
  The younger thrust the elder from his right:
  Since which, thou *Jove*, injuriously hast held
  The Heavens rule from *Titans* sonnes by might;
  And them to hellish dungeons downe hast feld:
Witnesse ye Heavens the truth of all that I have teld.

28

Whil'st she thus spake, the Gods that gave good eare
  To her bold words, and marked well her grace,
  Beeing of stature tall as any there
  Of all the Gods, and beautifull of face,
  As any of the Goddesses in place,
  Stood all astonied, like a sort of Steeres;
  Mongst whom, some beast of strange and forraine race,
  Unwares is chaunc't, far straying from his peeres:
So did their ghastly gaze bewray their hidden feares.

29

Till having pauz'd awhile, *Jove* thus bespake;
  Will never mortall thoughts ceasse to aspire,
  In this bold sort, to Heaven claime to make
  And touch celestiall seates with earthly mire?
  I would have thought, that bold *Procrustes* hire,
  Or *Typhons* fall, or proud *Ixions* paine,
  Or great *Prometheus*, tasting of our ire,
  Would have suffiz'd, the rest for to restraine;
And warn'd all men by their example to refraine:

30

But now, this off-scum of that cursed fry,
  Dare to renew the like bold enterprize,
  And chalenge th'heritage of this our skie;
  Whom what should hinder, but that we likewise
  Should handle as the rest of her allies,
  And thunder-drive to hell? With that, he shooke
  His Nectar-deawed locks, with which the skyes
  And all the world beneath for terror quooke,
And eft his burning levin-brond in hand he tooke.

31

But, when he looked on her lovely face,
  In which, faire beames of beauty did appeare,
  That could the greatest wrath soone turne to grace
  (Such sway doth beauty even in Heaven beare)
  He staide his hand; and having chang'd his cheare,
  He thus againe in milder wise began;
  But ah! if Gods should strive with flesh yfere,
  Then shortly should the progeny of Man
Be rooted out, if *Jove* should doe still what he can:

32

But thee faire *Titans* child, I rather weene,
  Through some vaine errour or inducement light,
  To see that mortall eyes have never seene;
  Or through ensample of thy sisters might,
  Bellona; whose great glory thou doost spight,
  Since thou hast seene her dreadfull power belowe,
  Mongst wretched men (dismaide with her affright)
  To bandie Crownes, and Kingdomes to bestowe:
And sure thy worth, no lesse than hers doth seem to showe.

33

But wote thou this, thou hardy *Titanesse*,
  That not the worth of any living wight
  May challenge ought in Heavens interesse;
  Much lesse the Title of old *Titans* Right:
  For, we by Conquest of our soveraine might,
  And by eternall doome of Fates decree,
  Have wonne the Empire of the Heavens bright;
  Which to our selves we hold, and to whom wee
Shall worthy deeme partakers of our blisse to bee.

34

Then ceasse thy idle claime thou foolish gerle,
  And seeke by grace and goodnesse to obtaine
  That place from which by folly *Titan* fell;
  There-to thou maist perhaps, if so thou faine
  Have *Jove* thy gratious Lord and Soveraigne.
  So, having said, she thus to him replide;
  Ceasse *Saturnes* sonne, to seeke by proffers vaine
  Of idle hopes t'allure mee to thy side,
For to betray my Right, before I have it tride.

35

But thee, O *Jove*, no equall Judge I deeme
　Of my desert, or of my dewfull Right;
　That in thine owne behalfe maist partiall seeme:
　But to the highest him, that is behight
　Father of Gods and men by equall might;
　To weet, the God of Nature, I appeale.
　There-at *Jove* wexed wroth, and in his spright
　Did inly grudge, yet did it well conceale;
And bade *Dan Phœbus* Scribe her Appellation seale.

36

Eftsoones the time and place appointed were,
　Where all, both heavenly Powers, and earthly wights,
　Before great Natures presence should appeare,
　For triall of their Titles and best Rights:
　That was, to weet, upon the highest hights
　Of *Arlo-hill* (Who knowes not *Arlo-hill*?)
　That is the highest head (in all mens sights)
　Of my old father *Mole*, whom Shepheards quill
Renowmed hath with hymnes fit for a rurall skill.

37

And, were it not ill fitting for this file,
　To sing of hilles and woods, mongst warres and Knights,
　I would abate the sternenesse of my stile,
　Mongst these sterne stounds to mingle soft delights;
　And tell how *Arlo* through *Dianaes* spights
　(Beeing of old the best and fairest Hill
　That was in all this holy-Islands hights)
　Was made the most unpleasant, and most ill.
Meane while, O *Clio*, lend *Calliope* thy quill.

38

Whylome, when *IRELAND* florished in fame
　Of wealths and goodnesse, far above the rest
　Of all that beare the *British* Islands name,
　The Gods then us'd (for pleasure and for rest)
　Oft to resort there-to, when seem'd them best:
　But none of all there-in more pleasure found,
　Than *Cynthia*; that is soveraine Queene profest
　Of woods and forrests, which therein abound,
Sprinkled with wholsom waters, more than most on ground.

39

But mongst them all, as fittest for her game,
 Either for chace of beasts with hound or boawe,
 Or for to shroude in shade from *Phœbus* flame,
 Or bathe in fountaines that doe freshly flowe,
 Or from high hilles, or from the dales belowe,
 She chose this *Arlo*; where shee did resort
 With all her Nymphes enranged on a rowe,
 With whom the woody Gods did oft consort:
For, with the Nymphes, the Satyres love to play and sport.

40

Amongst the which, there was a Nymph that hight
 Molanna; daughter of old father *Mole*,
 And sister unto *Mulla*, faire and bright:
 Unto whose bed false *Bregog* whylome stole,
 That Shepheard *Colin* dearely did condole,
 And made her lucklesse loves well knowne to be.
 But this *Molanna*, were she not so shole,
 Were no lesse faire and beautifull than shee:
Yet as she is, a fairer flood may no man see.

41

For, first, she springs out of two marble Rocks,
 On which, a grove of Oakes high mounted growes,
 That as a girlond seemes to deck the locks
 Of som faire Bride, brought forth with pompous showes
 Out of her bowre, that many flowers strowes:
 So, through the flowry Dales she tumbling downe,
 Through many woods, and shady coverts flowes
 (That on each side her silver channell crowne)
Till to the Plaine she come, whose Valleyes shee doth drowne.

42

In her sweet streames, *Diana* used oft
 (After her sweatie chace and toilesome play)
 To bathe her selfe; and after, on the soft
 And downy grasse, her dainty limbes to lay
 In covert shade, where none behold her may:
 For, much she hated sight of living eye.
 Foolish God *Faunus*, though full many a day
 He saw her clad, yet longed foolishly
To see her naked mongst her Nymphes in privity.

43

No way he found to compasse his desire,
  But to corrupt *Molanna*, this her maid,
  Her to discover for some secret hire:
So, her with flattering words he first assaid;
  And after, pleasing gifts for her purvaid,
  Queene-apples, and red Cherries from the tree,
  With which he her allured and betraid,
  To tell what time he might her Lady see
When she her selfe did bathe, that he might secret bee.

44

There-to hee promist, if shee would him pleasure
  With this small boone, to quit her with a better;
  To weet, that where-as shee had out of measure
Long lov'd the *Fanchin*, who by nought did set her,
  That he would undertake, for this to get her
  To be his Love, and of him liked well:
  Besides all which, he vow'd to be her debter
  For many moe good turnes than he would tell;
The least of which, this little pleasure should excell.

45

The simple maid did yield to him anone;
  And eft him placed where he close might view
  That never any saw, save onely one;
Who, for his hire to so foole-hardy dew,
  Was of his hounds devour'd in Hunters hew.
  Tho, as her manner was on sunny day,
  Diana, with her Nymphes about her, drew
  To this sweet spring; where, doffing her array,
She bath'd her lovely limbes, for *Jove* a likely pray.

46

There *Faunus* saw that pleased much his eye,
  And made his hart to tickle in his brest,
  That for great joy of some-what he did spy,
He could him not containe in silent rest;
  But breaking forth in laughter, loud profest
  His foolish thought. A foolish *Faune* indeed,
  That couldst not hold thy selfe so hidden blest,
  But wouldest needs thine owne conceit areed.
Babblers unworthy been of so divine a meed.

47

The Goddesse, all abashed with that noise,
  In haste forth started from the guilty brooke;
And running straight where-as she heard his voice,
Enclos'd the bush about, and there him tooke,
Like darred Larke; not daring up to looke
On her whose sight before so much he sought.
Thence, forth they drew him by the hornes, and shooke
Nigh all to peeces, that they left him nought;
And then into the open light they forth him brought.

48

Like as an huswife, that with busie care
  Thinks of her Dairie to make wondrous gaine,
  Finding where-as some wicked beast unware
  That breakes into her Dayr'house, there doth draine
  Her creaming pannes, and frustrate all her paine;
  Hath in some snare or gin set close behind,
  Entrapped him, and caught into her traine,
  Then thinkes what punishment were best assign'd,
And thousand deathes deviseth in her vengefull mind:

49

So did *Diana* and her maydens all
  Use silly *Faunus*, now within their baile:
  They mocke and scorne him, and him foule miscall;
  Some by the nose him pluckt, some by the taile,
  And by his goatish beard some did him haile:
  Yet he (poore soule) with patience all did beare;
  For, nought against their wils might countervaile:
  Ne ought he said what ever he did heare;
But hanging downe his head, did like a Mome appeare.

50

At length, when they had flouted him their fill,
  They gan to cast what penaunce him to give.
  Some would have gelt him, but that same would spill
  The Wood-gods breed, which must for ever live:
  Others would through the river him have drive,
  And ducked deepe: but that seem'd penaunce light;
  But most agreed and did this sentence give,
  Him in Deares skin to clad; and in that plight,
To hunt him with their hounds, him selfe save how hee might.

51

But *Cynthia's* selfe, more angry than the rest,
  Thought not enough, to punish him in sport,
  And of her shame to make a gamesome jest;
  But gan examine him in straighter sort,
  Which of her Nymphes, or other close consort,
  Him thither brought, and her to him betraid?
  He, much affeard, to her confessed short,
  That 'twas *Molanna* which her so bewraid.
Then all attonce their hands upon *Molanna* laid.

52

But him (according as they had decreed)
  With a Deeres-skin they covered, and then chast
  With all their hounds that after him did speed;
  But he more speedy, from them fled more fast
  Than any Deere: so sore him dread aghast.
  They after follow'd all with shrill out-cry,
  Shouting as they the heavens would have brast:
  That all the woods and dales where he did flie,
Did ring againe, and loud reeccho to the skie.

53

So they him follow'd till they weary were;
  When, back returning to *Molann'* againe,
  They, by commaund'ment of *Diana*, there
  Her whelm'd with stones. Yet *Faunus* (for her paine)
  Of her beloved *Fanchin* did obtaine,
  That her he would receive unto his bed.
  So now her waves passe through a pleasant Plaine,
  Till with the *Fanchin* she her selfe doe wed,
And (both combin'd) themselves in one faire river spred.

54

Nath'lesse, *Diana*, full of indignation,
  Thence-forth abandond her delicious brooke;
  In whose sweet streame, before that bad occasion,
  So much delight to bathe her limbes she tooke:
  Ne onely her, but also quite forsooke
  All those faire forrests about *Arlo* hid,
  And all that Mountaine, which doth over-looke
  The richest champian that may else be rid,
And the faire *Shure*, in which are thousand Salmons bred.

Mutabilitie

55

Them all, and all that she so deare did way,
  Thence-forth she left; and parting from the place,
  There-on an heavy haplesse curse did lay,
  To weet, that Wolves, where she was wont to space,
  Should harbour'd be, and all those Woods deface,
  And Thieves should rob and spoile that Coast around.
  Since which, those Woods, and all that goodly Chase,
  Doth to this day with Wolves and Thieves abound:
Which too-too true that lands in-dwellers since have found.

CANTO VII

Pealing, from Jove, *to* Natur's *Bar,*
  bold Alteration *pleades*
Large Evidence: but Nature *soone*
  her righteous Doome areads.

1

AH! whither doost thou now thou greater Muse
  Me from these woods and pleasing forrests bring?
  And my fraile spirit (that dooth oft refuse
  This too high flight, unfit for her weake wing)
  Lift up aloft, to tell of heavens King
  (Thy soveraine Sire) his fortunate successe,
  And victory, in bigger noates to sing,
  Which he obtain'd against that *Titanesse*,
That him of heavens Empire sought to dispossesse.

2

Yet sith I needs must follow thy behest,
  Doe thou my weaker wit with skill inspire,
  Fit for this turne; and in my feeble brest
  Kindle fresh sparks of that immortall fire,
  Which learned minds inflameth with desire
  Of heavenly things: for, who but thou alone,
  That art yborne of heaven and heavenly Sire,
  Can tell things doen in heaven so long ygone;
So farre past memory of man that may be knowne.

3

Now, at the time that was before agreed,
  The Gods assembled all on *Arlo* hill;
  As well those that are sprung of heavenly seed,
  As those that all the other world doe fill,
  And rule both sea and land unto their will:
  Onely th'infernall Powers might not appeare;
  Aswell for horror of their count'naunce ill,
  As for th'unruly fiends which they did feare;
Yet *Pluto* and *Proserpina* were present there.

4

And thither also came all other creatures,
  What-ever life or motion doe retaine,
  According to their sundry kinds of features;
  That *Arlo* scarsly could them all containe;
  So full they filled every hill and Plaine:
  And had not *Natures* Sergeant (that is *Order*)
  Them well disposed by his busie paine,
  And raunged farre abroad in every border,
They would have caused much confusion and disorder.

5

Then forth issewed (great goddesse) great dame *Nature*,
  With goodly port and gracious Majesty;
  Being far greater and more tall of stature
  Than any of the gods or Powers on hie:
  Yet certes by her face and physnomy,
  Whether she man or woman inly were,
  That could not any creature well descry:
  For, with a veile that wimpled every where,
Her head and face was hid, that mote to none appeare.

6

That some doe say was so by skill devized,
  To hide the terror of her uncouth hew,
  From mortall eyes that should be sore agrized;
  For that her face did like a Lion shew,
  That eye of wight could not indure to view:
  But others tell that it so beautious was,
  And round about such beames of splendor threw,
  That it the Sunne a thousand times did pass,
Ne could be seene, but like an image in a glass.

7

That well may seemen true: for, well I weene
  That this same day, when she on *Arlo* sat,
  Her garment was so bright and wondrous sheene,
  That my fraile wit cannot devize to what
  It to compare, nor finde like stuffe to that,
  As those three sacred *Saints*, though else most wise,
  Yet on mount *Thabor* quite their wits forgat,
  When they their glorious Lord in strange disguise
Transfigur'd sawe; his garments so did daze their eyes.

8

In a fayre Plaine upon an equall Hill,
  She placed was in a pavilion;
  Not such as Craftes-men by their idle skill
  Are wont for Princes states to fashion:
  But th'earth her self of her owne motion,
  Out of her fruitfull bosome made to growe
  Most dainty trees; that, shooting up anon,
  Did seeme to bow their bloosming heads full lowe,
For homage unto her, and like a throne did shew.

9

So hard it is for any living wight,
  All her array and vestiments to tell,
  That old *Dan Geffrey* (in whose gentle spright
  The pure well head of Poesie did dwell)
  In his *Foules parley* durst not with it mel,
  But it transferd to *Alane*, who he thought
  Had in his *Plaint of kindes* describ'd it well:
  Which who will read set forth so as it ought,
Go seek he out that *Alane* where he may be sought.

10

And all the earth far underneath her feete
  Was dight with flowres, that voluntary grew
  Out of the ground, and sent forth odours sweet;
  Tenne thousand mores of sundry sent and hew,
  That might delight the smell, or please the view:
  The which, the Nymphes, from all the brooks thereby
  Had gathered, which they at her foot-stoole threw;
  That richer seem'd than any tapestry,
That Princes bowres adorne with painted imagery.

11

And *Mole* himselfe, to honour her the more,
　Did deck himself in freshest faire attire,
　And his high head, that seemeth alwaies hore
　With hardned frosts of former winters ire,
　He with an Oaken girlond now did tire,
　As if the love of some new Nymph late seene,
　Had in him kindled youthfull fresh desire,
　And made him change his gray attire to greene;
Ah gentle *Mole*! such joyance hath thee well beseene.

12

Was never so great joyance since the day,
　That all the gods whylome assembled were,
　On *Hæmus* hill in their divine array,
　To celebrate the solemne bridall cheare,
　Twixt *Peleus*, and dame *Thetis* pointed there;
　Where *Phœbus* self, that god of Poets hight,
　They say did sing the spousall hymne full cleere,
　That all the gods were ravisht with delight
Of his celestiall song, and Musicks wondrous might.

13

This great Grandmother of all creatures bred
　Great *Nature*, ever young yet full of eld,
　Still mooving, yet unmoved from her sted;
　Unseene of any, yet of all beheld;
　Thus sitting in her throne as I have teld,
　Before her came dame *Mutabilitie*;
　And being lowe before her presence feld,
　With meek obaysance and humilitie,
Thus gan her plaintif Plea, with words to amplifie;

14

To thee O greatest goddesse, only great,
　An humble suppliant loe, I lowely fly
　Seeking for Right, which I of thee entreat;
　Who Right to all dost deale indifferently,
　Damning all Wrong and tortious Injurie,
　Which any of thy creatures doe to other
　(Oppressing them with power, unequally)
　Sith of them all thou art the equall mother,
And knittest each to each, as brother unto brother.

15

To thee therefore of this same *Jove* I plaine,
   And of his fellow gods that faine to be,
   That challenge to themselves the whole worlds raign;
   Of which, the greatest part is due to me,
   And heaven it selfe by heritage in Fee:
   For, heaven and earth I both alike do deeme,
   Sith heaven and earth are both alike to thee;
   And, gods no more than men thou doest esteeme:
For, even the gods to thee, as men to gods do seeme.

16

Then weigh, O soveraigne goddesse, by what right
   These gods do claime the worlds whole soverainty;
   And that is onely dew unto thy might
   Arrogate to themselves ambitiously:
   As for the gods owne principality,
   Which *Jove* usurpes unjustly; that to be
   My heritage, *Jove's* self cannot deny,
   From my great Grandsire *Titan*, unto mee,
Deriv'd by dew descent; as is well knowen to thee.

17

Yet mauger *Jove*, and all his gods beside,
   I doe possesse the worlds most regiment;
   As, if ye please it into parts divide,
   And every parts inholders to convent,
   Shall to your eyes appeare incontinent.
   And first, the Earth (great mother of us all)
   That only seems unmov'd and permanent,
   And unto *Mutability* not thrall;
Yet is she chang'd in part, and eeke in generall.

18

For, all that from her springs, and is ybredde,
   How-ever fayre it flourish for a time,
   Yet see we soone decay; and, being dead,
   To turne again unto their earthly slime:
   Yet, out of their decay and mortall crime,
   We daily see new creatures to arize;
   And of their Winter spring another Prime,
   Unlike in forme, and chang'd by strange disguise:
So turne they still about, and change in restlesse wise.

19

As for her tenants; that is, man and beasts,
  The beasts we daily see massacred dy,
  As thralls and vassalls unto mens beheasts:
  And men themselves doe change continually,
  From youth to eld, from wealth to poverty,
  From good to bad, from bad to worst of all.
  Ne doe their bodies only flit and fly:
  But eeke their minds (which they immortall call)
Still change and vary thoughts, as new occasions fall.

20

Ne is the water in more constant case;
  Whether those same on high, or these belowe.
  For, th'Ocean moveth stil, from place to place;
  And every River still doth ebbe and flowe:
  Ne any Lake, that seems most still and slowe,
  Ne Poole so small, that can his smoothnesse holde,
  When any winde doth under heaven blowe;
  With which, the clouds are also tost and roll'd;
Now like great Hills; and, streight, like sluces, them unfold.

21

So likewise are all watry living wights
  Still tost, and turned, with continuall change,
  Never abyding in their stedfast plights.
  The fish, still floting, doe at randon range,
  And never rest; but evermore exchange
  Their dwelling places, as the streames them carrie:
  Ne have the watry foules a certaine grange,
  Wherein to rest, ne in one stead do tarry;
But flitting still doe flie, and still their places vary.

22

Next is the Ayre: which who feeles not by sense
  (For, of all sense it is the middle meane)
  To flit still? and, with subtill influence,
  Of his thin spirit, all creatures to maintaine,
  In state of life? O weake life! that does leane
  On thing so tickle as th'unsteady ayre;
  Which every howre is chang'd, and altred cleane
  With every blast that bloweth fowle or faire:
The faire doth it prolong; the fowle doth it impaire.

23

Therein the changes infinite beholde,
  Which to her creatures every minute chaunce;
  Now, boyling hot: streight, friezing deadly cold:
  Now, faire sun-shine, that makes all skip and daunce:
  Streight, bitter storms and balefull countenance,
  That makes them all to shiver and to shake:
  Rayne, hayle, and snowe do pay them sad penance,
  And dreadfull thunder-claps (that make them quake)
With flames and flashing lights that thousand changes make.

24

Last is the fire: which, though it live for ever,
  Ne can be quenched quite; yet, every day,
  Wee see his parts, so soone as they do sever,
  To lose their heat, and shortly to decay;
  So, makes himself his owne consuming pray.
  Ne any living creatures doth he breed:
  But all, that are of others bredd, doth slay;
  And, with their death, his cruell life dooth feed;
Nought leaving but their barren ashes, without seede.

25

Thus, all these fower (the which the ground-work bee
  Of all the world, and of all living wights)
  To thousand sorts of *Change* we subject see.
  Yet are they chang'd (by other wondrous slights)
  Into themselves, and lose their native mights;
  The Fire to Aire, and th'Ayre to Water sheere,
  And Water into Earth: yet Water fights
  With Fire, and Aire with Earth approaching neere:
Yet all are in one body, and as one appeare.

26

So, in them all raignes *Mutabilitie*;
  How-ever these, that Gods themselves do call,
  Of them doe claime the rule and soveraintie:
  As, *Vesta*, of the fire æthereall;
  Vulcan, of this, with us so usuall;
  Ops, of the earth; and *Juno* of the Ayre;
  Neptune, of Seas; and Nymphes, of Rivers all.
  For, all those Rivers to me subject are:
And all the rest, which they usurp, be all my share.

27

Which to approven true, as I have told,
  Vouchsafe, O goddesse, to thy presence call
  The rest which doe the world in being hold:
  As, times and seasons of the yeare that fall:
  Of all the which, demand in generall,
  Or judge thy selfe, by verdit of thine eye,
  Whether to me they are not subject all.
  Nature did yeeld thereto; and by-and-by,
Bade *Order* call them all, before her Majesty.

28

So, forth issew'd the Seasons of the yeare;
  First, lusty *Spring*, all dight in leaves of flowres
  That freshly budded and new bloosmes did beare
  (In which a thousand birds had built their bowres
  That sweetly sung, to call forth Paramours):
  And in his hand a javelin he did beare,
  And on his head (as fit for warlike stoures)
  A guilt engraven morion he did weare;
That as some did him love, so others did him feare.

29

Then came the jolly *Sommer*, being dight
  In a thin silken cassock coloured greene,
  That was unlyned all, to be more light:
  And on his head a girlond well beseene
  He wore, from which as he had chauffed been
  The sweat did drop; and in his hand he bore
  A boawe and shaftes, as he in forrest greene
  Had hunted late the Libbard or the Bore,
And now would bathe his limbes, with labor heated sore.

30

Then came the *Autumne* all in yellow clad,
  As though he joyed in his plentious store,
  Laden with fruits that made him laugh, full glad
  That he had banisht hunger, which to-fore
  Had by the belly oft him pinched sore.
  Upon his head a wreath that was enrold
  With eares of corne, of every sort he bore:
  And in his hand a sickle he did holde,
To reape the ripened fruits the which the earth had yold.

31

Lastly, came *Winter* cloathed all in frize,
　Chattering his teeth for cold that did him chill,
　Whil'st on his hoary beard his breath did freese;
　And the dull drops that from his purpled bill
　As from a limbeck did adown distill.
　In his right hand a tipped staffe he held,
　With which his feeble steps he stayed still:
　For, he was faint with cold, and weak with eld;
That scarse his loosed limbes he hable was to weld.

32

These, marching softly, thus in order went,
　And after them, the Monthes all riding came;
　First, sturdy *March* with brows full sternly bent,
　And armed strongly, rode upon a Ram,
　The same which over *Hellespontus* swam:
　Yet in his hand a spade he also hent,
　And in a bag all sorts of seeds ysame,
　Which on the earth he strowed as he went,
And fild her womb with fruitfull hope of nourishment.

33

Next came fresh *Aprill* full of lustyhed,
　And wanton as a Kid whose horne new buds:
　Upon a Bull he rode, the same which led
　Europa floting through th'*Argolick* fluds:
　His hornes were gilden all with golden studs
　And garnished with garlonds goodly dight
　Of all the fairest flowres and freshest buds
　Which th'earth brings forth, and wet he seem'd in sight
With waves, through which he waded for his loves delight.

34

Then came faire *May*, the fayrest mayd on ground,
　Deckt all with dainties of her seasons pryde,
　And throwing flowres out of her lap around:
　Upon two brethrens shoulders she did ride,
　The twinnes of *Leda*; which on eyther side
　Supported her like to their soveraine Queene.
　Lord! how all creatures laught, when her they spide,
　And leapt and daunc't as they had ravisht beene!
And *Cupid* selfe about her fluttred all in greene.

35

And after her, came jolly *June*, arrayd
  All in greene leaves, as he a Player were;
  Yet in his time, he wrought as well as playd,
  That by his plough-yrons mote right well appeare:
  Upon a Crab he rode, that him did beare
  With crooked crawling steps an uncouth pase,
  And backward yode, as Bargemen wont to fare
  Bending their force contrary to their face,
Like that ungracious crew which faines demurest grace.

36

Then came hot *July* boyling like to fire,
  That all his garments he had cast away:
  Upon a Lyon raging yet with ire
  He boldly rode and made him to obay:
  It was the beast that whylome did forray
  The Nemæan forrest, till th'*Amphytrionide*
  Him slew, and with his hide did him array;
  Behinde his back a sithe, and by his side
Under his belt he bore a sickle circling wide.

37

The sixt was *August*, being rich arrayd
  In garment all of gold downe to the ground:
  Yet rode he not, but led a lovely Mayd
  Forth by the lilly hand, the which was cround
  With eares of corne, and full her hand was found;
  That was the righteous Virgin, which of old
  Liv'd here on earth, and plenty made abound;
  But, after Wrong was lov'd and Justice solde,
She left th'unrighteous world and was to heaven extold.

38

Next him, *September* marched eeke on foote;
  Yet was he heavy laden with the spoyle
  Of harvests riches, which he made his boot,
  And him enricht with bounty of the soyle:
  In his one hand, as fit for harvests toyle,
  He held a knife-hook; and in th'other hand
  A paire of waights, with which he did assoyle
  Both more and lesse, where it in doubt did stand,
And equall gave to each as Justice duly scann'd.

39

Then came *October* full of merry glee:
  For, yet his noule was totty of the must,
  Which he was treading in the wine-fats see,
  And of the joyous oyle, whose gentle gust
  Made him so frollick and so full of lust:
  Upon a dreadfull Scorpion he did ride,
  The same which by *Dianaes* doom unjust
  Slew great *Orion:* and eeke by his side
He had his ploughing share, and coulter ready tyde.

40

Next was *November*, he full grosse and fat,
  As fed with lard, and that right well might seeme;
  For, he had been a fatting hogs of late,
  That yet his browes with sweat, did reek and steem,
  And yet the season was full sharp and breem;
  In planting eeke he took no small delight:
  Whereon he rode, not easie was to deeme;
  For it a dreadfull *Centaure* was in sight,
The seed of *Saturne*, and faire *Nais*, *Chiron* hight.

41

And after him, came next the chill *December:*
  Yet he through merry feasting which he made,
  And great bonfires, did not the cold remember;
  His Saviours birth his mind so much did glad:
  Upon a shaggy-bearded Goat he rode,
  The same wherewith *Dan Jove* in tender yeares,
  They say, was nourisht by th'*Idæan* mayd;
  And in his hand a broad deepe boawle he beares;
Of which, he freely drinks an health to all his peeres.

42

Then came old *January*, wrapped well
  In many weeds to keep the cold away;
  Yet did he quake and quiver like to quell,
  And blowe his nayles to warme them if he may:
  For, they were numbd with holding all the day
  An hatchet keene, with which he felled wood,
  And from the trees did lop the needlesse spray:
  Upon an huge great Earth-pot steane he stood;
From whose wide mouth, there flowed forth the Romane floud.

43

And lastly, came cold *February*, sitting
 In an old wagon, for he could not ride;
 Drawne of two fishes for the season fitting,
 Which through the flood before did softly slyde
 And swim away: yet had he by his side
 His plough and harnesse fit to till the ground,
 And tooles to prune the trees, before the pride
 Of hasting Prime did make them burgein round:
So past the twelve Months forth, and their dew places found.

44

And after these, there came the *Day*, and *Night*,
 Riding together both with equall pase,
 Th'one on a Palfrey blacke, the other white;
 But *Night* had covered her uncomely face
 With a blacke veile, and held in hand a mace,
 On top whereof the moon and stars were pight,
 And sleep and darknesse round about did trace:
 But *Day* did beare, upon his scepters hight,
The goodly Sun, encompast all with beames bright.

45

Then came the *Howres*, faire daughters of high *Jove*,
 And timely *Night*, the which were all endewed
 With wondrous beauty fit to kindle love;
 But they were Virgins all, and love eschewed,
 That might forslack the charge to them foreshewed
 By mighty *Jove*; who did them Porters make
 Of heavens gate (whence all the gods issued)
 Which they did dayly watch, and nightly wake
By even turnes, ne ever did their charge forsake.

46

And after all came *Life*, and lastly *Death*;
 Death with most grim and griesly visage seene,
 Yet is he nought but parting of the breath;
 Ne ought to see, but like a shade to weene,
 Unbodied, unsoul'd, unheard, unseene.
 But *Life* was like a faire young lusty boy,
 Such as they faine *Dan Cupid* to have beene,
 Full of delightfull health and lively joy,
Deckt all with flowres, and wings of gold fit to employ.

47

When these were past, thus gan the *Titanesse*;
    Lo, mighty mother, now be judge and say,
    Whether in all thy creatures more or lesse
CHANGE doth not raign and beare the greatest sway:
For, who sees not, that *Time* on all doth pray?
But *Times* do change and move continually.
So nothing here long standeth in one stay:
    Wherefore, this lower world who can deny
But to be subject still to *Mutabilitie?*

48

Then thus gan *Jove*; Right true it is, that these
    And all things else that under heaven dwell
    Are chaung'd of *Time*, who doth them all disseise
Of being: But, who is it (to me tell)
That *Time* himselfe doth move and still compell
To keepe his course? Is not that namely wee
Which poure that vertue from our heavenly cell,
    That moves them all, and makes them changed be?
So them we gods doe rule, and in them also thee.

49

To whom, thus *Mutability*: The things
    Which we see not how they are mov'd and swayd,
    Ye may attribute to your selves as Kings,
And say they by your secret powre are made:
But what we see not, who shall us perswade?
But were they so, as ye them faine to be,
Mov'd by your might, and ordred by your ayde;
    Yet what if I can prove, that even yee
Your selves are likewise chang'd, and subject unto mee?

50

And first, concerning her that is the first,
    Even you faire *Cynthia*, whom so much ye make
    Joves dearest darling, she was bred and nurst
On *Cynthus* hill, whence she her name did take:
Then is she mortall borne, how-so ye crake;
Besides, her face and countenance every day
We changed see, and sundry forms partake,
    Now hornd, now round, now bright, now brown and gray:
So that *as changefull as the Moone* men use to say.

51

Next, *Mercury*, who though he lesse appeare
  To change his hew, and alwayes seeme as one;
  Yet, he his course doth altar every yeare,
  And is of late far out of order gone:
  So *Venus* eeke, that goodly Paragone,
  Though faire all night, yet is she darke all day;
  And *Phœbus* self, who lightsome is alone,
  Yet is he oft eclipsed by the way,
And fills the darkned world with terror and dismay.

52

Now *Mars* that valiant man is changed most:
  For, he some times so far runs out of square,
  That he his way doth seem quite to have lost,
  And cleane without his usuall sphere to fare;
  That even these Star-gazers stonisht are
  At sight thereof, and damne their lying bookes:
  So likewise, grim Sir *Saturne* oft doth spare
  His sterne aspect, and calme his crabbed lookes:
So many turning cranks these have, so many crookes.

53

But you *Dan Jove*, that only constant are,
  And King of all the rest, as ye do clame,
  Are you not subject eeke to this misfare?
  Then let me aske you this withouten blame,
  Where were ye borne? some say in *Crete* by name,
  Others in *Thebes*, and others other-where;
  But wheresoever they comment the same,
  They all consent that ye begotten were,
And borne here in this world, ne other can appeare.

54

Then are ye mortall borne, and thrall to me,
  Unlesse the kingdome of the sky yee make
  Immortall, and unchangeable to bee;
  Besides, that power and vertue which ye spake,
  That ye here worke, doth many changes take,
  And your owne natures change: for, each of you
  That vertue have, or this, or that to make,
  Is checkt and changed from his nature trew,
By others opposition or obliquid view.

55

Besides, the sundry motions of your Spheares,
So sundry waies and fashions as clerkes faine,
Some in short space, and some in longer yeares;
What is the same but alteration plaine?
Onely the starrie skie doth still remaine:
Yet do the Starres and Signes therein still move,
And even it self is mov'd, as wizards saine.
But all that moveth, doth mutation love:
Therefore both you and them to me I subject prove.

56

Then since within this wide great *Universe*
Nothing doth firme and permanent appeare,
But all things tost and turned by transverse:
What then should let, but I aloft should reare
My Trophee, and from all, the triumph beare?
Now judge then (O thou greatest goddesse trew!)
According as thy selfe doest see and heare,
And unto me addoom that is my dew;
That is the rule of all, all being rul'd by you.

57

So having ended, silence long ensewed,
Ne *Nature* to or fro spake for a space,
But with firme eyes affixt, the ground still viewed.
Meane while, all creatures, looking in her face,
Expecting th'end of this so doubtfull case,
Did hang in long suspence what would ensew,
To whether side should fall the soveraigne place:
At length, she looking up with chearefull view,
The silence brake, and gave her doome in speeches few.

58

I well consider all that ye have sayd,
And find that all things stedfastnes doe hate
And changed be: yet being rightly wayd
They are not changed from their first estate;
But by their change their being doe dilate:
And turning to themselves at length againe,
Doe worke their owne perfection so by fate:
Then over them Change doth not rule and raigne;
But they raigne over change, and doe their states maintaine.

59

Cease therefore daughter further to aspire,
  And thee content thus to be rul'd by me:
  For thy decay thou seekst by thy desire;
  But time shall come that all shall changed bee,
  And from thenceforth, none no more change shall see.
  So was the *Titaness* put downe and whist,
  And *Jove* confirm'd in his imperiall see.
  Then was that whole assembly quite dismist,
And *Natur's* selfe did vanish, whither no man wist.

The VIII. Canto, *unperfite*

1

When I bethinke me on that speech whyleare,
  Of *Mutability*, and well it way:
  Me seemes, that though she all unworthy were
  Of the Heav'ns Rule; yet very sooth to say,
  In all things else she beares the greatest sway.
  Which makes me loath this state of life so tickle,
  And love of things so vaine to cast away;
  Whose flowring pride, so fading and so fickle,
Short *Time* shall soon cut down with his consuming sickle.

2

Then gin I thinke on that which Nature sayd,
  Of that same time when no more *Change* shall be,
  But stedfast rest of all things firmely stayd
  Upon the pillours of Eternity,
  That is contrayr to *Mutabilitie*:
  For, all that moveth, doth in *Change* delight:
  But thence-forth all shall rest eternally
  With Him that is the God of Sabbaoth hight:
O that great Sabbaoth God, graunt me that Sabaoths sight.

FINIS